ROB NEYER'S

BIG BOOK OF
BASEBALL LINEUPS

A Complete Guide to the Best, Worst, and
Most Memorable Players to Ever Grace the Major Leagues

ROB NEYER

A FIRESIDE BOOK
Published by Simon and Schuster
New York   London   Toronto   Sydney   Singapore

FIRESIDE
Rockefeller Center
1230 Avenue of the Americas
New York, NY 10020

For information regarding special discounts for bulk purchases,
please contact Simon & Schuster Special Sales at
1-800-456-6798 or business@simonandschuster.com

Designed by Ruth Lee

Manufactured in the United States of America

10   9   8   7   6   5   4   3   2   1

Library of Congress Cataloging-in-Publication Data

Neyer, Rob.
Rob Neyer's big book of baseball lineups : a complete guide to
the best, worst, and most memorable players to ever grace the
major leagues / Rob Neyer.
        p.   cm.
Includes bibliographical references and index. Baseball players—
Rating of—United States. Baseball teams—United States—
Miscellanea.   I. Neyer, Rob.   II. Title.
GV875.A1N496   2003
796.357'02—dc21   13060597

ISBN 0-7432-4174-6

This book is for Bill James,
to whom I owe practically everything.

CONTENTS

BIG BOOK OF
BASEBALL LINEUPS

INTRODUCTION

Some of you may prefer to skip these next few pages. Just dive right in. And I wouldn't blame you for a Manhattan minute.

But my editor's a pretty sharp guy—more on him in the acknowledgments—and he thinks that all sorts of baseball fans will wind up with this book in their hands. He also thinks that this introduction should speak to all of those different sorts, from the casual fan to the SABR (Society for American Baseball Research) member who spends much of his spare time poring over microfilm of baseball's early history.

If you are a casual fan—maybe you'd never heard of this Rob Neyer character until now, or never read a baseball book—my advice is to start with your favorite team and enjoy the memories. When you see who I've picked as the franchise's worst defensive third baseman, close your eyes and try to see him at the hot corner, a ball bouncing off his chest or his throw sailing into the stands behind first base. Of course, if I picked some guy who last played in 1914, you're probably going to have a tough time with this particular exercise. But you get the point. My hope is that even if your interest doesn't range far afield from your favorite team, you'll find some names that evoke fond memories. Or even not so fond, because those have their place, too.

I suppose if this book has a target audience, it's the fans who are not obsessed (like I am) with baseball, but who check the standings every day in August, enjoy a trip to the ballpark more than a few times a year, and probably have played Rotisserie or tabletop baseball at some point. You probably watch *Baseball Tonight*, and you think Peter Gammons is something close to God.

You're the sort of fan who has to buy this book if it's going to sell, because there are a *lot* of you out there. Millions of you.

And if you're one of those SABR guys—or rather, if you're one of *us* SABR guys, because of course I'm one, too—then I suspect you'll find something to argue about on virtually every page.

Chuck Tanner once said, "Baseball's just an opinion." I disagree with Tanner, because reducing something to "opinion" means that there's no right answer, and if I didn't think there were right answers, I wouldn't have bothered with this book. That said, I'm certainly aware that all of *my* answers aren't right, and you're going to become aware of that, too. I'm pretty easy to reach, so if you want to argue about something, I'll be ready. I'll be posting some of these arguments at www.robneyer.com, and if I'm lucky enough to publish another edition of this book someday, I'm sure I'll have a long list of new people to thank.

Why did I write this book, and what's in it?

I wrote it because I wanted to read it, and what's in it is just about everything that I could think to put in it.

Not specific enough? Okay.

You want books that rate players? No problem. There are enough to stock a good-sized bookcase. The "problem" is that all the players in all those books are compared to each other. I mean, there are certainly plenty of good reasons to compare Lou Gehrig to Jimmie Foxx, or Eddie Collins to Joe Morgan. There are plenty of books that do this well, and I probably own all of them. But there's another kind of book that nobody's written, a book that compares Lou Gehrig to Don Mattingly, and Eddie Collins to Nellie Fox. When you tell the story of baseball, as often as not you're telling the story of the *teams*, and so I figured there must be room in the bookcase for one book that compares players to their *teammates*.

And that's what this is. You'll have to look elsewhere if you want to know who was better, Gehrig or Foxx. But if you want to know who played better for the White Sox, Collins or Fox . . . well, you've come to the right place.

What's in it? Every team that's been around since at least 1977 gets the full treatment. What's the full treatment? An all-time team, a runner-up team, a single-season team, an all-rookie team, an all-homegrown team, an all-traded-away team, an all-defense team, an all-lousy-defense team, an all-bust team, and an all-used-to-be-great team. Most of the time, the full treatment also includes an all-nickname team. These various teams are accompanied by text sidebars, and each chapter concludes with a longer essay (more about the sidebars and essays later).

The four most recent expansion teams get something less than the full treatment, simply because there's not as much material to work with.

There is also some variation in format among franchises that have moved. In a few cases, where the franchise's first home didn't last long, I considered both homes in one chapter. The only notable instance is with the Rangers, who spent more than a decade in Washington before moving to Arlington. One could certainly make a case for *not* combining them, but the fact is that the great majority of the franchise's interesting players have played in Texas. So there wasn't a lot to be gained by considering the Rangers alone, and then doing a separate chapter on the franchise's entire history.

That is, however, what I did with six other franchises: the Athletics, Braves, Dodgers, Giants, Orioles, and Twins. In the chapters on the other twenty-four franchises, I also included a list of great seasons and great managers. For these six, I held off on the great seasons and great managers until the chapter on the entire franchise.

Got that? This will make sense once you actually see it all laid out.

THE TEAMS: I was pretty strict about picking a left fielder, a center fielder, and a right fielder for each lineup, as opposed to simply picking three outfielders. A couple of years ago, the *Boston Globe* published the All-Centennial Red Sox team, as selected by the newspaper's readers. The three outfielders? Ted Williams, Carl Yastrzemski, and Jim Rice. Three left fielders.

To me, that's not a team. It's a collection of talent. Which is fine, but I think teams are more interesting than collections of talent. So I don't care how good somebody is; if he was a left fielder, I'm not going to slot him in right.

One big question was, how much is enough? What's better, one great year or three good ones? Three great years, or six good ones? Six great years, or twelve good ones? I didn't answer these questions with any sort of precision. I did decide that for a player to be considered for a franchise's Number One or Number Two team, he had to have spent at least three seasons with the club (I often broke this rule for designated hitters, as few players spend more than a season or two in that role with the same team). And I generally came down on the side of excellence. Three great seasons are better than six good ones . . . but not necessarily better than *nine* good ones.

When filling out the Homegrown lineup, I considered only players who got their professional start (or very nearly) with the team in question. So while Joe DiMaggio never belonged to a major-league franchise other than the Yankees, I don't consider him "homegrown," as he was the property of the San Francisco Seals for about three years before the Yankees paid the Seals $25,000 (and five forgotten players) for his contract.

That's an easy case. However, the professional origins of many pre-1950 players are murky, and when I was unable to make a clear (or nearly clear) determination, I erred on the side of caution.

When filling out the Traded-Away lineup, I considered what the players did *after* the deal. That is to say, I wasn't interested in how good a player had *been*, but rather in how good he would *be*. My source for the dates of most pre-1984 trades was Joe Reichler's *Baseball Trade Register* (Macmillan, 1984). For trades since then, I relied on various editions of *The Sporting News Baseball Register*.

When determining the value of the players—and of course, most of the book is about the value of the players—I relied on both the readily available statistics and Bill James's Win Shares, which were published in his book *Win Shares* (STATS Publishing, 2002). Though I rarely mention Win Shares anywhere in the book but here, I consulted them often, especially when making the tough calls (and there were a lot of them). While my reliance on Win Shares has undoubtedly led to some mistakes on my part, I'm certain that I'd have made far *more* mistakes if I had *not* relied on Win Shares to the extent that I did.

THE TIMES: I chose to start this little exercise with the twentieth century. I could list a number of reasons why, but if you're a fan of the nineteenth century, my reasons would ring hollow. If it's any consolation, I suspect that my decision had only a tiny effect on who actually got into the book. And if it's any further consolation, I'll take a look, on my Web site, at who *did* get left out.

THE SIDEBARS: Within each team chapter are a number of sidebars, which are intended to illuminate the short notes that accompany the listed players. When deciding what to write about, my rule was, "Will my ideal reader already know this?" And if the answer was yes, then I tried to think of something else to write about. So, within the Yankees chapter, you're not going to find an essay on what set Babe Ruth apart from his contemporaries, or about how great DiMaggio was in center field, because I figure you already know about Ruth and DiMaggio. What you will find is a short essay about the defensive greatness of third baseman Clete Boyer, because he's been largely forgotten due to his contemporary, Brooks Robinson.

THE ESSAYS: At the end of each chapter is a longer essay, in which I wrote about whatever struck my fancy. The only rule was that there weren't any rules.

THE REGULARS: After the teams are . . . right, more teams. Actually, they're the same teams, but presented far differently. I thought it would be fun to see the regulars for each franchise, position by position, year by year, in a huge chart. So that's what we did, and we've presented them in a fashion that's supposed to make it easy to evaluate the stability, or lack thereof, for each franchise at each position over the years.

Otherwise, they're unadorned. But I think you'll find these listings interesting if you take the time, and I'll probably be doing the same.

SOURCES: There were hundreds of them, too many to list here. My primary source for statistics was *The All-Time Baseball Handbook* (STATS, Inc., 2000), because that tome uses the official definition of on-base percentage. My sources for the lists of regulars for each franchise were *Total Baseball* and *The Sports Encyclopedia: Baseball*.

The Web site Retrosheet.org was immensely helpful in a number of ways, and Baseball-Reference.com was exceptionally useful for finding statistics for players with particular teams. . . . Wait a minute. That's not strong enough. Without Baseball-Reference.com, I would have missed my deadline by six months rather than three. So, thank you, Sean Foreman (and one of these days, all that hard work's going to make you rich).

For information on nicknames, I consulted Don Zminda's *From Abba Dabba to Zorro: The World of Baseball Nicknames* (STATS Publishing, 1999) and James K. Skipper's *Baseball Nicknames: A Dictionary of Origins and Meanings* (McFarland & Co., 1992). The latter of those books is out of print and extremely difficult to find, and I'm indescribably grateful to John Skipper for loaning me a copy of his late brother's masterpiece.

At the end of each chapter, I list sources that were particularly helpful with that particular team.

Okay, now you can dive in.

PART ONE
TODAY'S THIRTY

ANAHEIM ANGELS

		YEARS	NOTES
	ALL-TIME		
DH	Don Baylor	1977–1982	Still able to play the outfield (sort of) and mostly played left field for Angels, but did see significant action as DH, including 65 games at "position" in 1979 MVP season.
C	Bob Boone	1982–1988	Couldn't hit at all, but there's not much competition here, and he did win three straight Gold Gloves and caught regularly for two of franchise's three division titlists.
1B	Wally Joyner	1986–1991	He was a fine player for a long time, but never really got any better than he'd been in his first two years, when he totaled 56 home runs and 217 RBI.
2B	Bobby Grich	1977–1986	The Angels have misspent a fair chunk of change on free agents over the years, but they got their money's worth with Grich, who was fantastic for eight years.
SS	Jim Fregosi	1961–1971	A six-time All-Star and the American League's best shortstop in the 1960s; after doing his duty in the field, provided the Angels great value as trade bait.
3B	Troy Glaus	1998–2002	Minor-league slugger hit just one home run in his first season (165 at-bats), but blasted 147 in his next four; decline in 2002 offset by *seven* postseason homers.
LF	Brian Downing	1978–1990	Once a catcher with moderate power, he hit the weights and started hitting home runs, then got hurt and became an outfielder; would lead off one day and hit clean-up the next.
CF	Jim Edmonds	1993–1999	Didn't look like a great prospect in the minors and hit only 5 homers in his first 112 major-league games, but somehow developed into power-hitting Gold Glover.
RF	Tim Salmon	1992–2002	Never quite became a superstar, due in part to various injuries, but for eight straight years he was consistently excellent and now holds the club's home-run record.
SP1	Chuck Finley	1986–1999	Never won 20 games, but was one of the more durable starters of the 1990s and easily ranks No. 1 on club's all-time list with 165 victories and 2,675 innings.
SP2	Nolan Ryan	1972–1979	In eight seasons, led American League in strikeouts seven times and tossed four no-hitters; career record with Angels was 138-121, not quite as good as his 3.07 ERA.
SP3	Frank Tanana	1973–1980	For the five seasons before he hurt his arm, Tanana was demonstrably better than his teammate Nolan Ryan; pure power with Angels, then had nice career throwing slop.
SP4	Mike Witt	1981–1990	Solid fastball and devastating curve came together for Witt in 1986, when he ranked behind only Roger Clemens; pitched perfect game on last day of '84 season.
RP	Troy Percival	1995–2002	Like Trevor Hoffman, began pro career as position player and became the most consistent closer in his league; Percival converted all 7 save chances in 2002 postseason.

The argument against Nolan Ryan as a *great* pitcher is that he was seldom great over the course of a single season. The same baseball writers (well, some of the same baseball writers) who elected Ryan to the Hall of Fame in a landslide never rated him as better than the second-best pitcher in his league; he finished second in the Cy Young balloting once (1973), and third twice.

What's more, it can reasonably be argued that Ryan was not, over a five-year span that represented a good chunk of his peak, even the best pitcher on his own *team*. From 1974 through 1978, Ryan went 82-75 (.522) with twenty-two shutouts and a 3.19 ERA. Those same five seasons, Frank Tanana went 82-59 (.582) with twenty-two shutouts and a 2.86 ERA.

Both of them were fine pitchers, of course. Interestingly enough, as much as they had in common, Ryan and Tanana didn't get along at all. After Ryan questioned Tanana's work habits in 1977, Tanana said, "In the overall picture, it doesn't matter who does or doesn't get along. He'll do his job and I'll do mine."

Frank Tanana had every bit of Nolan Ryan's ability. But he didn't have Ryan's work habits and, more to the point, he didn't have the *extremely* rare ability to sustain a huge early workload without getting hurt.

So why did Bobby Bonds play for so many different teams, anyway?

We could try to answer this question in any one of seven chapters, as Bonds spent two seasons or fewer with seven different teams, after spending the *first* seven years of his career with the Giants. It's easy to say that eight teams didn't want Bonds, but of course it's just as true that eight teams *did* want him. Among the players traded *for* Bobby Bonds were Bobby Murcer, Mickey Rivers, Ed Figueroa, Brian Downing, and Claudell Washington. So again, why so many teams?

The Giants traded him to the Yankees because they got tired of the strikeouts. The Yankees traded him to the Angels because he and Billy Martin didn't get along. The Angels traded him to the White Sox because if they'd kept him, he'd have left as a free agent after the '78 season and they'd have received nothing in return. The White Sox traded him (after twenty-six games) to the Rangers for the same reason. The Rangers traded him to the Indians because the owner wanted to dump salary. The Indians sold him to the Cardinals because Bonds hated Cleveland. The Cardinals released him because he suddenly stopped hitting. And the Cubs released him because he didn't start again.

All of which is to say, there's no one reason. It just worked out that way.

NO. 2			
		YEARS	NOTES
DH	Chili Davis	1988–1990 1993–1996	Mostly an outfielder (and not a very good one) in his first stint, then came back in '93 and became one of the league's top designated hitters.
C	Bob Rodgers	1961–1969	An original Angel, and spent his entire nine-year career with franchise; returned as manager in August of '91 but fired in '94 after a couple of fifth-place finishes.
1B	Rod Carew	1979–1985	Came aboard when Angels offered *him* $4 million (over five years) and his *team* four players, among them Ken Landreaux; Carew good, but never great, with Angels.
2B	Bobby Knoop	1964–1969	Remembered for his brilliant defense, but Knoop could hit a little, too; 11 triples and 17 HR in 1966 were his best numbers, but he was solid from '65 through '68.
SS	Dick Schofield	1983–1992 1995–1996	Like his old man, didn't hit much, but also like his old man, could flash the leather, and was slick enough to play nearly every day in six different seasons for Halos.
3B	Doug DeCinces	1982–1987	With Ripken coming up, Orioles deemed DeCinces expendable . . . but Ripken became a SS and O's were left without a 3B while DeCinces starred for Angels.
LF	Garret Anderson	1994–*2002*	Perpetually described as underrated, and so eventually became overrated, but still a good player; Leon Wagner (1961–63) was better, but not for nearly as long.
CF	Fred Lynn	1981–1984	Played horribly in his first season after signing big free-agent deal, but followed up with three fine seasons, and played in three All-Star Games as Angel.
RF	Bobby Bonds	1976–1977	Didn't play regularly for even two full seasons, but RF has been a particularly unstable position for the Angels, and Lee Stanton just didn't do enough in his four years.
SP1	Dean Chance	1961–1966	Franchise's first real star, and if he hadn't spent so much time hanging around with Bo Belinsky, he might rank higher than eighth on franchise list with 74 victories.
SP2	Mark Langston	1990–1997	Prototypical power pitcher with great fastball and big curve, combined with Mike Witt on no-hitter in his first start for Angels, and an All-Star from 1991 through '93.
SP3	Clyde Wright	1966–1973	In 1970, the curveball artist pitched in the All-Star Game, tossed a no-hitter, and won 22 games (still the franchise record); low K rate eventually did him in.
SP4	Kirk McCaskill	1985–1991	Power pitcher started like gangbusters, suffered arm problems for two years, then revived career as finesse artist and won 45 games in his last four years.
RP	Bryan Harvey	1987–1992	Threw one of the most devastating splitters in the game, and led AL with 46 saves in 1991; suffered elbow injury in '92 and was grabbed by Marlins in expansion draft.

SINGLE SEASON

		YEARS	NOTES
DH	Frank Robinson	1973	Turned thirty-eight on August 31, but still had one great season left and this was it: 30 homers, 97 RBI, and 861 OPS.
C	Lance Parrish	1990	At thirty-three, erstwhile Tigers star played nearly as well for Halos in 1990 as he ever had; 24 homers and 70 RBI in 133 games.
1B	Don Mincher	1967	It doesn't look like much—.273-25-76—but in context it's excellent; beaning in '68 got him banished to Pilots.
2B	Bobby Grich	1979	After two injury-plagued seasons, Grich finally gave Angels their money's worth; just as valuable as MVP Don Baylor.
SS	Jim Fregosi	1964	At twenty-two, hit 8 home runs, drew 72 walks, and played solid defense; played nearly as well in '67 and won Gold Glove.
3B	Doug DeCinces	1982	His first season with Angels was the best of his career, as he established career highs in every stat that matters.
LF	Darin Erstad	2000	After batting .253 in '99, jumped to .355 (with 950 OPS); just edges Baylor in '79, when the MVP DH'd in 65 games.
CF	Albie Pearson	1963	Little speedster batted .304, drew 92 walks, and was the best defensive outfielder in the American League.
RF	Tim Salmon	1995	In one of his rare years of good health, finished among league leaders in batting (.330), on-base (.429), and slugging (.594).
SP	Dean Chance	1964	Great, MVP-caliber season: AL-best 20 victories, 11 shutouts, and amazing 1.65 ERA; beat out Koufax for Cy Young.
RP	Ken Tatum	1969	Came out of nowhere to go 7-2 with 22 saves and 1.36 ERA in 86 innings; fastballer allowed just one homer all season.

ALL-ROOKIE

		YEARS	NOTES
C	Bob Rodgers	1962	Hitting stats unimpressive, but Buck's 150 games behind the dish were more than anybody else in the majors.
1B	Wally Joyner	1986	"Wally World" became a sensation in Anaheim, but there was a sad ending as infection knocked him out of ALCS.
2B	Jerry Remy	1975	Didn't hit much, but was as good with the glove as anybody in the league after Grich (who replaced Remy three years later).
SS	Gary DiSarcina	1992	Like Remy, not any kind of hitter, but played nearly every game and gave the club great defense up the middle.
3B	Carney Lansford	1978	One of the few outstanding hitting prospects developed by Angels in 1970s, batted .294 with 20 steals as rookie.
LF	Garret Anderson	1995	Batted .321 with 16 homers in only 106 games, and finished second to Marty Cordova in very close RoY balloting.
CF	Devon White	1987	It was '87, so White hit 24 homers, more than he would hit in any of the succeeding seasons of his long career; played a lot in RF.
RF	Tim Salmon	1993	Smacked 31 homers and knocked in 95 runs to become first—and so far, only—Rookie of the Year in Angels history.
SP	Dean Chance	1962	Spent two months in the bullpen, yet still managed to pitch 207 innings and win 14 games with a 2.96 ERA.
RP	Ken Tatum	1969	Pitched poorly in spring training but won job anyway, then went 7-2 with 22 saves and 1.36 ERA in 87 innings.

Not many players have done what Darin Erstad did.

In 1999, the ex-Nebraska star batted .253 and rapped out only 148 hits in 142 games, which was something of a disappointment considering his .295 career average entering that season. But in 2000, Erstad more than made up for any disappointment with a .355 batting average and 240 hits. Erstad's 92-hit improvement set a "record" for a player who racked up at least 500 at-bats in both seasons.

And then in 2001, he gave most of those hits right back. Hindered by a strained knee ligament, Erstad batted .258 with 163 hits (and nine homers). Those three seasons have to rank among the oddest-looking up-and-down stories ever.

Erstad was (and is) immensely talented. But something the onetime Cornhusker punter never seemed to learn is that baseball isn't football; it's a marathon rather than a sprint, and if you give 110 percent on every play, you'll wind up having only eighty or ninety percent to give. And eighty percent of Darin Erstad just isn't good enough to play every day in the majors. In 2002, he proved that it was 2000 rather than 2001 that was likely the fluke. Yet during the season, the Angels rewarded Erstad with a four-year contract extension for $32 million.

And when they won the World Series, some people actually thought it was *because* of Erstad.

For the great part of the 1970s and '80s, somebody looking at the young players in the Angels' farm system might logically have said, "Hell, there's nobody down there who's going to help us much. If we're going to win anything in the next five years, we're going to have to find the players somewhere else." To see how bare the cupboard was, just look at the best players *traded* by the Angels over the years. Andy Messersmith became a superstar (if only briefly) after getting traded, but otherwise the best Angels traded in the 1970s and '80s became good players but not great ones. The talent simply wasn't there.

For many years, the Angels were accused of trying to buy a pennant (and indeed they did buy a few division titles). One could reasonably argue that the Angels should have spent all that money on player development rather than free agents. But that would have meant a *plan* that included not contending for a few years. And given the age of owner Gene Autry and the feeling that the franchise had to compete with the Dodgers, *planning* to not compete simply wasn't an option.

HOMEGROWN			
		YEARS	NOTES
C	Bengie Molina	1998–*2002*	Wasn't drafted but reached the majors with Angels . . . as did his kid brother José, also a catcher, in 2001.
1B	Wally Joyner	1986–1991	BYU product selected in '83 with third-round pick Angels got because Yankees signed Don Baylor.
2B	Mark McLemore	1986–1990	Enjoyed his best season in 2001, when he was a thirty-six-year-old utility man for a team that won 116 games.
SS	Jim Fregosi	1961–1971	Actually started with Red Sox, but Angels grabbed him in expansion draft after one season in (very) low minors.
3B	Troy Glaus	1998–*2002*	San Diego's second-round pick in '94 didn't sign, and after three years at UCLA was third overall pick in '97.
LF	Garret Anderson	1994–*2002*	Native of Los Angeles area was Angels' fourth-round pick in 1990, then took a few years to show some power.
CF	Jim Edmonds	1993–1999	Seventh-round pick in 1988, out of California's Diamond Bar High School.
RF	Tim Salmon	1992–*2002*	Phoenician drafted in 1986 by Braves but didn't sign; three years later, taken in third round by Angels.
SP	Frank Tanana	1973–1980	The thirteenth overall pick in the '71 draft lost his great fastball in mid-career but still managed to win 240 games.
RP	Troy Percival	1995–*2002*	Sixth-round pick in 1990 as a *catcher* . . . batted .203 in 29 games, became a pitcher, and destiny was fulfilled.

TRADED AWAY			
		TRADED	NOTES
C	Phil Nevin	March 29, 1999	Traded to Padres for a bucket of sunflower seeds; Angels weren't first club to give up on him, but still . . .
1B	Jason Thompson	April 1, 1981	Played only four months for Angels before traded to Pirates, for whom he enjoyed a big 1982.
2B	Mark McLemore	August 17, 1990	Sent to Tribe in deal that netted Angels a catcher named Ron Tingley; Damion Easley also given away.
SS	Dickie Thon	April 1, 1981	With Burleson aboard, Thon traded to Astros for a used Forsch . . . all too typical of early-'80s Angels.
3B	Carney Lansford	December 10, 1980	Might have worked out if both Rick Burleson and Butch Hobson hadn't been complete busts.
LF	Dante Bichette	March 14, 1991	I'm not Dante's biggest fan, but even I'll admit that trading him for Dave Parker didn't work out.
CF	Devon White	December 2, 1990	Traded after a terrible season, became key part of Jays squad that won two World Series; also, Jim Edmonds.
RF	Tom Brunansky	May 12, 1982	Angels sent Bruno *and* $400K to Twins for reliever Doug Corbett and 2B Rob Wilfong; typical of Angels.
SP	Andy Messersmith	November 28, 1972	With 3B Ken McMullen, went to Dodgers for Frank Robinson and four others; Robinson did play well.
RP	Roberto Hernandez	August 2, 1989	Sixteenth pick in the '86 draft struggled in minors as starter, so Angels sent him to White Sox for OF Mark Davis.

GOLD GLOVE			
		YEARS	**NOTES**
C	Bob Boone	1982–1988	Regarded around the league as the thinking man's catcher, and was still playing at high level in his late thirties.
1B	Jim Spencer	1968–1973	With good range and great hands, won his only Gold Glove in 1970, at twenty-three; beats out Joyner and Snow.
2B	Bobby Knoop	1964–1969	Played Gold Glove–quality defense from the moment he stepped on the field, and eventually won three of them.
SS	Dick Schofield	1983–1992 1995–1996	Never won a Gold Glove or really deserved one, but his defense kept him in the game for a long time.
3B	Aurelio Rodriguez	1967–1970	Not as great as advertised—and such a poor hitter that he shouldn't have been playing—but he was very good.
LF	Garret Anderson	1994–1998 2001–2002	He's been mostly a left fielder because the Angels have been blessed with Jim Edmonds and now Erstad, but could play any of the outfield spots.
CF	Jim Edmonds	1993–1999	Two Gold Gloves, and in 1997 he made one of the all-time great catches; Gary Pettis also outstanding.
RF	Bobby Bonds	1976–1977	Like his son, had the range for center field; unlike his son, had the arm for right field and was one of the best.
P	Mark Langston	1990–1997	Did virtually everything well and finished his career with seven Gold Gloves.

IRON GLOVE			
		YEARS	**NOTES**
C	Earl Averill	1961–1962	A catcher in name only, but kept position warm until Buck Rodgers arrived; did hit with some authority.
1B	Mo Vaughn	1999–2001	Fits nicely with peers like Mike Sweeney, Frank Thomas, Brad Fullmer, and Ryan Klesko . . . ah, baseball today.
2B	Torey Lovullo	1993	Played only 91 games at 2B in his only season with Angels, but club has long tradition of fine defense here.
SS	Dave Chalk	1973–1974 1976–1978	Not a bad third baseman, but played shortstop regularly in three different seasons and really shouldn't have.
3B	Paul Schaal	1964–1968	Ranks among the very worst defensive third basemen ever, among those with long careers.
LF	Leon Wagner	1961–1963	Very few outfielders so bad have been allowed to play so many games there; think Greg Luzinski, Jeff Burroughs.
CF	Junior Felix	1991–1992	Speed allowed him to outrun some of his mistakes, but not nearly enough of them; strong but erratic arm.
RF	Chili Davis	1988	In his only season as the Angels' right fielder, Davis made 19 errors and posted .942 fielding percentage.
P	Chuck Finley	1986–1999	A complete disaster once the ball left his hand; as one fan remembers, "Stiff-legged, awkward, clueless, brutal."

Leon "Daddy Wags" Wagner was born before his time; if he'd come along in the early 1970s rather than the early 1960s, he'd have made one hell of a designated hitter.

As it was, the Angels just had to put up with his adventures in left field, because he was the best hitter they had. On April 13, 1961, just two days after their first-ever game, the Angels traded Lou Johnson—who would become a pretty good player in his own right—to the Dodgers for Leon Wagner. That turned out to be one of the best deals a first-year expansion club ever made, as Wagner led the Angels in homers in each of his first three seasons: twenty-eight in 1961, thirty-seven (the club record for twenty years) in 1962, and twenty-six in 1963.

He didn't make any friends in the front office, though. To finance a clothing store he opened on Crenshaw Boulevard in Los Angeles— the slogan was "Get your rags from Daddy Wags"—Wagner plied management with requests for loans. And in December of 1963, negotiations for a new contract became so acrimonious that Wagner was traded to Cleveland for a journeyman pitcher named Barry Latman and thirty-six-year-old slugger Joe Adcock. When he heard about the trade, Wagner commented, "I have nothing against Cleveland, but I'd rather have been traded somewhere in the United States."

Granted, Dante Bichette's not the greatest player who ever lived. But one of the many stupid things the Angels did in the early 1990s was jettisoning Bichette, thus leaving a big hole in the DH slot that wasn't filled until Chili Davis returned to the club in 1993.

Prior to the 1991 season, the Angels traded Bichette to the Brewers for Dave Parker, who by then was pushing forty. Coming off a solid 1990 season with Milwaukee, Parker had never suffered through a truly bad season. Not until coming to Anaheim, that is. Jackie Autry would later say of Parker, general manager Mike Port, and manager Doug Rader, "Mike Port hired Doug Rader, and Doug Rader told us that Dave Parker would be the mortar holding up the clubhouse walls when the wind started to blow in July."

When July rolled around, Dave Parker had six home runs and a .222 batting average. By the time September rolled around, Rader had been fired. And when September 7 rolled around, Dave Parker was released. With Bichette gone, the Angels traded for Hubie Brooks to take some of the DH at bats in 1992 . . . and he was just as bad as Parker.

		YEARS	NOTES
		ALL-BUST	
DH	Dave Parker	1991	Unmitigated disaster; manager Pat Corrales asked for forty-year-old slugger, and he got 637 OPS in 119 games.
C	Todd Greene	1996–1999	He crushed minor-league pitching, but couldn't stay healthy with Halos and left club with .281 OBP.
1B	Mo Vaughn	1999–2001	Disney's first big move was to sign the Hit Dog, but for most of his tenure he was more dog than hit.
2B	Damion Easley	1992–1996	Batted .313 as sophomore, then just .212 over next three seasons before going to Detroit, where he thrived.
SS	Rick Burleson	1981–1986	Played brilliantly in '81, then tore rotator cuff and got paid a lot of money for doing very little.
3B	Gary Gaetti	1991–1993	Terrible for two years after signing four-year deal for $11.4 million; traded, and suddenly his bat came alive.
LF	Rick Reichardt	1964–1970	Got a huge bonus, started slow, then suffered debilitating illness just when it looked like he'd become a star.
CF	Jay Johnstone	1966–1970	Decent with the glove but rarely met a pitch he didn't like; .294 OBP and 26 homers in five seasons.
RF	Von Hayes	1992	Only thirty-three, but the former Phillies star was done, batting .225 with 4 homers in 94 games to close career.
SP	Ken Hill	1997–2000	Angels initially gave him $16.5 million for three years, and they got only 22 wins in four seasons.
RP	Mark Holzemer	1993 1995–1996	You gotta hand it to the Angels: they let the lefty pitch in 42 games, the result of which was an 8.31 ERA.

		YEARS	NOTES
		USED-TO-BE-GREAT	
DH	Frank Robinson	1973–1974	Other candidates: Reggie Jackson (1982–1986), Eddie Murray (1997), Cecil Fielder (1998), Dave Parker.
C	Lance Parrish	1989–1992	Still had the old power, and in 1990 he led all major-league catchers with 24 home runs.
1B	Joe Adcock	1964–1966	In his *last* season, at thirty-eight, Adcock slugged .576 in 231 at-bats; Ted Kluszewski also finished with Angels.
2B	Harold Reynolds	1994	Longtime Mariner finished career with Angels; .312 OBP and .290 slugging average before joining ESPN.
SS	Bert Campaneris	1979–1981	In 1965 *against* the Angels, Campy had become the first major leaguer to play all nine positions in one game.
3B	Eddie Yost	1961–1962	"Walking Man" could still walk, but couldn't hit or field; Malzone and Wallach also finished with Angels.
LF	George Hendrick	1985–1988	Enjoyed something of a resurgence as part-timer in '86, but hit the wall in '87 and was hopeless in '88.
CF	Vada Pinson	1972–1973	If the second half of his career had been anything like the first half, he'd be in the Hall; .304 OBP as Angel.
RF	Reggie Jackson	1982–1986	Actually, he was still great, at least in '82 when he led AL with 39 homers and played 139 games in RF.
SP	Luis Tiant	1982	At forty-one (perhaps), El Tiante pitched his last major-league game for Angels; 2-2 with 5.76 ERA in 30 innings.
RP	Hoyt Wilhelm	1969	Baseball's first Hall of Fame reliever spent five months with Angels, posted 2.47 ERA before traded to Braves.

		YEARS	NOTES
M	"Joe College" Bobby Winkles	1973–1974	Longtime head coach at Arizona State also became known by some as "Dr. Strange Moves."
DH	"The Incredible Hulk" Brian Downing	1978–1990	Downing was one of the first players to bulk up with weights; incidentally, looked like Christopher Reeve.
C	"The Immortal Azcue" Joe Azcue	1969–1970 1972	Picked up the nickname while playing for Cleveland, when for a while everything he hit was a line drive.
1B	"Wally World" Wally Joyner	1986–1991	Named for the fictional amusement park in *Vacation*, because Angels played so close to Disneyland.
2B	"The Iron Pony" Sandy Alomar	1969–1974	Either because he played in 648 straight games, or because he twice played 162 in a season for Angels.
SS	"Little Duck" Dick Schofield	1983–1992 1995–1996	His dad Dick, a major leaguer for 19 years, was "Ducky," so of course young Dick was "Little Duck."
3B	"Rat" Gary Gaetti	1991–1993	It wasn't until he dumped the curly locks and shaved the mustache that we finally learned what animal Gaetti best resembled.
LF	"Daddy Wags" Leon Wagner	1961–1963	Slogan for his short-lived L.A. haberdashery was, "Get Your Rags from Daddy Wags."
CF	"Mighty Mite" Albie Pearson	1961–1966	At 5'5" and 145 pounds, he was hardly bigger than a minute, but for three years he was one of the mightier leadoff men in the game.
RF	"Disco Dan" Dan Ford	1979–1981	Supposedly because Ford had a financial interest in one *and* because he danced to beat of his own drummer.
SP	"Super Dude" Rudy May	1965–1974	Courtesy of Mickey Rivers; May liked it so much, he had "Super Dude" emblazoned on his T-shirts.
RP	"King Arthur" Art Fowler	1961–1964	Still pitching brilliantly at forty-one, and also known as "The Hummer" for his crackling fastball.

TOP FIVE SEASONS

YEAR 2002   **RECORD** 99-63
BEST HITTER Garret Anderson
BEST PITCHER Jarrod Washburn
NOTES Supposed to finish last, won the World Series instead.

YEAR 1979   **RECORD** 88-74
BEST HITTERS Don Baylor, Bobby Grich
BEST PITCHERS Dave Frost, Nolan Ryan
NOTES After twenty-eight seasons, finally a postseason berth.

YEAR 1982   **RECORD** 93-69
BEST HITTER Doug DeCinces
BEST PITCHER Geoff Zahn
NOTES Came within two runs of reaching World Series.

YEAR 1986   **RECORD** 92-70
BEST HITTERS Brian Downing, Wally Joyner
BEST PITCHER Mike Witt
NOTES Less said about October, the better.

YEAR 1962   **RECORD** 86-76
BEST HITTERS Billy Moran, Leon Wagner
BEST PITCHER Dean Chance
NOTES In only their second season, roared into third place.

TOP FIVE MANAGERS

MANAGER Gene Mauch
YEARS 1981–1982, 1985–1987
RECORD 379-332 (.533)
NOTES Little ball brought two division titles.

MANAGER Mike Scioscia
YEARS 2000–*2002*
RECORD 256-230 (.527)
NOTES It's early, but preliminary signs are *very* good.

MANAGER Bill Rigney
YEARS 1961–1969
RECORD 625-707 (.469)
NOTES Suffered through a lot of strangeness.

MANAGER Doug Rader
YEARS 1989–1991
RECORD 232-216 (.518)
NOTES No titles, but Angels were always competitive.

MANAGER Jim Fregosi
YEARS 1978–1981
RECORD 237-249 (.488)
NOTES Resume includes first- and sixth-place finishes.

Is there anything better than when your passions come together?

I love baseball, of course, and for some inexplicable reason I also love *National Lampoon's Vacation* (the first one in the series; the rest are drivel). It's about this buffoon who drives his family across the country and . . . well, you know the rest. Still, I wonder what people are going to think in fifty years, when they see that Wally Joyner's nickname was "Wally World." Will they know that *Vacation* was released in 1983, and that Chevy Chase's character was taking his family to Wally World, which was a stand-in for Disneyland, which sat not far from the California Angels' ballpark, which was home to rookie sensation Wally Joyner in 1986?

I don't know. But what I do know is that the Marty Moose song from *Vacation* drives my wife absolutely crazy (and not in the good way), so here it is:

Whoooo's the . . . moosiest
moose we know?
   Marty Moose!
Who's the star of our favor-ite
show?
   Marty Moose!
M is for Merry, we're merry you
see,
O is oh gosh, oh golly, oh gee,
S is for super-fun family glee,
E is for everything you want to
be-e-e-e
   "What's that spell?"
Marty Moose, Marty Moose,
Marty Moose
   "Yu-up, that's me!"

NO GUARDIAN ANGELS HERE

The Curse of the Bambino gets all the attention, but if Orange County were a major media center, "The Curse of the Singing Cowboy" might have entered the vernacular by now. Because over the last three or four decades—until 2002, that is—no team in baseball suffered worse luck than the Angels.

- Outfielder Ken Hunt hit twenty-five home runs in 1961. In 1962, while in the on-deck circle getting warmed up, he broke his collar bone and never played again.
- Ken McBride was named to the American League All-Star team in each of the Angels' first three seasons, in which he won thirty-six games with a 3.46 ERA. But in 1964 he suffered neck and back injuries in a car accident, and won only four more games in the major leagues.
- In 1964, the Angels signed Wisconsin All-American Rick Reichardt for $200,000. Reichardt, also a football star, was supposed to be the next Mickey Mantle. And at the All-Star break in 1966, his first full season, Reichardt had sixteen homers and forty-four RBI. But he was also suffering severe headaches and occasional fainting spells, and before long doctors removed one of his kidneys. Though he would later enjoy some solid seasons for the Angels and White Sox, he never played quite so well as he had in that first half of the '66 season, when he was twenty-three years old.
- In the first winter of free agency, Gene Autry opened the safe and spent $2 million on Joe Rudi and $1.5 million on Bobby Grich . . . and both were lost for most of their first season, Rudi with a broken hand and Grich with a herniated disc he suffered when lifting an air conditioner.
- Continuing their spending spree, the Angels signed Twins outfielder Lyman Bostock to a $2.2 million deal after the '77 season. Bostock got off to a horrible start in '78—he batted just .147 in April—and offered to return his salary to the club. Instead the money went to charity, and Bostock batted .318 the rest of the way. But with seven games to play and the Angels in Chicago, Bostock went to Gary, Indiana, to visit friends and family. And that night, he was shot dead while sitting in the backseat of a car. His assailant was trying to kill somebody else.
- It looked like one of their best moves. After the 1980 season, the Angels traded for Red Sox shortstop Rick Burleson. In 1981, in addition to maintaining his status as the league's most valuable defensive player, Burleson also enjoyed his best season with the stick. And then in 1982, he tore his rotator cuff in spring training and never played regularly again.
- October 12, 1986. Game five of the American League Championship Series. Only one victory stands between the California Angels and their first trip to the World Series, and going into the ninth they've got a 5–2 lead over the Red Sox, with their best pitcher, Mike Witt, on the mound. But with one out, ex-Angel Don Baylor hit a two-run homer, on a full count, to make the score 5–4. Witt retired Dwight Evans on a pop-up. One out away. But with Rich Gedman due up, manager Gene Mauch yanked Witt in favor of Gary Lucas. And Lucas, who hadn't hit a batter in four years, plunked Gedman with his very first pitch. The rest is history, of course, as the Angels lost that game and the next two.
- In his very first regular-season game, Mo Vaughn—who'd recently been gifted with a six-year, $80 million contract—toppled into a dugout while pursuing a foul ball and sprained his ankle. After missing two weeks, he came back and put together a couple of decent seasons . . . but missed the entire 2001 season with a torn biceps.

And those are just the lowlights. The Angels have to lead the world in players killed or maimed in auto accidents. Bottom line, this franchise suffered from lousy management for a majority of its history. But there was an awful lot of lousy luck, too. If any team ever deserved to win a World Series, it was the Angels.

I'm grateful to Dave Zybert, Noah Lemas, and especially to Ashby Jones for their editorial suggestions. Sources for this chapter include Ross Newhan's The Anaheim Angels *(Hyperion, 2000).*

ARIZONA DIAMONDBACKS

		YEARS	NOTES
ALL-TIME			
C	Damian Miller	1998–2002	One of the game's most consistent players, Miller would, year in and year out, bat around .270 with a .340 OBP and .440 slugging percentage.
1B	Mark Grace	2001–*2002*	Erubiel Durazo would own this spot if he'd been given the job, but the Diamondbacks do like their veterans . . . and you can't argue with winning the World Series.
2B	Jay Bell	1998–2002	Signed to provide veteran stability, and certainly did that, but also came through with bizarre numbers in 1999: 38 home runs, 112 RBI, and 132 runs scored.
SS	Tony Womack	1999–*2002*	One of the fastest men in the game, led NL with 72 steals in 1999 and with 14 triples in 2000, then played brilliantly down the stretch in 2001.
3B	Matt Williams	1998–*2002*	Like Bell, acquired before the franchise's first season to provide stability and respectability, and even with the ups and downs, he delivered.
LF	Luis Gonzalez	1999–*2002*	Pretty good player with Astros, Cubs, and Tigers became superstar after hooking up with D'backs when he was thirty-one; rapped World Series–winning hit in 2001, of course.
CF	Steve Finley	1999–*2002*	Following a bad year with Padres, joined D'backs and got his career going again, swatting 69 homers and scoring 200 runs in his first two seasons.
RF	Danny Bautista	2000–*2002*	Came in trade shortly after twenty-eighth birthday, and topped .300 in each of his first two seasons; fine glove, and knocked in 5 runs in Game 6 of 2001 World Series.
SP1	Randy Johnson	1999–*2002*	After winning one Cy Young award in his first 11 seasons, joined D'backs when he was thirty-five and started winning Cy Youngs *every year.*
SP2	Curt Schilling	2000–*2002*	In 2001, he and Big Unit gave Arizona the best one-two combination that anybody could remember, and the pair practically won the World Series all by themselves.
SP3	Brian Anderson	1998–2002	The Diamondbacks' first pick in the expansion draft, and the club's best pitcher in that first season, going 12-13 with a 4.33 ERA for a team that lost 97 games.
SP4	Omar Daal	1998–2000	Got off to a brutal start in 2000 before getting traded, but in '98 and '99 he went 24-21 with 3.32 ERA, and tossed club's first shutout (7/30/98); fooled 'em with slow stuff.
RP	Byung-Hyun Kim	1999–*2002*	As a submariner who actually throws *hard*, Kim is unique among his contemporaries; prone to wildness and gopher balls, but phenomenal strikeout rate heals all.

There are, of course, any number of amazing things about Randy Johnson. But in the context of the Arizona Diamondbacks, what's most amazing has been Johnson's consistency. In his first three seasons with the club, the Big Unit posted ERA's "ranging" from 2.48 through 2.64. In each of the three seasons, he started either thirty-four or thirty-five games (and it would have been thirty-five each season if he hadn't sat out his last scheduled start in 2001 to prepare for the postseason). In each of the three seasons, he led the National League in strikeouts, with the numbers ranging from 347 to 327. And Johnson's Win Shares for those three seasons? Twenty-six, twenty-six . . . and twenty-six.

Johnson put together a similarly consistent set of three seasons nearly a decade earlier. In 1990, 1991, and 1992, he led the American League in walks each season, won between twelve and fourteen games each season, and posted an ERA between 3.65 and 3.98 each season. But while he was certainly consistent, he certainly was not great. The greatness would come in 1995 and 1997, but it wasn't until he combined the greatness with consistency that Johnson cemented his eventual spot in the Hall of Fame.

There are a lot of things to remember about the 2001 season.

One thing that's often forgotten, though, is that the Diamondbacks came very close to not even *reaching* the postseason. The D'backs finished only two games ahead of the Giants in the National League West, and their ninety-two wins wouldn't have been enough for the Wild Card if they'd finished in second place.

And another thing that's forgotten is that before the season, D'backs general manager Joe Garagiola, Jr., made two moves, both of them questionable at the time, that helped make the difference.

Reggie Sanders was thirty-three years old, coming off a terrible season with the Braves, and Garagiola signed him for the bargain-basement price of $1.5 million for one season. Sanders hit thirty-three homers in 126 games.

Mark Grace was thirty-six years old, coming off a so-so season with the Cubs, and Garagiola signed him to a two-year deal worth six million bucks. I thought Garagiola was a lunatic, considering that he already had Erubiel Durazo on the payroll. But Grace played about as well as he always had, and Durazo gave the D'backs the greatest pinch hitter in the game.

Nobody talks about Garagiola, and he's certainly done a lot of things that I wouldn't have done. But you can't argue with the results.

		YEARS	NOTES
SINGLE SEASON			
C	Damian Miller	2001	On Sept. 22, he collected his 100th hit and D'backs became only seventh NL team in history with nine 100-hit men.
1B	Mark Grace	2001	Batted .298 during regular season and started Game 7 rally with leadoff single against Mariano Rivera.
2B	Jay Bell	1999	In his first season at 2B, enjoyed career year with bat, starting All-Star Game and hitting 38 HR with 112 RBI and 132 runs.
SS	Jay Bell	1998	Homered in the last game of the season to reach 20; played the last 15 games at his new position, second base.
3B	Matt Williams	1999	Player of the Month in April, started the All-Star Game, and wound up with 142 RBI, destroying his previous best.
LF	Luis Gonzalez	2001	Who knew? At thirty-three, hit 57 homers, 26 more than he ever had before, and finished season with World Series–clinching hit.
CF	Steve Finley	2000	Hit 27th homer on July 21, but finished with just 35 due to back and hand injuries; won second straight Gold Glove.
RF	Reggie Sanders	2001	Just a Diamondback for one season, but clubbed career-high 33 homers—16 of them against NL West clubs.
SP	Randy Johnson	2001	Not enough room here . . . 372 strikeouts, 2.49 ERA, third straight Cy Young, and *three* wins over Yanks in Series.
RP	Byung-Hyun Kim	2001	Maybe the World Series should disqualify him, but he posted 2.94 ERA in regular season and was nearly perfect in NLCS.

		YEARS	NOTES
GOLD GLOVE			
C	Damian Miller	1998–2002	Strong and accurate throwing arm, and of course in 2001 he happened to catch the two best pitchers in the league.
1B	Mark Grace	2001–2002	Even at thirty-seven, the four-time Gold Glove winner still one of the league's best.
2B	Jay Bell	1998–2002	Slowing down at SS, Bell made the switch to 2B late in the '98 season and became at least competent.
SS	Tony Womack	1999–2002	Interesting role reversal, as when Womack was a Pirate he shifted to second so Bell could stay at shortstop.
3B	Matt Williams	1998–2002	A few years past his prime, but then again he doesn't have any competition at all.
LF	David Dellucci	1998–2002	Doesn't throw particularly well, but does have excellent range and could play center field for some teams.
CF	Steve Finley	1999–2002	Won Gold Gloves his first two seasons with club, got great jumps and threw accurately, if not powerfully.
RF	Danny Bautista	2000–2002	Speedy enough to play CF and strong enough for RF, but will occasionally let loose a wild throw.
P	Brian Anderson	1998–2002	Solid fielder with one of the game's best moves to first base; tied for league lead in pickoffs in '98 and 2000.

STUMBLING TO GLORY

Sometimes, as they say, it's better to be lucky than good.

And while Bob Brenly certainly had some good players in the 2001 World Series, he was also very, very lucky. Because Brenly probably did as many stupid things as a manager can do and still *win* a World Series.

One of the odd things about the Series was this: Brenly made two terrible moves with his pitching staff, and yet he got blasted by the baseball writers just once . . . and that was for a move that actually made sense.

Going into the Series against the dynastic Yankees, the big question was, would Brenly get four starts from his aces, or five? Actually, there was another big question, too: if Brenly would ask Randy Johnson or Curt Schilling to start three games, which one? They totaled virtually the same number of innings during the regular season, and Johnson's ERA was significantly better during the regular season. But where Johnson was number one in the National League, Schilling was number two. Both were well rested; the Diamondbacks had knocked out the Braves on October 21, six days before the first game of the World Series.

Brenly chose Schilling for the opener. It was a questionable decision, but Brenly probably deserved the benefit of the doubt on that one; presumably, he knew which of his aces was better equipped to start twice on three days' rest.

Schilling was great in Game 1, the Yankees weren't. After four innings, the Diamondbacks led 9–1. After five innings, the Diamondbacks still led 9–1. Schilling had his *W* in the bag. Time to turn this one over to the pen, and get an early start on resting up for Game 4.

But Schilling pitched on.

After six innings, the Diamondbacks still led 9–1.

And Schilling pitched on.

Finally, in the bottom of the seventh, Brenly did what he should have done in the bottom of the fifth: he replaced his starter with a pinch hitter. Curt Schilling left the game after throwing 102 pitches.

Johnson started Game 2 and fired a three-hit shutout. Brian Anderson and a pair of relievers pitched well in Game 3, but Roger Clemens and Mariano Rivera pitched better.

So three days after Game 1, it's Schilling's turn again in Game 4. He was great . . . but after seven innings he was also gassed. Brenly took him out, the game tied at one run apiece. Arizona took a 3–1 lead in the top of the eighth, but then with two outs in the bottom of the ninth, Tino Martinez tied the game with a two-run homer off Byung-Hyun Kim. The Diamondbacks didn't score in the tenth. And then, with two outs (of course) in the bottom of the tenth, Derek Jeter hit *another* homer off Kim to end the game.

The media jumped on Brenly for taking Schilling out of the game. That wasn't fair; Brenly had ample evidence that Schilling was indeed tiring. A smaller portion of the media jumped on Brenly for sending Kim out for the tenth, his third inning. That might have been fair; he'd pitched three full innings in a game just once all season, and that was way back on May 18.

But what everybody somehow missed was Brenly's *big* mistake, which was letting Schilling pitch seven innings in Game 1. If Schilling had pitched just five or six innings in the opener, isn't it *likely* that he could have gone more than seven innings in Game 4? If Schilling had lasted eight innings in Game 4, isn't it *likely* that Kim would have finished off the Yankees in the ninth? Kim retired five of the first six Yankees he faced, four of them on strikeouts. (Of course, all this assumes that Schilling couldn't have pitched the ninth inning himself. And if he'd thrown twenty-five or thirty fewer pitches in Game 1, maybe he could have.)

Okay, so Brenly screwed up. He didn't rest his pitcher when he had the chance, and it probably cost him a World Series game. But Brenly's a smart fellow, and so he learned from his mistake, right?

Nope. Brenly made almost *exactly* the same mistake in Game 6.

But I'm getting ahead of myself. The Yankees won Game 5 when Kim gave up another walk-off homer. Some probably criticized Brenly for going to Kim again, just twenty-four hours after he got blasted in Game 4. But unless he was tired, there wasn't any reason to dump him from his normal role. It just didn't work out.

Randy Johnson hadn't started Game 5, because Brenly figured—correctly, I thought—that if the Big Unit could start just once more, he might as well start on four days rest rather than three. As it turned out, though, even Randy *Jones*—yes, even at fifty-one years of age—probably could have beaten the Yankees in Game 6, because the Diamondbacks scored fifteen runs in the first four innings.

Fifteen. So did Brenly get Johnson out of the game, in case he was needed for relief duties in Game 7?

Nope. The D'backs led 15–0 after five innings. Johnson pitched on. The D'backs led 15–0 after six innings. Johnson pitched on. Finally, in the bottom of the seventh, Brenly did what he should have done in the fifth inning; he replaced his starter with a pinch hitter. Johnson had thrown 103 pitches, limiting—and perhaps *eliminating*—his usefulness as a reliever in Game 7.

Schilling started the finale, again on three days' rest. And again he pitched well, shutting out the Yankees for six innings before wavering in the seventh; the Yanks scored once to tie the game (Roger Clemens pitched well, too). New York took the lead in the eighth when Alfonso Soriano led off with a home run. After an out and a single, Miguel Batista replaced Schilling, and Batista got Jeter to hit into a fielder's choice. With left-handed-hitting Paul O'Neill up next, Brenly went to the mound and summoned . . . Randy Johnson from the bullpen.

Which raises the question, if Brenly was even *considering* using Johnson in relief, then why on earth did he let Johnson throw 103 pitches in Game 6? Fortunately for Brenly, Johnson showed no ill effects in Game 7, retiring all four hitters he faced. And the rest, as they say, is history.

Bob Brenly made two great decisions in the 2001 World Series. He chose Curt Schilling to start three games, and he sent Randy Johnson to the bullpen in Game 7. But those great decisions were nearly undone by his ridiculous obeisance to the notion that it's somehow unmanly for a starting pitcher to come out of a game simply because his team has a huge lead.

Randy Johnson, Curt Schilling, and some guy we couldn't afford to airbrush out of the photo
Courtesy Arizona Diamondbacks

ATLANTA BRAVES

		YEARS	NOTES
C	Javy Lopez	1992–2002	Greg Maddux didn't like to pitch to him; but then, neither did enemy pitchers; .478 career slugging percentage made him No. 2–hitting catcher in NL after Piazza.
1B	Fred McGriff	1993–1997	Can't pin Atlanta's October flops on the Crime Dog; in postseason games he homered every 17 AB and his 993 OPS was 108 points *better* than his regular-season mark.
2B	Glenn Hubbard	1978–1987	Great-field, no-hit player who placed first or second in range factor each year from '82 to '87, and should have won two or three Gold Gloves rather than zero.
SS	Jeff Blauser	1987–1997	If you could live with his inconsistent hitting and his consistently mediocre defense, Blauser could be a big help with his mid-range power.
3B	Chipper Jones	1993–2002	Career got started a year late, as he tore a knee ligament early in '94 and missed that season, but he's still got a decent shot at the Hall of Fame, left field and all.
LF	Rico Carty	1966–1972	An even more injured version of Tony Oliva, Carty played more than 150 games only once in his 15-year career and missed all of 1968 with tuberculosis.
CF	Dale Murphy	1976–1990	Came to majors as a catcher, shifted to first base, and was finally moved to CF by Bobby Cox in 1980; won back-to-back MVP's and played in seven All-Star Games.
RF	Hank Aaron	1966–1974	Aaron did play a lot of first base and left field in Atlanta, but he also hit 335 HR for Braves after move, as Fulton County helped make up for Milwaukee's County.
SP1	Greg Maddux	1993–2002	Nearly a decade ago, I dubbed Maddux "The Smartest Pitcher Who Ever Lived," and he's done nothing since to make me regret that label.
SP2	Phil Niekro	1966–1983 1987	Knuckleballer began and ended his career with Braves, and most of his best seasons were buried by less-talented teammates; tops Atlanta list with 268 wins.
SP3	Tom Glavine	1987–2002	Since beginning his professional career nearly 20 years ago, has hit the Disabled list exactly *never*; only Glavine and Robin Roberts have led majors in starts six times.
SP4	John Smoltz	1988–2002	In his best season, Smoltz won more games—24—than Maddux or Glavine ever did; elbow woes eventually cost him spot in rotation and already-slim Hall chances.
RP	Gene Garber	1978–1987	Sidearmer with great change-up still holds franchise record with 141 saves, and he stopped Pete Rose's 44-game hitting streak with a sloppy strikeout.

John Smoltz was something of a late bloomer.

To be sure, he showed great early promise. In his first full season, Smoltz posted a 2.94 ERA in twenty-nine starts. Three years later, in 1992, Smoltz went 15-11 with a 2.85 ERA. But after eight seasons, it would have been hard to make a convincing argument that Smoltz was a great pitcher. His career statistics after the 1994 season included ninety wins, eighty-two losses, and a 3.53 ERA. Even worse, he underwent elbow surgery that off-season.

Then again, maybe elbow surgery was all that he'd been missing. Because when Smoltz returned in 1995, he became a star. From '95 through '99, Smoltz went 79-38 with a 2.77 ERA, all the more impressive considering what the hitters were doing in those years.

Then he got hurt again. Another elbow injury. Smoltz missed the entire 2000 season, and could pitch only fifty-nine innings in 2001. Nevertheless, following that season—in which Smoltz saved ten games, the first ten saves of his career—the Braves rewarded him with a new three-year contract for thirty million dollars. "Madness!" I thought (and wrote). But if there's one thing the Braves know, it's pitching. And in 2002, the National League's second-best closer was . . . John Smoltz.

✍Isn't it wonderful when perception meets reality?

It's generally assumed that if a player *looks* great with the glove, then of course he *is* great. If you think about it, there's no logical reason why this must be so. There are hitters with beautiful swings—Travis Lee comes to mind—who aren't great hitters. There are pitchers who throw awesome pitches, but aren't great pitchers. So why couldn't there be fielders who make amazing plays, but aren't great fielders?

The answer, of course, is that there are. Omar Vizquel is one of those, but I don't mean to pick on him. There have been plenty of Gold Glovers over the years who were good, but not great.

Andruw Jones is great, though. It's a truism in baseball that "fielding stats don't mean anything," and it's actually true . . . to a point. If you just look at the raw stats, you can certainly be fooled, so a lot of people just choose to ignore them altogether. And fielding stats can be tricky even if you look at them with some sophistication. So what I look for are players with great defensive stats *and* great defensive reputations.

And that's Andruw Jones. Bobby Cox says that Jones is the best he's seen since Willie Mays, and the numbers suggest that Jones is the best since Willie Mays. At least.

		YEARS	NOTES
		NO. 2	
C	Joe Torre	1966–1968	Very good hitter during era when catchers didn't produce a lot; two NL catchers had 100+ RBI seasons in the '50s and '60s: Campanella three times, and Torre twice.
1B	Chris Chambliss	1980–1986	Chambliss is one of two Braves over the past 100 years to start at first for at least five straight seasons; Cepeda had better seasons but was the regular for only two years.
2B	Felix Millan	1966–1972	Good fielder, so-so hitter who epitomized middle infielders in the '60s and '70s; Braves gave up on him too early, getting Buzz Capra in bad exchange with Mets.
SS	Rafael Ramirez	1980–1987	Raffy put up a couple of freaky stats during his pretty average career: he hit into 21 double plays in '85 and was thrown out stealing in 17 of his 31 attempts in '84.
3B	Darrell Evans	1969–1976 1989	Never got the credit as a fielder or hitter that he deserved; just a .246 average as a Brave, but OBP was still better than batting champ/teammate Ralph Garr's.
LF	Ryan Klesko	1992–1999	Always seemed to be more defined by expectations than by what he actually produced; fifth on Braves' all-time OPS list and hit three homers in '95 World Series.
CF	Andruw Jones	1996–*2002*	Fantastic player who hits home runs, steals bases, and plays defense like nobody since Mays; youngest player (nineteen) in World Series history to hit a home run. ✍
RF	David Justice	1989–1996	Key player as Braves transformed themselves from TBS filler to legit team; played more postseason games (112) than any other player, 46 of them with Braves.
SP1	Pat Jarvis	1966–1972	Dependable starter behind Niekro, thanks to good fastball and curve; Mets hammered him for 6 runs in critical Game 3 that decided 1969 NLCS.
SP2	Kevin Millwood	1997–2002	Looked like the next Smoltz in 1999, when he went 18-7 and tossed a one-hitter; shoulder problems diverted his path to stardom, but he bounced back nicely in 2002.
SP3	Denny Neagle	1996–1998	NL's only 20-game winner in '97 went 38-19 as a Brave; of his 7 career shutouts, 6 came with Atlanta even though he made only 71 of his 279 career starts for them.
SP4	Carl Morton	1973–1976	Started pro career as outfielder in Braves' system, was Rookie of the Year with Expos, returned to Atlanta and won as many games (48) as Niekro from '73 through '75.
RP	Mark Wohlers	1991–1999	Gave up the big homer to Leyritz in '96, but that same season he set franchise record with 39 saves and he's No. 2 on the franchise list with 112.

		YEARS	NOTES
SINGLE SEASON			
C	Javy Lopez	1998	Set franchise highs for catcher with 34 homers and 106 RBI, and beginning on August 29 homered in four straight games.
1B	Hank Aaron	1971	Yes, first base. In '71, Aaron played 60 games in the outfield and 71 at 1B; 47 homers and NL-best .669 slug.
2B	Davey Johnson	1973	After hitting 5 home runs with Orioles in '72, joined Braves and hit *43* homers . . . then back down to 15 bombs in '74.
SS	Jeff Blauser	1997	Coming off three subpar seasons, batted .308 with 17 home runs and 70 walks; power disappeared with Cubs in '98.
3B	Chipper Jones	1999	Like Terry Pendleton in '91, Chipper won MVP; Chipper's big edge with bat trumps Pendleton's big edge with glove.
LF	Rico Carty	1970	Crashed into public consciousness with .366 batting average, tops in National League; 101 RBI, too.
CF	Dale Murphy	Pick	MVP Awards in 1982 and '83 (when Braves contended), and was almost exactly as good in '84 and '85 (when they didn't).
RF	Hank Aaron	1969	Put together one of his greatest seasons—44 homers and .607 slugging—to lead Atlanta to first postseason berth.
SP	Greg Maddux	1995	Not easy to choose, but in '95 he went 19-2 with unbelievable 1.63 ERA to capture unprecedented fourth straight Cy Young.
RP	Gene Garber	1982	Recorded career-high 30 saves with 2.34 ERA for division winners, and the real plus is that he also pitched 119 innings.

		YEARS	NOTES
ALL-ROOKIE			
C	Earl Williams	1971	Couldn't really catch, but he hit 33 homers so they lived with him back there; 72 games at catcher, 73 at corners.
1B	David Justice	1990	A lovely surprise, as Justice's doubles power in the minors transmogrified into homers power in the majors.
2B	Ron Gant	1988	No, he couldn't play second base any more than your grandma could; what he *could* do was hit 19 homers in 146 games.
SS	Rafael Furcal	2000	Made the jump from Class A to winning Rookie of the Year honors, impressive even if he *wasn't* nineteen (which he wasn't).
3B	Chipper Jones	1995	Just edges Bob Horner, largely on strength of .364 average and 8 RBI in 14 postseason games.
LF	Ryan Klesko	1994	Limited by both the strike and Bobby Cox's platoon, Klesko hit 17 homers in only 245 at-bats.
CF	Andruw Jones	1997	Hit 18 homers, played defense like nobody, and set an odd record with only 55 singles in 150 (or more) games.
RF	Jermaine Dye	1996	He didn't play all that much, but is literally the only candidate and did slug .459 in 98 games, 292 at-bats.
SP	Craig McMurtry	1983	Didn't have great stuff, but came to majors with four pitches and veteran smarts, and won 15 games with 3.09 ERA.
RP	Kerry Ligtenberg	1998	Wohlers is hurt? No problem; we'll just take this refugee from the Prairie League and he'll save 30 games for us.

When it comes to pitchers, Braves manager Bobby Cox and pitching coach Leo Mazzone will be remembered for the big stars: Maddux, Glavine, and Smoltz. And to be sure, Cox and Mazzone should be commended for developing Glavine and Smoltz, and for keeping Maddux healthy enough to win nearly three hundred games (so far).

However, I think that Cox and Mazzone don't get nearly enough credit for their ability to build bullpens. A few somewhat random highlights . . .

In 1991, Juan Berenguer, Mike Stanton, Kent Mercker, and Marvin Freeman combined for thirty-one saves and a 2.66 ERA in 264 innings. In 1993, change-up artist Greg McMichael—not even considered much of a prospect before the season—took over as closer in late July and finished with nineteen saves and a 2.06 ERA. In 1998, with Mark Wohlers going through a career crisis, the Braves turned to Kerry Ligtenberg, who saved thirty games. The next season, Ligtenberg was hurt . . . but nobody noticed, because John Rocker saved *thirty-eight* games.

More recently, Cox and Mazzone have gotten wonderful work from Mike Remlinger, Chris Hammond, John Smoltz, and of course Tim Spooneybarger. Mazzone has his own ideas about conditioning the arms of relief pitchers, but just as important are his and Cox's ability to *see* which pitchers can thrive in the bullpen.

Two facts.

In 2001, the Braves finished *thirteenth* in the National League with 729 runs.

In 2001, Bret Boone and Ryan Klesko combined for sixty-seven home runs and 254 runs batted in.

And here's a third fact: in 1999, both Boone and Klesko were property of those same Atlanta Braves. But should the Braves have kept Boone and Klesko? And just as important, *could* they have?

On December 22, 1999, the Braves traded Boone, Klesko, and minor-league pitcher Jason Shiell to San Diego for Quilvio Veras, Wally Joyner, and Reggie Sanders. In 2000, Boone and Klesko collectively earned thirty-eight Win Shares at a cost of $9.6 million; Veras, Joyner, and Sanders earned twenty-six Win Shares at a cost of slightly more than ten million dollars.

Big edge for Padres . . . after which it's hard to figure, because Boone became a free agent and signed with Seattle, for whom he enjoyed his career year. Sanders also became a free agent, signed with Arizona at a substantial pay cut, and had a great year for the Diamondbacks.

We already know what Boone and Klesko did in 2001. Limited by injuries, Veras didn't play well for the Braves. So, all things considered, the Braves would have been better off keeping Boone and Klesko. However, there's no way to know if either would have played as well if they'd stayed in Atlanta.

HOMEGROWN			
		YEARS	NOTES
C	Javy Lopez	1991–*2002*	Native of Puerto Rico excelled in volleyball while attending Academia Cristo Rey.
1B	Gerald Perry	1983–1989	Uh, not exactly a position of organizational strength, though Klesko and Justice both could fit here.
2B	Felix Millan	1966–1972	Puerto Rican drafted from A's after his first pro season (1964), and established himself in majors four years later.
SS	Jeff Blauser	1987–1997	Rafael Furcal might one day take this spot, but at this moment he's still a few years behind Blauser.
3B	Chipper Jones	1993–2001	The Braves grabbed him with the first pick in '90 draft because they didn't want to pay Todd Van Poppel.
LF	Ryan Klesko	1992–1999	Fifth-round pick in '89, hit 2 HR in first 42 pro contests but in '93 dropped 22 bombs in 98 minor-league games.
CF	Dale Murphy	1976–1990	Gotta go with Murphy, of course, but in a few years Andruw Jones should be making a bid.
RF	David Justice	1989–1996	Just another great Cincinnati ballplayer; Braves' fourth-round pick in '85 out of small Kentucky college.
SP	Tom Glavine	1987–*2002*	Outstanding hockey player drafted by L.A. Kings, but signed with Braves as second-round draft pick instead.
RP	Mark Wohlers	1991–1998	How did the Red Sox let him get away? Wohlers a Mass. native, grabbed by Braves in eighth round of '88 draft.

TRADED AWAY			
		TRADED	NOTES
C	Vacant	—	The Braves have never traded a catcher who later made a good accounting of himself.
1B	Darrell Evans	June 13, 1976	Traded to Giants in midst of his worst season; Braves did get a good year of Willie Montanez in deal.
2B	Bret Boone	December 22, 1999	Went to S.D. with Klesko in blockbuster that netted Reggie Sanders, Quilvio Veras, and Wally Joyner.
SS	Denis Menke	October 8, 1967	Looked like superstar in '64, but Braves gave up on him three years later; two big years for Astros.
3B	Joe Torre	March 17, 1969	Cards got Torre (whose stats skyrocketed) and Braves got Cepeda (who did have one big year left in him).
LF	Dusty Baker	November 17, 1975	Looked great in '76, as Dusty played terribly for Dodgers; not so good afterward, when he starred.
CF	Brett Butler	October 21, 1983	Part of a terrible deal that sent Butler *and* Brook Jacoby to Cleveland for Len Barker.
RF	Gary Matthews	March 25, 1981	Straight up for young Bob Walk, and both players still had plenty of good ball to play.
SP	Joe Niekro	April 6, 1975	Braves could have had *both* Niekros in their primes, but instead they sold Joe to Astros for 35 grand.
RP	Ron Reed	May 28, 1975	Ex-NBAer had always been a starter, but in '76 he began long run as one of NL's top relievers.

GOLD GLOVE			
		YEARS	**NOTES**
C	Eddie Perez	1995–2001	One of the slowest men in the game, but he had some power and Greg Maddux loved pitching to him.
1B	Sid Bream	1991–1993	Acquired for express purpose of shoring up defense, and Braves reached World Series in his first season.
2B	Mark Lemke	1988–1997	Glenn Hubbard was also outstanding; he and Lemke rank among the greatest ever, for any franchise.
SS	Walt Weiss	1998–2000	Historically, a weak spot for Braves; Weiss old but still good, made game-saving play in Game 3 of 1999 NLDS.
3B	Clete Boyer	1967–1971	In his prime, just as good as Brooks but stuck in the same league; garnered his one Gold Glove in 1969.
LF	Ralph Garr	1969–1975	Not a *good* left fielder, exactly, but there ain't much to choose from and at least he could outrun his mistakes.
CF	Andruw Jones	1996–*2002*	Your eyes don't deceive, Bobby Cox . . . Jones really *is* the greatest defensive center fielder since Willie Mays.
RF	Brian Jordan	1999–2001	Has to be classed as disappointment with the bat, but speed and strength of ex-NFLer made for great D.
P	Phil Niekro	1964–1983 1987	My pick is Niekro, who won five Gold Gloves and employed one of the game's great pickoff moves.

IRON GLOVE			
		YEARS	**NOTES**
C	Dale Murphy	1976–1979	Over four seasons, Murphy caught 85 games and developed mental block about throwing to pitcher.
1B	Mike Lum	1973–1975 1979–1980	Solid outfielder, but in his sixth season the Braves moved him to first base with ill effects.
2B	Ron Gant	1987–1988	After this didn't work, they tried him at third base in '89, with even worse results; born an outfielder.
SS	Marty Perez	1971–1974	After three years, Braves figured out that he wasn't a shortstop . . . and they gave the job to Larvell Blanks?
3B	Chipper Jones	1995–2001	A great hitter, so everybody agreed to ignore the obvious defensive inadequacies for seven years.
LF	Rico Carty	1964–1972	Converted catcher started career as liability, and various injuries over the years didn't exactly help.
CF	Mack Jones	1961–1963 1965–1967	Plenty of speed for center, but lacked instincts for the position; helluva hitter, though.
RF	Gary Sheffield	*2002*	Tough choice between him and Jeff Burroughs; both preferred to save themselves for more important work.
P	Terry Forster	1983–1985	Being a "fat tub of goo" didn't seem to affect his pitching one bit, but he couldn't field or hold runners.

A lot of people aren't going to buy Phil Niekro as the Braves' best-fielding pitcher. Yes, he won five Gold Gloves. But Greg Maddux won *thirteen* Gold Gloves (through 2002), including ten while a Brave, becoming as automatic as Jim Kaat once was.

Maddux was perennially one of the easiest pitchers to run against in the game, though, especially from 1993 through 1996, when runners with larceny in their hearts were successful slightly more than eighty percent of the time. Shouldn't shutting down the running game be considered when evaluating a pitcher's defensive contribution? Of course it should.

On the other hand, should the knuckleballing Niekro be held accountable for the passed balls and wild pitches? No, I don't think so. Passed balls and wild pitches should certainly be considered when one is evaluating Niekro's overall contribution, but I do not think they are germane to a discussion of his *defense*.

Maddux did pile up a ton of assists, but the great majority of those came after he made a good pitch that resulted in an easy comebacker. He was, and still is, a fine defender with good reflexes and an accurate arm, but I cannot in good conscience rubber-stamp all those Gold Gloves without a good reason.

In 1979, the Braves used their first pick—the fourth overall—in the June draft to select outfielder Brad Komminsk. In his very first professional at-bat, Komminsk hit a home run. In his second pro season, he hit twenty home runs. In his third pro season, he was named the Carolina League's Most Valuable Player. In his fourth pro season, he hit twenty-eight home runs.

When Komminsk opened his fifth pro season, with the Braves' Triple-A farm club, he was still only twenty-two years old, and all he did was bat .334 with twenty-four homers—and, lest we ignore an important skill, seventy-eight walks—in only 117 games. So when he played in his first major-league game on August 14, 1983, there was every reason to think he'd become a star.

It didn't happen. Komminsk spent most of 1984 and all of 1985 with the big club, but didn't hit. In 1986, the Braves sent him back to Triple-A, where he played a lot of third base and still didn't hit. In fact, aside from a nice year (1987) with the Brewers' Triple-A team in Denver, Komminsk never really hit again. After leaving the Braves, Komminsk played in the majors for five different franchises, each of them hoping he'd get back to where he'd been in his early twenties. Which he never did, finishing his career with a .218 batting average.

ALL-BUST

		YEARS	NOTES
C	Jody Davis	1988–1990	An All-Star with the Cubs in 1984 and '86, came to the other superstation team and batted .161 in 92 games.
1B	Nick Esasky	1990	Signed as free agent after solid 1989 with Red Sox, then played only 9 more MLB games because of vertigo.
2B	Damaso Garcia	1987–1988	Came to Atlanta with Bobby Cox, and totaled 7 hits in two seasons, for which he was paid cool $1.4 million.
SS	Larvell Blanks	1975	He played 141 games, including 129 at SS; spent another five seasons in majors, but never played that much again.
3B	Vinny Castilla	2002	More proof that Schuerholz ain't perfect; they moved Chipper to LF, and gave Castilla eight million dollars?
LF	Brad Komminsk	1983–1986	Fourth overall pick in '79 draft ran up impeccable track record in minors, but never found his stroke in majors.
CF	Oddibe McDowell	1990	Hit like gangbusters after coming over in mid-season '89, but batting average dropped 61 points in '90.
RF	Brian Jordan	1999–2001	Some will quibble, but the Braves signed Jordan for an immense amount of money and got an average player.
SP	Len Barker	1983–1985	Getting hammered in Cleveland, but Braves gave up Brett Butler and Brook Jacoby for him anyway.
RP	Bruce Sutter	1985–1988	After 45 saves in 1984, signed with Braves for $10 million and totaled 40 saves in four years before retiring.

USED-TO-BE-GREAT

		YEARS	NOTES
C	Ted Simmons	1986–1988	Last three seasons, even though he couldn't really hit anymore and didn't belong in the field at all.
1B	Wally Joyner	2000	At thirty-eight, was signed to spell Galarraga, and posted OBP (.365) right in line with career mark.
2B	Julio Franco	2001–2002	Of course, he never played an inning at second for Braves but, way back when, he was an All-Star 2B.
SS	Zoilo Versalles	1971	Finished career with .191 batting average—albeit with a touch of power—in 66 games as 3B/SS.
3B	Darrell Evans	1989	Braves never should have let him get away in the first place, but at forty-two he didn't have a whole lot left.
LF	Bernard Gilkey	2001	One of the all-time up-and-down careers ended with only 106 at-bats, and zero in postseason.
CF	Jim Wynn	1976	Statistically, the ultimate destination of Wynn's career: 17 homers, 127 walks . . . and .207 batting average.
RF	Ken Griffey	1986–1988	Did his best work for Reds and Yanks, but did bat .308 with pop in '86 after coming over in mid-season deal.
SP	Phil Niekro	1987	After nearly four seasons in American League, returned to make one last start for Braves, on September 27.
RP	Hoyt Wilhelm	1969–1970 1971	In '70, his only (almost) full season with Braves, posted 3.10 ERA in 78 innings . . . at forty-eight.

THE NAME OF THE GAME IS BLAME

Last summer in *Sports Illustrated*, Tom Verducci wrote, "Over the last decade . . . in which the Braves have won 10 straight division titles but only one World Series championship, playoff opponents have survived Atlanta's elite starters and feasted on its unreliable bullpen."

Verducci's got a wonderful way with words, but occasionally his facility with facts leaves something to be desired. So I thought I'd check. . . . Can we lay the Braves' failure to win more than one World Series at the foot of the bullpen?

To answer this question, I focused on the Braves' postseason losses; that is, every postseason game they lost from 1991 through 2002. There are forty-nine of them, and I entered the pitching lines for every Braves pitcher in each of those forty-nine games, with one sheet for the starters and another for the relievers.

Rather than bore you with more unnecessary details of the process, I'll get right to the product: Atlanta's relievers have not, on the whole, pitched poorly in the postseason. Actually, that's not putting it kindly enough. I suspect that if I checked all of the Braves' postseason games, rather than just the losses, I'd find that Atlanta's relievers have pitched damn close to brilliantly. But even in the losses, they've been pretty good. Here are the stats for the relievers *and* the starters in those forty-nine postseason losses:

	Innings	Hits/9	W/9	K/9	ERA	Losses
Starters	281	9.6	3.9	7.2	4.55	35
Reliefers	142	7.5	5.2	7.7	3.41	14

Even when you consider the inherent advantage relievers have in ERA—because they're not responsible for inherited runners—it's hard to argue that the relievers have been any worse than the starters. But again, that's not fair. Given the competition, both the relievers *and* the starters have generally pitched well, especially considering that we're considering only the losses.

Of course, those stats don't tell the whole story. But if you go through those forty-nine losses, game by game, you'll find that for every awful performance by the bullpen, there have been a couple of awful performances by a starter.

So where does this notion come from, that the relievers are to blame? Part of it, I think, is that Atlanta's starters are *so* good during the regular season, and of course baseball's all about pitching (isn't it?), so who does that leave? Right, the bullpen.

The bigger reasons, though, are two games and two home runs. In Game 6 of the 1991 World Series, Kirby Puckett beat the Braves with a home run off Charlie Leibrandt. In Game 4 of the 1996 World Series, Jim Leyritz helped beat the Braves with a home run off Mark Wohlers.

I'm sure you remember . . . and that's the problem, isn't it? Forty-nine losses in the postseason, and we remember those two.

But if you really want to blame somebody, then blame Atlanta's hitters for not scoring enough runs, or blame Atlanta's general manager for not getting better hitters. But leave the relief pitchers alone, because they've been getting a bum rap.

I'm grateful to Royce Webb for his editorial suggestions.

In 1955, the Baltimore Orioles signed two high-school third basemen who would enjoy long careers in the major leagues.

Wayne Causey, from Ruston, Louisiana, was inked to a deal that paid him a $35,000 signing bonus. Brooks Robinson, from Little Rock, Arkansas, was inked to a deal that paid him more than $30,000 less. And it was probably the best thing that ever happened to him.

At the time, there was this idiotic rule that if you paid a guy more than $4,000 to sign a professional contract, then you had to place him on the major-league roster and keep him there for two years. And that's why Wayne Causey was playing for the Baltimore Orioles when he was eighteen. In three seasons, he played in 135 games . . . and batted .187 with two homers and fourteen RBI. Causey finally went to the minors, was traded to the Kansas City Athletics, and wound up having a decent career with them and the White Sox.

Brooks, on the other hand, got his four grand and went straight to the Piedmont League, where he belonged. He moved up the ladder quickly but he moved at his own pace, and he became the star that Wayne Causey was supposed to become.

BALTIMORE ORIOLES

		YEARS	NOTES
ALL-TIME			
DH	Harold Baines	1993–1995 1997–1999 2000	Maryland native also served three tours with White Sox, and is one of two players in history to play three times with two teams (Bobo Newsom's the other).
C	Rick Dempsey	1976–1986 1992	Yankees castoff wound up catching regularly for O's for 10 years; MVP of '83 World Series thanks to .385 average and five extra-base hits, but defense his forte.
1B	Eddie Murray	1977–1988 1996	Switch-hitter finished with 504 home runs, even though he never hit 35 in a season; in '96, joined Mays and Aaron as only players with 500 homers and 3,000 hits.
2B	Bobby Grich	1970–1976	Stuck behind Davey Johnson for two years, but once he got the job he was the best-hitting *and* -fielding second baseman in the league for four seasons.
SS	Cal Ripken	1981–2001	Add it all up—the defense, the home runs, the Durability with a capital "D"—and there should be little doubt that he's among three greatest SS ever.
3B	Brooks Robinson	1955–1977	With the exception of 1964, he wasn't ever really a great hitter, but he played forever and you've probably heard something about his defense.
LF	Brady Anderson	1988–2001	Played a lot in center, too, but range more suited to one of the corner slots; he had power and patience, and gave the O's one great season and a lot of good ones.
CF	Paul Blair	1964–1976	Had some decent seasons at the plate and once hit 3 homers in one game, but defense was Blair's long suit, as he won eight Gold Gloves and deserved them all.
RF	Frank Robinson	1966–1971	One of the game's best and toughest players; Orioles started going to the World Series the season he arrived, and stopped the season after he left. Coincidence?
SP1	Jim Palmer	1965–1984	Now remembered mostly for his squabbles with Earl Weaver and the underwear ads, rather than for the great fastball, three Cy Youngs, and *eight* 20-win seasons.
SP2	Mike Mussina	1991–2000	Went 147-81 in his 10 seasons with O's, and never had anything like a bad year; threw all the pitches and there wasn't anybody smarter this side of Greg Maddux.
SP3	Dave McNally	1962–1974	From '68 through '71, went 87-31 with a 2.82 ERA; threw solid fastball and one of the league's best curves; traded to Expos for Ken Singleton and Mike Torrez.
SP4	Mike Cuellar	1969–1976	With Palmer and McNally, gave Orioles the best staff in the game; in eight seasons with O's, went 143-88 with 3.18 ERA and won 23 in '69 to share Cy Young with McLain.
RP	Gregg Olson	1988–1993	Served as O's closer for only five seasons, but devastating curve resulted in 160 saves, easily the franchise record; Rookie of the Year in 1989.

		NO. 2	
		YEARS	**NOTES**
DH	Ken Singleton	1975–1984	Took over as the full-time DH in '82; by that point he was painfully slow and grounded into 66 double plays in his last three seasons.
C	Gus Triandos	1955–1962	Stuck behind Yogi in New York, came to O's in *eighteen-player* deal and gave them power; hit 55 homers in 1958 and '59 to earn a spot on "Home Run Derby" (he lost).
1B	Boog Powell	1961–1974	The big fella wasn't real mobile, but he had soft hands around the bag and he could hit the ball a mile; named to four straight All-Star teams (1968–71).
2B	Roberto Alomar	1996–1998	A truly great hitter, of course—on-base ability and speed, plus power rare for middle infielder—and while with O's his defense actually matched its reputation.
SS	Mark Belanger	1965–1981	Reached base only occasionally and had no power at all, but the best defensive shortstop of the 1970s was key piece of three World Series teams.
3B	Doug DeCinces	1973–1981	Had to wait a couple of extra years because O's wouldn't let Brooks go, but at twenty-six he did establish himself as a solid defender and a mid-range power threat.
LF	Don Buford	1968–1972	Fine leadoff man and almost impossible to double up, though limited defensively; stats mysteriously plummeted in '72 and off he went to Japan.
CF	Al Bumbry	1972–1984	Vietnam veteran grabbed Rookie of the Year honors, played great defense, and wound up setting franchise record with 252 steals; struggled badly in October.
RF	Ken Singleton	1975–1984	Switch-hitter came to O's in one of the more lopsided deals in history, and gave club productive combination of power and patience.
SP1	Milt Pappas	1957–1965	Pitching in majors at eighteen, and career record nearly identical to Don Drysdale's, though Pappas's peak wasn't as high; threw one of the game's great sliders.
SP2	Mike Flanagan	1975–1987 1991–1992	From 1977 through '84, no American Leaguer pitched more innings or started more games; threw the last pitch in Memorial Stadium, striking out Travis Fryman.
SP3	Scott McGregor	1976–1988	Spent entire MLB career with Orioles, and from 1978 through '84 went 108-63 with 3.57 ERA; best pitch was a slow curve, nicely complementing high-80s fastball.
SP4	Dennis Martinez	1976–1986	Had a world of stuff, but struggled badly his last four seasons in Baltimore; career didn't really take off until he was traded to Montreal and stopped drinking. ✎
RP	Dick Hall	1961–1966 1969–1971	Came to the majors as outfielder with Pirates and became one of the game's greatest control pitchers; with Orioles, went 65-40 with 2.89 ERA and 58 saves.

✎ Dennis Martinez pitched in the major leagues until he was forty-three, by which point he was *the* most popular man in his native land.

For a while, though, it looked like he was going to piss it all away.

Orioles scout Roy Poitevint discovered Martinez in Nicaragua, and what he discovered was an eighteen-year-old string bean, six feet tall and maybe 140 pounds dripping wet, who nevertheless threw plenty hard and already had a major-league curveball. In Martinez's first two pro seasons, mostly in the Class A Florida State League, he went 31-11 with a 2.34 ERA. The next year, 1976, Martinez led the Triple-A International League in just about everything, then pitched great in a September cup of coffee with the Orioles.

Scott McGregor recalled, "Dennis was amazing. When he threw on the side [between starts], Flanagan and Palmer and I would run out and watch him. We'd go, 'Please, God, let us throw like this.' He had no idea what he was doing, but he had the best arm of all of us."

From 1977 through 1982, Martinez won 81 games and lost 55. But then from 1983 through 1985 he went 26-36 with a 5.46 ERA. Martinez was an alcoholic and got help after the '83 season, but it wasn't until 1987 that he became a quality pitcher again. And by then, he was an Expo.

🗨Ron Hansen could have been Cal Ripken.

No, he wouldn't have played in a gazillion straight games. But you want a power-hitting shortstop who plays Gold Glove defense? That could have been Ron Hansen. And for a few years, it was.

A third baseman coming out of high school, Hansen shifted to shortstop his first season as a pro, 1956, after one of the Orioles' hot short-stop prospects broke a leg. Hansen made a lot of errors at his new position, but he also batted .289 . . . and missed the entire 1957 sea-son with a slipped disk in his back. He came back in 1958 and played poorly, then re-bounded with a fine perfor-mance in 1959; elevated to Class AAA despite his prior struggles, Hansen hit eight-een homers and led PCL shortstops in putouts and as-sists.

The next spring, Hansen won the everyday shortstop job. He was twenty-two years old, and he played bril-liantly: twenty-two homers, eighty-six RBI, and Gold Glove–caliber defense. His hitting slipped badly in 1961, but his defense re-mained great. Then came 1962, a complete disaster, as he batted just .173 when he wasn't wearing a U.S. Army uniform.

The Orioles traded him to Chicago for Luis Aparicio. Hansen found his stroke in 1964, hitting 20 homers, and continued to play top-notch defense. But in '66 he slipped another disk, and was never the same.

		YEARS	NOTES
SINGLE SEASON			
DH	Eddie Murray	1977	At twenty-one, hit 27 homers and slugged .470 while playing 160 games, and won Rookie of the Year honors.
C	Chris Hoiles	1993	Everybody hated his defense, but for two years this guy was a great-hitting catcher.
1B	Eddie Murray	Pick	Murray's 1983 might be the best choice because O's won the World Series, but his adjusted OPS's from 1981 through '84 read 156, 156, 156, and . . . 156.
2B	Bobby Grich	1974	Broke through at the plate with 19 homers and 82 RBI, and was easily best defensive second baseman in the league.
SS	Cal Ripken	1983	He was actually a bit better with the bat in 1984 and '91, but in '83 the Orioles won the World Series, which does count.
3B	Brooks Robinson	1964	In a season that was, it should be said, a bit out of character, Brooks hit 28 homers, led AL with 118 RBI, and was MVP.
LF	Boog Powell	1964	Yes, Boog was once a left fielder, and one of the best; hit 39 homers and topped league with .606 slugging percentage.
CF	Brady Anderson	1996	One of the all-time fluke (or something) seasons; hit 50 homers and slugged .637, *far* exceeding other career bests.
RF	Frank Robinson	1966	First season with O's was best of his career: hit for Triple Crown (.316-49-122) and led O's to first World Series.
SP	Jim Palmer	1975	The greatest of his many great seasons: 23-11 with career-best 2.09 ERA, resulting in his second Cy Young (of three).
RP	Stu Miller	1965	Throwing slow, slower, and slowest, saved 24 games *and* won 14, with brilliant 1.89 ERA in 119 innings.

		YEARS	NOTES
ALL-ROOKIE			
DH	Eddie Murray	1977	Rookie DH'd despite solid skills with glove, because veteran Lee May wasn't ready to move off first base.
C	Dan Graham	1980	Hit .278 with 15 homers in 86 games, then batted .176 in '81 and was never seen again.
1B	Jim Gentile	1960	Slugged .500 and made All-Star team as twenty-six-year-old rookie; as sophomore in '61, hit 46 homers and drove in 141.
2B	Davey Johnson	1966	Hadn't quite learned to hit yet, but did play solid defense for Bal-timore's first pennant winners.
SS	Ron Hansen	1960	Better than Ripken in 1982? Yep. Hansen's OPS was 781, Ripken's was 792, and Hansen was better with the glove.🗨
3B	Craig Worthington	1989	Okay, so he slugged only .384. But he did hit 15 homers, drove in 70 runs, drew 61 walks . . . and there's nobody else.
LF	Al Bumbry	1973	Played only 110 games, but batted .337, led AL with 11 triples, and copped Rookie of the Year honors.
CF	Paul Blair	1965	Sent to Triple-A in mid-season to work on his hitting, but even then his defense reminded people of Curt Flood.
RF	Curt Blefary	1965	Rookie of the Year slugged .470 and drew 88 walks in 144 games; played well in '66 before swing fell apart.
SP	Wally Bunker	1964	His victories matched his age, as the nineteen-year-old went 19-5 with a 2.69 ERA; it was all downhill from there, and fast.
RP	Gregg Olson	1989	In his first full season as pro, took over as closer in May and wound up with 27 saves and 1.69 ERA.

HOMEGROWN		
	YEARS	**NOTES**
DH Don Baylor	1970–1975	No. 2 pick in '67 signed for $7,500; shoulder injury kept him from playing college football (or throwing well).
C Andy Etchebarren	1962 1965–1975	The man with one very large eyebrow got an $85,000 signing bonus when he signed with Orioles in 1961.
1B Eddie Murray	1977–1988 1996	O's spent $16,000 and their third-round pick on Murray in 1973; RH-hitting catcher became switch-hitting 1B.
2B Bobby Grich	1970–1976	Recruited to play quarterback at UCLA, but was eighteenth player selected in '67 draft and signed for $40,000.
SS Cal Ripken	1981–2001	A great pitcher in high school, was last of club's three second-round picks in 1978 and signed for $20K bonus.
3B Brooks Robinson	1955–1977	Orioles beat out the Giants and Reds for Robinson, who got a $4,000 salary and a major-league contract.
LF Boog Powell	1961–1974	Hey, he *was* a left fielder for three years; signed for $25,000 bonus after O's and Cards colluded.
CF Steve Finley	1989–1990	O's got him with thirteenth-round pick in '87 draft after his senior season at Southern Illinois.
RF Tito Francona	1956–1957	Pennsylvanian didn't do much with O's, but later had some big years for Tribe and enjoyed 15-year career.
SP Jim Palmer	1965–1984	Palmer's folks didn't like Paul Richards, then the Astros GM, so he signed with Orioles for $40K instead.
RP Armando Benitez	1994–1998	Granted, he gave up some big homers. But the Dominican who signed in 1990 could really bring it.

TRADED AWAY		
	TRADED	**NOTES**
DH Don Baylor	April 2, 1976	Sent Baylor and Mike Torrez to Oakland for Ken Holtzman and one year of Reggie; didn't quite pay off.
C Mickey Tettleton	January 11, 1991	Power-hitting catcher with patience traded straight up to Tigers for Jeff M. Robinson, who won 4 games.
1B Mike Epstein	May 29, 1967	Destroyed minor-league pitchers for two years to quickly reach majors, but O's already had Boog.
2B Davey Johnson	December 30, 1972	Talk about dealing from strength: Davey one of AL's best 2B, but the O's had Grich, who was better.
SS Ron Hansen	January 14, 1963	Gave the White Sox three solid seasons before a ruptured spinal disk destroyed his ability to hit.
3B Doug DeCinces	January 28, 1982	Didn't really blossom until going to the Angels in strange deal that brought Disco Dan Ford to O's.
LF Lou Piniella	March 10, 1966	Traded to Cleveland for Cam Carreon; but then, a *lot* of teams didn't want Piniella in the 1960s.
CF Steve Finley	January 10, 1991	Sent to Houston with Curt Schilling *and* Pete Harnisch for Glenn Davis. For more, see sidebar.
RF Frank Robinson	December 2, 1971	Basically traded to clear a spot for Baylor, who didn't play particularly well in '72 as O's finished third.
SP Curt Schilling	January 10, 1991	Yes, it was a terrible trade for the O's, but it's probably worth noting that the Astros quickly dumped him, too.
RP José Mesa	July 14, 1992	Always a starter for O's, got off to lousy start and sent to Indians for somebody named Kyle Washington.

On January 10, 1991, the Orioles made the worst trade in franchise history.

Coming to Baltimore: Astros first baseman Glenn Davis.

Going to Houston: Orioles outfielder Steve Finley and Orioles pitchers Pete Harnisch and Curt Schilling.

You know what happened with those guys. Davis, hampered by back problems, struggled terribly in three seasons before retiring. Finley later became one of the best center fielders in the National League, Harnisch turned into a pretty good pitcher, and Schilling won more than 150 games after leaving the Orioles.

But wait, it gets worse. With the Orioles taking on Davis's $3.275 million salary, management was instructed to cut salary somewhere else. And so, a day after trading for Davis, the Orioles did something really stupid: they traded Mickey Tettleton to Detroit for Jeff Robinson, who went 4-9 with a 5.18 ERA for the O's and was released. Meanwhile, Tettleton turned into a hitting machine. Sure, he wasn't much with the glove, but the O's could have used a DH with numbers like Tettleton posted.

At the time of the trade for Davis, it looked pretty good to me. But then, I didn't know about Glenn Davis's back. Neither did the Orioles, apparently, and it cost them dearly, as did their cheapness with Tettleton.

It's not so easy to pick the Orioles' greatest defensive shortstop, and it's really tough to find the Orioles' worst defensive shortstop.

In the 1960s, the two best defensive shortstops in the American League were Ron Hansen and Luis Aparicio. The Orioles had both of them.

In the 1970s, the best defensive shortstop in the American League was Mark Belanger. The Orioles had him.

In the middle 1980s—well, at least from 1983 through 1986—the best defensive shortstop in the American League was Cal Ripken. The Orioles, of course, had him.

Hansen didn't win a Gold Glove in either of his two seasons as the regular, but that was only because Aparicio, still with the White Sox, had a headlock on them. Aparicio won Gold Gloves with the O's in 1964 and '66, and he should have won in '65. With Belanger knocking on the door, the O's traded Little Looie back to the White Sox after the '67 season. Belanger grabbed his first Gold Glove in 1969, and eventually had eight of them in his trophy room (or atop his mantel, or wherever he kept them). Ripken won a couple in the early '90s, but those were due to his reputation and his fielding percentage; he was at his best earlier. And Ripken was succeeded by Mike Bordick, who was very good though not consistently great.

GOLD GLOVE

		YEARS	NOTES
C	Rick Dempsey	1976–1986 1992	Great throwing arm his most obvious attribute, but he was accomplished in every phase of the glove game.
1B	Tony Muser	1975–1977	Very little statistical evidence of his defensive prowess . . . but why else would Weaver have kept him around?
2B	Roberto Alomar	1996–1998	Always acrobatic but didn't become the *best* defensive second baseman around until he teamed with Ripken.
SS	Mark Belanger	1965–1981	Some years his bat so anemic that he shouldn't have been playing, but mostly the tradeoff was worth it.
3B	Brooks Robinson	1955–1977	Garnered *sixteen straight* Gold Gloves (1960–1975) and actually deserved about half of them, no mean feat.
LF	Brady Anderson	1990–1995	Regular for five seasons in left field, where his range and strong arm made him one of the best.
CF	Paul Blair	1964–1976	For five years, 1969 through '73, Blair was the best defensive outfielder in the league; eight Gold Gloves.
RF	Joe Orsulak	1988–1992	Excellent on the fundamentals, and in 1991 he recorded Orioles record 22 baserunner kills (assists).
P	Mike Mussina	1991–2000	Fielded as smartly as he pitched, was almost impossible to run on, and won four Gold Gloves.

IRON GLOVE

		YEARS	NOTES
C	Earl Williams	1973–1974	Absolutely brutal behind the plate, and played a bunch of games at first base just to get his bat in the lineup.
1B	Randy Milligan	1989–1992	Catchers Gus Triandos and Earl Williams were awful when they played first, and Boog was immobile at the end.
2B	Delino DeShields	1999–2001	Arrived as a second baseman, but so shaky afield that he left (in trade to Cubs) as a left fielder.
SS	Melvin Mora	2000–2002	The team of Aparicio, Belanger, and Ripken hasn't ever had a bad defensive shortstop for more than a season.
3B	Wayne Gross	1984–1985	Would have made a great platoon DH for the 2001 Oakland A's, but his defense was simply gross.
LF	Curt Blefary	1965–1968	Fine hitter his first few seasons, then mysteriously lost his swing; nicknamed "Clank" for defensive problems.
CF	Larry Harlow	1975–1979	When Al Bumbry broke his leg in '78, Harlow forced into action in center, for which he didn't have the speed.
RF	Larry Sheets	1984–1989	The complete package: poor instincts, lead in his shoes, and he couldn't throw.
P	Gregg Olson	1988–1993	Shaky with the glove, and generally hopeless at holding runners; oftentimes, catcher didn't bother throwing.

ALL-BUST		YEARS	NOTES
DH	Ron Kittle	1990	Onetime Rookie of the Year spent two months with Orioles, batted .164 with 2 homers in 22 games.
C	Dave Duncan	1975–1976	Good defense, but not nearly good enough to make up for a bat that made Rick Dempsey look like Babe Ruth.
1B	Glenn Davis	1991–1993	Complete disaster, as back problems robbed him of power and mobility before he could really get going.
2B	Alan Wiggins	1985–1987	Stolen-base wizard with Padres, came to O's and, beset by off-field problems, declined each year.
SS	Juan Bell	1989–1991	Supposed to move Ripken off shortstop—*yeah, right*—but instead he batted .167 and got traded to Phillies.
3B	Ryan Minor	1998–2000	Onetime hoops star at Oklahoma was supposed to supplant Cal at third, but hit .185 with 3 HR in 87 games.
LF	Dave Nicholson	1960, 1962	Got $100,000 signing bonus, but in two seasons batted .178 and struck out in nearly half his at-bats.
CF	Brady Anderson	1998–2001	After solid '97, signed *five*-year deal for $31 million and gave the Orioles one big year and two good ones.
RF	Albert Belle	1999–2000	Signed $65 million contract for five years, but played only two before degenerative hip injury ended career.
SP	Ben McDonald	1989–1995	First overall pick in '89 draft won only 58 games as Oriole, never more than 14 in a season.
RP	Norm Charlton	1998	Ray Miller thought he'd "fixed" Charlton in spring training; result was 6.94 ERA in 35 innings.

USED-TO-BE-GREAT		YEARS	NOTES
DH	Harold Baines	2000	His third stint with his hometown club; also played for the White Sox three different times.
C	Terry Kennedy	1987–1988	Former Padres All-Star posted .289 OBP in two seasons, and played his part in Orioles' 0-21 start in '88.
1B	Will Clark	1999–2000	Still a fine hitter in his mid-thirties, but traded to the Cardinals in 2000 for minor-league 3B José León.
2B	Delino DeShields	1999–2001	Opened the '90s as budding star with Expos, ended them trying to keep his career afloat with Orioles.
SS	Rick Burleson	1987	Conquered back woes to put together decent year for Angels in '86, but followed up with .209 average for O's.
3B	Brooks Robinson	1975–1977	After a decent '74 campaign, completely stopped hitting in '75, which helped cost O's a shot at title.
LF	Phil Bradley	1989–1990	He *was* great for a few years in Seattle, and played well in '89 for O's but stopped hitting in '90, his last season.
CF	Fred Lynn	1986–1988	Former nine-time All-Star could still play; hit 23 homers in each of his three full seasons in Baltimore.
RF	Albert Belle	1999–2000	Posted great numbers (941 OPS, 117 RBI) in '99 before hip problems got bad in 2000, his last season.
SP	Ed Lopat	1955	At thirty-seven, Yankees star waived to Baltimore for last hurrah, went 3-4 with 4.22 ERA in 49 innings.
RP	Harvey Haddix	1964–1965	Longtime National League starter finished as reliever with O's and was outstanding in '64 (5-5, 2.31 ERA).

In 1952, Dizzy Trout retired with 170 American League victories on his résumé. He could still pitch, but he was thirty-seven years old, he'd been offered a job broadcasting Tigers games, and in those days an old ballplayer had to think about his future.

Fast-forward to the late summer of 1957. The broadcasting gig ended two years earlier, and Trout is a forty-two-year-old Detroit restaurateur who hasn't pitched in five years (the occasional sandlot game notwithstanding). But he wants to pitch again. And Orioles manager Paul Richards a) caught Trout in Detroit during his best years, 1943 through '46, and b) is also the Orioles' *general* manager. So with the O's fighting to finish in the first division—that is, in fourth place or higher—Trout is welcomed when he asks Richards for a tryout.

And it turns out that Ol' Diz can still throw hard, about as hard as Ray Moore, who's reputedly the fastest pitcher on the Oriole staff. So Richards signs Trout, who heads off to Vancouver for a few warm-up outings . . . and then on September 2, with the rosters expanded, Dizzy Trout, all forty-two years and 225 pounds of him, is back in the major leagues.

Unfortunately, that's as good as the story gets. Trout pitched to only five hitters in his comeback, four of them hit safely, and the Orioles finished fifth.

BROKEN WINGS

How many great arms did the Orioles develop in the late 1950s and early '60s?

Consider this: Bo Belinsky and Dean Chance weren't considered outstanding prospects, and were allowed to slip away, virtually unnoticed.

And this: Between 1957 and 1960, the Orioles came up with six outstanding young major-league pitchers. In 1966, the Orioles won their first American League pennant, then swept the vaunted Dodgers in the World Series. And they did it without even one of those pitchers they'd developed six and seven years earlier.

From 1955 through '61, the Orioles were run, both on and off the field, by Paul Richards, who had been a great defensive catcher in the major leagues in the 1930s and '40s. It's quite possible that there's never been a catcher better at working with pitchers. Richards couldn't hit at all, and so he spent only seven full seasons in the major leagues. Nevertheless, he was credited with playing a big role in the development of many outstanding pitchers, including Hal Newhouser and Dutch Leonard.

All of which is to say, Richards thought he knew pitchers. And he probably did; after all, they didn't call him the Wizard of Waxahachie for nothing. But catching them is one thing, and managing them is quite another.

In the late 1950s and early 1960s, Richards and the Orioles came up with a wondrous crop of young pitchers. So wondrous, they got two nicknames: "Baby Birds" and "Kiddie Korps." There were five of them, and all five showed great potential at the major-league level before or during their Age 22 seasons:

	Year	Age	IP	W-L	ERA
Milt Pappas	1959	20	209	15-9	3.27
Jerry Walker	1959	20	182	11-10	2.92
Jack Fisher	1960	21	198	12-11	3.41
Chuck Estrada	1960	22	209	18-11	3.58
Steve Barber	1961	22	248	18-12	3.33

No Cy Young candidates here, but try to remember how many pitchers in their early twenties have performed this well in the last few seasons.

Now, let's fast-forward just a few years, to 1964:

	Year	Age	IP	W-L	ERA
Milt Pappas	1964	25	252	16-7	2.97
Jerry Walker	1964	25	10	0-1	4.66
Jack Fisher	1964	25	228	10-17	4.23
Chuck Estrada	1964	26	55	3-2	5.27
Steve Barber	1964	25	157	9-13	3.84

Pappas was still excellent. Walker had pitched a 16-inning complete game late in 1959, and in 1961—by then he was in Kansas City—suffered an elbow injury that spelled the end of his career. Fisher hung around for a while, but in 1964 he was pitching for the Mets and never got back to where he'd been. Estrada, having suffered a serious elbow injury, was at the end of the line. Barber did pitch well in both 1965 and '66, after which his career pretty much went in the toilet.

You can probably guess what I think happened. I think they threw too many innings before their arms had fully developed. Walker threw 182 innings when he was twenty, and never threw as many in one season again. Fisher threw 198 innings when he was twenty-one, and though he did become a workhorse after joining the Mets in 1964, he never pitched as *well*. Estrada threw 209 innings when he was twenty-two, 212 innings when he was twenty-three, 223 innings when he was twenty-four . . . and the grand total of 119 innings after he turned twenty-five. Steve Barber threw 248 innings when he was twenty-two, only 140 innings when he was twenty-three (because of National Guard duty), and 259 innings when he was twenty-four . . . and reached 200 innings in a season only once more in his career.

The funny thing is, Richards was occasionally criticized for *babying* his young pitchers. Or at least one of them.

Milt Pappas reached the majors when he was eighteen, pitching in four games late in the 1957 season. He turned nineteen the following May, and spent most of the season in the starting rotation. But Richards put Pappas on strict pitch limits: first eighty, and then ninety. In his autobiography, Pappas recalled,

> When I look back at what Paul did for me, taking me out of a ball game when I had thrown 90 pitches, I believe he prolonged my career by five or six years. I never had any real arm problems, and I thank him for it.
>
> I had a shutout going one time. I was winning, 8–0, and it's the eighth inning against Kansas City. I reached 90 pitches, and out he walks. I looked at him and I said, "What are you doing?"
>
> "Take a shower."
>
> "Come on, I've got a shutout."
>
> "You're gone. The bullpen is coming in."
>
> I took a shower.

As best I can tell, that game was in 1960, when Pappas was still only twenty years old. However, the facts don't really square with Pappas's memory. He pitched 11 complete games in 1960, and he'd pitched *fifteen* complete games in 1959—second most in the American League—leading one to wonder, how do you pitch twenty-six complete games in two seasons if you're on a ninety-pitch limit? In *From 33rd Street to Camden Yards*, John Eisenberg's excellent oral history of the Orioles, Eisenberg writes that Pappas was actually limited to eighty pitches per start in 1960, but all those complete games simply don't support that notion.

Somehow, though, that supposed eighty-pitch limit is what people remember. Later in his career, Pappas got the reputation as a guy who couldn't finish his games. Dick Williams told Eisenberg, "Pappas was a guy Paul really babied. The pitch limit hurt him later on, although he had a good career. Later on in his career, no matter who was the manager, when he got to that eighty-pitch limit, it was like he hit a brick wall."

When you ask Pappas's teammates about him, the typical reaction is that he was a prick who didn't want to pitch. Well, I can't speak to the first of those, but in addition to completing fifteen games in 1959 (second in the league), he also completed eleven in 1960 (eighth), eleven in 1961 (eighth), eleven in 1963 (tenth), thirteen in 1964 (third), and nine in 1965 (tenth). From 1959 through 1965, Pappas completed seventy-nine games . . . *more than all but one other pitcher in the American League*. Does that sound to you like a guy who didn't want to pitch?

Pappas's complete games dropped off to six in 1966 and five in 1967 . . . but by then he was a) pitching for the Reds, and b) twenty-seven and twenty-eight years old. You know what I think? I think that Pappas—his nickname was "Gimpy"—was disliked by most of his teammates. And over the years, they've unconsciously exaggerated his limitations to the point where he's popularly remembered as a pitcher who didn't really want to be on the mound in the eighth and ninth innings. But the *facts* are that Pappas pitched sixteen full seasons in the major leagues, and in eight of those seasons he completed at least nine of his starts.

That was a lot more than I expected to write about Pappas. My points are

1. If Pappas *was* babied, it certainly didn't hurt him; he enjoyed a far better career than any of the other Baby Birds, and
2. He probably wasn't babied all that much, anyway.

In fact, aside from a brief stretch when Pappas was nineteen, I don't believe that Richards babied his young pitchers at all. Further, I believe that the combination of bringing them to the majors at such tender ages and *not* babying them goes a long way toward explaining why only Pappas won as many as a hundred games in his career. In his book *Super Scout: Thirty-five Years of Major League Scouting*, longtime Orioles employee Jim Russo wrote,

> With Paul, we led the major leagues every year in, of all things, tonsillectomies. Paul was from the old school that said, "There's got to be poison in your system if you've got an injury." When our young pitchers would come up with shoulder problems, Paul would tell our team doctor, "Doc, these kids are having shoulder and arm problems. Better check those tonsils out real close." We had more kids having their tonsils removed than any other club, and it was all silly and unnecessary. The only thing wrong with those kids was they were throwing too much. . . .
>
> Paul's teaching ability was genius. But he had another side that was just plain dumb. Say we're in spring training and a young kid goes three innings in an exhibition game. On most clubs, he goes out and does some running, then goes in and showers. Not on our club. We had some great young arms—Milt Pappas, Chuck Estrada, Jack Fisher, Jerry Walker—they called them "the Kiddie Corps," and that was an outstanding staff. . . .
>
> But with Paul, one of those kids would pitch in an exhibition game and, instead of running and a shower, it was to the bullpen to work on either an extra pitch or the slip pitch. And nobody's keeping track of how many pitches they're throwing. We're not talking about veterans here. We're talking about nineteen- and twenty-year-old arms. Everybody calls Paul a genius, and he was a real smart man. But how can you lose track of that?

And the really amazing thing was, it didn't really hurt the Orioles. After the 1965 season, the O's traded Pappas to the Reds for Frank Robinson. They figured they could spare Pappas, because Barber was still pitching well, and in the previous few years they'd also come up with Wally Bunker *and* Dave McNally *and* Jim Palmer. And in 1966, they swept the Dodgers in the World Series. By then, however, Richards was long gone.

I'm grateful to Eddie Epstein and Bob Haynie for their editorial suggestions. Sources for this chapter include John Eisenberg's From 33rd Street to Camden Yards: An Oral History of the Baltimore Orioles *(Contemporary Books, 2000), Brent Kelley's* Baseball's Biggest Blunder: The Bonus Rule of 1953–1957 *(McFarland, 1997), Milt Pappas's* Out at Home *(Angel Press of Wisconsin, 2000), and Jim Palmer and Jim Dale's* Together We Were Eleven Foot Nine *(Andrews and McNeel, 1996).*

BOSTON RED SOX

		YEARS	NOTES
ALL-TIME			
DH	Jim Rice	1974–1989	Rice played 119 more games at DH than Yaz did; it's often said that the Wall cost Rice a ton of home runs, but he hit significantly better at Fenway than elsewhere.
C	Carlton Fisk	1969–1980	His 162 homers beats the two next-best Sox catchers combined (Rich Gedman and Sammy White) by 16; Fisk played more games in Chicago, but was better in Boston.
1B	Jimmie Foxx	1936–1942	Foxx and Albert Belle are the only two players to hold the single-season HR record for two different franchises, *and* Foxx beats Boggs's career OBP by a single point.
2B	Bobby Doerr	1937–1944 1946–1951	A marginal Hall of Famer, but he's the only great second baseman to spend much time with Sox; Pete Runnels was the only other to even finish in the top 10 in an MVP vote.
SS	Nomar Garciaparra	1996–*2002*	One Red Sox who can't wait to play in October again; Nomar's career postseason stats: .383-7-20 in just 47 at-bats, and only injuries can keep him from Cooperstown.
3B	Wade Boggs	1982–1992	The Red Sox have won an AL-most 23 batting titles, one more than the Tigers; Boggs only American Leaguer to collect at least 200 hits in seven straight seasons.
LF	Ted Williams	1939–1942 1946–1960	Struck out far less often than any other member of the 500-homer club, and the evidence at hand suggests that he did a few other nice things at the plate, too.
CF	Tris Speaker	1907–1915	Career OPS with Red Sox ranks behind only Williams in franchise history *and* he's one of the greatest defensive center fielders in the game's history.
RF	Dwight Evans	1972–1990	Led the AL in OPS twice, and steadily improved his offense throughout career—his best years came at twenty-nine and thirty-five—and totaled 14 RBI in 14 World Series games.
SP1	Roger Clemens	1984–1996	Best pitcher in the world for seven years, before the injuries started coming in 1993; won three Cy Youngs with Sox, and who guessed he'd win three more?
SP2	Pedro Martínez	1998–*2002*	Not as durable as Clemens or Young, but if the mythic all-time Red Sox need to win one game, he's my pitcher if he's close to completely healthy.
SP3	Cy Young	1901–1908	Did his best work in the pre-1901 National League, but baseball's all-time winner also led the American League in victories in each of the loop's first three seasons.
SP4	Joe Wood	1908–1915	"Can I throw harder than Joe Wood? Listen, my friend, there's no man alive who can throw harder than Smoky Joe Wood."—Walter Johnson, 1912
RP	Dick Radatz	1962–1966	"The Monster" was overpowering in his first three seasons—40-21 with 78 saves and a 2.18 ERA—then completely fell apart: 12-22, 4.54 ERA after 1964.

What would baseball be without freaky coincidences? One of my favorites is that if you list every major-league player in alphabetical order, Hank Aaron comes first. Another is that Aaron and Babe Ruth both scored exactly 2,174 runs. Another is that Jeff Bagwell and Frank Thomas were born on the same day in the same year.

And here's a new one (at least to me): Cy Young and Roger Clemens posted nearly identical records for the American League's Boston franchise. Young won 192 games and lost 112. Clemens won 192 games and lost 111.

In another way, they're opposites. Young pitched for Boston at the beginning of the twentieth century, near the end of his career. Clemens pitched for Boston near the end of the twentieth century, at the beginning of his career.

There is, of course, one more connection between the two burly righthanders. The Cy Young Award is named after Cy Young, and Clemens has won six Cy Young Awards. There is a chance that Randy Johnson will someday match Clemens's record of six Cy Youngs. But the chances are better that Roger Clemens's name will forever by linked with Cy Young's in something like exclusive fashion.

How good was Babe Ruth, exactly? If he hadn't become an outfielder, would he eventually have been elected to the Hall of Fame as a pitcher?

Ruth pitched full-time for only three seasons, 1915 (when he was twenty) through 1917. Over that span, he won sixty-five games and lost thirty-three, with a 2.02 ERA. Only two pitchers posted lower ERA's over those three seasons: Pete Alexander (1.54) and Walter Johnson (1.88). On the other hand, Johnson and Alexander were both eight years older than Ruth.

The Babe totaled eighty Win Shares before he turned twenty-three, and it would be wonderful if we could find a contemporary or near-contemporary who enjoyed the same success at the same age. The closest is probably Johnson, who totaled seventy-two Win Shares before he turned twenty-three. There's also Joe Wood (Ruth's teammate for two seasons), who got an early start—he debuted when he was eighteen—and totaled *ninety-one* Win Shares before he turned twenty-three.

Wood hurt his arm the season after he turned twenty-three, and of course the same thing might have happened to Ruth. I think the odds were in Ruth's favor, though. I think he had a better chance of following Johnson's career path than Wood's. And so I think that Babe Ruth would be in the Hall of Fame no matter which position he'd played.

		YEARS	NOTES
	NO. 2		
DH	Carl Yastrzemski	1961–1983	A regular for *twenty-three years*, and primarily a DH for the last five of those; 1979 was his best season at the "position," and really just hanging around for the next four years.
C	Wally Schang	1918–1920	Stalwart with A's and Yankees, too, but his two best seasons were with Sox; best catcher of his time, and should be in the Hall of Fame rather than Ray Schalk.
1B	Mo Vaughn	1991–1998	Stole 1995 AL MVP—Edgar Martinez and Albert Belle were both more worthy—making Sox the only team with an MVP in every decade from 1930s to 1990s.
2B	Pete Runnels	1958–1962	Shifted to first base his last two years with Sox, but made a couple of All-Star teams playing second; not great with the glove, but hit for average and walked.
SS	Johnny Pesky	1942 1946–1952	Led AL in hits as rookie, went into the service for three years, and led AL in hits his first two seasons after coming back; injuries hastened early end of career.
3B	Jimmy Collins	1901–1907	Player/manager for first modern World Series winner; only Red Sox 3B in top 10 for homers more than once, and universally regarded as top fielder of his time.
LF	Carl Yastrzemski	1961–1983	Did you know that in addition to his years playing left field and (at the end) DH, Yaz also played regularly in center field one season, and 765 games at first base?
CF	Fred Lynn	1974–1980	It's a little silly to argue for Dom DiMaggio as a Hall of Famer, considering that Lynn was actually the better player and hasn't received any support at all.
RF	Harry Hooper	1909–1920	A civil engineer by trade, Hooper was enticed to sign with Sox by offer of $2,850 *and* a job working on new Fenway Park; didn't get the job . . . but didn't need it.
SP1	Lefty Grove	1934–1941	Managed to go 105-62 for Sox, even though he lost his great fastball early in his tenure; recorded his 300th (and last) victory on July 25, 1941.
SP2	Mel Parnell	1947–1956	Fenway inflated his ERA's and kept him from being recognized as one of the best pitchers of his era, but that's exactly what he was from 1948 through '53.
SP3	Babe Ruth	1914–1919	On top of his 89-46 regular-season record, Ruth went 2-0 with a 0.87 ERA in two World Series; case can be made that he'd have been a Hall of Fame pitcher, too.
SP4	Luis Tiant	1971–1978	Tiant and Clemens are the only Sox pitchers to win 20 games three times in the last 90 years; threw a bewildering assortment of pitches from just as many angles.
RP	Ellis Kinder	1948–1955	Started more than he relieved in three of his seasons, but came out of pen to save 91 games and win 39 more; change-up artist pitched brilliantly into his early forties.

SINGLE SEASON

		YEARS	NOTES
DH	Jim Rice	1977	Everybody remembers the MVP in 1978 (mostly as left fielder), but in '77 Rice led AL with 39 homers and .593 slug.
C	Carlton Fisk	1972	His rookie season was probably his best; his stats looked better in other seasons, but '72 was a tough year for hitters.
1B	Jimmie Foxx	1938	Set team records for homers (50) and RBI (175) that still stand; Fenway friendly, with 35 of 50 HR coming at home.
2B	Bobby Doerr	1948	Doerr (27) and SS Vern Stephens (29) both out-homered Williams (25); '44 also excellent, but a wartime season.
SS	Nomar Garciaparra	2000	On July 20, his batting average stood at .403, leading to the inevitable "Will he?" stories; finished with AL-best .372.
3B	Wade Boggs	1987	Twenty-four homers? If he'd maintained his '87 HR rate for his entire career, he'd have finished with 401 homers rather than 118.
LF	Ted Williams	1941	Yes, maybe he played better in 1942 and 1946, but it's awful hard to ignore a batting average that starts with a 4.
CF	Tris Speaker	1912	Joe Wood's 34 wins and Speaker's greatest year proved unbeatable as Sox began brilliant seven-year run.
RF	Ted Williams	1939	Williams's rookie season was his only season in right, but it's still the best season by a Red Sox right fielder.
SP	Joe Wood	1912	Only 22, Wood won 34 games and beat Walter Johnson in the biggest pitching matchup to that point . . . and maybe since.
RP	Ellis Kinder	1953	"Old Folks" turned 39 in July, but still managed to lead AL with 69 games pitched, 27 saves, and 10 relief wins.

ALL-ROOKIE

		YEARS	NOTES
DH	Jim Rice	1975	Actually played 90 games in left field, and most years he'd have been Rookie of the Year. Had to get him in somehow.
C	Carlton Fisk	1972	Local kid makes good, slugs .538 with league-high 9 triples and is unanimous choice as Rookie of the Year.
1B	Walt Dropo	1950	Exploded upon scene with 144 RBI, tied for league lead and one short of the all-time rookie record.
2B	Jody Reed	1988	Took over at second base in late June, and batted .293 with a pair of game-winning suicide squeezes.
SS	Johnny Pesky	1942	Batted .331 and topped AL with 205 hits . . . and spent the next three seasons playing for Uncle Sam.
3B	Wade Boggs	1982	After he topped .300 in five straight minor-league seasons, Sox finally gave him a job and he batted .349 in 104 games.
LF	Mike Greenwell	1987	In a great year for hitters, cracked 56 extra-base hits in 412 at-bats and slugged .570, drawing raves from Ted Williams.
CF	Fred Lynn	1975	Talk about your foreshadowing . . . as a September call-up in 1974, Lynn batted .419 over 15 games.
RF	Ted Williams	1939	He was only twenty but he was already damn near the greatest hitter that ever walked down the street; .327-31-145.
SP	Babe Ruth	1915	Sign of things to come, as twenty-year-old with the great fastball went 18-8 with 2.44 ERA in 32 games.
RP	Dick Radatz	1962	From the first moment he stepped on the field, Radatz was the best reliever in the AL and would remain so for three years.

As everyone reading this probably knows, Fred Lynn was the first player to be named Rookie of the Year and MVP in the same season (the feat was duplicated by Ichiro Suzuki in 2001). But did you know that Lynn was *not* the unanimous Rookie of the Year choice?

Not quite. One of the two Boston voters—according to the *Boston Globe,* it was George Bankert of the Quincy *Patriot Ledger*—split his vote between Lynn and teammate Jim Rice.

Purely in terms of performance, there's really no comparison between the two of them.

Yes, they played in virtually the same number of games, and they both stole ten bases while being caught five times, and they both hit slightly more than twenty home runs (twenty-two for Rice, twenty-one for Lynn), and they both drove in slightly more than one hundred runs (105 RBI for Lynn, 102 for Rice).

But Lynn batted .331 to Rice's .309, Lynn hit forty-seven doubles to Rice's twenty-nine, and Lynn drew sixty-two walks to Rice's thirty-six. Oh, and Lynn won a Gold Glove (and deserved it). Rice did play well enough in left field, but he also DH'd in fifty-four games.

Lynn and Rice were teammates and friends, so giving Rice half of a Rookie of the Year vote was "nice." But it didn't make much sense.

As SABR member Maxwell Kates notes, in 1988 the Red Sox set a record that won't ever be broken. Facing off against the Athletics in Game 1 of the American League Championship Series, the Red Sox featured ten starters who were developed in the organization. That's right, ten: all nine guys in the lineup, plus the starting pitcher.

In these days of peripatetic professional athletes, that would be almost impossible, but even in the 1980s it was probably unique. Free agency had become a big part of the game a decade earlier, yet five of the homegrown starters in Game 1 were drafted in the 1970s (or in the case of Dwight Evans, in 1969).

For the sake of posterity, here's that Game 1 lineup: CF Ellis Burks (first round, 1983), 2B Marty Barrett (first round, 1979), C Rich Gedman (signed as undrafted free agent, 1977), LF Mike Greenwell (sixth round, 1982), 3B Wade Boggs (seventh round, 1976), DH Jim Rice (first round, 1971), RF Dwight Evans (fifth round, 1969), SS Jody Reed (eighth round, 1984), 1B Todd Benzinger (fourth round, 1981). And on the mound, a kid from Texas named Roger Clemens (first round, 1983).

Unfortunately, the Sox lost Game 1, as well as Games 2, 3, and 4. They got swept by the A's, just as they'd get swept by the A's in 1990, too.

HOMEGROWN

		YEARS	NOTES
DH	Jim Rice	1974–1989	Club's first pick in '71 draft moved up fast and won Triple Crown (.337-25-93) in last minor-league season.
C	Carlton Fisk	1971–1980	Beloved in Boston for both his gritty play and his New England roots; second pick in January '67 draft.
1B	Jeff Bagwell	—	Boston-born and grew up in Connecticut, batted .323 with scad of doubles in two minor-league seasons.
2B	Jody Reed	1987–1992	*Jody Reed?* Yeah, Jody Reed. He wasn't great, but the Sox just haven't developed many good second basemen.
SS	Nomar Garciaparra	1996–*2002*	Batted .372 in three seasons at Georgia Tech, played in 1992 Olympics, and was Sox's first pick in '92 draft.
3B	Wade Boggs	1982–1992	Seventh-round pick in '76 spent six seasons in the minors because of deficiencies in power and defense.
LF	Carl Yastrzemski	1961–1983	Long Island native almost signed with Yankees, but went to Notre Dame instead and eventually signed with Sox.
CF	Reggie Smith	1966–1973	Drafted out of Twins organization after first pro season and eventually played in seven All-Star Games.
RF	Dwight Evans	1972–1990	Fifth-round pick in 1979 and the very next year took MVP honors in the International League.
SP	Roger Clemens	1984–1996	All-American at U. of Texas, won deciding game of 1983 College World Series; nineteenth pick in '83 draft.
RP	Sparky Lyle	—	Sox stole Lyle from O's after his first pro season, in which he struck out 95 Class A hitters in 68 innings.

TRADED AWAY

		TRADED	NOTES
C	Wally Schang	December 15, 1920	His best years were mostly behind him, but he'd last another decade and play in three World Series for Yanks.
1B	Jeff Bagwell	August 31, 1990	Red Sox got 22 fine innings from Larry Andersen; Astros got a Hall of Fame career from Bagwell. 'Nuff said.
2B	Buddy Myer	December 15, 1928	They *had* him . . . and then they let him get away, to the Nats for five players (some of whom actually helped).
SS	Roger Peckinpaugh	January 10, 1922	Spent only two weeks as property of Sox before going to Senators in a three-team deal; MVP in 1925.
3B	Joe Dugan	July 23, 1922	Jumpin' Joe wasn't a great player, but he did play third base for five Yankee teams that reached World Series.
LF	George Stone	January 16, 1905	Americans traded their top prospect for aging slugger Jesse Burkett; Stone became big star with Browns.
CF	Tris Speaker	April 12, 1916	When Spoke refused to take a big pay cut, Sox traded him to Indians for two players and $50,000.
RF	Babe Ruth	January 3, 1920	You were expecting someone else? Harry Frazee sold Ruth to the Yanks, but *not* because he needed the dough.
SP	Red Ruffing	May 6, 1930	After going 39-96 (!) for Sox in six-plus seasons, went to Yankees and somehow turned into a Hall of Famer.
RP	Sparky Lyle	March 22, 1972	Sox traded one of the league's best relievers (Lyle) for a 32-year-old, singles-hitting first baseman (Danny Cater).

		YEARS	NOTES
GOLD GLOVE			
C	Rick Ferrell	1933–1937	One of a dozen catchers in the Hall of Fame, and we can safely say that he didn't make it on strength of his bat.
1B	Dave Stapleton	1980–1986	In the ninth inning of Game 6 of the 1986 World Series, the best defensive 1B in team history was on the bench.
2B	Bobby Doerr	1937–1944 1946–1951	His double-play partner Johnny Pesky said, "Doerr wasn't good, he was simply great."
SS	Rick Burleson	1974–1980	Funny how nobody remembers that "Rooster" was the best everyday glove man in the league for five years.
3B	Jimmy Collins	1901–1907	Universally recognized as the inventor of "modern" third-base technique . . . and he could *play*, too.
LF	Duffy Lewis	1910–1917	Played the embankment in front of the left-field fence with such skill, they named it "Duffy's Cliff."
CF	Tris Speaker	1907–1915	Nobody played shallower than Speaker, the Willie Mays of his time; DiMaggio, Piersall, and Lynn also great.
RF	Trot Nixon	1996–*2002*	Wait a minute . . . Nixon's better than Harry Hooper and Jackie Jensen and *Dwight Evans?* Yes, he is.
P	Carl Mays	1915–1919	Holds franchise record for assists by a pitcher, with 122 in 1918 . . . and the second and third spots as well.

		YEARS	NOTES
IRON GLOVE			
C	Scott Hatteberg	1995–2001	Guilty with an explanation (Sox pitchers didn't worry about runners), but Hatteberg just couldn't throw.
1B	Dick Stuart	1963–1964	Good Lord, was he awful. Yes, Stuart was every bit as horrible as everybody said he was.
2B	Felix Mantilla	1963–1965	Hit 18 homers and made All-Star team in '65, but didn't have a position and was out of the majors a year later.
SS	Jackie Gutierrez	1983–1985	An atrocious fielder and a zero at the plate, Gutierrez was one of the worst players in recent memory.
3B	Butch Hobson	1975–1980	Sometimes fielding percentage doesn't tell the whole story, but with Hobson maybe it does; he was that bad.
LF	Smead Jolley	1932–1933	Batted .305 in four seasons, but spent sixteen seasons in the minors because he simply couldn't play defense at all.
CF	Braggo Roth	1919	A poor right fielder, installed in center field after joining Sox in 1919 and didn't change his true glove ways.
RF	Ike Boone	1923–1925	Like Jolley, a fine hitter (and minor-league superstar) whose glove cost him a long big-league career.
P	Matt Young	1991–1992	Quite possibly the worst since the invention of TV, and never met a grounder he couldn't turn into an adventure.

Don Zimmer's autobiography runs 286 pages, which leaves room for hundreds of Zim's wonderful stories. Zimmer found only fifty-six words, however, to explain why he let Butch Hobson play 133 games at third base in 1978.

Those fifty-six words: ". . . Hobson had bone chips in his elbow which he had to continually rearrange between pitches. I got a lot of criticism for keeping Hobson in the lineup every day because he was committing a lot of throwing errors. But the man hit 17 homers and knocked in 80 runs. Who else was going to do that?"

The Red Sox did have a terrible bench; Jack Brohamer and Frank Duffy were the only other qualified third basemen on the roster, and neither of them could have come close to matching Hobson's modest production (.312 OBP, .408 slugging percentage). The Sox had Dave Stapleton in Pawtucket, but he couldn't hit, either.

Red Sox general manager Haywood Sullivan made some great deals prior to the 1978 season. He acquired Mike Torrez, Dennis Eckersley, and Jerry Remy, all of whom played key roles in a ninety-nine-win season. But Sullivan's inability to acquire a third baseman who actually could throw a baseball helped cost the Red Sox the pennant. Zimmer may not have been the greatest manager in the world, but I don't think he had much of a choice here.

It's a fundamental part of human nature, I suspect. When we have a lot of something, we don't value any of it. Or at least not enough of it.

That's what happened to Red Sox general manager Dan Duquette in the late twentieth century. Thanks to Fenway Park and a media market that encompasses most of New England, Duquette had a lot of money to play with. And it would take more space than I've got here to detail how badly he wasted it. In shorthand, though . . . $24 million for four years of José Offerman; $8.6 million for two really bad years of Troy O'Leary; $7 million for three years of Darren Lewis; $6.3 million for an awful year of Ramón Martínez; $6.25 million for a year of Mike Lansing . . . and these are just the "highlights."

Duquette's inability to make intelligent financial choices, in addition to costing him a lot of money, also cost him a lot of freedom. When you're paying a player like José Offerman six or seven million bucks for the season, it's very difficult to cut him, even after you've realized that he's doing more to hurt than help.

It's not that teams like the Red Sox can't afford to blow money on players like José Offerman and Mike Lansing. It's that they can't afford to also blow roster spots on them.

ALL-BUST			
		YEARS	NOTES
DH	Jack Clark	1991–1992	Did well enough in '91, but in '92 he suffered series of nagging injuries and didn't homer even once at Fenway.
C	Marc Sullivan	1982 1984–1987	Sure, it's *possible* that this .186 hitter didn't spend parts of four years with Sox because his old man ran the club.
1B	Tony Clark	2002	Coming off a pretty good year with Tigers and looked like good bet, but was a *complete* waste of $5 million.
2B	José Offerman	2000–2002	He played well in 1999, but the next three seasons were full of anemic hitting, ugly defense, and wasted millions.
SS	Don Buddin	1956–1961	Got a huge bonus to sign with Sox out of high school, later symbolized franchise's woes as "Bootin' Buddin."
3B	Wilton Veras	1999–2000	Supposedly one of the fruits of the Duke's farm system, and posted .297 OBP with 2 homers in 85 games.
LF	Jesse Burkett	1905	Future Hall of Famer didn't play *poorly* in his last season, but he cost the Bostons future star George Stone.
CF	Carl Everett	2000–2001	Outstanding hitter in 2000, just fair in 2001 . . . and one hell of a distraction during most of both seasons.
RF	Mel Almada	1936–1937	After decent rookie campaign in '35, slumped badly in '36 and got traded to Nats after slow start in '37.
SP	Jim Lonborg	1968–1970	After winning 22 in '67, tore up his knee skiing that winter and totaled 17 wins over next three seasons.
RP	Greg Harris	1994	After four good years, posted 8.28 ERA and managed to blow 4 saves before drawing his release in late June.

USED-TO-BE-GREAT			
		YEARS	NOTES
DH	Orlando Cepeda	1973	Everybody thought the DH was invented for guys like Cepeda, and he took to the job like a fish to water.
C	Elston Howard	1967–1968	Nine-time All-Star with Yankees finished with Sox, and struggled terribly with bat down the stretch in '67.
1B	Tony Perez	1980–1982	Pretty good as everyday first baseman in 1980 before showing his age the next couple of years.
2B	Max Bishop	1934–1935	Even at the end of his career, "Camera Eye" still an on-base master and posted .424 OBP as utility man.
SS	Lou Boudreau	1951–1952	Still relatively young but just a shadow of his former self, played sparingly in '52 while managing the club.
3B	Ken Keltner	1950	Gary Gaetti (2000) hung around longer, but Keltner—who ended his career with 13 games for Sox—was better.
LF	Al Simmons	1943	Got a shot because so many kids were working for Uncle Sam, but batted just .203 with one homer in 40 games.
CF	Willie McGee	1995	Two-time National League batting champ spent his only full AL season with Sox and batted .285 as part-timer.
RF	Andre Dawson	1993–1994	DH'd mostly, but the extra rest didn't do anything for his stick, as he batted .260 and drew 26 walks in 196 games.
SP	Tom Seaver	1986	At forty-one, posted 3.80 ERA in 16 starts, but September knee injury kept him out of postseason in his last hurrah.
RP	Dennis Eckersley	1998	Twenty years earlier, he'd won 20 games for Sox, and came back to set record with 1,071 games pitched.

ALL-NAME

		YEARS	NOTES
M	"Tollway Joe" Joe Morgan	1988–1991	In a previous life, he drove a snowplow on the Massachusetts Turnpike.
DH	"The Baby Bull" Orlando Cepeda	1973	His dad, known as "the Babe Ruth of Puerto Rico," was also nicknamed "The Bull."
C	"Pudge" Carlton Fisk	1969–1980	Solid when we saw him, but he was 5'4" and weighed 155 pounds when he was in the eighth grade.
1B	"Dr. Strangeglove" Dick Stuart	1963–1964	Stuart was the worst-fielding 1B in the game, Kubrick's masterpiece was released in '64, and the rest is history.
2B	"Pete" Thomas Runnels	1958–1962	His father and older brother were also nicknamed "Pete," which led to some confusion in the Runnels household.
SS	"Rooster" Rick Burleson	1974–1980	Shortened from "Red Rooster," invented by coach Johnny Pesky due to Burleson's "cocky and competitive spirit."
3B	"Chicken" Wade Boggs	1982–1992	Among the many rituals that kept Boggs hyperfocused, one was chicken for lunch. Every single day.
LF	"Splendid Splinter" Ted Williams	1939–1942 1946–1960	Just one of many given him over the years, the others including "Teddy Ballgame," "The Kid" and "Thumper."
CF	"The Little Professor" Dom DiMaggio	1940–1942 1946–1953	Joe and Vince were both big, strapping fellows who hit the ball a mile; Dom looked like Radar O'Reilly.
RF	"Carl Reggie Smith" Reggie Smith	1966–1973	Derisively given Smith for his attempts to "act like a white man"—Yastrzemski—"trapped in a black man's body."
SP	"Spaceman" Bill Lee	1969–1978	Referring to the Apollo program, catcher John Kennedy said, "We have our own spaceman right over there."
RP	"The Monster" Dick Radatz	1962–1966	Michigan State graduate was smarter than his nickname sounds; at 6-6 and 265, perhaps the first scary reliever.

TOP FIVE SEASONS

YEAR 1912 **RECORD** 105-47
BEST HITTER Tris Speaker
BEST PITCHER Smoky Joe Wood
NOTES Beat Giants in Series thanks to Snodgrass Muff.

YEAR 1903 **RECORD** 91-47
BEST HITTERS Patsy Dougherty, Jimmy Collins (Manager)
BEST PITCHER Cy Young
NOTES Pilgrims win first modern World Series over Pirates.

YEAR 1915 **RECORD** 101-50
BEST HITTER Tris Speaker
BEST PITCHER Rube Foster
NOTES So good they didn't even need Babe in the Series.

YEAR 1967 **RECORD** 92-70
BEST HITTER Carl Yastrzemski (MVP)
BEST PITCHER Jim Lonborg
NOTES Impossible Dream created cathedral at Lansdowne and Yawkey.

YEAR 1916 **RECORD** 91-63
BEST HITTERS Larry Gardner, Harry Hooper
BEST PITCHER Babe Ruth
NOTES Topped unlikely Dodgers for second straight championship.

TOP FIVE MANAGERS

MANAGER Bill Carrigan
YEARS 1913–1916, 1927–1929
RECORD 489-500 (.494)
NOTES His nickname was "Rough," but he held the Sox together.

MANAGER Joe Cronin
YEARS 1935–1947
RECORD 1071-916 (.539)
NOTES Had the first shot at Jackie Robinson, but blew it.

MANAGER Jimmy Collins
YEARS 1901–1906
RECORD 455-376 (.548)
NOTES Did quite well until stuck with an idiot owner.

MANAGER Jimy Williams
YEARS 1997–2001
RECORD 414-352 (.540)
NOTES King of the unorthodox, but mostly made it work.

MANAGER Joe Morgan
YEARS 1988–1991
RECORD 301-262 (.535)
NOTES It's a shame he never got another shot to manage.

Perhaps enough time has passed since Ted Williams's passing that we can examine some of the myths surrounding his career.

First, there's 1941. The way the story goes, Williams entered the last day of the season batting .400, but played the season-ending doubleheader even though it could have cost him a measure of immortality. Except Williams actually was batting .3995, and most people at the time would *not* have rounded that figure up, and given him credit for hitting .400.

Now, about Williams's military career. As everybody knows, Williams served for three seasons during World War II *and* for most of two seasons during the Korean conflict. Those five "missed" seasons are often held up as proof of Williams's selfless patriotism.

But if Williams hadn't enlisted during World War II, he'd certainly have been drafted. And when Williams was recalled to duty in 1952, he resented it. As he wrote in his autobiography, "In my heart I was bitter about it, but I made up my mind I wasn't going to bellyache. I kept thinking one of those gutless politicians someplace along the line would see that it wasn't right and do something."

I'd have been bitter, too. I just think it's a little strange to hold up Williams as the paragon of patriotism because of something for which he showed so little enthusiasm.

SUSPICIOUS SERIES

It's commonly believed that the Black Sox scandal in 1919 was something of an isolated event, the product of too many rogue ballplayers who just happened to play for the Ebenezer Scrooge of baseball owners.

But as anyone who has studied the Dead Ball Era knows all too well, the 1919 World Series was *not* all that out of the ordinary; prior to 1919, a *number* of baseball games—and yes, World Series games—were tainted by at least the suspicion of chicanery. And while it's quite possible, and perhaps even likely, that the suspicions weren't always warranted, it's also true that 1) the mere existence of the suspicions suggests that something funny was going on at least some of the time, and 2) there were probably conspiracies to throw games that were *not* suspected, or at least not to the point where suspicion crept into the press coverage.

We don't have to go fishing for suspicion, though, because there was plenty out in the open. Just looking at the Red Sox, there were serious questions about each of the franchise's first two World Championships.

In 1903, after two years of all-out war, the National and American Leagues settled their differences, and as the season neared its conclusion, the owners of the two championship clubs agreed to meet in a "world's series." Pirates owner Charley Dreyfuss had his players under contract through October 15, but Boston owner Henry Killilea had a big problem: his players were under contract only through September 30, while the world's series was supposed to start on the first day of October.

So Killilea would have to pay the players something extra; the question was how much. After a fair amount of contentious negotiating, the parties finally agreed: the players would receive two weeks' pay, plus half of Killilea's gate receipts.

There was a big problem with this arrangement, though . . . it meant the longer the series lasted, the more money the players (and, of course, the owners) would make. And before the series even started, speculation was rife that the players and/or the owners might conspire to ensure the best-of-nine series actually lasted eight or nine games.

And wouldn't you know it, the series lasted eight games. That winter, writing in *Reach's Official Base Ball Guide*, Francis Richter opined, "The entire series was played grandly, cleanly, squarely and without friction, and there was not the slightest taint of scandal."

(Richter was a brilliant editor, but when it came to scandal he generally turned a blind eye to the obvious. This is a man who would write, sixteen years later, "[A]ny man who insinuates that the 1919 World's Series was not honorably played by every participant therein not only does not know what he is talking about, but is a menace to the game quite as much as the gamblers would be if they had the ghost of a chance to get in their nefarious work." Harumph.)

Cy Young started the opener for Boston, and he retired leadoff man Ginger Beaumont in good order. Then Fred Clarke fouled out to the catcher. Following which, as Glenn Stout writes in *A Red Sox Century*, "[I]n the next few moments, the Boston Americans, the pride of the American League, played the absolute worst baseball of their three-year existence, handing the game to Pittsburgh in a manner that seemed suspicious then and seems even more so now. The very first game of the very first 'world's series' was, in all likelihood, thrown by Boston."

Without getting into the gory details, the Pirates scored four runs after two were out in the first inning, and wound up winning 7–3. What's more, it's quite possible that both teams were in on the fix. The Red Sox won the second game, 3–0, which evened things up and allowed everyone to carry on as if the first two games hadn't happened.

Except, of course, that in addition to ensuring that at least four more games would be played, the players also could have made a tidy profit betting on the first game, or perhaps the first two games.

Anyway, it's likely that the rest of the series was on the up-and-up, and the Americans won in eight games.

In 1912, the Red Sox beat the Giants in the first game of the World Series. After a 6–6 tie in the second game, the Giants evened the Series with a victory in Game 3. But the Sox won the next two, and with ace Smoky Joe Wood rested enough to start Game 6, the smart money was on Boston to close out the Series without much trouble.

But that sixth game was scheduled for New York, and if the Red Sox won, lucrative pay-days back in Boston—site of Game 7 and perhaps Game 8 (if necessary)—would be lost. Quite possibly with this in mind, Red Sox president James McAleer ordered manager Larry Stahl to start Buck O'Brien instead of Wood.

O'Brien, who may have been hung over, gave up five runs in the first inning. For his troubles, he was hung with the loss *and* was physically assaulted . . . first by Joe Wood's brother—who lost a hundred bucks betting on the Sox—and later by Wood himself.

The Red Sox, who had quite likely bet on themselves to win Game 6, quite possibly bet on themselves to lose Game 8. Which they did, as Smoky Joe Wood—the best pitcher on the planet during the regular season—gave up six runs in the first inning. The Giants won going away, 11–4, and there would be one more game.

To determine the site of the deciding contest, a coin was flipped. John McGraw called "Heads." The coin came up tails. It would be Fenway Park, again. There would be no giant windfall for McAleer, however. As Stout writes in *Red Sox Century* (the primary source for this article), "On October 6, 1912, Fenway Park was barely half full for what many would later describe as the greatest World Series game of the Dead Ball Era. The events of the previous day kept the crowd sparse, and more than a few writers observed that the empty seats were ample evidence of a profound lack of faith on the part of the Boston fans."

Not lack of faith that the Red Sox would win, but rather lack of faith that the Red Sox would *try* to win. Fortunately, they did try to win, and took the Series with an improbable two-run rally in the bottom of the tenth, highlighted by Fred Snodgrass's famous muff of a lazy fly ball. And as Stout writes, "Good thing, for his error has since served to obscure the events surrounding game seven."

All this isn't meant as an indictment of Boston's American Leaguers. It's just that their pre-1919 World Series have been scrutinized more than anybody else's. There's good reason to believe that the Red Sox weren't alone. We'll never know how many Series were compromised by unscrupulous players and owners. But the answer is quite likely higher than zero.

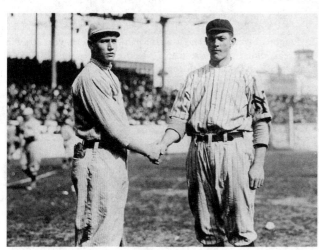

I'm grateful to Bill Nowlin for his editorial suggestions. The sources for this chapter include Glenn Stout and Richard A. Johnson's Red Sox Century *(Houghton Mifflin, 2000).*

Joe Wood and Jack Tesreau before Game 1. And they couldn't be happier.
National Baseball Library, Cooperstown, New York

In 1985, the Cubs drafted a couple of *hitters:* Rafael Palmeiro in the first round, Mark Grace in the twenty-fourth round. Aside from the presumably vast difference in their signing bonuses, Palmeiro and Grace had, or at least would come to have, a great deal in common.

They were born almost exactly three months apart, in 1964. At this moment, they're both still playing in the major leagues. They've collected roughly the same number of hits, they've got roughly the same lifetime batting averages, and they've drawn roughly the same number of walks. They've both been outstanding defensive players for most of their careers.

And it was apparent, early on, that there wasn't room for both of them at Wrigley Field. Grace was always a first baseman, and while Palmeiro saw plenty of action in the outfield, most everybody figured he'd end up at first. Which he did; since leaving the Cubs, Palmeiro hasn't played even a single inning anywhere else on the field.

So did the Cubs keep the right first baseman? No, they didn't. There's a huge difference between Palmeiro and Grace: Palmeiro's going to finish his career with more than five hundred home runs, and Grace won't reach two hundred.

They kept the wrong guy, and why? For want of a "closer."

CHICAGO CUBS

		ALL-TIME	
		YEARS	NOTES
C	Gabby Hartnett	1922–1940	Joe McCarthy managed Dickey and he managed against Cochrane, but said, "I rated Gabby the perfect catcher, a manager's dream . . . I must take Hartnett as the best."
1B	Mark Grace	1988–2000	Not much power, but a solid batting eye, great glove, and more hits than anybody else in the 1990s; media loved him, teammates sometimes a bit less effusive.
2B	Ryne Sandberg	1982–1997	Fantastic blend of power and speed, and collected nine straight Gold Gloves to boot; only blots on his career are relative brevity and Wrigley Field.
SS	Ernie Banks	1953–1971	Only a shortstop from '53 through '61, but showed great power and won MVP awards in '58 and '59; with wrecked knees, just okay for a decade as first baseman.
3B	Ron Santo	1960–1973	Great glove and bat, and incredibly durable, averaging 159 games per year from '61 through '71; not quite the fielder Brooks was, but the best all-around 3B of his era.
LF	Billy Williams	1959–1974	Famous for his swing and, according to Durocher, "was everything that Banks was supposed to be . . ."; set (since-broken) NL record with 1,117 straight games.
CF	Hack Wilson	1926–1931	No, he wasn't much with the glove, and yes, his peak was short, calling his Hall of Fame credentials into question. But for five years, Hack was awesome.
RF	Sammy Sosa	1992–2002	Hard work and hitting coach Jeff Pentland changed Sosa; he walked 115 times in his first 2,006 appearances, and 116 times in 693 PA's in 2001 alone.
SP1	Mordecai Brown	1904–1912 1916	Dominating pitcher who won 148 games over a six-year 20+ win streak; didn't win more than 20 before or after; sub-2.00 ERA each season from 1906 through '10.
SP2	Ferguson Jenkins	1966–1973 1982–1983	Averaged 39 starts a year from '67 to '73 while posting six straight 20-win seasons; nobody threw more innings in the twentieth century without making it to the postseason.
SP3	Pete Alexander	1918–1926	His best years came with Phillies, but he did win his third and final pitcher's Triple Crown with the Cubs in 1920; reached 20 wins with three different franchises.
SP4	Greg Maddux	1986–1992	Rookie on bad '86 team that featured four great pitchers, all of them at the wrong part of their careers; Eckersley, Sutcliffe, Moyer, and Maddux were combined 20-33.
RP	Bruce Sutter	1976–1980	Started in Chicago, where he became first master of split-finger fastball, and was the first pitcher used something like a modern "closer"; 133 saves with 2.39 ERA.

		YEARS	NOTES
NO. 2			
C	Johnny Kling	1900–1911	In 1922, John McGraw and Wilbert Robinson both named "Noisy" one of the two greatest-ever catchers; fine thrower and hit just fine for the times.
1B	Frank Chance	1898–1912	Didn't shift to 1B until his fifth season, then was the best in the NL for five years. Also managed, of course, and was one of the toughest customers in the game.
2B	Billy Herman	1931–1941	At his peak, 1935 through '37, was arguably the best player in the National League; excellent fielder with patience and power, and famous for his brainy play.
SS	Joe Tinker	1902–1912 1916	Among the Tinker-Evers-Chance trio, Tinker was the worst hitter, the best fielder, and the least deserving of his plaque in the Hall of Fame.
3B	Stan Hack	1932–1947	Patient and fast . . . why is George Kell in the Hall of Fame, and Stan Hack is not? There's no good reason, and Smiling Stan's case for the Hall is better than just that.
LF	Hank Sauer	1949–1955	Great hitter who didn't get a shot until he was thirty-one, then played in majors until he was forty-two; MVP in 1952, and probably not as bad with the glove as people think.
CF	Andy Pafko	1943–1951	Mostly remembered as a Boy of Summer, but as a Cub he posted an 830 OPS and twice knocked in 100 runs; they never should have let him get away.
RF	Kiki Cuyler	1928–1935	Speedy Hall of Famer's best years came with the Cubs, batting ahead of Hack Wilson; edges Andre Dawson, who was well past his peak by the time he was a Cub.
SP1	Hippo Vaughn	1913–1921	Vaughn (1918) and Alexander (1920) gave the Cubs two pitching Triple Crown wins in three years. He won 143 games between 1914 and 1920, and won only 3 afterward.
SP2	Charlie Root	1926–1941	Lost in the fuss about whether he gave up the called shot to Ruth in 1932 is that Root had a terrible Series record in general, going 0-4 with a 6.75 ERA in 28 innings.
SP3	Lon Warneke	1930–1936 1942–1943	Neck and neck with Dizzy Dean for the best NL pitcher in the '30s to hail from Arkansas; for the decade, Dean was 147-80, 2.96 ERA, and Warneke 144-85, 3.23.
SP4	Ed Reulbach	1905–1913	Big Ed led NL in winning percentage three straight seasons (1906–08); only pitcher to start both games of a doubleheader and throw shutouts in each (9/26/1908).
RP	Lee Smith	1980–1987	Giant power pitcher followed Bruce Sutter as Cub closer; in eight seasons, saved 180 games with 2.92 ERA, all thanks to overpowering high heat.

To this point, exactly two relievers have been elected to the Hall of Fame: Hoyt Wilhelm and Rollie Fingers. Wilhelm made it in 1986, on his eighth try. Fingers made it six years later.

Wilhelm pitched effectively for nearly twenty years, and piled up every record that a relief pitcher could pile up. Fingers racked up 341 saves, which stood as the record until 1992, when Jeff Reardon and Lee Smith both passed him. In 1993, Smith zoomed past Reardon, and he finished his career with 478 saves. Among active closers, Trevor Hoffman is closest to Smith, but he's still three great seasons away from catching the big man.

Lee Smith became eligible for election to the Hall of Fame in 2003, and it's safe to say that his candidacy was met with something less than overwhelming enthusiasm. Of the 496 ballots cast by voting members of the BBWAA, only 210—42 percent—listed Smith. Seventy-five percent is required for election. Smith got one more vote than Gossage but fifty-six fewer than Bruce Sutter. Considering that Sutter still fell far short of election, it seems unlikely that Smith will make it anytime soon.

And I'm not sure if that's fair or not. It's hard to argue that Smith was one of the hundred greatest pitchers of all time . . . but on the other hand, he *does* hold the career record for saves.

Bottom line, Lee Smith was rarely a great pitcher. But he was a very good one for a long time, and that's been enough to get a lot of players a ticket to Cooperstown.

Kerry Wood isn't the Cubs' greatest rookie pitcher, even though in 1998 he went 13-6, struck out twenty Astros in one game, and was named Rookie of the Year in the National League.

"Toothpick Sam" Jones isn't the Cubs' greatest rookie pitcher, even though in 1955 he pitched in the All-Star Game, tossed a no-hitter, and led the Cubs with fourteen victories.

"Tornado Jake" Weimer isn't the Cubs' greatest rookie pitcher, even though in 1903 he won twenty games and posted a 2.30 ERA.

Why? Because of an amazing run of four rookie pitchers that began in 1905 with Ed Reulbach and ended in 1912 with Larry Cheney. Tossing Jack Pfiester (1906) and King Cole (1910) into the mix, the quartet collectively went 84-36 with a 1.92 ERA as rookies.

Reulbach became a star, of course, but the other three didn't fare quite so well. Pfiester did lead the league with a 1.15 ERA in 1907, but he couldn't handle the high workloads of the era, and last pitched in 1911. Cole won eighteen games in his second season, fifteen games thereafter. And after winning 26 games as a rookie, Cheney won forty-one games over the next two seasons, but only forty-eight thereafter (and most of those for the Dodgers).

		SINGLE SEASON	
		YEARS	NOTES
C	Gabby Hartnett	1930	Hit 37 homers; other seven NL starting catchers combined for 39. Rich Wilkins only other Cub catcher with 30-HR season.
1B	Frank Chance	1906	Easily his best season as a player . . . *and* he managed the Cubs to 116 wins in the regular season.
2B	Rogers Hornsby	1929	At thirty-three, enjoyed his last great season, winning the MVP and propelling the Cubs to the World Series.
SS	Ernie Banks	1959	Second straight MVP season; he'd hit slightly better in '58, but had a better year with the glove in '59.
3B	Ron Santo	1964	Finished eighth in MVP voting but had a better year in every regard than winner Ken Boyer; also excellent in '67.
LF	Billy Williams	1972	Had his best offensive year as his defense began to slip, setting career highs for both slugging and OPS at age thirty-four.
CF	Hack Wilson	1930	One of baseball's most famous seasons, as Wilson hacked his way to 191 RBI, still the all-time record.
RF	Sammy Sosa	2001	Everybody outside Chicago missed it because of Bonds, but Sosa hit 64 homers and led NL with 146 runs and 160 RBI.
SP	Ferguson Jenkins	1971	In Gibson's and then Seaver's shadow for years, but finally broke through with 24 wins, 263 K's, and only 37 walks.
RP	Bruce Sutter	1977	With devastating splitter, K'd 129 hitters in 107 innings with a 1.34 ERA, and was first Cub to save more than 30 in a season.

		ALL-ROOKIE	
		YEARS	NOTES
C	Randy Hundley	1966	After two cups of coffee with Giants, joined Cubs and hit 19 homers while playing 149 games.
1B	Ray Grimes	1921	Batted .321 as rookie and .354 as sophomore, but slipped a disk in 1923 and career went to hell in a hurry.
2B	George Grantham	1923	Did some nice things with the stick, but also made 55 errors to earn his forever-after nickname: "Boots."
SS	Charlie Hollocher	1918	Led National League in hits (161) and total bases (202), and helped Cubs to their first pennant since 1910.
3B	Ryne Sandberg	1982	"Hey, let's try the kid at third base!" The power not there yet, but he did smack 33 doubles and steal 32 bases.
LF	Hack Miller	1922	Billed as the strongest man in major-league history, and batted .352 with .511 slugging average as twenty-eight-year-old rookie.
CF	Jerome Walton	1989	Edged fellow Cub outfielder Dwight Smith for Rookie of the Year Award; neither of them ever played as well again.
RF	Scot Thompson	1979	Rick Reuschel's brother-in-law platooned with Mike Vail for a spell and batted (empty) .289 in 128 games.
SP	Larry Cheney	1912	Part of an amazing run of rookie starters that began with Ed Reulbach in 1905; Cheney 26-10 with 2.85 ERA.
RP	Willie Hernandez	1977	Make fun of the Cubbies if you want, but in the space of two seasons they came up with Hernandez *and* Sutter (1976).

HOMEGROWN		YEARS	NOTES
C	Bob O'Farrell	1915–1925 1934	Signed out of high school, enjoyed two big seasons before losing job to Hartnett, later MVP with Cards.
1B	Rafael Palmeiro	1987–1988	Cubs' first-round pick in 1985 after starring at Mississippi State with Will Clark and Bobby Thigpen.
2B	Glenn Beckert	1965–1973	Initially signed with Red Sox, but Cubs drafted him after his initial season in the low minors.
SS	Don Kessinger	1964–1975	At Ole Miss, Kessinger was all-conference in both baseball and basketball; signed with Cubs for $25,000.
3B	Ron Santo	1960–1973	Seattle high-school product signed for a $20,000 bonus, even though the Reds were offering $80,000.
LF	Lou Brock	1961–1964	Fudging some here; Brock played in right field for Cubs, and Billy Williams (below) spent most of career in left.
CF	Cy Williams	1912–1917	Played football at Notre Dame, signed by Cubs and brought straight to the majors after he graduated.
RF	Billy Williams	1959–1974	Like Aaron and McCovey, a product of Mobile, Ala.; signing bonus was a train ticket to Class A.
SP	Greg Maddux	1986–1992	Second-round draft pick in 1984, out of Valley High School in Las Vegas; great gamble, Cubbies …
RP	Lee Smith	1980–1987	Second-round pick performed miserably as starter, but reached Wrigley quickly after shifting to bullpen.

TRADED AWAY		TRADED	NOTES
C	Smoky Burgess	October 4, 1951	With Bob Borkowski, traded to Reds for a couple of guys who combined to play 23 games for Cubbies.
1B	Rafael Palmeiro	December 5, 1988	Everybody *knew* he would hit, but Cubs sent him and Jamie Moyer to Texas for Wild Thing and five bodies.
2B	Eddie Stanky	June 8, 1944	Traded during '44 season for Bob Chipman, who won 47 games afterward; Stanky became great leadoff man.
SS	Dick Bartell	December 6, 1938	Cubs traded Bartell, an outfielder, and a catcher to Giants for a shortstop, an outfielder, and a catcher.
3B	Eric Hinske	March 28, 2001	In 2000, hit 20 homers with 78 walks in Double-A … and traded to A's for Miguel Cairo and Scott Chiasson.
LF	Lou Brock	June 15, 1964	In St. Louis, the most common sentiment was, "Why in hell didn't the Cards get more for Broglio?"
CF	Cy Williams	December 26, 1917	Two weeks after Phillies stupidly traded Pete Alexander to Cubs, Phillies smartly got Williams *from* Cubs.
RF	Joe Carter	June 13, 1984	Long-term, trading Carter didn't work … but short-term, it got them Sutcliffe and a division title.
SP	Joe Niekro	April 24, 1969	With two others to S.D. for Dick Selma, who would be packaged in ill-advised deal for Callison (see above.)
RP	Dennis Eckersley	April 3, 1987	After a poor season (6-11, 4.57) as starter, Eck was dumped off to A's for three guys you never heard of.

The Cubs haven't made a lot of great deals over the years, but they haven't made a lot of bad ones, either. Even Lou Brock for Ernie Broglio … what a lot of people forget is 1) Brock's only position was left field, and the Cubs already had a pretty good player there, and 2) Brock wasn't a great player, anyway. He did enjoy some great seasons with the Cardinals, of course, some borderline MVP-level seasons. But most years, he was merely very good, with his great speed and good batting average balanced somewhat by a moderate number of walks and poor defense.

When it comes to poor trades, the Cubs' one weak spot is relief pitchers; well, that and the late 1960s/early 1970s.

The list of pitchers who became bullpen stalwarts *after* being traded by the Cubs is amazingly long. There's Eckersley, of course. But the Cubs also traded Ron Perranoski in 1960, Donnie Moore in 1979, Bruce Sutter in 1980, Jay Howell and Bill Caudill in 1982, and Willie Hernandez in 1983.

In 1969, the Cubs gave away Joe Niekro and Oscar Gamble. In 1971, they traded Ken Holtzman for Rick Monday. And in 1972, they traded Billy North—one of the game's best center fielders for the rest of the decade—to Oakland for reliever Bob Locker, who gave them one excellent season before his arm gave out.

In 1962, Cubs second baseman Ken Hubbs ran away with the Rookie of the Year award, garnering nineteen of the twenty votes. Hubbs hated to fly but he was a brave man, so he took flying lessons and got his license. On February 13, 1964, just a week before spring training, Hubbs and a friend took off in the middle of a Utah snowstorm, and crashed onto an ice-covered part of Lake Utah. Both men lost their lives. Hubbs was barely twenty-two years old.

It's now been nearly four decades since Ken Hubbs passed from this earthly plane, so perhaps now it's okay to ask: Was he really a great player, and if not, would he have become one, as so many people associated with the Cubs believe?

Hubbs *was* a great defensive second baseman, the best in the game not named Mazeroski.

The problem was that Ken Hubbs couldn't hit. As a rookie, he led the National League in strikeouts *and* ground-ball double plays, slugged .346, and posted a .299 on-base percentage. The next year he was worse: .322 slugging percentage, .285 OBP. Hubbs was so good with the glove that he reached the majors when he was twenty, but he obviously wasn't ready to hit major-league pitching, and probably should have spent at least two more seasons in the minors. Absent those two seasons, it's unlikely that he'd have ever become a decent hitter.

GOLD GLOVE

		YEARS	NOTES
C	Johnny Kling	1900–1911	According to John McGraw, "nobody . . . could throw better than Kling." Regular with four pennant-winners.
1B	Mark Grace	1988–2000	He collected four Gold Gloves with Cubs, and that's a fair measure of his contributions with the glove.
2B	Ryne Sandberg	1982–1994 1996–1997	Ryno's the obvious choice, but Billy Herman and Ken Hubbs and Manny Trillo were all brilliant, too.
SS	Joe Tinker	1902–1912	It's become fashionable to downplay the greatness of the famous double-play combo, but they really *were* great.
3B	Ron Santo	1960–1973	Sixties an amazing decade for third basemen, with Santo and K. Boyer in NL, Robinson and C. Boyer in AL.
LF	Jimmy Slagle	1902–1908	Played in left field his first three years with Cubs, then finally went to center field, where he belonged.
CF	Jigger Statz	1922–1925	Fantastic defender who played 3,473 games as a professional, more than any other player in history.
RF	Kiki Cuyler	1928–1935	In his prime, speedy and strong-armed, and good enough to play nearly as many games in center as in right field.
P	Claude Passeau	1939–1947	Top glove man of his time, and still holds MLB record with 273 consecutive chances without an error.

IRON GLOVE

		YEARS	NOTES
C	Tyler Houston	1996–1999	Second pick in '89 draft flopped with Braves, but got back on track as sometime catcher for Cubs.
1B	Dale Long	1957–1959	Long wasn't horrible, but first-base defense has generally been a strong point for the Cubs over the years.
2B	George Grantham	1922–1924	Let's put it this way . . . sportswriters didn't call him "Boots" because he preferred high-riding footwear.
SS	Chuck Wortman	1916–1918	Quite possibly the worst SS to play more than a thousand innings, and he really doesn't have any competition.
3B	Bill Serena	1949–1954	Had such a great arm that they toyed with idea of making him a pitcher, but didn't have any range at all.
LF	Lou Novikoff	1941–1944	If you're going to play the outfield at Wrigley, it's better if you *don't* have a serious phobia regarding the ivy.
CF	Hack Wilson	1926–1931	What the hell was Hack doing in center field, anyway? Joe McCarthy must have known something we don't.
RF	Keith Moreland	1982–1986	Summing up: "Moreland is a catcher who is trying his best to play the outfield."—*The Scouting Report: 1984*
P	Mitch Williams	1989–1990	Didn't get many chances, which was good because the left fielder had a better shot at snagging a comebacker.

		ALL-BUST	
		YEARS	**NOTES**
C	Todd Hundley	2001–2002	After consecutive 24-homer seasons in L.A., signed big four-year deal with Cubs and couldn't even bat .200.
1B	Chuck Connors	1951	Significantly better as a *Rifleman* than as a batsman; in 66 games, Dodgers castoff batted .239 with a pair of homers.
2B	Ted Sizemore	1979	Proved that his terrible stats in '78 weren't a fluke, and dispatched to Boston before season's end.
SS	Rabbit Maranville	1925	Came over from Pirates in blockbuster deal, then played only 75 games due to broken leg and failed as manager.
3B	Gary Scott	1991–1992	Hailed as "the next Ron Santo" and handed job without benefit of Class AAA, then batted .160 in 67 games.
LF	Steve Henderson	1982	Everybody loved his tools and he played well in '81 after coming over in Kingman deal, but slumped badly in '82.
CF	Adolfo Phillips	1966–1969	Leo Durocher said of Phillips: "He's got as much ability as Willie Mays," but he was out of the majors at twenty-eight.
RF	Chuck Klein	1934–1936	He wasn't terrible, but neither was he the same hitter in Wrigley that he'd been in the Baker Bowl.
SP	Ernie Broglio	1964–1966	One of the most famous busts of all, going 7-19 for Cubs after coming from Cardinals in trade for Lou Brock.
RP	Jim Brewer	1960–1963	Eventually became one of league's best with Dodgers, but 4-13 with 5.66 ERA in four seasons with Cubs.

		USED-TO-BE-GREAT	
		YEARS	**NOTES**
C	Roger Bresnahan	1913–1915	Longtime Giant and future Hall of Famer also managed the club in 1915, his last year as player.
1B	Fred McGriff	2001–2002	Came over in August deal for stretch run, and played brilliantly while nearly everybody else slumped.
2B	Davey Lopes	1984–1986	Actually played mostly in LF, and was successful on 67 of 77 steal attempts despite advanced age (39–41).
SS	Larry Bowa	1982–1985	Ryne Sandberg was a *throw-in* on the deal that brought Bowa from the Phillies to the Cubs. . . .
3B	Ron Cey	1983–1986	Who knows? If Cubs hadn't acquired Cey, Ryno might still be remembered as a third baseman today. . . .
LF	Ralph Kiner	1953–1954	Back was killing him by then, but he still had some pop; in '53 he slugged .529 in 117 games with Cubs.
CF	Bobby Bonds	1981	After awful season with Cardinals in 1980, got a chance to redeem himself . . . and batted .215 in 45 games.
RF	Johnny Callison	1970–1971	Rapped 19 homers in '70 before slumping badly in '71; finished with a couple of seasons in the Bronx.
SP	Robin Roberts	1966	After five-plus solid seasons in Baltimore and Houston, came to Cubs and posted 6.14 ERA in 11 games.
RP	Goose Gossage	1988	Just one of his many late-career stops, and his worst season since '73; 13 saves and 4.33 ERA in 44 innings.

Two Hall of Fame managers, and two Hall of Fame talents in center field.

One Hall of Fame manager got his Hall of Fame talent to play like a Hall of Famer. The other didn't.

The first pair was Joe McCarthy and Hack Wilson.

According to Charlie Grimm, McCarthy "was quite a psychologist. He could get Hack crying like a baby. Wilson would go through a wall for him." McCarthy took over as Cubs manager in 1926, and from that season through 1930, Wilson's slugging percentage increased every season, culminating in his .723 figure—not to mention fifty-six homers and 191 RBI. McCarthy was fired at the end of the 1930 season . . . and in 1931, Wilson's stats plunged. He staged a nice comeback in 1932 with the Dodgers, but quickly went downhill after that.

The second pair was Leo Durocher and Adolfo Phillips. Of the latter, Fergie Jenkins said, "He had great talent and did things easily, without struggling or strenuous effort. He had a strong arm, he could run, and he hit for both power and average. One-handed, he could hit the ball out of the ballpark. . . ."

Phillips played well in the first half of 1967, but his career went straight downhill after that. Durocher once compared Phillips to Willie Mays; if only Durocher had handled Phillips in 1968 nearly as well as he'd handled Mays in 1951.

In 1963, Sandy Koufax won twenty-five games, lost five, and was rewarded with the first of his three Cy Young Awards. In 1963, Sandy Koufax was the best pitcher on the planet.

Well, him or Dick Ellsworth.

Koufax won twenty-five games, but he won them for a team that won ninety-nine. Ellsworth won twenty-two games for a team that won eighty-two.

Koufax posted a league-best 1.88 ERA, but he posted that ERA while pitching half his games in the best pitcher's park in the National League. Ellsworth posted a 2.11 ERA while pitching half his games in one of the best hitter's parks in the National League. You have to give Koufax the edge because he pitched a few more innings and struck out quite a few more hitters. But Ellsworth was right there.

What made Ellsworth's season all the more impressive was that he'd just *lost* twenty games the previous season, despite throwing one of the league's best sinkers. He also threw a curveball and a change-up, but a lot of people credited Ellsworth's success in 1963 to a refined slider. Whatever the difference, it didn't really take. Ellsworth lost eighteen games in 1964, went 14-15 in 1965, and led the majors with twenty-two losses in 1966. He pitched well (16-7, 3.03) for the Red Sox in 1968, but his career petered out quickly after that.

	ALL-NAME		
		YEARS	NOTES
M	"Leo the Lip" Leo Durocher	1966–1972	Popularized by writers Will Wedge and Ford Frick; Babe Ruth called him "the All-American Out."
C	"Gabby" Charles Hartnett	1922–1940	Tagged by sportswriters because he wouldn't say a word to them; also known as "Old Tomato Face."
1B	"The Peerless Leader" Frank Chance	1898–1912	Commonly called "Husk," took over as manager of the club in 1905 and led Cubs to four pennants.
2B	"The Crab" Johnny Evers	1902–1913	Initially called "The Crab" because of how he gripped the ball, but became famous for sour personality.
SS	"Mr. Cub" Ernie Banks	1953–1971	And you can't hear or say "Mr. Cub" without also hearing or saying, "Let's play two!"
3B	"Smiling Stan" Stanley Hack	1932–1947	A lot of nicknames are "opposites," but not this one, as Stan really did smile a lot.
LF	"The Mad Russian" Lou Novikoff	1941–1944	A likeable sort who led various minor leagues in hitting, but flaky as hell and never consistently hit in the majors.
CF	"Jigger" Arnold Statz	1922–1925	He was a great golfer, and the most appealing theory ties "Jigger" to a golf club of the same name.
RF	"Swish" Bill Nicholson	1939–1948	Did lead NL in strikeouts once, but not to be confused with Dave Nicholson (no relation), who K'd every day.
SP	"Three Finger" Mordecai Brown	1904–1912 1916	Like a lot of nicknames, this one not as popular as another, less colorful moniker; in this case, "Miner."
RP	"Dirt" Dick Tidrow	1979–1982	Got this while pitching for Yankees, for the way he got his uniform dirty during pregame fielding drills.

TOP FIVE SEASONS	
YEAR	1907 RECORD 107-45
BEST HITTERS	Frank Chance, Jimmy Sheckard
BEST PITCHERS	Orval Overall, Miner Brown
NOTES	After '06 disappointment, came back to smash Tigers in Series.
YEAR	1906 RECORD 116-36
BEST HITTERS	Frank Chance, Harry Steinfeldt
BEST PITCHERS	Three Finger Brown
NOTES	Shocked in Series, but 116 wins is 116 wins.
YEAR	1908 RECORD 99-55
BEST HITTER	Joe Tinker
BEST PITCHER	Three Finger Brown
NOTES	Another World Series, another drubbing of Cobb's Tigers.
YEAR	1935 RECORD 100-54
BEST HITTERS	Augie Galan, Billy Herman
BEST PITCHERS	Lon Warneke, Bill Lee
NOTES	Three one-run losses to Tigers in Series spelled defeat.
YEAR	1984 RECORD 96-65
BEST HITTER	Ryne Sandberg (MVP)
BEST PITCHER	Rick Sutcliffe
NOTES	*Cubs win! Cubs win! Cubs win!*

TOP FIVE MANAGERS	
MANAGER	Frank Chance
YEARS	1905–1912
RECORD	768-389 (.664)
NOTES	Highest winning percentage in major-league history.
MANAGER	Charlie Grimm
YEARS	1932–1938, 1944–1949, 1960
RECORD	946-782 (.547)
NOTES	Managed Cubs to a couple of World Series.
MANAGER	Joe McCarthy
YEARS	1926–1930
RECORD	442-321 (.579)
NOTES	How—O how!—did they let him get away?
MANAGER	Gabby Hartnett
YEARS	1938–1940
RECORD	203-176 (.536)
NOTES	Never got to manage after he stopped playing.
MANAGER	Leo Durocher
YEARS	1966–1972
RECORD	535-526 (.504)
NOTES	Just a shadow of his former self, but did some nice things.

SLAMMIN' SAMMY SO-SO

When it comes to baseball, writing about what's already happened is a lot easier than writing about what's *going* to happen. Because baseball players are something more than amalgamations of physical attributes and past performance. They're also humans, and humans are unpredictable as hell.

Shortly after the 1997 season, I wrote an article in which I argued that Sammy Sosa was greatly overrated. I even made up a new nickname for him: "Sammy So-So." Actually, I probably shouldn't take credit for that, because 1) some writer in Chicago probably was there before me, and 2) in light of what's happened since, the nickname doesn't exactly reflect positively on my ability to forecast the future.

What could cause such a gross error on my part? A couple of things, I think; one of them excusable, one of them not so excusable.

First, the not so excusable . . . I made a classic error in my evaluation when I placed a greater weight on the just-ended season than on the rest of Sosa's recent career. Add up Sosa's statistics from 1994 through 1996, and you get some impressive results: .334 on-base percentage (good), .534 slugging percentage (great). But in 1997, Sosa slumped to a .300 OBP and .480 slugging percentage. He'd signed a huge contract extension during that season, and when I focused on his '97 stats instead of what had come before, I may have been reacting to that contract more than anything.

Anyway, after 1997 I happily exclaimed, "See, I told you that Sammy's inability to control the strike zone would get him in trouble!" I saw what I wanted to see, while ignoring the three previous good—not great, but very good—seasons. Sosa wasn't the great player that everyone told me he was, and so I didn't give him credit for being the very *good* player that he actually was.

All that said, there simply wasn't any good reason to think that Sammy Sosa would, at the relatively advanced age of twenty-nine, become one of baseball's biggest stars. Haven't you wondered how that happened? I know that I have. And the answer can be found in *Sosa: An Autobiography*, ghostwritten by Marcos Breton and published in 2000. How *did* Sosa jump from thirty-six home runs and thirty-six unintentional walks in 1997 to sixty-six and fifty-nine in 1998?

In 1997, hitting coach Jeff Pentland joined the Cubs. As Pentland says in Sosa's book,

> The two things that really stood out were [Sosa's] attitude and his aggressiveness. He is about as aggressive a person as I've ever been around. I've always felt as a coach that the more aggressive the player is, the better, because it's your job as a teacher to harness that aggression to where it's productive. At that point Sammy was aggressive, but he was wildly aggressive.
>
> And there was no direction or control of that aggression. His holes in his swing were off the plate—you could get him to chase balls. In other words, he was lacking in his ability to read pitches, which I think is critical. Obviously, the guys who do it best are the best hitters in the game: Barry Bonds, Gary Sheffield, and Jeff Bagwell. Those guys have tremendous ability to identify pitches when they are batting.

My memories of Sammy Sosa from all those pre-1998 seasons boil down to two things: Harry Caray moaning about Sosa missing the cutoff man, and Sosa striking out while taking a mighty cut at a slider in the dirt. Now, it's one thing for a hitting coach to recognize a hitter's deficiencies; it's a far rarer thing for a hitter himself to recognize his deficiencies, and possess both the desire and the ability to significantly improve.

But at the close of the 1997 season, Sosa had just signed the fat new contract and he had suffered through a subpar (for him) season, and the combination just might have been exactly what he needed. Well, that and Jeff Pentland, who said, "The important thing about hitting is that it's like opening up a flower. When it's there and the petals are all folded in, you don't know how beautiful it might be. What I made Sammy aware of was that there was a lot of finesse and softness in hitting."

But again, Sosa himself had to want to change, and by all accounts he did. "In spring training of that year," Sosa remembered, "when Jeff Pentland and I would meet daily to discuss hitting, we set out many goals because we thought it could be a special season. So we talked a lot about me taking more walks. We talked about me hitting the ball to the opposite field . . . We talked technique. We talked game strategies and identifying the pitches. We talked about my footwork, where I held the bat, how I held the bat, how I swung the bat . . . But going into that season, Jeff and I never—ever—talked about home runs . . . Home runs were the furthest thing from my mind."

Specifically, Pentland reconstructed Sosa's swing. Sosa dropped his arms, and changed his footwork to include a revised "tap step," and the result was, as Pentland says, "that Sammy would begin to use his legs better than anybody in the big leagues . . . Sammy was learning that power was actually more coordination and timing than brute strength."

And the rest, as they say, is history.

I'm grateful to Geoff Reiss for writing a number of the player comments, and to Al Yellon, Jason Brannon, and Bob Bojanowski for their editorial suggestions. Sources for this chapter include Peter Golenbock's Wrigleyville: A Magical History Tour of the Chicago Cubs *(St. Martin's Press, 1996) and Warren Brown's* The Chicago Cubs *(Putnam, 1946).*

CHICAGO WHITE SOX

		YEARS	NOTES
		ALL-TIME	
DH	Greg Luzinski	1981–1984	Finally able to play his natural position after years in NL, and solid for three seasons; one of only two men to hit three balls out of old Comiskey Park in one season.
C	Carlton Fisk	1981–1993	Ranks fourth on Sox all-time HR list; Sox the only original AL team whose top 10 career home run list is made up entirely of post-WWII players.
1B	Frank Thomas	1990–*2002*	Very close to a right-handed-hitting version of Ted Williams, until injuries began to take control of his career in the late 1990s; atrocious with the mitt.
2B	Eddie Collins	1915–1926	The best hitter on the 1919 team who didn't throw the Series still ended up hitting worse (.226) than three (Jackson, Weaver, and Gandil) who were in on the fix.
SS	Luke Appling	1930–1943 1945–1950	His 2,422 games with White Sox ranks first by more than 300; famous for his ability to foul off pitches at will, and for playing well at advanced age.
3B	Robin Ventura	1989–1998	Beginning in 1957, the Sox used 51 different third basemen until Ventura finally arrived; the over-under for the next 32 years is 57½ (Joe Crede notwithstanding).
LF	Joe Jackson	1915–1920	Hit 12 HR in 1920, one fewer than in the three previous years combined; was young enough when banished (thirty) that his power stats would have benefited from lively ball.
CF	Fielder Jones	1901–1908	Singles hitter with good batting eye was there for the first American League season, and managed Sox to their first championship in 1906.
RF	Harold Baines	1980–1989 1996–1997 2000–2001	In 1989, shortly after being traded to Rangers, became third active player to have his number (3) retired; first career home run came against Jim Palmer.
SP1	Ed Walsh	1904–1916	One of thirteen children in family of coal miners, learned spitball from pitch's supposed inventor, and for years rivaled Walter Johnson as the league's best pitcher.
SP2	Ted Lyons	1923–1942 1946	Suffering dead arm in 1931, developed knuckleball and wound up winning 260 games; in 1942, when he was forty-one, started 20 games and completed all 20 of them.
SP3	Billy Pierce	1949–1961	He's listed at 160 pounds, yet twice led the AL in K's per 9 innings and is Sox's all-time K leader; went 15-8 against Whitey Ford and Bob Lemon.
SP4	Red Faber	1914–1933	He and fellow HOF'er Burleigh Grimes were among last three pitchers to throw legal spitters; Grimes had more wins (270–254), Faber the better ERA (3.15–3.53).
RP	Hoyt Wilhelm	1963–1968	Didn't get to the Sox until he was forty (!) and threw 675 innings with a 1.92 ERA; best year was '67, when he went 8-3 with 1.31 ERA and 12 saves.

Defenders of Shoeless Joe Jackson would have us believe that while Jackson did take $5,000 from the gamblers, he didn't really *want* the money. And more to the point (we're told), he played his best in the 1919 World Series, leading all hitters with a .375 batting average and a .563 slugging percentage. Thus, Jackson's only real crime—and it was a slight one (so the argument goes)—was his failure to inform the authorities that some of his teammates were attempting to throw the Series.

In the first five games of the World Series, Jackson collected six base hits but was hitless with runners in scoring position. He drove in one run in Game 6 and two more in Game 7, but those were games that everybody was trying to win. He knocked in three runs in Game 8, but the first RBI came when the Sox already trailed 5–0, and the second and third came when they were losing 10–1 in the eighth.

Jackson's hitting stats don't prove his guilt, but neither do they prove his innocence. More damning, actually, was his 1920 admission that he'd given the Reds several runs with sloppy defense in left field. Taken together, the evidence suggests that while Jackson might have been a bit less guilty than a few of his co-conspirators, he was also something less than innocent.

It's not so controversial, rating Carlton Fisk as the franchise's greatest catcher. But Sherm Lollar ahead of Ray Schalk for the number-two slot?

Schalk was a *great* defensive catcher, and it's his glove—and perhaps his clean sox—that got him into the Hall of Fame. He weren't much of a hitter, though. Granted, Schalk spent the first six or seven years of his career in a pitcher's era, but he didn't hit in the 1920s, either.

Sherm Lollar wasn't Schalk's equal behind the plate . . . but he *was* one hell of a defensive catcher, thanks in large part to the tutelage of Paul Richards (a great defensive catcher in his day, he managed Lollar in 1953 and '54). Lollar led the American League in fielding percentage five times, he was one of the greatest ever at preventing (avoiding?) passed balls, and he won three Gold Gloves.

And Lollar could hit a little, too. His OBP with the Sox was twenty-one points higher than Schalk's (.361–.340) and his slugging percentage was eighty-seven points higher (.403–.316). In 1959, when the Sox won their first pennant since 1919, Lollar hit eleven home runs at Comiskey Park; Schalk hit eleven home runs in his career.

Yes, I know that defense is important for catchers. But Schalk's small edge *behind* the plate just doesn't make up for Lollar's big edge *next* to it.

NO. 2			
		YEARS	NOTES
DH	Frank Thomas	1990–*2002*	Rough adjustment to full-time DH role in 1998, hitting a career low .265; took to the role in 2000, though, and finished close second to Giambi for AL MVP.
C	Sherm Lollar	1952–1963	Good hitter who developed into solid defender after joining the White Sox, his fourth major-league club; one of the more underrated players of his time.
1B	Dick Allen	1972–1974	Didn't even make it through three full seasons, but when he played he was a one-man wrecking crew; despite missing 34 games in '74, only AL player with 30 homers.
2B	Nellie Fox	1950–1963	He and Eddie Collins both won AL MVP awards after hitting 2 homers, the fewest number a nonpitching MVP has hit in a season.
SS	Luis Aparicio	1956–1962 1968–1970	Fox and Aparicio finished one-two in the 1959 AL MVP voting, the only time double-play partners have done that; top stolen-base threat in the league during first stint.
3B	Willie Kamm	1923–1931	A career .281 hitter, and considered so great defensively that in 1964 his glove was put on display in the Hall of Fame; master of the ol' hidden-ball trick.
LF	Minnie Minoso	1951–1957 1960–1961	Chicago's first black major leaguer debuted for the Sox on May 1, 1951, and hit a 415-foot homer in his first at-bat; Mickey Mantle hit his first homer in the same game.
CF	Chet Lemon	1975–1981	Lemon was good, though far from great. . . . After a century in business it's fair to expect more here than a .288 hitter with medium power; just edges Johnny Mostil.
RF	Magglio Ordoñez	1997–*2002*	Sort of snuck up on everybody; didn't establish himself as a great prospect until winning American Association MVP award in his sixth pro season.
SP1	Eddie Cicotte	1912–1920	Posted first 20-win season at age thirty-three in 1917, and went on to win 90 games in his final four seasons; knuckleball pioneer would be in Hall if not for 1919.
SP2	Doc White	1903–1913	Only Sox pitcher to rack up double-figure victories in nine straight seasons, and in September of 1904 he tossed five straight shutouts.
SP3	Wilbur Wood	1967–1978	From 1971 through '74, Wood won 130 games and averaged 347 innings; only White Sox other than Red Faber to win 20 games in four straight seasons.
SP4	Thornton Lee	1937–1947	Won 22 in 1941; only Sox to win 20 between 1937 and 1955, and only ALer that season aside from Dimaggio and Williams to get first-place vote for MVP.
RP	Roberto Hernandez	1991–1997	Power pitcher with imposing presence was at his best in 1996, when he pitched in the All-Star Game; saved 165 games for White Sox before going to Giants.

SINGLE SEASON		
	YEARS	**NOTES**
DH Frank Thomas	1991	In his first full season, led American League with 138 walks and .453 OBP; also hit 32 homers and slugged .553.
C Sherm Lollar	1959	Named to All-Star team for fifth time in six seasons, and led Sox with 84 RBI as club won its first pennant since 1919.
1B Dick Allen	1972	An unbelievable performance in first year with Sox: 37 homers and 113 RBI to lead AL; just edges Thomas in '97.
2B Eddie Collins	1915	Sox benefited from Mack's dissolution of Athletics, as Collins batted .332 and topped American League with 119 RBI.
SS Luke Appling	1936	Batted .477 in September to finish at .388, the highest batting average in franchise history.
3B Robin Ventura	1996	Won his fourth Gold Glove and hit 34 homers, then the most *ever* by a left-handed hitter in a White Sox uniform.
LF Albert Belle	1998	Disappointed in '97 after signing huge free-agent deal, but came back in '98 with 49 HR and 152 RBI (team records).
CF Fielder Jones	1908	His best season came when he was thirty-seven . . . after which, he promptly retired to the lumber business in Oregon.
RF Harold Baines	1984	Baines played forever, but 1984 was the only season in which he led his league in anything: .541 slugging percentage.
SP Ed Walsh	1908	In 464 innings, topped AL with 40 wins, 11 shutouts, 6 saves, and 269 strikeouts . . . and went 4-1 in last 10 days of season.
RP Goose Gossage	1975	Back when relievers were real men, Goose pitched *142 innings* with 1.84 ERA, and topped AL with 26 saves.

ALL-ROOKIE		
	YEARS	**NOTES**
C Ray Schalk	1913	No sort of hitter yet, but he did a great job behind the plate and there really aren't any other viable candidates here.
1B Frank Thomas	1990	Played only 60 games and didn't figure in Rookie of the Year balloting, but slugged .529 with .545 OBP.
2B Ray Durham	1995	Heralded prospect cracked 27 doubles and 6 triples; made 4 errors in first 6 games, but only 11 the rest of the way.
SS Ozzie Guillen	1985	At twenty-one, arrived in the majors fully formed: fantastic glove, but virtually zero plate discipline or power.
3B Pete Ward	1963	He was only twenty-three but never played quite so well again, due mostly to a series of injuries (the worst of them a hernia).
LF Ron Kittle	1983	Scout Billy Pierce's prize discovery, the big slugger went deep 35 times to garner Rookie of the Year honors.
CF Tommie Agee	1966	Stats—.273-22-86, 44 steals—superficially unimpressive, but Comiskey in '66 was *very* tough; Rookie of the Year.
RF Smead Jolley	1930	Legendary for his fielding misadventures, but the man could certainly hit; as rookie, batted .313 and slugged .492.
SP Reb Russell	1913	Armed with a new curve, Russell went 22-16; arm woes soon killed career, but he returned to majors years later as a hitter.
RP Salome Barojas	1982	Plucked from the Mexican League after six seasons, went straight to majors and set club's rookie record with 21 saves.

You'd think that Kenesaw Mountain Landis might have given Dickie Kerr a break. After all, while roughly a third of his teammates were doing whatever they could to lose the 1919 World Series, the rookie Kerr started two games and won both, permitting just three earned runs in nineteen innings.

Kerr's performance wasn't a complete fluke, either. He'd posted a 2.88 ERA during the regular season, and in 1920 he won twenty-one games (and saved five more) while compiling a 3.37 ERA. After winning nineteen games in 1921—albeit with an unimpressive ERA—Kerr asked for a $500 raise. The White Sox wouldn't give it to him, so Kerr signed with a semipro team . . . and got suspended by Landis.

Landis did eventually let Kerr off the hook—after Kerr had abstained from playing any professional baseball at all for an entire year—but the little lefty didn't have anything left, and posted a 5.15 ERA in thirty-seven innings in 1926, his last major-league season. And many years later, Kerr became somewhat famous as the minor-league manager who convinced Stan Musial to give up pitching, and instead concentrate on hitting (though Kerr didn't actually do any such thing).

Rarely, if ever, has a team followed up a pennant with as many idiotic moves as the White Sox made after the 1959 season.

Maybe if the Sox had won the World Series instead of losing to the unimpressive Dodgers, things would have been different. But the Sox did lose, and Bill Veeck panicked. On December 6, in two separate deals, Veeck traded Norm Cash, John Romano, and Johnny Callison for Minnie Minoso, Gene Freese, and a bunch of bodies. Minnie was pushing forty by then, but he gave the Sox two good seasons. Freese was, a year later, used to acquire Juan Pizarro. Meanwhile, Cash, Romano, and Callison combined to play thirty-seven more years in the major leagues.

Wait, there's more. The next April 5, exactly two weeks before the Sox's first game, Veeck sent Earl Battey *and* Don Mincher *and* $150,000 to the Senators for first baseman Roy Sievers. Sievers played quite well for two seasons (after which the Sox discarded him). But Battey was the second-best catcher in the American League in the 1960s, and Mincher was one of the league's top power hitters.

Those post-1959 moves might not have cost the White Sox any pennants, but they certainly didn't help them win any, either.

	HOMEGROWN		
		YEARS	NOTES
DH	Harold Baines	1980–1989 1996–1997	Also 2000–2001; first overall pick in '77 draft after being personally scouted by Sox owner Bill Veeck.
C	Brian Downing	1973–1977	Wasn't drafted, but then, who knew he'd one day become baseball's "Incredible Hulk"?
1B	Frank Thomas	1990–*2002*	Like Ventura the June before, a first-round pick, and like Ventura, Thomas blew through the minors.
2B	Ray Durham	1995–2002	Never great, but always good (and in the lineup), drafted in fifth round out of a Charlotte high school.
SS	Luis Aparicio	1956–1962 1968–1970	Fellow Venezuelan Chico Carrasquel recommended Aparicio . . . and then Little Looie took Chico's job.
3B	Robin Ventura	1989–1998	First-round pick in '88 made history with 58-game hitting streak at Oklahoma State.
LF	Don Buford	1963–1967	Sox didn't know what they had, and so they kept fooling around with Buford in the infield.
CF	Mike Cameron	1995–1998	Why haven't the White Sox won a World Series since 1917? For a partial answer, keep reading. . . .
RF	Magglio Ordoñez	1997–*2002*	. . . Shouldn't the White Sox have developed at least a few outstanding outfielders *before* the 1990s?
SP	Ted Lyons	1923–1942 1946	Went straight from Baylor University to the majors, and never spent a single day in the minor leagues.
RP	Bobby Thigpen	1986–1993	Fourth-round pick in '85 reached majors in second pro season, set MLB record with 57 saves in 1990.

	TRADED AWAY		
		TRADED	NOTES
DH	Brian Downing	December 5, 1977	Still a catcher, and wouldn't become an OF, DH, and great hitter for a few years yet; Sox got Bobby Bonds.
C	Earl Battey	April 5, 1960	Horrible deal sent Battey *and* Don Mincher *and* big dough (for the time) to Senators for Roy Sievers.
1B	Norm Cash	December 6, 1959	Sox got two good years of Minnie Minoso but lost 15 years of Norm Cash, so it wasn't the best deal ever.
2B	Ray Durham	July 25, 2002	We don't have any idea what Durham's career will look like in 10 years, but he's got little competition.
SS	Luis Aparicio	January 14, 1963	Great deal for Sox, who got Looie's replacement (Ron Hansen) *and* Hoyt Wilhelm; Aparicio returned for 1968.
3B	Bobby Bonilla	July 23, 1986	Sox grabbed him from Pirates in Rule 5 draft, then traded him back a year and a half later.
LF	Don Buford	November 29, 1967	First a second baseman, then a third baseman with Sox, became left fielder and OBP machine with Orioles.
CF	Tommie Agee	December 15, 1967	Rookie of the Year in 1966 dropped off in '67, which was all general manager Ed Short needed to see.
RF	Sammy Sosa	March 30, 1992	Hey, who knew? In two seasons with Sox, Sosa batted .227 and walked just slightly more often than Ironsides.
SP	Tommy John	December 2, 1971	Deal for Dick Allen looked great for a couple of years, but of course John outlasted Allen by quite a bit.
RP	Rich Gossage	December 10, 1976	The Sox got a fine season from Richie Zisk; a bunch of other teams got nearly two good decades from Gossage.

GOLD GLOVE

		YEARS	NOTES
C	Ray Schalk	1912–1928	The AL's best defensive catcher for about a decade, and supposedly the first to back up 1B on ground balls.
1B	Joe Kuhel	1938–1943	After four years of watching Zeke Bonura wave at ground balls, Sox fans were thrilled with Kuhel's skills.
2B	Nellie Fox	1950–1963	Started career as first baseman in A's system, but eventually became best second baseman in the league.
SS	Ron Hansen	1963–1967 1968–1969	Before a serious back injury took over his career in 1966, Hansen was the top glove man in the majors.
3B	Willie Kamm	1923–1931	Best third baseman in the AL for about a decade; William Curran compared his grace to Gene Kelly's.
LF	Al Simmons	1933–1935	"There never was a greater left fielder in going to the line and holding a double to a single."—Joe Cronin
CF	Mike Kreevich	1935–1941	Good wheels and a great arm; plenty of competition here, including Felsch, Mostil, Tucker, Agee, and Singleton.
RF	Jim Rivera	1952–1961	Famous for his hustle, and saved Game 5 in '59 Series with brilliant catch after entering game to play defense.
P	Ted Lyons	1923–1942 1946	In 1933, described as "one of the greatest fielding pitchers in the history of the majors . . ."

IRON GLOVE

		YEARS	NOTES
C	Mike Squires	1980, 1984	You just have to mention a first baseman who caught two games . . . left-handed.
1B	Frank Thomas	1990–*2002*	Terrible, but 1) he hit better when he was playing 1B, and 2) 1B defense doesn't really matter that much anyway.
2B	Jorge Orta	1972–1979	Quite possibly the worst defensive second baseman *ever* to play as many games there (689) as he did.
SS	Alan Bannister	1976–1978	Well, it was better to have him there than nobody . . . but he and Orta were historically awful up the middle.
3B	Kenny Williams	1988	Noble experiment that failed spectacularly, as Williams made 14 errors in 32 games *and* stopped hitting.
LF	Johnny Dickshot	1944–1945	Born John Oscar Dicksus, nicknamed "Ugly" . . . *and* he couldn't play defense? Some guys get all the luck.
CF	Myril Hoag	1941–1942 1944	Decent enough in the corners, but miscast in center and played there only because of the war; Jeff Abbott bad, too.
RF	Smead Jolley	1930–1932	Great hitter in the PCL but couldn't catch a cold in the outfield; immensely popular with the fans, though.
P	James Baldwin	1995–2001	Generally looked half-asleep, and didn't start a double play until his sixth season in the majors.

For one glorious summer, the White Sox featured the worst keystone combination in major-league history.

What's glorious about that? In 1977, the Sox set a franchise record with 1,657,135 paying customers. All those fans gained national attention for demanding a curtain call every time a White Sox player homered. And there were a lot of curtain calls, as the Sox obliterated their franchise record with 192 homers, leading to the nickname, "South Side Hit Men." All that offense gave the Sox a five-and-a-half-game lead in the American League on July 31, and as late as August 19 they were still in first place.

The Sox eventually finished a dozen games off the pace. But many White Sox fans still remember 1977 as the most exciting summer of their lives.

Now, about that keystone combination . . . Shortstop Alan Bannister led the American League with forty errors. Jorge Orta committed "only" nineteen miscues, but his .970 fielding percentage was the worst in the league among second basemen who played more than seventy-five games. As a team, the White Sox turned 125 double plays, fewest in the league.

The Sox actually had decent defense in the outfield, and at the infield corners. But they didn't have much pitching, and they didn't get any defense at all from the guys around second base.

On Opening Day of the 1998 season, Queens native Mike Caruso was 1) still a few weeks shy of his twenty-first birthday, and 2) the starting shortstop for the Chicago White Sox.

Caruso, a former second-round draft pick, spent 1997 in Class A and batted .311 with a couple of teams. He came to camp with the White Sox the following spring, and became the youngest player in nearly forty years to make the club's Opening Day roster.

Caruso led all American League rookies with a .306 batting average, and finished third in Rookie of the Year voting. It was an empty .300—only fourteen walks and twenty-eight extra-base hits—but it certainly was something to build on. That's not what happened, though. Caruso's shaky defense didn't get any better, his batting average dropped to .250, and at twenty-two Mike Caruso was basically washed up.

In both of his major-league seasons, Caruso was the hardest player in the league to strike out. Unfortunately, he also was one of the hardest to walk and he didn't have any power. As a hitter, Caruso was essentially another Ozzie Guillen, but Caruso wasn't the fielder that Guillen was. And if you've got Ozzie Guillen's bat but you don't have Ozzie Guillen's glove, then you can't play.

ALL-BUST

		YEARS	NOTES
DH	George Bell	1992–1993	His two years were bad enough—.278 OBP and .396 slugging—and the Sox gave up Sammy Sosa to get him.
C	Joel Skinner	1986	GM Hawk Harrelson sent Fisk to left field and installed Skinner behind plate, but he batted .201 and got traded.
1B	Chick Gandil	1919	There's no way to know for sure, but it seems unlikely the Series would have been fixed without him.
2B	Ron Santo	1974	Safe to say the move to second base didn't work out so well, as Santo batted .221 with only 5 homers all season.
SS	Bill Cissell	1928–1932	Lasted four seasons as regular, but didn't hit for beans after costing Sox something like $150,000.
3B	Chris Snopek	1997	Showed great promise in minors, then batted .218 with little power in first (and only) shot at regular duty.
LF	Tommy Davis	1968	Supposed to put Sox over the top after the near-miss in '67, but scored only 30 runs in 132 games.
CF	Jay Johnstone	1972	After decent '71 season—.260 with 16 homers as part-timer—crashed with .188 average and lost his job.
RF	Rocky Colavito	1967	Just two seasons removed from leading AL in RBI, batted .221 with 3 homers in 60 games as Sox fell short in race.
SP	Scott Ruffcorn	1993–1996	Considered one of the game's great pitching prospects, but went 0-5 with 9.71 ERA in 12 games.
RP	Whit Wyatt	1933–1936	Before making four All-Star teams with Dodgers, went 11-18 with 5.90 ERA in four seasons with Sox.

USED-TO-BE-GREAT

		YEARS	NOTES
DH	José Canseco	2001	Like him or not, the man could still hit, and walloped 9 homers in only 66 at-bats against lefties.
C	Sandy Alomar, Sr.	2001–2002	Six-time All-Star—and yes, I know he really wasn't that good—played sparingly because of injuries; nothing new.
1B	Hal Trosky	1944, 1946	Retired for two years because of migraine headaches, then came back for a couple of poor seasons with Sox.
2B	Ron Santo	1974	Sox already had Melton at 3B, so they tried to make a 2B out of Santo; it didn't work, and he never played again.
SS	Don Kessinger	1977–1979	First Santo, then Kessinger, who still couldn't hit but did manage in 1979 until resigning in early August.
3B	Bob Elliott	1953	Came over from Browns in mid-season, but change of scenery didn't help; also, Vern Stephens and George Kell.
LF	Tim Raines	1991–1995	Beginning in 1993, stole 40 straight bases to shatter the American League record.
CF	Kenny Lofton	2002	After a decade with Tribe, signed with Sox and posted .348 OBP in 93 games before getting traded to Giants.
RF	Harry Hooper	1921–1925	The Red Sox sent most of their stars to the Yankees, but the White Sox got Hooper, who still had plenty left.
SP	Steve Carlton	1986	Sox were second team on Carlton's list as he quickly ran through clubs willing to take a chance.
RP	Sparky Lyle	1982	Pitched in 11 games for the Sox, and his only save for the club was No. 238—and the last—of his long career.

	ALL-NAME	YEARS	NOTES
M	"Pants" Clarence Rowland	1915–1918	Showed up one day wearing big brother's pants, and the nickname stuck through six decades in the game.
DH	"Big Hurt" Frank Thomas	1990–*2002*	White Sox broadcaster Hawk Harrelson invented a lot of nicknames, and this was probably the best of them.
C	"Cracker" Ray Schalk	1912–1928	No, he wasn't from Dixie; Chicago-area native claimed that he didn't know how he got the moniker.
1B	"Ozark Ike" Gus Zernial	1949–1951	Hollywood Stars broadcaster Fred Haney came up with this one, after a popular cartoon character.
2B	Cass Michaels	1943–1950 1954	Changed his baseball name to Cass Michaels in 1944; before that he was Casimir Eugene Kwietniewski.
SS	"Old Aches and Pains" Luke Appling	1930–1943 1945–1950	Played into his early forties and was also a notorious hypochondriac; also known as "Luscious Luke."
3B	"Psycho" Steve Lyons	1986–1990	Came by "Psycho" fair and square, and parlayed his reputation into a lucrative TV career.
LF	"The Polish Prince" Richie Zisk	1977	Homered his first time up with the club, and became instant fan favorite in Pole-heavy Chicago.
CF	"Dutch" Edward Zwilling	1910	Alphabetical list of major-league players begins with Hank Aaron . . . and ends with Dutch Zwilling.
RF	"Jungle Jim" Jim Rivera	1952–1961	Product of a New York ghetto spent ten years in an orphanage, and played like there was no tomorrow.
SP	"Doc" Guy Harris White	1903–1913	Successful composer also practiced dentistry until he'd pitched three full seasons in the majors.
RP	"Old Tilt" Hoyt Wilhelm	1963–1968	He was old—forty-five by the time he left Chi—and he tilted his head to one side; any more questions?

TOP FIVE SEASONS

YEAR 1906 **RECORD** 93-58
BEST HITTERS George Davis, Fielder Jones, Frank Isbell
BEST PITCHERS Doc White, Ed Walsh
NOTES Hitless Wonders shocked 116-win Cubs in World Series.

YEAR 1917 **RECORD** 100-54
BEST HITTERS Eddie Collins, Joe Jackson, Hap Felsch
BEST PITCHER Eddie Cicotte
NOTES Sox topped Giants in Series as Red Faber won thrice.

YEAR 1959 **RECORD** 94-60
BEST HITTER Nellie Fox
BEST PITCHERS Early Wynn, Bob Shaw
NOTES After forty years, back in Series but lost to Dodgers.

YEAR 2000 **RECORD** 95-67
BEST HITTER Frank Thomas
BEST PITCHER Keith Foulke
NOTES Top record in league, but swept by M's in Division Series.

YEAR 1983 **RECORD** 99-63
BEST HITTER Carlton Fisk
BEST PITCHERS Rich Dotson, LaMarr Hoyt
NOTES First postseason berth since '59, dropped LCS to Orioles.

TOP FIVE MANAGERS

MANAGER Al Lopez
YEARS 1957–1965, 1968–1969
RECORD 840-650 (.564)
NOTES Only one pennant, but Sox were nearly always competitive.

MANAGER Fielder Jones
YEARS 1904–1908
RECORD 426-293 (.592)
NOTES Took over in center field in 1903, as manager a year later.

MANAGER Jimmy Dykes
YEARS 1934–1946
RECORD 899-940 (.489)
NOTES Managed seventeen full seasons in majors, never finished higher than third.

MANAGER Pants Rowland
YEARS 1915–1918
RECORD 339-247 (.578)
NOTES Thirty Sox managers since Rowland *haven't* won a World Series.

MANAGER Tony La Russa
YEARS 1979–1986
RECORD 522-510 (.506)
NOTES No "genius" yet, but took Sox to first postseason since 1959.

A lot of people don't like Ken Harrelson as a broadcaster.

That's not really saying anything, because you can find a lot of people who don't like *any* broadcaster. Well, maybe there's nobody who doesn't like Ernie Harwell. But you know what I mean. Baseball broadcasters are like broccoli: everybody's got an opinion.

I think Harrelson's pretty good, at least when he's not talking about his most recent trip to the golf course. But whether you like him or you don't, I think you *have* to admire what he's done for the lost art of nicknaming.

Back in the old days, every broadcaster or baseball writer worth his salt just assumed that part of his job was the assigning of nicknames. Bob Broeg came up with "Stan the Man," Mel Allen came up with "Old Reliable," etc. Now, though, everybody basically punts.

Everybody except Ken "Hawk" Harrelson. As Don Zminda points out in *From Abba Dabba to Zorro: The World of Baseball Nicknames,* Harrelson has "come up with several enduring nicknames, including Black Jack (Jack McDowell), The Big Hurt (Frank Thomas), The Little Hurt (Craig Grebeck), The Deacon (Warren Newson), and The Little Bulldog (Greg Hibbard)." And Hawk also popularized Lance Johnson's nickname: "One Dog."

So you don't have to like Hawk Harrelson. But you gotta give him credit.

SINKING SOX

Something that a lot of people don't know—though you probably do—is that it took nearly a year for the Black Sox scandal to break. With the exception of Chick Gandil, all of the conspirators came back and played with the White Sox in 1920, and most of them played brilliantly. But in late September, Cicotte, Jackson, and Lefty Williams all confessed to the grand jury, and all seven remaining conspirators were suspended. At that point, the Sox trailed the first-place Indians by just a half-game, but bereft of most of their stars, the Sox finished the season two games off the pace. So their chances of winning in 1920 were severely compromised.

But did the scandal have a significant impact on the franchise's future, *after* 1920? It is, of course, difficult to answer that question with any great precision.

Cicotte turned thirty-six in the middle of the 1920 season, but the other suspended stars were still in their late twenties or (very) early thirties, so there's every reason to think the Sox would have been quite competitive in 1921 and beyond, absent the suspensions.

With the suspensions, though, the White Sox were forced to rebuild. Had the Sox been broken up a decade earlier, Comiskey would likely have received some "help" restocking his club, because for the first twenty-odd years of the American League's existence, President Ban Johnson's primary interest was in beating the National League rather than promoting fair competition within his own league. But by 1921, 1) Johnson's power had been greatly diminished, and 2) Johnson and Comiskey hated each other's guts. So no help would come from that quarter. Comiskey would have to rebuild with his own resources.

It's often been written that Comiskey's health began to fail in the wake of the Black Sox scandal, and I don't have any reason to believe that's not true. However, Comiskey lived for another decade, and in the meantime he didn't exactly scrimp when it came to acquiring players for his club. In 1922, third baseman Willie Kamm batted .342 for San Francisco out in the Pacific Coast League. A number of clubs were interested in Kamm's services, and Comiskey "won" the auction with a bid of $100,000, a new record. As Warren Brown later wrote,

> . . . it took the publication of photostatic copies of the check, as well as an exhibition of the canceled original, to make some of the skeptical believe (a) that a minor-league player could be worth that much and (b) that Comiskey would pay it. After the airing given the wage scale of some of the players during the "Black Sox" hearings there had been a change of mind with many regarding Comiskey's once generally accepted free and easy way with money.

Not long after purchasing Kamm's contract, the Sox signed Ted Lyons off the Baylor University campus, and of course Lyons became one of the great pitchers of the next twenty years. Five years later, Comiskey again turned to the Pacific Coast League, paying the Portland club $75,000 cash *and* four ballplayers valued at $50,000 in exchange for a shortstop named Bill Cissell. Like Kamm, Cissell was supposedly a great defensive player with a pretty good bat.

As it turned out, Cissell was a good defensive player with a pretty terrible bat, and he didn't perform anywhere near as well as advertised. In fact, though he's largely forgotten today, Cissell gained a fair degree of ill fame in his time. As one recent book says, "Bill Cissell, a shortstop–second baseman, gained grim preternatural status among fans as the Cissell Curse when he disappointed expectations of an all-star career, took to the bottle, wandered around Comiskey Park for some years as a part-time day laborer, then ended up dying of malnutrition."

That's more than I planned on telling you about Bill Cissell. The point here is that Comiskey (and his business manager, Harry Grabiner) didn't simply throw in the towel after 1920. Comiskey invested heavily in the future of the franchise, in terms of both players and the physical plant (prior to the 1927 season, Comiskey financed a major overhaul of his ballpark).

If not for the suspension of six of their best players, the White Sox would likely have competed with the Yankees for American League pennants from 1921 through 1923, and perhaps beyond. But while I do believe that Comiskey's failing health hurt his franchise's fortunes, I'm not at all sure that it's appropriate to attribute Comiskey's failing health to the Black Sox; after all, Comiskey was old man. I think his health would have suffered in the 1920s even if the Sox had won the 1919 World Series, and I think the Sox would have suffered right along with him. If there's one thing that baseball history teaches us, it's that franchises generally suffer without strong leadership. And it's a fact that once Comiskey's strength wavered, the White Sox were left without strong leadership for decades.

I am especially grateful to Don Zminda for his editorial suggestions. Sources for this chapter include Richard C. Lindberg's The White Sox Encyclopedia *(Temple University Press, 1997) and Bob Broeg's* Super Stars of Baseball *(The Sporting News, 1971).*

Charles Comiskey. "Hey, look! I just screwed somebody else!"
National Baseball Library, Cooperstown, New York

Slotting Pete Rose as the Reds' No. 1 left fielder is little more than a convenience. He played virtually the same number of games with Cincinnati at three positions: 643 games in left field, 629 games at third base, 622 games at second base. Rose could easily rank as not only the franchise's No. 1 left fielder, but also its No. 1 third baseman, and No. 2 second baseman, and No. 2 right fielder (he also played 559 games in right field).

I've listed Rose as a left fielder for three reasons. One, he obviously played slightly more games at that position than any other. And two, it allows me to get the best players into the top two lineups. Because if you slot Rose as the franchise's No. 1 third baseman, Bill Werber gets bumped from the No. 2 slot at that position, and the No. 2 slot in left field goes to . . . well, probably Wally Post, who wasn't as good (though he was with the club for about twice as long).

That second reason also explains why I've got Frank Robinson in right field rather than left. He actually played about a season's worth of games more in left than right for the Reds, because he didn't throw well (though he was a fine outfielder otherwise).

CINCINNATI REDS

		YEARS	NOTES
C	Johnny Bench	1967–1983	Was catching every day for the Reds when he was 19, and if his knees hadn't given out he'd be everyone's pick for the greatest catcher of them all.
1B	Tony Perez	1964–1976 1984–1986	Six 100-RBI seasons for Reds, later returned to club and batted .328 in 1985, when he was 43; played nearly as many games in first stint at third base as first base.
2B	Joe Morgan	1972–1979	The greatest second baseman ever, a five-time Gold Glover who led his league in OBP four times and scored more than 100 runs in each of his first six seasons in Cincy.
SS	Barry Larkin	1986–*2002*	Best-hitting shortstop of his era—yes, even better than Cal Ripken—and only his inability to stay in the lineup for 150 games per season kept him from superstardom.
3B	Heinie Groh	1913–1921	Played second base for a couple of years before switching to third, became outstanding defender and one of the league's best hitters for six years.
LF	Pete Rose	1963-1978 1984–1986	Is Rose overrated? Yes and no. He was never the best player in the league and rarely even the best on his team. But he was very very good for a very very long time.
CF	Edd Roush	1916–1925	Like Groh, came from and went back to Giants but did best work with Reds; batting titles in 1917 and '19, and was outstanding defensively for most of his career.
RF	Frank Robinson	1956–1965	Truly great from the moment he reached the majors, with his only weakness a poor throwing arm that got him stuck at first base or in left field for a few years.
SP1	Bucky Walters	1938–1948	A converted third baseman with great sinker and slider, he topped National League in wins three times; 49-21 over '39 and '40 as Reds won two pennants.
SP2	Paul Derringer	1933–1945	Coming straight overhand, kept 'em guessing with mostly fastballs and curves, and the occasional knuckler; seven times an All-Star.
SP3	Dolf Luque	1918–1929	He was small—5'7" and 160 pounds—but the right-hander from Havana won 154 games for Reds, thanks mostly to a great curve he later taught to Sal Maglie.
SP4	Eppa Rixey	1921–1933	At 6-5 and 210 pounds, huge for his time; lefty never pitched in the minors after graduating from Univ. of Virginia with degree in chemistry; finesse with power.
RP	Clay Carroll	1968–1975	Came from Braves in a trade and became most reliable member of Captain Hook's Big Red Machine bullpen; had all the pitches, starting with fastball.

		YEARS	NOTES
		NO. 2	
C	Ernie Lombardi	1932–1941	Virtually immobile behind the plate, but he could certainly hit; batted .311 with Reds and it might have been .351 if he weren't the slowest player in the game.
1B	Ted Kluszewski	1947–1957	From 1953 through 1956, "Big Klu" and his massive biceps—remember, he basically invented the sleeveless jersey—hit 171 homers with only 140 strikeouts.
2B	Lonnie Frey	1938–1943 1946	Born Linus Reinhard Frey, but nicknamed "Lonnie," "Junior," and "Leopard"; easily the best defensive 2B in the National League before he got drafted.
SS	Dave Concepción	1970–1988	The NL's best defensive SS in the 1970s and also a solid hitter for most of the decade; performance fell off badly in '80s, otherwise he'd be in the Hall of Fame.
3B	Bill Werber	1939–1941	Valuable member of the "Jungle Club" infield—Werber was "Tiger"—that helped Reds win pennants in '39 and '40; scored 220 runs in those two seasons.
LF	George Foster	1971–1981	Everybody remembers 1977, of course, but that was just one of seven great seasons he gave the Reds; solid with the glove until fairly late in his career.
CF	Vada Pinson	1958–1968	He could hit, he could run, he could play defense, and looked like a Hall of Famer until he was 27, when his bat went away for no apparent reason.
RF	Ken Griffey, Sr.	1973–1981	Not much power, but hit for average and played well in right field, so just edges Ival Goodman (1935–1944); strangest Senior stat: only 6 HBP in nine seasons.
SP1	Noodles Hahn	1899–1905	Debuted a week before his 20th birthday and was spent before he turned 27, but those were seven great years; 127-91 with 2.52 ERA while a Red.
SP2	Jim Maloney	1960–1970	Might have been fastest in game before sore arm killed his career, pitched *three* no-hitters, all with Reds; in prime, went 117-60 with 2.90 ERA (1963–69).
SP3	Pete Donohue	1921–1930	One of the great workhorses of his time; with excellent change-up and brilliant control, twice led NL in innings pitched and thrice won 20 games.
SP4	José Rijo	1988–1995 2001–*2002*	Reached majors at 19 with Yankees, later came to Reds and posted six straight sub-3.00 ERA seasons; after five-year absence from majors, came back in 2001.
RP	John Franco	1984–1989	New York native known as longtime Met, but started with Reds and pitched brilliantly for six seasons: 42-30 with franchise-record 148 saves and 2.49 ERA.

Want to guess how many starting pitchers have won fewer than 100 games, yet pitched in six All-Star Games?

I don't know, either. But I do know that Ewell Blackwell is one of them. Yes, Blackwell pitched in six All-Star Games as a Red. So why isn't he listed as one of the Reds' eight greatest starters of all time? Well, the big problem is his record; he was 79-77 with Cincinnati. Blackwell was, it should be said, better than a .500 pitcher; in 1946 he went 9-13 despite a 2.45 ERA, and in 1950 he was just 17-15 despite a 2.97 ERA.

So he was certainly a hell of a pitcher. With his long arms, sidearm motion, and outstanding fastball, they called Blackwell "The Whip" (Red Smith once described him as "a fly rod with ears"). He scared right-handed hitters to death. But those six All-Star Games are nearly as misleading as Blackwell's record. He pitched in the 1948 All-Star Game in the middle of a season in which he finished 7-9 with a 4.54 ERA. He pitched in the 1949 All-Star Game in the middle of a season in which he went 5-5 with a 4.23 ERA.

Blackwell was a great pitcher at times, but he wasn't a *good* pitcher for long enough to rank among the Reds' eight greatest ever. I've got him tenth, right behind Johnny Vander Meer.

Teammates Danny Graves and Scott Williamson have one man to thank for their presence on these lists: Jack McKeon. Sure, Graves and Williamson were both fine pitchers. But as much as the quality of their work, it's the quantity of that work that brought them distinction. And if McKeon hadn't been their manager, they certainly wouldn't have worked as often.

McKeon took the helm of the club in late July of 1998. He was sixty-six years old, the oldest manager in the majors, and had first managed in 1973. Back then, top relief pitchers commonly worked 100-plus innings per season, and McKeon didn't buy into the modern practice limiting great firemen to seventy-five or eighty innings.

To be sure, there were some analysts—and yes, I was one of them—who predicted that all that work would take its toll on McKeon's bullpen stalwarts. Well, Williamson pitched two seasons for the Reds, and then he broke down, the victim of an elbow injury. On the other hand, Graves and Scott Sullivan (another workhorse) have, at this writing, shown no ill effects; in 2001, Sullivan became the first pitcher in history to lead the major leagues in relief innings in four straight seasons. McKeon, though, was gone by then. Despite his successes, the Reds replaced him with Bob Boone prior to the 2001 season . . . and the Reds promptly dropped from contender to also-ran.

		SINGLE SEASON	
		YEARS	NOTES
C	Johnny Bench	1972	Won MVP Award in '70 and '72, was just a touch better in '72, thanks to 40 homers and career-best 100 walks.
1B	Ted Kluszewski	1954	Big Klu hit 49 homers and struck out 35 times while batting .326; also topped NL with 141 RBI and .642 slugging.
2B	Joe Morgan	1975	You want Little Joe in 1975 or '76? Both seasons he was MVP after leading NL in OBP and winning Gold Glove.
SS	Barry Larkin	1996	Somehow named MVP in 1995, but actually played better in '96, with career highs in homers (33) and slugging (.567).
3B	Heinie Groh	1917	Swinging his famous bottle bat, topped National League with 182 hits, 39 doubles, and .385 on-base percentage.
LF	George Foster	1977	Hard to believe now, but Foster, with 52 homers, was the only major leaguer to top 50 HR in the 1970s *or* the 1980s.
CF	Cy Seymour	1905	A star pitcher in 19th century, but in 1905 led NL in hits, doubles, triples, RBI, batting, and slugging; fine fielder, too.
RF	Frank Robinson	1962	He was the MVP in 1961, but this was his best in Cincy: NL-best 134 runs, 51 doubles, 1045 OPS.
SP	Bucky Walters	1939	One of the great seasons ever, as Walters led NL with 27 wins, 2.29 ERA, 31 complete games, and 319 innings.
RP	Danny Graves	2000	Because he wasn't used like a "modern" reliever, recorded 30 saves *and* won 10 games, courtesy of Jack McKeon.

		ALL-ROOKIE	
		YEARS	NOTES
C	Johnny Bench	1968	Like Pudge Rodriguez 23 years later, Bench recognized as game's top defensive catcher the moment he arrived.
1B	Doc Hoblitzel	1909	Only 20 and would play regularly for nine more seasons, but his rookie season was his best: .364 OBP and .418 slugging.
2B	Pete Rose	1963	Didn't set the world on fire, but played good defense over 157 games, scored 101 runs . . . and of course he hustled.
SS	Barry Larkin	1987	Actually, he missed being a rookie by a few games, but is the only rookie or near-rookie to play well at SS for Reds.
3B	Chris Sabo	1988	Broke in with great defense, uniform-dirtying not seen since the days of Charlie Hustle, and funny-looking goggles.
LF	Frank Robinson	1956	One of the great rookie seasons: 38 homers, .558 slugging percentage, and league-leading 122 runs. Unanimous RoY.
CF	Vada Pinson	1959	Made the All-Star team and led National League with 131 runs and 47 doubles; he'd have better years, but not many.
RF	Mike Mitchell	1907	Mitchell's numbers don't look great—.292-3-47—but for a pitcher's year like 1907, they were excellent.
SP	Elmer Riddle	1941	Went 19-4 and topped NL in winning percentage and ERA (2.24), but was 26 and never pitched nearly as well again.
RP	Scott Williamson	1999	Working for old-timer McKeon, pitched 93 innings and recorded 19 saves *and* 12 victories.

HOMEGROWN

		YEARS	NOTES
C	Johnny Bench	1967–1983	Reds' second-round pick in 1965; he didn't do much in his first year as pro, but hit 22 homers in his second.
1B	Ted Kluszewski	1947–1957	Gridiron star at Indiana Univ. signed with Reds for $15,000 bonus; won batting titles first two years as pro.
2B	Pete Rose	1963–1978 1984–1986	Signed for $7,000 bonus, $400 per month, and an extra $5,000 . . . if he someday spent a month in the majors.
SS	Barry Larkin	1986–*2002*	The club's second-round pick in 1982, but local native didn't sign . . . so they used their first pick on him in '85.
3B	Tony Perez	1964–1976 1984–1986	Cuban native signed in 1960, and like Bench struggled initially but exploded as sophomore pro (.348-27-132).
LF	Hal McRae	1968–1972	Drafted out of Florida A&M in sixth round of '65 draft; injuries derailed his career with Reds.
CF	Vada Pinson	1958–1968	Memphis native dominated Class A in his first full season as pro, reached majors when he was 19.
RF	Frank Robinson	1958–1965	Signed out of high school—where he played hoops with Bill Russell and baseball with Vada Pinson—for $3,500.
SP	Jim Maloney	1960–1970	In his first two pro seasons, fireballing Fresno native struck out 341 hitters in 349 innings.
RP	Jeff Montgomery	1987	Ninth-round draft pick in '83; smart enough to earn a degree in computer science from Marshall University.

TRADED AWAY

		TRADED	NOTES
C	Ernie Lombardi	February 7, 1942	Nearly 34 and ran like he was 64, but the big guy could still hit, and batted .330 for the Braves in '42.
1B	Joe Adcock	February 16, 1953	Sent to Braves as part of four-team deal that netted Rocky Bridges for Reds.
2B	Bret Boone	November 10, 1998	Boone *and* Mike Remlinger went to Braves for Denny Neagle, Michael Tucker, and Rob Bell.
SS	Leo Durocher	May 7, 1933	Fine defensive shortstop for years afterward, but the Reds got Paul Derringer from St. Louis in the deal.
3B	Harry Steinfeldt	March 1906	Sent to Cubs for Hans Lobert and Jake Weimer, and became stalwart on league's best team for five years.
LF	Hal McRae	November 30, 1972	Reds got Richie Scheinblum and Roger Nelson, who never did anything; McRae a great DH for a decade.
CF	Curt Flood	December 5, 1957	One of the franchise's worst, with Flood going to Cards for two pitchers who combined for zero wins.
RF	Frank Robinson	December 9, 1965	Deal immortalized in *Bull Durham* as "Frank Robinson for Milt Pappas," but Reds got more (if not enough).
SP	Christy Mathewson	December 15, 1900	Traded to Giants for Amos Rusie, who had zero wins ahead of him, while Matty still had 373 to go.
RP	Jeff Montgomery	February 15, 1988	Dominant reliever in minors, then struggled as starter for two seasons so Reds gave him to Royals.

Finally, a chance to write about Ted Kluszewski . . .

In the entire history of the major leagues, seven players have finished a season with forty or more home runs and forty or fewer strikeouts. And three of the players—the last three, actually—are Ted Kluszewski. In 1953, he hit forty homers and struck out thirty-four times. In 1954, he hit forty-nine homers and struck out thirty-five times. In 1955, he hit forty-seven homers and struck out forty times. (He might have done it in 1956, too, if he'd been healthy. Kluszewski hit thirty-five homers and struck out thirty-one times in 138 games.)

It's been written that Kluszewski's home runs jumped because in 1953, the Reds pulled in the Crosley Field fences, but Philip J. Lowry's *Green Cathedrals*, the definitive source on ballpark dimensions, doesn't really support that notion. There was a change, but it wasn't a major alteration.

From 1949 through 1952, Kluszewski hit thirty-one homers at home, and thirty-one on the road. From 1953 through 1956, he hit 104 homers at home, and sixty-nine on the road. So while Crosley Field certainly helped Kluszewski, it's clear that Kluszewski helped Kluszewski, too.

Big Klu hit thirty-five home runs in 1956, when he was thirty-two. Plagued by back problems, he would hit only thirty-four homers the rest of his career.

For the first fifty or so years of the twentieth century, if you asked someone involved with baseball to name the greatest defensive first baseman ever, the odds were very good that he'd quickly respond with "Hal Chase." When Babe Ruth selected his all-time team—not based on defense, but on everything—he named Chase. It's mostly speculation, of course, but I suspect that if Chase hadn't gotten himself into so many troubles, he would have received a great deal of support for the Hall of Fame. . . . And he wasn't a particularly good hitter. People who saw him considered Chase a virtual wonder at first base, and this was at a time when first basemen were called upon to contribute quite a lot, because teams bunted so often.

So how can I call Chase the *worst* defensive first baseman in franchise history? Well, for one thing, his defensive stats were uniformly terrible, easily the worst in the National League. Even if you look at his defensive stats with an incredibly sophisticated method, they're still terrible. And then there's this: it's generally assumed that Chase, for his own reasons, wasn't trying particularly hard to make all of the plays. Let's say he purposefully kicked away ten or twenty plays per season . . . wouldn't that make him the worst defensive first baseman in the league?

GOLD GLOVE			
		YEARS	NOTES
C	Johnny Bench	1967–1983	Could both catch and throw with the best ever; won first of 10 straight Gold Gloves as rookie.
1B	Frank McCormick	1937–1945	Remembered for his big RBI years (1939 and '40), but also the NL's best defensive first baseman.
2B	Lonnie Frey	1938–1943 1946	Erstwhile poor shortstop became league's top defensive second baseman; especially good going to his left.
SS	Roy McMillan	1951–1960	Easily the game's top defensive shortstop for most of the 1950s, and a pretty good batting eye, to boot.
3B	Heinie Groh	1913–1921	Still holds single-season record for highest fielding percentage by NL third baseman, which is pretty amazing.
LF	Frank Robinson	1956–1965	Played left field for four seasons, didn't throw well but got to everything, and always knew what he was doing.
CF	Eddie Milner	1980–1986 1988	Seymour, Roush, Geronimo were all great, but Milner would have been a perennial Gold Glover if he'd hit better.
RF	Ken Griffey, Sr.	1973–1981	Outstanding in right field, and when he got a shot to play center in '81 he did quite well.
P	Bucky Walters	1938–1948	Played third base until he was 25, and so truly was a sort of "fifth infielder" after moving to the mound.

IRON GLOVE			
		YEARS	NOTES
C	Eddie Taubensee	1994–2000	Good thing he could hit; couldn't throw at all, or block low pitches; one of the all-time worst defensive catchers.
1B	Hal Chase	1916–1918	But he did enjoy his best-ever year with the bat in 1916, and when he *tried* to play defense, he looked great.
2B	Juan Samuel and Bip Roberts	1993	Samuel played 70 games at second base, Roberts 64 games, but neither of them belonged in the infield.
SS	Otto Bluege	1933	With Durocher traded to Cards, Ossie's baby brother pressed into service for 96 games and was awful.
3B	Dan Driessen	1973–1974	This didn't work out too well, so the Reds wound up trading Tony Perez to open up first base for Driessen.
LF	Joe Adcock	1950–1952	Something of a joke around the league, but couldn't play 1B because Ted Kluszewski was already there.
CF	Chick Hafey	1933–1937	With his eyesight getting worse and his hitting stats heading south, Reds kept putting him out there anyway.
RF	Dante Bichette	2000	Actually quite good fundamentally, but by then he was so bulky that he could hardly move.
P	Rob Dibble	1988–1993	With all those strikeouts nobody really noticed, but Dibs couldn't hold runners and he was an awful fielder.

ALL-BUST			
		YEARS	NOTES
C	Jerry Zimmerman	1961	Granted, the Reds did win the pennant, but rookie Zimmerman posted off-the-charts *483 OPS* in 76 games.
1B	Pete Rose	1984–1986	The manager was also a 44- and 45-year-old first baseman who couldn't hit, a shame given the guys left on the bench.
2B	Pokey Reese	1997–2001	GM Jim Bowden refused to include Pokey in the Griffey trade . . . and two years later, he was expendable.
SS	Woody Woodward	1968–1971	Hey, it wasn't *his* fault he absolutely could not hit; anyway, he looked fantastic in Reds livery.
3B	Willie Greene	1992–1998	Phenom finally established himself after five years, but Reds couldn't live with all the K's and E's.
LF	Kal Daniels	1986–1989	Had as much hitting talent as anybody in franchise history, but knee problems devastated his career.
CF	Taylor Douthit	1931–1933	Former defensive standout with Cardinals stopped hitting the moment he joined the Reds, and quickly lost job.
RF	Paul Householder	1980–1984	He was bad in '81 and '83, but in '82 he was atrocious, with frightening stats including a .265 OBP.
SP	Jack Armstrong	1988–1991	Entered 1990 All-Star Game, which he started, with 2.28 ERA, but just 5.96 after that, and traded not long after.
RP	Ray Washburn	1970	Longtime Cardinal stalwart finished career in Cincy with 6.92 ERA in 66 innings (Reds reached Series anyway).

USED-TO-BE-GREAT			
		YEARS	NOTES
C	Johnny Kling	1913	Former Cubs great came aboard for one season and hit his career hitting marks almost exactly.
1B	Pete Rose	1984–1986	After five years with Phillies and one with Expos, returned to play first base and manage the club.
2B	Bill Doran	1990–1992	Joined Reds for late stretch in September of '90 and batted .373 in 17 games; more or less the regular in '91 and '92.
SS	Joe Tinker	1913	First link of Cubs' DP trio managed Reds to seventh place but posted some of the best hitting stats of his career.
3B	Buddy Bell	1985–1988	After playing terribly in 1985 for Rangers and Reds, came back with two fine seasons.
LF	Wally Berger	1938–1940	Four-time All-Star CF with Braves spent two full seasons with Reds and could still wallop the ol' horsehide.
CF	Ken Griffey, Jr.	2000–*2002*	It wasn't supposed to happen this way, as Junior came home and went from great to merely good.
RF	Harry Heilmann	1930, 1932	Longtime Tigers star gave the Reds one fine season before arthritis in wrists ended his career.
SP	Christy Mathewson	1916	In first year managing club, pitched one game and won it, despite allowing 15 hits and 8 runs in 9 innings.
RP	Lee Smith	1996	Just one year removed from 37-save season with Angels, pitched moderately well in middle relief for Reds.

Perhaps it's not fair to classify Kal Daniels as a bust, given what he was able to accomplish. But he could have accomplished so much more. . . .

After his first three seasons, in which he played 322 games, Daniels sported a 937 career OPS; .410 OBP, .527 slugging average. He turned twenty-five late in that third season and was, at that moment, one of the greatest hitters on the planet. True, he wasn't much in left field—as they once did with Ted Williams, critics complained that Daniels spent too much time thinking about hitting—but he did run well, stole sixty-eight bases in those 322 games.

Daniels had the hitting ability of a Hall of Famer, but unfortunately he also had Tony Oliva's knees. Worse, maybe. Daniels underwent five knee operations before he turned twenty-six, and it was pretty much all downhill from there. After a slow, injury-plagued start in 1989, the Reds traded him and Lenny Harris to the Dodgers for Tim Leary and Mariano Duncan. His speed gone, Daniels nevertheless could still hit, and he drove in ninety-four runs for the Dodgers in 1990. That was his last hurrah, though, and Daniels was out of the majors before he turned thirty.

The 1939 and 1940 Reds infield, aside from ranking among the greatest infields of all time, is one of the few infields to have a nickname: "the Jungle Club."

The quartet came together on March 16, 1939, when Connie Mack sold third baseman Bill Werber to the Reds. Werber was both intelligent and intense, a real hustle guy, and when he threw the ball around the infield after an out, he really zipped it. Soon, shortstop Billy Myers and second baseman Lonnie Frey followed suit, making a big show of jumping around on the balls of their feet, etc. As Werber later remembered, "Lonnie had liver-colored birthmarks over much of his body and he was lithe and graceful, so . . . I began calling him the Leopard." Myers wanted a nickname, too, so Werber dubbed Myers "Jaguar" and himself "Tiger."

First baseman Frank Mc-Cormick desperately wanted to join the "Jungle Club," but the other guys didn't think he hustled enough. McCormick set about to change his ways (according to Werber, at least), and after a month or so, Werber told McCormick he was in the club . . . as "the Hippopotamus." McCormick sulked about that, but Werber was just kidding; McCormick became "Wildcat" instead, and the Jungle Club was complete.

ALL-NAME			
		YEARS	NOTES
M	"Captain Hook" George "Sparky" Anderson	1970–1978	Believe it or not, Earl Weaver was called "Captain Hook" before Sparky (George), but it didn't stick.
C	"The Schnozz" Ernie Lombardi	1932–1941	What can we say? You simply have to see the biggest nose in baseball to believe it.
1B	"Big Klu" Ted Kluszewski	1947–1957	At 225 pounds when he came up, ex-linebacker made the sleeveless look fashionable.
2B	"Mighty Mite" Miller Huggins	1904–1909	140-pounder commonly called "Hug," but this one was a lot more fun for the sportswriters.
SS	"Jaguar" Billy Myers	1935–1940	Just one component of the Jungle Infield, invented by third baseman Billy Werber.
3B	"Spuds" Chris Sabo	1988–1993 1996	First player to wear goggles and faintly resembled Spuds McKenzie, a dog who pitched beer on TV.
LF	"Charlie Hustle" Pete Rose	1963–1978 1984–1986	Hung on Rose by Whitey Ford when he sprinted to 1B after walking during a spring-training game.
CF	"Neon Deion" Deion Sanders	1994–1995 1997, 2001	Wherever he went, cameras followed; however, neither of his good seasons came with the Reds.
RF	"Greasy" Earle Neale	1916–1920 1921–1922	Got the nickname as a kid, later elected to both college and pro football's Halls of Fame as coach.
SP	"The Pride of Havana" Dolf Luque	1918–1929	He really was born in Havana, and became the first native Spanish speaker to become a star in the U.S.
RP	"The Nasty Boys" Dibble, Myers, Charlton	1990–1991	They were together for only two years, but might be the only bullpen to earn a popular nickname.

TOP FIVE SEASONS	
YEAR 1975	RECORD 108-54
BEST HITTER Joe Morgan	
BEST PITCHERS Don Gullett and Gary Nolan	
NOTES Beat Red Sox in one of the greatest World Series.	
YEAR 1976	RECORD 102-60
BEST HITTER Joe Morgan	
BEST PITCHER Rawly Eastwick	
NOTES Big Red Machine rolled over Yankees in World Series.	
YEAR 1940	RECORD 100-53
BEST HITTER Frank McCormick, Bill Werber	
BEST PITCHER Bucky Walters	
NOTES Reds won World Series for last time in 35 years.	
YEAR 1939	RECORD 97-57
BEST HITTERS The "Jungle Club" infield	
BEST PITCHER Bucky Walters	
NOTES Swept by dynastic Yankees in World Series.	
YEAR 1919	RECORD 96-44
BEST HITTERS Edd Roush, Heinie Groh	
BEST PITCHER Dutch Ruether	
NOTES World Series is, of course, remembered for the losers.	

TOP FIVE MANAGERS	
MANAGER Sparky Anderson	
YEARS 1970–1978	
RECORD 863-586 (.596)	
NOTES Only as good as his players, but that's true of *most* managers.	
MANAGER Bill McKechnie	
YEARS 1938–1946	
RECORD 747-632 (.542)	
NOTES Managed three franchises to World Series, did best work in Queen City.	
MANAGER Pat Moran	
YEARS 1919–1923	
RECORD 425-329 (.564)	
NOTES One of the great short managerial careers.	
MANAGER Fred Hutchinson	
YEARS 1959–1964	
RECORD 446-375 (.543)	
NOTES Reds came out of nowhere to win flag in '61, won even more in '62.	
MANAGER Davey Johnson	
YEARS 1993–1995	
RECORD 204-172 (.543)	
NOTES Took team in disarray to division titles in both full seasons.	

963 TO 10

Every franchise makes big mistakes from time to time, but has any franchise discarded more great pitchers than the Reds? Consider this: the franchise held title to Christy Mathewson and Jesse Haines and Claude Osteen and Mike Cuellar before any of them registered even one of their combined 964 major-league victories. And how many of those 964 victories came for the Reds?

One.

That's right. The Reds had 964 wins in their hands, and they let all 963 of them get away. And in the deals for those four pitchers, the Reds received three pitchers . . . who won ten games for the Reds, which puts the Reds 953 victories in the hole.

How did they manage to give away so much pitching talent?

Jesse Haines and Mike Cuellar just got away.

When Haines debuted with the Reds in 1918, two days before his twenty-fifth birthday, he didn't yet have the hard knuckleball that would eventually get him into the Hall of Fame. He could pitch, though, and did well in his first outing. After which the Reds released him.

Haines spent 1919 in the minors, joined the Cardinals in 1920 and wound up winning 210 games for them in eighteen seasons.

Cuellar opened the 1959 season with the Reds, but after just four innings was sent back to Havana (where the Cuban native had pitched in 1957 and '58). He eventually was released by Cincinnati, and didn't get back to the majors until 1964, with the Cardinals.

Like Cuellar, Osteen pitched briefly for the Reds in 1959. After signing for a big bonus in 1957, he actually pitched in three games when he was seventeen, then went down to the minors. He made it back to the big club in '59, but only for a couple of games, then pitched in 20 games for the '60 club but fared poorly. And then near the end of the '61 season, most of which Osteen again spent in the minors, the Reds sent him to the Senators for cash and a player to be named later. That player turned out to be pitcher Dave Sisler, the son of Hall of Fame first baseman George Sisler. Dave was thirty, and won four games in 1962, his last season in the majors. Osteen won eight games for the Senators, and would eventually become one of the great workhorses in the game. He never led his league in innings pitched, but in 1963 he did begin a string of ten straight seasons in which he started at least thirty-three games. Like Haines, Osteen was never really a *great* pitcher, but like Haines he was a very good pitcher for quite some time.

Dumping Cuellar and Osteen may have cost the Reds a couple of pennants. In 1964, they finished one game out of first place, and that same season, Osteen posted a 3.33 ERA in thirty-six starts for the Senators (Cuellar pitched brilliantly in the minors for a couple of months, but was just fair as a reliever for the Cardinals). In 1969, they finished four games out of first place; that same season, Osteen went 20-15 for the Dodgers and Cuellar went 23-11 for the Orioles.

Mathewson was an odd case. While the deal that sent him to the Giants for Amos Rusie is frequently remembered as a terrible trade, the truth is that it wasn't so much a trade as it was a setup, pure and simple. After Matty got off to a great start in 1900 with the Norfolk Mary Janes of the Virginia League, Giants owner Andrew Freedman made a deal with Norfolk owner E. H. Cunningham. The Giants would take Mathewson, and if they liked him, by October 15 they'd pay Cunningham $2,000 (a fair amount of money for a ballplayer in those days).

Matty struggled in his six-game tryout, but when October 15 rolled around, Freedman hadn't sent Mathewson back to Norfolk *or* paid Cunningham the two grand. Freedman offered $1,000. Cunningham declined. Assuming that Mathewson was safely back in the fold, Cunningham then sold Matty's contract to Toronto. Or at least he thought he did. As Fred Eisenhammer and Jim Binkley write in *Baseball's Most Memorable Trades,*

Little did Cunningham know, but Freedman had already hatched a plot to keep Mathewson in New York at a minimal cost. To make it all work, he contacted his old pal John Brush, who was owner of the Cincinnati Reds as well as a stockholder in the Giants.

Freedman and Brush were about to play what was referred to at the time as "syndicate baseball," and Cunningham was going to be caught out in left field. As noted in an article in *Sporting Life*, Cunningham received notice on December 19 that the Giants were returning Mathewson to Norfolk. The following day, Cincinnati drafted Mathewson for the paltry $100 fee required by the Virginia League . . . Brush then sent Mathewson back to New York in exchange for Amos Rusie—a hard-throwing pitcher who had already won 246 games but had not played in two years—to complete a deal made on December 15.

So the whole thing wasn't a trade at all, but rather a scheme to save Freedman $2,000 (or $1,000, depending on how you look at it). And it worked to perfection, at least for the Giants. Mathewson, of course, became the best pitcher in the National League for roughly a decade. Meanwhile, Rusie's comeback lasted three games and twenty-two innings, and resulted in zero wins and an 8.59 ERA. And if you think that baseball owners today are a greedy, pernicious lot . . . well, they've got nothing on their counterparts from a century ago.

(Mathewson did return to the Reds in 1916, as their manager, and recorded a victory in his first and only appearance as a pitcher in a Cincinnati uniform.)

I'm grateful to Doug Dennis and Pierre Bergeron for their editorial suggestions.

**It's 1916, and Christy
Mathewson is wearing a
Reds uniform. Finally.**
*National Baseball Library,
Cooperstown, New York*

CLEVELAND INDIANS

		YEARS	NOTES
DH	Andre Thornton	1977–1987	Generally remembered as a first baseman (at least by me), but DH'd more while in Cleveland, even though (the stats suggest) he was at least a decent fielder.
C	Jim Hegan	1941–1957	Had a little power but mostly helpless at the plate; *behind* the plate, though, nobody was better, and Hegan was widely considered the top glove man of his time.
1B	Jim Thome	1991–2002	Originally a lousy defensive third baseman, but switched to first and became a superstar with his punishing combination of power and patience.
2B	Nap Lajoie	1902–1914	Lajoie was so good that from 1903 to 1911, the team was unofficially renamed the "Naps"; has there been another MLB player who enjoyed that honor?
SS	Lou Boudreau	1938–1950	Let's see . . . fantastic defensive shortstop with great stick, also managed the club for nine seasons . . . nice combo, even if he was slower than pond water.
3B	Al Rosen	1947–1956	Played only seven full seasons, but ranked as game's best third baseman for most of them before back woes and boos drove him into retirement.
LF	Albert Belle	1989–1996	The first Indian to hit 50 homers, Belle became a devastating hitter and perennial All-Star after changing his name from Joey to Albert.
CF	Tris Speaker	1916–1926	Also the Red Sox's No. 1 center fielder; like Lajoie and Boudreau, longtime Tribe player-manager, and led club to first World Championship in 1920.
RF	Joe Jackson	1910–1915	Actually a better player with Tribe than ChiSox; has third-highest career batting average (.356) but is the only player in the top 17 not to have won a batting title.
SP1	Bob Feller	1936–1941 1945–1956	Led the AL in wins 6 times, and did so in 3 different decades; struck out 348 batters in 1946, at a time when K's were about a third less common than today.
SP2	Addie Joss	1902–1910	Pitched one-hitter in debut, died two days after his 31st birthday from meningitis; with great control of sharp curve and fastball, won 92 games from 1905 through '09.
SP3	Stan Coveleski	1916–1924	Very good pitcher, marginal Hall of Famer; with 215 wins, spitballer tied with Jim Perry for 78th place on the all-time list.
SP4	Bob Lemon	1946–1958	Converted outfielder is only man in baseball history to win World Series games as both pitcher and manager; also hit 37 homers and often used as pinch hitter.
RP	Doug Jones	1986–1991 1998	Perhaps the only premier closer who relied to such a great degree on his change-up; saved 112 games from '88 through '90 for team that twice finished sixth.

The story of how Nap Lajoie became a Cleveland Indian is worth telling, because 1) most people consider Lajoie the *greatest* Indian, and 2) until recently, everybody got the story wrong.

By the close of the 1900 season, Phillies second baseman Lajoie ranked as baseball's biggest star; they called him "the King." At the time, however, a league rule stipulated that no player could be paid more than $2,400 per season.

Good money for the day . . . but significantly less than the $4,000 per season that Philadelphia Athletics owner/manager Connie Mack offered Lajoie, shortly after the founding of the American League in 1901. So Lajoie jumped, and was all-everything in the new league's first season. But on Opening Day in 1902, Lajoie received a telegram: the Phillies had been granted an injunction that prohibited him from playing for the Athletics. Lajoie sat out for a couple of months, during which it was determined that the injunction was limited to Pennsylvania.

It's long been accepted that Mack then essentially gave Lajoie to Cleveland Blues owner Charles Somers, who had helped finance the Athletics. But researcher Norman Macht has discovered that because Lajoie's contract had been invalidated by the courts, he actually became a free agent. He could sign anywhere he liked. And he liked Cleveland.

Aside from starting pitchers—five longtime Indian starters are in the Hall of Fame—center field has been the franchise's strongest position. Selecting Tris Speaker as Cleveland's greatest center fielder isn't too tough, but for the number-two spot we have to choose between two Hall of Famers. And it's not an easy choice.

In this corner you've got Earl Averill, with 268 Win Shares in ten seasons as the everyday center fielder. In that corner you've got Larry Doby, with 216 Win Shares in eight seasons as the everyday center fielder. Averill averaged 26.8 Win Shares per season. Doby averaged 27.0 Win Shares per season.

Doby faced slightly better competition than Averill, but Averill lasted a couple of seasons longer than Doby. Averill was named to six All-Star teams; Doby was named to seven All-Star teams.

I could pick Averill because he's got that two-season edge, but even that's not fair, because after two seasons in Chicago, Doby returned to Cleveland and played well as a part-timer in 1958.

I could pick Doby because he batted .318 with a key home run in the 1948 World Series, but he also batted .125 in the 1954 World Series (Averill never played in a postseason game for the Indians).

In the end, I went with Averill because of those two extra seasons. But you could probably have talked me out of it.

NO. 2

		YEARS	NOTES
DH	Rico Carty	1974–1977	There may never have been a player as well-suited to DH as Carty, but unfortunately he was born about ten years too early; batted .303 in 430 games with Tribe.
C	Steve O'Neill	1911–1923	A lesser version of Jim Hegan, O'Neill went on to a successful managerial career, winning over 1,000 games as well as the 1945 World Series (with Detroit).
1B	Hal Trosky	1933–1941	Among the top six AL HR hitters in each of his first four seasons; due to migraines, career already on the wane when he briefly retired, and it didn't un-wane afterward.
2B	Roberto Alomar	1999–2001	Found his power upon joining club, averaging .323-21-103 in three seasons as Indian, during which he and Omar put on spectacular show around keystone.
SS	Joe Sewell	1920–1930	A freakishly good contact hitter, he struck out only 25 times in 1923 and '24 while racking up 215 RBI; four top 10 MVP finishes from 1923 through '27.
3B	Ken Keltner	1937–1949	Good hitter and fielder, widely regarded as the top American League third baseman of his era, and a seven-time All-Star . . . but not quite a Hall of Famer.
LF	Jeff Heath	1936–1945	Extreme up-and-down player. From 1940 to 1942 he slugged .399, .586, and .442; if somebody did that today, we'd all be wondering if he was on the juice.
CF	Earl Averill	1929–1939	Starting CF for 10 straight seasons, and only Speaker had greater longevity; borderline Hall of Famer, with late start and injuries limiting his career MLB numbers.
RF	Manny Ramirez	1993–2000	Outstanding hitter who combined power and strike-zone judgment from the beginning of his career; only Indian to lead league in OPS two straight seasons.
SP1	Mel Harder	1928–1947	Pitched in four straight All-Star Games (1934–1937) and is the only pitcher to pitch more than 10 All-Star innings without allowing a run; 582 games tops franchise list.
SP2	Early Wynn	1949–1957 1963	He'd have knocked down his own grandma if she crowded the plate; won 163 games in nine seasons with Tribe, then returned in '63 for career win No. 300.
SP3	Sam McDowell	1961–1971	The rap was that he wasn't as good as he should have been . . . but he was still pretty damn good, averaging 275 K's per season from 1965 through 1975.
SP4	Mike Garcia	1948–1959	Learned curve from Harder in 1949 and refined it in '51, which gave him two great pitches: the curve and an outstanding hard sinker; was merely good after 1954.
RP	José Mesa	1992–1998	The Indians successfully converted him from starter to closer with brilliant (albeit short-lived) success; saved 101 games from 1995 to 1997.

	SINGLE SEASON		
		YEARS	NOTES
DH	Andre Thornton	1982	After disastrous '81, installed as DH and responded with 32 homers and career highs in RBI (116) and walks (109).
C	Johnny Romano	1961 1962	Strange as it seems, "Honey" posted two best seasons by a Tribe catcher, and consecutively; 46 homers, 161 RBI.
1B	Jim Thome	2001	Walloped 49 homers, and in the process took over as franchise's all-time leader; also 124 RBI and 111 walks.
2B	Nap Lajoie	1910	Yes, he batted .426 in 1901, but the league was a lot tougher in 1910, when he batted .384 with 51 doubles.
SS	Lou Boudreau	1948	Let's see ... Hall of Fame shortstop enjoying biggest season, while also managing his club to World Championship.
3B	Al Rosen	1953	Hit 43 homers—the record for an AL third baseman until 2000—and fell just one base hit short of Triple Crown; 145 RBI.
LF	Albert Belle	1995	Downright scary: in only 143 games, became first major leaguer to reach 50 homers and 50 doubles in a season.
CF	Tris Speaker	1920	Wasn't quite as good with the bat as he was in 1916, but in 1920 Speaker also managed Tribe to World Series victory.
RF	Joe Jackson	1911	His first full season was best of many great ones, as he batted .408 with power and stole 41 bases.
SP	Addie Joss	1908	Topped AL with 1.16 ERA and pitched perfect game against Ed Walsh in late stages of three-team pennant race.
RP	José Mesa	1995	In first season as closer, converted 46 of 48 save chances, posted 1.13 ERA, and finished runner-up in Cy Young vote.

	ALL-ROOKIE		
		YEARS	NOTES
DH	Joe Charboneau	1980	Rookie of the Year and national sensation at 25, "Super Joe" was a complete bust before he turned 26.
C	Sandy Alomar	1990	Won Gold Glove, and became third unanimous choice for AL Rookie of the Year, joining Carlton Fisk and Mark McGwire.
1B	Hal Trosky	1934	Rookie season his best—35 homers, 142 RBI—but he starred through '40, if overshadowed by Gehrig and Greenberg.
2B	Ray Mack	1940	Tribe nearly won pennant, and rookie Mack was one of the big reasons why; All-Star batted .283 with 12 homers.
SS	Joe Sewell	1921	After sparking Indians to flag in September of '20, came back in '21 to bat .318 with 80 walks and only 17 strikeouts.
3B	Al Rosen	1950	Got cups of coffee in previous three seasons, broke through as rookie with 37 homers to lead American League.
LF	Joe Vosmik	1931	Batted .381 and .397 in two minor-league seasons, arrived with Indians at 21 and batted .320 with career-high 117 RBI.
CF	Earl Averill	1929	After tearing up the Pacific Coast League for three years, tore up the American League; first ALer to homer in first at-bat.
RF	Homer Summa	1923	No power, no glove, but he could put the bat on the ball; batted .328 as rookie and .303 in seven seasons with Tribe.
SP	Gene Bearden	1948	Knuckleballing war hero won 20 games, including one-game playoff for pennant, then tossed shutout in World Series.
RP	Doug Jones	1987	Pitched well—3.15 ERA in 91 innings—but not until '88 did the change-up artist break through with 37 saves.

At the conclusion of the 1962 season, Johnny Romano's career statistics included a .280 batting average, a .373 on-base percentage, and a .478 slugging percentage. He'd hit forty-six home runs over the previous two seasons. Not to put too fine a point on it, but Romano was the best-hitting catcher in the major leagues.

And he was only twenty-eight years old.

But he suffered a broken hand early in the 1963 season, missed forty-two games, and wound up with terrible numbers. He got off to a great start in 1964 ... but in early May, got nailed on the same hand by a Milt Pappas fastball. It wasn't broken this time, but he missed some time and wound up playing only 106 games (in which he hit nineteen home runs). Romano still had his power, but he just stopped hitting for average.

His first four seasons, he batted .294, .272, .299, and .261. His next four, he batted .216 (in 1963), .241, .242, and .231. This decline was likely due to the hand injuries.

Granted, Romano didn't help himself much. In February 1965, he made some disparaging comments about Indians' management—he didn't think he'd been playing enough—and got traded to the White Sox. Romano continued to hit homers and draw walks for two seasons with the Sox, but his career ended abruptly in 1967 with the Cardinals.

From 1960 through 1970, Detroit Tigers first baseman Norm Cash hit 293 home runs, scored 837 runs, and drove in 883 runs. Over those same eleven seasons, the Cleveland Indians' regular first basemen were Vic Power, Tito Francona, Fred Whitfield, Bob Chance, Whitfield again, and Tony Horton. Without checking, I'm pretty sure that they did not, as a group, hit 293 home runs, score 837 runs, or drive in 883 runs.

And what a lot of people don't remember is that Norm Cash was, for a few cold months, a Cleveland Indian.

On December 6, 1959, the Indians traded four players, the most notable of them Minnie Minoso, to the White Sox for third baseman Bubba Phillips, catcher Johnny Romano, and twenty-five-year-old first baseman Norm Cash. So far, so good.

But then Indians general manager Frank Lane made another deal (they didn't call him "Trader" for nothing). Just prior to Opening Day of the 1960 season, Lane sent Cash to Detroit for twenty-five-year-old third baseman Steve Demeter.

After the trade, Demeter batted five times in the majors, without a hit. Cash batted 6,593 times in the majors, and got 1,793 hits.

Based on their minor-league stats, there was little reason to think that Cash would become a quality major leaguer and Demeter would not. But that's exactly what happened.

HOMEGROWN

		YEARS	NOTES
C	Jim Hegan	1941–1942 1946–1957	Signed by Cy Slapnicka out of a Massachusetts high school, where he also starred in basketball and football.
1B	Jim Thome	1991–*2002*	Not bad for a 13th-round selection; believe it or not, he hit zero homers in first professional season (186 at-bats).
2B	Carlos Baerga	1990–1996 1999	Puerto Rican looked like a Hall of Famer for a few years, then suddenly became ordinary for no apparent reason.
SS	Lou Boudreau	1938–1950	Great hoopster at University of Illinois, but lost college eligibility after signing with Tribe for $5,000.
3B	Al Rosen	1947–1956	Didn't arrive for good until 1950 because Ken Keltner had a lock on third base.
LF	Albert Belle	1989–1996	Set all sorts of career records at LSU, then chosen by Indians in Round 2 of 1987 June draft.
CF	Rick Manning	1975–1983	Second player selected in '72 draft and got $65,000 signing bonus; better as a broadcaster than a player.
RF	Manny Ramirez	1993–2000	Grew up in Manhattan, not far from Yankee Stadium, but Tribe grabbed him with their first pick in '91 draft.
SP	Bob Feller	1936–1941 1945–1956	Cy Slapnicka, the most devious scout ever, illegally signed 17-year-old Feller and got away with it.
RP	Jim Kern	1974–1978	Took him nine years to reach the majors to stay, but then he became one of the best in the game for seven years.

TRADED AWAY

		TRADED	NOTES
DH	Pedro Guerrero	April 4, 1974	Still only 17 years old, but that season he batted .316 in the Northwest League; would've been a great DH.
C	Sherm Lollar	December 20, 1946	Starred in Triple-A, then traded to Yankees in deal for Gene Bearden, later became star with White Sox.
1B	Norm Cash	April 12, 1960	Trading Cash to Detroit for Steve Demeter didn't look so bad then, but turned into one of Tribe's worst deals.
2B	Jeff Kent	November 13, 1996	Turned into a lousy deal: essentially, Kent, José Vizcaíno and Julian Tavarez to S.F. for Matt Williams.
SS	Jay Bell	March 25, 1989	Sent to Pirates for SS Felix Fermin in a "challenge trade" that obviously didn't work out so well for Tribe.
3B	Graig Nettles	November 27, 1972	Indians smart enough to get him from Twins, and dumb enough to trade him to Yankees.
LF	Joe Carter	December 6, 1989	Nice deal for Tribe, who gave up Carter but got Sandy Alomar and Carlos Baerga from Padres.
CF	Brian Giles	November 18, 1998	May wind up ranking as one of three worst deals in franchise history: Giles straight up for Ricardo Rincón.
RF	Joe Jackson	August 21, 1915	Just the best of many candidates, as Tribe also traded Rocky Colavito, Jeromy Burnitz, and Roger Maris.
SP	Tommy John	January 20, 1965	John *and* Tommie Agee traded to White Sox in three-way deal that brought Colavito back to Cleveland.
RP	Hoyt Wilhelm	August 23, 1958	Sold to Orioles for the waiver price; sure, he was only 2-7 at the time, but he also had a 2.49 ERA.

		YEARS	NOTES
GOLD GLOVE			
C	Jim Hegan	1941–1942 1946–1957	He wrote the book on catching . . . literally: *Jim Hegan's Secrets of Catching* (G. P. Putnam & Sons, 1968).
1B	George Stovall	1904–1911	As a flashy fielder with weak stick, wiry Stovall a virtual mirror of his predecessor, Piano Legs Hickman.
2B	Roberto Alomar	1999–2001	Teamed with Omar Vizquel to perhaps form the most spectacular—if not the best—DP combo ever.
SS	Lou Boudreau	1939–1950	Like Cal Ripken, Boudreau was a great athlete—albeit a slow one—with great instincts and intelligence.
3B	Ken Keltner	1938–1949	Famous for his habit of looking at the baseball—"counting the stitches"—before throwing to first base.
LF	Joe Vosmik	1930–1936	Hometown boy made good in left with fine instincts and an excellent throwing arm for the position.
CF	Joe Birmingham	1906–1914	Not much of a hitter, but a brilliant fielder with legendary throwing arm; took over as manager in 1912.
RF	Rocky Colavito	1955–1959 1965–1967	For all of the Rock's skills, defense wasn't really one of them, but it's not been a good position over the years.
P	Orel Hershiser	1995–1997	Getting up there in years, but still one of the best in the business, quick to the plate and quick off the mound.

		YEARS	NOTES
IRON GLOVE			
C	Gary Alexander	1978–1980	In '79, his last season as a catcher, he led the league with 18 errors despite catching only 91 games.
1B	Eddie Morgan	1928 1930–1933	Two big years, but he stopped hitting in '32 and his glove certainly wasn't going to carry his bat.
2B	Chick Fewster	1924–1925	Generally an outfielder before hooking up with Tribe, and it certainly showed when he tried to play second.
SS	John Gochnauer	1902–1903	What a prize . . . batted exactly .185 in each of his two seasons, and in 1903 he led AL with *98 errors.*
3B	Al Smith	1954–1957	Fine hitter and decent corner outfielder, but in his four years with Tribe he fielded just .915 at third base.
LF	Leon Wagner	1964–1968	Described by Terry Pluto as "bizarre" in left field; caught balls one-handed and didn't bother calling for anything.
CF	Pat Seerey	1943–1947	Never the regular, but did play 88 games in CF for Tribe, who've traditionally had good or great defense there.
RF	Hal Peck	1947–1949	Played 97 games in the outfield in '47, convincing Indians to make him a full-time pinch hitter afterward.
P	Paul Shuey	1994–2002	Couldn't hold runners, motion left him in poor fielding position, and he prayed that the ball wasn't hit his way.

There are people who think that Omar Vizquel is the best defensive shortstop in baseball history.

I don't know any of these people *personally*, but I do know they're out there because I get e-mail from them, and I hear them talking while I'm watching baseball games on TV. And if you're one of these people, I'm here to tell you that it just ain't true.

Oh, Vizquel is certainly a *good* shortstop. But just looking at the men who have played shortstop for the Indians, Vizquel isn't as good as Lou Boudreau. Nor is Vizquel as good as Terry Turner, Joe Sewell, George Strickland, or Larry Brown. Nevertheless, there are actually people—you know who you are—who think that if Ozzie Smith is in the Hall of Fame, then by gosh so should be Omar Vizquel, someday.

There's a simple reason for this misconception. While Vizquel may not *be* great, he certainly does *look* great. And there's absolutely nothing wrong with that. If you give me a choice between watching Omar Vizquel play shortstop or Miguel Tejada play shortstop, I'll take Vizquel with nary a second thought. Because watching baseball is supposed to be fun, and there are few things more fun than watching Vizquel play shortstop.

But if I'm building a team, I want the guy who makes *more* plays, not the guy who makes *prettier* plays.

No franchise can touch the Indians when it comes to ex-great pitchers. In addition to Cy Young, the list of other immortals employed by Cleveland at (or very near) the ends of their careers includes Hal Newhouser, Satchel Paige, Steve Carlton, and Phil Niekro.

And for a brief spell in 1987, Carlton and Niekro were teammates.

In 1986, Carlton had pitched terribly for the Phillies and Giants, but rebounded with a 3.69 ERA in 10 starts with the White Sox. He signed with Cleveland the next spring, and on June 20 he won the 328th game of his long career. Ten days later, Phil Niekro won the 317th game of *his* long career. Oddly enough, both pitchers would win exactly one more game; Niekro with the Indians on July 20, Carlton with the Twins on August 8.

Anyway, both Niekro and Carlton opened the 1987 season with the Indians. Carlton was traded to Minnesota on July 31, and Niekro was traded to Toronto eight days later. And if my figuring is correct, those four months they spent together was the first time in baseball history that one team employed two pitchers with at least 300 wins under their belts.

Another, related, statistical note: the Indians' collective 5.28 ERA that season was the highest posted by an American League team since 1953 (Washington Senators, 5.33).

ALL-BUST			
		YEARS	NOTES
DH	Russell Branyan	1998–2002	You had to love his power, but it came at a pretty steep price, and Tribe finally tired of all those K's.
C	Sandy Alomar	1990–2000	Strange to list a six-time All-Star here, but he spent many months on the DL and wasn't a good hitter.
1B	Keith Hernandez	1990–1991	Utter disaster: Hernandez batted .200 in first season of big two-year deal, then didn't play at all in '91.
2B	Carl Lind	1929–1930	Played all but one game and batted .294 as rookie in '28, then caught bug in Cuba and never was the same.
SS	Mark Lewis	1991–1994	Second overall pick in '88 draft never became better than adequate with either the wood or the leather.
3B	Max Alvis	1965–1969	Another manifestation of the Curse: spiral meningitis reduced him from budding star to just adequate.
LF	Joe Charboneau	1981–1982	Rookie of the Year in 1980 batted .211 over next two years, making him one of all-time one-season wonders.
CF	Alex Cole	1992	In his first two seasons, batted .296 with 67 steals, then traded after batting .206 in first 41 games of '92.
RF	Harvey Kuenn	1960	Made the All-Star team and batted .308 in 126, not nearly good enough for the man traded for the Rock.
SP	Gene Bearden	1949–1950	After posting league-best 2.43 ERA as rookie in '48, struggled terribly in '49 and '50 and got traded.
RP	John Rocker	2001	Was pitching well for Braves, but completely fell apart and lost job as closer shortly after joining Tribe.

USED-TO-BE-GREAT			
		YEARS	NOTES
DH	Frank Robinson	1974–1976	Joined Tribe late in '74, took over as manager in '75 and occasionally wrote his own name on the lineup card.
C	Lance Parrish	1993	Played only 10 games all season, but would go on to play with two other teams before hanging up the spikes.
1B	Keith Hernandez	1990	You have to wonder what Tribe was thinking, considering that Hernandez already looked like he was done.
2B	Billy Martin	1959	He zipped through six teams in five seasons after Yanks dumped him, and the Indians were the third.
SS	Tony Fernandez	1997	After a year on DL, came back as 2B; did fairly well but made critical error in Game 7 of World Series.
3B	Bill Melton	1977	Hit 89 home runs from 1969 to 1971 with White Sox, but at 32 he managed zero homers in 133 AB for Tribe.
LF	Ralph Kiner	1955	The power was still there—18 homers in 321 at-bats—but back problems made this his last season.
CF	Pete Reiser	1952	Last gasp in one of the all-time lost careers; batted .136 in 34 games, most of them as pinch hitter.
RF	Sam Rice	1934	Not including player-managers, no other 44-year-old hitter has played so much in a season: 335 at-bats.
SP	Cy Young	1909–1911	He was 42 in aught-nine, but still managed to win 19 games with a 2.26 ERA for a sixth-place club.
RP	Dick Radatz	1966–1967	Did save 10 games in '66, but he also went 0-3 with 4.61 ERA as the old heat just wasn't there anymore.

	ALL-NAME		
		YEARS	NOTES
M	"The Boy Manager" Lou Boudreau	1942–1950	Lobbied for job as Tribe manager when he was only twenty-four years old . . . and got it.
DH	"Human Rain Delay" Mike Hargrove	1979–1985	He wasn't the first to take his own sweet time getting into the box, but he might be the first to get a nickname for it.
C	"Honey" Johnny Romano	1960–1964	As a baby, family looked at him and said, "Isn't he a honey!" (I call one of my grandmothers "Honey," too.)
1B	"Piano Legs" Charlie Hickman	1902–1904	Stocky fellow—5'8" and 185 pounds—supposedly had thick legs, like those of a piano.
2B	"Bad News" Odell Hale	1931 1933–1940	As in, bad news for pitchers; picked up nickname as first-year pro, when he hit 23 homers in Cotton States League.
SS	"Cotton Top" Terry Turner	1904–1918	See, if this were the old days, Omar Vizquel would have a good nickname, something like "Barehand."
3B	"Flip" Al Rosen	1947–1956	In junior high, Rosen was the pitcher—the "flipper"—for his softball team; he became "Flip," and it stuck.
LF	"Bedford Sheriff" Elmer Flick	1902–1910	He was from Bedford, Ohio; there's no evidence that he was a sheriff, but that's never stopped anybody before.
CF	"Rock of Snohomish" Earl Averill	1929–1939	Oddly enough, baseball's other famous Earl—Torgeson—also hailed from Snohomish, Washington.
RF	"Shoeless Joe" Joe Jackson	1910–1915	Details of invention are murky at best, but W. P. Kinsella knew a great title when he saw one.
SP	"Rapid Robert" Bob Feller	1936–1941 1945–1956	Close call between "Rapid Robert" Feller and "Sudden Sam" McDowell, who had almost identical stuff.
RP	"Macho" Ernie Camacho	1983–1987	Ernie never won a junior-lightweight championship, but Hector never saved 23 games in one season.

TOP FIVE SEASONS	
YEAR 1920	**RECORD** 98-56
BEST HITTER	Tris Speaker
BEST PITCHERS	Jim Bagby, Stan Coveleski
NOTES	Edged Black Sox for pennant, then topped Dodgers in Series.
YEAR 1948	**RECORD** 97-58
BEST HITTER	Lou Boudreau (manager)
BEST PITCHERS	Bob Lemon, Gene Bearden
NOTES	Survived one-game playoff with Red Sox, beat Braves in Series.
YEAR 1954	**RECORD** 111-53
BEST HITTERS	Bobby Avila
BEST PITCHERS	Mike Garcia, Bob Lemon, Early Wynn
NOTES	Set league record for wins, then swept by Giants in Series.
YEAR 1995	**RECORD** 100-44
BEST HITTER	Albert Belle
BEST PITCHERS	José Mesa, Dennis Martinez
NOTES	Won 100 despite short season, lost World Series to Braves.
YEAR 1997	**RECORD** 86-75
BEST HITTERS	David Justice, Jim Thome
BEST PITCHERS	Charles Nagy
NOTES	So-so during regular season, but took Marlins to Game 7.

TOP FIVE MANAGERS	
MANAGER	Mike Hargrove
YEARS	1991–1999
RECORD	721-591 (.550)
NOTES	If only he understood young pitchers like he did hitters . . .
MANAGER	Al Lopez
YEARS	1951–1956
RECORD	570-354 (.617)
NOTES	Overshadowed by Stengel, whom he'd once played for.
MANAGER	Tris Speaker
YEARS	1919–1926
RECORD	617-520 (.543)
NOTES	Not nearly as good when he didn't have himself to manage.
MANAGER	Lou Boudreau
YEARS	1942–1950
RECORD	728-649 (.529)
NOTES	See comment on Speaker.
MANAGER	Joe Gordon
YEARS	1958–1960
RECORD	184-151 (.549)
NOTES	Traded to the Tigers, straight up for Jimmy Dykes.

At least one source says that Odell Hale "was named Bad News by enemy pitchers." But according to the 1940 edition of the *Baseball Register,* the nickname "[w]as given him by sports writers in Cotton States League."

That would have been in 1929, Hale's first professional season. He played third base for Alexandria, and batted .324 with twenty-three home runs. In his second pro season, Hale hit eight home runs. In his third—including twenty-five games with the Tribe—Hale hit *two* home runs. In 1932, the Indians farmed Hale back to Toledo, where he batted .333 with seven homers and 110 RBI (and perhaps most impressive, thirty-six doubles and twenty-two triples).

Hale won a regular job with the Indians in 1933, and hit ten home runs . . . all of them on the road; he's one of only eleven players in major-league history to hit at least ten homers on the road, but none at home.

Hale wasn't a bad fielder, but his two memorable defensive plays were both miscues of sorts. In 1935, Joe Cronin shot a line drive that caromed off the head of Hale, who was playing third base. The ball bounced to shortstop Bill Knickerbocker, who started a triple play. And on the last day of the 1936 season, Hale didn't make a play at third base that he might have, and Johnny Allen's fifteen-game winning streak was history.

TAKING A "REST"

When Ted Williams went to his greater reward last summer, a lot of people revisited the question, "What kind of stats would Williams have piled up if he hadn't served in both World War II and the Korean War?"

Of course, Bob Feller served in World War II, too. I mean, he *really* served. On December 7, 1941, Feller was driving to a meeting with Indians management, hoping to sign his contract for 1942. He heard about Pearl Harbor on the radio, though, and when he arrived at the meeting he told his employers he'd be enlisting in the navy immediately. He did, and after a spell of easy duty, volunteered for combat. He saw plenty of it, too, while serving as chief of an antiaircraft gun crew aboard the USS *Alabama*. Feller was discharged in 1945, early enough to start nine games for the Indians.

He'd missed the better part of four seasons, and as Feller and so many other great players returned to the game, the speculation began. As Feller said in his most recent autobiography,

> Then people began to wonder how we would have done if the war hadn't come along . . . Eventually, an analyst in Seattle, Ralph Winnie, sat down at his computer and figured out the answers.
>
> He took our individual stats for the last three years before our military services and our first three years after the war, then averaged them out on a per-season basis and projected them across the war years.
>
> . . . In pitching, Winnie discovered that Warren Spahn would have had the third highest number of victories instead of fifth . . .
>
> In my case, Winnie projected that I would have won 107 more games, finishing with 373 wins instead of 266, with another 1,070 strikeouts, five no-hitters instead of three and 19 one-hitters instead of 12. He calculated that I would have finished with the sixth most wins in history instead of 28th and the seventh most shutouts instead of 29th.

Reasonable enough . . . but not particularly illuminating. First of all, the Spahn analysis doesn't work at all, because Spahn didn't win even one game in the major leagues before the war. In 1942, he posted a 5.74 ERA without a decision in sixteen innings. What's more, one can make a convincing argument that World War II actually *helped* Spahn. He pitched effectively in 1963, when he was forty-one years old. It's possible, and perhaps even likely, that taking three years "off" during the war was good for his arm.

And you know, the same may have been true for Feller. Like Spahn but unlike most ballplayers, Feller actually spent more of his service time in war zones than on baseball diamonds. He threw 1,448 innings in the majors before he turned twenty-three, and it's reasonable to wonder if his arm wasn't hanging by a thin thread by 1942. Maybe he needed the rest.

What's more, Feller's arm wore out long before its time, anyway. His last great season was 1947, when he was still only twenty-eight years old. Feller pitched effectively for another eight years, but he wasn't the dominating pitcher that he'd been. I believe that if not for World War II, Feller's decline simply would have begun three or four years earlier than it did. And that it's just as likely that he'd have won *fewer* games in his career, as more.

I'm grateful to Geoff Reiss for writing many of the player comments, and also to Steve Schulman and Adam Ulrey for their editorial suggestions. Sources for this chapter include Franklin Lewis's The Cleveland Indians *(Putnam, 1949), Terry Pluto's* The Curse of Rocky Colavito *(Simon and Schuster, 1994), and Bob Feller and Bill Gilbert's* Now Pitching, Bob Feller *(Birch Lane Press, 1990).*

COLORADO ROCKIES

		YEARS	NOTES
ALL-TIME			
C	Jeff Reed	1996–1999	He was the regular for just one season, but he easily out-hit Joe Girardi and Kirt Manwaring, and he wasn't *that* bad with the glove.
1B	Todd Helton	1997–*2002*	Helton, the eighth pick in the 1995 draft, is still the only great player developed by the Rocks; first player in MLB history to rap 100 extra-base hits in two straight seasons.
2B	Eric Young	1993–1997	First batter in franchise history, and a few days later hit Rockies' first HR in Colorado; played a lot of left field in his first three seasons, led NL with 53 steals in '96.
SS	Neifi Perez	1996–2001	Put in context, his hitting stats were simply atrocious during his years with the club, but he also happened to be one of the better defensive shortstops in the game.
3B	Vinny Castilla	1993–1999	In both 1996 *and* 1997, Castilla batted .304 with 40 home runs and 113 RBI; he's the only player in history to duplicate his Triple Crown stats in consecutive seasons.
LF	Dante Bichette	1993–1999	Sure, it would've been nice if he'd drawn the occasional walk; we shouldn't quibble, though, considering he leads Rockies in hits (1,278), doubles (270), and RBI (826).
CF	Ellis Burks	1994–1998	Played slightly more left field than center, but the only alternative is OBP-challenged Juan Pierre, and Burks left Colorado with nifty .579 slugging pct. for Rocks.
RF	Larry Walker	1995–*2002*	Always had trouble staying in the lineup, but when healthy he was all-around brilliant: average, power, speed, smarts, and terrific defense in right field.
SP1	Pedro Astacio	1997–2001	Tops the Rockies in wins (53), strikeouts (749), innings (827), shutouts (13), and nobody else is close; showed just how good he was after getting out of Coors.
SP2	Armando Reynoso	1993–1996	The 58th pick in the expansion draft, and a good one; plenty of DL time limited him to 30 wins in four years, but 4.65 ERA positively sparkling for Rockies.
SP3	Kevin Ritz	1994–1998	First things first . . . in five seasons, Ritz racked up a 5.20 ERA. That's the bad news. Good news is that he won more than he lost, including 17 wins in 1996.
SP4	John Thomson	1997–2002	Suffered disastrous (1-10, 8.04) 1999, then missed all of 2000 while recovering from shoulder surgery, but with 27 career wins he's sixth on the franchise list.
RP	Steve Reed	1993–1997	They never let him have the saves, but the righty submariner pitched in 329 games, posted a 3.68 ERA, and is the only Rockie to pitch effectively year to year.

I'm writing this early in the morning of August 3, 2002. At this exact moment, Larry Walker's career statistics include a .399 on-base percentage and a .577 slugging average.

Every eligible player with a slugging average higher than .577 is in the Hall of Fame. In fact, every eligible player with a slugging average higher than .534—there are eighteen of them—is in the Hall of Fame. So you could say that Walker's got one hell of a cushion. If he can just keep his slugging average from dropping forty-three points in the next four or five years, then he's got one hell of a shot at getting a plaque in Cooperstown.

Except I'm not at all sure that he does. Or that he should.

Larry Walker's got two things working against his argument for the Hall of Fame.

First, there's Coors Field. A lot of people, even people who know better, like to say, "Larry Walker can hit anywhere." That's true, I suppose, but it's also true that he hits a hell of a lot *better* in Denver than he does anywhere else. He's posted those wonderful numbers while playing a lot of his games in the best hitter's park ever, and all of his games in the best hitter's era ever.

The other problem is, there aren't enough of those games. Walker's played more than 150 games only once in his career. So he ain't no Hall of Famer.

Oddly enough, the Colorado Rockies have enjoyed some fine relief seasons. This was especially true in 1995, when the Rockies reached the postseason thanks largely to a fantastic bullpen. Darren Holmes and Curtis Leskanic combined for twelve wins, twenty-four saves, and a 3.33 ERA in 165 relief innings. Bruce Ruffin missed four months with an elbow injury, but before getting hurt he saved eleven games and posted a 2.12 ERA in thirty-four innings. And submarining righty Steve Reed posted a 2.14 ERA in eighty-four innings as the club's primary setup man. Taken together, the quartet racked up thirty-eight saves with a 2.83 ERA in 283 innings, and I'd argue that their collective performance ranks as one of the all-time great seasons by a bullpen.

Those guys were all talented, but of course that season was something of a fluke, especially when you consider where they did half their pitching. That group pitched almost exactly the same number of innings in 1996, but their collective ERA jumped from 2.83 to 4.54 (Leskanic suffering the most).

Hey, here's an interesting question . . . Is the bullpen more important for the Rockies, because their starters get knocked out early so often? Or is it less important, because the Rockies don't play as many close games as does a typical team?

SINGLE SEASON

		YEARS	NOTES
C	Jeff Reed	1997	Don Baylor, in his infinite wisdom, let Reed play in only 90 games, but he still managed 17 home runs and 47 RBI.
1B	Todd Helton	2000	Like Boston's Nomar Garciaparra, flirted with .400 for a spell but wound up at .372 to capture his loop's batting title.
2B	Eric Young	1996	After dabbling in center field for three years, finally went to second base full-time, scored 113 runs and played good D.
SS	Neifi Perez	2000	Played every game, cracked 60 extra-base hits, and (as usual) displayed Gold Glove–quality defense.
3B	Vinny Castilla	1997	Better glove in '96 and bigger stick in '98, but '97 was his best combination; could have picked any of the three, though.
LF	Ellis Burks	1996	After struggling with injuries for years, played healthy all season and led NL with 142 runs and .639 slugging pct.
CF	Juan Pierre	2001	Historically, weak position for franchise but Pierre (temporarily) changed that; .327 average and 46 steals.
RF	Larry Walker	1997	Became first Canadian to win MVP, thanks to 49 homers, .366 batting average, 130 RBI . . . and yes, Coors Field.
SP	Pedro Astacio	1999	Pay no attention to that 5.04 ERA or those 38 home runs allowed; his 17 wins were the real deal.
RP	José Jimenez	2000	After washing out as starter with Cards, became reliever with Rocks and went 5-2 with 24 saves and pretty 3.18 ERA.

TRADED AWAY

		TRADED	NOTES
C	Brad Ausmus	July 26, 1993	Before he reached majors, traded to San Diego in deal for two pitchers—Hurst and Harris—who were busts.
1B	Greg Colbrunn	July 30, 1998	Prototypical professional hitter batted .311 in four months before going to Braves in deadline deal.
2B	Eric Young	August 19, 1997	Grabbed from Dodgers with 11th pick in expansion draft, traded back to Dodgers for Pedro Astacio.
SS	Neifi Perez	July 25, 2001	Errr, ummm . . . He's been terrible since leaving, but he'll probably hang around for at least a few years.
3B	Jeff Cirillo	December 15, 2001	In two years, batted .320 but didn't show much power, so dispatched to Seattle for three young arms.
LF	Ellis Burks	July 31, 1998	Deadline deal didn't work out so well, as Burks didn't suffer much of a post-Coors drop-off at all.
CF	Vacant	—	Nobody, though the Devil Rays did blow their second pick in the expansion draft on Quinton McCracken.
RF	John Vander Wal	August 31, 1998	In '95, batted .347 and set NL record with 28 pinch-hits; finally blossomed after leaving Rocks.
SP	Andy Ashby	July 27, 1993	Who knew? Ashby was PTBNL in trade with Padres after going 0-4 with 8.50 ERA in 54 innings.
RP	Dave Veres	November 16, 1999	Part of big deal that sent Darryl Kile to St. Louis and brought José Jimenez to Denver.

GOLD GLOVE			
		YEARS	**NOTES**
C	Henry Blanco	1999	Amazing arm, can throw with anybody, but he doesn't hit like Ivan Rodriguez so nobody knew.
1B	Todd Helton	1997–*2002*	Galarraga got the nickname, but Helton was by far the better fielder, easily one of the best of his time.
2B	Mike Lansing	1998–2000	Back troubles made him just a shadow of the player he'd been, but still a fine defender, at least in '98.
SS	Neifi Perez	1996–2001	Anybody surprised? Still have to wonder how bad his hitting stats would have been in a real ballpark.
3B	Jeff Cirillo	2000–2001	Never quite hit like the Rockies thought he would, but at least Cirillo's sterling defense survived his relocation.
LF	Jeffrey Hammonds	2000	Had the speed for center field, if not the instincts, and gave Rockies one year of all-around quality.
CF	Juan Pierre	2000–2002	Great speed serves him well in the garden; it's just too bad he doesn't get to use it on the bases more often.
RF	Larry Walker	1995–*2002*	Looks a little blocky, but there's no right fielder in the game with better instincts, and of course he can throw.
P	Mike Hampton	2001–2002	Widely regarded as the most athletic pitcher in the National League, accomplished with glove and bat.

IRON GLOVE			
		YEARS	**NOTES**
C	Ben Petrick	1999–*2002*	There was never much question about his stick, but his glove drove his managers nuts and limited his at-bats.
1B	Andres Galarraga	1993–1997	Nobody's going to believe this, but "Big Cat" really wasn't that good; he just didn't have a lot of range.
2B	Nelson Liriano	1993–1994 1998	Todd Walker's got the rep, but he wasn't quite as bad as all that, and Liriano was worse than we thought.
SS	Freddie Benavides	1993	How bad was he? Opening Day shortstop made 11 errors in 48 games, so they replaced him with Vinny Castilla.
3B	Charlie Hayes	1993–1994	Not really fair because Hayes wasn't *bad*, but he wasn't as good as Castilla or Cirillo.
LF	Howard Johnson	1994–1995	At the end of the line as hitter and totally miscast as an outfielder, but played 75 games in garden for Rockies.
CF	Alex Cole	1993	Great wheels and decent OBP, but so shaky with the glove that he never could hold down a regular job.
RF	Dante Bichette	1993–1998	Wasn't actually as bad as he looked, but suffers badly in comparison to Walker, the club's other right fielder.
P	José Jimenez	2000–2002	"Jimenez doesn't do much to help himself and seems oblivious to the details of defense."—Tracy Ringolsby

Neifi Perez never became the star that I thought he might become. His minor-league stats, while not overwhelming, were impressive enough, especially after he got to Colorado Springs (the Rockies' Class AAA affiliate). True, C-Springs is a great place to hit, and what we didn't know then, but do now, is that Perez was a couple of years older than we thought. Whatever the reason, Perez never cleared the .300 mark with the Rockies, which is pretty bad when you consider his home ballpark.

He was, however, a wonderful shortstop. In 1998, Rey Ordoñez won the Gold Glove, but Perez deserved it. In 1999, Ordoñez won again and deserved to, but Perez was right behind him. In 2000, with Ordoñez on the DL most of the season, Perez was clearly the best shortstop in the league (and the majors) and this time he did win the Gold Glove. In 2001, Expos shortstop Orlando Cabrera played brilliantly and won the Gold Glove. Perez wouldn't have won it anyway, because he got traded to Kansas City in July and didn't play particularly well for either the Royals or the Rockies. For a three-year stretch, though, he was probably as good as anybody in the world.

SO WHAT'S THE PROBLEM?

Saying the Rockies have pitching problems is like saying Enron had accounting problems. Saying the Rockies have pitching problems is like saying Andy Dick and Robert Downey Jr. have substance-abuse problems. Saying the Rockies have pitching problems is like saying Ray Charles and Stevie Wonder have vision problems.

Did I mention that the Rockies have pitching problems?

Actually, the Rockies pitchers aren't as bad as they look (well, some of them are). The real "problem" is that the Rockies are always looking for starting pitchers who can post a sub-5.00 ERA for them, and there probably aren't more than two or three people on the planet who could do that in consecutive seasons. Armando Reynoso is the only starter in franchise history with two sub-5.00 ERA seasons (minimum 162 innings), and those seasons came three years apart (1993 and 1996).

The other problem is that they haven't developed any quality starting pitchers of their own. Not one. Zero. Armando Reynoso came out of the Braves' system. Pedro Astacio came from the Dodgers. Kevin Ritz came from the Tigers. Curtis Leskanic played in the Indians' and Twins' organizations before the Rockies got him. At this writing, the franchise leader among pitchers actually signed by the Rockies is John Thomson, selected in the seventh round of the 1993 draft. Thomson won exactly twenty-seven games—and lost forty-three— before the Rockies traded him to the Mets during the 2002 season.

There was a ray of hope in 2002, when portly Jason Jennings won sixteen games to earn the National League's Rookie of the Year award. That's just one season, though, and anyway Jennings is just one pitcher. It's a good start, but it's just a start.

Building a pitching staff through the farm system isn't easy. But you've got to do better than this. Because when you don't, you wind up doing desperate things. Like signing Mike Hampton to an eight-year contract for $121 million.

Even now, two years into the deal, it looks strange. *Eight-year contract.* Who signs a twenty-eight-year-old pitcher to an eight-year contract? Rockies general manager Dan O'Dowd, that's who.

At the time, I didn't criticize O'Dowd for that shocking deal. At least I don't think I did. I think I raised the same questions anybody else would have raised, while also expressing admiration for O'Dowd's willingness to try something bold. After all, everybody knew the Rockies needed to pitch better. Hampton was coming off two straight fine seasons, in which he'd combined for thirty-seven wins and only fourteen losses. And he was great at inducing ground balls, a skill that some have theorized is key if a pitcher is to consistently pitch well in Denver.

Hampton was a complete disaster, of course. The Rockies traded him after the 2002 season, but they'll be feeling the financial pain for years to come. And with that knowledge— ain't hindsight great?—we can see just how stupid it was to commit so much money on Hampton's contract. This is a classic case of the possible benefits paling next to the possible damage. We're now just two years into the contract—six to go!—and it's the first thing you think about when you think about the Rockies. Dan O'Dowd almost certainly wakes up every morning with thoughts of Hampton's contract, and thoughts of Hampton's contract probably keep him from falling asleep at night, too. The Rockies have already spent $16.5 million, they've received virtually nothing in return, and there's no telling how they're going to fix this.

I'm grateful to Rod Nelson for his editorial suggestions.

DETROIT TIGERS

		YEARS	NOTES
DH	Rusty Staub	1976–1979	Made All-Star team as Tigers' RF in '76 but didn't hit much after shifting to DH in '77, notwithstanding his 121 RBI in '78 (thank you, Ron LeFlore).
C	Bill Freehan	1961–1976	Fine defensive catcher with good power, but suffered great misfortune of playing his best seasons in the Era of the Pitcher, otherwise he'd be a Hall of Fame candidate.
1B	Hank Greenberg	1930–1941 1945–1946	Thanks to World War II and 1936 injury, played only nine full seasons—eight of them with Tigers—but still managed to hit 331 home runs.
2B	Charlie Gehringer	1924–1942	Great defensive second baseman and he could hit, too; or as Mickey Cochrane said, "He says 'hello' opening day, 'goodbye' closing day and, in between, hits .350."
SS	Alan Trammell	1977–1996	His reputation suffers by comparison to Cal Ripken (and to a lesser extent, Ozzie Smith), but Tram had a Hall of Fame career and it's really a shame that nobody noticed.
3B	George Kell	1946–1952	Doesn't really deserve his Hall of Fame plaque, but he did enjoy most of his good seasons in Detroit, and made five straight All-Star teams beginning in '47.
LF	Bobby Veach	1912–1923	Veach, Cobb, and Sam Crawford (below) gave the Tigers arguably the greatest outfield in the game's history; Veach led AL in RBI three times.
CF	Ty Cobb	1905–1926	For something like half a century, it was Cobb—and not Ruth—who was considered the game's greatest player ever; when he was passed, it was by Willie Mays.
RF	Al Kaline	1953–1974	Kaline's career suffers from comparisons to his rookie season (fairly) and Roberto Clemente (unfairly), but he was a great hitter and one of the great glove men.
SP1	Hal Newhouser	1939–1953	It's true that he benefited from pitching during World War II, but he also enjoyed some brilliant seasons *after* the war; as scout, *begged* Astros to draft Derek Jeter.
SP2	Mickey Lolich	1963–1975	Remembered for girth more than anything, but let's not forget that he had a great sinker, won 207 regular-season games for Tigers, and went 3-0 in '68 World Series.
SP3	Tommy Bridges	1930–1943 1945–1946	He won 194 games for Tigers, and his "jughandle curve" was famous; catcher Birdie Tebbetts described him as "a guy with the best curveball in the history of baseball."
SP4	Jack Morris	1977–1990	His argument for Cooperstown doesn't cut the mustard, but he was one of the great innings-eaters of the late 20th century, and went a decade without missing his turn.
RP	John Hiller	1965–1970 1972–1980	After four seasons with club, Toronto native suffered heart attack 1971, signed on as BP pitcher in '72 . . . and became game's best reliever in '73; 125 career saves.

It's nothing but an accident of baseball history that Denny McLain is remembered more often than Mickey Lolich.

Well, maybe not an accident. After all, McLain did pitch brilliantly in 1968. He won thirty-one games, and nobody has won more than twenty-seven in a season since.

That season, Lolich posted a 3.19 ERA, which looks pretty good unless you know that the *league* ERA that season—the Year of the Pitcher—was 2.98. Lolich was just the third-best starter on the Tiger staff, behind McLain and Earl Wilson.

Until the World Series, in which Lolich pitched three complete games—including Game 7 on two days' rest—and won all three of them. Just as McLain is the last pitcher to win thirty games in one season, Lolich is the last pitcher to win three starts in one World Series.

But it's McLain who's remembered, even though he wound up winning 131 games to Lolich's 217. Why? Well, those thirty-one victories are the biggest reason. But it's also because of what they did *after* their careers. All Lolich did was open up a donut store. Meanwhile, McLain engaged in all sorts of illegal activities, and wound up doing some hard time.

See, sometimes crime really *does* pay.

A friend of mine, Jason Brannon, recently spent a few weeks nursing an obsession with players who enjoyed great seasons that didn't include even a single home run. And in the midst of this obsession, Jason brought Donie Bush to my attention.

Saying that Bush didn't have a lot of power is a little like saying that Tricky Dick Nixon didn't have a lot of scruples. He was a Tiger for fourteen full seasons, and in those fourteen seasons he hit exactly nine home runs . . . and five of those were of the inside-the-park variety.

Anyway, according to Jason, Bush put together three of the greatest homer-free seasons in major-league history. In 1909, Bush didn't hit a home run, but he did draw eighty-eight walks, he did steal fifty-three bases, he did score 114 runs, and he did play excellent defense.

That was the best one, but he also fared well without any circuit clouts in 1914 and 1917.

Oh, and in case you're wondering, the *best* zero-homer seasons of the twentieth century were posted by Eddie Collins in 1912 and Tris Speaker in 1915. Collins scored 137 runs. Speaker's was anomalous, as he had excellent power. He just didn't happen to hit any homers that season, during which he batted .322, scored 108 runs, and played brilliantly in center field.

		YEARS	NOTES
		NO. 2	
DH	Kirk Gibson	1993–1995	His best season came with the Dodgers, but after five seasons away, gritty Gibson returned to hometown club and finished career with three solid seasons.
C	Lance Parrish	1977–1986	Like most catchers, he faded early, but in eight seasons as the regular, Parrish garnered six All-Star berths and topped 20 homers just as often.
1B	Norm Cash	1960–1974	Granted, the one big season was one of the all-time flukes, but Cash was very good for a long time, and few remember that he was an outstanding defensive player.
2B	Lou Whitaker	1977–1995	Isn't it amazing how fast Whitaker and Trammell have faded from memory? Perhaps it's because they were followed by so many big-hitting middle infielders.
SS	Donie Bush	1908–1921	Little guy who didn't have any power at all, but in five of his first six seasons he led the league in walks; decent with the glove, but couldn't turn the double play at all.
3B	Travis Fryman	1990–1997	Aside from Kell and Fryman, this has not been a strong position for the Tigers over the years; hit between 18 and 22 homers in six of his seven full seasons.
LF	Willie Horton	1963–1977	Perhaps the most beloved player in Tigers history, the Detroit native played in four All-Star Games and took to the streets to discourage rioters in the summer of '67.
CF	Chet Lemon	1982–1990	Fine all-around player who did everything well except steal bases; edges Barney McCosky and Ron LeFlore, who played better but didn't last nearly as long.
RF	Sam Crawford	1903–1917	Great spot for Tigers, with Hall of Famers Kaline, Crawford, and Harry Heilmann accounting for 31 years in a span of 69 years.
SP1	Dizzy Trout	1939–1952	During World War II, the only AL pitcher Trout's equal was his teammate Hal Newhouser; Trout never pitched as well again, but his fastball carried him to 161 wins.
SP2	George Mullin	1902–1913	Toledo native chose Tigers over Dodgers, stands second on franchise list with 209 victories, and posted 1.86 ERA in seven World Series games; pitched no-hitter in 1912.
SP3	Hooks Dauss	1912–1926	Did *you* know that Dauss, famous for his curveball, is the Tigers' all-time leader in pitching wins? I didn't, either, but nobody's topped his 222, or is going to anytime soon.
SP4	Wild Bill Donovan	1903–1912 1918	Went 25-4 in 1907 to set AL record for winning pct. That stood until 1931; winless in 4 Series starts before winning Game 2 in '09, but then shelled in Game 7.
RP	Mike Henneman	1987–1995	Skinny right-hander ranked as one of the league's top relievers for seven straight seasons, thanks to solid repertoire including sinker, forkball, and slider.

SINGLE SEASON

		YEARS	NOTES
DH	Kirk Gibson	1994	Truncated season, of course, but Gibby slugged career-high .548 in second season of his return to hometown team.
C	Bill Freehan	1968	A truly brilliant season with both bat and glove, and he finished behind only teammate Denny McLain in MVP vote.
1B	Norm Cash	1961	The most famous fluke season in baseball history; Cash batted .361 in '61, just .264 the rest of his career.
2B	Charlie Gehringer	1934	You could take your pick of his great seasons, but this was probably the greatest: AL-best 134 runs, brilliant defense.
SS	Alan Trammell	1987	He enjoyed plenty of good seasons, but this was his only truly *great* season: 28 homers, 109 runs, 105 RBI.
3B	Eddie Yost	1959	In his first season as Tiger, "The Walking Man" paced AL with 135 walks (typical) *and* 115 runs (atypical).
LF	Matty McIntyre	1908	Yep, Matty McIntyre. It was the Dead Ball Era, and Matty led the American League with 104 runs scored.
CF	Ty Cobb	1911	Pulled out of a hat; true, he hit .420, but Ty was just as great in 1910 and '12, and then again from 1915 through '17.
RF	Ty Cobb	1909	Already the best player in the league, Cobb broke out in 1909 with .377 batting average, 76 steals, and AL-leading 9 homers.
SP	Hal Newhouser	1946	Yes, Prince Hal actually pitched his best *after* the boys came home; topped AL with 26 wins, 1.94 ERA, and 9.7 BR/9.
RP	John Hiller	1973	In his first full season after recovering from '71 stroke, won 10 games and set MLB record with 38 saves.

ALL-ROOKIE

		YEARS	NOTES
C	Matt Nokes	1987	Yes, I know it was 1987. But 32 homers in 461 at-bats is pretty impressive even if you're playing on Mars in 1930.
1B	Dale Alexander	1929	Batted .331 in the majors, and started career with .343 average and AL-high 215 hits as 26-year-old rookie.
2B	Lou Whitaker	1978	In their first season together, Sweet Lou won Rookie of the Year Award with 21 votes, and Trammell got 3.
SS	Harvey Kuenn	1953	Not much with the glove, then or later, but led the American League with 209 hits (and again with 201 hits in 1954).
3B	Rudy York	1937	Fudging a bit here, as York played only 41 games at 3B, but he hit 35 homers—18 in August alone—in only 375 at-bats.
LF	Dick Wakefield	1943	Signed for astronomical $52,000 bonus out of Univ. of Michigan, then led AL with 200 hits and 38 doubles as rookie.
CF	Barney McCosky	1939	Batted .311 and scored 120 runs; excellent player who lost three seasons of his prime to World War II.
RF	Ira Flagstead	1919	Oddly, the Tigers' all-time position hasn't supplied an outstanding rookie; Flagstead batted .331 in 97 games.
SP	Mark Fidrych	1976	For a summer, "The Bird" was the most famous player in the world; 19-9 as rookie, 10-10 the rest of his "career."
RP	Chuck Seelbach	1972	Won 9 games and saved 14, including pennant-clincher against Red Sox; shoulder injury in '73 killed his career.

In 1976, Mark Fidrych struck out only ninety-seven hitters in 250 innings. It didn't matter, because he allowed only 217 hits, fifty-three walks, and twelve home runs. But as we've learned over the last few years, the number of hits a pitcher allows is largely a function of how many batters he strikes out. Fidrych allowed 217 hits in his 250 innings, a very low number of hits for a pitcher who didn't strike out many batters. Statistically, the most similar pitcher to Fidrych—including their ages—is Bill Stafford, and Stafford's career petered out pretty quickly. Focusing only on age, innings, home runs allowed, walks, and strikeouts, the two most similar pitchers to Fidrych are Rich Nye (1967) and Dave Fleming (1992). Not exactly household names.

On the other hand, if Fidrych was "hit-lucky" in 1976, then he was hit-lucky in 1977 and 1978, too. He was able to start only fourteen games over those two seasons . . . but when he did pitch, he was outstanding. In those fourteen starts, Fidrych went 8-4 with a 2.80 ERA. We can fool around with the numbers 'til the cows come home, but the fact is that we'll never *know* how good Fidrych could have been, absent the arm injury. And that's the real shame, isn't it?

You gotta feel for Randy Smith.

He served as the Tigers' general manager for six seasons, and the Tigers didn't win more games than they lost in even one of those seasons. Overall, Smith's Tigers won 411 games and lost 560, for a .423 winning percentage. The Tigers did open a new ballpark during Smith's tenure . . . and in Comerica Park's second season, the Tigers dropped to ninth in the league in attendance. Essentially, Randy Smith presided over a disaster.

Smith deserves a small bit of credit for one thing, though . . . Bernie Williams very nearly became a Detroit Tiger. It happened after the 1997 season, which the Tigers concluded with a surprisingly good 79-83 record. Meanwhile, Williams had just one season left on his contract, and the Yankees weren't convinced he deserved a long-term deal for big dollars.

So the Tigers and Yankees worked out a deal: Detroit would get Williams, and New York would get minor-league pitchers Mike Drumright and Roberto Duran. The deal was done . . . and then it wasn't. Supposedly, Steinbrenner killed it. The Yankees won 114 games in 1998, and the Tigers lost ninety-seven.

Getting Bernie Williams wouldn't have saved Randy Smith's reputation, any more than getting Brian Giles saved Cam Bonifay's reputation. But it sure as hell would have helped.

HOMEGROWN			
		YEARS	NOTES
C	Bill Freehan	1961–1976	Signed for $100,000 bonus, which his dad didn't let him have until he'd graduated from the University of Michigan.
1B	Hank Greenberg	1930–1940 1945–1946	Bronx native coveted by Yanks, but he didn't want to get stuck behind Gehrig and signed with Tigers for $9,000.
2B	Charlie Gehringer	1924–1942	Tigers scouted him on the recommendation of Bobby Veach, who was tipped off by a hunting buddy.
SS	Alan Trammell	1977–1996	San Diego native drafted in second round by Tigers and didn't spend even two full seasons in minors.
3B	Travis Fryman	1990–1997	Detroit got Fryman with 30th pick in '87 draft, which they got as compensation for losing Lance Parrish to Phillies.
LF	Willie Horton	1963–1977	Was raised in inner-city Detroit, homered in Tiger Stadium at 16, and got $50,000 signing bonus at 18.
CF	Ron LeFlore	1974–1979	Now *that's* scouting: in 1973, LeFlore was in a maximum-security prison; in '74, he was in center field.
RF	Al Kaline	1953–1974	Signed for $30,000, earned a spot in the lineup when he was 19, and never spent a day in the minor leagues.
SP	Hal Newhouser	1939–1953	Detroit native signed for $400 bonus; minutes later, the Indians offered $15,000 and a new car for his dad.
RP	John Hiller	1965–1970 1972–1980	Discovered on the sandlots in Toronto—Tigers country, in those days—and signed as free agent in 1962.

TRADED AWAY			
		TRADED	NOTES
C	Nig Clarke	August 11, 1905	Anybody know what happened? Tigers bought Clarke from Cleveland on Aug. 1, and sold him back on the 11th.
1B	Wally Pipp	January 7, 1915	Went to Yankees for waiver price; remembered now for losing his job, but he was a fine player for a long time.
2B	Frank Bolling	December 7, 1960	Outstanding fielder who enjoyed a few nice seasons after going to Milwaukee Braves in six-player deal.
SS	Kid Elberfeld	June 10, 1903	Sent to Yankees in a deal quite likely engineered by Ban Johnson to strengthen the league's newest team.
3B	Howard Johnson	December 7, 1984	Straight up for Walt Terrell, who won 47 games and ate a lot of innings over the next three seasons.
LF	Heinie Manush	December 2, 1927	After off year, traded to Browns and batted .378 with MLB-high 241 hits in 1928; eventually elected to HoF.
CF	Baby Doll Jacobson	August 8, 1915	Pipp and Jacobson was a lot of talent to discard in one year, but then, scoring runs wasn't really the problem.
RF	Ben Oglivie	December 9, 1977	Awful trade: Tigers got pitcher Jim Slaton from Brewers, and he returned to Milwaukee as free agent a year later.
SP	Billy Pierce	November 10, 1948	Sent Pierce *and* $10K to White Sox for catcher Aaron Robinson . . . whom they waived three years later.
RP	Phil Regan	December 15, 1965	Tigers got Dick Tracewski, who flopped; Dodgers got Regan, who twice led National League in saves.

GOLD GLOVE

		YEARS	NOTES
C	Paul Richards	1943–1946	Fantastic fielding stats and one of the smartest men to play the game; credited with developing Newhouser.
1B	Norm Cash	1960–1974	Never won a Gold Glove and probably never deserved to, but was consistently excellent for a decade.
2B	Charlie Gehringer	1924–1942	Made all the plays, but especially adept at fielding slow rollers and drag bunts, then getting his man at first base.
SS	Billy Rogell	1930–1939	"He's the only player I ever knew who could catch a bad hop . . . I don't know how he did it."—3B Marv Owen
3B	Aurelio Rodriguez	1971–1979	A truly terrible hitter, but thought to be so good with the glove that he played more than 2,000 games.
LF	Bobby Veach	1912–1923	With a right fielder's arm and a center fielder's legs, Veach could have played anywhere.
CF	Chet Lemon	1982–1990	Great speed gave him great range, and he threw well, too; Barney McCosky (1939–1942) also outstanding.
RF	Al Kaline	1953–1973	He may not have been Clemente, but Kaline made fewer errors, threw great, and won 10 Gold Gloves.
P	Jack Morris	1977–1990	Never won a Gold Glove, but excelled in all phases of the defensive game.

IRON GLOVE

		YEARS	NOTES
C	Matt Nokes	1986–1990	The easy choice, if not necessarily the best one; like Mike Piazza, Nokes was a bit better than he looked.
1B	Cecil Fielder	1990–1996	Aside from the fact that he couldn't actually move, Big Cecil wasn't really so bad around the bag.
2B	Ralph Young	1915–1921	A weak link for seven seasons, Young didn't contribute much with the glove *or* the bat.
SS	Eddie Lake	1946–1950	Not a bad wartime player, but joined *postwar* Tigers and was probably the worst defensive SS in the league.
3B	Dean Palmer	1999–*2002*	Always shaky on the grounders, a shoulder injury in 2000 reduced Palmer to something like a disaster.
LF	Bob Fothergill	1922–1930	Played about as well as you'd expect of a guy who stood 5-10, weighed 230 pounds, and was nicknamed "Fatty."
CF	Harvey Kuenn	1958–1959	Ex-shortstop completely miscast in center field, and never played there regularly again after 1958.
RF	Melvin Nieves	1996–1997	The guy had power, but K'd 315 times in 236 games and couldn't get out of his own way in the outfield.
P	Mark Redman	2001–2002	Maybe it was just a bad year, but in 2002 Redman made 6 errors in his 31 starts.

I think you'd be hard-pressed to find a third baseman with a longer career and a weaker bat than Aurelio Rodriguez's. He played in the major leagues for sixteen full seasons, and yet not a single one of those seasons were *good* seasons, hitting-wise.

That's just strange. Even guys like Clete Boyer and Bert Campaneris got lucky once in a while. Not Rodriguez, though. His *best* season with the stick was 1970, when he posted a .302 on-base percentage and a career-high .420 slugging percentage. Rodriguez was only twenty-two that season, and it looked like the Tigers might be getting a rising star when they traded for him that winter.

Hardly. Rodriguez never hit as well again, and while he was durable and annually ranked as one of the best glove men in the league, he was such a terrible hitter that for about half of his years in Detroit, he really shouldn't have been playing. In fact, he wasn't really a *great* defensive player. He was very good, but not really any better than contemporaries like Graig Nettles or Buddy Bell or George Brett.

Aurelio Rodriguez was a Tiger for nine years, in which the club won one division title. It's certainly not his fault—if you want to blame somebody, blame the Orioles and the Yankees—but the Tigers did stick with their defensive specialist for far too long.

At the end of August 1906, the Detroit Tigers were hurting.

In mid-July, nineteen-year-old Ty Cobb left the Tigers after suffering what was likely an emotional and physical breakdown. In Cobb's absence, Davy Jones took over in center field, but nobody was immediately added to the roster.

Enter Big Sam Thompson.

In the nineteenth century, Thompson had starred in the National League, first for the Detroit Wolverines and then for the Philadelphia Phillies. Suffering from an aching back, Thompson called it quits after the 1898 season.

For a while, at least. As Norman Macht wrote in *Baseball's First Stars,* "When Detroit returned to the majors in 1901 via the new American League, Thompson became friendly with part-owner Frank Navin while working as a deputy U.S. marshall and court bailiff. He kept in shape by playing in amateur leagues, and late in the 1906 season, when a rash of injuries left the Tigers shorthanded, Thompson, now 46, agreed to play the outfield."

Thompson made his American League debut on August 31. He played right field and knocked in two runs as the Tigers topped the St. Louis Browns, 5–1. That was as good as it got, though. Cobb returned to the lineup a few days later, and Thompson finished with seven hits and three RBI in eight games.

ALL-BUST		YEARS	NOTES
DH	Bip Roberts	1998	Previously a good bet to hit .300, but batted .248 in 34 games and played a big part in getting Buddy Bell fired.
C	Frank House	1950–1951 1954–1957	Signed for $75,000 and a couple of cars, but spent two years in the service and never really panned out.
1B	Ray Knight	1988	East champs sign (by-then) weak-hitting 3B and assign him to 1B . . . wanna guess what happens next?
2B	Chris Pittaro	1985	The original Torey Lovullo (below); Sparky Anderson said Pittaro would take over from Whitaker (he didn't).
SS	Tom Veryzer	1973–1977	Just fair with the glove and absolutely brutal with the bat, yet somehow turned his skills into a 12-year career.
3B	Torey Lovullo	1988–1989	Sparky billed him as the second coming of Mickey Mantle; instead, he batted .167 in 41 games with Tigers.
LF	Dick Wakefield	1946–1949	Still good, but nothing like what he'd been in '43 and '44, *after* signing for $52K and *before* going into the army.
CF	Al Simmons	1936	Batted .327, but numbers down from his years in Philly, and he and skipper Mickey Cochrane didn't get along.
RF	J. W. Porter	1955–1957	In '55 he was the big story in spring camp, but batted empty .231 in parts of three seasons.
SP	Mark Fidrych	1977–1980	Was 250 innings in '76 too much? We'll never know for sure; we do know that he won only 10 more games.
RP	Matt Anderson	1998–*2002*	Throws 100, but after five seasons the No. 1 pick in '97 draft still hasn't quite harnessed that amazing stuff.

USED-TO-BE-GREAT		YEARS	NOTES
DH	Frank Howard	1972–1973	Position was invented for guys like him, and in his last season he slugged .463 in 85 games.
C	Wally Schang	1931	Backstop for six pennant winners finished up with Tigers and batted .184 in 30 games, at ripe age of 41.
1B	Gregg Jefferies	1999–2000	It was strange, watching that once-great talent, just trying to hang on before he'd even turned 35.
2B	Del Pratt	1923–1924	Went from regular with Red Sox to part-timer with Tigers in an awful hurry; not one of manager Ty's faves.
SS	Johnny Pesky	1952–1954	Former Red Sox great played shortstop in '52, second base in '53, and pinch hitter in '54; .367 OBP w/Tigers.
3B	Eddie Mathews	1967–1968	Finished career as pinch hitter with World Champs, and saw action in two Series games that fall.
LF	Earl Averill	1939–1940	His back was killing him, but he did okay after coming over from Tribe in '39, before crashing in '40.
CF	Fred Lynn	1988–1989	Acquired for failed stretch run in '88; still had some pop, but not enough to make up for low batting average.
RF	Sam Thompson	1906	Former National League great with Detroit and Philly came back to play 8 games when he was 46!
SP	Wilbur Cooper	1926	Pirates' all-time winner spent 14-plus seasons in NL before joining Tigers, and went 0-4 in 8 games.
RP	Roy Face	1968	Pitched grand total of 1 inning for Tigers, after spending most of the season pitching well for Pirates at age 40.

ALL-NAME

		YEARS	NOTES
DH	"Gates" William Brown	1963–1975	Many think this refers to prison gates—he was recruited out of prison—but he got the name as a little boy.
C	"Birdie" George Tebbetts	1936–1947	". . . 'Birdie' Tebbetts is 'Birdie' because he's always a-hollerin' like a little ol' canary bird."—Dizzy Dean
1B	"Stinky" Harry Davis	1932–1933	So named by his Rochester teammates in 1928, because he bore a resemblance to a cartoon character of same name.
2B	"Mechanical Man" Charlie Gehringer	1924–1942	"All you do is wind him up on Opening Day and he runs on and on all season."—Doc Cramer
SS	"Topper" Emory Rigney	1922–1925	Origin of nickname unknown; serious beaning in 1925 helped cut short what looked like a promising career.
3B	"Soldier Boy" John Murphy	1903	We don't know why they called him "Soldier Boy," nor even which way he batted and threw.
LF	"Fats" Bob Fothergill	1922–1930	Anybody else miss the honesty of the old-style nicknames? Fothergill was 5'10" and 230-some pounds.
CF	"Georgia Peach" Ty Cobb	1905–1926	Cobb hailed from Roylston, Georgia; nickname invented by Detroit sportswriter Joe Jackson in 1906.
RF	"Wahoo Sam" Sam Crawford	1903–1917	It's so damn *easy* to use a player's hometown in his nickname . . . so why don't we do it anymore?
SP	"Yankee Killer" Frank Lary	1954–1964	When he's remembered, it's for 28-13 mark against Yanks; also hung with nicknames "Taters" and "Bulldog."
RP	"Señor Smoke" Aurelio Lopez	1979–1985	This one speaks for itself; he didn't always know where the ball was going, but he always threw it hard as hell.

TOP FIVE SEASONS

YEAR 1968 **RECORD** 103-59
BEST HITTER Bill Freehan
BEST PITCHER Denny McLain (MVP)
NOTES Topped Cardinals to conclude long, hot, violent summer.

YEAR 1935 **RECORD** 93-58
BEST HITTER Hank Greenberg (MVP)
BEST PITCHERS Tommy Bridges, Schoolboy Rowe
NOTES Bridges pitches Tigers to first World Series title.

YEAR 1984 **RECORD** 104-58
BEST HITTERS Alan Trammell, Kirk Gibson
BEST PITCHER Willie Hernandez (MVP, Cy Young)
NOTES Started 16-1 and 35-5, finished with World Series walk.

YEAR 1945 **RECORD** 88-65
BEST HITTER Roy Cullenbine
BEST PITCHER Hal Newhouser (MVP)
NOTES Greenberg returns in July, Tigers win in October.

YEAR 1907 **RECORD**
BEST HITTER Ty Cobb
BEST PITCHER Ed Killian
NOTES First of three straight pennants *and* three straight Series defeats.

TOP FIVE MANAGERS

MANAGER Hughie Jennings
YEARS 1907–1920
RECORD 1131-972 (.538)
NOTES Three pennants in first three seasons, and none thereafter.

MANAGER Sparky Anderson
YEARS 1979–1995
RECORD 1308-1218 (.518)
NOTES Eventually became something of a caricature.

MANAGER Steve O'Neill
YEARS 1943–1948
RECORD 509-414 (.551)
NOTES In addition to '45 flag, three second-place finishes.

MANAGER Mickey Cochrane
YEARS 1934–1938
RECORD 348-250 (.582)
NOTES Serious beaning in '37 killed him as player *and* manager.

MANAGER Mayo Smith
YEARS 1967–1970
RECORD 363-285 (.560)
NOTES Famed for making a shortstop out of Mickey Stanley in '68.

From 1955 through 1961, the New York Yankees won six pennants in seven seasons. And during those seven seasons, Tigers right-hander Frank Lary went 27-10 with a 3.04 ERA against the Yankees. Lary did his best work against the Bombers in 1958 and '59, when he started fourteen games and won twelve of them.

How did he do it? According to Lary, "That whole team was geared for power, but since the Yankees didn't steal, I could concentrate more on the man at the plate. Forget about that guy on first, he's not going anywhere . . . Whereas teams like the White Sox with Fox, Aparicio, Jim Landis, and Jim Rivera running all the time could drive me to distraction."

More to the point, Lary had four good pitches: fastball, slider, sinker, change-up. And as Lary told author Richard Lally, "I threw a hard slider, didn't break real big, maybe five or seven inches, but I could change speeds on it, even easier than I did my fastball. That threw a lot of Yankees sluggers off."

You know, we'll never have another Yankee Killer again. The Tigers and Yankees used to face off twenty-two times per season, which allowed Lary to start against them seven or eight times in a season. But now, with so many more teams and the five-man rotation, pitchers just don't pitch against the Yankees often enough to kill them.

HOW QUICKLY THEY FORGET . . .

For some reason, in baseball, children are always "youngsters." So for you *youngsters* out there with designs on the Hall of Fame, my best advice is, "Don't hang around with Pete Rose, and don't grow up to become a Detroit Tiger."

Since the 1950s, the Tigers have featured a number of outstanding players, yet only one of them, Al Kaline, has even sniffed the hallowed halls in Cooperstown.

- Norm Cash wasn't a great player—well, he was great in 1961—but he is one of the top twenty or twenty-five first basemen of all time. Cash's first shot at the Hall of Fame came in 1980 . . . and it was also his last, as he garnered exactly six votes and fell off the ballot.
- Bill Freehan is one of the ten or fifteen greatest catchers of all time. Freehan's first shot at the Hall of Fame came in 1982 . . . and it was also his last, as he garnered *two* votes and fell off the ballot.
- Darrell Evans is one of the dozen or so greatest third basemen of all time. Evans's first shot at the Hall of Fame came in 1995 . . . and it was also his last, as he garnered eight votes— hey, at least he did better than Cash and Freehan—and fell off the ballot.

But if what happened to those guys doesn't make sense, then what happened to Alan Trammell and Lou Whitaker must qualify as some sort of a crime.

When Trammell and Whitaker were playing together it was generally assumed that one day they'd both be in the Hall of Fame. In fact, it was commonly hoped that they'd retire at the same time, so they could go into the Hall as they'd played for so long: together.

Trammell became eligible for the Hall of Fame in 2002. If you study the issue with any sort of sophistication, it's pretty clear that Trammell, like Freehan and Evans, ranks among the all-time greats at his position. And with seventy-five percent of the vote necessary for election to the Hall, Trammell received 15.7 percent.

But Trammell's lucky, because at least he got to stay on the ballot for another shot in 2003. If five percent of the ballots don't include your name, you're gone forever (or until they change the rules again, whichever comes first). Lou Whitaker did not enjoy such good fortune. Eligible for the Hall a year earlier than Trammell, Whitaker received *fifteen* votes . . . slightly less than three percent of the ballots cast, and so he was eliminated from future consideration. Lou Whitaker, an excellent player who easily ranked as the American League's top second baseman for roughly a decade. Fifteen votes.

So what's going on here? Are those damned Hall of Fame voters prejudiced against players from the Motor City?

I don't think so. Rather, I think that the Tigers' Hall of Fame candidates have simply been victimized by circumstances. Nobody knows how good Cash and Freehan were because many of their best seasons came in the middle and late 1960s, when the pitchers had the upper hand. Nobody knows how good Evans was because a great deal of his value came from all the walks, and it's just *now* that baseball writers are beginning to understand that the base on balls isn't something that just "happens" to the batter.

And Trammell and Whitaker? They had the great misfortune to retire approximately five years before middle infielders started hitting forty-plus homers in a season with alarming regularity. What looked like Hall of Fame numbers in the 1980s don't look all that great now, early in the twenty-first century.

All of this constitutes an explanation, not an excuse. It's always seemed to me that in exchange for the privilege of deciding who gets into the Hall of Fame, the voters have a responsibility to educate themselves at least to the point of knowing that Bill Freehan and Darrell Evans were great players. Unfortunately, most voters don't take their duties seriously. Or maybe they do, but just don't know how to apply that seriousness to the relatively simple task of analyzing the performance of baseball players.

I'm grateful to Dave Raglin and Mark Pattison for their editorial suggestions. The sources for this chapter include Pattison and Raglin's Detroit Tigers Lists and More *(Wayne State University Press, 2002), Fred Lieb's* The Detroit Tigers *(Putnam, 1946), and Richard Lally's* Bombers: An Oral History of the New York Yankees *(Crown, 2002).*

Hey, we're going to the Hall of Fame! (Aren't we?)
Detroit Tigers

The expansion draft is not usually the best place to acquire front-line talent, due to the simple fact that teams don't generally expose front-line talent in the expansion draft.

Jeff Conine played baseball at UCLA, where he was a pitcher, and not a particularly good one. But Kansas City Royals scout Guy Hansen liked Conine anyway . . . as a hitter, so the Royals drafted him in the fifty-eighth round of the '87 June draft.

That was one of the great draft picks in history. Conine zipped through the farm system in good order, and in 1992 he clubbed twenty homers in 110 games for Kansas City's Triple-A affiliate. And that November, the Royals didn't protect him in the expansion draft. Rather, they protected utility infielder David Howard and relief pitcher Bill Sampen.

We might describe the Marlins' selection of Conine as one of the great expansion draft picks in history . . . but if they were really that smart, they wouldn't have waited until the twenty-second pick.

It should be said that this expansion draft wasn't like the ones that had come before. A *number* of fine players were available. In addition to Conine, the Marlins got Trevor Hoffman, Bryan Harvey, Carl Everett, and Robert Person (though only Conine and Harvey actually played well for Florida).

FLORIDA MARLINS

		YEARS	NOTES
		ALL-TIME	
C	Charles Johnson	1994–1998 1901–*2002*	University of Miami product was Fish's first pick in '92 draft, and won Gold Glove as rookie in '94; went to Dodgers in '98 trade, then came home as free agent in '01.
1B	Derrek Lee	1998–*2002*	Dumping Kevin Brown's salary on the Padres didn't help in the short term, but in 2000, ex-Padre Lee developed into one of the top first basemen in the league.
2B	Luis Castillo	1996–*2002*	Got off to slow start with Marlins, but in 2000 he batted .334 with 66 steals, and in 2002 he put together a 35-game hitting streak (which ended with him on deck).
SS	Edgar Renteria	1996–1998	In three seasons, batted .288 and swiped 89 bases; more notably, in 1997 he delivered game-winning hits in two postseason games, including Game 7 of World Series.
3B	Mike Lowell	1999–*2002*	Epitome of consistency was a gift from the Yankees, via McGriff-like trade for three pitchers who've combined for exactly one major-league victory since.
LF	Jeff Conine	1993–1997	Played 162 games in franchise's inaugural season, still ranks atop Marlins' all-time list in a few categories, and will forever be remembered as "Mr. Marlin."
CF	Preston Wilson	1998–2002	Poor man's Bobby Bonds: power, speed, and strikeouts . . . lots and lots of strikeouts, but he didn't let the K's bother him and played well in center field.
RF	Gary Sheffield	1993–1998	He's been gone a few years now, but still sits atop the franchise list with 122 homers, and his career marks for OBP (.426) and slugging (.523) are safe for now.
SP1	Kevin Brown	1996–1997	Only two seasons, but we make allowances for the young franchise, and Brown won 33 games, plus 2 more in '97 NLCS (but got hammered in World Series).
SP2	Ryan Dempster	1998–2002	Made the All-Star team in first full season (2000), and tops franchise list with 42 victories (yes, only 42); traded to Reds during disappointing 2002.
SP3	Pat Rapp	1993–1997	An original Marlin, and in 1994 and '95 he combined for 21-15 mark with solid 3.62 ERA; dropped to 8-16, 5.10 in '96 and traded to Royals in '97.
SP4	Alex Fernandez	1997–2000	Miami native won 17 games in '97, but missed most of the next three seasons with a shoulder injury and got paid a big chunk of change in the process.
RP	Robb Nen	1993–1997	Took over as closer in '94 after Bryan Harvey got hurt, and converted 15 straight save chances; in '97, saved 35 games to finish second in Rolaids Relief Man rankings.

		SINGLE SEASON	
		YEARS	**NOTES**
C	Charles Johnson	1997	Won (and deserved) third straight Gold Glove, setting record for errorless games (123) by catcher in a season; also, 19 HR.
1B	Derrek Lee	2002	After two decent seasons, got a chance to start every day and responded with 27 homers, 98 walks, and 19 steals.
2B	Luis Castillo	2000	Fantastic season in the leadoff slot, posting .418 on-base percentage and stealing MLB-most 62 bases.
SS	Edgar Renteria	1997	After the season, received "San Carlos Cross of the Order of the Great Knight," Colombia's highest honor, from president.
3B	Bobby Bonilla	1997	One of three big free agents for Fish in '97, set team record with 39 doubles and started game-winning rally in Game 7.
LF	Cliff Floyd	2001	Established career bests in everything worth besting, and also set franchise mark with 123 runs scored.
CF	Preston Wilson	2000	Became 30th 30-30 MLB player, with 31 HR and 36 SB; could have done more, but held out late to avoid setting K record.
RF	Gary Sheffield	1996	Finally healthy for a full season, set personal bests with 161 games, 42 homers, 120 RBI, 118 runs, 142 walks.
SP	Kevin Brown	1996	Finished second in Cy Young vote after leading NL with 1.89 ERA and 3 shutouts; won 17 games despite two weeks on DL.
RP	Bryan Harvey	1993	Arguably a bit short of Robb Nen's '96 season, but Harvey provided instant credibility to franchise with 45 saves.

		ALL-ROOKIE	
		YEARS	**NOTES**
C	Charles Johnson	1995	Got off to slow start with bat, but wound up hitting .251 with 11 homers and picked up his first Gold Glove after season.
1B	Orestes Destrade	1993	After four seasons in Japan, Miami native came home and led Marlins with 20 homers and 87 RBI.
2B	Quilvio Veras	1995	Marlins had to give up Carl Everett to get him, but Veras stole 56 bases, scored 86 runs, and posted .384 OBP.
SS	Edgar Renteria	1996	Recalled from Triple-A on May 9 and batted .334 after All-Star break, including 22-game hitting streak.
3B	Mike Lowell	1999	Underwent testicular-cancer surgery February 21, but got back in time to hit 12 homers and knock in 47 runs in 97 games.
LF	Jeff Conine	1993	Didn't find his power until the next season, but did bat .292 and play all 162 games for first-year Fish.
CF	Preston Wilson	1999	With 26 home runs and .502 slugging percentage, led all MLB rookies in both categories.
RF	Mark Kotsay	1998	Kotsay's 721 OPS wasn't anything to write home about, but he did tie for NL lead with 20 outfield assists.
SP	Livan Hernandez	1997	Cuban émigré won 9 games during the regular season, then racked up 4 more victories in LCS and World Series.
RP	Matt Mantei	1998	Didn't arrive until May 20 and later spent two weeks on DL, but topped club with 9 saves and K'd 63 in 55 innings.

I'm no expert in psychology. I did take Intro to Psychology in high school, but I was seventeen and the class came immediately after lunch, and so my only memories of that course are of the lovely Laura Gentry and trying desperately to stay awake.

And maybe if I knew more about psychology, I'd get what the big deal is with strikeouts. Entering the 2000 season, the major-league record for strikeouts by a hitter in a single season was 189, set by Bobby Bonds in 1970 (a great season for him, otherwise). On September 24 against the Rockies, Preston Wilson struck out three times. That gave him 185 K's for the season and the Marlins still had six games left, so it was apparent that Wilson would almost certainly break Bonds's record if he continued to play.

Marlins manager John Boles said he didn't want Wilson to break that record, and so he held him out of the lineup for a couple of games. Wilson finished with 187 strikeouts.

To me, there's no shame at all in breaking the strikeout record, because that simply means that you're good enough to play enough games to break it. And Wilson was very good in 2000: thirty-one home runs, team-record 121 RBI. And in my admittedly uneducated mind, it's a shame he didn't get the chance to do even better.

Trading Quilvio Veras worked out eventually, but it was one of general manager Dave Dombrowski's few post-1996 moves that didn't pay an immediate dividend.

Shortly after the '96 season, Dombrowski traded Veras to San Diego for Dustin Hermanson, a right-handed pitcher. Hermanson would become a solid major-league starter, but at that point his career consisted of thirty-four relief appearances in which he'd posted an embarrassing 7.35 ERA. By the following March, the Marlins were well stocked with pitchers, so Dombrowski sent Hermanson and outfielder Joe Orsulak—the Marlins had plenty of outfielders, too—off to Montreal for Cliff Floyd.

In 1997, these deals didn't look too good. Veras, who'd struggled in '96 after a fine rookie campaign, found his game again in San Diego. Floyd, still suffering the after-effects of a horrible wrist injury he suffered in 1995, batted .234 (albeit with good power and patience) in sixty-one games. And Veras's primary replacement at second base, rookie Luis Castillo, clearly wasn't ready.

There was, of course, a very happy ending to this story: Cliff Floyd became a fine major-league hitter, and Luis Castillo eventually became a pretty good player, too. Oh, and the Marlins won the World Series.

TRADED AWAY			
		TRADED	NOTES
C	Mike Piazza	May 22, 1998	After playing the grand total of five games with Fish, traded to Mets for Preston Wilson and others.
1B	Jeff Conine	November 20, 1997	First loss in the post-championship salary purge, as Conine sent to Royals for a marginal pitching prospect.
2B	Quilvio Veras	November 21, 1996	Straight up to Padres for Dustin Hermanson, who was passed along to the Expos for Cliff Floyd.
SS	Edgar Renteria	December 14, 1998	Part of the ongoing fire sale, sent to Cardinals for three minor leaguers after making All-Star team in '98.
3B	Todd Zeile	July 31, 1998	Salary dump, as Zeile delivered to Rangers for two "prospects" who've yet to reach the majors.
LF	Moises Alou	November 11, 1997	Signed for five years, played only one before going to Astros in deal for three guys who didn't do nothin'.
CF	Carl Everett	November 29, 1994	Did well in Triple-A but deemed a problem, suspended for a month, and mailed to Mets for Quilvio Veras.
RF	Gary Sheffield	May 15, 1998	Part of huge deal that sent him, Bobby Bonilla, Charles Johnson, and others to Dodgers for Piazza and Zeile.
SP	Al Leiter	February 6, 1998	Well, at least this salary dump eventually had a happy ending, as Marlins got A. J. Burnett in deal with Mets.
RP	Trevor Hoffman	June 24, 1993	Sent to San Diego in deal that worked out for both clubs, as Marlins got Sheffield in return.

GOLD GLOVE			
		YEARS	NOTES
C	Charles Johnson	1994–1998 2001–2002	Ranks behind only Pudge Rodriguez among his peers, and many observers thought CJ called a better game.
1B	Jeff Conine	1997	Conine was one of the great racquetball players in the country, and his agility came in handy around the bag.
2B	Luis Castillo	1996–2002	Shoulder injuries left him reluctant to dive to his left, but quickness and arm make him strong up the middle.
SS	Edgar Renteria	1996–1998	A bit overrated, but looked pretty on the double play and did play brilliantly when it mattered (in 1997).
3B	Mike Lowell	1998–2002	A liability when he started, but worked his ass off and became one of the league's better defenders.
LF	Moises Alou	1997	Marlins got better at two positions when Alou replaced Conine in LF and Conine replaced Colbrunn at 1B.
CF	Chuck Carr	1993–1995	Chucky couldn't hit or throw, but Chucky could run and Chucky could chase down those fly balls.
RF	Mark Kotsay	1997–2000	It's the strong-armed Kotsay by default, as Gary Sheffield and Darrell Whitmore were both butchers.
P	Kevin Brown	1996–1997	He did everything well, which was good because his mid-90s sinkers turned into a lot of ground balls.

ALL-BUST

		YEARS	NOTES
C	Steve Decker	1993–1995	Onetime hot prospect with Giants batted .203 in limited action over three seasons.
1B	Orestes Destrade	1994	Following serviceable '93, got off to horrible start in '94 and finished his final season at .208-5-15.
2B	Bret Barberie	1993–1994	Hit 3 homers off Saberhagen in spring game, but never topped 5 in regular season and awful with the glove.
SS	Alex Gonzalez	2000	Batted exactly .200 in 2000 . . . and that included career-high 13-game hitting streak in which he batted .333.
3B	Josh Booty	1996–1998	"Tools" are great, but ideally they're possessed by someone who can actually play baseball.
LF	Nigel Wilson	1993	Florida's first pick in the expansion draft went 0-for-16 in his brief stint with the big club.
CF	Todd Dunwoody	1997–1999	One of franchise's prize prospects and got 670 at-bats with Marlins, but showed little ability in majors.
RF	Darrell Whitmore	1993–1995	Named No. 1 prospect in PCL, but batted .204 in 76 games with Fish and barely heard from again.
SP	Alex Fernandez	1998–2001	Suffered torn rotator cuff during 1997 NLCS and never came close to getting back to where he'd been.
RP	Kurt Miller	1994–1997	Fifth pick in '91 draft (by Pirates) so he kept getting chances, but posted 7.45 ERA in 74 innings with Fish.

USED-TO-BE-GREAT

		YEARS	NOTES
C	Darren Daulton	1997	Finished career on fine note, coming to Marlins in July and batting .262 in 52 games for Series winners.
1B	Orestes Destrade	1993–1994	After becoming Randy Johnson's first-ever K victim, Cuban starred in Japan, with 154 homers in four years.
2B	Vacant	—	Generally, the Marlins haven't been real eager to bring aboard ex-superstars just for the sake of doing it.
SS	Walt Weiss	1993	Doesn't really qualify here, as he wasn't *great* before 1993 and did enjoy some good seasons *after* 1993.
3B	Terry Pendleton	1995–1996	Played very well in 1995, but hit the wall in '96 and traded to Braves with sub-.300 OBP.
LF	Tim Raines	2002	At 42, Florida native came back for one last season, but batted just .191 and the good moments were few.
CF	Jim Eisenreich	1997–1998	Always one of my favorite players, but his days of great contact hitting were mostly over by now.
RF	Andre Dawson	1995–1996	Signed at a nominal salary, Dawson slugged .434 in 1995, when he was 40.
SP	Charlie Hough	1993–1994	Ancient knuckleballer threw the first pitch and earned the first win in franchise history.
RP	Alejandro Peña	1995, 1996	An odd career, as Pena posted ERA's in the threes for 12 straight seasons beginning in 1981.

On May 1, 1997, *USA Today*'s Rod Beaton wrote of Josh Booty, "He is playing baseball better than ever. He has been a productive power hitter for Class AA Portland (Maine) in the Eastern League, a notoriously pitcher-friendly league." This left aside the salient facts that 1) Booty's home ballpark, Portland's Haddock Field, was a fantastic park for power hitters, and 2) power was the *only* positive in Booty's game.

Wait, this gets better. A few months later, on September 19, Beaton wrote, ". . . the critics of Florida third base prospect Josh Booty (.210, 20 homers, 60 RBI at Class AA) have no sense of history. Booty, once the nation's top college quarterback recruit, is a great fielder with power. Buddy Bell, Steve Buechele and Graig Nettles had long careers with Booty-esque skills."

Sense of history? I won't go into great detail here, but neither Bell nor Buechele nor Nettles played *anything* like Josh Booty in the first few years of their pro careers. Bell did hit .229 in his first professional season, but 1) he was seventeen that summer, and 2) that .229 was better than Booty hit in *any* of his first three pro seasons.

Josh Booty quit playing baseball after the 1998 season, and did what he should have done in the first place: he played football at LSU.

CORRECTING THE RECORD

There haven't been many books written about the Marlins. In fact, there's only one that I know about: Dave Rosenbaum's *If They Don't Win It's a Shame: The Year the Marlins Bought the World Series*. It's one of the better books of its kind, and it's a bit of a shame that not many people care enough about the Marlins to have read it.

I don't think the subtitle is completely fair, though.

It's true that, prior to the 1997 season, the Marlins committed $89 million in long-term contracts to six free agents, including Alex Fernandez (five years, $35 million), Moises Alou (five years, $25 million), and Bobby Bonilla (four years, $23.3 million).

That sounds like a lot of money, and it was (back in those old days). The Marlins carried a hefty payroll in 1997. But what's often lost, I think, is the fact that the Marlins' $48 million (or thereabouts) season-opening payroll was *lower* than that of five teams in the American League, and lower than that of the Braves in the National League. What's more, the Reds, Cardinals, Dodgers, and Rockies weren't far behind.

The Baltimore Orioles opened the 1997 season with a $55 million payroll, roughly seven million higher than the Marlins. If the Orioles had won the World Series, do you think anyone would have accused them of "buying" a championship? Probably not. The Cleveland Indians opened the '97 season with a $54 million payroll. If the Indians had won the World Series—which, of course, they very nearly did—would anyone have accused them of "buying" a championship? Probably not.

So why do the Marlins get such a bum rap? Two reasons, I think.

One, they didn't win like expansion franchises are "supposed" to win. Previously, expansion franchises had attempted to build from within, and in the process most of them endured losing season after losing season. Prior to free agency, of course, they didn't have much of a choice. But most recently, the expansion Mariners and Blue Jays had eschewed expensive free agency, trusting instead in their farm systems (it worked for the Jays and didn't work for the M's). So maybe it didn't sit well with the baseball writers, seeing these upstart Marlins spend their way into contention.

And two, it wasn't so much that the Marlins spent a lot of money, it was that they spent a lot of it at once. Very rarely had any franchise signed up three premier free agents in one off-season, and I guess that offended the writers, too.

But the facts are that the Marlins' payroll was *not* out of line with most of the other clubs with postseason aspirations, and the team *was* well-positioned for the future. If owner Wayne Huizenga hadn't taken the money and run, there's no reason why the Marlins couldn't have challenged the Braves for National League East primacy for the next two or three seasons, at least.

Oh, before I let the Marlins go, I wanted to clear up another misconception about the 1997 club. That was the last season of Gary Sheffield's contract, but shortly after the season started, Sheffield got a huge extension: $61 million over six years.

In a photo caption for his book, Dave Rosenbaum compares Sheffield to Kevin Brown and writes, "Gary Sheffield's relationship with the media was far more amicable, even though the big stick he carried didn't cause much damage to opposing pitchers."

In the 1998 *Baseball Guide*, Dan Graziano of the *Palm Beach Post* labeled Sheffield the Marlins' biggest disappointment, writing, "Right fielder Gary Sheffield, who received a staggering six-year, $61 million contract extension . . . struggled all season at the plate, hitting .250 with 21 homers and 71 RBIs."

If only we could all struggle like Sheffield did. Granted, by his own standards it wasn't a great season; in 1996, Sheffield had hit .315 with forty-two homers and 120 RBI (which of course is why he got the big new contract). And he did spend two weeks on the Disabled List with a sprained left thumb. But rather than focus on what Sheffield did not do in 1997, why not focus on what he *did* do?

He drew 121 walks, *forty-eight more than anybody else on the team.*

He posted a .424 on-base percentage, *forty-six points better than anybody else on the team.*

He posted an 870 OPS, *highest on the team.*

Sheffield also scored eighty-six runs, four off the team lead, and his twenty-one homers were second. He was, by almost any objective measure, right there with Moises Alou as one of the two most productive hitters on the team.

I'm grateful to Jon Sciambi for his help with this chapter, the sources for which include Dave Rosenbaum's If They Don't Win It's a Shame: The Year the Marlins Bought the World Series *(McGregor Publishing, 1998).*

**Throw me a fastball.
I dare you.**
Courtesy Florida Marlins

Craig Biggio is *unique*.

People throw "unique" around like it's nothing, but "unique" does not mean "rare"; it means "one of a kind." And Craig Biggio meets the dictionary definition, because there's never been another player like him.

Biggio was a catcher at Seton Hall and a good one, and in 1987 the Astros spent their first-round draft pick (twenty-second overall) on him. In his first pro season, Biggio batted .375 in Class A. In his second pro season he skipped Double-A, batted .320 in three months of Triple-A, and finished by catching fifty games for the big club.

Speed had always been a big part of Biggio's game—he stole 56 bases in those first two professional seasons—but everybody knows what catching does to a fellow's legs, and nobody in Houston was thrilled at the prospect of their young hare transmogrifying into a tortoise. In 1991, his third full season with the Astros, Biggio batted .295 and made the All-Star team as a catcher. But in the next-to-last series of the year, he played three games at second base. And when Opening Day rolled around in 1992, Craig Biggio was officially a second baseman. He eventually became a very good *defensive* second baseman, winning a few Gold Gloves. And he's the only one of his kind.

HOUSTON ASTROS

ALL-TIME			
		YEARS	NOTES
C	Alan Ashby	1979–1989	Switch-hitter was the first Astro to homer from both sides of the plate in one game; caught no-hitters from Ken Forsch, Nolan Ryan, and Mike Scott.
1B	Jeff Bagwell	1991–*2002*	Nice trade, as the Astros gave up a month of 37-year-old middle reliever Larry Andersen and got one of the six or eight greatest first basemen of all time.
2B	Craig Biggio	1988–*2002*	First player ever to successfully switch from catching to playing in the middle of the infield, and should pop right into the Hall of Fame as a second baseman.
SS	Craig Reynolds	1979–1989	Houston native couldn't hit a lick or run particularly well, but his glove kept him in the majors for 13 full seasons (and parts of two more).
3B	Doug Rader	1967–1975	Never made an All-Star team, but he was a regular for seven years and was considered NL's top defensive third baseman; later, longtime coach and manager.
LF	José Cruz	1975–1987	Wonderful player, perhaps robbed of Hall of Fame numbers by the Astrodome; enjoyed his two best seasons after reaching his mid-30s.
CF	Cesar Cedeño	1970–1981	Drew early comparisons to Mays and actually deserved them, but career petered out after he turned 30, some say because of something that happened off the field.
RF	Terry Puhl	1977–1990	Never developed the power some thought he might, but was intelligent and aggressive on the bases, played a solid right field, and just about everybody liked him.
SP1	Mike Hampton	1994–2000	In six seasons, left-hander with variety of fastballs never posted a losing record or an ERA worse than league average; traded to Mets with 82-62 record as Astro.
SP2	Nolan Ryan	1980–1988	Pitched for the Astros longer than any other team; most remembered for 1987, when he went 8-16 despite leading the league with a 2.76 ERA.
SP3	J. R. Richard	1971–1980	Took years to establish himself, but finally became a star with overpowering stuff in late '70s; 10-4 with 1.90 ERA in 1980 when he suffered stroke that ended his career.
SP4	Don Wilson	1966–1974	One of the most feared pitchers around, tossed two no-hitters and was once lifted after eight no-hit innings; lifetime 3.15 ERA, but lifetime tragically ended after '74 season.
RP	Dave Smith	1980–1990	Power pitcher with bevy of complementary pitches took time to establish himself as a closer, but made a couple of All-Star teams and temporarily sits atop franchise's all-time saves list, with 199.

		YEARS	NOTES
NO. 2			
C	Johnny Edwards	1969–1974	Didn't hit much but considered fine defensively; won a couple of Gold Gloves before coming to Astros, then set consecutive errorless games streak (138) *with* Astros.
1B	Glenn Davis	1984–1990	Like a lot of guys, was hurt by the Astrodome; in his seven seasons with Astros, he hit 94 homers on the road but only 72 at home.
2B	Joe Morgan	1963–1971 1980	Obviously would rank No. 1 if he'd spent his career with Astros; missed most of the 1968 season with knee injury; played well in 1980 return, when he was 36.
SS	Dickie Thon	1981–1987	Played good defense, *and* had power and speed, but a severe beaning by Mike Torrez in 1984 cost him a year-and-a-half; didn't play regularly again until 1989, with Phils.
3B	Ken Caminiti	1987–1994 1999–2000	Decent power and acrobatic defense, but unfortunately fans didn't see the best of Caminiti until he confronted his alcoholism *and* got traded to Padres.
LF	Bob Watson	1966–1979	Playing out of position, but the Astros had Lee May at first base; beats out Luis Gonzalez, and is most famous for supposedly scoring MLB's millionth run.
CF	Jimmy Wynn	1963–1973	"Jimmy . . . was Willie Mays at the same age, but he just had a different agenda, and because of that he never progressed."—Joe Morgan
RF	Kevin Bass	1982–1989	Played in his only All-Star Game in '86, when the Astros reached Game 6 of NLCS, in which Bass made last out; good speed and strong arm in right field.
SP1	Mike Scott	1983–1991	Was just 14-27 with Mets, but learned devastating splitter from Roger Craig and went 86-49 for Astros from 1985 through '89 and won Cy Young in '86.
SP2	Joe Niekro	1975–1985	Didn't join Astros until he was 31, at which point he refined knuckleball and wound up winning 144 games for Astros, a franchise record that's not threatened.
SP3	Larry Dierker	1964–1976	Debuted for Astros on his 18th birthday and enjoyed his best season when he was 22; finished with 137 wins with Houston, No. 2 behind Niekro on all-time list.
SP4	Ken Forsch	1970–1980	Never won more than 12 games in a season with Astros and was a rotation starter in only five seasons, but pitched consistently well and tossed no-hitter in 1979.
RP	Billy Wagner	1995–*2002*	Always had the overpowering fastball, then learned a killer slider from Randy Johnson; struggled terribly in 2000 with injury, but came back strong in 2001.

Everybody gets "The Cesar Cedeño Story" wrong.

Cedeño arrived in 1970, and he looked like The Next Big Thing.

However, following the 1973 season, Cedeño was convicted, in the Dominican Republic, of involuntary manslaughter in a tragedy involving his girlfriend. He paid a small fine and walked free, but his early decline is often blamed on the difficulty of dealing with his girlfriend's death and the attendant abuse from hecklers.

There's a big problem with this story, though . . . Cedeño actually played quite well from 1974 through '77. Then, after missing most of '78 with an injury and struggling in '79, Cedeño bounced back with a fine 1980. At that point, he was *still* on a Hall of Fame path. The dividing line in Cedeño's career is not 1973/1974; it's 1980/1981.

So what happened between 1980 and 1981? Consult *The Ballplayers* or *Baseball: The Biographical Encyclopedia,* as I initially did, and you'll remain mystified, because everybody seems to forget that in Game 3 of the NLCS in 1980, Cedeño stepped awkwardly on first base while trying to beat a double-play relay, and suffered a compound fracture of his right ankle.

That's a bitch of an injury. Cedeño was only twenty-nine years old, but he'd never be the same. Manslaughter didn't kill his career; a broken ankle did.

In 1991, the Astros made a decision that would have a big impact on their future and a huge impact on the future of another organization.

The previous fall, they'd made one of the great trades in the history of the game, sending relief pitcher Larry Andersen to the Red Sox for minor leaguer Jeff Bagwell. The only "problem" was that Bagwell played third base, and the Astros already had a third baseman that they liked quite a lot, guy named Ken Caminiti. They could shift Bagwell to first base, but they already had Glenn Davis, one of the league's best. They could put off the decision for a year, and simply send Bagwell to Class AAA. This was the most obvious solution, as Bagwell hadn't spent a day in Triple-A, and hadn't showed home-run power in Double-A.

The Astros had one more option. They could trade Glenn Davis, and hand first base to Jeff Bagwell. That's what they did, of course, and Bagwell 1) was the Rookie of the Year in 1991, and 2) became the game's best first baseman.

I often wonder, though, if Bagwell could have been a great third baseman, too. Caminiti never really developed in Houston, and after his departure the Astros ran through third basemen like Steinbrenner used to run through managers. It's hard to argue with success, but still I can't help but wonder. . . .

		YEARS	NOTES
SINGLE SEASON			
C	Craig Biggio	1991	Biggio's last year as catcher was also the *best* year by an Astros catcher; edges Joe Ferguson in '77 because of speed.
1B	Jeff Bagwell	1996	Bagwell's season of seasons: led NL with 48 doubles, scored 111 runs and drove in 120, even stole 21 bases.
2B	Craig Biggio	1997	Played every game and scored 146 runs, most in the National League since 1932; also grabbed Gold Glove.
SS	Dickie Thon	1983	Just an amazing season: great defense and solid offensive stats across the board, including 20 homers and 34 steals.
3B	Ken Caminiti	1992	No Astros 3B has ever had an MVP-type season, but in '92 Caminiti slugged .441 and posted .350 OBP.
LF	José Cruz	1984	The ageless wonder set career highs in runs and RBI, posting virtually identical stats as he had the previous season.
CF	Jimmy Wynn	1969	He hit 33 homers, drew NL-best 148 walks, played solid defense, and so may have been the best player in the league.
RF	Jimmy Wynn	1972	Scored career-high 117 runs and drove in 90 in last big year with Astros; just edges Rusty Staub's 1967 season here.
SP	Mike Scott	1986	The best 18-10 season ever; he led NL with 275 innings, 306 K's, and 2.22 ERA, and pitched no-hitter to clinch West title.
RP	Hal Woodeshick	1963	Sinkerballer recorded only 10 saves, but he also won 11 games and posted 1.97 ERA in 114 innings.

		YEARS	NOTES
ALL-ROOKIE			
C	Mitch Meluskey	2000	Close to a 900 OPS in 117 games, but his glove was weak, the Astros lost 90 games, and so Meluskey became a Tiger.
1B	Jeff Bagwell	1991	Didn't spend a day in Class AAA, but posted .387 OBP, drove in 82 runs, and garnered Rookie of the Year honors.
2B	Joe Morgan	1965	Hint of things to come, as he stole 20 bases, scored 100 runs, and topped National League with 97 walks.
SS	Sonny Jackson	1966	Just like Morgan in '65, Jackson finished second in Rookie of the Year vote; 49 steals tied then-MLB record for rookies.
3B	Bob Aspromonte	1962	One of two rookies in franchise history to see significant time at third base; played 149 games and hit 11 homers.
LF	Luis Gonzalez	1991	Hot prospect played 137 games and showed promise, but .320 OBP and .433 slugging didn't foretell long-term future.
CF	Cesar Cedeño	1970	Played in only 90 games, but batted .310 and stole 17 bases . . . and he was only 19 years old for the entire season.
RF	Lance Berkman	2000	After destroying minor-league pitchers for a few years, finally got his shot and didn't miss: .388 OBP, .561 slugging.
SP	Roy Oswalt	2001	Opened season in minors and started only 20 games, but wound up 14-3 with 2.73 ERA for first-place Astros.
RP	Charlie Kerfeld	1986	Fat, bespectacled fireballer went 11-2 for division winners; career fell completely apart afterward.

		YEARS	NOTES
C	Jerry Grote	1963–1964	Signed as free agent with Colt .45s, and actually hit—something he wouldn't do later—in the minors.
1B	John Mayberry	1968–1971	Sixth player selected in 1967 draft, when he was just 17, and signed for reported $40,000 bonus.
2B	Joe Morgan	1963–1971 1980	After a year at Oakland City College, signed with Colts scout Bill Wight for $3,000 bonus and $500 per month.
SS	Sonny Jackson	1963–1967	His first season as a regular would be his best, even though he was only 21; seven seasons with Braves.
3B	Ken Caminiti	1987–1994 1999–2000	Unfortunately for the Astros, Caminiti's greatness lasted for exactly the four years he was in San Diego.
LF	Luis Gonzalez	1990–1995 1997	Floridian attended South Alabama, fourth-round pick in '88; sadly, most of his power came with other teams.
CF	Jimmy Wynn	1963–1973	Actually got his starts with the Reds, but Astros grabbed him in minor-league draft after his first pro season.
RF	Rusty Staub	1963–1968	Reportedly received $100,000 bonus to sign with Astros in 1961, before they'd actually played a game.
SP	J. R. Richard	1971–1980	The second player selected in 1969 draft and signed for $100K, supposedly so good in high school he never had to pitch from stretch.
RP	Dave Smith	1980–1990	Eighth-round pick in '76 out of San Diego St.; a starter all the way through minors, with just middling success.

HOMEGROWN (table title)

TRADED AWAY

		TRADED	NOTES
C	Jerry Grote	October 19, 1965	Sent to Mets for cash and pitcher Tom Parsons, who'd just gone 1-10 in his last MLB season.
1B	John Mayberry	December 2, 1971	Traded to Royals for pitchers Lance Clemons and Jim York, neither of whom did much afterward.
2B	Joe Morgan	November 29, 1971	Worst deal in franchise history; Astros manager Harry Walker labeled Morgan a "troublemaker."
SS	Vacant	—	It's a good thing, that they haven't traded a good short-stop . . . and a bad thing that they haven't *had* to.
3B	Ken Caminiti	December 8, 1994	Just one component of a *12-player deal* with Padres; Caminiti enjoyed his biggest seasons in San Diego.
LF	Manny Mota	April 2, 1963	Then–Colt .45s sent Mota and cash to Pirates for outfielder Howie Goss; Mota never batted for Colts.
CF	Kenny Lofton	December 10, 1991	To Tribe for Taubensee; imagine the 1990s lineup that could have been: Lofton-Biggio-Bagwell . . .
RF	Bobby Abreu	November 8, 1997	Astros didn't trade him, but neither did they bother protecting him in the 1993 expansion draft.
SP	Curt Schilling	April 2, 1992	Straight up to Phillies for Jason Grimsley, who spent a season in Tucson, then got released.
RP	Todd Jones	December 10, 1996	Sent to Tigers in nine-player deal, and saved 132 games in four full seasons in Detroit.

The Astros first reached the postseason in their nineteenth season. No other National League expansion team's fans have ever waited so long. And the hell of it is, they probably could have made it six or eight years earlier.

It's not until just now that I realized how badly the Astros screwed up in the early 1970s. This is an organization that held title, as late as 1970, to an amazing collection of hitting talent. And within four years, they pissed most of it away.

In 1974 and '75, Joe Morgan, Jimmy Wynn, John Mayberry, and Rusty Staub were all big stars. For other teams. Meanwhile, their old spots on the depth chart were filled by names like Rob Andrews, Wilbur Howard, and Greg Gross.

How did it happen? Well, it's a truism of baseball analysis that screwed-up organizations tend to assume that if they're losing, it's because their best players aren't good enough. And the tendency was even more pronounced in Houston, where the Astrodome made great hitters look good, and good hitters look average. And truth be told, there were some black/white issues at work, too. Manager Harry Walker considered Morgan a "troublemaker," which probably says more about Walker than Morgan. And things were never the same for Staub after he used a racial slur that you weren't supposed to use, even then.

In 2000, a twenty-six-year-old catcher named Mitch Meluskey batted .300 with fourteen home runs and an 888 OPS in 117 games. Also in 2000, a thirty-one-year-old catcher named Brad Ausmus batted .266 with seven home runs and a 722 OPS in 150 games.

Care to guess which catcher Jeff Bagwell and Craig Biggio wanted behind the plate in 2001? Right . . . they picked the old guy who can't hit. Oh, did I mention that Ausmus had been their teammate in 1997 and '98? Bagwell and Biggio wielded a fair amount of influence with management, and on December 11, 2000, the Astros traded three players, including Meluskey, to Detroit for three players, including Ausmus.

Ausmus hit like a little girl in 2001. On the other hand, the Astros' pitching did improve, so it must have been Ausmus, right? Well, maybe. Houston's two worst pitchers in 2000 had been José Lima (6.65 ERA) and Chris Holt (5.35). Holt went to Detroit in the deal for Ausmus, and Lima was even worse for the Astros in 2001 before he went to Detroit, too. Scott Elarton was the Astros' best starter in 2000, and he actually regressed in 2001, eventually being traded to Colorado.

For now, though, the trade looks great. Because not only did the Astros return to the postseason—after finishing fourth in 2000—but Meluskey missed the entire 2001 season and most of 2002 with injuries.

GOLD GLOVE			
		YEARS	NOTES
C	Brad Ausmus	1997–1998 1set2001–*2002*	Lack of power kept him from playing every day, but glove and arm have kept him in the majors for a long time.
1B	Glenn Davis	1984–1990	Played multiple positions in minors, but worked very hard and became outstanding defensive first baseman.
2B	Craig Biggio	1988–*2002*	Switched from catcher to second base in 1992, and eventually became a fine defensive player.
SS	Craig Reynolds	1979–1989	Lousy hitter so he eventually lost his job to Dickie Thon, but was an outstanding defensive player.
3B	Doug Rader	1967–1975	Caminiti was good, but Rader was better and won five Gold Gloves in his seven seasons as a regular.
LF	Al Spangler	1962–1965	Once described as an "outfield slickster," which might be stretching things . . . but hey, this *is* left field.
CF	Gerald Young	1987–1992	Very fast, never won a Gold Glove but deserved at least two; defense declined as hitting did the same.
RF	Terry Puhl	1977–1990	He was fast enough to play center field, and in 1979 didn't make a single error in 152 outfield games.
P	Mike Hampton	1994–2000	Generally considered the most athletic pitcher in the league; great move and very tough to run on.

IRON GLOVE			
		YEARS	NOTES
C	Mitch Meluskey	1998–2000	Best-hitting catcher in franchise history, but team's vets didn't care much for his glove or his personality.
1B	Eddie Mathews	1967	The 35-year-old third baseman had very nearly never played first base in his life before, and it showed.
2B	Art Howe	1976–1982	Nominally the regular in 1977 and '78, switched to the corners and for very good reasons.
SS	Julio Lugo	2000–*2002*	Good hitter, but so shaky afield that Astros compelled to keep José Vizcaíno around; killer errors in 2001 NLCS.
3B	Sean Berry	1996–1998	So bad that he couldn't stay in the lineup, even though he was the best-hitting third baseman they had.
LF	Bob Watson	1966–1979	He was a catcher in the minors and a first baseman after Lee May left Houston, which speaks volumes.
CF	Carl Warwick	1962–1963	Right in the middle as the Colts' inaugural outfield did *very* little defensively; shifted to right field in '63.
RF	Greg Gross	1973–1976	Lasted three years as regular in right, though limited range and weak arm eventually turned him into PH.
P	Brian Williams	1991–1994	Good athlete and quick off the mound, but showed tendency to botch the routine plays.

ALL-BUST		YEARS	NOTES
C	Eddie Taubensee	1992–1993	He cost the Astros Kenny Lofton, and didn't hit for them like he had before and would later.
1B	Denis Menke	1971	Playing second and short, hit 29 homers in previous three seasons, then shifted to 1B in '71 and hit *one* homer.
2B	Dave Rohde	1990–1991	Got the first shot at replacing Billy Doran, but batted .165 in 88 games, opening door for Biggio at second base.
SS	Sonny Jackson	1967	After batting .292 with 49 steals as rookie, dropped to .237 and 22, and was traded to Braves.
3B	Chris Truby	2000–2001	Came to majors with solid minor-league résumé, but posted unacceptable .288 OBP in 126 games.
LF	Wilbur Howard	1974–1978	Speedster did steal 32 bases in 1975, but .285 career on-base percentage didn't merit six years in majors.
CF	Gerald Young	1987–1992	125 steals in first three seasons, but defense and hitting both plummeted in what should have been his prime.
RF	Eric Anthony	1989–1993	Astros waited for five years, but all they got for their troubles was a .224 batting average and 673 OPS.
SP	José Lima	2000–2001	After winning 21 games in 1999, dropped to 7-16 with 6.65 ERA the very next season, Astros' first in Enron.
RP	John Hudek	1995–1997	Saved 16 games as rookie, but injuries limited him to 13 saves and 5.17 ERA over next three seasons.

USED-TO-BE-GREAT		YEARS	NOTES
C	Gus Triandos	1965	Former power-hitting catcher with Orioles finished in Houston with 24 games, 2 homers, and .181 average.
1B	Eddie Mathews	1967	He was "only" 35, but the future Hall of Fame third baseman was but a mere shadow of his former self.
2B	Nellie Fox	1964–1965	Hall of Famer spent his last two seasons in Houston, and enthusiastically tutored Joe Morgan in defense.
SS	Denis Menke	1968–1971 1974	He was very good from '68 through '70, but never matched brilliant '64 with Braves.
3B	Buddy Bell	1988	With Caminiti back in the minors after a shaky '87, Astros needed somebody for just a season.
LF	Tommy Davis	1969–1970	He'd play six more seasons with five other teams, but his days as a great player were already far past.
CF	Tommie Agee	1973	After three solid years with Mets, slumped in '72 and came over in trade; passed along to Cards in August.
RF	Kevin Bass	1993–1994	Came back after four seasons away and enjoyed one of his best years as 35-year-old part-timer in '94.
SP	Robin Roberts	1965–1966	In two partial seasons, former Phillies workhorse and future Hall of Famer went 8-7 with outstanding 2.77 ERA.
RP	Mike Henneman	1995	Detroit's all-time saves leader came over in August, pitched 21 innings, and saved 8 games.

It's said that pitchers are unpredictable, and they are. But absent injuries, they're really not *that* unpredictable. The ERAs and the wins and losses might go up and down, but the basic skills—strikeouts, walks, keeping the baseball in the ballpark—are actually pretty consistent.

And then there's Jose Lima. From 1995 through 1997, Lima, pitching for the Tigers and the Astros, went 9-21 with a 6.14 ERA. His strikeout-to-walk ratio in those seasons was actually pretty good, though, and the Astros didn't give up on him.

Their faith paid off when Lima went 16-8 in 1998 and 21-10 in 1999. In those two seasons, Lima struck out 356 batters and walked 76.

There was a small fly in the ointment, though: Lima did allow sixty-four home runs over those two seasons.

In 2000, the Astros moved into cozy Enron Field. And Jose Lima fell completely apart. Before getting traded to Detroit in June of 2001, Lima went 8-18 with a 6.79 ERA. More telling, in 249 innings he gave up sixty home runs.

At first, escaping Enron seemed to help Lima some. He started eighteen games in 2001 for the Tigers, and went just 5-10 but with a not-so-embarrassing 4.71 ERA. Then again, cavernous Comerica Park was the best pitcher's park in the American League, yet Lima somehow managed to give up twenty-three home runs in 113 innings. And then in 2002 the roof caved in—again—as he posted an ERA (7.77) that looks like a really big airplane.

Baseball's got a strange little rule, whereby you can get credit for playing in a game without ever actually playing in a game.

Confused? This comes up from time to time when a pinch hitter is announced, the other team changes pitchers, and then somebody pinch-hits for the pinch hitter. Well, in the official records the first pinch hitter, the one who never actually batted, still gets credited with a "game" simply because he was announced.

This doesn't happen with pitchers very often, because if a pitcher is announced he is required to actually pitch to at least one batter. Unless he's hurt. Which is what happened to Larry Yount, Robin's big brother, on September 15, 1971. With the Astros trailing the Braves 4–1 in Houston, Yount was summoned from the bullpen to pitch the top of the ninth inning. It would be his first major-league appearance . . . and his last. After throwing a few warm-up pitches, Yount felt something in his elbow pop. He told his manager, and was removed before throwing a single pitch in anger. The injury wasn't serious, but it was enough to keep Yount out of action for the rest of the season, and he never did make it back to the majors. So while Larry Yount is listed in the baseball encyclopedias, his name is accompanied by just one, solitary statistic: 1 Gm.

ALL-NAME			
		YEARS	NOTES
C	"Skip" Alfred Jutze	1973–1976	How's this for excitement? His dad called him "Skip," for no particular reason.
1B	"Bags" Jeff Bagwell	1991–*2002*	I promise, these are going to start getting a lot more interesting any minute now. . . .
2B	"Pigpen" Craig Biggio	1988–*2002*	His batting helmet might have been the most disgusting in all of Organized Baseball.
SS	"Sonny" Roland Jackson	1963–1967	Boyhood name that fit his small stature; at 5'9" and 155 pounds, he made a nice match for "Little Joe" Morgan.
3B	"The Red Rooster" Doug Rader	1967–1975	Wore his red hair long, with shock sticking out from back of his cap, reminding teammates of Foghorn Leghorn.
LF	"The Bull" Bob Watson	1966–1979	Built like a linebacker, and got the nickname from a coach in high school.
CF	"Toy Cannon" Jimmy Wynn	1963–1973	Small—5'10" and 160—but oh so powerful, which supposedly inspired the fans to invent this one.
RF	"Rusty" Daniel Staub	1963–1968	*Le Grand Orange* would come later; when Staub was born, nurses immediately dubbed him "Rusty."
SP	"Turk" Dick Farrell	1962–1967	According to *The Sporting News*, "Inherited name from father who was called Turk for unknown reason."
RP	"Ferrum Fireballer" Billy Wagner	1995–*2002*	Yes, I just made this up. But shouldn't a pitcher like Wagner have an evocative nickname?

TOP FIVE SEASONS		
YEAR	1986	RECORD 96-66
BEST HITTER	Kevin Bass	
BEST PITCHER	Mike Scott (Cy Young)	
NOTES	If only they could've got the ball to Scott in a Game 7 . . .	
YEAR	1980	RECORD 93-70
BEST HITTERS	Cesar Cedeño, José Cruz	
BEST PITCHERS	Vern Ruhle, Joe Niekro	
NOTES	Their first postseason, and they took the Phillies to the very limit.	
YEAR	1998	RECORD 102-60
BEST HITTER	Craig Biggio	
BEST PITCHERS	Mike Hampton, Shane Reynolds	
NOTES	Maybe the best Astros ever, but they ran into Kevin Brown.	
YEAR	1999	RECORD 97-65
BEST HITTER	Jeff Bagwell	
BEST PITCHER	Mike Hampton	
NOTES	Beat Braves in Game 1 of DCS, then got skunked.	
YEAR	2001	RECORD 93-69
BEST HITTERS	Lance Berkman, Jeff Bagwell	
BEST PITCHERS	Wade Miller, Roy Oswalt	
NOTES	Another Division Series, another wipeout for Killer B's.	

TOP FIVE MANAGERS	
MANAGER	Larry Dierker
YEARS	1997–2001
RECORD	448-362 (.553)
NOTES	From the pitcher's mound to the dugout to the top of the charts.
MANAGER	Bill Virdon
YEARS	1975–1982
RECORD	544-522 (.510)
NOTES	The Yankees' loss (firing, actually) was Astros' gain.
MANAGER	Hal Lanier
YEARS	1986–1988
RECORD	254-232 (.523)
NOTES	Division title in first season, but all downhill from there.
MANAGER	Harry Walker
YEARS	1968–1972
RECORD	355-353 (.501)
NOTES	If only he could have gotten along with Joe Morgan . . .
MANAGER	Terry Collins
YEARS	1994–1996
RECORD	224-197 (.532)
NOTES	Three seasons, three second-place finishes.

KILLING THE KILLER B'S

The Killer B's are the biggest flop in postseason history.

There, I said it. I didn't even bother with any of that pesky research. I just threw it out there, and now I'm going to defend it to the death, in the grand tradition of baseball writers everywhere. . . .

The Killer B's, of course, consist of Craig Biggio, Jeff Bagwell, and Derek Bell (1997–1999) or Lance Berkman (2000–2002, and counting). They've been the engine that's powered the Astros to four postseason berths in the last six years . . . and they've been the engine that's sputtered and died in each of those four postseasons.

How bad have they been? To get the ugliest picture, you have to look at them as a group.

	Games	AB	2B	3B	HR	RBI	OBP	Slug
Chilly B's	40	144	1	0	1	6	.253	.167

Forty games and 144 at-bats is almost exactly equivalent to one-fourth of a regular season, and those numbers are so bizarre that it's worth going into some small detail:

- The lone double was struck by Biggio on October 4, 1998, in Game 4 of the Division Series against San Diego. The Astros lost that game 6–1, and were eliminated.
- The lone home run was struck by Bell on October 1, also in 1998, in Game 2 of that same series. The Astros won that one, 5–4, with a run in the bottom of the ninth.
- Bagwell's got four of the six runs batted in, with Biggio and Bell claiming one apiece.
- Bagwell doesn't have a single extra-base hit in forty-six at-bats, but he does sport the "highest" batting average (.174) and, thanks to twelve walks, the highest on-base percentage (.367) by quite a bit.

Granted, Derek Bell wasn't a great player. But the odds against these four players combining for a .139 batting average over forty collective games must be incredibly high. The odds against any *one* of them batting .139 over forty games must be fairly high. And that's true even when we acknowledge that of the Astros' four Division Series, three came against the Braves, and in the other (1998) they had to face Kevin Brown twice.

So how can we explain that .139 batting average (and two extra-base hits)? I think it's been plain old shitty luck. Even beyond the shitty luck of going against the Braves three times. I think the Astros have generally run into the Braves on days when the Braves starters happened to be at the top of their games. If you assume that's true, and you also assume that the Killer B's were *not* at the top of theirs, then you can understand how some of the best hitters in the game could have failed so miserably when the chips were down.

There will be people who say that Biggio and Bagwell choked, especially if they don't break the hex before it's too late. But you know, Willie Mays hit only one home run in eighty-nine postseason at-bats. And nobody's calling *him* a choker.

I'm grateful to Bill Gilbert, Tal Smith, and Claudia Perry for their editorial suggestions. Sources for this chapter include Joe Morgan and David Falkner's Joe Morgan: A Life in Baseball *(W. W. Norton, 1993).*

The most interesting thing about the Royals' all-time lineup is that virtually all of them played together, as eight of the nine non-pitchers (and ten of fourteen including the pitchers) were on the club in 1977. And this was a very good team, if not a great one. From 1975 through 1980, the Royals didn't win a World Series, but they did win three American League West titles and 557 regular-season games (the Yankees, Orioles, and Reds all won a few more over that span).

What characterized the Royals of that era, just as much as quality, was stability. Frank White manned second base for fifteen years. Amos Otis manned center field for fourteen years. George Brett manned third base for thirteen years. Hal McRae was the DH for thirteen years (including most of a season in left field). Fred Patek manned shortstop for nine years. As a kid watching the Royals, I just assumed that every team was like this, with stable lineups for years and years. Of course it's unheard of now, but even in the 1970s very few teams had the Royals' stability, with five players in key roles for at least nine straight seasons.

KANSAS CITY ROYALS

		YEARS	NOTES
DH	Hal McRae	1973–1987	Game's greatest DH before Edgar Martinez, and retired with virtually every record for the "position" after 15 seasons with club; stolen from Reds in lopsided trade.
C	Darrell Porter	1977–1980	Only four years in Kansas City, but named to three All-Star teams and ranked as one of AL's best-hitting catchers; one of Whitey Herzog's all-time favorites.
1B	John Mayberry	1972–1977	Swiped from Astros in lopsided trade. Eventually left under a cloud, but he gave the Royals six seasons, three of them very good ones; twice led AL in walks.
2B	Frank White	1973–1990	Kansas City native literally helped build Royals Stadium, then won eight Gold Gloves and spent his entire 18-year career in his hometown.
SS	Fred Patek	1971–1979	Only 5'4", but stole 336 bases as Royal and sparkled with the glove; enduring image is Patek crying in the dugout after Game 5 of 1977 ALCS (I cried, too).
3B	George Brett	1973–1993	The jewel of the franchise, of course, and the only longtime Royal to reach Hall of Fame; arguably the second-greatest third baseman of all, after Schmidt.
LF	Willie Wilson	1976–1990	The fastest player of late '70s and early '80s, and perfectly suited to artificial turf in Royals Stadium; performance dropped when he tried to hit the ball over the fence.
CF	Amos Otis	1970–1983	Incredibly underrated, and accomplished in all facets of the game: hitting, baserunning, and fielding; swiped from the Mets in another lopsided trade.
RF	Danny Tartabull	1987–1991	Lousy fielder and injury-prone; but man, could he ever hit a baseball, and was rare Royal with plate discipline. Not a bad guy but never really seemed to fit in.
SP1	Bret Saberhagen	1984–1991	Cy Young Awards in 1985 and 1989; fragility and overwork resulted in alternating years of success, but he had as much talent as anybody not named Clemens.
SP2	Kevin Appier	1989–1999	Lousy support resulted in 114-89 record and masked great career; he posted 3.46 ERA as Royal, thanks to funky, Gossage-like motion and devastating splitter.
SP3	Dennis Leonard	1974–1986	From 1975 through '80 he won 107 games, tops in the American League. Right-handed power all the way, but like a lot of guys, he was overworked.
SP4	Paul Splittorff	1970–1984	Still the franchise's all-time leader with 166 wins, the stylish lefty relied on an average fastball and great control; last good season came in '83, when he was 36.
RP	Dan Quisenberry	1979–1988	Game's best closer from '80 through '85; submariner led AL in saves in five of those six seasons, and never threw anything resembling a fastball.

		YEARS	NOTES
		NO. 2	
DH	Chili Davis	1997	A Royal for just one season, but the pickings at DH are slim; other options are George Brett and Bob Hamelin, and they're already all over this chapter.
C	Mike Macfarlane	1987–1994 1996–1998	From 1991 through '94, ranked as one of the American League's best-hitting catchers, though nobody noticed; at least 14 HBP four times, resulting in solid OBP.
1B	Mike Sweeney	1995–2002	Came up as catcher, but switched to first base and played in three All-Star Games (so far); only moderate plate discipline keeps him from true greatness.
2B	Cookie Rojas	1970–1977	Despite underwhelming hitting stats, named to four straight All-Star teams. Tutored Frank White, and remembered for bringing credibility to franchise.
SS	U L Washington	1977–1984	Very little competition, as Royals have been searching for a long-term solution at shortstop since Patek left. Switch-hitting probably killed rather than helped him.
3B	Kevin Seitzer	1986–1991	Good enough to move Brett off third base, Rookie of the Year runner-up in '87 enjoyed three more fine seasons before knee problems and fielding woes got him gone.
LF	Bo Jackson	1986–1990	Vastly overrated, of course, but he was a very good player in 1989 and 1990 (before the football injury), and always seemed to be doing *something* interesting.
CF	Carlos Beltran	1998–*2002*	Made a big splash as Rookie of the Year in 1999, but actually played far better in both 2001 and '02; his many skills include historic percentage as base stealer.
RF	Jermaine Dye	1997–2001	In 2000, first Royal voted to All-Star team by fans since Bo Jackson in '89 . . . but traded to Oakland in '01, for same reasons that Damon went to the Athletics.
SP1	Mark Gubicza	1984–1996	Always stingy with the gopher ball, Gubicza went 20-8 with 2.70 ERA in 1988, his best season; kept ball down with sinking fastball and slider.
SP2	David Cone	1986 1993–1994	K.C. native posted 5.56 ERA in '86; won 27 games and Cy Young Award in his second, two-year stint. Would obviously rank higher if he'd been around a bit longer.
SP3	Steve Busby	1972–1980	Pitched regularly in only three seasons, but those seasons included 56-41 record and two no-hitters; was worked hard, career destroyed by arm injuries.
SP4	José Rosado	1996–2000	Unimposing 37-45, but got poor support from his mates and pitched in two All-Star Games; not blessed with great stuff, but fearlessly threw inside heat to righties.
RP	Jeff Montgomery	1992–1999	At retirement after 1999, ranked ninth on MLB's all-time saves list, with 304; just might be the only great four-pitch closer in history.

The transformation of the Royals from model franchise to laughingstock took roughly a decade. It essentially began with the signing of Mark Davis after the 1989 season, and was completed at the dawn of the twenty-first century, when first Johnny Damon and then Jermaine Dye were sent to Oakland because the Royals weren't interested in paying the going rate for star baseball players.

In fairness, the Royals were fairly well stocked in the outfield, so it wasn't hard to justify getting rid of Damon and Dye. The problem was that the Royals didn't get nearly enough for them, and that both deals looked really, really bad to the fans. For the first twenty-some years of the franchise's existence, ownership wasn't shy about spending money on ballplayers, but that changed after Ewing Kauffman died in 1993. Then economy became the watchword, and the game's new economics soon left the Royals with a payroll that reflected the franchise's low ticket prices—fans in Kansas City wouldn't stand for anything else—and paltry local TV and radio revenues. It's often said that you *can* compete with limited financial resources, and to a point that's true. But the margin for error is significantly smaller, and the truth is that there are simply not enough good owners and smart general managers to go around.

In *Play by Play: 25 Years of Royals on Radio*, Royals broadcaster Denny Matthews, who's been with the Royals since the beginning, wrote of the team's first season, "Around the infield were Chuck Harrison, Jerry Adair, Jack Hernandez and Joe Foy."

Well, Chuck Harrison did play 55 games at first base, but a guy named Mike Fiore played *91* games at first base. Harrison was very bad (.276 OBP, .296 slugging), Fiore was very good (.420 OBP, .428 slugging).

In each of his first three pro seasons, Fiore led his minor league in walks. That was just Class A, but in two-plus years of Double- and Triple-A, Fiore posted a .400 OBP and slugged .464, in a pitcher's era. But the Orioles were loaded with fine prospects, and so the Royals were able to pluck Fiore in the expansion draft.

He spent all of 1969 with the inaugural Royals, and nobody on the club had a higher OBP. But he wasn't much with the glove, and when he got off to a bad start in 1970 the Royals traded him to Boston for Tommy Matchick. Fiore never did find his stroke again. He played four seasons after 1969, mostly as a pinch hitter, and managed just a .288 OBP and a .195 slugging percentage. That solid '69 campaign was *not* a fluke, but something happened to Mike Fiore.

		YEARS	NOTES
	SINGLE SEASON		
DH	Hal McRae	1982	Set team record with 133 RBI; seemed like every time runners were on base, he ripped a double into the gap.
C	Darrell Porter	1979	101 runs, 112 RBI, AL-leading .429 OBP; granted, his pitchers struggled, costing the Royals the division title.
1B	John Mayberry	1975	The best hitter in the American League, with .416 OBP and .547 slugging, and league-most 23 homers on the road.
2B	Frank White	1986	Hit 22 homers, slugged .465, and won seventh Gold Glove; also homered off Mike Scott in All-Star Game.
SS	Jay Bell	1997	In his only year as Royal, hit 21 homers and drove in 92 runs, both of them easily club records for a shortstop.
3B	George Brett	1985	No, he didn't hit .390. But he was healthy all season, played brilliantly down the stretch, and won his only Gold Glove.
LF	Willie Wilson	1980	Led AL with 133 runs, 230 hits, and 15 triples, and stole 79 bases; also won his only Gold Glove.
CF	Amos Otis	1978	Brilliant all-around season, including 22 HR, career-high .525 slugging, 32 steals, and typical great defense.
RF	Al Cowens	1977	Easily his best season: 112 RBI, .525 slugging, and his only Gold Glove; finished second in MVP vote to Rod Carew.
SP	Bret Saberhagen	1989	Captured his second Cy Young Award thanks to league-leading 23 victories and 2.16 ERA.
RP	Dan Quisenberry	1983	Pitched 139 innings, recorded 45 saves, and posted 1.94 ERA; relievers have won Cy Youngs with far less.

		YEARS	NOTES
	ALL-ROOKIE		
DH	Bob Hamelin	1994	K.C.'s first Rookie of the Year since '69, but career quickly fizzled for the powerful "Hammer."
C	Brent Mayne	1991	Royals' No. 1 draft pick in 1989 didn't hit much but showed good plate discipline, and his pitchers liked him.
1B	Mike Fiore	1969	Piniella was the Rookie of the Year, but Fiore posted better OBP and slugging percentage (.428, albeit in less action).
2B	Carlos Febles	1999	Half of "Dos Carlos," Royals' impressive rookie duo in 1999; career derailed by various injuries, and he'll soon be forgotten.
SS	Mendy Lopez	1998	Default pick; terrible hitter who played only 74 games as rookie, but no rookie has ever played more SS for Royals.
3B	Kevin Seitzer	1987	The man who moved George Brett off third base looked like a future star with 207 hits, 80 walks, and All-Star berth.
LF	Lou Piniella	1969	Rookie of the Year in a weak field, Piniella was 25 years old and already with his fifth ML organization.
CF	Carlos Beltran	1999	Nearly unanimous Rookie of the Year after becoming only eighth rookie to reach 100 runs and 100 RBI in one season.
RF	Jon Nunnally	1995	Okay, so 14 homers (and 86 strikeouts) in 303 at-bats isn't any great shakes; guess you had to be there.
SP	Steve Busby	1973	Busby's record (16-15, 4.23) nothing special, but he tossed a no-hitter and threw 238 innings.
RP	Tom Gordon	1989	Went 7-7 with 3.99 ERA in 16 starts, but sparkled with 10-2 record and 3.14 ERA in 33 relief appearances; great curve.

HOMEGROWN

		YEARS	NOTES
DH	Bob Hamelin	1993–1997	Recruited by Notre Dame as linebacker; hit 31 homers in one season for Rancho Santiago JC; No. 2 draft pick in '88.
C	Mike Macfarlane	1987–1994 1996–1998	Fourth-round pick out of University of Santa Clara in 1985, gave the Royals a few solid years with stick.
1B	Mike Sweeney	1995–2002	A 10th-round draft pick, Sweeney was a catcher in the minors, and in the majors through the '98 season.
2B	Frank White	1973–1990	Wasn't drafted, but instead became the only graduate of the unique Royals Academy to star in majors.
SS	U L Washington	1977–1984	Not drafted, signed as free agent out of Murray State for the Royals Academy.
3B	George Brett	1973–1993	Second-round pick in 1971, selected immediately after the Phillies took Mike Schmidt.
LF	Bo Jackson	1986–1990	No. 1 pick in the NFL draft; then the Royals gambled a fourth-round MLB pick, which paid off nicely.
CF	Willie Wilson	1976–1990	Eighteenth overall pick in 1974 draft, supposedly was a catcher in high school, and a great football player.
RF	Al Cowens	1974–1979	Just the one big season (1977), but as an 84th-round pick in 1969, he was a steal.
SP	David Cone	1986 1993–1994	Grew up just a few miles from Royals Stadium, and a third-round pick out of high school in '81 draft.
RP	Dan Quisenberry	1979–1988	Undrafted, signed as free agent in 1975 after attending three different colleges.

TRADED AWAY

		TRADED	NOTES
DH	Cecil Fielder	February 4, 1983	In his first year as pro, swatted 20 homers in 69 games, after which they traded him for . . . Leon Roberts?
C	Don Slaught	January 18, 1985	Went to Rangers in four-team deal in which Royals acquired Jim Sundberg; played 13 more seasons.
1B	Ken Phelps	January 19, 1982	Minor-league star traded to Expos for Grant Jackson; .484 slugging percentage in majors after leaving K.C.
2B	Terry Shumpert	December 13, 1994	Supposed to replace Frank White at second base; failing that, became jack of all trades for Rockies.
SS	Bill Pecota	December 11, 1991	Never actually the regular shortstop, but Pecota was the best utility infielder the Royals ever had.
3B	Joe Randa	December 13, 1996	Traded to Pittsburgh in deal for Jay Bell and Jeff King; Royals got him back two years later, from Mets.
LF	Lou Piniella	December 7, 1973	Sent to Yankees in deal that left Royals with a void in left field until Willie Wilson won the regular job.
CF	Johnny Damon	January 18, 2001	Part of three-team deal that didn't really work for *anybody;* Damon struggled but so did other principals.
RF	Jermaine Dye	July 25, 2001	On the verge of becoming expensive, Dye traded to A's where he joined ex-Royals Giambi and Damon.
SP	David Cone	March 27, 1987	Sent to Mets in one of all-time worst trades. Later reacquired, and eventually traded *again* for peanuts.
RP	Jeff Shaw	December 9, 1992	Never pitched for Royals; signed to free-agent deal and traded to Expos a month later for Mark Gardner.

The 1970s Royals were built with a series of lopsided trades that brought Fred Patek, Amos Otis, Hal McRae, Darrell Porter, and John Mayberry to Kansas City, all of them in exchange for players who did virtually nothing of consequence after leaving the Royals.

Unfortunately, the most lopsided trade in franchise history went the other way. On March 27, 1987, the Royals traded David Cone and catcher Chris Jelic to the Mets, and received catcher Ed Hearn and pitchers Rick Anderson and Goose Gozzo. Cone was coming off a season in which he'd pitched well (8-4, 2.79) for Triple-A Omaha, but the Royals had routinely been developing outstanding pitchers, so perhaps general manager John Schuerholz regarded Cone as surplus.

Of course, Cone wound up with a better career than any pitcher the Royals have ever developed, with the possible exception of Bret Saberhagen. Ed Hearn, supposedly the big prize in the deal, had backed up Gary Carter for one season and batted .265 with decent peripheral stats. After the trade, he played in thirteen major-league games.

Later, the Royals got Cone back. He won the Cy Young Award in 1994 . . . and the Royals traded him to the Blue Jays for Chris Stynes and a couple of guys who never escaped the minor leagues. Fool me once, shame on you. Fool me twice . . .

It's been suggested that if Bill Mazeroski is a Hall of Famer, well then by golly Frank White should be, too. After all, Mazeroski was regarded as the best defensive second baseman of his time and garnered eight Gold Gloves, and White was regarded as the best defensive second baseman of his time and garnered eight Gold Gloves. Their hitting stats are roughly comparable, and in fact they contributed virtually the same number of runs to their teams over the courses of their long careers.

So is Frank White a Hall of Famer? No, he's not. The fact that White won as many Gold Gloves as Mazeroski doesn't mean he was just as valuable defensively, any more than the fact that Cy Williams won more home-run titles than Lou Gehrig makes Williams the better power hitter. While it's true that Mazeroski's amazing defensive statistics were due, in part, to the pitchers on his teams, it's also true that Mazeroski was, indeed, the greatest defensive second baseman ever, or at least the greatest who played for more than a few years. White, meanwhile, may well rank among the five or ten greatest ever. But if Mazeroski was the greatest and just *barely* gained election to the Hall, where does that leave White? With scores of other players: great, certainly, but not quite great enough to merit the game's highest honor.

		YEARS	NOTES
GOLD GLOVE			
C	Jim Sundberg	1985–1986	Six-time Gold Glover, the last of them in 1981, four years before he joined Royals; edges Bob Boone here.
1B	Wally Joyner	1992–1995	Very slick, had a throw for every occasion; Offerman was even better, but played only 96 games at first base.
2B	Frank White	1973–1990	Eight-time Gold Glover; not great on the double play, but expert at cutting off would-be singles to right field.
SS	Freddie Patek	1971–1979	Baltimore's Belanger was winning the Gold Gloves, but Patek had good range and surprisingly strong arm.
3B	Greg Pryor	1982–1986	Brett's backup for five years, and an outstanding third baseman who played 105 games there in 1984.
LF	Willie Wilson	1976–1990	Couldn't throw for beans, but his wheels allowed him to outrun occasional mistakes; fine CF, too, after Otis.
CF	Amos Otis	1970–1982	It never looked like he was working hard, yet he made all the plays; three Gold Gloves.
RF	Jermaine Dye	1997–2001	Lacked great speed, but threw well, made a habit of the diving catch, and won a Gold Glove in 2000.
SP	Bret Saberhagen	1984–1991	Fielded like he pitched: without great *style*, but with great intelligence and skill.

		YEARS	NOTES
IRON GLOVE			
C	Don Slaught	1982–1984	Bat kept him in the majors for 16 years, glove kept him from being an everyday player.
1B	Willie Aikens	1980–1983	His numbers aren't actually *terrible* . . . which is a great object lesson in not always trusting the numbers.
2B	Luis Alicea	2001–*2002*	You had to see him every day to really appreciate him, as he did something stupid in virtually every game.
SS	Kurt Stillwell	1988–1991	Stillwell's defensive stats were uniformly terrible, partly due to the pitchers and partly due to poor range.
3B	Paul Schaal	1969–1974	One big year with the bat, but his defensive stats were consistently awful; replaced by George Brett.
LF	Mark Quinn	1999–*2002*	Lousy instincts, often looked bad while going after fly balls . . . and was even worse on the liners.
CF	Jim Eisenreich	1988–1992	Not really fair, as Eisenreich didn't play a lot of center field, and wasn't bad when he did play there.
RF	Danny Tartabull	1986–1991	An absolutely atrocious defensive player, took bad routes to batted balls and couldn't throw at all.
P	Tom Gordon	1988–1995	Occasionally forgot to cover first base, but did improve his defense as he went along.

ALL-BUST		YEARS	NOTES
DH	Bob Hamelin	1993–1996	Rookie of the Year in '94, he batted .168 in '95 and was gone in 1997; suffered from chronic back pain.
C	Ed Hearn	1987–1988	Royals gave up David Cone to get Ed Hearn, who played in 13 games for Kansas City.
1B	John Mayberry	1972–1977	How can the franchise's greatest first baseman also appear on this list? See for yourself . . .
2B	José Lind	1993–1995	Won a Gold Glove with Pirates in 1992, but lasted just one year as regular with the Royals.
SS	Neifi Perez	2001–2002	Allard Baird made a lot of mistakes in his first two years as GM, but trading for Perez was the worst of them.
3B	Gregg Jefferies	1992	Onetime Mets bust didn't blossom until joining the Cardinals (and switching to first base) in 1993.
LF	Michael Tucker	*2002*	If trading for Neifi was the worst, signing Tucker to a two-year deal for millions is a strong runner-up.
CF	Bo Jackson	1986–1990	Played well and made the magazine covers, but got hurt playing football just as he was peaking in baseball.
RF	Clint Hurdle	1977–1981	Made the cover of *SI* as "Royal Phenom" prior to 1978, but injuries and immaturity killed his career.
SP	Storm Davis	1990–1991	After going 35-14 over two seasons with A's, went 10-19 in two seasons with Royals.
RP	Mark Davis	1990–1992	Signed as free agent after Cy Young season (44 saves) with Padres; 7 saves in three seasons as Royal.

USED-TO-BE-GREAT		YEARS	NOTES
DH	Harmon Killebrew	1975	Whose idea was this? Killebrew and Pinson (see below) kept Royals from competing for division title in '75.
C	Jim Sundberg	1985–1986	Six Gold Gloves with Texas, smashed bases-loaded triple in Game 7 of '85 ALCS with Royals.
1B	Wally Joyner	1992–1995	Joyner played well enough for the Royals, both with the bat and glove, but the days of Wally World were over.
2B	José Lind	1993–1995	Always a terrible hitter, Lind's Gold Glove defense disappeared in K.C. and so did his playing time.
SS	Greg Gagne	1993–1995	Starter for both of Minnesota's World Series winners, brought his still-solid defense to K.C.
3B	Gary Gaetti	1993–1995	Rejuvenated career as Royal, hit 35 home runs in '95 after getting a new contact-lens prescription.
LF	Kirk Gibson	1991	Just edges Sleepy Kevin McReynolds, by virtue of his MVP with the Dodgers in 1988.
CF	Omar Moreno	1985	Spent September with the Royals, filling in for the injured Willie Wilson (and no, he was never really "great").
RF	Vada Pinson	1974–1975	What the hell were they thinking? Once a fine player, but by the mid-'70s Pinson clearly didn't have anything left.
SP	Gaylord Perry	1983	Royals were Perry's eighth, and last, major-league team; he went 4-4 with 4.27 ERA at age 45.
RP	Hoyt Wilhelm	1969	Hall of Famer was selected by Royals in expansion draft . . . but immediately traded to the Angels.

John Mayberry was only twenty-six in 1975, but he never played nearly so well again.

Mayberry signed with the Astros in 1967, when he was eighteen, and quickly established himself as a power hitter who hit for a decent average and walked more often than he struck out. Mayberry played poorly in a pair of major-league trials, however, and after the '71 season the Astros gave him to the Royals for a couple of pitchers you never heard of. He went right into K.C.'s lineup and was immediately the best hitter on the club, beginning a four-year stretch climaxed by his superb '75 season.

In '76 he slumped horribly, his OPS plummeting nearly 300 points. He improved a bit in '77, but showed up for Game 4 of the ALCS hung over, played poorly, and got benched for Game 5. Whitey Herzog insisted that Mayberry be traded, and so off he went to Toronto. Bill James has written that Mayberry "was never the same player again" after leaving Kansas City, but that's not exactly right, as he was actually better during his four seasons as a Blue Jay than he'd been in his last two seasons as a Royal. It's true, though, that his three best seasons came before he turned twenty-seven, and before the Royals started winning division titles.

Amos Otis belongs in the Hall of Fame.

Preposterous, you say?

Amos Otis was, during the 1970s, the best center fielder in the game. (Well, him or Cesar Cedeño. But I'm convinced Otis was just slightly better, which is all that matters for the purposes of this particular argument.)

And if Amos Otis was the best center fielder of the 1970s, isn't that enough, all by itself, to qualify him for Cooperstown?

No, you're right; of course it isn't. Otis was a fine player for quite a long time, but he wasn't really a *great* player, not year in and year out.

Which brings me to Mark Grace (yes, in a chapter about the Royals). Like Otis, Grace was a very good player for quite a long time. And like Otis, Grace was rarely great. Actually, Grace was never great, though he was slightly more consistent than Otis, which made him approximately as valuable as Otis over the course of his career.

But there are people who want to put Mark Grace in the Hall of Fame, and their argument is always the same: "Mark Grace had more hits in the 1990s than anybody else."

To which I respond, "That's a nice little piece of trivia. But it doesn't have a whole hell of a lot to do with whether or not he belongs in the Hall of Fame. And if you want to know why it doesn't, just look at Amos Otis."

ALL-NAME

		YEARS	NOTES
M	"Milk and Cookies" Tony Muser	1997–2002	Gained after he suggested his players should ease up on the milk and cookies, and drink more booze instead.
DH	"Hammer" Bob Hamelin	1993–1996	Folk hero for a while, and had the cool nickname that a folk hero has to have.
C	"Duke" John Wathan	1976–1985	He could talk like John Wayne, but didn't manage like the movie Duke (presumably) would have.
1B	"Bye-Bye" Steve Balboni	1984–1988	A relic of his minor-league days, in honor of his long homers; his teammates called him "Bones," though.
2B	"Cookie" Octavio Rojas	1971–1977	His nickname was "Cuqui" in Spanish, but of course we Anglos weren't having any of *that*.
SS	U L Washington	1977–1984	The interesting thing here is that the *U* and *L* are not initials, per se; that's his name: U L.
3B	"Joker" Joe Randa	1995–1996 1999–*2002*	Hung on him by Pirates broadcaster Bob Walk, because his natural smile makes him look like the Joker.
LF	"Sweet Lou" Lou Piniella	1969–1973	If you've seen him play or manage over the last 30 years, you know this was for his swing, and not his personality.
CF	"A.O." Amos Otis	1970–1983	One of my favorite childhood memories is the chants of "A-O, A-O!" when Otis came up at Royals Stadium.
RF	"Bull" Danny Tartabull	1987–1991	Contrary to popular opinion, *not* because he played defense like a male bovine wearing skates.
SP	"Flash" Tom Gordon	1988–1995	. . . In the grand tradition of virtually every player in history with that last name, but at least he did throw hard.
RP	"Duck" Marty Pattin	1974–1980	In honor of his famous impressions of Donald Duck; you think he and Wathan ever put on shows together?

TOP FIVE SEASONS

YEAR	1985	RECORD	91-71
BEST HITTER	George Brett		
BEST PITCHER	Bret Saberhagen		
NOTES	Nine years after Chambliss, how sweet it is.		

YEAR	1980	RECORD	97-65
BEST HITTER	George Brett		
BEST PITCHER	Larry Gura		
NOTES	I still say they were better than the Phillies.		

YEAR	1977	RECORD	102-60
BEST HITTER	George Brett, Al Cowens		
BEST PITCHER	Dennis Leonard		
NOTES	Franchise's best club ever? Meet the Yankees.		

YEAR	1976	RECORD	90-72
BEST HITTER	George Brett		
BEST PITCHER	Dennis Leonard, Al Fitzmorris		
NOTES	First title soiled by Littell and Chambliss.		

YEAR	1978	RECORD	92-70
BEST HITTER	Amos Otis		
BEST PITCHER	Larry Gura, Dennis Leonard		
NOTES	Another October, another loss to the #@$ Yankees.		

TOP FIVE MANAGERS

MANAGER	Whitey Herzog
YEARS	1975–1979
RECORD	410-304 (.574)
NOTES	If only he could have gotten along with the owner . . .

MANAGER	Dick Howser
YEARS	1981–1986
RECORD	404-365 (.525)
NOTES	Guided Royals to their only World Championship.

MANAGER	Jack McKeon
YEARS	1973–1975
RECORD	215-205 (.512)
NOTES	Didn't realize that Brett and White could play. . . .

MANAGER	Jim Frey
YEARS	1980–1981
RECORD	127-105 (.547)
NOTES	Fine manager when everything going right.

MANAGER	Hal McRae
YEARS	1991–1994
RECORD	286-277 (.508)
NOTES	Didn't like to play the kids, and it got him fired.

SO WHO'S THE *REAL* KING?

A few years ago, baseball researcher Bruce Markusen named his All-Time Kansas City Royals Team for bigbadbaseball.com, and when I sat down to make my own choices for this book, I wound up agreeing with each of his . . . save one. For manager, Markusen selected Dick Howser, commenting, "Led the franchise to its only world championship in 1985. Like 'Quiz,' died much too young."

Bruce tends toward sentiment more than I do, and I suspect that sentiment—which pops up in his comment about Howser dying too young—played at least a small part in his selection of Howser. Cold-hearted bastard that I am, I'd like to evaluate the Royals' two greatest managers without the sentiment, because I generally find that sentiment gets in the way of clear-headed analysis; as a character in a movie once noted, "Passion is the enemy of precision."

Anyway, here's a simple comparison of the two:

	Years	Record	Postseason
Herzog	1975–1979	410-304, .575	3 AL West titles
Howser	1981–1986	404-365, .524	2 AL West titles, 1 World Championship

Both Herzog and Howser took over the Royals in the middle of a season. Herzog replaced Jack McKeon on July 24, 1975, and guided the club to a 41-25 (.621) record the rest of the way (the Royals finished a strong second, behind Oakland). Howser replaced Jim Frey 20 games into the "second half" of the abominable 1981 season, and the Royals earned a postseason berth by going 20-13 (.606) the rest of the way (they were swept by Oakland in the first round of the playoffs).

Both Herzog and Howser managed the Royals for only four full seasons. Herzog was fired after the '79 season because 1) he couldn't beat the Yankees in October, and 2) he couldn't get along with the man who signed his paychecks. Howser, of course, was forced to retire in the middle of the 1986 season because of the brain tumor that took his life the following June. He was only fifty-one.

In Herzog's four seasons, the Royals finished first three times, and second once. In Howser's four seasons, the Royals finished first twice, and second twice. In 1979, Herzog's only second-place campaign, the Royals finished three games behind the California Angels. In 1982, Howser's solid second-place campaign—in '83, the Royals also finished second but with a 79-83 record—the Royals finished three games behind the California Angels.

In *The Bill James Guide to Baseball Managers*, James presented two statistical methods for rating managers. The Accomplishment Count method awards points for various accomplishments, tied to both regular-season records and the postseason. By this method, Herzog tops Howser 11–9. The Expected Wins method arrives at the number of games the team might have been expected to win in a given season, given both the team's past performance and the pronounced tendency of all teams to drift toward a .500 record. If we would expect a team to win 71 games and it wins 81, then the team's manager would get a +10 for that season. By this method, Herzog tops Howser by a wider margin, +17 to +3.

Statistics aside, some will argue that for all of Herzog's accomplishments in Kansas City, he wasn't able to do what Howser did: get the Royals to the World Series, and then win it. And to be sure, Howser managed brilliantly in first getting the Royals to the postseason in both 1984 and 1985, and then upsetting both the Blue Jays and the Cardinals in October of '85. But let's remember that when Howser took over in 1981, it was still Herzog's team, the lineup that Herzog had developed: Brett, White, McRae, Wilson . . . these were the stars, and all of them came of age under Herzog. What's more, it was Herzog who plucked Dan Quisenberry off the scrap heap in 1979. Now, I certainly don't *know* that Herzog would have been smart enough to make Quisenberry his closer in 1980, as Jim Frey did, but given Herzog's success with his bullpens over the years, I think it's a pretty safe guess.

Howser's biggest contribution, in my mind, is tied to the development of the Royals' rotation in 1985. Arguably the best rotation of the 1980s, it was composed of Bret Saberhagen, Charlie Leibrandt, Danny Jackson, Mark Gubicza, and Bud Black, none of whom had established themselves as major-league pitchers before working for Howser. I don't know exactly *how* he did it, but he did it and he deserves a great amount of credit for doing it. That said, Herzog accomplished similar things with a group of young starters that included Dennis Leonard, Larry Gura, and Rich Gale (along with veterans Paul Splittorff and Al Fitzmorris).

No doubt, Dick Howser was a fine manager. But there's little question in my mind that Whitey Herzog was better. The team that Herzog (and general manager Joe Burke) built remained among the American League's elite for another five years after Herzog left. But the team that Herzog (and, it should be said, general manager John Schuerholz) built sank to mediocrity just one season after winning the World Series.

Howser's number 10 has been retired, because he left us too early. Without Herzog, though, Howser's teams wouldn't have been what they were.

I'm grateful to Rany Jazayerli and Bill James for their editorial suggestions.

The King
*National Baseball Library,
Cooperstown, New York*

LOS ANGELES DODGERS

		ALL-TIME	
		YEARS	**NOTES**
C	Mike Piazza	1992–1998	The best-hitting catcher in the history of the game (with the possible exception of Josh Gibson) and, believe it or not, aside from a poor arm he wasn't that bad with the glove.
1B	Steve Garvey	1969–1982	Okay, so he didn't walk a lot and couldn't throw . . . but he *was* a fine hitter for a decade and a four-time Gold Glover; growing up, idolized Gil Hodges.
2B	Davey Lopes	1972–1981	A speedy center fielder in the minors, but switched to second base just before reaching the majors, eventually became a decent defender; four-time All-Star.
SS	Maury Wills	1959–1966 1969–1972	The game's premier base stealer and the first $100,000 shortstop; loved L.A. and spent a lot of time hobnobbing (among other things) with the show people.
3B	Ron Cey	1971–1982	With 228 homers, ranks fifth on franchise's all-time list, and behind only Eric Karros among L.A. players; worked hard and became good with the glove.
LF	Gary Sheffield	1998–2001	Not much defensively and rarely content, but one of the game's truly great hitters; ranks No. 1 on franchise's all-time list in OBP (.424) *and* slugging percentage (.573).
CF	Willie Davis	1960–1973	Excellent defensive player who won three Gold Gloves and deserved at least that many, 1966 World Series notwithstanding; a fast runner and a different thinker.
RF	Raul Mondesi	1993–1999	Dominican dropped out of school after the sixth grade and learned to play baseball with a milk carton for a glove and a tree limb for a bat.
SP1	Sandy Koufax	1955–1966	After Dodgers moved to Chavez Ravine in 1963, he was 111-34 with 1.86 ERA; great fastball *and* overhand curve made him close to unhittable in Dodger Stadium.
SP2	Don Sutton	1966–1980 1988	In his first 15 years as a Dodger, Sutton *never* pitched fewer than 210 innings in a season, and with 233 wins he tops the franchise's all-time list.
SP3	Don Drysdale	1956–1969	The big right-hander with the overpowering fastball didn't like hitters who crowded the plate, and he led the league in HBP five times.
SP4	Orel Hershiser	1983–1994 2000	Led the league in innings pitched three straight years (1987–1989) and was never the same afterward, but one of the game's greatest during the later 1980s.
RP	Jim Brewer	1964–1975	Pitched before the modern closer was invented, but ranks third on the franchise saves list (125), and the screwballer worked far more innings than the guys ahead of him.

In 1972, Bill Russell (a converted center fielder) took over as the Dodgers' regular shortstop. In 1973, Davey Lopes (a converted center fielder) took over as the Dodgers' regular second baseman, and Ron Cey as the Dodgers' regular third baseman.

Steve Garvey was still out in the cold, though. He'd been more or less the regular at third base in '71 and '72, but his throwing problems got out of hand—in '72, Garvey made 28 errors in only 85 games at third base—so when the '73 season opened, he was on the bench. And that's mostly where he stayed for nearly three months. As June hurried toward July, Garvey was on both the bench and the trade block.

But near the end of the month, left fielder Von Joshua got hurt, and then fourth outfielder Manny Mota pulled a hamstring. First baseman Bill Buckner could run and throw, so manager Walt Alston sent Buckner to left field.

That left first base open. Garvey debuted there on June 23. The infield was set, and it wouldn't change for another eight-and-a-half years.

From 1982 through 1987, Fernando Valenzuela averaged 265 innings per season. He pitched into the late 1990s with a variety of clubs, but was never anything like the pitcher he'd been in his early and middle twenties.

From 1985 through 1989, Orel Hershiser averaged 251 innings per season. He pitched into the late 1990s with the Dodgers, Indians, Giants, and Mets, but was never anything like the pitcher he'd been in his middle and late twenties.

From 1990 through 1991, Ramón Martínez averaged 227 innings per season. He pitched into the late 1990s with the Dodgers and Red Sox, but was never anything like the pitcher he'd been in his early twenties.

Through 1987, Valenzuela's career ERA was 3.08; after 1987, it was 4.29.

Through 1989, Hershiser's career ERA was 2.69; after 1989, it was 4.17.

Through 1991, Martínez's career ERA was 3.15; after 1991, it was 3.84.

Hershiser's career pivoted on a severe shoulder injury that cost him most of the 1990 season. Neither Valenzuela nor Martínez suffered serious injuries that required major surgery, but both obviously lost a great deal of their stuff after the heavy workloads early on.

I say they were abused by their manager. Tommy Lasorda would, I suspect, disagree. And as Chuck Tanner used to say, baseball's just an opinion.

NO. 2			
		YEARS	NOTES
C	John Roseboro	1957–1967	Just edges Mike Scioscia, but they were comparable players and caught roughly the same number of games for the Dodgers; Roseboro had a huge collection of bats.
1B	Eric Karros	1991–2002	Not as consistent as Garvey, but both were productive right-handed hitters who played good defense; Karros L.A.'s all-time HR leader, with no challenger in sight.
2B	Steve Sax	1981–1988	Will always be remembered for being the first to contract Steve Sax Disease, but he wasn't *that* bad and was actually quite similar to Lopes, his predecessor.
SS	Bill Russell	1969–1986	Almost never had anything like a good year with the bat, but one-time outfielder became a solid defender and held the job for a dozen years.
3B	Jim Gilliam	1958–1966	Jackie's replacement at second base in Brooklyn moved to third when Dodgers moved, and took to it immediately; solid glove and on-base skills.
LF	Dusty Baker	1976–1983	Tommy Davis's two best years were better than Baker's best, but Dusty had a lot more good ones; he and Reggie Smith gave Dodgers two-thirds of a great outfield.
CF	Brett Butler	1991–1994 1995–1997	Great bunter and on-base man, sort of a modern-day Richie Ashburn without the great defense; L.A. native achieved lifelong dream when he signed with Dodgers.
RF	Reggie Smith	1976–1981	Played only 542 games with Dodgers, but many of his teammates considered him their MVP in 1977 and '78; benefited from the promotion of Tommy Lasorda.
SP1	Andy Messersmith	1973–1975 1979	Pitched only three full seasons for Dodgers, but went 53-30 with 2.51 ERA; fastballer was never the same after throwing league-most 322 innings in '75.
SP2	Fernando Valenzuela	1980–1990	We may never know how old he was, or how good he might have been if Lasorda hadn't slagged his arm, but for a few years Fernandomania was all the rage.
SP3	Claude Osteen	1965–1973	Overshadowed by teammates like Koufax, Drysdale, Sutton, and Messersmith, but a fine pitcher who posted 0.86 ERA in three World Series starts for Dodgers.
SP4	Ramón Martínez	1988–1998	Lasorda strikes again. Martínez enjoyed a wonderful career for the Dodgers—123 wins, 3.45 ERA—but it could, *should*, have been so much better.
RP	Ron Perranoski	1961–1967 1972	Dodgers got him from the Cubs for Don Zimmer, which of course was a great trade; threw a great sinker, and served as club's pitching coach from 1981 through '94.

SINGLE SEASON

		YEARS	NOTES
C	Mike Piazza	1997	Set L.A. Dodger records with .362 batting average (NL record for a catcher), 40 homers, .638 slugging percentage.
1B	Eddie Murray	1990	After disappointing first season with Dodgers, native Los Angeleno came through with his last great campaign.
2B	Steve Sax	1986	Leadoff man batted career-high .332, stole 40 bases, and played pretty good defense.
SS	Maury Wills	1962	Played all 165 games and ran wild on the bases, with record-setting 104 steals (didn't deserve his MVP, though).
3B	Pedro Guerrero	1983	Everybody rags about his defense, but Pete was easily the best hitter for a team that won the division.
LF	Tommy Davis	1962	One of the all-time fluke seasons: 230 hits, .346 batting average, and *154 RBI* . . . and he finished third in the MVP vote.
CF	Jimmy Wynn	1974	A great player's last great season; in his first year in L.A., paced NL champs in every important hitting stat.
RF	Shawn Green	2001	Set franchise record with 49 homers, and ended 415-game playing streak—best in league—on Yom Kippur.
SP	Sandy Koufax	1966	His last season was his best: career-high 27 wins, 317 K's, and 1.73 ERA that was brilliant even considering the context.
RP	Mike Marshall	1974	Today the numbers don't look real: 15 wins, 21 saves, a 2.42 ERA, *106 games and 208 innings* . . . all in relief.

ALL-ROOKIE

		YEARS	NOTES
C	Mike Piazza	1993	Hit 35 homers to destroy record for rookie catchers on his way to becoming 13th Dodger to win Rookie of the Year honors.
1B	Eric Karros	1992	Shared first base with Kal Daniels and Todd Benzinger for 38 games, but wound up with 20 HR and 88 RBI.
2B	Jim Lefebvre	1965	A real strength over the years; like Lefebvre, Dodger 2B Steve Sax and Ted Sizemore also Rookies of the Year.
SS	Mariano Duncan	1985	Not much with the bat or the glove, but he did steal 38 bases and played nearly every day for a division-winning club.
3B	Ron Cey	1973	Club finally gave up on Garvey at 3B, and Cey settled in for the next decade; 15 homers, 74 walks, and excellent glove.
LF	Todd Hollandsworth	1996	The fifth straight Dodger to be named Rookie of the Year, but in all honesty it was a weak year for rookies.
CF	Tommy Davis	1960	Batted .276 with decent power, but plagued by lack of plate discipline that would characterize his entire career.
RF	Raul Mondesi	1994	Third straight Dodger RoY, and unanimous choice after hitting .306 with 16 homers and 16 assists in short season.
SP	Fernando Valenzuela	1981	Sure, it was a short season, but he went 13-7, won thrice in the postseason and was the biggest story in the game.
RP	Steve Howe	1980	In thin year for rookies, Howe's 17 saves and 2.66 ERA in 85 innings were enough for Rookie of the Year.

If you're making a list of underachieving teams, the Dodgers of the late twentieth and early twenty-first centuries have to rank somewhere near the top.

In 1996 the Dodgers won ninety games and grabbed the Wild Card, but were swept by Atlanta in the Division Series . . . and at this writing, they have not played a postseason game since. That's seven seasons without a trip to the playoffs, for a franchise that annually spends as much money as any team in the National League.

What happened? The short answer is that the organization stopped producing talent. Beginning in 1992, the Dodgers churned out five straight National League Rookies of the Year, which of course was (and is) unprecedented. But the well has been almost completely dry since then, thanks in large part to a number of premium draft choices wasted on pitchers with great arms who couldn't throw strikes.

From 1997 through 2001, thirty-seven different players received at least one measly fifth-place vote for Rookie of the Year. Not one of them was a Dodger. Granted, the Dodgers weren't the only team without a candidate over that span; neither the Brewers nor the Giants nor the Padres had any, either. But it's one hell of a comedown for a team that used to produce young stars so regularly.

Stupid trades. With one obvious exception, the Dodgers have made very few of them since moving to Los Angeles. On November 19, 1993, they traded Pedro Martínez to the Montreal Expos for Delino De-Shields. But even that one looks stupid only in hindsight. DeShields was a twenty-four-year-old second baseman with a .368 OBP and 187 steals in just four seasons. Pedro Martínez had all the potential in the world, but how many pitchers with all the potential in the world actually turn into Pedro Martínez?

The Dodgers have also traded a number of good first basemen, but it's hard to say they shouldn't have. Jim Gentile could obviously hit, but in the late 1950s the Dodgers had a lot of guys who could obviously hit. When Frank Howard got traded, he'd been playing the outfield but didn't really belong there, and the Dodgers had Ron Fairly and Wes Parker on hand to play first base. Same thing with Dick Allen and Bill Buckner, "outfielders" blocked by Steve Garvey at first base. It turned out that Paul Konerko couldn't play third—he did try—and the Dodgers weren't going to move Eric Karros.

Those guys were all traded, and among the players received by the Dodgers were Claude Osteen, Tommy John, Rick Monday, and Jeff Shaw. So the club made out okay.

HOMEGROWN			
		YEARS	NOTES
C	Mike Piazza	1992–1998	Everybody knows the story: as a favor to Lasorda, Dodgers took him with 1,385th pick in '88 draft.
1B	Steve Garvey	1969–1982	All-American third baseman also played football at Michigan State, signed with Dodgers for $40K bonus.
2B	Davey Lopes	1972–1981	Drafted by Dodgers in 1968, then went back to school and earned bachelor's degree in education a year later.
SS	Maury Wills	1959–1966 1969–1972	Spent eight years in the minors and reached the majors only after learning to switch-hit.
3B	Ron Cey	1971–1982	Third-round pick in '68; spent an extra season in Triple-A because club still screwing around with Garvey at 3B.
LF	Tommy Davis	1960–1966	Born in Brooklyn and signed in 1956, two years before the Dodgers moved 2,500 miles to California.
CF	Willie Davis	1960–1973	In his only two minor-league seasons, led California and Pacific Coast Leagues in batting avg., hits, runs, steals.
RF	Raul Mondesi	1993–1999	Fans wish he'd been more consistent, but Dodger Stadium cost him more than a few hits over the years.
SP	Sandy Koufax	1955–1966	Scouted by Al Campanis and signed for $14,000 bonus and $6,000 salary, sent straight to majors as bonus baby.
RP	John Wetteland	1989–1991	Lost temporarily in the Rule 5 draft, but Tigers couldn't see into the future and gave him back.

TRADED AWAY			
		TRADED	NOTES
C	Mike Piazza	May 15, 1998	Him and Todd Zeile to Marlins for Gary Sheffield, Bobby Bonilla, Charles Johnson, and two bodies.
1B	Frank Howard	December 4, 1964	Take your pick, as Dodgers also traded away Jim Gentile, Dick Allen, Bill Buckner, and Paul Konerko.
2B	Davey Lopes	February 8, 1982	Traded to A's for scrub to make room for Sax; was almost 37 but played another six years.
SS	José Offerman	December 17, 1995	Okay, so it turned out he wasn't actually a shortstop . . . to Royals for lefty reliever Billy Brewer.
3B	Ron Cey	January 20, 1983	Still had a few good years in him, but the Dodgers were looking to get younger and Pedro Guerrero was ready.
LF	Tommy Davis	November 29, 1966	Only 27 but his big years were far behind him; did hang around for another decade, though.
CF	Larry Hisle	October 26, 1972	Dodgers parked Hisle in Albuquerque for a season before trading him to Cards, who traded him to Twins.
RF	Raul Mondesi	November 8, 1999	Didn't actually play that well after going to Toronto, and will likely be replaced here by Gary Sheffield.
SP	Pedro Martínez	November 19, 1993	True, young pitchers are dicey . . . but Pedro for Delino won't go down as one of the club's best moves.
RP	John Wetteland	November 25, 1991	After establishing himself as minor-league closer, traded to Reds, who immediately traded him to Expos.

GOLD GLOVE

		YEARS	NOTES
C	Steve Yeager	1972–1985	His arm was just as good as Bench's; Charles Johnson even better, but only a Dodger for a few months.
1B	Wes Parker	1964–1972	One of the greatest glove men of all time, won six straight Gold Gloves before retiring while still on top.
2B	Charlie Neal	1956–1961	Only the regular for a few years, but always good and in 1959 he was the best in the league.
SS	Maury Wills	1959–1966 1969–1972	Deserved the Gold Gloves he won in 1960 and '61; career numbers dragged down by his last few years.
3B	Ron Cey	1971–1982	The winner by default, as the Dodgers haven't had an outstanding glove at third base since Jackie Robinson.
LF	Dusty Baker	1976–1983	Once had the speed for center and the arm for right, and remained a fine defender after moving to left.
CF	Willie Davis	1960–1973	Remembered for missing a couple of fly balls in the '66 Series, but won three Gold Gloves and deserved them.
RF	Raul Mondesi	1993–1999	Dropped off badly his last couple of years, but from '95 through '97 he might have been the best in the league.
SP	Fernando Valenzuela	1980–1990	He looked soft, but was an excellent hitter and a fine defender who even played a few innings in the field.

IRON GLOVE

		YEARS	NOTES
C	Todd Hundley	1999–2000	Threw out only 19 percent of attempting base stealers and finished last in fielding percentage both seasons.
1B	Greg Brock	1982–1986	He wasn't bad at all, but the Dodgers have generally had great or good defense at first base.
2B	Juan Samuel	1990–1992	The Phillies and Mets had the right idea, putting him in the outfield; eventually became a first baseman.
SS	José Offerman	1990–1995	How bad was he? He was the worst defensive shortstop *ever* to play more than 5,000 innings at the position.
3B	Steve Garvey	1970–1972	Simply couldn't throw, and he fielded .922 in 191 career games at third base.
LF	Billy Ashley	1992–1997	Minor-league slugger looked lost in the outfield, and he didn't hit enough in the majors to carry his glove.
CF	Ken Landreaux	1981–1987	Good wheels, but got poor jumps, was tentative on balls hit in front of him, and didn't throw well.
RF	Frank Howard	1958–1964	Walt Alston was a pretty sharp guy, but why he had Hondo in right and Fairly at first remains a mystery.
SP	Alejandro Peña	1981–1989	Slow delivery limited his ability to hold runners at first base, and error-prone as well.

If you're a baseball player, there are two places you don't want to embarrass yourself: New York, because that's where most of the caustic sportswriters live; and Los Angeles, because that's where most of the comedy writers live.

And wouldn't you know it, a number of Dodgers have embarrassed themselves.

Steve Garvey was the first. Due to an old football injury, Garvey really couldn't throw at all, which led wags to say, "When Steve Garvey plays third base, it's Ball Night at Dodger Stadium."

Next came Steve Sax, who developed the inconvenient inability to make the most routine throws to first base. This was in 1983, so people said that Sax was the only man on earth who could overthrow the Ayatollah. And of course, he got a disease named after him.

Then came José Offerman, a heralded shortstop prospect who, as it turned out, wasn't actually a shortstop. He played 115 or more games at the position in three seasons, and he led the National League in errors all three seasons. It got so bad that when somebody riddled you, "How do you spell Offerman?" the correct answer was "O-F-F-E-E-E-E-E . . ."

Other players in recent memory have suffered serious defensive problems, but Chuck Knoblauch is the only non-Dodger to suffer such public ignominy.

In 1980, reliever Steve Howe was the National League's Rookie of the Year. Nervous about the press conference, Howe snorted some cocaine. It wasn't the first time, nor would it be the last; by 1982, he was snorting two grams of coke per week. At the end of that season, he checked into rehab, but it didn't take. In late May of 1983, he checked into rehab again. Howe rejoined the club a month later, continued to pitch brilliantly . . . and missed a team flight in September. The team suspended him for the rest of the season, and Bowie Kuhn later suspended him for the entire 1984 season.

Howe returned in 1985, but pitched poorly in limited duty, and the Dodgers released him on July 3. That fall, Tom Niedenfuer gave up decisive ninth-inning home runs in Games 5 and 6 of the NLCS, and the Cardinals went to the World Series instead of the Dodgers. If Steve Howe had been able to overcome his addiction, things might have been different.

And of course there was Darryl Strawberry, who, upon signing a five-year, $20 million contract, announced that he was a born-again Christian and would never drink again. After one great season, Strawberry sank back into the depths of substance abuse, and hit ten home runs in two seasons before the Dodgers finally gave up on him.

ALL-BUST			
		YEARS	NOTES
C	Todd Hundley	1999–2000	Batted .207 in '99, came back with solid numbers in 2000, but throwing woes drove fans to distraction.
1B	Greg Brock	1982–1986	Slugged .600 in four minor-league seasons, but never came close to filling Garvey's big spikes.
2B	Juan Samuel	1990–1992	He was what he was, but his "great tools" led people to expect so much more. . . .
SS	José Offerman	1990–1995	Dodgers did a lot of dumb things in the 1990s, and force-feeding Offerman was one of the dumbest.
3B	Bob Bailey	1967–1968	Decent hitter with Pirates and Expos before and after, but batted exactly .227 in both seasons as Dodger.
LF	Billy Ashley	1992–1997	In 1994, batted .345 with 37 homers in Triple-A, but strikeouts ate him alive in the majors.
CF	Devon White	1999–2000	His stats weren't terrible—732 OPS—but they certainly didn't justify the outlay of $6.5 million.
RF	Darryl Strawberry	1991–1993	L.A. native signed big five-year deal as free agent, then gave the Dodgers one good year and two poor ones.
SP	Darren Dreifort	1994–2002	Dodgers gave him crazy contract after 2000, and then he missed half of 2001 and *all* of 2002.
RP	Steve Howe	1980–1985	One of the game's great relievers, but drugs cost him entire 1984 season, and Dodgers finally dumped him in '85.

USED-TO-BE-GREAT			
		YEARS	NOTES
C	Gary Carter	1991	Yet another pitcher's park for Carter, in a long parade of them; caught 68 games and pinch-hit quite a bit.
1B	Eddie Murray	1997	L.A. native who'd played for club from 1989 through '91 returned for 9 games, 7 AB and 2 singles.
2B	Willie Randolph	1989–1990	Played against Dodgers in three World Series, came to club years later and posted .365 OBP in 171 games.
SS	Zoilo Versalles	1968	Just three years removed from MVP season with Twins, batted .195 and traded to Indians for a body.
3B	Ken Boyer	1968–1969	Mets castoff (!) came over from White Sox and played well in '68, but struggled early in '69 and that was it.
LF	Cesar Cedeño	1986	After batting .434 with Cards the previous September, got one last shot but batted empty .231 in 37 games.
CF	Eric Davis	1992–1993	L.A. native picked Dodgers for his comeback, but things didn't work out (though he did enjoy big seasons later).
RF	Rocky Colavito	1968	Longtime American League star played poorly in '67 but Dodgers signed him anyway; .204 in 40 games.
SP	Juan Marichal	1975	Finished his career with 2 starts for his old nemeses, and got hammered in both of them.
RP	Hoyt Wilhelm	1971–1972	On July 10—just a few weeks shy of his 50th birthday—pitched then-record 1,070th (and last) game of his long career.

BREAKING 'EM UP

They had a good run. But on February 8, 1982—twenty years ago to the day, as I write this—the Los Angeles Dodgers broke up baseball's longest-running infield. Just a few months after beating the hated Yankees in the World Series, the Dodgers traded Davey Lopes, who was thirty-six and had batted .206 during the regular season, to Oakland for a minor-league second baseman named Lance Hudson.

That deal wasn't about Lance Hudson (who would spend not a single day in the major leagues). It was about Steve Sax, a twenty-two-year-old second baseman who had batted .346 at Double-A in '81 before skipping Triple-A and debuting with the Dodgers in August.

A year later, Steve Garvey and Ron Cey were gone, too.

The 1982 season was the last of Garvey's six-year contract. On November 3, he turned down the Dodgers' final offer: $5 million for four years. On December 21, he signed with the Padres for $6.6 million guaranteed over five years. That season, Dodger farmhand Greg Brock had batted .310 with 44 home runs for Albuquerque, and many members of the Dodgers' front office were perfectly happy with the thought of Brock taking over for Garvey.

On January 19, 1983, the Dodgers traded Cey to the Cubs for outfielder Dan Cataline and pitcher Vance Lovelace. Purely in terms of talent exchanged, this ranks as one of the worst deals in franchise history, as Cey still had a few productive years left, while neither Cataline nor Lovelace ever played in the majors. But Pedro Guerrero had hit 32 home runs for the Dodgers in '82, and was slated to shift from the outfield to third base.

The front office had a plan, and the fans didn't seem to care so much as long as the replacements came through. The veteran players, predictably enough, weren't quite as sanguine about all the changes, and they still aren't.

Steve Yeager says, "I could never figure it out. Why do you win the World Series and then disassemble your champions? Maybe the front office felt they wouldn't skip a beat. Well, they did skip a beat. They couldn't find a third baseman after Cey. And Greg Brock was no Steve Garvey."

Ron Cey says, "I was very upset with it. I felt like I could have stayed here longer, kept producing longer, and all of us could have been together longer. Maybe won a couple more World Series.

Steve Garvey says, "I've always felt they broke us up too soon. Probably four or five years sooner than they had to. Because we all played pretty good baseball for other teams."

All that's fine. It's certainly true that the Dodgers spent more than a decade looking for a long-term solution at third base after Cey left. But let's look at those five seasons after Lopes was traded.

In 1982, with the old infield intact aside from Lopes, the Dodgers finished one game out of first place. Lopes enjoyed a nice comeback in Oakland, but he wasn't anywhere near as good as Steve Sax, the National League's Rookie of the Year.

In 1983, with only Russell still in the fold, the Dodgers finished in first place. Garvey's replacement, Greg Brock, was a huge disappointment. But Pedro Guerrero, who took over at third base for Cey, was one of the best hitters in the league. (Or as Guerrero was fond of saying, "I can fucking hit.") He struggled with the glove, of course, but it wasn't until 1984 that things got so bad that he had to change positions.

In 1984, the Dodgers finished fourth, thirteen games behind Garvey's Padres, who beat Cey's Cubs in the playoffs. But Garvey played poorly, Cey was just okay, and by then Lopes had moved to the outfield because he simply couldn't play second base anymore. There's absolutely no reason to think that the three ex-Dodgers could have lifted their old club from fourth place to first place.

In 1985, with neither Garvey nor Cey doing much for their teams, the Dodgers finished in first place again.

In 1986, the Dodgers plummeted to fifth place. But Garvey was awful in San Diego, while Cey and Lopes (who had joined Cey in Chicago), though still productive, were reduced to part-time duty. Again, there's little the trio of ex-Dodgers could have done in Los Angeles.

The Dodgers certainly *could* have kept the old infield together, and I suppose they *might* have won just as many division titles. But considering the ages of the players involved and the amount of money they'd have wanted, it would have been gross negligence if management *had* kept them together.

Continuity is great, but winning is a hell of a lot better.

I'm grateful to Bob Timmermann for his editorial suggestions. Sources for this chapter include Steve Delsohn's True Blue *(William Morrow, 2001), Tommy Lasorda and David Fisher's* The Artful Dodger *(Arbor House, 1985), Don Drysdale's* Once a Bum, Always a Dodger *(St. Martin's Press, 1990), Sandy Koufax's* Koufax *(Viking Press, 1966), Steve Garvey's* Garvey *(Times Books, 1986), and Phil Regan's* Phil Regan *(Zondervan, 1968).*

Cey, Russell, Lopes, Garvey. They say that breaking up is hard to do, but sometimes it just can't be helped.
Los Angeles Dodgers, Inc.

MILWAUKEE BREWERS

		YEARS	NOTES
DH	Paul Molitor	1991–1994	Became full-time DH his last 2 years in Milwaukee, and enjoyed two of his best three seasons; games by position as Brewer: 3B 791, DH 418, 2B 400, SS 57, OF 50.
C	Charlie Moore	1973–1986	He spent 14-plus years in the majors, and was generally a good-hitting catcher except for three mid-career seasons in which he was a poor-hitting right fielder.
1B	Cecil Cooper	1977–1987	Stolen from Red Sox for George Scott, batted .302 as a Brewer—third best behind Cirillo and Molitor—and garnered four straight top 10 MVP finishes, 1980–83.
2B	Jim Gantner	1976–1992	Entire 1,801-game career came as a good-fielding, weak-hitting Brewer; more games (1,449) at second base than the next three Brewers (Garcia, Viña, Molitor) combined.
SS	Robin Yount	1974–1984	Hall of Famer's career stats look something like Phil Niekro's: a couple of incredible seasons (MVP for Yount in both) mixed with a lot of good ones.
3B	Paul Molitor	1978–1990	Amazing progression as a postseason player; from '81 to '93 his postseason averages went .250, .316, .355, .391, and culminated with a 12-for-24 World Series.
LF	Ben Oglivie	1976–1986	Up-and-down player who hit above .300 and below .245 twice in a 5-year period. Brewers got him for Jim Slaton, who ended up coming back to Milwaukee a year later.
CF	Robin Yount	1985–1993	Came up when he was 18 and played more games (243) as teenager than anybody, and was the last active player to have been a teammate of Hank Aaron's.
RF	Jeromy Burnitz	1996–2001	Truth be told, Burnitz never had anything like a *great* year; instead he was solid in each of his five seasons as a regular, balancing plenty of K's with plenty of homers.
SP1	Teddy Higuera	1985–1994	The closest thing to a superstar pitcher in franchise history, Higuera went 69-38 in his first four seasons before injuries overwhelmed his career.
SP2	Mike Caldwell	1977–1984	Joined Brewers after washing out of NL; in first full season, spitballer went 22-9 with AL-best 23 complete games; in second, led AL with .727 (16-6) winning pct.
SP3	Jim Slaton	1971–1977 1979–1983	Evolved from staff workhorse—5 straight years with 30 or more starts—to swing man. Pitched in 8 postseason games, posting 2.01 ERA in 13 innings.
SP4	Bill Wegman	1985–1995	Pretty average pitcher whose control (2 walks per 9 innings) kept him from getting regularly waxed; not to be confused with photographer who takes ironic dog photos.
RP	Dan Plesac	1986–1992	Burst on the scene with 124 saves between '86 and '90, got hurt and has mustered only 31 more as a setup guy over the next 11 years.

When Robin Yount was eighteen years old, he reached the majors for good.

When Yount was twenty-two years old, he retired in favor of a prospective career as a professional golfer. Or at least that's what he told everybody. Actually, Yount was pissed at the Brewers because they were thinking about making him a center fielder due to his erratic defense at shortstop. He eventually returned to the club after being assured he could play whichever position he liked.

When Yount was twenty-six years old, he won the MVP Award as a shortstop.

When Yount was thirty-three years old, he won the MVP Award as a center fielder.

So everybody was right. Yount was good enough to play in the major leagues when he was eighteen, he was good enough to play shortstop, and he was good enough to play center field.

Incidentally, Yount was only the third player to win MVPs at two different positions, but his feat was easily the most impressive. Hank Greenberg won as a first baseman (1935) and a left fielder (1940), while Stan Musial won as a right fielder (1943 and '48) and a first baseman (1946). Yount played two key defensive positions, and he played them both well.

It's one of the most surprising statistics I've ever run across.

In 1971, the Milwaukee Brewers led the American League with twenty-one shutouts.

That might not strike you as *that* surprising, until I tell you that the Brewers finished last in the American League West—yes, the Brewers played in the West in 1970 and '71—with a 69-92 record. So in nearly a third of their victories, the Brewers didn't allow any runs at all.

You might guess that the Brewers didn't score a lot of runs, and you'd be right. With 534 runs scored, the Brewers did worse than every team but the Angels.

Where did all those shutouts come from? Marty Pattin led the Crew with five, and was followed closely by Bill Parsons and Jim Slaton, with four apiece. Skip Lockwood pitched one shutout, which leaves nine combined shutouts. Without checking, some of the credit for those nine extra whitewashes probably goes to reliever Ken Sanders, who led the league with thirty-one saves and posted a 1.92 ERA over 136 innings.

As a group, Milwaukee's pitchers were not great. They finished the season with a 3.39 ERA, just a bit better than the league average. In 1972, Sanders and Parsons and Lockwood all slumped, and Pattin and Slaton were pitching elsewhere. The Brewers spun fourteen shutouts, just eighth in the league.

NO. 2			
		YEARS	NOTES
DH	Dave Parker	1990	His last full-time gig resulted in reasonably productive season (21-92-.289); other notable short-term occupants of DH slot include Aaron, Simmons, and Hisle.
C	Darrell Porter	1971–1976	The Brewers gave up on Porter's high OBP/occasional power after a bad year in '76; he eventually played a pivotal role in beating Milwaukee in the '82 Series.
1B	George Scott	1972–1976	A big man with big power, he enjoyed his two best offensive seasons as a Brewer and won a Gold Glove each year he played in Milwaukee.
2B	Fernando Viña	1995–1999	Everyone wants a claim to fame . . . or, failing that, something else; Viña is the Brewers' all-time HBP leader with 58, beating Gantner's 52 and Yount's 48.
SS	José Valentín	1992–1999	With Valentín, you had to take the good with the bad; in '96, he hit 24 homers and struck out 145 times, and showed good range at short but made 37 errors.
3B	Jeff Cirillo	1994–1999	The Brewers have enjoyed run of good third basemen; Cirillo heads a list that includes Tommy Harper, Don Money, Sal Bando, Gary Sheffield, and Kevin Seitzer.
LF	Johnny Briggs	1971–1975	Greg Vaughn's the obvious choice because of his long tenure, but Briggs, now mostly forgotten, posted the highest adjusted OPS for a career in franchise history.
CF	Gorman Thomas	1973–1983 1986	Tempting to mistake Thomas as a Dave Kingman–like, big homer/big K player, but he also drew a ton of walks, was solid with the glove, and a likeable guy.
RF	Sixto Lezcano	1974–1980	Always left the party too early, playing for Brewers, Cards, and Padres the year *before* each made it to the postseason; outstanding throwing arm.
SP1	Chris Bosio	1986–1992	Rarity among modern pitchers, as three times he posted a save and a shutout in the same season; thanks to lousy run support, he twice lost twice as many as he won.
SP2	Lary Sorensen	1977–1980	Among the zillion players included in the big Brewers/Cardinals trade; terrific control, and odd spelling of first name was tribute to Tigers pitcher Frank Lary.
SP3	Moose Haas	1976–1985	Gritted out 91 wins with the Brewers. At 6'0" and 180 pounds, one of the more unlikely guys named "Moose" in the game, though he *was* an accomplished martial artist.
SP4	Marty Pattin	1970–1971	Threw 5 shutouts in '71 when he, Slaton, and Bill Parsons combined for 13 (more than the Orioles' four 20-game winners totaled that year).
RP	Rollie Fingers	1981–1985	Milwaukee might have won the '82 World Series had Fingers not been hurt; missed '83 season due to injury, but came back to post 1.96 ERA in '84.

		YEARS	NOTES
SINGLE SEASON			
DH	Paul Molitor	1987	His career highs in OBP and slugging both came in '87, and he stole 45 bases in 55 tries; also excellent in 1991.
C	Ted Simmons	1983	'83 was Simba's final roar and the only time he hit above .300 or had more than 100 RBI as a Brewer.
1B	Cecil Cooper	1980	Overshadowed by Brett, but batted .352 with league-best 122 RBI and won the first of his two Gold Gloves.
2B	Paul Molitor	1979	Played only a few years at 2B before being moved to protect him from injury; set still-standing team record with 16 triples.
SS	Robin Yount	1982	MVP; Cooper, Gantner, Yount, and Molitor gave the '82 Brewers the best AL infield since WWII. At least.
3B	Paul Molitor	1982	Molitor just edges Tommy Harper (1970) on the strength of fine postseason stats, including 9 runs scored.
LF	Ben Oglivie	1980	Topped AL with 41 homers, also batted .304, slugged .563, and drove in 118 runs; all four figures were career highs.
CF	Robin Yount	1989	One last great MVP season for the Hall of Famer; the very next year, he became a completely ordinary ballplayer.
RF	Sixto Lezcano	1979	Total career year, with career marks for every category but triples and walks; 2nd in AL OPS and won his only Gold Glove.
SP	Mike Caldwell	1978	Nobody noticed because Guidry was going 25-3, but Caldwell won 22 games and led AL with 23 complete games.
RP	Rollie Fingers	1981	Posted 1.04 ERA and 28 saves in abbreviated season, edged Rickey Henderson out of MVP and easily won Cy Young.

		YEARS	NOTES
ALL-ROOKIE			
DH	Joey Meyer	1988	Picture a less athletic Steve Balboni. Meyer hit 11 homers in 312 AB's, then fizzled in '89, never to return to the majors.
C	Darrell Porter	1973	His 16 homers in '73 compare pretty favorably to the 9 that *all* Brewer catchers combined for in 1971 and '72.
1B	Vacant	—	Billy Jo Robidoux the only rookie to play much first base for Crew, and he batted .227 with one homer in 56 games.
2B	Ronnie Belliard	1999	After slow start in Triple-A, recalled in May and wound up leading NL rookies in batting average (.295) and walks (64).
SS	Pat Listach	1992	Probably didn't deserve to win RoY over Lofton; Listach's rookie year was the only remotely good one of his career.
3B	Jeff Cirillo	1995	Old for a rookie, Cirillo was 25 when he got the job; decent freshman numbers (.277-9-39) took a huge jump in 1996.
LF	Greg Vaughn	1989	Did well in 38 games—.265-5-23—but his real rookie season was 1990, and he didn't play nearly so well that year.
CF	Bobby Coluccio	1973	Batted just .224, but also hit 15 homers in 124 games; only 21, but never played nearly so well again.
RF	Matt Mieske	1994	It's hard to believe, but the Brewers have *never* enjoyed a *good* full season from a rookie outfielder. Not even one.
SP	Teddy Higuera	1985	Stocky Mexican lefthander looked like another Fernando Valenzuela, throwing five pitches and winning 15 games.
RP	Doug Henry	1991	In just half a season, saved 15 games, and allowed only one homer and four runs in 36 innings; 27 years old.

If you're wondering why Pete Vuckovich's name doesn't show up as having the best single season for a Milwaukee starter—in fact, he wouldn't have ranked among the top *four*—let me answer that question with a related statement: There's never been a better example of the BBWAA's sick fascination with wins and losses than the 1982 balloting for the American League Cy Young Award.

Oh, it's not that Vuckovich had a bad year. His 3.34 ERA was sixth best in the American League, his eighteen victories were second best, and his .750 winning percentage was tied for first best (with Jim Palmer, who went 15-5 compared to Vuckovich's 18-6).

But you know, sixth best in ERA really ain't that great. Vuckovich started only thirty games all season. He gave up 234 hits in 224 innings. He walked nearly as many batters (102) as he struck out (105). Oh, and did I mention that County Stadium was a pitcher's park?

Vuckovich won the Cy Young Award because he won eighteen games for a team that finished in first place. But he wasn't as good that season as Dave Stieb (17-14, 3.25 with a bad team) or Dan Quisenberry (9-7 with thirty-five saves) or half a dozen other pitchers.

Trading Darrell Porter and Jim Colborn to the Royals for Jamie Quirk, Jim Wohlford, and Bob McClure is obviously one of the stupidest things the Brewers have ever done.

Oddly enough, the three players the Brewers got in the deal nearly lasted longer in the majors than either Porter or Colborn. Quirk hung around forever (through the '92 season, actually) as a utility man. Wohlford got the reputation as a "professional hitter" even though he really couldn't hit, and hung around through 1986. And McClure, a left-handed pitcher—pay attention, Mom and Dad—never won more than twelve games in a season, but pitched in the majors until 1993, when he was forty-one years old.

Meanwhile, Porter last played in 1987, Colborn in 1978. Still, it was a terrible deal for the Brewers, because Porter was a hell of a player for seven or eight years after leaving.

Colborn lasted just one full season (1977) after the deal, but he won eighteen games for the best Royals team ever, and he provided me with my first baseball thrill.

I was ten years old that spring. There weren't nearly as many games on TV back then, and I have a vivid memory of sitting in the kitchen at my dad's house, listening on the radio as Colborn nailed down a no-hitter against the Rangers. It was the Royals' third, and my first.

		HOMEGROWN	
		YEARS	NOTES
DH	Paul Molitor	1978–1992	Third player selected in '77 June draft, signed for $100K and played only 64 games in the minor leagues.
C	Darrell Porter	1971–1976	Fourth player selected in '70 June draft, and in his second pro season hit 24 homers and was summoned to big club.
1B	John Jaha	1992–1998	14th-round pick in '84 took his time, but established himself with .344-30-133 season with El Paso in '91.
2B	Jim Gantner	1976–1992	12th-round pick in '74 reached majors two years later, and wound up playing for Crew until he was nearly 40.
SS	Robin Yount	1974–1993	Third player selected in '73 draft—noticed a pattern in the 1970s yet?—and handed MLB job when just 18.
3B	Jeff Cirillo	1994–1999	11th-round pick quickly established himself as prospect by hitting .350 with 10 bombs in Pioneer League.
LF	Greg Vaughn	1989–1996	An argument for nature over nurture: Vaughn's cousins include major leaguers Mo Vaughn and Jerry Royster.
CF	Gorman Thomas	1973–1983 1986	The Seattle Pilots' very first draft pick, 21st overall in 1969, and showed big-time power in the minors.
RF	Sixto Lezcano	1974–1980	Native of Puerto Rico not subject to draft, signed as free agent in 1970.
SP	Jim Slaton	1971–1977; 1979–1983	Best thing that happened to the Pilots in '69 was drafting Slaton in 14th round; well, that and *Ball Four*.
RP	Doug Jones	1982	Pitched 3 innings for big club in 7 years, granted free agency, signed with Indians, became a star fireman.

		TRADED AWAY	
		TRADED	NOTES
C	Darrell Porter	December 6, 1976	From the Dept. of What Were They Thinking: Porter and starter Jim Colborn to Royals for three spare parts.
1B	Vacant	—	I can't confirm that the Brewers have ever traded a first baseman at all, let alone a *good* first baseman.
2B	Fernando Viña	December 20, 1999	After brilliant '98 season, missed most of '99 with variety of injuries, then deemed expendable. Oops.
SS	José Valentín	January 12, 2000	He and Cal Eldred both played well for White Sox after going over for Jaime Navarro and John Snyder. Oops.
3B	Gary Sheffield	March 27, 1992	Everybody knew he'd be good, but injury-plagued '91 made it easier to get rid of petulant problem child.
LF	Greg Vaughn	July 31, 1996	Blasted 31 homers in first four months, but was in last year of contract so Brewers sent him to San Diego.
CF	José Cardenal	December 3, 1971	Looked like he might be washed up so Brewers dumped him, but he came back with some fine seasons for Cubs.
RF	Kevin Bass	September 3, 1982	Bass one of three players—and the only good one—sent to Angels to complete trade for Don Sutton.
SP	Al Downing	February 10, 1971	Pitched well (3.34) for Crew but went just 2-10, then won 20 games for Dodgers the very next year.
RP	Mike Marshall	November 21, 1969	First the Pilots wouldn't let Marshall throw his great screwball, and then they sold him to the Astros.

GOLD GLOVE		YEARS	NOTES
C	Henry Blanco	2000–2001	Weak bat made it tough to keep him in lineup, but he threw amazingly well, just as good as Pudge Rodriguez.
1B	George Scott	1972–1976	Scott won six Gold Gloves and deserved most of them, but in all honesty, he didn't have much competition.
2B	Jim Gantner	1978–1992	After five years as utility man, settled at second base in 1981 and quickly became one of the best.
SS	José Valentín	1992–1999	Yount was pretty good, but his Gold Glove in 1982 was won almost entirely with his bat, as sometimes happens.
3B	Jeff Cirillo	1994–1999	Fantastic defensive player all the way around, and in 1998 he tied National League record by starting 45 double plays.
LF	Geoff Jenkins	1998–2002	Refreshing change after a long line of butchers running from Johnny Briggs to Ben Oglivie to Greg Vaughn.
CF	Gerald Williams	1996–1997	Outstanding center fielder blocked by Bernie Williams with Yanks and Andruw Jones with Braves.
RF	Matt Mieske	1993–1997	Reached majors on strength of his bat; never really hit as expected, but was a fine, strong-armed outfielder.
P	Bob McClure	1977–1986	Best move to first base in the game, so good that he often surprised his first baseman and confused the umpires.

IRON GLOVE		YEARS	NOTES
C	Dave Nilsson	1992–1994 1999	Apparently, the problem was that when Australians throw to second, the ball spins counterclockwise. . . .
1B	John Jaha	1992–1998	His usefulness to Brewers decreased significantly when they bolted to the league without the DH.
2B	Ron Belliard	1998–2002	Had all the tools and was pretty good when he came up, but as the weight went up the range went down.
SS	Tim Johnson	1973–1974	He didn't see combat in Vietnam or play decent defense at shortstop; even worse than Gary Sheffield.
3B	Dale Sveum	1986 1990–1991	In 1986, Sveum made 26 errors at third, which wouldn't be terrible . . . except he played only 65 games there!
LF	Ben Oglivie	1976–1986	Ran okay and threw well enough, but range limited by his unwillingness to leave his favorite grassy spot.
CF	Von Joshua	1976–1977	He wasn't actually bad, but the Brewers haven't ever had a regular center fielder who wasn't at least decent.
RF	Charlie Moore	1982–1984	Converted from catcher to RF to keep his bat in the lineup . . . but he didn't hit or field like a right fielder (great arm, though).
P	Jaime Cocanower	1983–1986	Sure, he was an extreme ground-ball pitcher, but 14 errors in 366 innings is still something special.

In 1999, Brewers general manager Sal Bando did something bold. The truth is that Bando made precious few bold moves in his tenure, let alone good ones. But putting Dave Nilsson behind the plate again was one of his best moments.

Nilsson came to the Brewers as a catcher, and the reviews were unanimous: he stunk at catching. After a few years of that, in 1995 Nilsson became an outfielder/DH/first baseman/occasional catcher. That went on for a few years . . . until 1999, when Bando took a chance and asked Nilsson to become a catcher again.

And it worked. At the All-Star break, catcher Dave Nilsson was hitting .311 with nineteen homers and fifty-two RBI. That's germane, because Nilsson also played in the All-Star Game, his first. His power dropped off in the second half, but his OBP went up . . . until late August, when he suffered a broken thumb that ended his season.

And after the season he retired. Not because of the injury, but because he simply wanted to spend more time back home in Australia. So barring a comeback—and I wouldn't rule one out, because he's still only thirty-three—Nilsson will go down as one of the few players to play his first All-Star Game in his last season. (In fact, he might be the only one; I can't figure out an easy way to check.)

Hank Aaron and Babe Ruth both scored 2,714 runs in the major leagues. But if not for a questionable decision by Brewers manager Alex Grammas in 1975, Aaron might have passed the Babe in that category, too.

In *The Ball Clubs* (Harper-Perennial, 1996), Donald Dewey and/or Michael Acocella wrote, "Grammas added insensitivity to the list of charges against him when he removed the slugger for a pinch-runner after a single in his last major league at bat. The pilot's intention had been to facilitate an ovation for Aaron as he left the field; the result was that the home run king was miffed at losing the chance to break a tie with Ruth for second place in career runs scored as pinch-runner [Jim] Gantner crossed the plate a few minutes later."

That's not how Aaron told the story, though. In his autobiography, *I Had a Hammer*—which was published before Dewey and Acocella's book, *and by the same publishing house*—Aaron remembered, "...when it came down to it, I didn't care very much about breaking another tie with Ruth. I sort of liked the idea of sharing something with the Babe, and I wasn't upset at all when Alex Grammas sent out Jim Gantner to run for me. I'm told I had a smile on my face as I trotted off the field."

ALL-BUST			
		YEARS	NOTES
DH	Larry Hisle	1978–1982	Signed six-year deal as free agent, and gave Brewers one great year and five injury-ravaged ones.
C	B. J. Surhoff	1987–1992	First player selected in 1985 draft wasn't actually so bad with glove, but didn't hit until moving to third base.
1B	Sean Berry	1999–2000	Came to Brewers as 3B with 810 career OPS, but shifted to 1B and was horrible: .272 OBP, .295 slugging.
2B	Ron Belliard	1998–*2002*	Top prospect battled weight, strikeouts, inconsistency, and finally lost his job in 2002.
SS	Tim Johnson	1973–1978	Handed regular job in '73 and was wall-to-wall awful: .213 batting, .259 OBP, .243 slugging, lousy defense.
3B	Gary Sheffield	1991	After breaking through with .294 average in '90, first-round pick crashed to .194 and plenty of DL time.
LF	Danny Thomas	1976–1977	Fantastic prospect did well in two brief stints, but was a head case and wound up hanging himself in 1980.
CF	Marquis Grissom	1998–2000	The genius of John Hart: after taking on Grissom's crazy contract, foisted it on Brewers just a year later.
RF	Glenn Braggs	1986–1989	Like a lot of Brewers prospects, he might have been overhyped due to Triple-A club being in Denver.
SP	Jim Abbott	1999	Two years after going 2-18 with Angels and one year after going 5-0 with ChiSox, went 2-8 with 6.91 ERA.
RP	Rob Dibble	1995	End of the road for Dibs, who walked 19 batters in 12 innings; baseball's loss, ESPN's gain.

USED-TO-BE-GREAT			
		YEARS	NOTES
DH	Hank Aaron	1975–1976	After nine seasons in Atlanta, moved back to the city where he started his career; hit last 22 HR as Brewer.
C	Brian Harper	1991	Past the point of being able to do anything behind the plate, but could still put the bat on the ball, and hit .291.
1B	Ted Simmons	1981–1985	All those years behind the plate took their toll, but Simba could still hit, especially in '82 and '83.
2B	Willie Randolph	1991	Actually, he still *was* great; in next-to-last season, batted career-high .327 and posted .424 OBP.
SS	Tony Fernandez	2001	After a season in Japan, played 28 games at third before moving on to finish career with Blue Jays, his first club.
3B	Sal Bando	1977–1981	With the old Mustache Gang scattering to the winds, Bando landed in Beer City and eventually ran the club.
LF	Tommy Davis	1969	Provided some National League respectability to first-year Pilots, but not a whole lot else.
CF	Marquis Grissom	1998–2000	Once a pretty good player, but by 1998 . . . well, let's just say this was one hell of a way to blow $15 million.
RF	Jimmy Wynn	1974	Played a total of 3 games for Brewers, going hitless in 3 at-bats, in his last major-league action.
SP	Don Sutton	1982–1984	Future Hall of Famer went 26-26 in two-plus seasons with Brewers; pitched brilliantly in September of '82.
RP	Mark Davis	1997	Close call here, with Rob Dibble's (1995) and Jim Kern's (1984–85) last gasps also strong contenders.

ALL-NAME

		YEARS	NOTES
C	"Simba" Ted Simmons	1981–1985	In honor of his long mane of hair, which he cut off after it caught fire while he was burning leaves.
1B	"Boomer" George Scott	1972–1976	Supposedly due to his power, and in 1975 he topped American League with 36 homers and 109 RBI.
2B	"Gumby" Jim Gantner	1976–1992	"Gantner was a master of 'gumming' things up with a mixed metaphor, a non sequitur, or the nonsensical."
SS	"Rockin' Robin" Robin Yount	1974–1993	Hey, it's the Brewers. If you want interesting nicknames, flip ahead to the Yankees chapter.
3B	"The Igniter" Paul Molitor	1978–1992	Okay, so he didn't draw a lot of walks. But when healthy, he could hit .300 and steal second base in his sleep.
LF	"Spiderman" Ben Oglivie	1978–1986	Long arms and skinny legs earned him nickname, but they also helped him hit 235 homers in the big leagues.
CF	"Stormin' Gorman" Gorman Thomas	1973–1983 1986	If you're too young to remember him, at least the nickname conjures an accurate image. . . .
RF	"Tiny" Mike Felder	1985–1990	For an outfielder—hell, for a late 20th-century *player*—he *was* tiny, at 5'8" and 160 pounds; 14 career homers.
SP	"Mr. Warmth" Mike Caldwell	1977–1984	Earned degree in sociology at N.C. State, but not one of the more pleasant Brewers and wore permanent scowl.
RP	Bob Gibson Jim Hunter	1983–1987 1991	Unfortunately, neither of these Brewers lived up to the promise of their illustrious pitcher names.

TOP FIVE SEASONS

YEAR 1982 **RECORD** 95-67
BEST HITTER Robin Yount
BEST PITCHERS Pete Vuckovich (Cy Young), Rollie Fingers
NOTES Hard to argue that Fingers's absence really cost Brewers the Series.

YEAR 1978 **RECORD** 93-69
BEST HITTERS Sal Bando, Larry Hisle
BEST PITCHER Mike Caldwell
NOTES First winning season a sideshow next to Red Sox and Yankees.

YEAR 1981 **RECORD** 62-47
BEST HITTER Cecil Cooper
BEST PITCHERS Rollie Fingers (Cy Young, MVP)
NOTES Best record in the East, and gave Yanks tussle in Division Playoff.

YEAR 1992 **RECORD** 92-70
BEST HITTER Paul Molitor
BEST PITCHERS Bill Wegman, Jaime Navarro
NOTES Finished only four games behind eventual World Champions.

YEAR 1979 **RECORD** 95-66
BEST HITTERS Sixto Lezcano, Paul Molitor, Gorman Thomas
BEST PITCHER Mike Caldwell
NOTES Only good for second place as O's ran away and hid.

TOP FIVE MANAGERS

MANAGER George Bamberger
YEARS 1978–1980, 1985–1986
RECORD 377-351 (.518)
NOTES Better than .500 in first three years, worse in last two.

MANAGER Harvey Kuenn
YEARS 1982–1983
RECORD 159-118 (.574)
NOTES Took over in middle of '82 and led "Harvey's Wallbangers" to World Series.

MANAGER Tom Trebelhorn
YEARS 1986–1991
RECORD 422-397 (.515)
NOTES Already fading from memory . . .

MANAGER Buck Rodgers
YEARS 1980–1982
RECORD 101-78 (.564)
NOTES Best thing he ever did was get fired in June of '82.

MANAGER Phil Garner
YEARS 1992–1999
RECORD 563-617 (.477)
NOTES Brewers shocked the world in Garner's first season, but he was just teasing.

One of the laments of the modern baseball fan is that teams just don't stay together like they used to. And it's true, they don't. I'm not sure it matters a whole hell of a lot to anybody but people like you and me, but I do miss those old days. As long as I live, if you ask me about the Brewers of the early 1980s I'll be able to remember almost everybody in the lineup: Cecil Cooper, Jim Gantner, Robin Yount, Don Money, Paul Molitor, Ben Oglivie, Gorman Thomas, and . . . Mark Brouhard, I think.

But if, twenty years from now, you ask a baseball fan—a serious baseball fan, I mean—about the Brewers of the early twenty-first century, what is he or she going to say? "Well, let's see . . . there was Richie Sexson, and Geoff Jenkins. And that pitcher from the Olympics who was supposed to be so great . . ."

Like I said, I don't know that any of this really matters much. I've got this . . . *thing* about connections to the past. I'm fascinated by old train stations and old highways and old baseball stadiums. I like old houses better than new houses, old neighborhoods better than new neighborhoods . . . and you know, I'm generally more interested in old baseball teams than new baseball teams. And so I'm glad that I still can see those old Brewers, and remember who they were.

THE CUPBOARD WAS BARE

Within the space of five years—and within a decade of the franchise's birth in Seattle—the Milwaukee Brewers produced two future Hall of Famers, and they were smart enough to keep both Robin Yount and Paul Molitor for quite a while. By way of comparison, no other expansion team has produced two Hall of Famers in its first ten years.

So why didn't Yount and Molitor play in the postseason more than twice? Because the Brewers had the same problem in the 1980s that they had in the 1990s, and that they've got now: an utter inability to develop, or trade for, quality starting pitchers.

When I was compiling the Brewers' home-grown lineup, I kept putting off filling that blank because I figured I must be missing somebody. The best Brewers pitcher is obviously Teddy Higuera, but should he really be considered home-grown? After all, the Mexican native spent four full seasons pitching for Ciudad Juárez. In 1983, his last season down there, Higuera led the Mexican League in just about everything. He was at least twenty-four years old, and while the Brewers deserve plenty of credit for acquiring Higuera, they didn't really develop him.

Next possibility is Jim Slaton. Now, Jim Slaton was a damn good pitcher, good enough to win 151 games and pitch in the major leagues for sixteen years. But after Slaton, there's a helluva drop-off. Bill Wegman, Moose Haas, Cal Eldred, Chris Bosio . . . all these guys were good pitchers, but you put them all together and they don't match what the Athletics have produced just in the last five years.

In fact, looking at the Brewers' pitching over the years, it's pretty amazing that they were as good as they were; from 1978 through 1982, only the Orioles won more games than the Brewers. How'd they do it? Those of you born before 1970 probably remember: they beat their opponents into submission. The Brewers led the American League in runs scored twice during those five years, and they were close to the top in the other three. This was fairly remarkable, considering that County Stadium favored the pitchers as much as any ballpark in the league.

The formula worked for five years. But in 1983, the veteran hitters started to show their age. The organization hadn't produced suitable replacements for guys like Ben Oglivie and Gorman Thomas, and the pitchers certainly weren't going to pick up the slack. Molitor and Yount were still in the primes of their careers, but they couldn't do it all by themselves. They needed a little help from the suits upstairs, and they didn't get it.

I'm grateful to Mat Olkin and Tom Rathkamp for their editorial assistance. Sources for this chapter include Daniel Okrent's Nine Innings *(Ticknor & Fields, 1985).*

Robin Yount and Paul Molitor
Courtesy of the Milwaukee Brewers Archives Library

MINNESOTA TWINS

		YEARS	NOTES
		ALL-TIME	
DH	Chili Davis	1991–1992	After three so-so years in Anaheim, joined Twins, became every-day DH, and revived his career with 29 homers and 93 RBI in Twins' championship season.
C	Earl Battey	1961–1967	Had trouble keeping his weight down and frequently suffered minor injuries, but four-time All-Star did everything well but run.
1B	Harmon Killebrew	1954–1974	Default position because it was his best, but he could also be listed as club's No. 1 third baseman; 549 homers with franchise . . . oh, and let's not forget his 1,505 walks.
2B	Rod Carew	1967–1978	As Twin, played nine seasons at second base and three at first. Greatest bat control of his time; Alan Bannister said, "He's the only guy I know who can go 4-for-3."
SS	Roy Smalley, Jr.	1976–1982 1985–1987	From '76—when he came from Rangers in trade for Bert Blyleven—through '80, Smalley's uncle Gene Mauch was also his manager; back problem slowed fine career.
3B	Gary Gaetti	1981–1990	Broke in with a bang, taking Charlie Hough deep to become third Twin to homer in first at-bat; hitting stats up and down, but his great glove never slumped.
LF	Larry Hisle	1973–1977	Remembered as a gimpy slugger, but before he got hurt he was a pretty good athlete who played 502 games in center field; in '76 and '77, knocked in 215 runs.
CF	Kirby Puckett	1984–1995	Best "bad-ball hitter" of his time, had no plate discipline but led AL in hits four times; six-time Gold Glover with a body and smile that little kids couldn't resist.
RF	Tony Oliva	1962–1976	Led AL in hits five times, doubles four times, batting average three times, and he was headed for the Hall of Fame until devastating knee injury in '71.
SP1	Bert Blyleven	1970–1976 1985–1988	The Dutchman won 149 games in his two stints with Twins, and his big curveball was one of the most impressive pitches of the 1970s.
SP2	Jim Kaat	1959–1973	The franchise has existed for more than a century, yet only two pitchers have won more than 150 games: Walter Johnson (417) and Jim Kaat (190).
SP3	Frank Viola	1982–1989	For two years, 1987 and '88, he was as good as anybody in the league; won twice in '87 World Series, including Game 7. Ranks fourth on Twins list with 112 wins.
SP4	Jim Perry	1963–1972	Gaylord's big brother didn't throw a spitball and he didn't win 300 games, but he was a hell of a pitcher and topped American League with 24 wins in 1970.
RP	Rick Aguilera	1989–1995 1996–1999	Spent a few months with Red Sox in '95, but returned in plenty of time for '96; his 254 saves with Twins is more than twice as many as No. 2 man on the list.

Baseball history is littered with the metaphorical corpses of pitchers with Hall of Fame talent who didn't come anywhere near the Hall of Fame because they got hurt.

But there are *not* a lot of analogous nonpitchers, guys who would obviously be in the Hall of Fame if they hadn't suffered a serious injury.

Tony Oliva is one of those guys, though; in fact, he might be the best of those guys. As one of the coauthors of *Baseball: The Biographical Encyclopedia* wrote of Oliva, "He could hit for average, he could hit with power, he could run, he could field, and, boy, could he throw." But Oliva was born with a serious weakness: a right leg that wasn't built for running and jumping. Oliva underwent knee surgeries in both 1966 and '67, but he kept on hitting. On June 29, 1971, though, he dove for a fly ball hit by Oakland's Joe Rudi and tore the cartilage in that same right knee. He was hitting .375 at the time and, limping through the rest of the season, finished at .337 to win his third batting title. But he was never the same.

Oliva played only ten games in 1972, then returned as a DH in 1973 and hung around until 1976. He earned approximately 210 Win Shares before he turned thirty-one, and approximately thirty-five after. With just one more big season, he'd be in the Hall.

Kent Alan Hrbek was born in Bloomington, Minnesota, on May 21, 1960. Exactly eleven months later, the Minnesota Twins hosted the expansion Washington Senators in the first Major League Baseball game ever played in the North Star State.

The Twins came of age in Bloomington—at Metropolitan Stadium—and so did Hrbek, who graduated from Kennedy High School in 1978. He planned to attend the University of Minnesota, but the Twins took him in the seventeenth round of the draft. Hrbek's agent asked the Twins for $30,000, and he got it after owner Calvin Griffith saw him put on a show in an American Legion game.

Hrbek spent nearly all of his first pro season on the disabled list. Things went better in 1980, though, as Hrbek hit nineteen homers with the Wisconsin Rapids in the Midwest League.

And then came 1981, a bad year for baseball but one hell of a year for Kent Hrbek. Moving up to Visalia in the Class A California League, Hrbek batted .379, hit twenty-seven homers, and knocked in 111 runs.

Hrbek spent September with the big club, and then, despite having not played a single game in Class AA or AAA, in 1982 he won the first-base job in spring training . . . and batted .301 with twenty-three homers to finish a strong second to Cal Ripken in the Rookie of the Year balloting.

		YEARS	NOTES
			NO. 2
DH	Paul Molitor	1996–1998	St. Paul native came home for final three seasons, and batted .341 with AL-leading 225 hits in 1996, despite turning 40 late that season.
C	Butch Wynegar	1976–1982	An All-Star his first two seasons, at ages of 20 and 21, but slumped horribly in his third season and never really played well again until leaving the Twins.
1B	Kent Hrbek	1981–1994	Minneapolis native spent entire career with Twins; had a lot of good years and never really had a bad one, but a lack of *great* years has left him underrated.
2B	Chuck Knoblauch	1991–1997	First-round pick in 1989 spent only two seasons in minors before making big club in '91, and batted .281 as rookie; eventually became great trade bait.
SS	Zoilo Versalles	1961–1967	"Zorro" wasn't any kind of hitter aside from his MVP season, but he played defense and did have some pop, and aces out Greg Gagne because of his stick.
3B	Corey Koskie	1998–2002	Batted .310 and .300 his first two seasons as regular, but broke through in '01 with 26 homers and 103 RBI; not bad for a 26th-round pick from Manitoba.
LF	Gary Ward	1979–1983	Ward was pretty good in '82 and '83 but then he went to Texas, and one could also reasonably argue for Dan Gladden, Marty Cordova, or Jacque Jones here.
CF	Jimmie Hall	1963–1966	Hit 98 homers and made two All-Star teams in his first four seasons, but stopped hitting by 30; nobody forgot his talent, though, and so he played for five other clubs.
RF	Bob Allison	1958–1970	Rookie of the Year while franchise still in Washington, but enjoyed some fine years in Minnesota, too; ex-footballer was the most feared baserunner in the League.
SP1	Camilo Pascual	1954–1966	Just as Blyleven featured the AL's best curveball in the 1970s, Pascual threw the league's best curve in the '60s; career took off when Senators became Twins in 1961.
SP2	Brad Radke	1995–2002	The late 1990s were tough on the Twins, but Radke was good throughout, and the franchise was smart enough to pay what it cost to keep him around.
SP3	Kevin Tapani	1989–1995	Came from Mets in deal that also netted Aguilera, with Twins giving up spent Viola; "Taps" went 16-9 with 2.99 ERA in '91, and started six straight home openers.
SP4	Eric Milton	1998–2002	Of the many fruits of Knoblauch deal, Milton's been the tastiest; not a lot of quality—his 1999 no-hitter aside—but didn't miss a start until his fifth season.
RP	Jeff Reardon	1987–1989	Twins were his third stop of seven, and he saved 104 games in three years; was outstanding only in 1988, with 42 saves and 2.47 ERA.

		YEARS	NOTES
DH	Chili Davis	1991	In first of two seasons as Twin, Davis rejuvenated his career with career-high 29 homers; also tied career high in RBI.
C	Earl Battey	1963	What more could you want? Battey hit career-high 26 homers, won his second of three Gold Gloves and made All-Star team.
1B	Rod Carew	1977	Didn't have a lot of power, didn't have a lot of power . . . but when you hit .388, you don't need a whole lot else.
2B	Chuck Knoblauch	1996	Numbers were eye-popping across the board: 140 runs, 98 RBI, 14 triples and 13 homers, .341 BA, and 45 steals.
SS	Zoilo Versalles	1965	In hindsight, his MVP shouldn't have been *that* surprising; he'd scored 94 runs and led league with 10 triples in '64.
3B	Gary Gaetti	1986	In nine full seasons with Twins, "The Rat" had two big years with the bat: '86 (.287-34-108) and '88 (.301-28-88).
LF	Harmon Killebrew	1964	Yes, he was slow. But in '64 Killebrew played 158 games in the outfield and topped AL with 49 home runs.
CF	Kirby Puckett	1988	A great season—234 hits, 24 homers, etc.—but Kirby had four other seasons that were just as good or close.
RF	Tony Oliva	1965	Why did the Twins win in 1965? Because Versalles (the MVP) and Oliva (runner-up) both had their biggest seasons.
SP	Bert Blyleven	1973	Only 20-win season (20-17) in his long career, and those 20 wins included league-leading 9 shutouts.
RP	Doug Corbett	1980	Yes, he was a rookie, but he was also 27 years old, and rode a nasty sinker to 23 saves and 1.98 ERA in 136 innings.

SINGLE SEASON

		YEARS	NOTES
DH	Randy Bush	1983	The *only* candidate here; spent entire 12-season career with Twins and batted against LHP exactly 100 times.
C	Butch Wynegar	1976	Only 20 years old, Wynegar became the youngest player to appear in an All-Star Game.
1B	Kent Hrbek	1982	Minneapolis native had great season—.301-23-92—and finished strong second to Cal Ripken in RoY voting.
2B	Chuck Knoblauch Rod Carew	1991 1967	Both were Rookies of the Year despite not playing all *that* well (though of course both later would).
SS	Zoilo Versalles	1961	After failing tryouts with Senators previous two seasons, got chance to play with move to Minn. and batted .280.
3B	John Castino	1979	Co–Rookie of the Year (with Alfredo Griffin) eventually became fine second baseman before back injury ended career.
LF	Marty Cordova	1995	Hit 24 homers to capture RoY honors, and played just as well in sophomore season before suffering from *junior* jinx in '97.
CF	Jimmie Hall	1963	Set American League rookie record with 33 homers, and everybody loved his defense, too; all downhill from there.
RF	Tony Oliva	1964	Rookie of the Year won batting title, and in '65 became first player ever to win batting titles in his first two seasons.
SP	Kevin Tapani	1990	Rookie starters not exactly a strength for Twins, as Taps is the best with his 12-8, 4.07 campaign.
RP	Doug Corbett	1980	He was 27 and would never better the 23 saves and 1.98 ERA posted in '80; relied on a "sinker" that some thought wet.

ALL-ROOKIE

There's no question but that Zoilo Versalles's MVP award in 1965 was anomalous; while he had better seasons with the glove, "Zorro" did significantly better with the bat in '65 than he ever had before or ever would again.

But did he deserve the MVP? After all, his .273 batting average wasn't anywhere among the league leaders. Nor was his .319 on-base percentage, or his .462 slugging percentage.

Based just on those numbers—which were about all I'd ever looked at—I figured it was just another of the BBWAA's many idiosyncratic choices. But now that I've actually *looked* at him . . .

Versalles played 160 games. He led the AL in runs scored (126), doubles (forty-five) and triples (twelve). He stole twenty-seven bases and was caught only five times. He was the leadoff man for a franchise that reached the World Series for the first time since 1933.

And he played shortstop. Far too often, the voters pay absolutely no attention to the defensive contributions of the candidates, which is why players like Juan Gonzalez and Mo Vaughn win awards they don't deserve. But in 1965, none of the big RBI men on the pennant contenders had big years. That left the door open for the shortstop with the good (but not great) hitting stats. And in 1965, Zoilo Versalles really was the best player in the league.

On May 8, 1998, Chuck Knoblauch played his first game in Minneapolis as a member of the New York Yankees. The previous winter, he'd demanded to be traded, so the Twins sent him to the Yankees for minor leaguers Eric Milton, Cristian Guzman, Brian Buchanan, Danny Mota, and cash.

Knoblauch was booed heavily during pregame warm-ups, he was booed for twenty-five seconds when he led off the game, and from there he was booed every time he touched the baseball or came close to touching the baseball.

Three years later, Knoblauch was still getting razzed during his Twin Cities visits, but by then the fans should have been showering him with rose petals. Because if Knoblauch hadn't wanted out of Minnesota, the Twins wouldn't have made their oh-so-surprising (if ultimately unsuccessful) run for the division title.

In 2001, Eric Milton went 15-7 with a 4.32 ERA.

In 2001, Brian Buchanan hit ten homers and slugged .497 in sixty-nine games.

In 2001, Cristian Guzman batted .302 and led the American League with fourteen triples despite spending a month on the disabled list.

And in 2001, Chuck Knoblauch, playing left field for the Yankees, batted .250, slugged .351, and scored only sixty-six runs in 137 games.

In more ways than one, Chuck Knoblauch is one of the best things that ever happened to the Minnesota Twins.

HOMEGROWN			
		YEARS	NOTES
DH	David Ortiz	1997–2002	He's had his problems, but the Dominican high-school graduate can hit the crap out of the ball.
C	Rick Dempsey	1969–1972	Twelfth-round pick in '67 spent better part of seven seasons in minors before establishing himself in majors.
1B	Kent Hrbek	1981–1994	Grew up watching Twins in Bloomington, was just 17th-round pick but jumped from Visalia to Twins in 1981.
2B	Rod Carew	1967–1978	After impressive tryout at Yankee Stadium, signed for $5K bonus and another $7,500 if he reached majors.
SS	Zoilo Versalles	1959–1967	Franchise's Cuba link began in 1940s, but didn't really pay off until 1960s with Pascual, Versalles, and Oliva.
3B	Gary Gaetti	1981–1990	Showed his power from the start, blasting 66 homers in his 341 minor-league games before reaching majors.
LF	Bob Allison	1958–1970	Kansas Jayhawk signed with Senators instead of Yankees because he thought he'd reach the majors faster.
CF	Kirby Puckett	1984–1995	Third overall pick in '82 draft batted .382 in first pro campaign, joined Twins for good early in '84.
RF	Tony Oliva	1962–1976	Signed out of Cuba by legendary scout Joe Cambria, then batted .410 in his first minor-league season.
SP	Bert Blyleven	1970–1976 1985–1988	Native of Holland drafted in third round, and just a year later he was 19 years old and pitching well for Twins.
RP	Jesse Orosco	—	Twins drafted him in '78 but sent him to Mets after he blew away Appy League hitters for three months.

TRADED AWAY			
		TRADED	NOTES
C	Rick Dempsey	October 27, 1972	Traded to Yankees for onetime super-prospect Danny Walton, who hit .176 in parts of two years with Twins.
1B	Rod Carew	February 3, 1979	He didn't win any more batting titles, but the master of the wand still had five .300 seasons left in him.
2B	Chuck Knoblauch	February 6, 1998	Sent to Yankees in exchange for four minor leaguers and cash, in what became a great deal for Twins.
SS	Jay Bell	August 1, 1985	Part of deal that brought Blyleven back; anyway, who knew that Bell would hit nearly 200 homers?
3B	Graig Nettles	December 10, 1969	One of four traded to Tribe for Luis Tiant and Stan Williams; would've been okay if Twins had kept Tiant.
LF	Gary Ward	December 7, 1983	Traded to Rangers for three players, none of whom did anything; he faded fast, but did hit 79 more homers.
CF	Ken Landreaux	March 30, 1981	Put together 30-game hitting streak in 1980 to become briefly famous, then traded to Dodgers.
RF	Dan Ford	December 4, 1978	Similar story to Ward's; the Twins didn't get much for him, but he'd given the Twins his best years.
SP	Bert Blyleven	June 1, 1976	All about the money, as Blyleven dispatched to Arlington for Roy Smalley, three other players, and $250,000.
RP	Jesse Orosco	December 8, 1978	Traded to Mets before he got a chance to pitch for Twins . . . and 24 years later, still pitching in the majors.

GOLD GLOVE			
		YEARS	**NOTES**
C	Earl Battey	1961–1967	Rough customer behind the plate, had a great arm and loved to pick runners off third base.
1B	Vic Power	1962–1964	Mientkiewicz is great, of course, but Power was one of *the* greats; Gene Larkin and Ron Coomer also excellent.
2B	Rob Wilfong	1977–1982	Knoblauch was very good before going to New York, but Wilfong's glove alone kept him in the league for 10 years.
SS	Greg Gagne	1985–1992	Physically unimpressive and never won a Gold Glove, but was brilliant and deserved at least two of them.
3B	Gary Gaetti	1981–1990	As good as anybody in the league for most of his career, and won 4 straight Gold Gloves beginning in 1986.
LF	Dan Gladden	1987–1991	Big-time hustler with good speed and decent arm, could have played decent center field if Kirby weren't around.
CF	Torii Hunter	1998–*2002*	Puckett deserved his six Gold Gloves, but Hunter has been brilliant since 1999.
RF	Tony Oliva	1964–1971	Great instincts, and before he got hurt he could run and throw with just about any right fielder in the league.
P	Jim Kaat	1959–1973	Won 16 Gold Gloves, 12 of them as a Twin; as a kid, imagined himself fielding like Bobby Shantz.

IRON GLOVE			
		YEARS	**NOTES**
C	Mark Salas	1985–1987	These three seasons he teamed with Tim Laudner, and both were essentially helpless against the running game.
1B	Danny Goodwin	1979–1981	Played 252 games in the majors, and DH'd in 150 of them, which pretty much says it all.
2B	Todd Walker	1996–2000	Probably not as bad as his reputation, but the Twins have virtually always had at least an average defender here.
SS	Ron Washington	1981–1986	More or less the regular in 1982, but from there his playing time decreased with each passing season.
3B	Harmon Killebrew	1955–1961 1966–1970	Harm didn't have any business playing anything but first base, but spent four years at third base anyway.
LF	Brant Alyea	1970–1971	Maybe just a tad worse than Killebrew in left field, and anyway one entry here for Harmon is probably enough.
CF	Larry Hisle	1973–1978	Twins kept using him in center, and he kept proving that he belonged in left.
RF	Bombo Rivera	1978–1980	He fielded like a "Bombo" should, but unfortunately he didn't hit that way, too.
P	Joe Decker	1973–1976	A survey of longtime Twins followers resulted in Decker, who was famous for his lack of control.

It's not really fair to suggest that Harmon Killebrew was born to DH. But while he played 969 games at first base—and was pretty good there—he also played 791 games at third base and 470 games in left field, and was awful in both spots.

So the question, I think, is, "Why didn't the Twins just install Killebrew at the initial sack and leave him there for a dozen or so years?"

Three reasons, but only one of them was good.

The good reason was Don Mincher. He could really hit, but he couldn't play anywhere but first base. So Killebrew had to move.

The bad reasons were Vic Power and Rich Reese.

Power played first base for the Twins in 1962 and '63, and of course he was one of the all-time greats . . . with the glove. But whatever defense Power gave the Twins at first base, Killebrew gave it back in left field. And Power didn't hit much (Mincher was on the roster, and he should have been playing first base if Killebrew wasn't going to).

If Power was a miscalculation, Reese was a disaster. He played well in 1969 to earn the full-time job at first base the following season, but slumped in 1970 and fell off the earth in 1971 and '72. And all the while, he, rather than Killebrew, was playing first base.

You'd have to search far and wide to find a player whose first two seasons were more similar, statistically, than Butch Wynegar.

In 1976, he totaled 534 at-bats and 139 hits; in 1977, he totaled 532 at-bats and 139 hits.

In 1976, he hit twenty-one doubles, two triples, and ten home runs; in 1977, he hit twenty-two doubles, three triples, and ten home runs.

Not too shabby for a kid who turned twenty-one during spring training in '77. After that '77 season—in which he played in his *second* All-Star Game—there wasn't any obvious reason to think that Wynegar wouldn't become a big star, maybe even a superstar.

Wynegar did not become a superstar, nor even a star. He completely stopped hitting in 1978, and didn't get back to where he'd been until 1982, which unfortunately was *after* the Twins had traded him to the Yankees. After a couple of years he stopped hitting for the Yankees, too, and by 1986—he was still only thirty years old—Wynegar was just hanging on, and went on the disabled list that season due to emotional stress.

		YEARS	NOTES
	ALL-BUST		
DH	David Ortiz	1999	He's doing fine now, of course, but spent nearly all of 1999 in the minors because of his poor work habits.
C	Butch Wynegar	1978–1982	Looked like a future superstar his first two years, but injuries and mysteries made him a huge disappointment.
1B	David McCarty	1993–1995	Third overall pick in '91 draft reached majors in just two years, then batted .226 with 3 homers in 167 games.
2B	Todd Walker	1996–2000	Eighth pick in '94 draft blew through minors, but struggled defensively and didn't get along with T.K.
SS	Houston Jimenez	1983–1984	He played in 144 games for the Twins, racking up 384 at-bats and a .195 batting average without a single homer.
3B	Brent Gates	1998–1999	Gates was a nice little player, but why on earth would Tom Kelly let him start 107 games at third base?
LF	Mickey Hatcher	1985–1986	Lousy as part-timer in '81 and '82, earned regular job in '83 '84, then combined for 678 OPS in '85 and '86.
CF	Darrell Brown	1983–1984	He didn't draw walks, or hit for power, or play great defense . . . but he did keep the position warm for Kirby.
RF	Dave Engle	1981–1982	After two seasons and .285 OBP, Twins realized that his "skills" might be more at home behind the plate.
SP	LaTroy Hawkins	1995–1999	Heralded prospect went 26-44 with *6.11 ERA* as starter before Twins finally sent him to the bullpen.
RP	Steve Howe	1985	Still had the amazing left arm, but also still had the coke problem and posted 6.16 ERA before relapse and release.

		YEARS	NOTES
	USED-TO-BE-GREAT		
DH	Paul Molitor	1996–1998	Like Winfield (below), a St. Paul native; came home to finish career and batted .341 with 225 hits in '96.
C	John Roseboro	1968–1969	Three-time All-Star with Dodgers was almost 35 when he joined Twins and didn't have a whole lot left.
1B	Vic Wertz	1963	At 38, onetime Tigers and Indians slugger finished career with .136 average in 35 games, mostly as PH.
2B	Tommy Herr	1988	Batted .250 against Twins in '87 World Series, came over and batted .263 *for* Twins in 86 games in '88.
SS	Chris Speier	1984	Hey, he really *was* great . . . for one season, way back in 1972 when he hit 15 homers and made the All-Star team.
3B	Dave Hollins	1996	He wasn't quite at the end of the line, but his only *great* seasons were with Phillies in 1992 and (especially) '93.
LF	Don Baylor	1987	Never actually played LF in late-season stint; that last happened in '86 when he played 3 games out there.
CF	Darrin Jackson	1997	Yes, we're stretching things quite a bit here . . . but DJ was *good* for the Padres in 1991, when he slugged .497.
RF	Dave Winfield	1993–1994	St. Paul native and Univ. of Minnesota product mostly DH'd with Twins, but did play 32 games in RF.
SP	Steve Carlton	1987–1988	Spent two-plus seasons trying to hang on with five different teams; 1-6 with 8.54 ERA as Twin.
RP	John Candeleria	1990	Onetime star starter for Pirates started just once for Twins; relieved in 33 games, went 7-3 with 3.39 ERA.

MISSING THE OBVIOUS

I have written about Bert Blyleven many times. Too many times, some might say.

But this is my book, and if I want to argue again that Blyleven belongs in the Hall of Fame, there's nobody who can stop me (except my editor, but I'm hoping that he won't).

Actually, I'm *not* going to try to convince you that Bert Blyleven belongs in the Hall of Fame. I *will* try to convince you that Blyleven was a great pitcher, a pitcher every bit as good as Nolan Ryan and Don Sutton, both of whom *are* in the Hall of Fame (oops, there I go again). Here are some basic stats for the three pitchers, along with one that's not so basic.

	Wins	Losses	WinPct	ERA	ERA+
Ryan	324	292	.526	3.19	111
Sutton	324	256	.559	3.26	108
Blyleven	287	250	.534	3.31	118

Ryan and Sutton both won 324 games, Blyleven "only" 287, though it's perhaps worth noting that Blyleven actually finished with a better winning percentage than Ryan. The three pitchers finished with comparable ERAs. But it's the last column to which I'd like to draw your particular attention. "ERA+" is a measure of a pitcher's ERA relative to the league average, *after* adjusting for his home ballparks.

Ryan's 111 ERA+ means, for example, that his 3.19 career ERA was, after making the adjustments, eleven percent better than league average. Similarly, Sutton, who spent the great majority of his career in a pitcher's league (the National) and a pitcher's park (Dodger Stadium), was about eight percent better than league average.

And the best of the group? Bert Blyleven, and it's not really close. He spent most of his career in the American League, and he never benefited from a great pitcher's park, as both Sutton and Ryan (Astrodome) did.

Ah, but Blyleven didn't win 300 games. He pitched for twenty-two seasons, and fell 13 victories short. He won 37 fewer games than both Ryan and Sutton. And as we all know, *the* measure of a starter's effectiveness is not how many runs he allows, but how many games he wins. Some pitchers "know how to win," and some don't, right? And maybe Blyleven just didn't know how to win.

Don't you believe it. Blyleven failed to win 300 games because he was unlucky and because, for most of his career, he didn't pitch for good teams. You don't think that Blyleven would have won 13 more games if he'd been with the Dodgers for sixteen years, as Sutton was? Blyleven pitched for twenty-two years, and only three of his teams reached the postseason. You don't think that a pitcher's team has anything to do with how many games he wins?

Don Sutton was a good pitcher for a long time, and a deserving Hall of Famer. But was he really a better pitcher than Bert Blyleven?

- Blyleven won 20 games once; Don Sutton won 20 games once.
- Blyleven finished in the top 10 in his league in ERA ten times; Sutton did it eight times.
- Blyleven finished in the top five in strikeouts thirteen times; Sutton did it three times.
- Blyleven finished in the top 10 in innings pitched eleven times; Sutton did it ten times.
- Blyleven finished in the top five in shutouts nine times; Sutton did it eight times.
- Blyleven pitched in eight postseason games, and went 5-1 with a 2.47 ERA; Sutton pitched in fifteen postseason games and went 6-4 with a 3.68 ERA.

Sutton's one advantage over Blyleven is the wins and losses, and this can be almost entirely attributed to one thing: Sutton spent most of his career pitching for good teams.

Frankly, this ain't rocket science. Any half-wit baseball writer (i.e. Hall of Fame voter) should be able to understand the difference between the National League and the American League, and the difference between Dodger Stadium and any of the five AL ballparks that Blyleven called home, and the difference between the Dodgers and the Twins. That Sutton's in the Hall of Fame while Blyleven has received little support is a testament to the stubbornness of baseball writers who choose to ignore the obvious.

Let me hasten to add that I absolutely do not mean to diminish the accomplishments of Don Sutton, who was a very good pitcher for a very long time. But where some people look at Bert Blyleven and see a poor man's Don Sutton, I look at Don Sutton and see a poor man's Bert Blyleven.

I'm grateful to John Sickels for his editorial suggestions.

Bert Blyleven in 1975
Minnesota Twins

MONTREAL EXPOS

		YEARS	NOTES
C	Gary Carter	1974–1984 1992	He didn't have a regular job until Dick Williams took over as manager in 1977, and Williams was smart enough to see what he had; it took six years, but he's finally in the Hall.
1B	Andres Galarraga	1985–1991 2002	With all due respect to Galarraga, his presence here says more about the Expos than it does about him; did enjoy a big year in 1988, but slumped badly in 1991.
2B	José Vidro	1997–*2002*	Switch-hitter not considered a great prospect in minors, but after establishing himself in majors, topped .300 with power each season from 1999 through 2002.
SS	Chris Speier	1977–1984	Solid defender and the scrappy sort that managers love; not much of a hitter but one of only four Expos to hit for the cycle (7/20/1978 vs. Braves).
3B	Tim Wallach	1980–1992	Homered in MLB debut, twice led NL in doubles, won three Gold Gloves, and served as team captain for a spell; of his 260 career homers, 204 came with Expos.
LF	Tim Raines	1979–1990 2001	Not that anybody knew it, but from 1984 through '87 Raines was the best player in the National League, and maybe the No. 2 leadoff man of all time.
CF	Andre Dawson	1976–1986	Dawson actually spent more time in center than right, and could do everything but draw a lot of walks; considered one of the game's hardest workers.
RF	Vladimir Guerrero	1996–*2002*	Statistically, through age 26 the players most similar to Guerrero were Willie Mays, Hank Aaron, and Frank Robinson; realistically, Vlad's not quite at their levels.
SP1	Steve Rogers	1973–1985	Montrealer his entire career and tops franchise list with 158 victories; won 3 games in '81 postseason, but lost heartbreaker to Dodgers in NLCS Game 5.
SP2	Dennis Martínez	1986–1993	Due in large part to alcoholism, his career was in the toilet with Orioles, but became a star after joining Expos, and on 7/28/91 he pitched 15th perfect game in MLB history.
SP3	Pedro Martínez	1994–1997	Only four seasons, but he went 55-33 and became the first—and the only, as things will probably turn out—Expo to win Cy Young (though .625 winning pct. pales next to .784 with Sox).
SP4	Bryn Smith	1981–1989	Sinkerballer with great control won 81 games, third-best on franchise list; went 18-5 in 1985, and Expos went 23-9 in his 32 starts.
RP	Jeff Reardon	1981–1986	Retired as all-time saves leader with 367, and 152 of them came with Expos; like most closers, relied on the fastball and whatever breaking pitch was working that day.

As I write this in April of 2002, the amazing Tim Raines is still playing in the major leagues, at forty-two years old. If this is Raines's last season, he'll be eligible for the Hall of Fame in 2007 ... and if he draws more than a nibble from the voters, I'll be shocked.

And that's a shame, because in six years Raines might be *the* best player not in the Hall of Fame (aside from Charlie Hustle and Shoeless Joe). He was, for a span of five seasons beginning in 1983, the most valuable player in the National League, among the five or six best players in the league in *each* of those seasons. Raines fell off some after that—he was never again anything like an MVP candidate—but he was very good for another seven or eight seasons.

Why doesn't anybody appreciate Raines? Two reasons. The first is walks, the second is Rickey Henderson. Raines posted a high batting average in a few seasons, but he drew walks in nearly *every* season. In eleven seasons as a regular, he drew at least seventy walks in ten of them. Even in the 1980s, most people realized that walks were good for a leadoff man, and Raines might have been the second-greatest leadoff man of all time ... but of course, the greatest was Rickey Henderson, Raines's exact contemporary. And so when people think of leadoff men, Raines is forgotten.

I've often described Greg Maddux as The Smartest Pitcher on Earth. However, Mike Marshall just might be The Smartest Man Who Pitched.

I won't try to explain the distinction, because then you'd realize that I'm just making this up as I go along. So, onward . . .

For a long time, pitchers threw two kinds of fastballs, which could basically be described as sinking and non-sinking. And it's likely that pitchers have been throwing the cut fastball for a long time, too, even if the term is fairly new. So that's three kinds of fastballs.

Well, Dr. Mike Marshall teaches his students *five* fastballs: "four seam Maxline Fastball, two seam Maxline Fastball, two seam Maxline Fastball with Maxline Sinker spin axis, four seam Torque Fastball and two seam Torque Fastball."

But wait, we're just getting started. Marshall also teaches his pitchers five types of breaking balls . . . and six types of *reverse* breaking balls. What's the difference between a breaking ball and a reverse breaking ball? "Breaking balls come off the inside of the tip of the pitcher's middle finger. Reverse breaking balls come off the outside of the tip of the pitcher's middle finger."

There's *much more* at Dr. Marshall's web site— drmikemarshall.com—which I highly recommend if you're interested in Marshall specifically or pitching generally.

NO. 2			
		YEARS	NOTES
C	Darrin Fletcher	1992–1997	Came over in great trade for Expos—Barry Jones to Phillies for Fletcher *and* cash—capping career in Montreal with 17 HR and .513 slugging pct. in 1997.
1B	Ron Fairly	1969–1974	After slumping terribly with Dodgers, added instant credibility in Expos' first season after arriving in deal involving Maury Wills; never great, but always good.
2B	Delino DeShields	1990–1993	Had some holes in his game—or rather, his glove—but you have to like a second baseman with a .360 OBP who swipes 45 or 50 bags every season.
SS	Spike Owen	1989–1992	He hardly ever struck out, wasn't ashamed about taking walks, and in 1990 set MLB record for shortstop with 63 errorless games to open season.
3B	Larry Parrish	1974–1980	Signed as undrafted free agent in 1972, and three years later was starting at third base; twice hit 3 homers in a game, but put everything together only in 1979.
LF	Moises Alou	1990–1996	Reached majors briefly in 1990, then missed all of '91 with shoulder injury before returning in '92 to play under father Felipe; batted .339 with 22 homers in 1994.
CF	Marquis Grissom	1989–1994	From 1991 through '93, was NL's biggest stolen-base threat, swiping 207 while being caught only 40 times; also the era's greatest defensive outfielder in prime.
RF	Larry Walker	1989–1994	More than anybody else, Walker symbolized the inability of ownership to keep the team together, as B.C. native signed with Rockies after batting .322 in '94.
SP1	Charlie Lea	1980–1984 1987	His peak was short but sweet: from 1982 through '84, Lea went 43-31 with 3.07 ERA; relied on throwing his curve at variety of speeds.
SP2	Javier Vazquez	1998–2002	According to Expos media guide, his repertoire consists of *rapide, courbe, glissante, et changement de vitesse*; in other words, fastball, curve, slider, and change-up.
SP3	Bill Gullickson	1979–1985	In 1980, set rookie strikeout record (since broken by Kerry Wood) with 18 K's against Cubs; his 72 wins with Expos makes him fourth on the list.
SP4	Steve Renko	1969–1976	Aside from a disastrous 1972 (1-10, 5.20) and an outstanding 1973 (15-11, 2.81), the ex-Jayhawk's time in Montreal distinguished mostly by his consistency.
RP	Mike Marshall	1970–1973	Liberated from Brewers during 1970 season, Marshall brought his screwball out of mothballs and pitched 416 innings, all in relief, from 1971 through '73.

		SINGLE SEASON	
		YEARS	**NOTES**
C	Gary Carter	1982	Not easy to pick just one, as he played brilliantly in four other seasons before going to Mets; 29 homers and great defense.
1B	Al Oliver	1982	A professional hitter's greatest season as a hitter; led NL with 204 hits, 43 doubles, 109 RBI, and .331 batting average.
2B	Mike Lansing	1997	Career highs with 45 doubles and 20 homers, and on May 7 became second NL 2B to homer twice in same inning.
SS	Orlando Cabrera	2001	And it's not even close. Cabrera played brilliant defense at shortstop—uncommon for Expos—and also slugged .428.
3B	Tim Wallach	1987	Early injury to Hubie Brooks forced Wallach into cleanup slot and he responded with 26 HR, NL-best 42 doubles, 123 RBI.
LF	Tim Raines	1985	Played in career-high 160 games, tied for 2nd in NL with .320 average, and ranked 2nd with 70 steals and 115 runs.
CF	Andre Dawson	1981	In short season, hit 24 HR, started All-Star Game, won his second Gold Glove, and runner-up to Schmidt in MVP vote.
RF	Vladimir Guerrero	Pick	It's just about impossible to choose between *four* of Guerrero's five full seasons; in 2002, he finished one homer shy of joining 40/40 club.
SP	Pedro Martínez	1997	After three solid seasons with Expos, broke through with 1.90 ERA to win Cy Young honors in last season with club.
RP	Mike Marshall	1973	Led league with 31 saves and *92 relief appearances*, and also won 14 games and pitched 179 innings.

		ALL-ROOKIE	
		YEARS	**NOTES**
C	Gary Carter	1975	Gene Mauch didn't think Carter could catch, so he played more right field than anything else; made All-Star team.
1B	Brad Fullmer	1998	There's not much competition and he did hit 44 doubles; two years later, he turned some of the doubles into homers.
2B	Delino DeShields	1990	Finished second in RoY vote behind Dave Justice, and just the 11th player in MLB history to open career with 4-hit game.
SS	Wil Cordero	1993	First Expo SS with 10 homers and 10 steals in same season, and made the All-Star team as sophomore in '94.
3B	Coco Laboy	1969	In first shot in majors, turned 30 shortly before All-Star Game and played 157 games, led club with 83 RBI.
LF	Tim Raines	1981	In truncated season, speedster led National League with 71 steals (in only 88 games) and ranked fifth with .394 OBP.
CF	Andre Dawson	1977	In the first season of baseball in Olympic Stadium, Dawson promised great things with his Rookie of the Year campaign.
RF	Moises Alou	1992	Actually played mostly in left, but did play 15 games in RF and batted .282 with 39 extra-base hits in 341 at-bats.
SP	Carl Morton	1970	Went 18-11 with a 3.60 ERA and captured Rookie of the Year honors; dropped to 10-18, 4.80 in 1971.
RP	Tim Burke	1985	As Jeff Reardon's setup man, employed sinker/slider combo on way to 9 wins and 2.39 ERA over 78 games and 120 innings.

I wouldn't want to do this too often, but I just have to bring to your attention how similar Tim Raines's 1985 and 1986 seasons were.

In 1985, Raines played 150 games; in 1986, 151 games.

In 1985, Raines rapped fifty-four extra-base hits; in 1986, fifty-four extra-base hits.

In 1985, Raines drew eighty-one walks and struck out sixty times; in 1986, seventy-eight walks and sixty strikeouts.

In 1985, Raines stole seventy bases and was caught nine times; in 1986, seventy steals and nine caught.

In 1985, Raines posted a .475 slugging percentage; in 1986, a .476 slugging percentage.

The only obvious differences between the two seasons were contextual. In 1985, Raines batted leadoff all season, so he scored 115 runs and drove in only forty-one; in 1986, he spent half the season batting third and scored "only" ninety-one runs but drove in sixty-two.

As you can see, choosing between these two seasons is close to impossible, but in the final analysis I chose 1985 because 1986 was a slightly better year for hitters around the majors. I could certainly see it the other way, though, because Raines hit significantly better in clutch situations in '86.

Randy Johnson *and* Pedro Martínez got away from the Expos. That's something. Johnson was still raw, but Martínez had already established himself as one of the game's best pitchers.

Most everybody knows that Pedro—who ranks just behind Johnson on the Traded Away team—was lost because the Expos didn't want to pay him the going rate for a brilliant starting pitcher with a few years of experience. Faced with losing him to free agency, Montreal sent Martínez to Boston in exchange for two fine pitching prospects, Tony Armas and Carl Pavano.

But what not everybody knows is that Pedro Martínez became an Expo in the first place because ownership didn't want to pay Delino DeShields the going rate for a top-flight second baseman with a few years of experience. Of course now it looks like one of the great steals of the century—or it would if the Expos had held on to Pedro for a few more years—but at the time, many were amazed that the Expos would trade one of the league's best second basemen for a rail-thin pitcher with exactly two major-league starts and ten major-league victories to his credit.

It's a shame when teams have to trade good players because they can't afford them. But if you know what you're doing, it doesn't have to be the end of the world.

HOMEGROWN			
		YEARS	NOTES
C	Gary Carter	1974–1984 1992	Could've played football at UCLA, but third-round pick in '72 draft signed with Spos five days after graduation.
1B	Andres Galarraga	1985–1991 2002	Signed out of Venezuela on Felipe Alou's advice, spent nearly seven full seasons in minor leagues.
2B	Tony Phillips	—	Drafted in 1978, spent two seasons in system before getting traded to Padres, who traded him to A's.
SS	Orlando Cabrera	1997–*2002*	Probably a bit of a stretch, but it's just hard to get excited about Mark Grudzielanek; native of Colombia.
3B	Tim Wallach	1980–1992	10th player selected in '79 June draft, spent just two seasons in minors and homered in first MLB at-bat.
LF	Tim Raines	1979–1990 2001, 2002	Two-sport star at Florida's Seminole High, fifth-round pick in '77 and Minor League Player of the Year in '81.
CF	Andre Dawson	1976–1986	Eleventh-round pick signed for $2,500, zipped through minors with .343 batting average and 41 HR in two years.
RF	Vladimir Guerrero	1996–*2002*	Followed his big (age, not size) brother Wilton from the Dominican Republic to the major leagues.
SP	Randy Johnson	1988–1989	Second-round draft pick out of USC in 1995, started only 10 games for Expos before ill-advised trade to M's.
RP	Ugueth Urbina	1995–2001	Venezuelan signed with Expos when he was 16, pitched well as starter before going to pen for good late in 1996.

TRADED AWAY			
		TRADED	NOTES
C	Gary Carter	December 10, 1984	Sent to Mets for four players . . . and it would have been a bad deal for Expos even if they'd gotten eight.
1B	Andre Thornton	December 10, 1976	Off to Cleveland for Jackie Brown; Expos, almost never strong at 1B, sure could have used him in '79.
2B	Delino DeShields	November 19, 1993	Great move for Expos, as they got Pedro Martinez *and* DeShields had already played his best ball.
SS	Mark Grudzielanek	July 31, 1998	Deadline deal sent Grudz and Carlos Perez to Dodgers for quartet of prospects including Ted Lilly.
3B	Tim Wallach	December 24, 1992	Traded to Dodgers after a couple of lousy years, but he eventually got it together and played well in 1994.
LF	Matt Stairs	June 8, 1993	Batted .333 with Harrisburg in 1991, but two years later Expos sold him to Chunichi Dragons.
CF	Marquis Grissom	April 6, 1995	Basically a salary dump, with Grissom going to Braves for Roberto Kelly, Tony Tarasco, and Esteban Yan.
RF	Ken Singleton	December 4, 1974	Part of a horrible deal that netted the Expos three players who never did anything for the franchise.
SP	Randy Johnson	May 25, 1989	The worst kind of deal: trading a future great to bolster roster for pennant run that's ultimately unsuccessful.
RP	John Wetteland	April 5, 1995	In deal concocted by two teams' owners, Wetteland *given* to Yankees for Grade C prospect and $1 million.

GOLD GLOVE

		YEARS	NOTES
C	Gary Carter	1974–1984 1992	Won three Gold Gloves and deserved them, amazing for a guy once considered a liability behind the plate.
1B	David Segui	1995–1997	Statistics good but not great; few of his peers looked more graceful making whatever throw necessary.
2B	Mike Lansing	1993–1997	One of the top two or three glove men in the league before congenital back problem got serious.
SS	Bobby Wine	1969–1972	There wasn't a better defensive SS in the league, but by then he just couldn't hit enough to hold the job.
3B	Tim Wallach	1980–1992	In 1992, manager Tom Runnels's ill-considered move to shift Wallach to 1B helped get him fired; 3 Gold Gloves.
LF	Rondell White	1993–2000	Played more in center, but did spend the better parts of '99 and 2000 in left, where his speed served him well.
CF	Marquis Grissom	1989–1994	Truly brilliant defender who won two Gold Gloves as Expo but should have won more.
RF	Larry Walker	1989–1994	Great instincts, fantastic arm, range of a center fielder . . . he just may have been one of the greatest ever.
P	Bill Lee	1979–1982	He always said that he liked ground balls because they're more democratic, and he was expert at fielding them.

IRON GLOVE

		YEARS	NOTES
C	Ron Brand	1969–1971	Well, if nothing else he had guts; at 5-7, one of the shortest everyday catchers in the 20th century.
1B	Brad Fullmer	1997–1999	One of the worst in history; Expos traded him to Ontario, where he played his natural position: DH.
2B	José Vidro	1997–2002	His bat could certainly carry his glove, but Vidro's going to end up in the outfield, and sooner than you think.
SS	Hubie Brooks	1984–1987	Wil Cordero (1992–1995) also a fine candidate, as his throwing problems forced him to the outfield in '95.
3B	Bob Bailey	1970–1974	Nicknamed "Beetle" because he fielded like a comic-strip character, and Bailey himself said, "I play hitter."
LF	Mack Jones Henry Rodriguez	1969–1971 1995–1997	Dead heat between these two, with Bob Bailey (1974) just good enough to avoid appearing here twice.
CF	Jerry White	1974–1978 1979–1983	Nominally the regular in 1976, but better suited to left field, which is why he's listed here.
RF	Vladimir Guerrero	1996–*2002*	Great athlete with plenty of range, but sloppy work on grounders and erratic throws led to far too many errors.
P	Jeff Juden	1996–1997	An Expos fan reports, "Juden was very awkward and couldn't find his ass with both hands and a map."

Larry Walker was a great right fielder. But at Dodger Stadium on April 24, 1994, Walker suffered one of the most embarrassing games that any right fielder's ever suffered.

It started in the bottom of the first. Dodgers center fielder Brett Butler doubled to right field. Walker fielded the ball on the warning track, turned to throw . . . at which point the ball slipped out of his hand, bounced off his shoulder and fell to the ground at his feet. Butler trotted to third base.

Things got worse—or at least funnier—in the third inning. With José Offerman on first base, Mike Piazza lifted a fly ball into foul territory down the right-field line. Walker made a running catch, and handed the ball to 11-year-old Sebastian Napier.

You see it every day on TV . . . except as Walker trotted toward his dugout, he saw Offerman speeding around second base—and realized that his catch was just the second out of the inning. He ran back to Napier, retrieved the ball and threw it back to the infield, by which time Offerman was standing on third base.

Walker was charged with errors on both plays, but the Expos lost 7–1 and all seven runs were earned. So Walker could laugh about it, saying after the game, "I saw a little kid sitting there and I tried to be Mr. Nice Guy, but I turned into Mr. Foolish."

In his book, Expos manager Dick Williams wrote, "Ellis Valentine was an extraordinary baseball player who became a thief. He stole from his own ability because of his lack of motivation and his unreliability. And he stole from his heart. Stole from his teammates' trust. Stole from everything important to him until he no longer had anything when he needed it. Like that great arm, that splendid bat, that will to win."

You read things like this—and I found many similar quotes—and you think that Valentine had plenty of talent but didn't do much with it. That's not really true, though. Maybe he should have been better, but he was damn good. When he was twenty-two he played in the All-Star Game; he hit twenty-five home runs that season (1977) and the next. After a moderate dropoff in 1979, Valentine played brilliantly in 1980 despite missing nearly half the year with injuries. It's been written that Valentine was "never the same" after getting beaned by Roy Thomas in May of '80, but that's not true; he actually hit better *after* coming back in July than he had before the beaning. It wasn't until 1981 that Valentine stopped hitting, for reasons that remain a mystery.

		YEARS	NOTES
ALL-BUST			
C	Tim Laker	1992–1993 1995	Came accompanied by huge expectations, but never did much of anything with the bat or the glove or the arm.
1B	Dan Driessen	1985	Played well after coming over in '84, but mysteriously lost his power in '85.
2B	Bret Barberie	1991–1992	Played well in minors and hit .353 in 57 games as rookie, but power disappeared in '92 and he was off to Marlins.
SS	Angel Salazar	1983–1984	Considered a fine defender, but batted *.166* with zero homers and 5 walks in 116 games and got cut loose.
3B	Shane Andrews	1995–1999	First-round pick was essentially handed job, but posted .294 OBP (albeit with some power) over five seasons.
LF	Rondell White	1993–2000	A fine player, of course, but could have been so much finer if he'd been able to stay in the lineup.
CF	Peter Bergeron	1999–*2002*	Still might save his career, but after two-plus seasons this once-promising prospect sported .305 career OBP.
RF	Ellis Valentine	1975–1981	"One wonders about talent like Ellis. There are those with far less talent doing much better."—Tim McCarver
SP	Dave McNally	1975	Acquired in deal that cost club Ken Singleton and Mike Torrez; retired after one poor year to test reserve clause.
RP	Graeme Lloyd	2000–2002	Jeffrey Loria just *had* to pay millions to a lefty setup man . . . then again, Loria *had* to do a lot of stupid shit.

		YEARS	NOTES
USED-TO-BE-GREAT			
C	Gary Carter	1992	After seven seasons and three teams, "Kid" returned to where it all began and batted .218 in 95 games.
1B	Pete Rose	1984	Oddly enough, ex-Reds Tony Perez and Dan Driessen both spent at least a season playing 1B for Expos, too.
2B	Dave Cash	1977–1979	All-Star in three previous seasons with Phillies, but never sniffed such status while toiling in Quebec.
SS	U L Washington	1985	Onetime Royal speedster stole only 6 bases in 68 games, but hit well enough to get a shot with the Pirates in '86.
3B	Graig Nettles	1988	He was 43 but the Expos signed him as a pinch hitter anyway; batted .172 with one homer in 80 games.
LF	Ron LeFlore	1980	Best years came in Detroit, but ex-con's one season in Montreal included NL-best 97 steals.
CF	Willie Davis	1974	Cost Expos Mike Marshall, and annoyed front office with continual demands for salary advances and loans.
RF	Felipe Alou	1973	Close to the end, played 19 games, batted .208 and hit 1 homer for the team he'd manage 20 years later.
SP	Dave McNally	1975	After seven straight solid (or better) seasons with O's, joined Expos and went 3-6 in injury-marred campaign.
RP	Lee Smith	1997	Hulking power pitcher saved five games in his final season, bringing total to MLB-record 478 saves.

ALL-NAME			
		YEARS	NOTES
C	"Kid" Gary Carter	1974–1984 1992	Mike Torrez started calling him "Kid" when he was 19, and they were still calling him "Kid" when he was 38.
1B	"Big Cat" Andres Galarraga	1985–1991 2002	Call him "the lesser Big Cat," because Johnny Mize—the first Big Cat—was better with both the glove and the bat.
2B	"Cool Breeze" Rodney Scott	1976 1979–1982	Got this from John Mayberry during his brief stint with the Royals, for his steady demeanor. As Scott later said, "I stay cool."
SS	"Spike" Spike Owen	1989–1992	No kidding, that really was his name: Spike Dee Owen, and fortunately it seemed to suit him.
3B	"Coco" José Alberto Laboy	1969–1973	What is it about "Coco" that people love so much? Absent it, nobody would remember the club's first third baseman.
LF	"Oh Henry!" Henry Rodriguez	1995–1997	After three-plus years of failing with Dodgers, came to Montreal and became a big star, if only briefly.
CF	"Games" Milton Bradley	2000–2001	I may actually have invented this one, but if I didn't, somebody else would, right?
RF	"Le Grande Orange" Rusty Staub	1969–1971	"Rusty" was a nickname, too, of course; and without it, he'd never have this more memorable moniker.
SP	"Skuz" Ross Grimsley	1978–1980	Would go for months with the same sweatshirt, and days without combing his hair or using deodorant.
RP	"Frenchy" Claude Raymond	1969–1971	Name may look pedestrian, but *Claude Raymond* was first French-Canadian to play for Expos.

TOP FIVE SEASONS	
YEAR 1981	**RECORD** 60-48
BEST HITTER	Andre Dawson
BEST PITCHERS	Steve Rogers, Scott Sanderson
NOTES	Lost NLCS to Dodgers in a heartbreaker.
YEAR 1979	**RECORD** 95-65
BEST HITTERS	Larry Parrish, Gary Carter
BEST PITCHERS	Bill Lee, Steve Rogers
NOTES	First season better than .500, and with apparent ease.
YEAR 1994	**RECORD** 74-40
BEST HITTERS	Moises Alou, Larry Walker
BEST PITCHERS	Ken Hill, John Wetteland
NOTES	On track for their best season ever, but labor war intervened.
YEAR 1980	**RECORD** 90-72
BEST HITTERS	Gary Carter, Andre Dawson
BEST PITCHER	Steve Rogers
NOTES	Eliminated from pennant race on season's last Saturday.
YEAR 2002	**RECORD** 83-79
BEST HITTERS	Vladimir Guerrero, Jose Vidro
BEST PITCHER	Javier Vazquez
NOTES	Supposedly on brink of extirpation, Expos played surprisingly well.

TOP FIVE MANAGERS	
MANAGER	Dick Williams
YEARS	1977–1981
RECORD	380-347 (.523)
NOTES	Brought them from respectable to contention.
MANAGER	Felipe Alou
YEARS	1992–2001
RECORD	691-717 (.491)
NOTES	Apathetic about plate discipline, but otherwise solid.
MANAGER	Gene Mauch
YEARS	1969–1975
RECORD	499-627 (.443)
NOTES	Expos horrible in '69, but respectable thereafter.
MANAGER	Buck Rodgers
YEARS	1985–1991
RECORD	520-499 (.510)
NOTES	Topped .500 in five of six full seasons.
MANAGER	Frank Robinson
YEAR	2002
RECORD	83-79 (.512)
NOTES	Returned to bench after decade away.

Claude Raymond—and when you pronounce his name, please try to sound like you took a semester of French in high school—is one of only three French Canadians to play for the Expos.

Raymond did his best work pitching out of the Houston bullpen in the mid-1960s. He posted a 2.98 ERA in three-plus seasons with the Colt .45's and Astros, and made the All-Star team in 1966 (but didn't pitch in the game). Raymond pitched well for the Braves in 1967 and '68, but got off to a rough start in 1969. The Expos, who were in their first season and certainly didn't have anything to lose, picked up the thirty-two-year-old right-hander on August 19. He pitched well enough the rest of that season, then came back in 1970 to record twenty-three saves, fourth most in the National League.

"Frenchy" was awful in 1971, dropped off the radar screen in 1972, but returned in 1973 as an analyst for the Expos' radio broadcasts. He switched over to TV in 1985, and held the job through the 2001 season. In 2002, after more than three decades out of uniform, Raymond was hired by the newly MLB-owned Expos as a "roving coach" (whatever that is).

The other French Canadians to play for the Expos were also pitchers: Denis Boucher (3-2, 3.83 ERA in 1993 and '94) and Derek Aucoin (two brief appearances in 1996).

PUTTING THE KID WHERE HE BELONGS

It's conceivable that by the time you read this, Gary Carter will already have been voted into the Hall of Fame. Unlikely. But conceivable. On the other hand, it's damn near inconceivable that he's not *already* in the Hall of Fame, given that he's been eligible for enshrinement since 1998.

For the most part, Hall of Fame arguments don't interest me all that much. Everybody's got his (or her) own pet candidate, and good luck trying to convince him (or her) that his (or her) favorite doesn't belong. The problem, of course, is that most fans don't really give a tinker's damn about the Hall of Fame as an *institution;* most fans care about the Hall of Fame merely as validation of their own biased evaluations of their favorite players.

Not to sound cynical or anything. But people get emotional about it, and it's very difficult to win hearts and minds when people are that emotional. That's why I don't spend a lot of time writing about the Hall of Fame. In this book, however, I've made two significant exceptions, because there are two omissions so obvious that they damage the *institution*.

Of course, I'm referring to Bert Blyleven and Gary Carter. I already wrote about Blyleven (page 137), and now I'm going to write about Carter.

I'll start with the end of the argument, because I know how it goes: Gary Carter is one of the ten greatest catchers in major-league history. And any player among the top ten at his position belongs, by almost anybody's definition, in the Hall of Fame.

Are we sure that Carter's in the top ten? Well, there are currently thirteen catchers in the Hall of Fame. One of them, Josh Gibson, played in the Negro Leagues. Another, Buck Ewing, played in the nineteenth century and caught only 636 games in his career.

That leaves eleven, including Roger Bresnahan, Rick Ferrell, Ernie Lombardi, and Ray Schalk. With all due respect to the memories of those men, none of them were great players. Bresnahan was probably the best, considering he played in the Dead Ball Era, when hits were hard to come by and catchers took a beating. Lombardi was an excellent hitter who couldn't really run or catch, and Ferrell and Schalk might charitably be described as "idiosyncratic" choices for the Hall.

That leaves seven: Johnny Bench, Yogi Berra, Mickey Cochrane, Roy Campanella, Carlton Fisk, Bill Dickey, and Gabby Hartnett. You want to argue that all seven of those guys are better than Carter? I got no problem with that. Even if Carter's only the eighth-best twentieth-century catcher eligible for the Hall of Fame, isn't that enough?

But you still haven't proved he's the eighth best! What about other catchers who are NOT in the Hall? Good point . . . but you'll have one hell of a time demonstrating that any of those other guys were *better* than Carter.

Ted Simmons? Great player, but not as good as Carter, and he hasn't received any Hall of Fame support at all.

Joe Torre? Again, great player. But of his twelve good seasons, only five came as a full-time catcher. I'm not even sure why he's considered a catcher in these discussions, as he played four hundred games more at other positions than he did as a catcher.

Bill Freehan? Thurman Munson? Elston Howard? Good players, but none of these men have received significant Hall of Fame consideration. Nor should they, save perhaps Freehan.

You still haven't proved anything. Are we just supposed to take your word for it, that Carter is really better than those guys? No, you're not supposed to take my word for it. Carter hit 324 home runs. Despite playing most of his career in pitcher's parks, his career on-base percentage (.335) and slugging percentage (.439) are both very comparable to Fisk's. He won three Gold Gloves, played in ten All-Star Games, and finished in the top six in MVP balloting four times. In thirty postseason games, he knocked in twenty-one runs.

I could go on, but do I really have to? There they are: Bert Blyleven and Gary Carter. If you care, *really care*, for the Hall of Fame as an institution, then instead of constructing intricate arguments for Dale Murphy or Jim Rice or Thurman Munson or Luis Tiant or Gil Hodges, you'll do whatever you can to get Blyleven and Carter elected. Because friends, when it comes to players from the 1970s and '80s, the line forms directly behind those guys. And it ain't much of a Hall of Fame without them.

POSTSCRIPT: Just before this book went to press, Gary Carter was elected to the National Baseball Hall of Fame. Praise be the BBWAA.

I'm grateful to Chuck Rosciam and especially Scott Lemieux for their editorial suggestions.

Gary Carter
National Baseball Library, Cooperstown, New York

The story of Dwight Gooden is often used as a cautionary tale: "You see, son? That's what happens if you take drugs."

What happened to Dwight Gooden is that he won 155 games before his twenty-ninth birthday, and only 39 games after. Most people figure that if only Doc could have stayed away from the blow, today he'd be working on his Hall of Fame induction speech.

Cocaine's obviously a horrible thing, but I don't think it does a great job of explaining Gooden's career. Yeah, he missed the first two months of the 1987 season after failing a drug test . . . and then he went 15-7 with a 3.21 ERA after returning to the rotation. In 1988, Gooden pitched in the All-Star Game and finished the season with eighteen wins and a 3.19 ERA. In 1989, he was 9-4 with a 2.89 ERA when he went on the DL in July with a shoulder injury.

And *that* was the turning point in Gooden's career. He was only twenty-four years old, but he was never the same pitcher again. Actually, there are three phases to Gooden's career. When he was nineteen and twenty, he was the best pitcher in the world (and was shamelessly overworked, as great young pitchers usually are). From twenty-one through twenty-four he was a very good pitcher. And after he turned twenty-five, Dwight Gooden was just another pitcher.

		ALL-TIME	
		YEARS	NOTES
C	Mike Piazza	1998–*2002*	Truth be told, he was slightly past his prime with the Mets . . . but the best-hitting catcher in MLB history still had plenty left for the Flushing fans.
1B	Keith Hernandez	1983–1989	Wasn't a regular after turning 33, but by then had more hits than six members of the 3,000-hit club had at same age, and was within striking distance of four others.
2B	Edgardo Alfonzo	1995–2002	From Ken Boswell to Wally Backman, the Mets have traditionally preferred bats to gloves at second; after shifting to the keystone in 1999, Alfonzo hit 85 homers in four seasons.
SS	Bud Harrelson	1965–1977	Not a lot of competition at short, with slick-fielding Harrelson the only Met shortstop ever named to an All-Star team; bonus points for starting a fight with Pete Rose.
3B	Howard Johnson	1985–1993	From the left side, Howard Johnson destroyed fastballs; Todd Worrell tried to disprove that basic truth, and gave up 4 homers in 11 at-bats to HoJo.
LF	Kevin McReynolds	1987–1991 1994	A very good player who was criticized for not being great; sports-talk radio flourished in NYC because of the number of callers who wanted to bust on him.
CF	Lee Mazzilli	1976–1981	When your team stinks, moments like Maz's '79 All-Star Game homer off Guidry matter a lot; the Mets parlayed him into Ron Darling and Howard Johnson.
RF	Darryl Strawberry	1983–1990	Aaron, Mays, McGwire, and Jackson all hit between 40 and 45 percent of their career homers before they were 30; Darryl? 84 percent. Phenomenal bat speed.
SP1	Tom Seaver	1967–1977 1983	His arrival was Mets' first leap toward legitimacy, and his departure in '77 triggered ice age that lasted until Davey arrived; record 16 opening-day starts in career.
SP2	Dwight Gooden	1984–1994	Gooden and Strawberry are forever linked for not having HoF careers, but the glass-half-full argument sees 343 homers, 194 wins, and six rings between them.
SP3	Jerry Koosman	1968–1978	Won 20 in '76, then lost 20 in '77 (even though his ERA was a quarter of a run below the NL average); five top-10 finishes among NL ERA leaders.
SP4	Al Leiter	1998–*2002*	When he came to the Mets, he was 32 and sported a 60-53 record; in five seasons since, he's 70-50 and clearly one of the game's best lefties.
RP	John Franco	1990–*2002*	New Yorker held up his end of the bargain, it wasn't his fault the Mets sank shortly after his arrival; his 268 saves in the 1990s ranked sixth in the majors.

		YEARS	NOTES
		NO. 2	
C	Gary Carter	1985–1989	If his peak years had come in New York rather than Montreal, his Cooperstown ticket would have been punched much faster; played brilliantly in '86 World Series.
1B	John Olerud	1997–1999	When adjusted for the era, his hitting stats are quite comparable to Hernandez's, but he wasn't in New York as long, nor was he Mex's equal with the glove.
2B	Ron Hunt	1963–1966	First Met to start an All-Star Game (1964) and it happened at Shea Stadium; as a Met, not yet into the freaky HBP thing, "only" 41 plunks in four seasons.
SS	Kevin Elster	1986–1992	Unspectacular but had a great glove and occasional power; Davey thought enough of Elster to put him on postseason roster in '86 despite only 30 career at-bats.
3B	Robin Ventura	1999–2001	Solid all-around player enjoyed the best year of his career in '99 before injuries plagued him for two years; struggled in postseason, batting just .161 in 87 at-bats.
LF	Cleon Jones	1963–1975	In his time, the poster child for enigmatic players, was key hitter on '69 team but didn't homer after August 10, then went 0-for-10 with runners on base during Series.
CF	Tommie Agee	1968–1972	Chunky, but an outstanding defensive center fielder who, just one year removed from a .217 campaign, led Mets in RBI in 1969 despite batting leadoff.
RF	Rusty Staub	1972–1975 1981–1985	Until 1985, he was the *only* Met to drive in 100 runs in a season; traded to Tigers after '75 season for Mickey Lolich, who was both overweight and over the hill.
SP1	David Cone	1987–1992	Went 80-48 for Mets and was involved in two great trades: Mets got him for Ed Hearn, and later they sent him to Toronto for Jeff Kent.
SP2	Jon Matlack	1971–1977	Rookie of the Year in '71 barely cleared .500 (82-81) as Met despite 3.03 ERA, second-best in franchise history; of those 82 wins, 26 were shutouts.
SP3	Sid Fernandez	1984–1993	Big guy with baffling delivery and great K rate had huge home-road splits with the Mets: 58-31 with 2.52 ERA at Shea, 40-47 and 3.81 everywhere else.
SP4	Rick Reed	1997–2001	Mets were his fifth organization and he had to spend a full season in Triple-A, but at 31 proved that he was a quality major-league starter.
RP	Jesse Orosco	1979–1987	Cost Mets Jerry Koosman, but he gave them 107 saves and 47 wins; brilliant in '86 postseason with *three* wins in NLCS and two saves in World Series, including Game 7.

Sid Fernandez was weird, mostly in a good way.

He didn't look anything like a baseball player; he looked like a pear with a cherry on top. He didn't throw particularly hard; he topped out at around ninety miles per hour with his fastball. He didn't get ground balls; in one unique 1988 game, he pitched an entire game in which not a single Mets fielder recorded an assist.

And you couldn't hit Sid Fernandez, at least not very often. From 1988 through 1990, El Sid gave up 6.4 hits per nine innings, and *nobody*—not Nolan Ryan or Roger Clemens or David Cone or Dave Stieb—gave up fewer. From 1988 through 1990, Fernandez struck out 8.7 batters per nine innings; only Ryan and Clemens did better. And while the rap on Fernandez was that he walked too many hitters, his control really wasn't bad. He walked fewer hitters per nine innings than Ryan, and he also walked fewer hitters than José Rijo and Mark Langston (two other high-strikeout, low-hit pitchers).

How did he do it? He was something called "sneaky fast," but that's understating the point because Fernandez may have been the all-time sneakiest fast. The way he threw, the ball just seemed to materialize out of his jersey, and the hitters had a devil of a time finding it in time to hit it.

When Opening Day of the 1973 season dawned, the Mets starting rotation included two former Rookies of the Year in Tom Seaver (1967) and Jon Matlack (1972), and one near Rookie of the Year in Jerry Koosman (finished second to Johnny Bench in 1968).

And none of them disappointed. Seaver posted a league-best 2.08 ERA to earn his second Cy Young Award. Koosman posted a 2.84 ERA, and Matlack posted a 3.20 ERA. And for good measure, George Stone, coming off a miserable season with the Braves, started 20 games and posted a 2.80 ERA.

Problem was, the Mets' fourth-best hitter wasn't nearly as good as the Mets' fourth-best pitcher. Rusty Staub led the Mets with a .361 OBP, John Milner led the Mets with a .432 slugging percentage, and as a team the Mets ranked last in the National League in slugging percentage and next-to-last in runs scored. Yes, Shea Stadium was a pitcher's park, but it wasn't *that* much of a pitcher's park. And yes, the Mets did win a division title and they did nearly win the World Series. But they're one of the worst teams to accomplish either feat, and it only happened because no other team in the East was able to win more than half its games.

		YEARS	NOTES
SINGLE SEASON			
C	Mike Piazza	2000	Why does this guy never get any MVP support? Did play just 136 games in 2000, but also hit 38 homers and slugged .614.
1B	Keith Hernandez	1984	You could make a great case for Olerud in '98, but Mex gets the nod because of his considerable leadership talents.
2B	Edgardo Alfonzo	2000	Both this *and* his 1999 campaign rank higher than those from any other Mets second baseman: great bat, good glove.
SS	Bud Harrelson	1971	Historically, the Mets' weakest position, and Harrelson's best really wasn't all that great; did win his only Gold Glove.
3B	Howard Johnson	1989	Best OPS of his career, stole 41 bases in 49 attempts, and deserved better than fifth place in MVP vote.
LF	Cleon Jones	1969	NLCS heroics push him just a shade past Kevin McReynolds (1988) and Bernard Gilkey (1996).
CF	Lee Mazzilli	1979	At 24, looked like New York's next big star, but '79 marked his best season and only All-Star appearance.
RF	Darryl Strawberry	1988	Second in MVP vote; four first-place votes to teammate Kevin McReynolds may have swung award to Kirk Gibson.
SP	Dwight Gooden	1985	Never quite the same, but did win 153 games *after* his amazing '85: 24-4, 268 K's, *1.53* ERA; Seaver owns next three spots.
RP	Jesse Orosco	1983	One of the greatest relief seasons ever, as Orosco posted 1.47 ERA while pitching 110 innings; won 13 games and saved 17.

		YEARS	NOTES
ALL-ROOKIE			
C	Mike Fitzgerald	1984	Good defensive catcher who handled the young staff and played well enough for the Expos to want him.
1B	Rico Brogna	1994	Only 39 games, but he batted .351 and the Mets have never had a rookie turn in a good, full season at first base.
2B	Ron Hunt	1963	Might have beat Pete Rose out for Rookie of the Year, but played on a bad team and lacked the catchy nickname.
SS	Kevin Elster	1988	Terrible hitter as rookie, but he gave the Mets outstanding defense they'd not seen since Bud Harrelson.
3B	Gregg Jefferies	1988 1989	Actually finished in top six in Rookie of the Year vote in both seasons, placing sixth in 1988 and third in '89.
LF	Steve Henderson	1977	Easily the best player Mets got for Seaver; lost Rookie of the Year to Dawson by just one first-place vote.
CF	Jay Payton	2000	Eleven Mets got RoY votes in 1980s, while just four got them in 1990s; kind of explains what happened to franchise.
RF	Darryl Strawberry	1983	N.Y. media badgered club into promoting him all spring; came up May 6 and was Rookie of the Year in a landslide.
SP	Jerry Koosman	1968	Posted 2.08 ERA over 263 innings and won 19 games for a team that lost 89 games and finished ninth.
RP	Roger McDowell	1985	Beats out Jeff Reardon in 1980 because he earned more saves (17–6) in more innings (127–110), and pitched for contender.

HOMEGROWN

		YEARS	NOTES
C	Todd Hundley	1990–1998	Career trajectory with Mets: overmatched, dangerous, hurt, Piazza, gone.
1B	Ed Kranepool	1962–1979	Career Met debuted at 17 and wound up playing for legendary managers Stengel, Hodges, Berra, and Torre.
2B	Edgardo Alfonzo	1995–*2002*	Venezuelan sidetracked by injuries for two years after shining in minors; brother Roberto a Mets farmhand.
SS	Bud Harrelson	1965–1977	Ordoñez won more Gold Gloves (3–1), but Bud was around longer and played in more All-Star Games (2–0).
3B	Hubie Brooks	1980–1984	Third overall pick in '78; rare baseball player to earn a college degree (health science, Arizona State).
LF	Kevin Mitchell	1986	Played four positions—including *shortstop* 24 times—and slugged .466 in '86; signed as nondrafted free agent!
CF	Amos Otis	1967, 1969	In his very first season after leaving Mets, earned All-Star berth and led American League with 36 doubles.
RF	Ken Singleton	1970–1971	Mets' first-round pick in '67 draft; didn't have the raw ability of Strawberry, but did have the better career.
SP	Tom Seaver	1967–1977 1983	The Mets didn't actually draft Seaver; they won a lottery after he'd been illegally signed by the Braves.
RP	Jeff Reardon	1979–1981	Close call between him and Rick Aguilera; the pair combined for 685 saves . . . 668 after leaving Mets.

TRADED AWAY

		TRADED	NOTES
C	Todd Hundley	December 1, 1998	Just two years after hitting 41 homers, traded to L.A. for Charles Johnson and Roger Cedeño.
1B	Rico Brogna	November 27, 1996	Traded to Phillies for pitchers Ricardo Jordan and Toby Borland, who combined for 1 win for Mets.
2B	Jeff Kent	July 29, 1996	Not as bad as trading Ryan, but Kent and Vizcaíno to Indians for Baerga and Espinoza not exactly a gem.
SS	Tim Foli	April 5, 1972	Sent to Expos in Rusty Staub deal; reacquired in 1977 and then traded once more in '79.
3B	Robin Ventura	December 7, 2001	After nearly forty seasons, the Mets finally traded a third baseman who did something afterward.
LF	Kevin Mitchell	December 11, 1986	Part of eight-player deal with Padres that essentially became Mitchell for Kevin McReynolds.
CF	Amos Otis	December 3, 1969	Joe Foy Joe Foy Joe Foy Joe Foy Joe Foy Joe Foy Joe Foy Joe Foy Joe Foy Joe Foy Joe Foy Joe Foy
RF	Ken Singleton	April 5, 1972	Another piece of deal for Staub; Mets outfield in late '70s could/should have been Singleton-Otis-Mazzilli.
SP	Nolan Ryan	December 10, 1971	True, the Mets had a surplus of great young arms . . . but for Jim Fregosi? The Common Wisdom is right.
RP	Jeff Reardon	May 29, 1981	He and Dan Norman to Expos for Ellis Valentine, who in '82 drew 5 walks in 111 games and was gone.

In 1966, the first year of the amateur draft, teams could draft college players after their sophomore seasons, and Reggie Jackson had just finished up a brilliant sophomore season at Arizona State. The Mets, having finished with the worst record in the majors in 1965, had the first pick in the draft. According to Jackson, Bobby Winkles (his baseball coach at ASU, and future coach and manager in Oakland) told him, "The Mets have the first pick, and there's no question in my mind that you should be the first pick. But I don't think they're going to take you."

"Why not?" Jackson asked.

"They're concerned you have a white girlfriend."

Jackson's future wife, Jennie Campos, was light-skinned. But her parents were Mexican, and Reggie—who himself boasted Spanish, Indian, and Irish heritage—didn't consider Jennie white. And even if she were "white" (whatever the hell that means), so what?

Draft day came, and the Mets took a catcher named Steve Chilcott, who never reached the majors. The Kansas City A's had the second pick and chose Reggie, who did reach the majors, and would eventually have his revenge. In 1973, Jackson's team beat the Mets in the World Series. And from 1977 through 1981, when Reggie's Yankees were routinely winning division titles, the Mets were finishing in last place more often than not.

Rey Ordoñez was born with a Gold Glove on his hand.

Or at least it seemed that way to most Americans, who never got a chance to see Ordoñez refining his defensive skills while he was growing up in Cuba.

But in 1993, Ordoñez defected, and after a short stint in the Northern League, the Mets won a lottery held to divvy up the rights to negotiate with Cuban defectors. After two full seasons in the minors, Ordoñez took over as the Mets' everyday shortstop in 1996. And from the day he arrived in the majors, Rey Ordoñez was a sensation, thanks mostly to ESPN. He had this move . . . a ball in the hole, he'd sprint over to make the play, stop himself by jamming his right knee into the ground, then pop up and make the peg to first. It looked great, of course, but the unorthodox technique was more than just flash; it allowed Ordoñez to get something extra on the throw, and quite often something extra makes the difference between a 6-3 and a base hit.

He couldn't hit, for most of his career he was older than we thought, and he was *not* the second coming of Ozzie Smith with the glove. But he *was* an outstanding fielder, one of the two or three best defensive shortstops in the game most years.

GOLD GLOVE			
		YEARS	NOTES
C	Jerry Grote	1966–1976	Played a key role in developing the great young starters; Charlie O'Brien would be No. 1 if he'd played more.
1B	Keith Hernandez	1983–1989	Begged enemy hitters to bunt, captained the infield, and certainly one of the greatest defensive first sackers ever.
2B	Brian Giles	1981–1983	Truly an outstanding defensive player, but couldn't hit at all and Davey wanted some offense from the position.
SS	Rey Ordoñez	1996–2002	The highlights are better than the numbers, but he's still excellent enough to rate ahead of Harrelson and Elster.
3B	Robin Ventura	1999–2001	So *that's* what a major-league third baseman looks like; great at starting around-the-horn double plays.
LF	Bernard Gilkey	1996–1998	Not as fast as he'd been with Cardinals, but still had speed and instincts, *Men in Black* notwithstanding.
CF	Tommie Agee	1968–1972	His time as a great defensive CF for Mets was brief, but he won a Gold Glove and probably deserved three.
RF	Ron Swoboda	1965–1970	It's not been a great spot for the Mets, but Swoboda was pretty good . . . and there *was* that big catch in the Series.
P	Ron Darling	1983–1991	Tremendous athlete, deadly accurate on throws to bases, and one of the best righty moves to first base in game.

IRON GLOVE			
		YEARS	NOTES
C	Mackey Sasser	1988–1992	His defense was poor *before* he became unable to throw the ball to the pitcher; just edges Choo Choo Coleman.
1B	Dave Kingman	1982	Played for a long time, but '82 was his only season as an everyday first baseman, and it got really ugly over there.
2B	Gregg Jefferies	1987–1991	How bad was he at second? By 24 he was at third base, and at 25 he discovered his natural position: first base.
SS	Frank Taveras	1979–1981	Not bad in '79—he came from Pirates in challenge trade for Tim Foli—but had no range at all the next two years.
3B	Howard Johnson	1985–1991 1993	Might have actually been better at shortstop than third, where concentration lapses resulted in a ton of errors.
LF	Frank Thomas	1962–1964	Once a fairly decent outfielder, but by '62 he was near the end of the line and couldn't really run at all.
CF	Howard Johnson	1992	After years of shaky work at short and third, Mets tried Hojo in center for 84 games; disaster of biblical scale.
RF	Al Luplow	1966–1967	Luplow is probably the least deserving of anybody here, but both he and Rusty Staub were liabilities in the field.
P	Glendon Rusch	1999–2001	Unsure of himself throwing to the bases, and not much of a pickoff move for a lefty.

ALL-BUST			
		YEARS	**NOTES**
C	Steve Chilcott	—	First overall pick in 1966 draft—just ahead of Reggie Jackson—but never played a game in the majors.
1B	Dave Kingman	1981–1983	Despite leading the NL in homers in '82, Kingman was dreadful in this, his second, go-round as Met.
2B	Carlos Baerga	1996–1998	Slugged just .373 as a Met, off nearly 150 points from his best in Cleveland; cost Mets Jeff Kent.
SS	Rey Ordoñez	1996–2002	We don't have a Ridiculously Over-Hyped Team, so instead we'll wedge Rey in here.
3B	Joe Foy / Jim Fregosi	1970 / 1972–1973	They only cost Mets Amos Otis and Nolan Ryan, giving new meaning to "F-word" around Shea.
LF	Vince Coleman	1991–1993	Supposed to make the faithful forget about Straw, which worked about as well as you'd think.
CF	Juan Samuel	1989	Trading Dykstra and McDowell for Samuel was the biggest personnel mistake the post-'86 Mets made.
RF	Ellis Valentine	1981–1982	Supposed to be a poor man's Dave Parker, but it turned out he was a poor man's Ollie Brown.
SP	The Class of '95	—	Wilson, Isringhausen, and Pulsipher were declared the second coming of Seaver, Ryan, and Koosman.
RP	Neil Allen	1979–1983	Never really had a closer's temperament, but at least he was useful as trade bait to get Keith Hernandez.

USED-TO-BE-GREAT			
		YEARS	**NOTES**
C	Yogi Berra	1965	The least funny thing Yogi ever said or did may have been playing 4 games for the Mets while a coach.
1B	Eddie Murray	1992–1993	Looked sleepy during his tenure in Shea, but did have the last 100-RBI season of his career in '93.
2B	Carlos Baerga	1996–1998	Supposed to be another steal like Hernandez, but he didn't hit and cost Jeff Kent rather than Neil Allen.
SS	Garry Templeton	1991	Career that started with such promise 15 years earlier ended with a thud, as he batted empty .228 in 80 games.
3B	Ken Boyer	1966–1967	A virtual dead heat with Joe Torre; both came to Mets a few years removed from MVP seasons with Cardinals.
LF	Rickey Henderson	1999–2000	He played like he was 30 in 1999, and like he was 50 in 2000 before going to Seattle and perking back up.
CF	Willie Mays	1972–1973	Hit a decisive homer in his first game as Met, and played well in '72 before collapsing the next season.
RF	Duke Snider	1963	Beats out Richie Ashburn, another once-great center fielder whose slower self played right field for the Mets.
SP	Warren Spahn	1965	Started 20 games and won 4 of them; famously said, "I played for Casey before and after he was a genius."
RP	Mike Marshall	1981	Of the two washed-up ex-Dodgers named Mike Marshall to play for Mets, he was the better.

Bill James ranks Willie Mays as the greatest center fielder in history, Duke Snider the sixth greatest, and Richie Ashburn the sixteenth greatest. All three, of course, spent time with the Mets at or (in the case of Snider) near the end of their careers. But while Snider and Ashburn were acquired, as much as anything, to add a veneer of old-style National League respectability to an infant franchise, Mays was obtained from the Giants in May of 1972 because he could still *play*.

The Mets just weren't scoring enough runs, and in 1971, though by then he was forty years old, Mays had led the National League with a .425 OBP. And in '72, after a slow start with San Francisco, he posted a .402 OBP in sixty-nine games with the Mets. It wasn't until 1973, when he was forty-two, that Mays fell apart at the plate.

Mays still worked hard, too. Tom Seaver wrote, "One thing that surprised me when he joined the Mets was how well thought-out his defensive play was . . . He'd come up to me with a list before a game I was pitching and ask me how I was going to pitch to each batter . . . I'd tell him in detail and he'd decide just what to do with each player in each circumstance . . . And if I looked around during the game, there he was, just where he said he'd be."

Hall of Famer Casey Stengel doesn't make this list of top five Mets managers. After all, Stengel's Mets won only thirty percent of their games before he was forced to retire after breaking his hip late in the evening of July 24, 1965.

All that's a matter of public record. What's funny, though, is that most of the things people *say* about Stengel aren't really true.

For example, it's routinely said that Stengel gave the Mets instant credibility, and that all by himself he brought fans to the Polo Grounds. However, the Mets did *not* draw particularly well in 1962. The Mets drew slightly more than 900,000 fans in 1962, seventh in the National League, which wasn't that good considering the size of the market (granted, by then the Polo Grounds weren't exactly a garden spot). Attendance didn't take off until 1964, Stengel's third season but Shea Stadium's first.

It's also said that Stengel was, by the time he managed the Mets, little more than a clown who frequently napped on the bench. I'm not so sure about that one, either. Robert Lipsyte covered the Mets for the *Times* that first spring, and he later remembered, "So there was a lot of hanging out with Stengel, and the one thing that happens when you hang out long enough with Stengel, you realize that he makes absolute sense."

ALL-NAME			
		YEARS	NOTES
U	"World" Kevin Mitchell	1986	Before he became a sluggardly slugger, Mets called him "World" because he could play any position.
C	"Choo Choo" Clarence Coleman	1962–1963 1966	Origins of his nickname are murky, and supposedly unknown even to Coleman himself.
1B	"Marvelous Marv" Marv Throneberry	1962–1963	Willingly became head clown for the worst team of the 20th century, and the fans loved him for it.
2B	"Hot Rod" Rod Kanehl	1962–1964	Stuck with Mets because Casey recalled him as old Yankee farmhand; in '62, did everything but pitch and catch.
SS	"Bud" Derrel Harrelson	1965–1977	His brother couldn't say "Derrel," so Derrel became "Bubba" and, eventually, "Bud."
3B	"Hojo" Howard Johnson	1985–1993	Listed here because Harry Caray said "Howard Hojo Johnson" many times during each Mets-Cubs game.
LF	"Sleepy Kevin" Kevin McReynolds	1988–1991 1994	Appears in print for the first time here; invented by Mets fan Jim Baker, because McReynolds looked that way.
CF	"Mookie" William Wilson	1980–1989	There's just something about "Mookie" . . . Letterman used to say "Mookie" all the time, for no reason at all.
RF	"Rocky" Ron Swoboda	1965–1970	Okay, so it ain't much, but Swoboda did make the great catch in the '69 Series. And it's better than "Straw."
SP	"Tom Terrific" Tom Seaver	1967–1977	Invented by New York sportswriters in 1969, while Seaver was winning first of three Cy Young Awards.
RP	"Tug" Frank McGraw, Jr.	1965–1974	According to 1970 *Baseball Register*, "Named by parents because he tugged on so many things as a baby."

TOP FIVE SEASONS	
YEAR	1969 RECORD 100-62
BEST HITTERS	Cleon Jones, Tommie Agee
BEST PITCHER	Tom Seaver
NOTES	By historical standards, their rise to top was speedy.
YEAR	1986 RECORD 108-54
BEST HITTER	Keith Hernandez
BEST PITCHER	Bob Ojeda
NOTES	Thank you, John McNamara and Bill Buckner.
YEAR	2000 RECORD 94-68
BEST HITTER	Edgardo Alfonzo
BEST PITCHER	Mike Hampton
NOTES	Disappointing finish to a wonderful season.
YEAR	1988 RECORD 100-60
BEST HITTER	Darryl Strawberry
BEST PITCHER	David Cone
NOTES	An early end to what should have been a dynasty.
YEAR	1973 RECORD 82-79
BEST HITTER	Rusty Staub
BEST PITCHER	Tom Seaver
NOTES	No, they weren't great . . . but they nearly won it all.

TOP FIVE MANAGERS	
MANAGER	Davey Johnson
YEARS	1984–1990
RECORD	595-417 (.588)
NOTES	Virtually overnight, turned a bad team into a good one.
MANAGER	Bobby Valentine
YEARS	1996–2002
RECORD	536-467 (.534)
NOTES	Sometimes a little too smart for his own good.
MANAGER	Gil Hodges
YEARS	1968–1971
RECORD	339-309 (.523)
NOTES	Quiet? Yes, but not afraid to let players know he was boss.
MANAGER	Yogi Berra
YEARS	1972–1975
RECORD	292-296 (.497)
NOTES	Probably should have succeeded Stengel in 1965.
MANAGER	Bud Harrelson
YEARS	1990–1991
RECORD	145-129 (.529)
NOTES	Mostly remembered for slagging Gooden's arm.

THE LOST GENERATION

Working on this book, there's one theme that keeps jumping out at me: *Bad things happen to good young pitchers*. And perhaps the best example is the Mets' so-called Generation K: Jason Isringhausen, Bill Pulsipher, and Paul Wilson.

Both Isringhausen and Pulsipher were dominant in the minors, and then both pitched well for the major-league Mets in 1995, after which the authors of *The Scouting Report: 1996* remarked, "Isringhausen began 1995 in Double-A. Now he's a staff ace in the big leagues . . . The Mets must watch his arm, though, as Jason has pitched 418 innings over the past two seasons."

Same book on Pulsipher: "Pulsipher had an uncomfortable September, when he was affected by a sprained elbow ligament. With the Mets out of the race, Bill sat out after September 11, but is reported to have fully recovered without any surgery . . . Bill will be just twenty-two this season and should continue to improve if he doesn't abuse his arm. Like Jason Isringhausen, he has had two straight years of over 200 innings at a tender age."

How does a professional pitcher abuse his own arm? I mean, I can certainly imagine how a *manager* might abuse a pitcher's arm, but I'm not sure how a pitcher himself would. Anyway, to these two impressive fellows the Mets would, in 1996, add the most impressive fellow of all, a twenty-three-year-old right-hander named Paul Wilson, who complemented his overpowering, mid-nineties fastball with a sharp slider. In '95, Wilson was the Pitcher of the Year in the Class AA Eastern League . . . and then he posted a 2.85 ERA in ten Triple-A starts. He struck out 194 hapless hitters in 187 minor-league innings while issuing only forty-four walks. John Sickels put Wilson on the cover of the *1996 Minor League Scouting Notebook*, and rated Wilson the game's No. 2 minor-league prospect (behind Johnny Damon).

So, heading into the '96 season the Mets had two kid pitchers who had pitched effectively in the majors, and another who ranked as *the* top pitching prospect in the minors.

And in 1996, the three of them combined for eleven wins, twenty-six losses, and a lovely 5.05 ERA. It often takes time for young pitchers to establish themselves, of course . . . but 1996 was as good as it got.

Isringhausen's ERA jumped to 4.77 in '96 as he suffered from a pulled rib-cage muscle, bone spurs in his elbow, and finally (and most seriously) a torn labrum. Two 130-plus pitch outings might (or might not have) played a part in Izzy's woes. Early in 1997, he suffered a broken wrist, and wound up missing most of the season. And then in January of 1998, Isringhausen underwent reconstructive surgery on his right elbow and spent the entire season recovering.

Pulsipher had pitched 201 minor-league innings in 1994, then 218 innings combined in Triple-A and the majors in 1995. In 1996, his ERA jumped to . . . actually, it dropped all the way to nothing, because Pulsipher didn't pitch even a single inning, due to a torn elbow ligament. He missed most of 1997, too, and then spent half of 1998 in the minors. And after getting traded to the Brewers, he spent half of 1999 on the DL with a lower back strain. The Brewers traded Pulsipher back to the Mets before the 2000 season, in which he spent a couple of weeks on the DL with the Mets, then another month on the DL (another back strain) after getting traded to the Diamondbacks.

Wilson, the crown jewel, had pitched 187 minor-league innings in 1995. Then, according to plan, he joined the big club's rotation at the beginning of the 1996 season. Wilson struggled, went on the DL with shoulder tendinitis in June, and came back with a 2-7 record in the second half of the season . . . after which he was diagnosed with a torn labrum that of course required surgery. In 1997, Wilson pitched 26 innings, all in the minors. In 1998, Wilson pitched 57 innings, all in the minors. In 1999, Wilson pitched precisely zero innings anywhere.

There were many, many people who thought that Isringhausen, Pulsipher, and Wilson could, and perhaps would, return the Mets to their mid-1980s glory. After 1995, Generation K combined for 14 wins, 33 losses, and a 5.54 ERA with the Metropolitans. Not exactly what anybody in Flushing had in mind.

Something good, however slight, did come out of all this. Dallas Green, who managed the Mets when Generation K arrived in the major leagues, showed a cavalier disregard for the fragility of young pitchers' arms. He made no bones about it. But when all three phenoms essentially had their careers destroyed—only Isringhausen eventually made it back to the majors and became a star, and that as a relief pitcher—it opened a lot of eyes, even among grizzled old baseball men who would much rather have remained blind.

I'm grateful to Geoff Reiss, who contributed many of the player comments in this chapter, the sources for which included Peter Golenbock's Amazin' *(St. Martin's Press, 2002) and Tom Seaver's* How I Would Pitch to Babe Ruth *(Playboy Press, 1974).*

**Left to right:
Bill Pulsipher, Paul
Wilson, and Jason
Isringhausen. Before
their arms fell off.**
Tom DiPace Photography

NEW YORK YANKEES

		YEARS	NOTES
			ALL-TIME
DH	Don Baylor	1983–1985	Baylor's the only Yankee to hold the job for more than a couple of years; batting average dropped each season, but he compensated by leaning into every inside pitch.
C	Yogi Berra	1946–1963	It's a shame that he's mostly remembered for what he said, rather than for how brilliantly he hit and caught, because he was one of the two or three greatest ever.
1B	Lou Gehrig	1923–1939	Not just the best first baseman in Yankee history, but the best first baseman in *baseball* history, and there's nobody currently active who's going to challenge him.
2B	Tony Lazzeri	1926–1937	First homer-hitting second baseman in the American League; best season was 1929, when Yankees did *not* win pennant. *Just* edges Willie Randolph here.
SS	Derek Jeter	1995–*2002*	Overrated with the glove, but his only competition here is the Scooter, and Jeter blows him away with the bat; Jeter, of course, made a lot of big plays in big games.
3B	Graig Nettles	1973–1983	A very good player, but underrated because of low batting average; power, walks, and great defense, and he was still playing every day when he was 42.
LF	Charlie Keller	1939–1943 1945–1952	Played like a Hall of Famer until he was 29, at which point back problems reduced him to part-time duty; spent all of 1944 and most of '45 in the service.
CF	Mickey Mantle	1951–1968	Oddly enough, often remembered for what he *wasn't* rather than for what he *was:* at his best, more valuable than any player in history, excepting Ruth and Bonds.
RF	Babe Ruth	1920–1934	List of his records may be getting smaller every year, but Babe still the greatest ballplayer who ever lived; played nearly as many games in left field as right.
SP1	Whitey Ford	1950 1953–1964	Went 9-1 as rookie in 1950, then spent two years in army; .690 career winning pct. is best of 20th century . . . and Stengel supposedly saved him for the good teams.
SP2	Red Ruffing	1930–1942 1945–1946	As Yankee, he won 231 and lost only 124 (.651), and was one of the great-hitting pitchers; drafted when he was 38, or the raw numbers would be even better.
SP3	Ron Guidry	1975–1988	Short and thin, but threw hard with a great slider; according to Bill Deane's research, Guidry was 84-26 under Billy Martin, 86-65 under other managers.
SP4	Lefty Gomez	1930–1942	Had a great fastball and twice led American League in wins and ERA, in 1934 and '37; remembered for his wit, but a marginal Hall of Famer.
RP	Mariano Rivera	1995–*2002*	Struggled as rookie starter, but among the elite relievers ever since; cut fastball practically unhittable, and he was nearly perfect in postseason until 2001 World Series.

Baseball's Greatest Lineups, published in 1952, ranked Joe DiMaggio as the fourth-greatest outfielder in history, behind only Cobb, Ruth, and Speaker. No mention of Mickey Mantle, but that was understandable considering that Mantle was then still a freckle-faced kid in his second season with the Yankees.

But twenty-five years later in *Sport Magazine's All-Time All Stars,* with the leagues split, there's still no sign of Mantle. Ruth's been moved to DH, Ted Williams has replaced Tris Speaker, but the other two AL slots are filled by DiMaggio and Cobb.

Neither Joe DiMaggio nor Mickey Mantle has played a game since then, but one thing has changed: we've gotten a little bit smarter, smart enough to understand just how great Mantle was. And he was, it turns out, greater than DiMaggio.

According to *Total Baseball,* DiMaggio's career OPS was fifty-six percent better than league average, after adjusting for his home ballpark. That's outstanding. But Mantle's OPS was *73 percent* better than league average, fifth-best of all time. DiMaggio may have been the best player in the American League four times, but Mantle may have been the best player in the American League *eight* times. At their best, Mantle was a little better than DiMaggio because he walked more often. And Mantle had more seasons at his best.

Allie Reynolds and Ed Lopat were joined in the pitching rotation, from 1948 through 1953, by Vic Raschi, and the trio became known as the Big Three. Over those six seasons, the Big Three combined for 307 wins and 143 losses, which works out to a .682 winning percentage. None of the three had a losing record even once in those six seasons, nor did any of them post an ERA higher than the American League average even once.

Granted, Yankee Stadium was one of the better pitcher's parks in the league, but even if you adjust for that, each of the Big Three was still better than average every year. They were so good that occasionally someone will argue that the Big Three should be elected to the Hall of Fame en masse, just like Tinker and Evers and Chance.

As great as Reynolds and Lopat and Raschi were, that overstates the case a bit. They *were* great, but it's hard to argue that any one of them was ever the best pitcher in the league, even for a single season. And once they were gone the Yankees didn't miss a beat. With Raschi gone in 1954, the Yanks won 103 games. And with Reynolds and Lopat gone in 1955, the Yanks won 96 games and yet another pennant.

		YEARS	NOTES
		NO. 2	
DH	Danny Tartabull	1992–1995	Signed to play RF, but the Yankees quickly realized his best spot was the batter's box, and so for two years he gave them solid production at DH; 845 OPS as Yank.
C	Bill Dickey	1928–1943 1946	Legitimately a *great* player from 1936 through '39, and a very good one the rest of the time; not as great as Berra, but he did teach Berra how to catch and throw.
1B	Don Mattingly	1982–1995	Great player for six years, before the back problems set in; 145 RBI and MVP Award in 1985, and he was just as good, RBI notwithstanding, in '84 and '86.
2B	Willie Randolph	1976–1988	Swiped from the Pirates in a brilliant deal for Yanks, gave them good defense, solid on-base skills, and speed; *just* edges Joe Gordon here.
SS	Phil Rizzuto	1941–1942 1946–1956	It's fashionable to downgrade Rizzuto, but he *was* an outstanding shortstop and he *did* miss three war years; had to wait forever to get into the Hall of Fame.
3B	Red Rolfe	1934–1942	Got a late start and an early finish, but he scored a ton of runs, got the job done at third base, and played every day for five World Series winners.
LF	Roy White	1965–1979	Brilliant all-around player, with only weakness a poor throwing arm; like Joe Cunningham and Cal Ripken, never could settle on one batting stance.
CF	Joe DiMaggio	1936–1942 1946–1951	What can you say that hasn't already been said? Is DiMaggio at least a bit overrated in some quarters? Yup. Was he a fantastic player? Better believe it.
RF	Reggie Jackson	1977–1981	In his thirties when he got to New York, but still had plenty in the tank and led AL with 41 homers in 1980; he and Billy Martin were the "Odd Couple" of the 1970s.
SP1	Allie Reynolds	1947–1954	Probably Casey Stengel's favorite pitcher, went 131-60 with Yankees, but served also as Casey's top relief ace so he didn't pile up a lot of starts or victories.
SP2	Eddie Lopat	1948–1955	"Steady Eddie" went 113-59 with Yankees; started as power pitcher with ChiSox, but in his prime he threw screwball and everything else but the kitchen sink.
SP3	Bob Shawkey	1915–1927	Won 168 games for Yanks, nearly half of them before they started winning pennants; relying mostly on two different curveballs, never really had a bad year.
SP4	Mel Stottlemyre	1964–1974	If he hadn't arrived in '64, would have accomplished the near-impossible: a decade with Yanks without reaching World Series; 35 or more starts 9 straight years.
RP	Goose Gossage	1978–1983	He's perhaps the greatest relief pitcher ever and he enjoyed his prime with the Yankees . . . but he was there for only six years, and so can't rate above Rivera.

		SINGLE SEASON	
		YEARS	**NOTES**
DH	Don Baylor	1983	Batted .303, hit 21 homers and knocked in 85 runs, and the big guy even stole 17 bases.
C	Yogi Berra	1954	Took his second (of three) MVP Awards even though the Yankees did *not* win a sixth straight pennant.
1B	Lou Gehrig	1927	Overshadowed by Ruth, but Gehrig slugged career-high .765 and topped AL with 52 doubles and 175 RBI.
2B	Joe Gordon	1942	Just edges Lazzeri (1929) and Willie Randolph (1980), but "Flash" only Yankee keystoner to win MVP Award.
SS	Phil Rizzuto	1950	Really did deserve his MVP; set career highs in virtually everything *and* played great defense for pennant winners.
3B	Red Rolfe	1939	In Yankees' greatest season, Rolfe led AL with 213 hits, 46 doubles, 139 runs, and played well with the glove, too.
LF	Babe Ruth	1921	Among the greatest seasons ever, along with Ruth's 1920 (below) and '23; topped AL in everything worth topping.
CF	Mickey Mantle	1956	It's not easy choosing among the Mick's best, but '56 included career highs in hits (188) and slugging pct. (.705).
RF	Babe Ruth	1920	His first season with the Yankees and his first as a full-time outfielder; hit 54 home runs, more than all but one *team*.
SP	Jack Chesbro	1904	Won 41 games (against 12 losses), most for any major-league pitcher since 1892; completed 48 of 51 starts.
RP	Joe Page	1949	Won 13 games and saved 27 more, with high heat and the occasional spitter; pitched horribly forever after.

		ALL-ROOKIE	
		YEARS	**NOTES**
DH	Kevin Maas	1990	Hit 10 HR in his first 77 at-bats, fastest ever, and finished with 21 HR in 254 at-bats; hit 44 homers the rest of his career.
C	Thurman Munson	1970	At 23, batted .302 with walks and mid-range power, and was named Rookie of the Year in a landslide.
1B	Lou Gehrig	1925	After cups of coffee in 1923 and '24, broke through with 20 homers; just edges Wally Pipp (his predecessor, of course).
2B	Tony Lazzeri	1926	At the conclusion of which, he just missed hitting a World Series–winning grand slam off Pete Alexander.
SS	Tom Tresh	1962	Shifted to the outfield in '63, was a near-star for five years, then dropped out of the majors before he turned 30.
3B	Billy Johnson	1943	Rewarded after solid rookie campaign with a draft notice, and didn't play again until the summer of '46.
LF	Joe DiMaggio	1936	The Yanks added Joe and advanced to Series for the first time since 1932; and yes, he played more LF than CF in '36.
CF	Earle Combs	1925	Purchased from Louisville for $50,000 and two players, speedy Combs stepped right into the lineup and produced.
RF	Bob Meusel	1920	Played 45 games at third base and a few games in left, too; later famous for his throwing arm; slugged .517 as rookie.
SP	Russ Ford	1910	Went 26-6 with a 1.65 ERA thanks largely to his "emery ball," a pitch that he supposedly invented.
RP	Wilcy Moore	1927	Did start 12 games, but rookie 30-year-old sinkerballer also led AL with 13 saves *and* 13 relief victories.

In 1910, Russ Ford was a rookie sensation, finishing second in the league with 26 wins and posting a 1.65 ERA. In 1911, Ford's victories dropped from 26 to 22 and his ERA rose from 1.65 to 2.27, but those apparent drop-offs were entirely attributable to things beyond his control.

Ford was famous for his spitballs, which did things that nobody had ever seen spitballs do. And for good reason, as Ford didn't actually throw a lot of spitballs, which were legal. His baffling pitches, everyone learned in 1913, were actually "emery balls."

In a 1935 interview published in *The Sporting News*, Ford finally revealed the long-held secrets of the emery ball. He'd "invented" the pitch in 1908. While he was warming up, a pitch got away from him and ricocheted off a wood beam, which scuffed the leather on the ball. The next time Ford threw, the ball broke crazily, and he quickly realized it was the scuff that caused the break. Eventually he started carrying a piece of emery paper to the mound with him, and a star was born. The star didn't shine for long, though. The combination of a sore arm and a new rule banning the emery ball ended Ford's career not long after it began, and he won only 51 major-league games—including 26 in the Federal League—after those first two seasons.

About a year after the Yankees traded Willie McGee for Bob Sykes, they traded outfielder Dave Collins, pitcher Mike Morgan, and minor-league first baseman Fred McGriff to the Blue Jays for reliever Dale Murray and minor-league pitcher Tom Dodd.

Murray had the virtue of being thirty-two years old, which at that point was something like a prerequisite if you wanted to play for the Yankees. He lasted two-plus seasons in New York and was out of the majors by 1985. Dodd never made it.

Collins gave the Jays a couple of good seasons, then moved on and played for four other teams. But here's the damning thing: as I write this, more than eighteen years after the trade, *Mike Morgan and Fred McGriff are still playing.*

Morgan never became a star, but the peripatetic right-hander did win 132 games (through 2002) after leaving the Yankees. McGriff, barely nineteen when the Yankees traded him, had just led the Gulf Coast League in homers, RBI, and walks. He reached the majors in 1986 and hasn't stopped hitting since. Yes, the Yankees had Mattingly at first base in the late 1980s, but at that point their DH slot was being filled by overpaid has-beens. Losing Fred McGriff didn't cost the Yankees any pennants, but it was symptomatic of the idiocy that resulted in a fourteen-year gap between postseason appearances.

HOMEGROWN			
		YEARS	NOTES
DH	Ron Blomberg	1969 1971–1976	The very first DH and a fine hitter for the few years he was healthy, though he couldn't hit left-handers at all.
C	Yogi Berra	1946–1963	Signed for $500 bonus, the same as his neighborhood pal Joey Garagiola got from the Cardinals.
1B	Lou Gehrig	1923–1939	Signed out of Columbia by scout Paul Krichell for $2,000 in his first pro season and $1,500 bonus.
2B	Joe Gordon	1938–1943 1946	Univ. of Oregon product starred in multiple sports and played violin before signing after his sophomore year.
SS	Derek Jeter	1995–*2002*	Sixth overall pick in 1992 draft; in '96 was first rookie to start at shortstop for Yanks on Opening Day since 1962.
3B	Red Rolfe	1934–1942	Only great Yankee third baseman who started with the club; signed after earning English degree at Dartmouth.
LF	Roy White	1965–1979	Signed out of Compton High in L.A., where he played with Reggie Smith, Don Wilson, Bobby Tolan, others.
CF	Mickey Mantle	1951–1968	Tom Greenwade signed Mantle for $1,100 and a paltry minor-league salary . . . Ain't scouts great?
RF	Charlie Keller	1939–1943 1945–1952	Krichell took care of the college kids, and so he inked University of Maryland product Keller to Yanks deal.
SP	Whitey Ford	1950 1953–1964	Yankees signed him for $7,000 after a "bidding war" in which the Red Sox offered $5,000, the Giants $6,000.
RP	Mariano Rivera	1995–*2002*	A Panama native so not subject to draft, and signed as free agent in 1990, a week after his seventeenth birthday.

TRADED AWAY			
		TRADED	NOTES
DH	Cliff Johnson	June 15, 1979	Sent to Tribe for Don Hood, who did pitch well; Johnson, though, still had a few years of heavy hitting in him.
C	Muddy Ruel	December 15, 1920	Yanks gave up Ruel and Del Pratt, but got Waite Hoyt and Wally Schang from the Red Sox.
1B	Fred McGriff	December 9, 1982	McGriff, Dave Collins, Mike Morgan, *and* cash to Jays for Tom Dodd and Dale Murray . . . jeepers creepers.
2B	Jerry Lumpe	May 26, 1959	After three part-time seasons with Yanks, played every day at 2B for seven seasons with A's and Tigers.
SS	Greg Gagne	April 10, 1982	Yankees gave up a couple of pitchers *and* Gagne for Roy Smalley, who lasted a bit more than two years in NYC.
3B	Mike Lowell	February 1, 1999	Signing Brosius and (eventually) trading Lowell worked in '98, but since then it's only hurt the Yanks.
LF	Lefty O'Doul	July 23, 1922	Still a pitcher in 1922; it wasn't until the late '20s that O'Doul made his mark as a slugger with the Phillies.
CF	Willie McGee	October 21, 1981	Yankees traded McGee to the Cardinals for Bob Sykes, a veteran who never pitched in the majors again.
RF	Jackie Jensen	May 3, 1952	The Yanks had Mantle, but why didn't they keep Jensen to play RF? He was better than what they had.
SP	Lew Burdette	August 30, 1951	Yanks traded Burdette *and* 50K to Braves for Johnny Sain in deal that came back to haunt them in '57 Series.
RP	Tippy Martinez	June 15, 1976	Part of 10-player deal with Orioles that also included Rick Dempsey and Scott McGregor.

		YEARS	NOTES
GOLD GLOVE			
C	Bill Dickey	1928–1943 1946	Yogi was outstanding, no question, but he learned most of what he knew from Dickey; Munson also a standout.
1B	Tino Martinez	1996–2001	A big upset over Mattingly, but Tino's numbers are so much better that I just couldn't go with the safe pick.
2B	Joe Gordon	1938–1943 1946	Joe McCarthy loved Gordon for many reasons, among them Gordon's brilliance when turning the double play.
SS	Phil Rizzuto	1941–1942 1946–1956	He's in the Hall of Fame because of his 1950 MVP, but it was his glove that made him occasionally great.
3B	Clete Boyer	1959–1966	Nettles was great, of course, but Boyer may be the greatest defensive third baseman who ever lived.
LF	Roy White	1965–1979	Ralph Houk called him "the best left fielder the Yanks have had in my experience," despite weak arm.
CF	Joe DiMaggio	1936–1942 1946–1951	Amazingly enough, Joe's brothers Dom and Vince were just as good; other NY standouts: Combs, Mantle, Rivers.
RF	Paul O'Neill	1994–2001	Until his last season, when he couldn't run, displayed good range to go with great instincts and solid arm.
P	Bobby Shantz	1957–1960	Guidry won five Gold Gloves, but Shantz was generally considered the best-fielding pitcher before Jim Kaat.

		YEARS	NOTES
IRON GLOVE			
C	Matt Nokes	1990–1994	Improved his defensive reputation with Yankees, but the truth is that he still was awful behind the plate.
1B	Ron Blomberg	1972–1973	The first DH, of course, which was fitting because few players in history needed the position more than he did.
2B	Chuck Knoblauch	1998–2000	Won Gold Glove the year before he became Yankee, then found himself unable to throw to first base in '99.
SS	Tom Tresh	1962	Regularly led his minor leagues in errors, and switched to outfield after winning Rookie of the Year Award at short.
3B	Ben Chapman	1930	Played 91 games at 3B (and 45 at 2B) as a rookie, and played so poorly that they made an outfielder of him.
LF	Chuck Knoblauch	2001	He's probably not *the* worst they've had, but as an apprentice at 32, had lousy instincts and couldn't throw.
CF	Joe Pepitone	1967–1968	Mantle took Pepi's spot at 1B, Pepi took Mantle's spot in CF . . . and returned to 1B the moment Mantle retired.
RF	Babe Ruth	1933–1934	He could still hit, of course, but the Babe's legs were practically useless and he cost the Yanks a lot of runs.
P	Rudy May	1974–1976 1980–1983	One of the worst in the league, and it was said, "He handles bunts as though they were live grenades."

In 1964, "third baseman" Clete Boyer played twenty-one games at shortstop for the pennant-winning New York Yankees; in all, Boyer played 162 games at short for the Yanks in his career. In *The Major League Baseball Handbook 1961*, Don Schiffer wrote of Boyer, "Very few in this fellow's class as a fielder, whether he's at shortstop or third base."

In other words, Clete Boyer had some serious range and a great arm. Which was a good thing, because not only did he play defense like a shortstop, most years he hit like one, too. If Clete had the hitting talent of his brother Ken, he'd be in the Hall of Fame (and if Ken had Clete's defensive abilities—not that he was far off—then *he* might be in the Hall of Fame).

Clete never won a Gold Glove in the American League because Brooks Robinson became an everyday third baseman before Boyer did, and once Brooks started winning the award, there weren't nobody going to take it away from him. But Gold Gloves aside, I haven't seen any evidence that Boyer wasn't just as good as Robinson. And he might have been better.

(By the way, Graig Nettles was brilliant with the glove, too. And like Boyer, Nettles deserved a few of the Gold Gloves that went to Brooks.)

For more than three weeks in 1980 (August 23 through September 15), the Yankee rotation consisted of Tommy John (37 years old), Gaylord Perry (41), Luis Tiant ("39"), Rudy May (36), and Tom Underwood (26). On September 16, Ron Guidry (30)—who'd been sent to the bullpen in mid-August after a few shaky starts—replaced Underwood. I don't know if it was the oldest rotation ever, but you'd be hard-pressed to find an older top four.

And this wasn't some lousy club signing geezers as gate attractions and mentors; this was a fine team fighting for a division title. The Yankees, of course, wound up winning 103 games and the division title. But it wasn't easy. When September dawned, the Yanks owned a skinny 1½-game lead over the Baltimore Orioles, who had just gone 21-8 in August. The Orioles went 24-10 from September 1 through the end of the season . . . but it wasn't nearly enough, as those decrepit starters helped the Yankees go 25-8 down the stretch and finish with a three-game edge over Baltimore.

		YEARS	NOTES
ALL-BUST			
DH	Ken Phelps	1988–1989	"What the hell did you trade Jay Buhner for? You don't know what the hell you're doing!"—Frank Costanza
C	Jake Gibbs	1962–1971	Star QB at Ole Miss got $100,000 bonus to sign, then converted from 3B to C but never did learn to hit.
1B	Johnny Sturm	1941	There was no finer manager than Joe McCarthy, but *why* did he let Sturm play 124 games . . . in the leadoff slot?
2B	Earle Gardner	1911–1912	After a three-year apprenticeship, got the everyday job in 1911 and couldn't handle it, posting 623 OPS.
SS	Rafael Santana	1988	At least most of the over-the-hill Yankees of the '80s could *once* hit; ex-Met didn't clear .300 in OBP or Slug.
3B	Rich McKinney	1972	Batted .215 and fielded .917 in 37 games; far worse, the Yankees traded Stan Bahnsen to the White Sox for him.
LF	Steve Kemp	1983–1984	Fine player in Detroit, but his power deserted him after signing big (for the time) free-agent deal.
CF	Bill Robinson	1967–1969	Hailed as "the next Mickey Mantle" (Murcer was still a short-stop), batted .206 with 16 homers in three seasons.
RF	Curt Blefary	1970–1971	Got his career back on track with Astros in '69, but came to New York and batted .210 in 120 games.
SP	Brien Taylor	—	No. 1 pick in '91 draft barely reached Class AA; finished pro career with 5.12 ERA and 352 walks in 436 innings.
RP	Wilcy Moore	1927–1929 1932–1933	After posting 2.28 ERA in his first season, racked up 4.35 mark in the rest of his time with Bombers.

		YEARS	NOTES
USED-TO-BE-GREAT			
DH	Darryl Strawberry	1995–1999	Five seasons but only 662 at-bats, due to his drug problems and bout with cancer; great as part-timer in '98.
C	Wilbert Robinson	1901–1902	Didn't play with Yankees, but the old National League Oriole played for the new AL Orioles before they moved to N.Y.
1B	John Mayberry	1982	A solid hitter for 10 years, but *stopped* hitting the day he arrived in New York, slugging .353 in 69 games.
2B	Sandy Alomar	1974–1976	Roberto and Sandy's pop was Yankees' everyday second baseman in 1975, spare part in '76.
SS	Bert Campaneris	1983	Granted, it was only 143 at-bats, but the 41-year-old batted a career-high .322 in his last season.
3B	Wade Boggs	1993–1997	After suffering through his first poor season in 1992, signed with Yankees and enjoyed a few good ones.
LF	Enos Slaughter	1954–1955 1956–1959	Old Cardinals great batted .304 as part-time player in 1958 when he was 42, then batted .172 when he was 43.
CF	Claudell Washington	1986–1988 1990	Yankees were his sixth team; he did for them what he'd done for the rest: one pretty good season, along with. . . .
RF	Ken Griffey, Sr.	1982–1986	Key component of Big Red Machine; started as right fielder with Yanks but played plenty in left, too.
SP	Gaylord Perry	1980	Came to club late in 1980 season, a month before his 42nd birthday, went 4-4 with worst ERA since '62.
RP	Jim Konstanty	1954–1956	Famous for 1950 MVP with Phils, but few remember his '55 season: 7-2 with 2.32 ERA and 11 saves.

	ALL-NAME		
		YEARS	NOTES
M	"The Old Professor" Casey Stengel	1949–1960	Of course, "Casey" itself is a nickname, after his hometown; also called "Doctor" by his friends.
DH	"The Hit Man" Mike Easler	1986, 1987	Career .293 hitter so he came by his nickname honestly; in his first year with Yanks, batted .302 in 146 games.
C	"Yogi" Lawrence Berra	1946–1963	All we know for sure is that his boyhood friends called him "Yogi"; early in his career, he was "Larry" to most.
1B	"The Iron Horse" Lou Gehrig	1923–1939	Early on, also called "Columbia Lou" and "Biscuit Pants," and Babe Ruth simply called Gehrig "Buster."
2B	"Poosh 'em Up" Tony Lazzeri	1926–1937	When Lazzeri played in Salt Lake City, an Italian restaurant owner told him to "poosh 'em up" (i.e. hit).
SS	"The Scooter" Phil Rizzuto	1941–1942 1946–1956	I've long believed that his other nickname was "The Glue Man," but I can't locate any evidence to support this.
3B	"Jumping Joe" Joe Dugan	1922–1928	Didn't get his nickname for acrobatic defensive play, but rather for his habit of going AWOL from his teams.
LF	"Twinkletoes" George Selkirk	1934–1942	Babe Ruth's successor in RF—he moved to left field later—ran on the balls of his feet, hence the nickname.
CF	"Yankee Clipper" Joe DiMaggio	1936–1942 1946–1951	Named after Pan Am's famous flying boat, but was the inventor Mel Allen, or Arch McDonald? Sources differ.
RF	"Mr. October" Reggie Jackson	1977–1981	Batted .357 with 10 homers and 24 RBI in five World Series; batted .227 with 6 homers in 45 LCS games.
SP	"Louisiana Lightning" Ron Guidry	1975–1988	He was a Cajun and he threw hard, which is just about all you need to know.
RP	"Grandma" Johnny Murphy	1934–1943 1946	Might be the only relief pitcher with three nicknames; also known as "Fireman" and "Fordham Johnny."

TOP FIVE SEASONS

YEAR 1998   **RECORD** 114-48
BEST HITTERS Scott Brosius, Derek Jeter, Bernie Williams
BEST PITCHER David Wells, David Cone
NOTES Capped perfect season with World Series sweep.

YEAR 1927   **RECORD** 110-44
BEST HITTERS Babe Ruth, Lou Gehrig (MVP)
BEST PITCHERS Wilcy Moore, Waite Hoyt
NOTES Team of teams swept Pirates in World Series.

YEAR 1939   **RECORD** 106-45
BEST HITTER Joe DiMaggio (MVP)
BEST PITCHER Red Ruffing
NOTES Swept Reds to win fourth straight Series.

YEAR 1923   **RECORD** 98-54
BEST HITTER Babe Ruth (MVP)
BEST PITCHER Joe Bush, Herb Pennock
NOTES After two tries, beat Giants to win first World Series.

YEAR 1937   **RECORD** 102-52
BEST HITTERS Joe DiMaggio, Lou Gehrig
BEST PITCHER Lefty Gomez
NOTES In first Subway Series since '23, Yanks beat Giants.

TOP FIVE MANAGERS

MANAGER Casey Stengel
YEARS 1949–1960
RECORD 1149-696 (.623)
NOTES In his dozen seasons, Yankees won *ten* pennants.

MANAGER Joe McCarthy
YEARS 1931–1946
RECORD 1460-867 (.627)
NOTES In 15 full seasons, Yanks won seven World Series.

MANAGER Miller Huggins
YEARS 1918–1929
RECORD 1067-719 (.597)
NOTES "Mighty Mite" handled Ruth as well as any man could.

MANAGER Joe Torre
YEARS 1996–*2002*
RECORD 685-445 (.606)
NOTES Nobody's ever packed so many into so few.

MANAGER Billy Martin
YEARS 1975–1979, 1983, 1985
RECORD 556-385 (.591)
NOTES He had his problems, but nobody better at turnaround.

You see a nickname like "Grandma" and you think "old," but they didn't call John Murphy "Grandma" because he was old. Teammate Pat Malone called Murphy "Grandma" because of his "incessant complaining about meals and accommodations."

Murphy graduated from Fordham in 1929, was signed by legendary Yankees scout Paul Krichell, and first reached the majors in 1932, still a few weeks shy of his twenty-second birthday. He pitched only three innings, then returned to the minors until 1934. He pitched quite well that season, going 14-10 with a 3.12 ERA, starting twenty games and relieving in twenty others.

Murphy continued to pitch well, but his starts dropped from twenty in 1934 to eight in '35, then from eight to five, from five to four, from four to two, and finally to zero in 1939. In 1937, he'd established a major-league record with twelve wins in relief, and then in '39 he saved nineteen games, the second-highest total up to that time.

Considered one of the most intelligent men on the roster, Murphy didn't throw particularly hard, but he did toss an overhand curveball that ranked among the best in the league. He served in World War II, came back in 1946 to pitch for the Yankees, then joined the Red Sox in 1947. In his last season, he posted a 2.80 ERA in thirty-two games.

MARSE JOE VS. THE OL' PERFESSOR

There are sixteen managers in the Hall of Fame. Four of those sixteen Hall of Fame managers guided the New York Yankees to World Championships. So which of them was the *greatest* Yankee manager?

We can summarily eliminate Bucky Harris from the competition. In his first year as skipper, he led the Yankees to a victory over the Brooklyn Dodgers in the 1947 World Series. In his second, he led the Yankees to a solid 94-60 record, but that was only good enough for third place, and Harris got fired.

Miller Huggins won't go so quietly, but go he must. Huggins managed the Yankees for twelve seasons, and in that span the Yanks won six American League pennants and three World Series. Great, but not great enough, as Huggins's Yankees also finished seventh, fourth, third twice, and second twice.

And it's with great reluctance that I eliminate Joe Torre from the competition, too. No, he's not in the Hall of Fame, but he will be someday. And at this writing, he's managed the Yankees to five American League pennants and four World Championships in seven years, a truly amazing run. While Torre's Yankees have benefited from an unprecedented financial advantage, I'm not going to make that argument here, because the Yankees enjoyed some mighty big advantages in the 1930s and the 1950s, too. Instead, I reluctantly eliminate Torre simply because he hasn't been there long enough.

That leaves two contenders: Joe McCarthy (1931–1946) and Casey Stengel (1949–1960). In fifteen full seasons, McCarthy's Yankees won eight pennants and seven World Series. In twelve full seasons, Stengel's Yankees won *ten* pennants and seven World Series. McCarthy managed the Yankees longer, but Stengel won more pennants and just as many World Series. McCarthy's best teams were better than Stengel's best teams, but their overall winning percentages with the Yankees are practically indistinguishable: .627 for McCarthy, .623 for Stengel.

So McCarthy's got an edge in career length, and Stengel's got an edge in what we might call "pennant percentage." Ignoring the very real possibility that McCarthy's teams might have faced tougher competition, these men look about as even as they could be.

Which leaves us with the subjective elements. And based on one subjective element, I rate Stengel just a *hair* better than McCarthy, because Stengel did more *managing*. McCarthy wrote out the same lineup, day after day after day. Stengel wrote out a *different* lineup, day after day after day. In fairness, McCarthy, like Stengel, was capable of great creativity with his pitching staff. But it seems to me that Stengel had to work just a little harder for all those pennants.

It's the unfortunate nature of comparisons that when you pick a "winner," you also have to pick a "loser." Joe McCarthy was anything but a loser. I think he's the greatest manager in baseball history. In *Yankee* history, though, he comes in second to the Old Professor.

I'm especially grateful to Richard Lally for his editorial suggestions. The sources for this chapter included Glenn Stout and Richard A. Johnson's Yankees Century: 100 Years of New York Yankees Baseball *(Houghton Mifflin, 2002).*

Oakland Athletics

		YEARS	NOTES
		ALL-TIME	
DH	Geronimo Berroa	1994–1997	After far too many years in the minors, he finally got a chance to play when he was 29 years old, and did what he was born to do: hit!
C	Terry Steinbach	1986–1996	Started '88 All-Star Game with .217 batting average, but homered to earn MVP honors; in 1996, set an American League record with 34 homers as catcher.
1B	Mark McGwire	1987–1997	Aside from an inexplicably poor '91 and injury-marred '93 and '94, he was consistently devastating, if not the sensation that he would become after going to St. Louis.
2B	Dick Green	1963–1974	With the exception of 1969, he was never more than adequate with the bat, but he was the top defensive second baseman in the American League for years.
SS	Miguel Tejada	1997–*2002*	In what seemed like the blink of an eye, went from being the fourth-best shortstop in the league to the league's MVP; from 2000 through '02, averaged 32 homers and 120 RBI per season.
3B	Sal Bando	1966–1976	Power-hitting third baseman and a decent defender, but best known for leadership; elected A's captain when just 24, and Don Baylor called him "a captain's captain."
LF	Rickey Henderson	1979-1984 1989-1993 1994-1995	Also played for the Athletics in 1998, giving him four separate stints with the club; baseball's greatest leadoff man also played for seven other teams in his *24* seasons.
CF	Dwayne Murphy	1978–1987	Fine defensive player with power who won six straight Gold Gloves (1980–1985), and finished in the top five in AL in walks three straight seasons (1980–1982).
RF	Reggie Jackson	1967–1975 1987	Made his lasting fame as a Yankee, but played for A's until he was almost 30 and was significantly better for them than anybody else.
SP1	Catfish Hunter	1965–1974	Won 161 games with franchise, including 131 with Oakland version, topping the list; in 1968, tossed AL's first perfect game since 1922; all fastballs and sliders.
SP2	Vida Blue	1969–1977	Oh, what could have been . . . In his first full season, won Cy Young *and* MVP Awards, but never pitched nearly so well again; overpowering fastball and curve.
SP3	Dave Stewart	1986–1992 1995	One of the first things La Russa did after taking over was make a starter of Stewart, who won nine of his first ten decisions; later enjoyed four straight 20-win seasons.
SP4	Bob Welch	1988–1994	Went 61-23 his first three seasons in Oakland—including 27-6 in 1990 that earned him the Cy Young—but fell off sharply in his remaining tenure with the A's.
RP	Dennis Eckersley	1988–1995	Started 2 games, relieved in 523 others, and recorded 320 of his 390 career saves for club; did it all with a fastball, a slider, and uncanny control.

It goes without saying that Dennis Eckersley's career was saved in 1987, when he joined the Oakland A's and was transformed, by the grace of Tony La Russa, from a starting pitcher into the game's dominant relief pitcher.

But *should* it go without saying?

From 1975 through 1982, Eckersley was one of the best starters in the American League, going 111-85 with a 3.43 ERA for the Indians and Red Sox. He pitched poorly for the Sox in '83, but bounced back brilliantly after getting traded to the Cubs in 1984. Over the rest of that season and 1985, Eckersley went 21-15 with a 3.06 ERA, thanks mostly to his amazing control.

He didn't pitch so well in 1986—6-11, 4.57—and shortly before Opening Day in 1987, the Cubs traded him to the A's for three minor leaguers who never became major leaguers. Eckersley opened the season in the bullpen, made a couple of uninspiring starts in May . . . and never started another game. He saved 16 games that season, then 45 more in 1988 as the A's won their first division title since 1981.

Though it's highly unlikely that Eckersley would have enjoyed a Hall of Fame career if he'd remained a starter, I do think he'd have continued to pitch, and pitch well, for at least a few more years.

When Jason Giambi, the second-best player in the American League, left the cash-poor Athletics for the cash-rich Yankees shortly after the 2001 season, virtually everyone attributed Giambi's decision to—you guessed it—cash.

I'm not sure it's that simple, though.

In their 2000 American League Division Series, the A's outscored the Yankees (23–17) but lost, due to one bad inning in the fifth game.

In their 2001 American League Division Series, the A's beat the Yankees in the first two games, then lost the third—and eventually the fourth and fifth—after Jason's little brother didn't slide in the bottom of the seventh.

Baseball players are amazing athletes, but asking a ballplayer for the big picture is like asking a tree to tell you about the forest; they can't do it, because they don't have any perspective. And while it's obvious to an objective observer that the A's could almost as easily have beaten the Yankees as lost, I suspect that it seemed to Jason Giambi (and at least some of his teammates) that the Yankees really were the better team, and that playing for the A's just meant more years of losing to the Yankees. Which ain't no fun. But it didn't have to happen the way it did, and if Oakland had gotten just two or three breaks in 2000 and 2001, Giambi might still be an Athletic.

		YEARS	NOTES
NO. 2			
DH	Harold Baines	1990–1992	Spent the great majority of his interminable career with Orioles and White Sox, but was an Athletic for two seasons and a month; hit 3 homers on May 7, 1991.
C	Mike Heath	1979–1985	Mostly an infielder in the minors, but became a decent catcher; one could argue for Gene Tenace, but his hitting didn't pick up until he started playing first base.
1B	Jason Giambi	1995–2001	The physical and emotional heart of baseball's biggest over-achievers, in terms of performance vs. payroll; 'twas a sad day when he left for Steinbrenner's millions.
2B	Tony Phillips	1982–1989 1999	Fit in perfectly with A's because he could play every position (which Tony La Russa liked) and draw a ton of walks (which Sandy Alderson liked).
SS	Bert Campaneris	1964–1976	Until Belanger and Grich came together in Baltimore, Campy and Dick Green were best keystone combo in the league; led AL in steals six times.
3B	Carney Lansford	1984–1992	The man could hit line drives all day long, which allowed him to play despite moderate power, patience, and defensive range; will likely be passed by Chavez soon.
LF	Joe Rudi	1967–1976 1982	Still remembered in Oakland (and Cincinnati) for his big catch in Game 2 of the '72 World Series; not the most gifted player, but his managers loved his work habits.
CF	Bill North	1973–1978	Outstanding defensive player who twice led AL in steals during his five full seasons with Athletics; frequently involved in locker-room brawls.
RF	José Canseco	1985–1992 1997	Don Baylor said, "Canseco possesses the most natural ability of any player I've ever seen," but Canseco rarely played quite as well as people thought he should.
SP1	Tim Hudson	1999–*2002*	Came to the majors pitching like a veteran—in his very first start, he struck out 11 Twins in 5 innings—and hasn't done anything different since.
SP2	Ken Holtzman	1972–1975	The unsung hero of the dynasty and the most famous Jewish pitcher since Koufax, Holtzman pitched a ton of innings and won 72 games in his four seasons.
SP3	Mike Moore	1989–1992	Like a lot of veteran starters, thrived under Tony La Russa and Dave Duncan; career-high 19 wins in '89, and team-high 17 wins in both '91 and '92.
SP4	Blue Moon Odom	1964–1975	Listing Hudson is a stretch, and we just couldn't justify Zito and Mulder yet, though in a couple of years they might well bump Moore and Odom (80-76, 3.53).
RP	Rollie Fingers	1968–1976	Didn't become a full-time reliever until 1972 (his fourth season), then averaged 10 wins, 21 saves, and 124 innings per season before going to San Diego.

SINGLE SEASON

		YEARS	NOTES
DH	John Jaha	1999	After a couple of injury-plagued seasons in Milwaukee, signed with A's and posted 970 OPS, including 35 homers.
C	Gene Tenace	1975	No, he wasn't much of a catcher. But in '75 he slugged .464 and got on base 40 percent of the time for a first-place team.
1B	Jason Giambi	2000	He won MVP Awards in both 2000 and 2001 with virtually identical contributions, then left for the big bucks.
2B	Dick Green	1969	Remembered as much for his weak stick as for his great glove, but in '69 he hit 12 homers and slugged .427, easily his best.
SS	Miguel Tejada	2002	His numbers were fantastic, but Tejada won the MVP going away thanks to his late-inning heroics during A's AL-record 20-game winning streak.
3B	Sal Bando	1969	Played every game, drew 111 walks, scored 106 runs, drove in 113; virtually identical to his brilliant '73 campaign.
LF	Rickey Henderson	1990	The Best of Rickey: tied career high with 28 homers *and* stole 65 bases *and* led major leagues with .439 on-base percentage.
CF	Dave Henderson	1988	Club had a nice run with Billy North, Dwayne Murphy, and Henderson, but it's been a while since they had a solid CF.
RF	Reggie Jackson	1969	In just his second full season, led AL with 123 runs and .608 slugging percentage; had 37 homers at All-Star break.
SP	Vida Blue	1971	One of his two 1970 victories was a no-hitter, and he followed that up with 24 wins, Cy Young and MVP Awards in '71.
RP	Dennis Eckersley	1990	Finished second (to Bobby Thigpen) with 48 saves, but *nobody* could match his *0.61 ERA* in 73 innings.

ALL-ROOKIE

		YEARS	NOTES
DH	Troy Neel	1993	Slugged .473 in 123 games, did about the same in '94, then escaped labor problems to enjoy nice career in Japan.
C	Terry Steinbach	1987	Batted .284 with 16 home runs in 122 games, and 2 of those homers came as a pinch hitter.
1B	Mark McGwire	1987	As a junior at USC, set Pac-10 record with 32 homers; as freshman at Oakland, set MLB rookie record with 49 homers.
2B	Brent Gates	1993	As rookie, batted .290 with 7 homers and 69 RBI, and would not better those or any other key stats the rest of his career.
SS	Walt Weiss	1988	Rookie of the Year despite anemic bat (.250-3-39), thanks to great defense and weak rookie class.
3B	Wayne Gross	1977	Even with two solid rookies (see next), the A's still managed to lose 98 games and finish behind the first-year Mariners.
LF	Mitchell Page	1977	Slugged .521 and was just nipped for Rookie of the Year Award by Eddie Murray; never played nearly so well again.
CF	Terrence Long	2000	Cost the A's Kenny Rogers—whom they couldn't really afford anyway—and gave them 104 runs and 80 RBI as rookie.
RF	Ben Grieve	1998	Totaled *160 RBI* at three levels in '97, then won Rookie of the Year Award in '98 with .288-18-89 (and 85 walks) campaign.
SP	Tim Hudson	1999	Went 11-2 with 3.23 ERA after reaching majors in early June; first 10-game winner drafted by A's since 1981 (Curt Young).
RP	Jeff Tam	2000	Because of a stupid rule, not technically a rookie, but posted 2.63 ERA and allowed only 3 homers in 86 innings.

For one season and one month, Mike Norris was one hell of a pitcher.

In 1973, the A's used their first-round draft pick, the twenty-fourth overall, to select Bay Area native Norris. He pitched well in his first two pro seasons, but didn't establish himself as a major leaguer until 1979. When the 1980 season opened, Norris was twenty-five years old and sported a 12-25 career record with a 4.68 ERA over 385 innings. Not exactly the stuff of which stars are made.

In 1980, though, Mike Norris was the best pitcher in the league, and didn't win the Cy Young Award only because the voters had (and still have) the misguided belief that a pitcher's record is more important than how well he actually pitches.

In 1981, he pitched great in April but was inconsistent the rest of the way, and a combination of arm problems and drug problems limited his effectiveness in 1982 and '83, after which he didn't pitch in the majors for quite some time. But after six years of pitching here and there and everywhere (actually, it was mostly with the San Jose Bees, a collection of castoffs), he made it back to the major leagues on April 11, 1990, when he shut out the Red Sox for two innings. He pitched pretty well in 14 games, but was released on July 15. The organization has never provided a specific reason for his release.

Okay, so Charlie didn't want to pay Reggie Jackson. Fair enough. But it was what Finley did *before* he traded Reggie that left the A's with a terrible outfield for two years.

In 1973, the club was loaded in the outfield, with Joe Rudi, Billy North, and Jackson. So in March, the A's traded twenty-three-year-old George Hendrick to Cleveland.

Two years later, Rudi was at first base, but left field was manned by a thrilling twenty-year-old player named Claudell Washington, who would hit .308 and steal 40 bases. So on June 15, 1975, nobody batted an eyelash when the A's traded minor-league outfielder Chet Lemon to the White Sox.

Well, by 1977 Rudi and Jackson and Washington (whose best season came when he was twenty) were all gone, and North missed most of the year with a broken finger. That season, Oakland's outfield consisted of Mitchell Page, Tony Armas, and Jim Tyrone. Only Page played well. A year later, it was Page and Armas again, along with Miguel Dilone and Joe Wallis. Again, only Page played well. The A's lost 191 games over those two seasons, while both Lemon and Hendrick were establishing themselves as stars for other teams.

In 1979, Rickey Henderson and Dwayne Murphy arrived, and for the next five years the franchise would boast one of the best outfields in the league.

HOMEGROWN			
		YEARS	NOTES
DH	Troy Neel	1992–1994	Couldn't field at all, but he could certainly hit, and might just as easily have enjoyed a decent career in the States.
C	Terry Steinbach	1986–1996	Ninth-round pick in '83 didn't catch a game until his third pro season, but was in the majors a year later.
1B	Mark McGwire	1986–1997	Drafted by Expos as a *pitcher* out of high school but didn't sign; 10th pick in '84 draft breezed through minors.
2B	Brent Gates	1993–1996	Perhaps Dick Green belongs here, but Green debuted with A's five years before they moved to Oakland.
SS	Miguel Tejada	1997–*2002*	Former shoeshine boy and garment worker in Dominican Republic signed for low, *low*, LOW bonus of $2,000.
3B	Sal Bando	1966–1976	Like Reggie Jackson, Bando was an Arizona State product who became a regular for the A's in 1968.
LF	Rickey Henderson	1979–1984 1989–93, etc.	Great RB in high school, had to be dragged into baseball; fourth-round pick signed for $10K with hometown team.
CF	Dwayne Murphy	1978–1987	Fifteenth-round pick in 1973 spent nearly five years in minors before becoming perennial Gold Glover.
RF	Reggie Jackson	1967–1975 1987	Went to Arizona State to play football, but left after his sophomore year when A's offered the big bonus.
SP	Catfish Hunter	1965–1974	He had a right foot full of shotgun pellets, but Charlie Finley personally signed him for $75,000 anyway.
RP	Rollie Fingers	1968–1976	Signed for $13,000 in 1964 as pitcher/outfielder; came up as starter, didn't move to bullpen full-time until 1972.

TRADED AWAY			
		TRADED	NOTES
M	Chuck Tanner	November 5, 1976	Yes, they traded the manager, Tanner going to the Pirates for catcher Manny Sanguillen and $100,000.
DH	Jeremy Giambi	May 22, 2002	Jason's little brother was born to DH, and should get the chance now that he's back in the American League.
C	Mickey Tettleton	—	A's actually *released* Tettleton (prior to '88 season), after which he hit 223 home runs for various teams.
1B	Mark McGwire	July 31, 1997	Played only four-and-a-half seasons after trade—two of them injury-marred—but still hit 220 more bombs.
2B	Manny Trillo	October 23, 1974	One of three players sent to Cubs for Billy Williams, who still had the sweet swing but not the sweet stats.
SS	Walt Weiss	November 17, 1992	Traded to Florida after a couple of poor seasons, and enjoyed nice years with Marlins, Rockies, and Braves.
3B	Eric Hinske	December 7, 2001	Prototypical Athletic, but blocked by Chavez . . . so why didn't Billy Beane move Hinske to first base?
LF	George Hendrick	March 4, 1973	With Rudi and North and Reggie, A's just didn't have room for another bat in the outfield.
CF	Chet Lemon	June 15, 1975	Traded to White Sox before he played a game for the A's, and wound up with an excellent 15-year career.
RF	Reggie Jackson	April 2, 1976	With Reggie holding out, A's swapped him to O's for Mike Torrez and Don Baylor; neither lasted long.
SP	Mike Morgan	November 3, 1980	Still only 21, sent to the Yankees for their second-string DP combo, Brian Doyle and Chicken Stanley.
RP	Don Stanhouse	March 4, 1972	Traded to Texas for Denny McLain, who won once for A's; years later, Stanhouse drove Earl Weaver crazy.

GOLD GLOVE

		YEARS	NOTES
C	Jim Essian	1978–1980 1984	His quick release compensated for so-so arm strength, and pitchers generally loved working with him.
1B	Mike Hegan	1971–1973	Dick Williams claimed Hegan "may have been the best-fielding first baseman ever," which is probably a bit of a stretch.
2B	Dick Green	1963–1974	Fielded so brilliantly in the 1974 World Series that some considered him the MVP even though he was hitless.
SS	Bert Campaneris	1964–1976	Actually began his pro career as a *catcher*; later became first in MLB history to play nine positions in one game.
3B	Scott Brosius	1991–1997	Outstanding even though he didn't become a full-timer at the position until he was 30.
LF	Joe Rudi	1967–1976 1982	He didn't deserve the three Gold Gloves, but was a solid outfielder with everything but speed.
CF	Billy North	1973–1978	Didn't throw well, but made up for it with great range; edges Dwayne Murphy, who won six Gold Gloves.
RF	Tony Armas	1977–1982	Didn't run well, but had good instincts and threw very well; played nearly as many career games in CF as RF.
P	Kenny Rogers	1998–1999	"Kenny Rogers is the best-fielding pitcher I have ever seen. It's like having an extra infielder."—Billy Beane

IRON GLOVE

		YEARS	NOTES
C	Dave Duncan	1964 1967–1972	Earl Williams (1977) was worse, of course, but he caught only 36 games with the club; also Tenace and Alexander.
1B	Jeff Newman	1976–1982	Horrible first baseman; for some unknown reason the A's wanted his "bat" in the lineup when he wasn't catching.
2B	Shooty Babitt	1981	Billy Martin told a peer, "If you ever see Shooty Babitt play second base for me again, I want you to shooty me."
SS	Rob Picciolo	1977–1982	Not much of a shortstop *and* he had the worst walk rate of his time, if not of all time.
3B	Wayne Gross	1976–1983 1986	He could hit a little and would have been a pretty decent player if only he could have fielded his position.
LF	Ben Grieve	1997–2000	Ranks with Glenallen Hill and Al Martin among the worst defensive outfielders of our time.
CF	Terrence Long	2000–*2002*	Good speed and decent arm but poor instincts, which left him more suited to left field than anywhere.
RF	Matt Stairs	1996–2000	People say you can't win with four DH's, but the A's had them all over the lineup and did just fine, thank you.
P	Buddy Groom	1996–1999	Rarely made an error, but that was mostly because he had so much trouble just getting leather on the ball.

You might think I'm exaggerating here, that the Athletics' regular outfield in 2000 certainly couldn't have been *that* bad, could it?

Well, yes, Grieve and Stairs and Long really were that bad.

Since 1900, only a dozen or so major leaguers as bad with the glove as Stairs and Grieve have been allowed to play as many games in the outfield as those two already have. Stairs had decent instincts and he could throw, but he moved like pond water. Grieve couldn't do much of anything out there. Stairs probably could have been a decent first baseman, but at just five-nine he was short for the position. Grieve was born a designated hitter (oddly enough, his father Tom was also something less than a defensive wizard).

Terrence Long could (and can) run, but his arm was (and is) just adequate, and he frequently got (and gets) tangled up when balls were (and are) hit directly toward him.

Bay Area baseball writers were obsessed with this stuff, and wrote countless columns instructing A's general manager Billy Beane to discard those sluggardly sluggers and get some defense into the outfield. But of course, Beane had the last laugh—not that the baseball writers learned anything—as the Athletics won a division title in 2000, acing out the Mariners by a half-game.

You probably know about Herb Washington, who "played" in ninety-two games for the A's in 1974 . . . all ninety-two games, every single one of them, as a pinch runner.

What you might not know is that the A's of that era employed another quite-strange method of roster management, most notably in September of 1972 as they tried to hold off the White Sox for the division title. On August 30, just before the deadline for setting your postseason roster, A's owner Charlie Finley traded for Dal Maxvill, a great defensive shortstop who couldn't hit a slow-moving balloon with a paddle.

What would the A's do with Maxvill, when they already had Bert Campaneris at shortstop, and slick-fielding Dick Green at second base? Finley and manager Dick Williams concocted a bizarre plan: the A's numerous second basemen, none of whom could hit, wouldn't be *allowed* to hit. Instead, every time the second baseman came up, Williams would send up a pinch hitter, who would then be replaced in the lineup by another second baseman, who would be bumped for a pinch hitter . . . you get the idea. Anyway, the bizarre plan seems to have worked, as the A's went 20-11 from September 1 through the end of the season and finished well ahead of the White Sox.

ALL-BUST			
		YEARS	NOTES
DH	Reggie Jackson	1987	Last hurrah might have cost A's division title, as he batted .220 and they finished 4 games out of first place.
C	A. J. Hinch	1998–2000	Third-round pick became No. 1 catcher in second pro season, but sub-.300 OBP soon made him a part-timer.
1B	Dick Allen	1977	His once-fearsome power nearly gone, played 54 games before being released after taking mid-game shower.
2B	Brent Gates	1993–1996	Club's first-round pick in '91 batted .290 as rookie in '93, but he never recovered from '94 wrist injury.
SS	Rob Picciolo	1977–1982 1985	In 607 games with A's, Picciolo drew 24 walks. Yes, you read right: 2-4. A month's work for Barry Bonds.
3B	Brook Jacoby	1991	Came over from Tribe in late July, and did as much as anybody to sink defending AL champs to fourth place.
LF	Don Baylor	1976	Hit on the left hand by a Dick Drago pitch on the second day of the season, and wound up slugging just .368.
CF	Johnny Damon	2001	Supposed to give the A's an all-around threat, but instead gave them little except his range in the outfield.
RF	Claudell Washington	1976	Played in 1975 All-Star Game when he was 20, but slumped in '76 and traded in '77.
SP	Vida Blue	1972	After winning Cy Young and MVP in 1971, held out in spring training and wound up with 6-10 record.
RP	Luis Vizcaíno	1999–2001	With great stuff, supposed to be the closer of the future, but racked up 5.61 ERA in 49 games over 3 seasons.

USED-TO-BE-GREAT			
		YEARS	NOTES
DH	Reggie Jackson	1987	Came home for one last season, and was pretty awful (699 OPS); edges Billy Williams (1975–76) here.
C	Brian Harper	1995	Played 11 games for the A's in '87, before his career got going, then came back for two more in '95.
1B	Willie McCovey	1976	*Before* his triumphant return to Giants, joined A's to finish an awful season he'd begun with the Padres.
2B	Joe Morgan	1984	Bay Area native finished career with A's and did well, posting .356 OBP, off his career mark but still fine.
SS	Dal Maxvill	1972–1973 1974–1975	One of the greatest defensive SS in history played 136 games for the A's, nearly all as defensive replacement.
3B	Ron Cey	1987	After four years in Chicago, returned to California and batted .221 in 45 games, often as Reggie's platoon partner.
LF	Rickey Henderson	1998	Came back for one last (?) stint, his fourth with club, and at 38 led American League with 118 walks and 66 steals.
CF	Willie Wilson	1991–1992	He could still go get the ball, but his .312 OBP and .325 slugging were just what declining Athletics didn't need.
RF	Felipe Alou	1970–1971	Played 145 outfield games but didn't play well, then traded to the Yankees in '71 for his last good season.
SP	Denny McLain	1972	Three years removed from his last good season, the fastball down to nothing, posted 6.04 ERA in 5 starts.
RP	Goose Gossage	1992–1993	Joined club when he was 40, gave them one good season (2.84 ERA in 38 innings) and one bad one (4.53 in 48).

THE LITTLE MOVE THAT BECAME A BIG ONE

On October 15, 1988, Athletics general manager Sandy Alderson signed a free-agent outfielder named William Lamar Beane III. Alderson did a great number of brilliant things in the fourteen years that he ran the franchise, but signing Billy Beane may well have been the *most* brilliant, in terms of its singular impact on the club's fortunes.

At that moment, Beane was twenty-six years old. His major-league statistics included a .212 batting average and nothing much to make that .212 look better. Granted, those numbers were compiled in fewer than 250 plate appearances, a small sample. But the truth was that Beane's performance in the *minor* leagues hadn't been particularly exciting, either. He spent three full seasons in Class AA, playing well only in the last of those seasons. Then he bounced around the various Class AAA leagues, playing just well enough to keep his career going; in 400 Triple-A games, Beane had batted .273 with a .326 OBP and .433 slugging percentage. Interestingly enough, the man who would one day become obsessed with plate discipline didn't draw many walks himself; about one for every four games.

This was something of a disappointment for a man who had, nine years earlier, been the Mets' first-round draft pick, the twenty-third player selected in the 1980 June draft. Beane did play a dozen games for the Minnesota Twins in 1987, but he didn't get a World Championship ring because the Twins were too cheap. In 1989 he did get a ring, playing in thirty-seven games for the major-league A's, who swept the Giants in the World Series (without any help from Beane, who didn't make the Series roster).

So why did the A's sign Beane? As Sandy Alderson, then the GM, told me in the spring of 2002, "I don't remember anything about that. I think Walt Jocketty, who was our assistant GM at the time, signed him to a Triple-A contract. As a player, just looking at the model we were following as a franchise, Billy didn't really fit."

The next spring, Beane was just short of twenty-eight years old, and he certainly could have kept playing. No, his career wasn't really going anywhere, but he had spent parts of each of the previous six seasons in the majors, and he'd recently added "Catcher" to his list of occupational duties. Beane could have spent the next three or four years, at least, bouncing around between Triple-A and the majors.

He wasn't having any of it. As Alderson recalled, "Billy heard that we had an opening for an advance scout. He walked into the office, basically retired on the spot, and said he wanted that job. And with the commitment he demonstrated, and the things we'd seen in him since he joined the team, we just thought he'd be the right guy. Billy was noticeably different from other players, in that he came across as being well-read, was certainly articulate, and seemed to be interested in the game beyond how it was played on the field. It wasn't a difficult decision."

Three years after hiring Beane as the club's major-league advance scout, Alderson promoted Beane to assistant general manager. And on October 17, 1997, Alderson left for a job with Major League Baseball, handing over the general manager's duties to Beane. In Alderson's last two seasons as GM, the A's went 78-84 and 65-97. In Beane's first two seasons as GM, the A's went 74-88 and 87-75. And as we all know, he was just getting started.

What sets Billy Beane apart from his peers?

He was one of the first baseball executives to understand that you should virtually *never* spend a high draft pick on a high-school pitcher. He was one of the first baseball executives to understand that "doing the little things" *is* little, compared to the big things like hitting home runs and drawing walks (and preventing your opponents from doing the same). He was one of the first baseball executives to understand that there's *plenty* of cheap hitting talent available, if only you know what to look for and where to look for it. And he was *the* first baseball executive to synthesize all of these empirical truths into a cohesive plan, and successfully implement them across a far-flung baseball organization. Even if Billy Beane retires tomorrow, he'll still deserve a place alongside Branch Rickey, John McGraw, Joe Burke, and Ed Barrow as one of the most successful franchise builders in the game's long history.

I'm grateful to Chris Kahrl for his editorial suggestions, and also to Sandy Alderson and Billy Beane for sharing their thoughts. Sources for this chapter include Bruce Markusen's Baseball's Last Dynasty: Charlie Finley's Oakland A's *(Masters Press, 1998), James A. Hunter and Armen Keteyian's* Catfish: My Life in Baseball *(McGraw-Hill, 1988), Bill Libby and Vida Blue's* Vida: His Own Story *(Prentice Hall, 1972), and Rickey Henderson's* Off Base: Confessions of a Thief *(HarperCollins, 1992).*

Young Slugger in Repose
Oakland Athletics

Master of His Domain
Oakland Athletics

PHILADELPHIA PHILLIES

			ALL-TIME
		YEARS	**NOTES**
C	Bob Boone	1972–1981	After earning psych degree at Stanford, became known as one of the game's smartest players; middle member of MLB's first three-generation family.
1B	John Kruk	1989–1994	An odd selection, perhaps, but 1B hasn't been a strong position for the Phils; key piece of '93 NL champs, and generally considered their most representative member.
2B	Tony Taylor	1960–1971 1974–1976	Came over from the Cubs via trade in May of 1960 and made All-Star team that summer; arguably the club's first outstanding second baseman since Nap Lajoie.
SS	Granny Hamner	1944–1959	All piss and vinegar, "Ham" played 150+ games in six straight seasons, made three straight All-Star teams, and fielded adroitly at both shortstop and second base. ✒
3B	Mike Schmidt	1972–1989	Truly great hitter *and* a 10-time Gold Glove winner, easily ranks as the game's greatest third baseman, and the game's best *player* between Mays and Bonds.
LF	Sherry Magee	1904–1914	Outstanding hitter and fielder, led league in RBI three times with Phils; like his teammate Roy Thomas, a great player who's been mostly forgotten.
CF	Richie Ashburn	1948–1959	Brilliant with the glove, though not as brilliant as you might think, looking at his raw stats; great leadoff man with two batting titles and three OBP titles.
RF	Johnny Callison	1960–1969	Remembered for his great arm, but also led the NL in triples twice and doubles once; three-time All Star, but vision went bad after 1965 and he was never the same.
SP1	Steve Carlton	1972–1986	Won four Cy Young Awards, with 23+ victories in each season; lefty relied on a deadly slider. "Hitting him was like trying to drink coffee with a fork."—Willie Stargell
SP2	Pete Alexander	1911–1917 1930	In first seven years as Phillie, went 190-88 with 2.12 ERA, and led league in IP six times; could throw his good fastball and sharp curve wherever he wanted.
SP3	Robin Roberts	1948–1961	Pitched for Phillies so nobody remembers, but Roberts was the NL's best pitcher in the early 1950s, starting five All-Star Games; fastball had great movement.
SP4	Curt Simmons	1947–1960	With Roberts, gave Phillies the NL's best pitching tandem of 1950s; threw with unorthodox, herky-jerky motion you wouldn't teach, but it worked for him.
RP	Tug McGraw	1975–1984	After two down years with Mets, screwballer joined Phillies and enjoyed a run of fine seasons, including brilliant work in Phils' *only* championship season.

✒ During World War II, baseball teams were willing to employ just about any white man with two arms and two legs (and in a couple of instances, not even that). On September 14, 1944, the Phillies signed seventeen-year-old Granville Hamner. He got into twenty-one games, and then he went back home and finished high school. It wasn't until 1948 that Hamner made it to the big leagues for good.

After a decade as a regular, Hamner was severely limited in 1958 and '59 by a knee injury. In 1960, still only thirty-three, he went back to the minors, playing mostly at third base but also pitching in seven games (three years earlier, suffering from a shoulder injury that limited his effectiveness as a hitter, he'd made an aborted attempt to become a pitcher). In 1961, Hamner went down a level, but this time managed his club . . . and pitched. Throwing mostly knuckleballs, he went 5-4 with a 3.43 ERA for Class A Portsmouth.

And in 1962, Hamner made it back to the major leagues as a knuckleball pitcher. He opened the season as player-manager in the minors, and went 10-4 with a league-best 2.03 ERA in twenty-two games. On July 28, he made his first appearance for the Kansas City A's and tossed two shutout innings. Hamner pitched poorly in his next two outings, though, and so ended his major-league career.

If you poll the good phans of Philadelphia and ask them to name the greatest shortstop in Phillies history, you'll have a landslide winner.

Larry Bowa.

He'll get more votes than everybody else combined. Which makes the lack of Bowa from my first *and* second Phillies teams look mighty strange. As Jayson Stark told me, "People in Philadelphia will really rebel over the omission of Bowa."

If there's one thing he's got over Granny Hamner and Dave Bancroft, it's longevity: Bowa was the Phillies' everyday shortstop for a dozen seasons, compared to only five for Hamner (who also played a lot of second base in those five seasons) and five for Bancroft.

The problem is that Bowa just wasn't very *good*. Don't get me wrong, he was a good player. But a *typical* season for Granny Hamner or Dave Bancroft was an *excellent* season for Larry Bowa.

What was "wrong" with Bowa? Well, nothing. Like I said, he was a good player. But his outstanding fielding percentages masked the fact that he didn't have a lot of range, and he was just decent with the glove. During his peak years, he'd usually bat between .275 and .300, but there weren't many walks or extra-base hits to pad his contribution.

If I weighted longevity just a bit more heavily, Bowa could be at the top where most of you probably think he belongs. But I don't, and so Bowa winds up third. A very *close* third. But third.

		YEARS	NOTES
			NO. 2
C	Andy Seminick	1943–1951 1955–1957	Had good power, and famous around the league for his ability to block home plate; "I think he was born to be a catcher."—Phillies pitcher Bubba Church
1B	Dolph Camilli	1934–1937	Nothing special in '34 and '35, then exploded in '36 and '37 before Phils traded him to Dodgers for . . . who knows? Whatever, it sure as shootin' wasn't enough.
2B	Dave Cash	1974–1976	Only a Phillie for three seasons, but he played virtually every game and was an All-Star all three years, but left after '76 season as one of first big-name free agents.
SS	Dave Bancroft	1915–1920	Fantastic fielder and not bad with the stick; one could also make a good case for Dick Bartell (short but sweet) or Larry Bowa (long but weak) in this spot.
3B	Dick Allen	1963–1969 1975–1976	From 1964 through 1972, there wasn't a more talented hitter on the planet. Period. And if he'd been healthier in both mind and body, that's how he'd be remembered.
LF	Del Ennis	1946–1956	Before Schmidt, Ennis was the club's all-time leader in homers and RBI . . . and like Schmidt, he was booed unmercifully, even though he was a native Philadelphian and knocked in more than 100 runs six times.
CF	Roy Thomas	1899–1908 1910–1911	The National League's top leadoff man for nearly a decade, topping loop in walks seven times in eight seasons; had almost zero power, but outstanding glove.
RF	Gavy Cravath	1912–1920	Failed trials with three different American League clubs before sticking with Phils, then became NL's premier home-run hitter, leading league six times.
SP1	Chris Short	1959–1972	Late in '63, came up with great curve that made him one of NL's best pitchers for the next five seasons, after which chronic back troubles limited him severely.
SP2	Jim Bunning	1964–1967 1970–1971	In 1964, pitched the first perfect game in league history, and in 1971 threw first pitch in Veterans Stadium; in first stint, good for 19 wins and 300 innings per annum.
SP3	Curt Schilling	1992–1999	Uneven tenure in Philly due to injuries; he didn't *really* blossom until going to the desert, but he did win 101 games with Phils, including 47 from '97 through '99.
SP4	Tully Sparks	1903–1910	According to Johnny Evers, Sparks was a master of the "slow ball," and in 1907 he went 22-8 with a 2.00 ERA; won only 95 games with Phillies, but 2.48 ERA with Phils ranks fourth all-time.
RP	Ron Reed	1976–1983	Notre Dame hoops star played in the NBA for a couple of seasons before focusing on baseball with Braves; served as fine complement to Tug McGraw for years.

SINGLE SEASON			
		YEARS	NOTES
C	Darren Daulton	1992 1993	Daulton's 1992 and '93 seasons are the *two* best for a Phillies catcher, and they were his best seasons, by far.
1B	John Kruk	1993	Almost identically productive in each of previous two seasons, but this one gets extra credit for the postseason.
2B	Dave Cash	1974	Cash was a hell of a player for a few years, but the Phillies have never had anything like an MVP candidate at second.
SS	Larry Bowa	1978	Virtually impossible to choose, as seven Phillie shortstops are essentially tied for the best season, but Bowa belongs here.
3B	Mike Schmidt	1980	Set career highs with 48 homers and 121 RBI; grabbed NL MVP, Gold Glove, and World Series MVP.
LF	Sherry Magee	1910	Magee's best of many fine seasons, as he led NL in runs, RBI, batting average, slugging percentage, and OBP.
CF	Lenny Dykstra	1993	One of the all-time great leadoff seasons, as Dykstra led NL in hits (194) and walks (129) *and* smacked 19 homers.
RF	Gavy Cravath	1915	Hit 24 homers, tops in the 20th century before Ruth; he and Alexander were the two best players in the league.
SP	Pete Alexander	1915	He'd been among the game's best since his rookie season, but in '15 he was *the* best, leading Phils to their first pennant.
RP	Jim Konstanty	1950	Junkballer went 16-7 with 2.66 ERA in 74 relief outings, and became first reliever to win an MVP Award.

ALL-ROOKIE			
		YEARS	NOTES
C	Bob Boone	1973	Already a polished defender when he arrived, Boone also hit 10 homers and knocked in 61 runs, fine figures for him.
1B	Willie Montanez	1971	Acquired from Cardinals after Curt Flood refused to report, and hit career-high 30 homers in 158 games as rookie.
2B	Juan Samuel	1984	Okay, so he showed less plate discipline than John Goodman; he also rapped out 70 extra-base hits *and* stole 72 bases.
SS	Jimmy Rollins	2001	Like Samuel, Rollins led NL in triples (12) and steals (46); the big difference was that Rollins could actually play D.
3B	Dick Allen	1964	Perhaps the greatest season ever by a rookie third baseman (though we shouldn't forget Scott Rolen's great 1997).
LF	Del Ennis	1946	Philadelphia boy's 17 home runs don't look all that great unless you know that Ralph Kiner led NL with 23.
CF	Richie Ashburn	1948	Suffered season-ending injury in late August, but before that he batted .333 and stole league-most 32 bases.
RF	Chuck Klein	1928	Debuted on July 30, and batted .360 with .577 slugging pct. the rest of the way . . . and that was just a hint.
SP	Pete Alexander	1911	One season removed from the Class B New York State League, won 28 games and tossed four straight shutouts.
RP	Ricky Bottalico	1995	Closer-in-training—he would take over in '96—posted 2.47 ERA and opponents batted .167 against him in 88 innings.

In 1992, the Phillies won forty-three percent of their games and finished sixth. In 1994, the Phillies won forty-seven percent of their games and finished fourth.

And in between, the Phillies won *sixty* percent of their games, finished first, and came pretty damn close to winning the World Series. At the time, the big story was the *personality* of the Phillies. They were a plain-talkin', tobacco-spittin', hard-livin' bunch of ballplayers, epitomized by their dynamic leadoff man, Lenny Dykstra. *Nails.*

But you know, if it was personality that won the pennant, why didn't the Phillies play nearly so well in 1992 or 1994? The answer, of course, is that the Phillies didn't win in '93 because of their great chemistry; they won because a huge number of their players enjoyed uncharacteristically great seasons. Just look at the Single-Season Lineup . . . *three* 1993 Phillies, and they weren't the only ones. Third baseman Dave Hollins had two great seasons in the majors, and one of them was 1993. Shortstop Kevin Stocker arrived from the minors in July, and batted .324 in seventy games; he finished his career with a .254 average. Tommy Greene won thirty-eight games in his career, and sixteen of them came in 1993.

Yes, trading Larry Bowa and Ryne Sandberg for (gulp) Ivan DeJesus is among the worst deals the Phillies ever made. But might we have made the same judgment on January 27, 1982, when the trade was consummated?

Defensively, Ryno was a question mark even after his fine rookie season, as he moved from third base to second base late in the 1982 season. In *The Scouting Report: 1983,* Tim McCarver commented, "Quick feet on defense. Cubs haven't had a great third baseman since Ron Santo, but Ryne could be it." Same book, Ralph Kiner said, "His range and pivot at second need improvement. . . ." So nobody was even sure where Sandberg would be playing, let alone that he'd win nine straight Gold Gloves.

But while there was no reason to think he'd become a Gold Glove second baseman or a National League MVP, there was ample reason to think that he would become an outstanding major-league baseball player. Just a twentieth-round draft pick in 1978, Sandberg batted .310 with eleven homers and twelve triples in his third professional season. He was twenty years old, and twenty-year-old middle infielders who hit like that in Class AA often become stars. He didn't play quite so well in Class AAA the next year, but using him as a throw-in with the sole aim of acquiring Ivan DeJesus was simply unconscionable.

HOMEGROWN			
		YEARS	NOTES
C	Bob Boone	1972–1981	Drafted in the 20th round out of Stanford as a third baseman, then taught to catch by Andy Seminick.
1B	Dick Allen	1963–1969 1975–1976	Mostly played third with the Phillies, of course, but wound up playing more at first in his career.
2B	Ryne Sandberg	1981	Advanced steadily through system as shortstop after Phils took him in 21st round of '78 June draft.
SS	Granny Hamner	1944–1959	Branch Rickey thought him too brash, so he signed with Phils and played 21 games with big club at 17.
3B	Mike Schmidt	1972–1989	Ohio Univ. grad (business administration) taken in second round of '71 draft, one pick after George Brett.
LF	Greg Luzinski	1970–1980	Phillies' first-round pick in '68 June draft was only 17, and was playing every day for Phils when he was 21.
CF	Richie Ashburn	1948–1959	Signed with Indians at 16, but he was too young and the deal was voided, so the Phils wound up with him.
RF	Del Ennis	1946–1956	Philadelphia boy figured on joining navy after high school, but signed with Phils for 50 bucks before leaving.
SP	Robin Roberts	1948–1961	Worked out for Braves and Phillies at Wrigley Field, and signed with Phils, who offered $25K bonus.
RP	Willie Hernandez	1983	Puerto Rican signed with Phils for $25K but drafted by Cubs before reaching majors; returned to Phils briefly.

TRADED AWAY			
		TRADED	NOTES
C	Smoky Burgess	April 30, 1955	One of three sent to Reds for three; Burgess eventually became the most famous pinch hitter in the game.
1B	Dolph Camilli	March 6, 1938	In return, Phils received Eddie Morgan, a first baseman who didn't play again in the majors . . . and $50,000.
2B	Ryne Sandberg	January 27, 1982	Ryno *and* Bowa for Ivan DeJesus looks a hell of a lot worse today than it did at the time.
SS	Dave Bancroft	June 8, 1920	To this day, the reasons for his departure are murky, but the cash-starved Phils did well in deal with Giants.
3B	Don Money	October 31, 1972	Part of seven-player deal that netted Jim Lonborg, who did give the Phils four good seasons.
LF	Irish Meusel	July 25, 1921	After benched for "indifference," sent to Giants for three players and $30K; 470 RBI over next 4 years.
CF	Larry Hisle	October 21, 1971	Straight up for Tommy Hutton, which didn't work out so well when Hisle became a star for the Twins.
RF	Chuck Klein	November 21, 1933	Another money-making deal for Phils, but it turned out that Klein's best days were behind him; returned later.
SP	Fergie Jenkins	April 21, 1966	The Phils got Larry Jackson, who did give them three solid seasons before retiring rather than play for Expos.
RP	Willie Hernandez	March 24, 1984	Immediately installed as Tigers closer, won Cy Young *and* MVP Awards as Detroit ran away with pennant.

		YEARS	GOLD GLOVE — NOTES
C	Bill Killefer	1911–1917	Regarded as a premier pitcher-handler and noted for the great accuracy of his throws.
1B	Rico Brogna	1997–2000	Close call for Rico over Frank McCormick, who was outstanding but only in Philly for one full season.
2B	Manny Trillo	1979–1982	Won three Gold Gloves in his four seasons, and in '82 he went 89 straight games without making an error.
SS	Dave Bancroft	1915–1920	Outstanding, and in the Hall of Fame on strength of defense . . . well, that and cronyism in Vets Committee.
3B	Mike Schmidt	1972–1989	It's true that players often win Gold Gloves with their bats, but Schmidt deserved at least half of his 10.
LF	Milt Thompson	1993–1994	Good enough to play CF for Phils in late '80s, came back for two seasons in '90s and played excellently in left.
CF	Garry Maddox	1975–1986	"Two thirds of the earth is covered by water; the other one third is covered by Garry Maddox."—Ralph Kiner
RF	Bake McBride	1977–1981	Certainly would have played center field on most teams, but shifted to right because of Maddox.
P	Jim Kaat	1976–1979	After winning 14 straight Gold Gloves in the American League, came to Phils and made it 16 straight.

		YEARS	IRON GLOVE — NOTES
C	Bill Atwood	1936–1940	After solid hitting stats as rookie, fell off the earth. How did he last five seasons? If you know, drop me a line. . . .
1B	Nick Etten	1941–1942	Fine wartime hitter whose best season actually came *before* the war, but couldn't get out of his own way at 1B.
2B	Les Mallon	1931–1932	Not a bad player in 1931, but played terribly both at the plate and in the field in '32, and lost his job.
SS	Frank Parkinson	1921 1923–1924	As a rookie, played 105 games at shortstop; as a sophomore, played 139 games at second base.
3B	Dick Allen	1964–1968	Great athlete but never took to third, and in 1969 the Phillies finally moved him to first base.
LF	Tony Curry	1960–1961	Yes, even worse than Luzinski; "When he picked up a baseball, the whole stadium scattered."—Clay Dalrymple
CF	Johnny Bates	1909–1910	Now forgotten, but a consistently outstanding NL hitter for nine years; not much in the outfield, though.
RF	Stan Benjamin	1939–1942	In 1941, his only season as a regular, the Phillies lost 111 games, and Benjamin helped in many different ways.
P	Seth Morehead	1957–1959	"Seth Morehead could no more handle a bunt than leap over City Hall. It was a fatal flaw."—David M. Jordan

Jack Clements doesn't fall within the scope of this book, but it's my book so I'm going to write about him anyway.

For a nineteenth-century catcher, Jack Clements played forever (1884–1900), and for most of that forever he played for the Phillies (1884–1897). All by itself, that sets Jack Clements apart. But Clements earned a far more significant distinction: he was the last left-handed catcher to play regularly in the major leagues. Eleven lefties—all of them in the nineteenth century— caught at least thirty-five games in the majors, but only three caught more than 200 games, and Clements, with 1,073, was the only one who caught more than 272. (I should note, however, that there are still a few catchers with significant careers for whom we don't know which hand they threw with.)

Clements was round-faced and built something like a squat fire hydrant, but in his prime he was one hell of a hitter. From 1894 through 1896 he batted .373 with power. Sure, it was a hitter's era, but not a lot of guys were doing what Clements did. And he wasn't bad with the glove, either. There's a huge prejudice against lefty catchers, but I've done some research on the subject, and for the life of me I don't see why a left-handed catcher couldn't do just fine, even today.

A lot of strange things happened in baseball during World War II, and one of the strangest was the transformation of Jimmie Foxx, Future Hall of Fame First Baseman, into Jimmie Foxx, Pitcher.

The end of Foxx's tenure as one of baseball's feared sluggers came quickly. In 1941, he batted .300 with nineteen homers and 105 RBI. He slumped badly in 1942, and retired. He came back in 1944 but didn't hit, and finished the season as player-manager of the Class B Piedmont Cubs. On September 5, for no particular reason that I can find, Foxx called upon himself to take the mound against Newport News . . . and he threw a six-hitter, allowing just one run.

Foxx returned to the majors in 1945 with the Phillies. He could still hit well enough to scare wartime pitchers, but various nagging injuries kept him from playing every day. He did, however, pitch a few scoreless innings in an exhibition game. That led to a few relief appearances in real games, and on August 19 he *started* against the Reds. Employing a fastball, change-up, screwball, and the occasional knuckler, Foxx tossed five shutout innings and gained credit for the Phillies' 4–2 victory.

Foxx started again on September 2, but didn't fare as well. He retired for good after the season, leaving the game with 534 home runs and a 1.52 ERA.

ALL-BUST			
		YEARS	NOTES
C	Al Lakeman	1947–1948	Phillies gave up Ken Raffensberger to get Lakeman, who couldn't run or throw and batted .160 in 87 games.
1B	Don Hurst	1933–1934	After leading NL with 143 RBI in 1932, held out in '33 and was never anything like the same player again.
2B	Sparky Anderson	1952	Yes, *that* Sparky Anderson; in his only MLB season, got into 152 games and batted .218 with 12 extra-base hits.
SS	Ted Kazanski	1953–1958	Hamner moved to 2B in '53 to make room for Kazanski, a decent fielder but an absolutely awful hitter.
3B	Rick Schu	1984–1987 1991	His minor-league stats weren't *that* good, but he got the fun job of replacing Mike Schmidt. Not for long, though.
LF	Harry Anderson	1959–1960	Played well as rookie in '57 and even better in '58, then stopped hitting in '59 and was out of the league by '61.
CF	J. D. Drew	—	Drew's agent *told* the Phils it would take $10 million to sign him; they drafted him anyway, but wouldn't pay.
RF	Von Hayes	1983–1991	Perhaps only in Philadelphia would a player this good—"Five for One," they called him—be booed like he was.
SP	Jim Owens	1960–1962	Went 12-12 with 3.22 ERA in 1959, but loved the nightlife and went 11-28 over the next three seasons.
RP	Mike Jackson	2000	Phils signed him for $3 million and wound up getting nothing when he hurt his shoulder on Opening Day.

USED-TO-BE-GREAT			
		YEARS	NOTES
C	Lance Parrish	1987–1988	Played until 1995 but was never really the same after leaving Detroit. Hit .215 in '88 but made All-Star team.
1B	Jimmie Foxx	1945	Only 37 but looked older, hit decently as part-timer . . . and also chipped in with a 1.59 ERA in 23 innings!
2B	Joe Morgan	1983	Joined old teammates Rose and Tony Perez as "The Wheeze Kids" advanced to the World Series.
SS	Dick Groat	1966–1967	Five-time All-Star with Pirates and Cardinals, Groat played his last full season with Phillies.
3B	Alvin Dark	1960	Onetime star shortstop with Giants, by 1960 Dark was on his last legs and playing third base.
LF	Ron Gant	1999–2000	Continuing his tour around the league, ex-Braves star hit 37 homers in 227 games for Phillies.
CF	Andy Van Slyke	1995	One of the game's very best players in 1992, but three years later playing out the string in 63 games with Phils.
RF	Dale Murphy	1990–1992	After 2½ bad seasons in Atlanta, Murphy came to Phillies but didn't improve; regular RF only in 1991.
SP	Pete Alexander	1930	Returned to Phillies after 12-year absence, but couldn't add to 373 career wins despite 9 appearances.
RP	Sparky Lyle	1980–1982	Big American League star from 1970s struggled with Phils, going 12-9 but posting 4.37 ERA in 92 games.

ALL-NAME			
		YEARS	**NOTES**
M	"Doc" James Prothro	1939–1941	One of his pitchers described the part-time dentist as "nervous as a cat in a room full of rocking chairs."
C	"Spud" Virgil Davis	1928–1933 1938–1939	As a boy, Davis thought eating potatoes would make him a better player . . . so he ate them at every meal.
1B	"Kitty" Bill Bransfield	1905–1911	Started out as "Kid," which became "Kiddy," which became "Kitty," which stuck.
2B	"Kid" Bill Gleason	1888–1891 1903–1908	Continuing the theme . . . Gleason got "Kid" early because he wore his cap on the back of his head like a kid.
SS	"Beauty" Dave Bancroft	1915–1920	There are competing explanations, but it seems that "Banny" was simply fond of saying "Beauty."
3B	"Puddin' Head" Willie Jones	1947–1959	Famous for his off-the-field "antics," and nicknamed after a song called "Wooden Head, Puddin' Head Jones."
LF	"Skates" Lonnie Smith	1978–1981	Got this one not because of his great speed, but due to all the slipping and sliding he did in left field.
CF	"Nails" Lenny Dykstra	1989–1996	Also the title of his "autobiography," which is quite possibly the worst book ever published in English.
RF	"Shake and Bake" Bake McBride	1977–1981	Of course, "Bake" itself was a nickname for the Missouri native, whose parents named him Arnold.
SP	"Losing Pitcher" Hugh Mulcahy	1935–1940 1945–1946	Wasn't actually a *bad* pitcher, but in four seasons as a workhorse he lost 76 games while winning only 40.
RP	"Wild Thing" Mitch Williams	1991–1993	The living embodiment of Charlie Sheen's character in *Major League*; problem was, Mitch wasn't acting.

TOP FIVE SEASONS	
YEAR	1980 **RECORD** 91-71
BEST HITTER	Mike Schmidt (MVP)
BEST PITCHER	Steve Carlton (Cy Young)
NOTES	Finally, a World Championship!
YEAR	1915 **RECORD** 90-62
BEST HITTER	Gavy Cravath
BEST PITCHER	Pete Alexander
NOTES	One-year wonders lost to Red Sox in Series.
YEAR	1950 **RECORD** 91-63
BEST HITTER	Del Ennis
BEST PITCHERS	Robin Roberts, Jim Konstanty (MVP)
NOTES	Whiz Kids swept by Yankees in World Series.
YEAR	1993 **RECORD** 97-65
BEST HITTER	Lenny Dykstra
BEST PITCHERS	Curt Schilling, Tommy Greene
NOTES	Mitch Williams, meet Joe Carter.
YEAR	1983 **RECORD** 90-72
BEST HITTER	Mike Schmidt
BEST PITCHER	John Denny (Cy Young)
NOTES	Wheeze Kids lose to Orioles in World Series.

TOP FIVE MANAGERS	
MANAGER	Gene Mauch
YEARS	1960–1968
RECORD	645-684 (.485)
NOTES	Nine years, but remembered for one week.
MANAGER	Pat Moran
YEARS	1915–1918
RECORD	323-257 (.556)
NOTES	Phils never should have let him get away.
MANAGER	Danny Ozark
YEARS	1973–1979
RECORD	594-510 (.538)
NOTES	Like Herzog in K.C., couldn't get over the hump.
MANAGER	Eddie Sawyer
YEARS	1948–1952, 1958–1960
RECORD	390-423 (.480)
NOTES	Low key, remembered by players as "the professor."
MANAGER	Jim Fregosi
YEARS	1991–1996
RECORD	431-463 (.482)
NOTES	Presided over those earthy-but-lovable '93 Phillies.

Giving up a devastating home run doesn't have to devastate your career.

Ralph Terry came back in 1962 and won twenty-three games. Mark Littell came back in 1977 and pitched well, then pitched brilliantly the next two years. Byung-Hyun Kim came back in 2002 and pitched better than he ever had before.

If you want to argue the other side, though, you've got Donnie Moore and Mitch Williams.

Moore came back in 1987 and spent most of it on the DL with a back injury. He came back in 1988 but pitched poorly, and what had happened in 1986 certainly didn't help. In 1989, shortly after getting cut from Kansas City's Triple-A farm club, Moore tried to kill his wife but failed, then killed himself.

Williams came back in 1994 and pitched horribly for the Astros, then pitched horribly for the Angels in 1995 and the Royals in 1997. He pitched thirty-seven innings after the 1993 World Series, and walked fifty-two batters. He'd always been wild, of course, but he'd rarely been so wild that he couldn't pitch effectively. Williams gets a bad rap now, but at the conclusion of the 1993 regular season he could boast 186 saves and a 3.39 career ERA.

Some make it back, and some don't. And if you want to predict who will do what, you'll have to look inside their heads rather than their numbers.

IMMATURITY? OR INJURIES?

In his book on the Hall of Fame, Bill James wrote that Dick Allen "did more to *keep* his teams from winning than anybody else who ever played major league baseball. And if that's a Hall of Famer, I'm a lug nut."

Bill softened a bit in his *New Historical Baseball Abstract*, saying, "Allen had baseball talent equal to that of Willie Mays, Hank Aaron, or Joe DiMaggio, and did have three or four seasons when he was as good a player as anyone in baseball, but lost half his career or more to immaturity and emotional instability."

Really? Allen became a regular in 1964, when he was twenty-two. He played until he was thirty-five, totaling 1,749 games. Jim Rice played nearly 2,100 games, Frank Robinson played 2,800 games, Hank Aaron played nearly 3,300 games.

Aaron was exceptionally durable, of course. Robinson was extraordinarily durable, too, but let's use him as our benchmark. If we assume that Allen's "immaturity and emotional instability" cost him part of his career, a more accurate estimate would be something like a third rather than half. But was it immaturity and emotional instability, or was it run-of-the-mill injuries?

In 1966, Allen dislocated his shoulder and played "only" 141 games.

In 1967, Allen suffered a serious hand injury while pushing a car and missed the last forty games of the season. There were all sorts of rumors about how he "really" hurt his hand, and the fans were rough on him.

In 1968, Allen wanted out of Philadelphia. But he played in 152 games, and in the Year of the Pitcher he hit thirty-three home runs.

In 1969, Allen *really* wanted out of Philadelphia, and it was a big problem. He was the biggest story in town, and it was bad for the club. He showed up late for one game and got fined. He showed up late for another, got suspended, and decided to retire instead of play another game for the Phillies. He did return—with the Phillies having promised they would trade him after the season—and wound up with fantastic numbers considering he played only 118 games. In terms of "immaturity and emotional instability," this was Allen's worst season.

In 1970, having been traded to the Cardinals, Allen got off to a fantastic start, but in the second week of August he tore a hamstring. Despite playing only one more game the rest of the way, he finished with thirty-four homers and 101 RBI in only 122 games.

In 1971, having been traded to the Dodgers, Allen played 155 games, and if you take Dodger Stadium into account, it was one of his best seasons.

In 1972, Allen played 148 games for the White Sox and ran away with the American League's MVP Award.

In 1973, he was playing nearly as well, but broke his leg in a collision at first base and was essentially out for the rest of the season, finishing with only 72 games.

In 1974, Allen was again playing brilliantly. On August 20, he was batting .310 and held huge leads over every other American Leaguer in both home runs and slugging percentage.

And that was essentially the end of Allen's career. He hung around for three more seasons with the Phillies and A's. But he just wasn't the same hitter. As Craig Wright pointed out in *The Baseball Research Journal* (Number 24, 1995), from the beginning of his career through August 20, 1974, Allen batted .300 with a 945 OPS. After that date, Allen batted .245 with a 735 OPS. There's no evidence that his sudden decline had anything to do with immaturity or emotional instability.

That's not to say that Allen didn't have his problems. He got traded too often for a man who could hit like he could. But we're talking about career length here, and I don't think his immaturity had much to do with the length of his career. He just got hurt, and so he didn't enjoy the sort of late career that most great hitters do. It's that, as much as all the other stuff, that has kept him out of the Hall of Fame.

I'm especially grateful to Jayson Stark for his editorial suggestions.

PITTSBURGH PIRATES

		YEARS	NOTES
		ALL-TIME	
C	Manny Sanguillen	1967–1976 1978–1980	"He was a free-swinging, dirty-uniform kind of guy, and he was always smiling. It made *you* smile just to look at him."—novelist Michael Chabon
1B	Willie Stargell	1962–1982	1979 season was his last as full-timer, but he went out in style: in 41 postseason at-bats he went .415-5-13 to sweep the regular-season, NLCS, and WS MVP Awards.
2B	Bill Mazeroski	1956–1972	The best pivot man in history is best remembered for game-winning homer in Game 7 of 1960 WS, but he also put away Game 1 with a two-run shot.
SS	Honus Wagner	1900–1917	Alex Rodriguez's only competition, Wagner led NL in OPS eight times; came to SS late, and in career played 372 games in outfield, 148 at first, 209 at third.
3B	Pie Traynor	1920–1937	John McGraw: "If I were to pick the greatest team player in baseball today, I would have to pick Pie Traynor." NL's greatest third baseman before Eddie Mathews.
LF	Barry Bonds	1986–1992	Best player of his era started in Pittsburgh, was NL's MVP in 1990 and '92 before signing with Giants; ran a lot as Pirate, averaging 45 steals a year from '90 to '92.
CF	Max Carey	1910–1926	Marginal Hall of Famer whose primary offensive weapon was stolen bases; Carey led National League in steals 10 times and still ranks 9th all-time with 738.
RF	Roberto Clemente	1955–1972	One of the most exciting players ever: he could run (10 or more triples 8 times), throw (he peaked at 27 assists in 1961), field (12 Gold Gloves) and hit (.317 career batting).
SP1	Wilbur Cooper	1912–1924	Almost completely forgotten now, but the smooth lefty with the sneaky fastball and the great pickoff move to third base tops franchise list with 202 career victories.
SP2	Babe Adams	1907 1909–1926	Enjoyed long career—he won 194 games, all of them with Pirates—but never surpassed fame gained as rookie for winning three games in 1909 World Series.
SP3	Sam Leever	1898–1910	Retired with .661 career winning percentage, No. 2 on franchise's all-time list, and nobody had a better winning percentage in the 1900s; relied on great curveball.
SP4	Bob Friend	1951–1965	"Warrior" went 73-94 during his first seven seasons as the Pirates won only 37 percent of their games; durable righty started at least 34 games each year from 1956 to 1965.
RP	Roy Face	1953–1968	He didn't invent the forkball but he certainly made it famous (or was it vice versa?), posting an amazing 18-1 record in 1959; still tops franchise list with 188 saves.

The Dodgers have Sandy Koufax, Dazzy Vance, and Don Drysdale. The Cardinals have Dizzy Dean and Jesse Haines. The Giants have Christy Mathewson, Carl Hubbell, and Juan Marichal. The Cubs have Mordecai Brown and Fergie Jenkins. The Braves have Phil Niekro, Greg Maddux, Tom Glavine, and Vic Willis. The Phillies have Pete Alexander and Steve Carlton. The Reds have Eppa Rixey.

Each of these seven National League franchises can claim at least one Hall of Fame pitcher who spent a long time pitching for them.

The only exception, of course, is the Pittsburgh Pirates. And while the Pirates have enjoyed the services of some fine pitchers, none of them has come *close* to getting a plaque in Cooperstown. Willis, of course, is in the Hall of Fame, and he won eighty-nine games for the Pirates. But he won many more games—62 more, to be precise—for the Boston Braves, so the Pirates can't really claim him.

And the Pirates can't squawk, either. Willis is somewhat marginal as a Hall of Fame candidate . . . but he's clearly better than any of the Pirates' best candidates: Wilbur Cooper, Babe Adams, and Sam Leever. What's more, those three starred for the Bucs in the first two decades of the twentieth century. Since then, the Pirates haven't had *anybody*, not for long anyway, who belongs in the Hall.

Bill James rates Andy Van Slyke the thirty-second greatest center fielder in baseball history, and Ginger Beaumont the thirty-ninth greatest. They were both fine defensive players, though they were different sorts of hitters. Van Slyke drew walks and hit for mid-range power, while most of Beaumont's value as a hitter was tied to his batting average.

In Beaumont's eight seasons with Pittsburgh, he earned 168 Win Shares, or twenty-one per season; his two best seasons were thirty Win Shares and twenty-eight Win Shares, in 1902 and 1903. In Van Slyke's eight seasons with Pittsburgh, he earned 166 Win Shares, or twenty-one per season; his two best seasons were thirty-five Win Shares and twenty-eight Win Shares, in 1992 and 1988. Dead heat.

But the Pirates of a century ago didn't play as many games as the Pirates of a decade ago. Beaumont averaged 21.8 Win Shares per 154 games, while Van Slyke averaged 20.5 Win Shares per 154 games. Is that enough to outweigh the timeline adjustment?

I have decided that it is. But that decision is based largely on the fact that while almost all of you know that Andy Van Slyke was a fine player, many of you probably don't know that Ginger Beaumont was fine, too. And both were finer than Lloyd Waner, who's in the Hall of Fame.

NO. 2			
		YEARS	NOTES
C	Tony Peña	1980–1986	Good power for a catcher, threw well, and had a style all his own; named to four All-Star teams and earned three Gold Gloves as Pirate.
1B	Elbie Fletcher	1939–1947	Not exactly a slugger, but he led NL in on-base pct. three straight seasons in the early 1940s; lost two prime seasons to the war, and wasn't the same afterward.
2B	George Grantham	1925–1931	Grantham and Claude Ritchey (1900–1906) both spent seven seasons with Pirates, and both were consistently good but never great; Ritchey the better fielder, by far.
SS	Arky Vaughan	1932–1941	Not only the Pirates' No. 2 shortstop, but—if you believe Bill James—*baseball's* No. 2 shortstop (though Alex Rodriguez certainly has something to say about that).
3B	Bill Madlock	1979–1985	Middling power, not many walks, not much defense . . . but he won two batting titles before dropping off badly in his last two seasons with the club.
LF	Ralph Kiner	1946–1953	One-dimensional? Kiner led National League in homers in each of his first seven years in the league *and* he averaged more than 100 walks per season.
CF	Ginger Beaumont	1899–1906	At his peak, a great leadoff man and just as good as Max Carey; first player to bat in the modern World Series (1903), and flied to center field against Cy Young.
RF	Paul Waner	1926–1940	A career .333 hitter, Waner won three batting titles and had doubles power; Wade Boggs and Tony Gwynn are the modern players Waner most resembles, statistically.
SP1	Deacon Phillippe	1900–1911	The mainstay of the staff topped 20 wins five times from 1900 through 1905; tossed 5 complete games and 3 victories in the 1903 World Series.
SP2	Vic Willis	1906–1909	Went 89-46 as a Pirate; though complete games were relatively common, Willis was particularly likely to go distance, completing 108 of 146 starts during brief stay.
SP3	Vern Law	1950–1967	Like Friend, came to Pirates when they were awful and was still around to play a big role when they got good; better winning percentage but poorer ERA than Friend.
SP4	Doug Drabek	1987–1992	Pirates got Drabek when the Yankees were still giving up future stars for nearly finished ones; Rick Rhoden won 28 games for Yanks, Drabek 92 for Bucs.
RP	Kent Tekulve	1974–1985	Durable and consistent, submariner saved 158 games for Bucs and was just a notch or two below his AL counterpart, Dan Quisenberry.

		YEARS	NOTES
SINGLE SEASON			
C	Jason Kendall	1998	Batted .327 with 51 walks, knocked in 75 runs, and stole 26 bases to set National League record for a catcher.
1B	Willie Stargell	1979	His best years came in LF; '79 wins because a) the Pirates have never had a great 1B and b) those stars were so cool.
2B	Bill Mazeroski	1966	Turned 161 DP's in 162 games; Glenn Beckert and Julian Javier were next best in the league, with 89 apiece.
SS	Honus Wagner	1908	Arguably the biggest offensive year of any shortstop, ever; led National League in OBP, slugging, steals, et cetera.
3B	Bobby Bonilla	1988	Before joining the Mets and George Fostering all over Shea, he was having a perfectly fine career knocking in lots of runs.
LF	Barry Bonds	1992	Set new career highs in HR (34!) and OBP (.456) during his final year as a Pirate; grabbed 2nd MVP and 3rd Gold Glove.
CF	Andy Van Slyke	1992	After Bonds and Van Slyke, something of a drop-off in right field: Alex Cole, Cecil Espy, and Gary Varsho.
RF	Roberto Clemente	1967	Dave Parker was great in '78, but Clemente was better with the glove and nearly as good with the stick.
SP	Wilbur Cooper	1920	The franchise's all-time winner won 24 games in '20, then pitched virtually as well in each of the next two seasons.
RP	Roy Face	1959	Okay, so his peripherals weren't the greatest . . . but geez, the guy went 18-1! And there weren't many vulture jobs, either.

		YEARS	NOTES
ALL-ROOKIE			
C	Manny Sanguillen	1969	Batted .303 and unveiled his unique catching style, looking "like a king crab trying to burrow himself into the earth . . ."
1B	Gus Suhr	1930	One of first rookies to drive in 100 runs (107), and the next Sept. he began eventual NL-record consecutive-game streak.
2B	Dots Miller	1909	Stats ain't much to look at, but he knocked in 87 runs and played great defense for World Champs.
SS	Glenn Wright	1924	Played 153 games and knocked in 111 runs, and played even better the next year for National League pennant winners.
3B	Bill Brubaker	1936	After sipping cups of coffee in previous four seasons, finally won regular spot and knocked in 102 runners.
LF	Kiki Cuyler	1924	Walks the only missing ingredient, as Hazen batted .354 with 16 triples and 32 steals in only 117 games.
CF	Lloyd Waner	1927	Joined his big brother (below) to form the greatest sibling-teammates combination in baseball (sports?) history.
RF	Paul Waner	1926	Arrived when he was 20 and was immediately superb, topping league with 22 triples and 118 Runs Created.
SP	Cy Blanton	1935	No raw kid, the 26-year-old speedballer won 18 games and led National League with 4 shutouts and 2.58 ERA.
RP	Diomedes Olivo	1962	Went 5-1 with 2.77 ERA in 62 games, which was pretty good for a *43-year-old* rookie from the Dominican Republic.

The Pittsburgh Pirates have never had a Rookie of the Year. The Pittsburgh Pirates have never had a Rookie of the Year. The Pittsburgh Pirates have never had a Rookie of the Year.

Did I mention that the Pittsburgh Pirates have never had a Rookie of the Year?

Sorry to be so obnoxious about it, but that's something that I hope sticks in your brain and stays there. Oh, they've come close. In 1982, second baseman Johnny Ray finished a very close second to Dodgers second baseman Steve Sax, and there's no obvious reason why Sax didn't instead finish a close second to Ray. Sax had a slight edge in on-base percentage, but Ray had a slight edge in slugging percentage, Ray played twelve more games than Sax, and Ray played better defense. Sax did steal forty-nine bases and played for a team that almost won a division title—the Dodgers finished one game behind the Braves—and it's probably those two things that gave him the award by just six points over Ray.

I should probably mention that if there'd been a Rookie of the Year award before 1947, Pirates would likely have won a bunch of them. Dots Miller, Jim Viox, Kiki Cuyler, both Waner brothers, Cy Blanton, Johnny Rizzo . . . all these men would have been strong Rookie of the Year candidates.

The two worst trades in franchise history both involve young middle infielders.

The Pirates traded Dick Bartell to the Phillies for shortstop Tommy Thevenow and pitcher Clyde Willoughby, and they traded Willie Randolph, Dock Ellis, and Ken Brett to the Yankees for Doc Medich.

Bartell had already spent three seasons with the Pirates, so it's not like they didn't know how good he was. Bartell was *clearly* a better hitter than Thevenow, and a better fielder as well. At the time of the trade, Willoughby's career stats included a 38-56 record and a 5.82 ERA. After the trade, Thevenow continued to not hit, and Willoughby went 0-2 before dropping from the majors forever.

Why did the Pirates trade Bartell? The way he tells it, owner Barney Dreyfuss just didn't like him, probably because Bartell had the temerity to hold out for a month before the 1930 season. According to Bartell, the last thing Drefuss said to him was, "I'll send you to a place, young man, where they will not even hear you when you ask for the kind of money you want."

Why did the Pirates trade Randolph? They wanted Medich—who'd won forty-nine games for the Yankees over the previous three seasons—and they already had Rennie Stennett at second base. It just didn't work out.

		YEARS	NOTES
HOMEGROWN			
C	Manny Sanguillen	1967–1976 1978–1980	Panamanian was traded to Oakland for a manager, but returned a year later and won Game 2 of the '72 Series.
1B	Willie Stargell	1962–1982	Grew up in Oakland and played on same high-school team with Tommy Harper and Curt Motton.
2B	Willie Randolph	1975	Most would presumably choose Mazeroski here, but Randolph was a demonstrably better player.
SS	Arky Vaughan	1932–1941	Yankees supposedly just missed signing him because scout Bill Essick detoured to see another kid prospect.
3B	Bob Elliott	1939–1946	Signed out of El Centro Junior College in California, then spent most of the next three summers starring in Savannah, Georgia.
LF	Barry Bonds	1986–1992	Sixth overall pick in '85 draft; some pedigree . . . his aunt Rosie, a hurdler, was member of '64 Olympic Team.
CF	Max Carey	1910–1926	His professional experience consisted of two seasons in the Class B Central League when Bucs grabbed him.
RF	Dave Parker	1973–1983	Taken in 14th round of draft in '70, then put the fear of God into pitchers in four different minor leagues.
SP	Bob Friend	1951–1965	Signed out of Purdue by Rickey, pitched decently for a few years, then led NL with 2.83 ERA in 1955.
RP	Kent Tekulve	1974–1985	Signed as free agent in 1969, then spent nearly seven seasons in the minors before finally making it for good.

		TRADED	NOTES
TRADED AWAY			
C	Tony Pena	April 1, 1987	Still had a few good years left and won Gold Glove in '91, but a great deal for the Pirates, who got Van Slyke.
1B	Charlie Grimm	October 27, 1924	Part of big deal that sent Grimm, Maranville, and Wilbur Cooper to Cubs for three players.
2B	Willie Randolph	December 11, 1975	Can't really blame the Pirates, as they already had Stennett . . . but Randolph *was* a great prospect.
SS	Joe Cronin	April 1, 1928	With Glenn Wright entrenched at short, Bucs sold Cronin to Kansas City, who sold him to Washington.
3B	Bob Elliott	September 30, 1946	After seven fine seasons with Pirates, traded to Boston and won MVP Award in his first season with Braves.
LF	Moises Alou	August 16, 1990	The PTBNL in deal that sent three young players to Expos in exchange for Zane Smith.
CF	Gus Bell	October 14, 1952	Great talent but didn't do a lot in three seasons with Bucs, and blossomed only after trade to Cincinnati.
RF	Kiki Cuyler	November 28, 1927	Got into a hassle with manager Donie Bush, and traded to Cubs with plenty of great years left in him.
SP	Dazzy Vance	1915	Sold to Yankees for a pittance, but didn't become *Dazzy Vance* until nearly seven years later.
RP	Gene Garber	October 25, 1972	He'd pitched brilliantly in Triple-A but was hammered (0-3, 5.61) in majors, so off to K.C. for Jim Rooker.

GOLD GLOVE

		YEARS	NOTES
C	Tony Peña	1980–1986	One of the game's best for nearly two decades, and three of his four Gold Gloves came with Bucs, 1983–1985.
1B	Charlie Grimm	1919–1924	Remembered for long career as player and manager with Cubs, but with Bucs he was top glove man in the league.
2B	Bill Mazeroski	1956–1972	Merely the greatest defensive second baseman of all time, and in 2001 he finally made the Hall of Fame.
SS	Honus Wagner	1901–1917	'Twas a different game; Hans didn't become an everyday shortstop until he was 29 . . . and then he became the best.
3B	Pie Traynor	1920–1935 1937	John McGraw: "I'll bet he ruined more base hits for my club than any other two infielders in the game."
LF	Barry Bonds	1986–1992	It's not easy to win a Gold Glove in left field, but Bonds did it three times as a Pirate (and five times with Giants).
CF	Omar Moreno	1975–1982	I selected Moreno because he's relatively modern, but Lloyd Waner and Max Carey were both great, too.
RF	Roberto Clemente	1955–1972	Twelve Gold Gloves; claimed to have inherited his throwing arm—"El Bazooka"—from his mother.
P	Wilbur Cooper	1912–1924	Famous for his pickoff move to third base, which he loved to work with Pie Traynor at the hot corner.

IRON GLOVE

		YEARS	NOTES
C	Don Slaught	1990–1995	There have certainly been worse, but Slaught probably the worst to play regularly for a few years.
1B	Dick Stuart	1952–1962	Stuart and the recent Frank Thomas were probably the two worst longtime first basemen ever.
2B	Jim Viox	1912–1916	Fielding stats were horrific; and yes, he was even worse than George "Boots" Grantham.
SS	Dick Cole	1951–1956	With Branch Rickey tinkering around, the Pirates' infield was just a big mess in the early '50s.
3B	Bobby Bonilla	1986–1991	He tried real hard, but, as Bill James wrote, "was no more a third baseman than he was an astronaut."
LF	Al Martin	1992–1999	He was fast, but he had a devil of a time getting a decent jump on batted balls and couldn't throw.
CF	Ralph Kiner	1946	Might not have been as bad as Branch Rickey later thought, but he didn't have any business in center field.
RF	Ham Hyatt	1909–1914	Ham's hands reduced him to bench status, but he served as premier pinch hitter for five seasons.
P	Bob Veale	1962–1972	Like a lot of guys with poor control—Veale led NL in walks four times—he had problems fielding his position.

Ralph Kiner, center fielder?

For part of one season, yes. As a rookie in 1946, Kiner played seventy-six games in center field (along with sixty-four in left). He actually opened that season as the regular in center, and played there regularly through July 21, when the Pirates wrapped up a home stand with a doubleheader. They were rained out on July 23, and when they played the first game of their road trip on July 24, Kiner played left, with Jim Russell shifting from left to center.

For the rest of that season and the nine more he played, Kiner never again saw action at any position other than left field.

Branch Rickey wrote of Kiner, somewhat famously, "Ruth could field. Our man cannot." And Rickey was right; Ruth was a pretty good outfielder (at least in his prime), while Kiner was a poor outfielder. But he wasn't *terrible*. He was good enough to play center field without completely embarrassing himself, and even after moving to left field permanently, he was a hell of a lot better than a lot of guys who have been sent out there over the years.

(Lest this be considered a dig at Branch Rickey, let history remember that Bill Mazeroski began his professional career as a shortstop. Rickey supposedly saw Maz make one play as a second baseman and said, "Leave that kid at second. He is now a second baseman.")

Among the *obvious* principles by which one *must* run a cash-poor franchise is this one: Don't sign mediocre players to multiyear contracts.

Pirates general manager Cam Bonifay committed that blunder . . . and then he committed it again, and again and again. And finally, when one of those idiotic signings *completely* exploded in his face, Bonifay got fired.

Bonifay will be remembered, I think, for two things, one of them good and one of them bad. The good was the trade that brought Brian Giles to Pittsburgh in exchange for Ricardo Rincón. The bad was signing free agent Derek Bell to a two-year deal worth nearly $10 million.

Bell, of course, was horrible. He played in forty-six games in 2001, batted .173, and was released—after threatening "Operation Shutdown"—shortly before the 2002 season began. But signing Bell was really just the logical end to Bonifay's team-building philosophy. Previously, Bonifay had spent actual money on has-beens and never-really-weres like Kevin Young, Pat Meares, Mike Benjamin, and Terry Mulholland.

And to what end? Getting the Bucs to the magical .500 mark? Well, it didn't work. Bonifay ran the show for eight years, and not even once did they win more than they lost.

ALL-BUST			
		YEARS	NOTES
C	Vic Janowicz	1953–1954	First Heisman Trophy winner (1950) to play baseball, signed for big dough and batted .214 in 83 games.
1B	Ed Konetchy	1914	Cardinals star supposed to break Bucs' first-base hex, but posted horrible numbers in his only season with club.
2B	Warren Morris	2000	Getting him from Rangers looked like great move for Cam Bonifay, but he slumped after solid rookie season.
SS	Eddie O'Brien	1953 1955–1958	Branch Rickey said of Eddie and twin brother Johnny, "They can't miss, I'll wager that." We'll take that bet.
3B	Art Howe	1974–1975	Future Astros stalwart batted .195 with 2 homers in 92 games with Pirates; traded to 'stros for Tommy Helms.
LF	Steve Kemp	1985–1986	Reported with sore shoulder, then lost regular job in July after hitting 2 homers in 181 at-bats.
CF	Dino Restelli	1949, 1951	Opened career with 9 homers in two weeks . . . and hit exactly 4 more over the rest of his (short) career.
RF	Derek Bell	2001	Signed for two years and nearly $10 million, finished Pirates career with 5 home runs and 13 RBI.
SP	Steve Blass	1973	After going 19-8 with 2.49 ERA in '72, went 3-9 with 9.85 ERA as Bucs finished 2½ games out of first place.
RP	Ray Krawczyk	1984–1986	First-round draft pick (by Red Sox) piled up K's in minors, but hammered (0-3, 8.45) in 26 MLB innings.

USED-TO-BE-GREAT			
		YEARS	NOTES
C	Lance Parrish	1994	Pirates were fifth of Parrish's six post-Detroit stops, and he batted .270 with 3 homers as Don Slaught's backup.
1B	Hank Greenberg	1947	After great '46 with Tigers, signed with Pirates and hit 25 homers with NL-best 104 walks in last MLB season.
2B	Wally Backman	1990	Ex-Met stalwart bounced back from a lousy year with Twins to post .374 OBP as part-timer for Bucs.
SS	Shawon Dunston	1997	Only with the club for a few weeks, but batted .394 and played shortstop every day for the last time in his career.
3B	Maury Wills	1967–1968	A shortstop his entire career, except for the two seasons in Pittsburgh; in mid-30s but still had plenty of speed.
LF	Amos Otis	1984	He lost it in a hurry; after ignominious departure from Royals, batted .165 in 40 games with Bucs.
CF	Freddie Lindstrom	1933–1934	Longtime Giant played center field for Pirates in '33 and left field in '34; one of the worst Hall of Famers.
RF	Dixie Walker	1948–1949	"The People's Cherce" in Brooklyn, but finished career in Pittsburgh and led NL with 13 pinch hits in 1949.
SP	Luis Tiant	1981	Joined Pirates after strike and went 2-5 in 9 starts, the highlight a complete-game four-hitter on September 15.
RP	Clem Labine	1960–1961	Joined Bucs late in '60 and pitched brilliantly (3-0, 1.48) down stretch before getting hammered in World Series.

	ALL-NAME		
		YEARS	NOTES
C	"Spanky" Mike LaValliere	1987–1993	He had a round face and a round body, but he hit .300 a couple of times and was happy to take a few pitches.
1B	"Kitty" William Bransfield	1901–1904	Bransfield had a large shock of hair that dangled over his eyes, in a style that some girls of his time wore.
2B	"No Touch" Bill Mazeroski	1956–1972	For his speed at making transfer on the double play; his teammates called him "Tree Trunk" for solidity on pivot.
SS	"Flying Dutchman" Honus Wagner	1900–1917	Oddly enough, "Honus" is actually a nickname, as was "Hans" . . . NL's greatest player was born John Wagner.
3B	"Pie" Harold Traynor	1920–1937	There are four known explanations for "Pie," one of which doesn't have anything at all to do with pie.
LF	"Big Poison" Paul Waner	1926–1940	There are competing versions of origin, with the brothers' nicknames supposedly invented in either . . .
CF	"Little Poison" Lloyd Waner	1927–1941 1944–1945	. . . Ebbets Field or the Polo Grounds by a New Yorker with an accent; physically, they were almost the same size.
RF	"Possum" George Whitted	1919–1921	According to Fred Lieb, Whitted loved to hunt and was raised in Carolina possum-hunting country.
SP	"Babe" Charles Adams	1907 1909–1926	The first notable "Babe" got nickname from women fans in Louisville, who shouted "Oh, you babe!" at him.
RP	"Bones" Kent Tekulve	1974–1985	At 6'4" and 175 pounds, the side-arming Tekulve looked all bones to the hitters.

TOP FIVE SEASONS
YEAR 1902 **RECORD** 103-36
BEST HITTER Honus Wagner
BEST PITCHERS Jack Chesbro, Jesse Tannehill
NOTES Amazing team, but World Series still a year away.
YEAR 1909 **RECORD** 110-42
BEST HITTER Honus Wagner
BEST PITCHER Howie Camnitz
NOTES Broke Cubs' streak and beat Tigers in World Series.
YEAR 1960 **RECORD** 95-59
BEST HITTERS Dick Groat, Don Hoak
BEST PITCHERS Vern Law (Cy Young), Bob Friend
NOTES Beat Yankees in the strangest World Series ever.
YEAR 1903 **RECORD** 91-49
BEST HITTER Honus Wagner
BEST PITCHERS Sam Leever, Deacon Phillippe
NOTES Topped Boston in first modern World Series.
YEAR 1971 **RECORD** 97-65
BEST HITTER Willie Stargell
BEST PITCHERS Steve Blass, Dock Ellis
NOTES In Clemente's swan song, beat Orioles in World Series.

TOP FIVE MANAGERS
MANAGER Danny Murtaugh
YEARS 1957–1964, 1967, 1970–1971, 1973–1976
RECORD 1115-950 (.540)
NOTES Among his virtues was apparent color-blindness.
MANAGER Fred Clarke
YEARS 1900–1915
RECORD 1422-969 (.595)
NOTES Pirates were better when he also played.
MANAGER Jim Leyland
YEARS 1986–1996
RECORD 851-863 (.496)
NOTES Assigned *roles*, and everybody knew who was boss.
MANAGER Chuck Tanner
YEARS 1977–1985
RECORD 711-685 (.509)
NOTES "What, me worry?" worked well for a few years.
MANAGER Donie Bush
YEARS 1927–1929
RECORD 246-178 (.580)
NOTES Only three seasons, but includes trip to World Series in '27.

What's in a name?

There was, for at least a few years, a persistent rumor going around that when the Veterans Committee met in 1967 to consider candidates for the Hall of Fame, the materials on Lloyd Waner accidentally included *Paul's* batting stats.

I think this gives the Veterans Committee far too much credit. Those old coots elected plenty of players just as undeserving as Little Poison without needing an excuse like "Oops! Somebody gave us the wrong statistics." Of course, it certainly didn't hurt Lloyd that his big brother was already in the Hall (and deserved to be).

When you hear the nicknames, "Big Poison" and "Little Poison," you just assume that Paul was bigger than Lloyd. But they were almost exactly the same size, right around five-nine and 150 pounds. Paul was "Big" because he was three years older, and also because he was a *lot* more dangerous. Paul finished his career with 605 doubles, 113 home runs, and a .473 slugging percentage. His little brother's totals in the same categories were 281, 27, and .393. Which is to say, they were completely different sorts of hitters. What's more, Paul (1,091) drew a *lot* more walks than Lloyd (420). Paul's kid brother was a good player for a long time, but putting him in the Hall of Fame was a mistake. One way or the other.

SOWING THE SEEDS

The early-1950s Pirates are legendary.

Legendarily bad.

In 1952, the Pirates lost 112 games, more than any National League team had managed to lose since 1935. The number-one catcher for those '52 Pirates was Joe Garagiola, and he later made a fine career out of running down not only his own career—oddly enough, he actually played well in '52—but also those awful Pirates. It wasn't just the '52 squad, either; the Bucs finished last in every season from 1952 through 1955.

And the architect of those wonderful collections of talent?

None other than Branch Rickey, the Hall of Fame executive who had built great dynasties in St. Louis and Brooklyn.

When Rickey is remembered today, of course, it's as the man who signed Jackie Robinson. Or as the man who invented the modern farm system. Most baseball fans don't have any idea that Rickey ran the Pirates for five years. And of those fans who do have some idea, most consider Rickey's tenure something of an embarrassment, the result of what happens when a brilliant thoroughbred isn't put out to pasture soon enough.

Rickey essentially ran the club from 1951 through 1955. Over those five seasons, the Pirates won 269 games and lost 501; essentially, they won thirty-five percent of their games with Rickey in charge. And that's pretty awful. The second-worst team in the National League over that period was the Cubs, but they managed to win forty-four percent of their games.

So what happened to Rickey's previously magical touch?

Well, he didn't fare too well when making trades. When writing about Rickey's deals, it's obligatory to list the following as disasters:

- On June 15, 1951, Rickey traded Wally Westlake and Cliff Chambers to the Cardinals for five players, including Joe Garagiola and Howie Pollet.
- On October 14, 1952, Rickey traded outfielder Gus Bell to the Reds for Cal Abrams, Joe Rossi, and Gail Henley.
- On December 26, 1953, Rickey traded infielder Danny O'Connell to the Braves for five players . . . and $100,000.
- On June 26, 1953, Rickey traded Ralph Kiner, along with Joe Garagiola, Howie Pollet, and Catfish Metkovich to the Cubs for six players . . . and $150,000.

Wally Westlake had been a fine player for the Pirates, but he was thirty years old, and Rickey generally didn't care much for players on the wrong side of thirty. And you know what? Westlake was terrible in 1952, and effective only in a part-time role afterward.

Bell was a decent young player, and blossomed after going to Cincinnati. When he played for the Pirates, though, both Rickey and manager Billy Meyer considered Bell to be somewhat lacking in desire. In 1953, after Bell had spent two full seasons in the major leagues, Rickey shipped him to the Pacific Coast League for a few weeks of reality therapy. As Rickey explained to the *Pittsburgh Sun-Telegraph*, "1) I want to win a pennant, 2) I want fellows on the club who can help me win it, 3) Bell can help me win it. He's capable of more ability than he's showing. It isn't that he's not trying. There are several things he has to get straightened out."

Rickey was right about Bell, who *was* capable of more ability than he'd shown. And who knows? If he'd stayed in Pittsburgh, maybe he never would have shown it.

Neither Rossi nor Henley ever did anything in the majors, but people forget that Abrams played well for the Pirates in 1953. In 1954, Rickey traded Abrams to the Orioles for pitcher Dick Littlefield, who won ten games for the Pirates that season. What's more, in

1956, Littlefield and Bobby Del Greco—a Rickey discovery—were traded to the Cardinals for Bill Virdon, who played a big role with the Pirates for years. Yes, trading Gus Bell was a clinker of a deal, but it wasn't quite as bad as people think.

Fifty years later, it's hard to understand why anybody made a fuss over Danny O'Connell. He'd played well as a rookie shortstop in 1950, but spent the next two years in the army. When he came back in 1953, he was twenty-six years old, and no longer deemed fit to play shortstop. O'Connell wound up spending ten seasons in the majors, but he never hit much, wound up at second base . . . and as you might recall, the Pirates found themselves a pretty good second baseman just a few years later. None of the five players the Pirates got for O'Connell did much of anything, but the deal really wasn't about players; it was about money, and Rickey got a hundred grand from the Braves.

And then, the Kiner deal. Rickey hated Kiner as a ballplayer; in 1952, he wrote Pirates owner John Galbreath a *fifteen-page* memo on Kiner's shortcomings. Rickey disliked Kiner for two reasons that everybody knows about—Kiner couldn't run, and by the early 1950s he was pretty lousy in left field—and one that nobody talks about: Kiner made a lot of money.

The Pirates were cash-starved. Kiner's salary was close to $100,000. Rickey received, in addition to six nondescript players, $150,000 cash when he dealt Kiner to the Cubs. Do the math, and it's pretty obvious why Rickey traded Kiner. He figured Kiner wouldn't be around when the Pirates finally became contenders, so he might as well milk Kiner for all he could, when he could.

That was 1953. By 1956, Kiner was out of the game, his career abbreviated by chronic back problems. Yes, Kiner *was* the Pirates at that time. And yes, the Pirates' attendance, already suffering badly, dropped to the bottom of the league after Kiner's departure. But given what we now know about his career, does anyone really want to argue that the organization would have been better off with Kiner finishing his career in Pittsburgh?

Looking at those four deals now, it seems to me that only the Bell trade might be considered truly bad. And even with that one, there are extenuating circumstances.

Still, Rickey's detractors had their evidence. When he assumed his new role as general manager shortly after the 1950 World Series ended, Rickey made the mistake of announcing a timetable.

"We're pointing toward 1955," he said. "That's when the bells will start ringing and the red wagon comes down the street. That's when Pittsburgh folks will shout, 'By George, this is it.' "

Five-year plans are a bad idea, as Nikita Khrushchev and Cam Bonifay would later prove in spectacular fashion. It's okay to *have* a five-year plan, in fact it's probably good to have one. But if you tell people you've got one, you're only setting yourself up for the big fall. And that's what happened to Rickey, who found himself with not enough talent and not enough money to make his plan work in anything like five years.

Then again, maybe the ol' Mahatma hadn't completely lost his bearings. Maybe Rickey simply miscalculated. Maybe he should have announced a *ten-year* plan instead. Because in 1960, the Pirates won their first World Championship since 1925. And that season,

- the Pirates' first baseman was Dick Stuart,
- their second baseman was Bill Mazeroski,
- their shortstop was Dick Groat,
- their left fielder was Bob Skinner,
- their right fielder was Roberto Clemente,
- their top starters were Vern Law and Bob Friend,
- and their relief ace was Roy Face.

All of these men either were acquired by the Pirates when Rickey was running the show, or came of age as major leaguers when Rickey was running the show. Most of the credit went to Joe Brown, who'd taken over as general manager after Rickey got fired. But what, exactly, did Brown do? Yes, he made a great trade when he acquired Bill Virdon from the Cardinals. But after 1960, the Pirates didn't seriously contend again until 1966, and they didn't reach the postseason again until 1970.

I'm not suggesting that Rickey did a *great* job in Pittsburgh. But if Rickey hadn't been running the Pirates in the early 1950s, it seems likely that they'd never have reached the World Series in 1960. And without Clemente, they might not have gotten there in 1971, either.

I'm grateful to Geoff Reiss for writing many of the player comments, and to Jack Moulds for his editorial suggestions. Sources for this chapter include Fred Lieb's The Pittsburgh Pirates: An Informal History *(Putnam, 1948) and Andrew O'Toole's* Branch Rickey in Pittsburgh *(McFarland & Co., 2000).*

With Branch Rickey close at hand, Duke's Dick Groat signs with Pirates on June 7, 1952. Two weeks later, he took over at shortstop.
National Baseball Library, Cooperstown, New York

St. Louis Cardinals

		YEARS	NOTES
			ALL-TIME
C	Ted Simmons	1968–1980	Fantastic hitter led Cards in OPS six times—only Musial and Hornsby did so more often—and he wasn't nearly as bad with the glove as his reputation suggests.
1B	Johnny Mize	1936–1941	Sometimes stats vividly represent a player's ability, and sometimes they're just freaky; in 1938 and '39, Mize hit 30 triples but didn't steal a single base.
2B	Rogers Hornsby	1915–1926	Best-hitting 2B ever, and the only player other than Ruth to lead his league in OPS six straight times; Cards parlayed him into 1,311 games worth of Frankie Frisch
SS	Ozzie Smith	1982–1996	Evolved from Ordoñez-like ability at the plate to being a pretty good hitter; defensive brilliance aside, his greatest moment may have been his homer in '85 NLCS.
3B	Ken Boyer	1955–1965	In 1964, became first NL third baseman to win MVP Award, and remained only one until Joe Torre in 1971, got old fast, hitting only 13 homers after turning 36.
LF	Stan Musial	1941–1963	"The Man" was a model of consistency: he hit 475 homers but never led the National League, and finished with 1,815 hits at home and 1,815 hits on the road.
CF	Curt Flood	1958–1942	So famous for challenging the reserve clause, people forget that he was truly amazing in center field, and a career .293 hitter, to boot.
RF	Enos Slaughter	1938–1942 1946–1953	Missed three years during World War II, but finished his career with a .300 average; "He is the greatest competitor ever to put on a big league uniform."—Bucky Harris
SP1	Bob Gibson	1959–1975	The greatest World Series performer ever? Went 7-2 with a 1.89 ERA and 92 K's in 81 innings *and* he's the only pitcher to win two Game 7's.
SP2	Dizzy Dean	1930–1937	From 1933 through '36, he averaged 25 wins and 7 saves per season; of his 150 career wins, 147 came before he turned 30, and of course he's not in the Hall for his record.
SP3	Larry Jackson	1955–1962	Consistently fine pitcher who'd have cleared 200 wins with ease, except he wouldn't pitch for Montreal; from '57 through '62, went 90-70 with 3.56 ERA.
SP4	Lon Warneke	1937–1942	He's primarily remembered for his long service with the Cubs, but Warneke went 83-49 in five-plus seasons and never had anything close to a losing record.
RP	Bruce Sutter	1981–1984	In four seasons as Cardinal, led National League in saves three times, thanks to devastating split-finger fastball and a great manager who knew exactly how to use him.

What is it about catchers that baseball writers don't get?

They missed on Gary Carter for five years, and they *really* missed on Ted Simmons. In 1994, his first year of Hall of Fame eligibility, Simmons garnered only seventeen votes out of a possible 456. And with that, he dropped off the ballot forever (at least according to the rules of the time).

Ted Simmons has more base hits to his credit than any player in history whose primary position was catcher. Only five catchers have more home runs than Simmons, and only *one* catcher (Yogi Berra) has more RBI. And by the way, he was good enough with the glove to *catch* more games than Berra, Johnny Bench, and all but seven other catchers.

Simmons did so poorly in the Hall of Fame voting that it's silly to ask why he wasn't elected; rather, we have to wonder why he came so *far* from election. There are two obvious reasons: defense, and decline. Simmons was, as Bill Deane has demonstrated, at least a decent defensive catcher. However, perhaps because of the way Simmons's career ended—as a DH/first baseman/pinch hitter for six years—he got the reputation as the big slow guy who couldn't do anything with the glove. And I guess that's what stuck with people.

I wish I still had the memo.

In 1990, I was working for Bill James, and Bill asked me to write something about Ray Lankford and Bernard Gilkey, two of the Cardinals' top prospects. They'd played together with Triple-A Louisville that season . . . actually, they'd both played exactly 132 games with Louisville that season, which seemed to make a comparison "baby simple" (as my friend Rob McQuown used to say).

And looking at their numbers with Louisville, I concluded that Gilkey was a) then the better player, and b) had the better future. After all, Gilkey had batted .295, drawn seventy walks, and stolen forty-five bases, while Lankford had batted just .260 with seventy walks and thirty steals.

I was wrong, though, and Bill told me so in memo form.

Bill saw that Lankford had more power, having cracked forty-three extra-base hits (including ten home runs) to Gilkey's thirty-seven (three homers). Bill saw that Lankford was nine months younger than Gilkey. And biggest of all—if I remember the memo correctly—Bill saw that while 1990 was Gilkey's best minor-league season to that point, it was Lankford's *worst.*

Gilkey did look like a better player, that one season. But you have to look at the bigger picture, and in the bigger picture Lankford was the better player before 1990 . . . and after.

NO. 2			
		YEARS	NOTES
C	Tim McCarver	1959–1969 1973–1974	Bonus baby didn't establish himself until 1963; probably not quite as good as he thinks he was, but certainly one of the NL's top defenders for at least a decade.
1B	Mark McGwire	1997–2001	In case you were stuck on an island with Tom Hanks or something . . . In his two healthy seasons, Big Mac hit 135 home runs and drew 295 walks.
2B	Frankie Frisch	1927–1937	Came over from Giants in huge trade because he couldn't get along with McGraw and Hornsby couldn't get along with Rickey; managed Cards to championship in 1934.
SS	Marty Marion	1940–1950	No, he probably didn't deserve that MVP Award in 1944—I guess you had to be there—but he's one of the greatest glove men ever, anchoring an outstanding defensive team.
3B	Whitey Kurowski	1941–1949	One of the game's top third basemen until separate arm injuries in 1948 and '49 destroyed his career; cracked decisive homer in Game 5 of 1942 World Series.
LF	Joe Medwick	1932–1940 1947–1948	Batted .379 with 5 RBI in 1934 Series, and in 1937 crashed his way to Triple Crown, feat that hasn't been matched in National League since.
CF	Ray Lankford	1990–2001	Left under something of a cloud, but with 222 home runs, ranks behind only Musial and Boyer; reputation suffers because his best season came as sophomore.
RF	George Hendrick	1978–1984	An aggressive line-drive hitter known for killing pitchers' mistakes; never great but always good; batted .294 and slugged .470 during tenure with club.
SP1	John Tudor	1985–1988 1990	If only he could have stayed healthy . . . in 1990, his last season, Tudor went 12-4 with 2.40 ERA; .705 career winning pct. (62-26) with Cards tops franchise list.
SP2	Jesse Haines	1920–1937	Won 210 games, second only to Gibson on franchise list; generally identified as a knuckleball pitcher, but his knuckler wasn't the conventional version of the pitch.
SP3	Harry Brecheen	1940 1943-1952	Granted, three of his good seasons came during World War II, but he twice led NL in shutouts *after* the war; relied on great control of screwball and curve.
SP4	Mort Cooper	1938–1945	With his brother Walker as battery-mate, totaled 65 victories from 1942 through '44, as Cardinals won three pennants and two World Series.
RP	Todd Worrell	1985–1992	With 129 saves, well behind Lee Smith (160) on franchise list, but Worrell pitched many more innings and posted better ERA; fastball/slider all the way.

SINGLE SEASON			
		YEARS	NOTES
C	Ted Simmons	1975	Slugged .491 and knocked in 100 runs on the nose . . . and was almost precisely as good in three other seasons.
1B	Mark McGwire	1998	Musial was great in '46, but didn't fare well in World Series . . . and of course, there's this little matter of 70 home runs.
2B	Rogers Hornsby	1922	He enjoyed nine or ten phenomenal seasons, but this was the phenomenalest: .401 average, 42 homers, 152 RBI.
SS	Ozzie Smith	1987	Won the Gold Glove, of course, and also posted a .392 OBP and scored 104 runs for the NL champions.
3B	Joe Torre	1971	An amazing season, certainly one of the greatest by *any* third baseman, Cardinal or otherwise; .363 batting avg., 137 RBI.
LF	Joe Medwick	1937	Hall of Famer's greatest season, as he grabbed Triple Crown with 31 homers, 154 RBI, and .374 battin' average.
CF	Stan Musial	1952	It's a testament to both Musial's talent and his versatility that he nearly makes this team at *three* different spots.
RF	Stan Musial	1948	Led the National League in virtually every category worth leading; significant action in left and center fields, too.
SP	Bob Gibson	1968	No, his 1.12 ERA is *not* the single-season record . . . but gosh, it was still pretty amazing, even for 1968.
RP	Lindy McDaniel	1960	One of the great relief seasons in the pre-closer era: 12 wins (with only 4 losses), 26 saves, and 2.09 ERA in 116 innings.

ALL-ROOKIE			
		YEARS	NOTES
C	Tim McCarver	1963	Only 21, batted .289 and flashed defense and intellect that would eventually make him a famous man.
1B	Johnny Mize	1936	He'd enjoy better seasons, but this one was pretty damn good: .329 batting average and 93 RBI in only 126 games.
2B	Don Blasingame	1956	"Blazer" didn't manage even one homer in 150 games, but he walked 72 times and played good defense at second and short.
SS	Solly Hemus	1951	Took over at shortstop from Marty Marion; didn't have Slats's glove (nobody did), but was a fine hitter for the position.
3B	Albert Pujols	2001	Unanimous choice for Rookie of the Year, but that understates the point; this was one of the best rookie seasons *ever.*
LF	Stan Musial	1942	In 1940, he was a star pitcher in the Florida State League; two years later, he batted .315 and scored 87 runs for NL champs.
CF	Homer Smoot	1902	League's best rookie in '02 and batted .300 on the nose over his first four seasons, but his eyesight went bad in '06.
RF	Wally Moon	1954	Batted .304 and scored 106 runs; remembered for his "Moon Shots" in L.A., but was actually a better player for Cards.
SP	Dizzy Dean	1932	Just 18-15 but led NL with 286 innings and 191 K's; two years later, brother Paul pitched brilliantly as a rookie, too.
RP	Todd Worrell	1986	Runaway Rookie of the Year choice after pacing National League with 36 saves; 2.08 ERA in 104 innings.

Dizzy Dean won only sixteen games in the major leagues after his twenty-eighth birthday. That's not very many . . . but it's more than his brother Paul won. "Daffy"—nobody who knew the younger Dean actually called him that—didn't win *any* games after he turned twenty-eight.

Who knows? Maybe it was hereditary. Maybe the Dean boys just weren't built to pitch a lot of innings. They could sure pitch, though. Everybody knows about ol' Diz; he's in the Hall of Fame. But consider . . .

In Dizzy's first two seasons, when he was twenty-two and twenty-three, he went 38-33 with a 3.17 ERA. In Paul's first two seasons, when he was twenty and twenty-one, *he* went 38-*23* with a 3.40 ERA. In terms of ERA relative to the league, Paul actually pitched *better* than Dizzy as a first- and second-year man (granted, Dizzy pitched more innings and so was more valuable than Paul).

One could reasonably argue that Paul had just as much *talent* as his more-famous brother—he pitched a no-hitter when he was twenty, and that same year he won two games in the '34 World Series—but there's one huge difference between them: Dizzy got hurt when he was twenty-seven, and Paul got hurt when he was only twenty-two. After winning those thirty-eight games his first two seasons, Paul won just a dozen more the rest of his career.

Marty Marion is still beloved in St. Louis, at least by the fans who remember him.

Garry Templeton is . . . well, let's just say he's not beloved by anybody, save perhaps his immediate family.

So I can predict with some degree of certitude that a significant number of Cardinals fans won't understand how I could possibly rank Templeton ahead of Marion among the club's home-grown talent. After all, wasn't Marion the greatest defensive shortstop of his time? (He was.) Wasn't he the National League's Most Valuable Player in 1944? (He was.) And what did Templeton ever do, aside from flipping Cardinals fans the bird and serving as trade bait for Ozzie Smith?

Quite a lot, actually. Rating Templeton ahead of Marion boils down to two things. One, Templeton was, in his prime, an outstanding defensive shortstop. And two, Templeton could hit and Marion could not.

Oh, there's also a three . . . A few of Marion's best seasons came during World War II, when the talent in the major leagues was not what it had been, or would be. Templeton, meanwhile, played in the 1970s and 1980s, when the National League featured an *abundance* of talent. I do rank Marion ahead of Templeton as a *Cardinals* shortstop because Marion spent more years in St. Louis. But career-wise, Templeton was the better player.

HOMEGROWN			
		YEARS	NOTES
C	Ted Simmons	1968–1980	A great high-school footballer who could have gone to any college, but signed with Cards as first-round pick.
1B	Johnny Mize	1936–1941	Devastating hitter who would be remembered as one of the all-time greats if not for World War II.
2B	Rogers Hornsby	1915–1926	Not signed originally by Cardinals, but they bought him and taught him to hit, and you know the rest of the story.
SS	Garry Templeton	1976–1981	The Cards' first-round pick in '73 draft had a brother who played in minors for three seasons.
3B	Ken Boyer	1955–1965	One of *six* Boyer boys who played pro ball, including three major leaguers; like Musial, started as pitcher.
LF	Stan Musial	1941–1963	Still a scrawny kid a few months shy of his seventeenth birthday, signed with Cards for $65 a month.
CF	Ray Lankford	1990–2001	L.A. native taken with club's third-round pick in '87 after stint at Modesto JC, where he starred as running back.
RF	Enos Slaughter	1938–1942 1946–1953	Signed with Cards in 1934 after attending a tryout camp run by his future manager, Billy Southworth.
SP	Bob Gibson	1959–1975	Tough call between him and Lefty, but Hoot enjoyed more big seasons . . . and there's all those World Series.
RP	Lindy McDaniel	1955–1962	Signed for $50,000 out of Abilene Christian College; two brothers, Von and Kerry Don, also pitched as pros.

TRADED AWAY			
		TRADED	NOTES
C	Walker Cooper	January 5, 1946	With Cooper still in the navy, owner Sam Breadon sold him to Giants for then-record $175,000.
1B	Johnny Mize	December 11, 1941	Four days after Pearl Harbor, Branch Rickey sent disgruntled Mize to Giants for three players and $50K.
2B	Rogers Hornsby	December 20, 1926	Rajah traded to Giants for Frankie Frisch and Jimmy Ring in the decade's biggest deal.
SS	Garry Templeton	December 10, 1981	One of the great "challenge" trades, one shortstop (Templeton) for another (Ozzie). Cards won.
3B	Todd Zeile	June 16, 1995	With Zeile headed for free agency, dumped to Cubs for Mike Morgan and a couple of bush leaguers.
LF	José Cruz	October 24, 1974	Sent to Astros in straight cash deal, and eventually—in his 30s—became player Cards thought he would.
CF	Andy Van Slyke	April 1, 1987	Club's first-round pick in '79 never won everyday job, blossomed after becoming full-timer in Pittsburgh.
RF	Larry Hisle	November 29, 1972	Before he played a game for Cards, traded to Twins for Wayne Granger, who totaled 5 wins afterward.
SP	Steve Carlton	February 25, 1972	Rick Wise was a pretty good pitcher, and won 113 games after the deal; then again, Lefty won 252.
RP	Hoyt Wilhelm	September 21, 1957	Cards had him for one season . . . and it happened to be his worst, so they sold him to Cleveland.

GOLD GLOVE			
		YEARS	NOTES
C	Mike Matheny	2000–*2002*	"The best blocker of balls in the dirt that I've ever seen."—Tim McCarver; Matheny has a great arm, too.
1B	Keith Hernandez	1974–1983	Arguably the greatest defensive first baseman ever, and handled relays from the outfield whenever possible.
2B	Red Schoendienst	1945–1956 1961–1962	Shortstop in the minors but blocked by Marion, became left fielder as rookie before settling in at second base.
SS	Ozzie Smith	1982–1996	The most valuable defensive player ever; Cards Marty Marion and Dal Maxvill also rank among all-time greats.
3B	Ken Boyer	1955–1965	Okay, so he wasn't as good as his little brother, but he *was* the best in the National League for a decade.
LF	Stan Musial	1941–1963	Yep, he could play some defense, too; more left field than anything, but good enough to play anywhere.
CF	Curt Flood	1958–1969	How good was Flood? Terry Moore was excellent, but Flood may have been better than Mays.
RF	Mike Shannon	1962–1966	Everybody who played with or against him remembers the great arm, but he could go and get the ball, too.
P	Bob Gibson	1959–1975	His follow-through left him in terrible fielding position . . . but he managed to win nine Gold Gloves anyway.

IRON GLOVE			
		YEARS	NOTES
C	Todd Zeile	1989–1990	Worth a shot, but by the end of Zeile's first full season in the majors, his future was obviously elsewhere.
1B	Pedro Guerrero	1988–1992	Couldn't throw the ball, couldn't catch the ball, and spent most of his time near the line to cut down on doubles.
2B	Cappy Charles	1908–1909	Cappy was born Charles Shuh Achenbach, he couldn't hit, and his fielding stats were atrocious.
SS	Art Butler	1914–1915	Art was born Arthur Edward Bouthillier, he couldn't hit, and his fielding stats were atrocious.
3B	Hector Cruz	1975–1976	In his first full season in majors, played 148 games at third base; afterward, no more than 21 in a season.
LF	George Barclay	1902–1904	They called him "Deerfoot" and he could certainly run, but he couldn't catch and he couldn't throw.
CF	Rip Repulski	1953	The regular in center field as a rookie, after which he became a liability, though less of one, in the corner spots.
RF	Tom Long	1915–1917	No glove, but in 1915 he did smack 25 triples, tops for a rookie in the 20th century.
P	Al Brazle	1943 1946–1954	I asked Bob Broeg, who's covered the Cards since WW II, and "Alpha Brazle" was the name that came to mind.

It's one of the oddities of baseball history that two of the 1960s' best defensive center fielders—they might have been *the* best—are often remembered for plays they did *not* make.

In Game 2 of the 1966 World Series, Willie Davis dropped two fly balls in the fifth inning, leading to three unearned runs. The Dodgers lost that game 6–0, and were swept by the Orioles in the Series. So it's not at all fair to suggest that Davis cost the Dodgers another championship. But when people picked a goat—as they always do—Davis got the horns.

In Game 7 of the 1968 World Series, Curt Flood got the horns. With two on and two out in the top of the seventh of a scoreless game, Tigers center fielder Jim Northrup lined a Bob Gibson fastball toward deep center. Flood's first few steps were in rather than out, and the ball sailed over his head for a two-run triple.

That put the Tigers ahead 2–0 (they'd eventually win, 4–1). Gibson wrote in his autobiography, "As we returned to the dugout, each of us struggling to keep our spirits alive, Flood stepped in next to me and said, 'I'm sorry. It was my fault.' I said, 'Like hell. It was nobody's fault.' What is often forgotten about that play is the fact that Northrup hit the damn ball four hundred feet."

For one last, glorious month, Cesar Cedeño flashed some of the wonderful talent that probably should have put him into the Hall of Fame.

As related in the Astros chapter, Cedeño played well in 1980 before suffering a severe ankle injury in the National League Championship Series. He came back in '81 but just wasn't the same. After the season, the Astros traded Cedeño to the Reds, and he played nearly every day for Cincinnati. But again, he wasn't the same. Cedeño batted .289, but hit only one triple and stole sixteen bases; in 1980, before he destroyed his ankle, he hit eight triples and stole *forty-eight* bases.

What followed were nearly three seasons in Cincinnati. His speed gone, the once-brilliant center fielder was reduced to playing first right field, and then left field and first base as a part-timer. As the 1985 season neared its conclusion, it looked like Cedeño was about done; on August 29, his batting average stood at .241 with three home runs in eighty-three games.

But the Cardinals were in a hot pennant race with the Mets, their first baseman got hurt, they took a flyer on Cedeño . . . and in twenty-eight games, he batted .434, hit six homers and drove in nineteen runs. The Cards finished three games ahead of the Mets, and they might not have done it without him.

		YEARS	NOTES
ALL-BUST			
C	Don Padgett	1940–1941	Ex-outfielder batted *.399* as part-time catcher in 1939, but dropped to .245 over next two seasons, his last as Card.
1B	Andres Galarraga	1992	Cards gave up Ken Hill to get Big Cat from Montreal, and he spent six weeks on DL and batted .243.
2B	Geronimo Peña	1990–1995	Had a world of talent, but injuries and (perceived) attitude kept him from ever becoming anything like a star.
SS	Don Kessinger	1976–1977	He wasn't *that* bad, but he couldn't really flash the leather anymore, and if his glove wasn't carrying his bat . . .
3B	Scott Cooper	1995	After two straight (albeit undeserved) All-Star berths with Red Sox, joined Cardinals and immediately tanked.
LF	Bobby Bonds	1980	After a dozen straight fine seasons, joined Cards—his fifth team in four seasons—and batted empty .203.
CF	Bobby Del Greco	1956	Great fielder but he simply didn't hit enough to play for a big-league club; batted .215, slugged .344 in 102 games.
RF	Alex Johnson	1966–1967	Batted .296 in two seasons before joining Cards and .313 in two seasons after leaving, but only .211 *with* Cards.
SP	Rick Ankiel	2001–*2002*	After spectacular flame-out in 2000 postseason—11 walks in 4 innings—hasn't found strike zone since.
RP	Mike Perez	1994	Earned closer role with two solid seasons, but lost it with 8.71 ERA over 31 injury-plagued innings.

		YEARS	NOTES
USED-TO-BE-GREAT			
C	Johnny Romano	1967	Power threat with Indians and White Sox closed out career with zero homers in 58 at-bats.
1B	Cesar Cedeño	1985	Far from the Gold Glove center fielder of yore, but he joined club in late August and batted .434 down stretch.
2B	Rogers Hornsby	1933	After six seasons away, returned to Cards and batted .325 in 46 games before leaving to manage Brownies.
SS	Alvin Dark	1956–1958	No longer great but still very good; in '57, his only full season with Cards, batted .290 and played solid defense.
3B	Bobby Bonilla	2001	Hadn't played *well* since helping Marlins to World Series victory in '97; batted .213 with Cards in swan song.
LF	Minnie Minoso	1962	After a pretty decent 1961 season with White Sox, came to Cards at 39 and batted .196 in 39 games.
CF	Tommie Agee	1973	A fine player just two seasons earlier with Mets, Agee was washed up at 30, batting .177 in 26 games.
RF	Bobby Bonds	1980	Some might argue for Maris here, but Bonds was the greater player; after solid '79, he simply stopped hitting.
SP	Dazzy Vance	1934	Pitched well but rarely in meaningful spots, winning a game and saving another in 19 appearances at age 43.
RP	Ellis Kinder	1956	The AL's top relief pitcher of the late '40s and early '50s saved 6 games before Cards waived him in July.

ALL-NAME

		YEARS	NOTES
C	"El Gato" Tony Peña	1987–1989	Picked up the nickname in his native Dominican Republic for—you guessed it—his catlike quickness.
1B	"Big Cat" Johnny Mize	1936–1941	Given to him by teammate Joe Orengo for his ability to snag bad-hop grounders during infield practice.
2B	"Creepy" Frank Crespi	1938–1942	According to Crespi, "It was because I could run almost full speed crouched for ground balls. . . ."
SS	"Slats" Marty Marion	1940–1950	At 6'2" and 170 pounds, looked like a slat when he turned sideways; also "Octopus" for his glovework.
3B	"Pepper" John Martin	1930–1940	Also known as "the Wild Horse of the Osage" and for the same reason: he was a 5'8" bundle of baseball energy.
LF	"Stan the Man" Stan Musial	1941–1944 1946–1963	Coined by St. Louis baseball writer Bob Broeg in Brooklyn; previously, he was "The Donora Greyhound."
CF	Homer Smoot	1902–1906	Spent four seasons as Cards' everyday center fielder, and hit three or four homers in each of them.
RF	"Country" Enos Slaughter	1938–1942 1946–1953	North Carolina native got his nickname in 1937 from Burt Shotton, his manager in Columbus.
SP	"Dizzy" Jay Hanna Dean	1930 1932–1937	Got his nickname while in the army, but explanations abound; all we know for sure about "Dizzy" is that it fit.
RP	"The Mad Hungarian" Al Hrabosky	1970–1977	Perhaps the best nickname of the 1970s; read his name and watch him pitch, and you had your explanation.

TOP FIVE SEASONS

YEAR 1942 **RECORD** 106-48
BEST HITTER Enos Slaughter
BEST PITCHER Mort Cooper (MVP)
NOTES Hey, who *says* the Yankees are unbeatable?

YEAR 1926 **RECORD** 89-65
BEST HITTER Les Bell
BEST PITCHERS Flint Rhem, Bill Sherdel
NOTES Ol' Pete Alexander strikes out Lazzeri in Game 6.

YEAR 1931 **RECORD** 101-53
BEST HITTER Chick Hafey
BEST PITCHER Wild Bill Hallahan
NOTES After losing to A's in 1930, Cards get revenge.

YEAR 1967 **RECORD** 101-60
BEST HITTER Orlando Cepeda (MVP)
BEST PITCHER Dick Hughes (Dick Hughes?)
NOTES Bob Gibson puts an end to the Impossible Dream.

YEAR 1982 **RECORD** 92-70
BEST HITTERS Lonnie Smith, Keith Hernandez
BEST PITCHER Joaquín Andujar
NOTES Game 7 comeback against Brewers for another Championship.

TOP FIVE MANAGERS

MANAGER Billy Southworth
YEARS 1929, 1940–1945
RECORD 620-346 (.642)
NOTES Finished first or second in all five full seasons.

MANAGER Whitey Herzog
YEARS 1980–1990
RECORD 822-728 (.530)
NOTES Nobody better at building a bullpen (among other things).

MANAGER Red Schoendienst
YEARS 1965–1976, 1980, 1990
RECORD 1041-955 (.522)
NOTES Two pennants, and always competitive.

MANAGER Frankie Frisch
YEARS 1933–1938
RECORD 458-354 (.564)
NOTES Two great seasons, but rode his starters hard.

MANAGER Eddie Dyer
YEARS 1946–1950
RECORD 446-325 (.578)
NOTES Championship in first season, followed by three second-place finishes.

Memory is a funny thing. Not funny ha-ha, but funny strange. You can't really trust your memory, no matter how vivid it might be. I do have a vivid memory of Al Hrabosky, though. It's roughly a quarter of a century old, but it's the single most vivid image I've got of a single relief outing.

I was nine or ten years old, and visiting my grandparents in Poplar Bluff, Missouri. Poplar Bluff is in the southeast part of the state, down by the bootheel. That's Cardinals country, and my grandparents were Cardinals fans (my uncle Marty was named after Marty Marion).

So the Cardinals were on TV one night, and some St. Louis pitcher fell behind the hitter, three balls and no strikes. Enter "The Mad Hungarian." I'd never seen him before, and what an impression he made. He had a Fu Manchu on his face. After taking the ball from the manager, he went behind the mound, put his head down for more than a few seconds, then *slammed* the ball into his glove before stalking back to the mound.

Then he blew away the hitter with three high fastballs. And I've never forgotten it.

Or at least I don't think I have.

SYMBOLS? OR JUST PLAIN OLD CHAMP-EENS?

Thanks to David Halberstam, the 1964 St. Louis Cardinals have become a symbol for something that goes far beyond baseball. The '64 Cardinals featured three black players in the starting lineup (four when ace starter Bob Gibson pitched). The '64 Yankees, who for most of the 1950s had resisted meaningful integration, generally featured one black player (Elston Howard) in the lineup (or two when number-three starter Al Downing pitched).

In October of 1964, the Cardinals beat the Yankees in the World Series, four games to three. And thus, a victory for the forces of integration over the forces of segregation. It all makes for a wonderful story, and Halberstam tells the story as only he can in his book, *October 1964* (Villard Books, 1994).

Except there wasn't anything revolutionary about the 1964 Cardinals. Yes, they had three black players in the starting lineup. So did the Cubs, and the Reds, and the Pirates (and Pittsburgh's top starter was black, too). The Braves often had four black players in the starting lineup. The Giants had five black regulars, and the Dodgers had *six*: second baseman Nate Oliver, shortstop Maury Wills, third baseman Jim Gilliam, center fielder Willie Davis, left fielder Tommy Davis, and catcher John Roseboro. The Cardinals certainly weren't ahead of the curve when it came to integration; they were smack-dab in the middle of the curve.

In fact . . . and I'm sorry, I know this chapter's supposed to be about the Cardinals . . . in fact, if you want to see a World Series that symbolized the changing of the guard, from lily-white American League to integrated National League, doesn't the 1963 Series make a lot more sense? In October 1963, the Dodgers featured five blacks in the starting lineup and *swept* the Yankees. Made them look bad. Outscored 'em twelve to four.

So why didn't Halberstam write *October 1963*. Because 1964 was a landmark year in the struggle for civil rights. It was in 1964 that three civil-rights workers were murdered in Mississippi. And it was not long before the World Series, that Lyndon Johnson signed the Civil Rights Act of 1964. So 1964 is a convenient backdrop for a story about the contrast between the baseball teams that understood the importance of integration and those that didn't.

Unfortunately—or fortunately, if you're like me and enjoy the randomness of it all—real life isn't convenient like that. In the real world, the random world, it was the *1963* World Series that said something had changed. It was the *1963* World Series in which the Yankees were swept four straight for the first time in twenty-eight trips to the Series.

If you're looking for meaning, wouldn't you first look at the Series in which the (almost) lily-white Yankees were swept four straight and badly outscored? That was 1963. In 1964, the Cardinals beat the Yankees by one game, and the Yankees outscored the Cardinals by one run.

That's not meaning. That's random.

I'm grateful to Geoff Reiss for writing many of the player comments, and to Lloyd Johnson for his editorial suggestions.

SAN DIEGO PADRES

		ALL-TIME	
		YEARS	**NOTES**
C	Terry Kennedy	1981–1986	Manager Dick Williams hated him—"He needed a diaper," Williams wrote—but Kennedy was a decent glove man and one of the game's best-hitting catchers.
1B	Fred McGriff	1991–1993	Came to San Diego in blockbuster deal and didn't disappoint; in 1992 he became only the second player in the 20th century to win a home-run title in both leagues.
2B	Roberto Alomar	1988–1990	Only 22 when he left the Padres and hadn't developed into the great hitter that he'd become, but still sits atop the club's list due to defense and 82 runs scored per season.
SS	Garry Templeton	1982–1991	He bears burdens of getting traded for Ozzie Smith *and* not matching supposed potential, and truth is that he was close to a zero with the bat for most of his time in S.D.
3B	Ken Caminiti	1995–1998	Who really knew? He went from 705 OPS in eight years with Astros to 924 OPS in four years with Padres; of course, the steroids probably helped a little bit.
LF	Gene Richards	1977–1983	Mostly forgotten now, but Richards batted .291 and stole 242 bases in seven years; one of just a few players of his era who choked up on the bat significantly.
CF	Steve Finley	1995–1998	Just like Caminiti, his career really took off after coming to Padres from Astros in huge trade; was Astrodome really *that* tough a place to hit?
RF	Tony Gwynn	1982–2001	Won eight batting titles, the first when he was 24 and the last when he was 37; in his prime, also a brilliant outfielder good for around 40 steals per season.
SP1	Randy Jones	1973–1980	Until Kevin Brown came along, Jones was the only star pitcher the Padres ever had; throwing an assortment of slow stuff, won 20 games in '75 and 22 in '76.
SP2	Eric Show	1981–1990	Tops the franchise victory list with 100, but more famous for giving up Pete Rose's 4,192nd hit, belonging to the John Birch Society, and dying of a drug overdose at 37.
SP3	Andy Benes	1989–1995	Looked like the Next Big Thing when he arrived in the majors as phenom, but his record never seemed to match his ability, due in part to poor run support.
SP4	Andy Ashby	1994–1999	When the Pads got Ashby, his major-league credentials included a 2-12 record and a 7.44 ERA in 133 innings, but after a shaky start he flourished in San Diego.
RP	Trevor Hoffman	1993–*2002*	Hell's Bells. Hoffman's best pitch was his devastating change-up, with which he racked up more saves with Padres than any other pitcher has for one team.

Anybody care to guess who owns the franchise record for pitching victories?

Eric Show, with 100 wins on the nose.

That's right, folks . . . only one Padres pitcher in thirty-five years has managed to reach triple digits. Three other teams entered the major leagues in 1969, when the Padres did. The Royals have six triple-digit winners, the Expos and Brewers both have two triple-digit winners. And looking at the Class of '77, the Blue Jays have four triple-digit winners, while the Mariners have only one. But Seattle's one is Randy Johnson (130 wins), who really can't be compared to Eric Show (and Jamie Moyer entered the 2003 season with 98 wins as a Mariner, so he'll probably have joined the club by the time you read this).

What does this tell us? It tells us that the Padres haven't developed any *great* pitchers, and it tells us that the Padres haven't held on to many of the good pitchers that they have developed. At this moment, the Padres boast a number of impressive young pitchers. And when it comes to young pitchers, this franchise is about due for some good luck.

It's generally true that high draft picks get more chances to succeed than low draft picks do. But it's also generally true that those extra chances don't amount to much.

Phil Nevin is one very obvious exception to the second of those general truths.

In 1991, the Houston Astros posted the worst record in the National League, which gave them the first pick in the 1992 amateur draft. They used that pick on Phil Nevin, a Cal State Fullerton product widely considered the best college hitter in the country. He was so polished that the Astros sent him straight to the Pacific Coast League, where Nevin batted .286 and hit ten homers in 123 games. The Astros had Caminiti at third base, so Nevin went back to Tucson in 1994 and posted virtually identical numbers to what he'd done in '93. Nevin was twenty-three, and his development seemed to have stalled. Less than a year later, the Astros traded Nevin to the Tigers, who decided that he'd never make it as a major-league third baseman. They turned him into an outfielder, then a catcher. They traded him to the Angels, for whom he batted .228 with little power. The Angels traded him to the Padres, who turned him back into a third baseman . . . and at the ripe old age of twenty-eight, Phil Nevin finally became a star.

		YEARS	NOTES
C	Benito Santiago	1986–1992	Had the great rookie season and later made four All-Star teams, but his .298 OBP as Padre obviously limited his contribution at the plate, if not behind it.
1B	Nate Colbert	1969–1974	One of the best expansion draft picks ever, and in 1972 double-header, Colbert set record with 13 RBI; that year, drove in 111 of the 488 runs scored by Padres.
2B	Quilvio Veras	1997–1999	Fragile and not much power, but outstanding with the glove, and a fine top-of-the-order hitter due to plate discipline and speed; beat out Jody Reed for job.
SS	Ozzie Smith	1978–1981	Not yet the hitter that he'd become, but Ozzie became the best defensive shortstop in the league the moment he arrived, and he could get around the bases in a hurry, too.
3B	Phil Nevin	1999–*2002*	Onetime bust as No. 1 draft pick and Astros catcher turned into All-Star third baseman after arriving in San Diego; peaked with 41 bombs and 126 ribs in 2001.
LF	Greg Vaughn	1996–1998	Only a Padre for two-plus seasons, but he hit 78 homers—50 of them in '98—and left field has been franchise's position of instability over the years.
CF	Kevin McReynolds	1983–1986	Outstanding in center field, at least in 1984 and '85, and in '86 he became a fine hitter with solid blend of average, power, and plate discipline.
RF	Dave Winfield	1973–1980	With all due respect to Nate Colbert, Winfield was the franchise's first great player, and in his fourth full season he became a perennial All-Star.
SP1	Gaylord Perry	1978–1979	He was a Padre for only two seasons, but spitballer went 33-17 for a team that was just 119-154 in the rest of its games during his tenure.
SP2	Ed Whitson	1983–1984 1986–1991	Left Padres for Yankees, but returned after fewer than two (disastrous) seasons; at his best in 1989 (16-11, 2.66) and '90 (14-9, 2.60) before arm fell off.
SP3	Bruce Hurst	1989–1993	Erstwhile Red Sox stalwart topped NL with 10 complete games in his first season with Padres, with 4 shutouts in his second, and went 55-38 in his tenure with club.
SP4	Andy Hawkins	1982–1988	Not the workhorse that his manager would have liked, but he pitched well in the '84 World Series and then opened the '85 season with 11 straight victories.
RP	Rollie Fingers	1977–1980	Like Fingers, ex–AL star Goose Gossage was a Padre for 4 years, but Fingers had more innings, more saves, and a cooler mustache.

NO. 2

SINGLE SEASON

		YEARS	NOTES
C	Terry Kennedy	1982	A great season that nobody really noticed, as Kennedy hit 21 homers and finished second in the league with 42 doubles.
1B	Jack Clark	1989	Better than Colbert's best, and Klesko's and McGriff's best? Yes, as Clark hit 26 homers and drew 132 walks.
2B	Roberto Alomar	1989	Second base hasn't been a strong position for Padres, and the young Alomar edges Wiggins in '84 because of his glove.
SS	Tony Fernández	1991	Another position that's not been great for Pads; Tony's two seasons are the two best by a shortstop in franchise history.
3B	Ken Caminiti	1996	Just an unbelievable season, in which Cammy was leader on the field and in the clubhouse for West champs.
LF	Greg Vaughn	1998	After a disappointing, injury-plagued 1997, Vaughn came back to set franchise record with 50 homers.
CF	George Hendrick	1977	Spent 18 seasons in the majors and this was his best, as he batted (career-high) .311 and drew (career-best) 61 walks.
RF	Tony Gwynn	1997	Great player who didn't actually have a lot of great *seasons*, but this was one of them: .372 average with 17 homers.
SP	Kevin Brown	1998	In his lone season as a Padre, won 18 games, pitched in All-Star Game, and often looked simply unhittable.
RP	Trevor Hoffman	1998	Hoffman finished with 53 saves and 1.48 ERA, and just barely edges out Mark Davis's 1989 Cy Young campaign.

ALL-ROOKIE

		YEARS	NOTES
C	Benito Santiago	1987	At 22, enjoyed his best season: .300 average, 18 homers, 21 steals, and rookie-record 34-game hitting streak.
1B	Nate Colbert	1969	The only real bright spot on a team that lost 110 games; led inaugural Padres with 24 homers and .482 slugging pct.
2B	Roberto Alomar	1988	He was only 20, which makes his 9 homers, 24 steals, and 84 runs scored look all the more impressive.
SS	Ozzie Smith	1978	Okay, so he only hit 1 homer; Ozzie also played Gold Glove-quality defense and stole 40 bases in 159 games.
3B	Vacant	—	This was *supposed* to be Sean Burroughs, but he wound up spending most of 2002 in Portland, Oregon.
LF	Gene Richards	1977	Speedster batted .290, stole 56 bases, *and* drew 60 walks to establish himself as one of the game's top leadoff men.
CF	John Grubb	1973	Before he became one of Sparky's favorite pinch hitters in Detroit, he was a quality center fielder in San Diego.
RF	Vacant	—	No rookie has played regularly in right field for the Padres, who of course have enjoyed both Winfield and Gwynn there.
SP	Mark Thurmond	1983	Joined rotation in late June and went 7-3 with 2.70 ERA in 18 starts; relied on good control with four average pitches.
RP	Luis DeLeón	1982	Rail-thin Puerto Rican posted 2.03 ERA in 102 innings thanks to lively heat, hard sinker, and sweeping slider.

Most of the time, the MVP is the guy who piles up big numbers for a first-place team, and Ken Caminiti's no exception. In 1996, Caminiti drove in 130 runs and played Gold Glove defense for a team that came out of nowhere to win its first division title in a dozen years.

But sometimes a candidate can help himself by doing something *special*. Kirk Gibson did that in 1988, when he went ballistic during spring training. And Caminiti did that in 1996.

August 18, to be precise. Caminiti's Padres and the New York Mets were in Monterrey, Mexico, for a three-game series. The Padres had won the first game but lost the second, falling into second place, a game behind the Dodgers.

Caminiti and his teammates really want to win that third game. Problem is, Caminiti can hardly walk. Violently ill from something he'd eaten the night before, moments before the game Caminiti is lying on the floor of the manager's office, taking his second liter of I-V fluids. At the last minute, he tells manager Bruce Bochy he can play. Just before his first at-bat, he wolfs down a Snickers . . . and hits a homer. Next time up, he hits a three-run homer. After striking out in the fifth, he can barely walk and is removed from the game. The Padres win, reclaiming a share of first place in the process. And Ken Caminiti locks up the MVP.

Nineteen hundred and eighty-one wasn't a good year for baseball, but it was one hell of a year for whoever was evaluating amateur hitters for the San Diego Padres.

In the first round, the Padres owned the sixth pick, which they used to select Kevin McReynolds, a junior out of the University of Arkansas. In the third round, the Padres selected Tony Gwynn, a junior out of San Diego State University. And in the secondary phase of the free-agent draft that same day, the Padres selected a hick from West Virginia named John Kruk.

Here's what those three did six years later, in 1987:

	OBP	Slug
Kruk	.410	.488
Gwynn	.447	.511
McReynolds	.364	.504

Friends, that's an impressive group of hitters. If you draft three guys like that every five or six years, you'll finish in first place every season. Of course, the Padres didn't enjoy all that talent for long. By 1987, McReynolds had already been sent to the Mets in an ill-advised trade, and Kruk wouldn't last long, either.

At least the Padres kept the right guy.

			HOMEGROWN	
		YEARS	NOTES
C	Benito Santiago	1986–1992	Puerto Rican native signed as free agent before the draft reached its long fingers into the Caribbean.
1B	John Kruk	1986–1989	Selected in secondary phase of '81 draft, and thrilled to sign when Padres offered a spectacular bonus of $2,500.
2B	Roberto Alomar	1988–1990	Like Santiago and his big brother and sometime teammate, Alomar hails from Puerto Rico.
SS	Ozzie Smith	1978–1981	Grew up in Watts, counted Eddie Murray among his high-school teammates, and signed for $5,000 bonus.
3B	Sean Burroughs	2002	A stretch, I'll admit, but it's either him or Luis Salazar, and the winner of that battle seems obvious even now.
LF	Kevin McReynolds	1983–1986	Sixth player drafted in '81, missed that season with knee injury, then absolutely tore up minors for two years.
CF	John Grubb	1972–1976	Stayed at Florida State long enough to gain his degree, then spent only two seasons in the minors.
RF	Dave Winfield	1973–1980	Selected in NFL, NBA, *and* MLB drafts; signed for $75K bonus, and given choice between hitting or pitching.
SP	Andy Benes	1989–1995	First overall pick in '88 draft reached majors for good after only 21 minor-league starts.
RP	Bob Patterson	1985	Lefty taken in 21st round of '82 draft, never approached stardom but pitched in majors for 13 seasons.

			TRADED AWAY	
		TRADED	NOTES
C	Sandy Alomar, Jr.	December 6, 1989	With Benito Santiago still a young man, Sandy, Chris James, *and* Carlos Baerga to Tribe for Joe Carter.
1B	Fred McGriff	July 18, 1993	With owner Tom Werner demanding cuts, sent to Braves for three prospects who never panned out.
2B	Roberto Alomar	December 5, 1990	Almost a year to the day after trading his big brother, Padres sent Roberto to Toronto in blockbuster deal.
SS	Ozzie Smith	February 11, 1982	Ozzie wanted $1 million per season, the Padres didn't want to pay him $1 million per season, so he had to go.
3B	Gary Sheffield	June 24, 1993	Like McGriff, traded for financial reasons, but at least the Padres got Trevor Hoffman from Marlins in deal.
LF	John Kruk	June 2, 1989	Lousy deal for Padres, who sent Kruk *and* Randy Ready to Phillies for Chris James.
CF	John Grubb	December 8, 1976	Played very few games in center after leaving San Diego, but he's a better choice than "Vacant."
RF	George Hendrick	May 26, 1978	Coming off fine '77 season, got off to slow start in '78 and traded to Cards for . . . Eric Rasmussen. Ouch.
SP	Joe Niekro	December 4, 1969	Not yet a real knuckleballer, Phil's little brother went 8-17 for Pads before getting traded to Cubs.
RP	Greg A. Harris	February 13, 1985	Ambidextrous journeyman sold to Rangers after season in which he posted 2.48 ERA in 54 innings.

GOLD GLOVE

		YEARS	NOTES
C	Brad Ausmus	1993–1996	It's debatable whether catchers have a big impact on ERA's, but his teammates loved how he called a game.
1B	Nate Colbert	1969–1974	Garvey was still great, but Colbert was incredibly underrated and deserved at least one Gold Glove.
2B	Roberto Alomar	1988–1990	Still learning, getting by mostly on his athleticism, but already one of the league's best.
SS	Ozzie Smith	1978–1981	Won first two of 13 straight Gold Gloves while a Padre, and deserved another for his rookie season. ✍
3B	Ken Caminiti	1995–1998	A bit erratic, but also acrobatic and fearless, and there wasn't anybody in the game with a stronger arm.
LF	Alan Wiggins	1981–1983	Terrible second baseman, but before that he put his fantastic speed to great use in the outfield.
CF	Kevin McReynolds	1983–1986	Put on weight later, but for the two years he played center for Padres, was one of NL's three best outfielders.
RF	Tony Gwynn	1982–1992	I'm talking about the pre-balloonish Tony Gwynn here; he was excellent for the first decade or so of his career.
P	Woody Williams	1999–2001	Williams was an all-conference shortstop at Univ. of Houston, and those skills showed up on the mound.

IRON GLOVE

		YEARS	NOTES
C	Mike Ivie	1971	Drafted as catcher but quickly washed out; it wasn't so much that he couldn't catch, but that he *wouldn't*.
1B	Ryan Klesko	2000–*2002*	Rare slugger who was probably less of a liability in left field than at first base.
2B	Mike Champion	1976–1978	According to Win Shares, *the worst* defensive second baseman to play the position regularly. By far. Yikes.
SS	Andujar Cedeño	1995–1996	You could live with his poor defense when he was hitting, but of course he didn't do much hitting in S.D.
3B	Chris Brown	1987–1988	Not bad early in his career, but by the time he joined the Padres, injuries had killed his defensive game.
LF	Al Martin	2000	Had good wheels, but routinely got poor jumps and couldn't really throw; in group with Glenallen Hill.
CF	Cito Gaston	1969–1971	Great hitting coach, good manager, decent hitter . . . but completely miscast in center field for three years.
RF	Oscar Gamble	1978	He had a fantastic arm, both strong and accurate; the problem was getting to the ball in the first place.
P	Joey Hamilton	1994–1998	For a righty, did a decent job holding runners, but was a clumsy fielder and frequently victimized by bunts.

✍ It's pretty amazing, really. Ozzie Smith and Roberto Alomar, both considered the greatest glove men at their positions during their careers, both got their starts with the San Diego Padres. Unfortunately for the Padres, neither Smith nor Alomar enjoyed their prime years in San Diego.

The Padres traded Ozzie to St. Louis when he was twenty-seven, and in fairness to then–Padres GM Jack McKeon, at that point it didn't look like Ozzie'd ever learn to hit. He was traded for Garry Templeton, and here's what each of them had done the previous season (1981):

	OBP	Slug
Ozzie	.294	.256
Garry	.315	.393

Oh, and Templeton was *younger* than Ozzie. So while the deal looks crazy now, who knew that Templeton would stop hitting, and Ozzie would start?

Alomar was just a kid, all of twenty-two years old, when he got dealt to the Blue Jays in what was probably the biggest trade of the 1990s. It doesn't look good now, of course, but the Padres picked up a couple of great players in Fred McGriff and Tony Fernández, and the deal was, over the next five years, almost exactly even. Alomar and McGriff were equally valuable, and Fernandez and Joe Carter were equally valuable.

I don't fault the Padres for trading Ozzie and Roberto; things just didn't work out so well.

Nobody's perfect. And Padres general manager Kevin Towers—one of the best GMs in the game—was never quite so far from perfect as when he acquired Randy Myers.

When August 6, 1998, dawned, the Padres were in first place, an even dozen games ahead of the second-place Giants. But the Padres didn't have a lefty relief specialist, and Towers wanted one. Desperately. Towers also wanted to keep the Atlanta Braves from getting one. Desperately.

Unfortunately, those twin desperations caused Towers to make what was probably the worst move of his career. Just the year before, in 1997, Myers had posted a career-best 1.51 ERA and led the American League with forty-five saves. In the first four months of the '98 season, he'd saved twenty-eight games for the Blue Jays (albeit with a 4.46 ERA). So the Padres got him, for the low price of two obscure minor leaguers . . . and a *big* chunk of change.

That's right. In addition to paying Myers's salary for the rest of the 1998 season, the Padres put themselves on the line for Myers's salary in 1999 ($6 million) and 2000 ($6.25 million). And what did the Padres get? Damaged goods. Myers pitched seventeen innings in 1998, zero innings in 1999, and zero innings again in 2000 (insurance did pick up a hefty chunk of the Padres' financial obligations).

		YEARS	NOTES
			ALL-BUST
C	Mike Ivie	1974–1977	First pick in 1970 draft developed mental block about throwing, and wound up catching only 9 MLB games.
1B	Keith Moreland	1988	After hitting 27 homers for Cubs in '87, joined Padres and managed only 5 bombs in 511 at-bats.
2B	Dave Cash	1980	Three-time All-Star with Phils in mid '80s, came to S.D. and posted career-lows .289 OBP and .280 slugging.
SS	Enzo Hernandez	1971–1977	A Padres fan was more likely to get hit by lightning than see Enzo get a big hit; in 2,324 at-bats, produced 113 RBI.
3B	Aurelio Rodríguez	1980	Always a lousy hitter, Rodríguez outdid himself in 89 games before getting sold to Yankees.
LF	Melvin Nieves	1993–1995	Supposed to be one of the prizes in the McGriff deal, showed some power but the strikeouts ate him alive.
CF	Shawn Abner	1987–1991	First overall pick in the '84 draft (by Mets), so he got chance after chance but posted 552 OPS with Padres.
RF	Joe Carter	1990	Yes, he drove in 115 runs. But that was due to the guys hitting ahead of him, as Carter's 681 OPS was ghastly.
CF	Ruben Rivera	1997–2000	Like Nieves, had power. Unlike Nieves, played great defense. But like Nieves, swung and missed far too often.
SP	Danny Jackson	1997	After rough start with Cardinals, joined Padres and went 1-7 with 7.53 ERA in 13 games; his last season.
RP	Randy Myers	1998	In terms of a poor ratio of innings pitched to money spent, Myers ranks as one of the all-time champions.

		YEARS	NOTES
			USED-TO-BE-GREAT
C	Randy Hundley	1975	Stalwart with Cubs in late '60s and early '70s, batted .206 with 2 homers in his one-year stint in San Diego.
1B	Willie McCovey	1974–1976	Great as part-timer in '74; other ex-greats who played 1B for Pads: Steve Garvey, Jack Clark, Wally Joyner.
2B	Glenn Beckert	1974–1975	Solid fielder and decent hitter with Cubs and a four-time All-Star, had nothing left by the time he joined Padres.
SS	Dickie Thon	1988	Thon's the only player who remotely qualifies here, but he'd play five more seasons for three other teams.
3B	Graig Nettles	1984–1986	Played well for a couple of seasons before collapsing in 1986, the summer in which he turned 42.
LF	Rickey Henderson	1996–1997 2001	In 2001, set MLB career records for walks and runs *and* set tone for new-look offense based on plate discipline.
CF	Willie Davis	1976	The 1970s Padres loved to look like the 1960s Dodgers, with Davis just one of many fine examples.
RF	Fred Lynn	1990	At 38, finished his career with 90 games for the Padres, and his 55 games in the outfield included 8 in right.
SP	Mickey Lolich	1978–1979	Pitched well (1.56) in '78 and developed a knuckleball for '79, but neither that nor his other pitches worked.
RP	Jack Baldschun	1969–1970	Like Podres, NL veteran went missing in '68; posted 8-2 record in two seasons despite unsightly ERA.

ALL-NAME		YEARS	NOTES
C	"Eye Chart" Doug Gwosdz	1981–1984	It's a shame he couldn't hit, because Gwosdz—that's pronounced "goosh"—was great behind the plate.
1B	"Crime Dog" Fred McGriff	1991–1993	The nickname we think is so nice, we decided it was okay if we used it thrice.
2B	"Bip" Leon Roberts	1986–1991	Origin supposedly unknown, but he needed a nickname because there was already a Leon Roberts in baseball.
SS	"Jump Steady" Garry Templeton	1982–1991	Given him by a cousin because of the way he jumped while dancing to Aretha Franklin's "Rock Steady."
3B	"Dirty Kurt" Kurt Bevacqua	1979–1980 1982–1985	In 1984, batted just .200 with 1 homer in regular season, then went 7 for 17 with 2 homers in World Series.
LF	"Bull" Al Ferrara	1969–1971	The Padres' first left fielder was also called "Kiki" by his family, because as a baby he kicked around a lot.
CF	"Cito" Clarence Gaston	1969–1974	And ever since, many fans have assumed that this native of San Antonio was born in some other country.
RF	"Downtown" Ollie Brown	1969–1972	In 1964, Brown hit 40 homers while playing for Fresno in the PCL, and many of them were hit toward downtown.
SP	"The Timid Texan" Andy Hawkins	1982–1988	Coined by Dick Williams, who said Hawkins "wouldn't fight the hitters if his snakeskin boots depended on it."
RP	"Baby Goose" Lance McCullers	1985–1988	Hard-throwing righty arrived in Gossage's second season, and bore a resemblance to the big Goose.

TOP FIVE SEASONS

YEAR 1984   **RECORD** 92-70
BEST HITTER Tony Gwynn
BEST PITCHER Goose Gossage
NOTES Fluky team ran into juggernaut Tigers in World Series.

YEAR 1998   **RECORD** 98-64
BEST HITTER Greg Vaughn
BEST PITCHER Kevin Brown
NOTES Postseason: Swept by Yankees in World Series.

YEAR 1996   **RECORD** 91-71
BEST HITTER Ken Caminiti (MVP)
BEST PITCHER Trevor Hoffman
NOTES Postseason: Lost to Cardinals in Division Series.

YEAR 1978   **RECORD** 84-78
BEST HITTER Dave Winfield
BEST PITCHERS Gaylord Perry, Rollie Fingers
NOTES In their 10th season, Pads finally got to .500.

YEAR 1989   **RECORD** 89-73
BEST HITTERS Jack Clark, Tony Gwynn
BEST PITCHER Mark Davis (CY), Bruce Hurst
NOTES In McKeon's only full season, three games out of first.

TOP FIVE MANAGERS

MANAGER Bruce Bochy
YEARS 1995–*2002*
RECORD 630-648 (.493)
NOTES Stays out of the headlines, just gets the job done.

MANAGER Dick Williams
YEARS 1982–1985
RECORD 337-311 (.520)
NOTES Real hard-ass who got Padres to their first World Series.

MANAGER Jack McKeon
YEARS 1988–1990
RECORD 193-164 (.541)
NOTES After eight seasons off the field, came back and did well.

MANAGER Greg Riddoch
YEARS 1990–1992
RECORD 200-194 (.508)
NOTES How come this guy never got another shot?

MANAGER Roger Craig
YEARS 1978–1979
RECORD 152-171 (.471)
NOTES Pads worse before he got there and after he left.

Do you believe that a catcher has a significant impact on a pitcher's performance?

Most of you reading this would answer in the affirmative. After all, the catcher calls the pitches (though on many teams, the pitches are called from the bench). And some catchers are expert at "framing" pitches (though the actual effect of this tactic is greatly exaggerated). And of course, there's the running game.

There's something odd about this, though . . . you'll have a devil of a time proving that who's behind the plate actually *does* have a significant impact on pitching statistics. That's not to say you could put Mo Vaughn behind the plate and it wouldn't matter. But the difference between any two *real* catchers is very hard to find, despite the best efforts of smarter men than I.

But on the other hand, you've got Doug Gwosdz. As Craig Wright observed in his brilliant book, *The Diamond Appraised* (1989), Gwosdz caught as a regular for four minor-league teams, and all four showed significant improvement in their team ERA's from the year before. And though Gwosdz was allowed to catch only 277 innings in the major leagues, his pitchers were essentially *thirty-three percent better* than might have been expected.

But Gwosdz batted .144 in sixty-nine major-league games, and that was that.

ENDING UP WITH ENZO

Tommy Dean. Jose Arcia. Enzo Hernandez. Derrel Thomas. Bill Almon.

Those are the men who played shortstop for the San Diego Padres before Ozzie Smith arrived in 1978. Mostly it was Hernandez, who played regularly for the better part of six seasons. And to be brutally honest, Enzo Hernandez has to rank among the worst players ever to play regularly for so many seasons. He was a terrible hitter, even for a shortstop. In those six seasons, he batted .225 with a .285 OBP and .267 slugging percentage. He did run pretty well, but wasn't on base nearly often enough for his speed to make much of a difference. The real problem, though, was that Hernandez wasn't much on defense, either. He was adequate, at best, and adequate isn't actually adequate when you're a complete zero with the stick.

And the hell of it was, the Padres could have had somebody good.

In July of 1968, the National League voted to expand into San Diego and Montreal. A banker named C. Arnholt Smith owned the minor-league San Diego Padres, and he got the new major-league franchise. Shortly afterward, Smith hired Buzzie Bavasi, then running the Dodgers, to run the new Padres. Bavasi wanted to stay with the Dodgers for a bit longer, but Dodgers owner Walter O'Malley told him that Phillies owner Bob Carpenter of the Phillies thought it would be a conflict of interest for Bavasi to stay on in Los Angeles. And so O'Malley wanted him out immediately.

Bavasi didn't understand how it could be a conflict of interest without one ballplayer in San Diego yet, and John Quinn, the Phillies' general manager, assured Bavasi that Carpenter didn't know anything about the situation. Then O'Malley asked Bavasi to stick around a few days so the Dodger players could give Bavasi a motorboat, after which Bavasi finally resigned.

But then, prior to the expansion draft in October, with Fresco Thompson in the hospital—Thompson was a long-time Dodgers executive who had taken over for Bavasi—O'Malley called Bavasi to ask for help preparing the list of forty players the Dodgers would protect in the Expansion Draft. Even though Bavasi was working for the Padres, he agreed to help O'Malley since Thompson was in the hospital.

Now *that* is a conflict of interest.

But wait, it gets worse. On the way to Dodger Stadium, Bavasi stopped at the hospital to visit Thompson. As Bavasi later related in his memoirs,

> I went up to see Fresco, and I told him I was doing his job for him, that I was going to Los Angeles to help Walter.
>
> "That's fine, Buzzie," Fresco said, "but who are you going to take in the draft?"
>
> "Bill Russell, Jeff Torborg, and Jim Brewer," I said, mentioning three players the Dodgers were not planning on protecting."
>
> "Oh, you can't do that, particularly Russell and Brewer. Russell's a fine prospect."
>
> "That's why I'm taking him," I said.
>
> "You can't do that," Fresco pleaded. "Buzzie, don't do that to me, really."
>
> ". . . OK, I'll do it for you . . ." I had spoken with the doctor, who had told me that Fresco was dying and that he wasn't going to make it. I knew I had to keep my promise.
>
> . . . I went to Dodger Stadium and met with Walter O'Malley and Walter Alston. I said, "You can't leave Brewer on the unprotected list. If you leave him there and I don't draft him, people are going to crucify me."
>
> Brewer had had 14 saves in 1968. I talked them into including Brewer on the protected list, which took the heat off me. Leaving Russell unprotected was OK, because nobody knew him at the time.

The Padres wound up drafting outfielders Al Ferrara and Jim Williams, and shortstop Zoilo Versalles, from the Dodgers. Ferrara gave the Padres a couple of good years, Williams barely played, and Versalles got traded to Cleveland for first baseman Bill Davis (who batted .175 in thirty-one games for the Padres).

Summing up . . . to run their team—and oversee their efforts in the Expansion Draft—the Padres hired a high-ranking employee of the Dodgers, perennial contenders with an enviable depth of talent in their organization. And the Padres came out of the draft with one ex-Dodger who helped them, and two who didn't.

From 1969 through 1973, Jim Brewer saved 103 games with a 2.38 ERA.

Bill Russell made the Dodgers' opening-day roster in 1969. And after three seasons in the outfield—the Dodgers still had Maury Wills at short—Russell took over as the club's everyday shortstop in 1972 and held the job for a dozen years.

Due to Bavasi's presence, the Padres employed a string of managers with historical ties to the Dodgers. But the Padres didn't employ nearly enough *players* with historical ties to the Dodgers. And what made this all the stranger is that when C. Arnholt Smith hired Bavasi, he'd given him a thirty-two percent interest in the franchise.

The San Diego Padres finished last in each of their first six seasons, and they'd have finished last even with Jim Brewer and Bill Russell, so not having those guys certainly didn't kill the Padres. But having them sure as hell would have helped.

Sources for this chapter include Dick Williams and Bill Plaschke's No More Mr. Nice Guy *(Harcourt Brace Jovanovich, 1990), and Buzzy Bavasi's* Off the Record *(Contemporary, 1987).*

Enzo Hernandez in 1971, a safe distance from the batter's box.
©*Bettmann–CORBIS*

Did you ever notice that teams rarely develop great relief pitchers on purpose?

Think about the best closers of the last decade or so.

Trevor Hoffman: drafted as a shortstop, and the Padres are his third team.

John Wetteland: Expos were his fourth team.

Troy Percival: began professional career as catcher.

And then there's Robb Nen, the subject of this little essay. He spent the better part of six years in the Rangers' organization, failing as a starting pitcher. In his first thirteen starts with Double-A Tulsa, he went 0-7 with a 5.60 ERA. He did pitch well in his first four starts in 1992, but missed the rest of the season with a nerve problem in his right shoulder.

Nevertheless, Nen opened the 1993 season with the big club. He got hammered, and then hammered again with Oklahoma City while rehabbing a strained groin. He still had that amazing right arm, however, and on July 17 the Marlins got him in a trade.

Florida moved him to the bullpen, which turned out to be a great move even though it didn't work immediately. In 1994, after injuries to Bryan Harvey and Jeremy Hernandez, Nen took over as closer and converted his first fifteen save chances.

The Giants got him in the Marlins' post-1997 fire sale, and everybody's been happy since.

SAN FRANCISCO GIANTS

		YEARS	NOTES
C	Tom Haller	1961–1967	Hit 27 homers in 1966, still the most for a Giant catcher since the move (Walker Cooper hit 35 in '47 for the New Yorkers); at 6'4", one of the biggest catchers of his day.
1B	Willie McCovey	1959–1973 1977–1980	He hit 469 home runs, still the S.F. record though probably not for long (thanks a lot, Barry); "Stretch" still holds NL record with 18 career grand slams.
2B	Jeff Kent	1997–2002	Arrived in S.F. and went on a tear with six straight 20-homer, 100-RBI seasons; better glove than most think, and only Giant middle infielder to win (modern) MVP.
SS	Rich Aurilia	1995–2002	Okay, so maybe not *all* of the slugging shortstops of his time ended up in the American League . . . though it's odd that other than Aurilia, all of them did.
3B	Matt Williams	1987–1996	Always seemed to play second fiddle to guys like Clark, Mitchell, and Bonds; not that we should feel sorry for him, but '94 strike cost him a good shot at 62 homers.
LF	Barry Bonds	1993–2002	Nobody had cracked the all-time single-season top 10 OPS list since Ted Williams, before Bonds put up No. 2 mark in 2001, then broke Ruth's record in 2002.
CF	Willie Mays	1951–1952 1954–1972	Played 140-plus games 15 straight years; preceded in CF by Bobby Thomson, followed by Garry Maddox, and only blot on amazing career is poor postseason numbers.
RF	Bobby Bonds	1968–1974	Terribly underrated, then and now, merely because he struck out a lot and followed in Mays's footsteps; first post-1900 player to hit a grand slam in first MLB game.
SP1	Juan Marichal	1960–1973	If not the best pitcher of his time (and he may have been that), certainly the most entertaining, throwing a wide variety of pitches with a wide variety of motions.
SP2	Gaylord Perry	1962–1971	Mastered the spitter while serving as a spot starter in 1964; of his 314 career wins, 134 came as a Giant, with the Indians distant runners-up at 70.
SP3	Jim Barr	1971–1978 1982–1983	Power pitcher quite effective from 1974 through '76, starting 97 games and posting 2.90 ERA; in 1972, retired 41 straight batters, spanning two starts.
SP4	Jack Sanford	1959–1965	Best year by far was 1962, when he went 24-7 and finished 2nd to Drysdale for the MLB-wide Cy Young award; pitched well vs. Yanks in Series, but lost twice.
RP	Robb Nen	1998–2002	If Mariano Rivera's the best closer in the game, Nen and Trevor Hoffman are right behind; all power, Nen employs an odd toe-tap in the midst of his delivery.

		YEARS	NOTES
C	Bob Brenly	1981–1988 1989	Oddly, before he won a World Series as manager, he was remembered mostly for the day he made four errors at third base (third base?) and hit a game-winning homer.
1B	Will Clark	1986–1993	One of the more underrated players of the last 20 years, earned four top-five MVP finishes from 1987 through 1991; outstanding hitter who did everything well.
2B	Robby Thompson	1986–1996	Amazingly consistent—in each of his first 7 seasons, he batted between .241 and .271—had a touch of power and great on the pivot, so Giants forgave him for all the K's.
SS	Chris Speier	1971–1977 1987–1989	Left S.F. the first time in strange challenge trade for Tim Foli, a player of remarkably similar age and ability; his fine rookie season helped Giants win division title.
3B	Darrell Evans	1976–1983	Great player, one of two eligible players with 400 homers *not* in the Hall of Fame, and according to Bill James "the most underrated player in baseball history, absolutely . . ."
LF	Kevin Mitchell	1987–1991	Tenure as regular left fielder lasted only three years, but in '89 he led National League with 47 homers and 125 RBI to beat out teammate Will Clark for MVP.
CF	Chili Davis	1981–1987	He ended up a DH, of course, but early on he was a decent CF, ran well and had some pop; Brett Butler, who replaced him in '88, had three good years as well.
RF	Jack Clark	1975–1984	With Bobby Bonds, Bobby Murcer, Clark and Chili Davis, Giants had quality in right for nearly 20 years; like Darrell Evans, under-appreciated while a Giant.
SP1	Mike McCormick	1956–1962 1967–1970	Timing is everything: Marichal won 154 games in 7-year stretch and didn't even sniff a Cy Young; McCormick had one pretty good year (1967) and got the plaque.
SP2	Vida Blue	1978–1981 1985–1986	Pitched well in three of his first four seasons, and in his second stint posted 3.27 ERA in '86 before failed drug test ended his career.
SP3	Bill Swift	1992–1994	Sinkerballer was a Giant for only three seasons, but in one of them he led National League with 2.08 ERA (1992), and in another he won 21 games (1993).
SP4	John Burkett	1987–1994	Like McCormick, shocked world with aberrant 22-win season (1993); unlike McCormick, Burkett went on to solid, if unspectacular, career afterward.
RP	Rod Beck	1991–1997	Plucked from Oakland's farm system for a song, showed good fastball and devastating splitter to great effect for two years and saved 48 games in near-miss '93.

It's fair, I think, to wonder if Dusty Baker did irreparable damage to Rod Beck's career.

In *The Scouting Report: 1994*, I wrote, "Beck's final stats [in 1993] were excellent, but they would have been even better if Baker hadn't overworked him late. In the last ten days of the season, Beck, obviously arm-weary, pitched eight times and threw four gopher balls."

From 1991 through 1993, Beck compiled a 2.37 ERA and struck out 211 hitters in 224 innings. From 1994 through 1996, Beck compiled a 3.56 ERA and struck out 129 hitters in 169 innings.

So let's assume that Baker did hurt Beck's career, by overworking him down the stretch in 1993. The next question is, was he justified?

I would argue that he was. When you have a shot at reaching the postseason—the Giants won 103 games, but finished a game behind the Braves—you have to do nearly everything you can to actually get there (short of trading top prospects for spare parts). What's more, in this era of free agency, it simply doesn't make a lot of sense for a manager to worry a lot about the long-term health of a pitcher, unless he knows that pitcher is going to be around for quite a while.

The bottom line, though, is that Beck never again pitched as well as he had in 1992 and 1993, when he was still a very young man.

When Jim Ray Hart is remembered, it's for two things: his rude introduction to the National League, and his fielding woes.

Hart debuted for the Giants on July 7, 1963, in the first game of a doubleheader against the Cardinals. Bob Gibson started the second game for St. Louis, and Gibson wasn't at all discriminating when it came to throwing at hitters; he broke Hart's shoulder blade. Hart returned to action on August 12 . . . and was beaned by Curt Simmons four days later. Hart didn't come back this time, and finished his first "season" with four hits in seven games. Welcome to the National League.

Then there was the fielding. As in, Jim Hart wasn't very good at it. He wasn't *terrible*, but he did have one terrible year; in 1965, Hart led the National League with thirty-two errors at third base. But generally he was poor rather than awful. He should have been a first baseman, but of course the Giants had McCovey. So he played third, and later left field, neither of them well.

What's forgotten in all of this is the most notable thing about Hart's career: he was one *hell* of a hitter. From 1965 through '67, Hart hit 116 home runs, slugged .501, and was amazingly consistent while doing those things. His career went into the tank soon afterward, however, because of injuries and perhaps alcohol.

		YEARS	NOTES
SINGLE SEASON			
C	Dick Dietz	1970	In his first crack at everyday duty, crashed through with .300 average, 22 homers, 109 walks, 107 RBI; back to earth in '71.
1B	Will Clark	1989	One of the greatest seasons nobody remembers; teammate Kevin Mitchell was MVP, but The Thrill was even better.
2B	Jeff Kent	2000	Edged teammate Bonds for MVP honors with .334 average, 33 homers, and 125 RBI; team-record 85 RBI at All-Star break.
SS	Rich Aurilia	2001	First Giants shortstop in All-Star Game since 1974, and first NL shortstop not named Ernie Banks to clear 35 homers.
3B	Jim Ray Hart	1967	Followed up three fine seasons with his best—.289-29-99, 77 walks—but never played nearly as well again.
LF	Barry Bonds	2001	Set MLB record with 177 walks, there was something about 73 homers . . . and the *next* season, set single-season OPS mark.
CF	Willie Mays	1965	Eleven years after winning his first MVP, won his second, thanks largely to career-high 52 homers.
RF	Bobby Bonds	1973	Hit career-high 39 homers, including NL record 11 to lead off game; peers selected him as MLB's Player of the Year.
SP	Juan Marichal	1966	Marichal boasts not only the best, but the *four* best single seasons by a San Francisco pitcher.
RP	Robb Nen	1998	In first season with Giants, converted 40 of 45 save chances, posted 1.52 ERA and K'd 110 hitters in 89 innings.

		YEARS	NOTES
ALL-ROOKIE			
C	Bob Schmidt	1958	Hit 14 homers and joined Cepeda (below), Willie Kirkland, and Jim Davenport as everyday rookies in Giants' first S.F. season.
1B	Orlando Cepeda	1958	Unanimous Rookie of the Year and fan favorite in Giants' first season on the coast; topped loop with 38 doubles.
2B	Robby Thompson	1986	After only three years in minors, skipped Triple-A and jumped right into starting lineup; batted .271 and scored 73 runs.
SS	Chris Speier	1971	Not much with the bat—he never really was—but played brilliant defense over 157 games for division winners.
3B	Jim Ray Hart	1964	Nice year for rookie third basemen in the NL, with Hart whacking 31 homers and Dick Allen being Dick Allen.
LF	Gary Matthews	1973	Ho-hum . . . just another outstanding outfielder developed by the Giants in the '60s and early '70s; batted .300 on the nose.
CF	Dan Gladden	1984	Edges Chili Davis (who played every day in '82) on the strength of his .351 batting average and 71 runs scored in 86 games.
RF	Bobby Bonds	1968	Came up in late June, and the numbers—.254-9-35, with 38 walks—don't dazzle . . . *until* you remember it was 1968.
SP	John Montefusco	1975	Went 15-9 to win RoY honors, then pitched almost exactly as well as sophomore before becoming quite ordinary for a decade.
RP	Elias Sosa	1973	Equaled franchise record with 71 appearances (since eclipsed), including 10 wins and 18 saves while posting 3.28 ERA.

		HOMEGROWN	
		YEARS	**NOTES**
C	Tom Haller	1961–1967	Illinois native got a P.E. degree at the U of I, and his brother Bill was an American League ump for 20 years.
1B	Willie McCovey	1959–1973 1977–1980	Signed by Giants scout Alex Pompez in 1955, and drove in 113 runs in 107 minor-league games that summer.
2B	Robby Thompson	1986–1996	A year and a half before the Giants got Thompson, the A's drafted him in the second round but he didn't sign.
SS	Chris Speier	1971–1977 1987–1989	UCSB product spent exactly one season in the minors before beginning his 19-season career in the majors.
3B	Matt Williams	1987–1996	Third overall pick in '86 draft, named All-American shortstop after junior season at UNLV.
LF	George Foster	1969–1971	Third-round pick in '68 hit 3 homers in his first pro season; did anybody predict that he'd one day hit 52?
CF	Garry Maddox	1972–1975	After one season in low minors, went to work for Uncle Sam, but moved up quickly after getting back to baseball.
RF	Bobby Bonds	1968–1974	In his first professional season, hit 25 home runs, stole 33 bases, and scored 103 runs in only 112 games.
SP	Juan Marichal	1960–1973	After nearly becoming a Yankee, the Dominican signed with the Giants for the grand sum of $500.
RP	Rod Beck	1991–1997	Drafted by A's, but traded to Giants after posting 5.20 ERA in 30 Class A games, then blossomed immediately.

		TRADED AWAY	
		TRADED	**NOTES**
C	Randy Hundley	December 2, 1965	Set with Tom Haller, Giants could spare Hundley, who gave the Cubs eight good years and a son.
1B	Jack Clark	February 1, 1985	After injury-plagued (but power-packed) '84 season, traded to Cardinals for a quartet of lesser lights.
2B	Bill Madlock	June 28, 1979	Got off to a slow start, and packaged with Lenny Randle in deal with Pirates for three young pitchers.
SS	Chris Speier	April 27, 1977	Pure challenge trade, with Speier going to Montreal for shortstop Tim Foli; Expos won the challenge.
3B	Matt Williams	November 13, 1996	Everybody in San Francisco hated this at the time, but you can't argue with a deal that gets you Jeff Kent.
LF	George Foster	May 29, 1971	For Frank Duffy and Vern Geishert; not one of the franchise's finer moments, and it would haunt them.
CF	Garry Maddox	May 4, 1975	The middle '70s were an ugly period in Giants history, and trading Maddox for Montanez didn't help.
RF	Felipe Alou	December 3, 1963	Felipe was the first of the Alou brothers to go; Matty followed two years later, Jesús four years after that.
SP	Gaylord Perry	November 29, 1971	He was 33 when the Giants traded him to Tribe, but still had 180 wins and 3.21 ERA left in the grease gun.
RP	Eddie Fisher	November 30, 1961	Included in deal with White Sox for Billy Pierce (who had something left) and Don Larsen (who didn't).

One of the hallmarks of an effective baseball executive, I think, is the ability to turn necessity into opportunity. When Brian Sabean took over as general manager of the Giants at the conclusion of the 1996 season, he came into what looked like a bad situation. He had a last-place team (the Giants had just finished 68-94), he had two superstars (Barry Bonds and Matt Williams) scheduled to make approximately seven million bucks apiece in 1997 . . . and he'd been ordered to cut the payroll to approximately thirty million dollars.

So if he kept both Bonds and Williams, he'd be spending half his money on two players. That's not good, no matter how good the players are. So Sabean had to trade one of his superstars, and he picked the lesser of them. As Sabean told me in 2002, "At that time, we had no choice. We literally had no choice."

Sabean sent Williams to Cleveland, and in return he received Jeff Kent *and* José Vizcaíno *and* Julian Tavarez *and* a million dollars, which he used to sign Darryl Hamilton. And those four players—along with J. T. Snow and a platoon of pitchers brought aboard just before the trading deadline—helped the Giants go from last place to first place in 1997, Sabean's very first season.

Hal Lanier never won a Gold Glove, but certainly ranked as one of the great defensive players of the 1960s. He simply had the misfortune to be competing with Bill Mazeroski when he played second base, and then with Dal Maxvill when he played shortstop.

The other thing was, Lanier couldn't hit. At all. Lanier was quite possibly *the worst* hitter ever to play at least one thousand games in the major leagues, not including pitchers.

This probably doesn't surprise anybody who followed baseball in the 1960s. What's surprising, though, is that Lanier was actually a pretty decent hitter in the minor leagues.

The son of Max Lanier, the old Cardinals pitcher, Hal signed with the Giants for $50,000 in 1961, and he batted .301 over his first three minor-league seasons. When the 1964 season opened, Lanier was only twenty-one years old and playing with Tacoma in the Pacific Coast League. And playing well; in mid-June he was batting .327 with seventeen doubles, and got summoned to the major leagues. He played almost every game the rest of the way, and batted .274.

Lanier would never do so well again. He batted just .226 in 1965, and that's what he was. Lanier played until 1973, he never batted higher than .233 again, and he finished with a .228 career batting average and eight *career* home runs.

GOLD GLOVE			
		YEARS	**NOTES**
C	Tom Haller	1961–1967	Big (6'4") for his time, well known for his abilities to block the plate, throw, and work with the pitchers.
1B	J. T. Snow	1997–*2002*	Probably didn't deserve all those Gold Gloves, but he is the best they've had and he certainly *looked* great.
2B	Hal Lanier	1964–1967	So brilliant at second base, after three years the Giants moved him to shortstop . . . and he was great there, too.
SS	Mike Benjamin	1989–1995	Could list Lanier here, but Benjamin was a little better, albeit as a part-timer due to (similarly) weak stick.
3B	Jim Davenport	1958–1970	As rookie, played third base in Giants' first game in San Francisco, and played brilliantly there for years.
LF	Barry Bonds	1993–*2002*	I happen to think he's been a bit overrated, but this *is* left field and he *did* win five Gold Gloves as a Giant.
CF	Willie Mays	1951–1952 1954–1972	Most remembered for his Catch in '54 Series and, oddly enough, that was his best *regular* season with the glove.
RF	Bobby Bonds	1968–1974	Both Bondses won multiple Gold Gloves . . . and yet neither spent much time in center during their careers.
P	Rick Reuschel	1987–1991	No, he didn't look great in the uniform, but he was one of the best fielders in the league and mastered the slide-step.

IRON GLOVE			
		YEARS	**NOTES**
C	Dick Dietz	1966–1971	From first to worst, as Dietz took over from Haller; fine hitter and strong arm, but erratic as hell with glove.
1B	Mark Carreon	1995–1996	Outfielder became a first baseman at 32, and the on-the-job-training didn't go particularly well.
2B	Joel Youngblood	1983	With a choice between Youngblood's bat and Brad Wellman's glove, Giants got worst of both worlds.
SS	Johnnie LeMaster	1975–1985	Well, he played 954 games at shortstop for the Giants, so apparently *somebody* thought he was good. He wasn't.
3B	Joel Youngblood	1983–1984	"Okay, so second didn't work . . . how's about third?" That didn't go real well, either, and Giants finally gave up.
LF	Hank Sauer	1957–1958	Even at 41, he could still hit, but whatever defensive abilities he'd once had were almost entirely gone.
CF	Marvin Benard	1995–*2002*	Benard's defensive shortcomings sent Brian Sabean around the bend, with Shinjo taking over in 2002.
RF	Glenallen Hill	1995–1997	Still no DH rule in the National League, so the Giants sent him out to right field, day after day after . . .
P	Robb Nen	1998–*2002*	Something like adequate with the glove, but utterly helpless when it comes to holding runners on first base.

		YEARS	NOTES
C	Steve Decker	1990–1992 1996	Heralded prospect batted just .215 in first go-round with club, then .230 with no power in second shot.
1B	J. R. Phillips	1993–1996	The expectations were probably too high for minor-league power hitter, but he batted just .194 in 133 games.
2B	Rennie Stennett	1980–1981	Coming off two horrible seasons with Pirates, but got a shot with Giants anyway; change of scenery didn't help.
SS	Rich Aurilia	1996	Got the job before he was ready and didn't manage even .300 in OBP or slugging pct; later busted out, of course.
3B	Ken Reitz	1976	Displaced on-base machine Steve Ontiveros, and posted .293 OBP without any power to compensate.
LF	Mark Leonard	1990–1992 1994–1995	Impeccable minor-league track record—average, walks, power— but he never got a real shot and didn't hit much.
CF	Jerry Martin	1981	Had showed some power with Cubs, but managed one homer in 107 road at-bats in his season with Giants.
RF	Eric Davis	2001	Supposed to platoon in right, but batted .205 and the Giants finished two games out of the money.
SP	Bud Black	1991–1994	His performance wasn't bad—34-32, 3.95 over four seasons— but his bank-breaking contract brought howls.
RP	Jim Poole	1996–1998	Pitched well down stretch in '96 to earn hefty two-year deal, then posted 6.39 ERA to earn his outright release.

USED-TO-BE-GREAT

		YEARS	NOTES
C	Gary Carter	1990	After terrible season with Mets in '89, slugged .406 in 92 games to show he still had something left.
1B	Reggie Smith	1982	Longtime outfielder with Red Sox, Cards, and Dodgers finished at first base with Giants and did quite well at 37.
2B	Joe Morgan	1981–1982	On the last day of the 1982 season, Morgan hit a dramatic homer to knock Dodgers out of pennant race.
SS	Dick Groat	1967	Ex-MVP and five-time All Star fell hard and fast, batting .171 in 34 games for Giants in his last season.
3B	Charlie Hayes	1998–1999	Played briefly for Giants at start of career, then again for two seasons near the very end.
LF	Joe Carter	1998	Played brilliantly down the stretch, but ended his career and Giants' season with last at-bat in Wild Card playoff.
CF	Duke Snider	1964	Didn't actually play even a single game in center, but it's just hard to think of him in right field (and a Giant?).
RF	Darryl Strawberry	1994	After nightmare season in L.A., Strawberry started his comeback with 29 productive games with Giants.
SP	Warren Spahn	1965	He was 44 and the *Mets* had just released him, but pitched pretty well (3-4, 3.39) in last MLB innings.
RP	Rich Gossage	1989	Just another stop on Goose's post-Padres tour; the next season, Quisenberry pitched 7 innings and got hammered.

Warren Spahn pitched in sixteen games for the Giants in 1965, and he pitched pretty well. This was something of a surprise, as Spahn had opened the season with the Mets, and gone 4-12 with a 4.36 ERA before they cut him loose. (A few years later, Spahn would note, "I'm probably the only guy who worked for Stengel before and after he was a genius.")

In those days, of course, if you couldn't pitch for the Mets, you probably couldn't pitch. Spahn could, though. He was forty-four, but hooked on with the Giants and posted a 3.39 ERA in sixteen games. Nevertheless, they didn't ask him back in 1966. After twenty-four years, it looked like Spahn was finally finished.

He wasn't ready to quit, though. Spahn signed on as pitching coach with the Mexico City Tigers, and he also wound up starting three games for the club, splitting two decisions. Some wondered why an all-time great like Spahn would hang on like he did, to which Spahn replied—rather wisely, I think—"I don't care what the public thinks. I'm pitching because I enjoy pitching."

Spahn got the last laugh. In addition to recording that last victory of his long professional career, Spahn saw his club beat the Mexico City Reds in a playoff for the Mexican League championship.

A GREAT *WHAT?*

You know what doesn't make a lot of sense? Referring to just about any city as a "great baseball town."

You hear that all the time, but it really doesn't mean anything. To me, a "great baseball town" would be one that supported its team through thick and thin, through the good times and the bad times and everything in between. And the truth is that, outside of post-1967 Boston and the North Side of Chicago, I don't see any cities that fit the bill.

In 2001, the Giants had a good team and a new ballpark, and they led the National League with 3,277,244 paying customers. Not that I have any quotes at hand, but I suspect that a variety of media types fell all over themselves talking about what a "great baseball town" San Francisco is.

Well, it wasn't that long ago—less than thirty years, which isn't long, really—that the Giants were *the* biggest joke in baseball. In 1974 and '75, they barely managed to draw one million fans . . . in the two years *combined*. Yes, you read that right. In 1974, the Giants drew approximately 520,000 fans; in '75, they bumped the attendance all the way up to 523,000. And perhaps it's worth noting that in '74, the World Champion Oakland A's didn't quite pull in 850,000 fans. So in 1974—and '75, too—the Athletics and Giants *together* drew less than half as many fans as the Giants did in 2001, all by themselves.

Things got so bad that in 1975, Horace Stoneham, the Giants' ancient owner, announced that he'd concluded an agreement to sell the franchise to a group that made no secret of its intention to move the Giants to Toronto. However, San Francisco mayor George Moscone employed a variety of tactics to hold up the sale, and in 1976 prospective owners Bob Lurie and Arthur Herseth came up with eight million dollars and a solemn promise to keep the Giants right where they were.

Nevertheless, the Giants still finished last in attendance in 1976, and last again in 1977. And then, in 1978, attendance skyrocketed by nearly 150 percent!

Why? Because the Giants got off to a 30-19 start and were in the thick of the pennant race until an August slide. And two years later? In 1980, only the Braves drew fewer fans than the Giants. Why? Because the Giants got off to a 6-15 start and were never a part of the pennant race.

It's fair to accuse Giants fans of being fickle . . . but can't we paint the fans in virtually every city with that same brush? If you chart attendance for *any* city, you'll find a *high* correlation between attendance and performance. The simple fact is that most people don't want to spend their money and their time on a game their favorite team is probably going to lose. And that's true in Minneapolis and New York and, yes, San Francisco, too.

If some statistician type is reading this, I'd love to see a study comparing attendance, performance, and market size, because I think we'd learn something interesting about whether or not there really *are* great baseball towns. For the moment, though, I'm agnostical on the subject.

I'm especially grateful to Rob Wood for his editorial suggestions.

SEATTLE MARINERS

		YEARS	NOTES
DH	Edgar Martinez	1987–2002	If not for his defensive limitations and the late start, he'd be an obvious choice for the Hall of Fame, but as a DH for most of his career, his chances don't look so hot.
C	Dan Wilson	1994–2002	The M's had to give up Bret Boone to get him, but he gave them solid glove and decent stick for a long time; holds MLB record with 42-AB postseason hitless streak.
1B	Alvin Davis	1984–1991	The franchise's first legitimate star, and so forever known as "Mr. Mariner"; mysteriously lost virtually all of his quick-wristed hitting ability after turning 30.
2B	Harold Reynolds	1983–1992	Pacific Northwest native (Eugene, Oregon) won three Gold Gloves, led the league with 60 steals in 1987, and made a couple of All-Star teams.
SS	Alex Rodriguez	1994–2000	He looks like a real good bet to become one of the two greatest shortstops who ever played the game (Honus Wagner being the other).
3B	Edgar Martinez	1987–2002	I would rather not list the same player twice, but Edgar did play 563 games at third base, and the No. 2 choice just wouldn't fit on this list.
LF	Phil Bradley	1983–1987	Still the only Mariners left fielder to make an All-Star team, and for a few years he looked like a star; in retrospect, his career makes sense, given the late start.
CF	Ken Griffey, Jr.	1989–1999	Gosh, what more can you say about him? Sure, his exit strategy was a little ugly, but for 10 years he gave it everything he had, and he had a hell of a lot to give.
RF	Jay Buhner	1988–2001	Came from Yanks in great trade for M's, and became big-time power threat with three straight 40-homer seasons. Lost most of final year to foot injury.
SP1	Randy Johnson	1989–1998	If not the greatest pitcher ever, or even of his era, certainly the greatest *big* pitcher in the game's long history; nearly unhittable when completely focused.
SP2	Jamie Moyer	1996–2002	With the exception of 2000 season, the lefty change-up artist— actually, he was a *master*—could do little wrong after joining Mariners: 98-48 record through 2002.
SP3	Mark Langston	1984–1989	Fondly remembered in Seattle not only for winning 19 games in 1987 and thrice leading the league in strikeouts, but also for serving as trade bait in Randy Johnson deal.
SP4	Freddy García	1999–2002	The tastiest fruit born of the Randy Johnson trade with Houston, he hit the ground running and was arguably the league's best pitcher by his third season.
RP	Kazuhiro Sasaki	2000–2002	Fan favorite had just an average fastball, but nasty forkball made him one of game's better closers from the very moment he arrived from Japan.

Edgar Martinez wasn't the greatest right-handed hitter of his era—that label goes to Frank Thomas—but Edgar isn't far behind. They've got some other things in common, too: both missed significant chunks of their careers with injuries, and both were, shall we say, *limited* as players when they weren't in the batter's box.

The biggest *difference* between them was that the White Sox knew what they had, and the Mariners didn't have the foggiest. Not long after his twenty-second birthday, Thomas was playing every day for the Sox. Martinez didn't nail down a regular job until he was twenty-seven, in part because the M's just couldn't bear to part with Jim Presley.

In 1999, with the Mariners preparing to move across the street into Safeco Field, Ken Griffey and Alex Rodriguez whined about the dimensions in the new ballpark. Meanwhile, Edgar told me, "We'll see what happens when we get over there." And in the club's first full season at Safeco, the thirty-seven-year-old topped the American League with 145 RBI.

He's not the greatest right-handed hitter of his era, nor is he the greatest Mariner . . . but I do believe that he'll always be my favorite in both categories. If they ever let me vote for the Hall of Fame—don't worry, it won't happen—I'll put a check mark in the box next to Edgar Martinez with nary a second thought.

One of the interesting things about this franchise is that while it's obviously produced a number of Grade A players, there haven't been many Grade B players, which is evident when you look at the No. 2 team. When composing these teams for most franchises, one runs into at least a few tough choices, but with the Mariners there aren't really *any* tough choices. At every position, virtually any seventy-three-year-old member of the BBWAA would arrive at exactly the same conclusion that I have, and there certainly aren't many other things that you can say that about.

Among the position players, only Alvin Davis and John Olerud made me pause to consider. Olerud certainly was the better defensive player, and he did pile up some nice numbers with the Mariners. But Davis was around for a long time—he's still billed as "Mr. Mariner" when he shows up at events—and for a few years his numbers were outstanding, when you adjust for the different levels of offense in the 1980s and the early twenty-first century.

I'll write more about this later, but what hurt the Mariners for a long time was their inability to develop or acquire enough Grade B players, players better than Greg Briley and Jim Presley and Al Cowens.

NO. 2			
		YEARS	NOTES
DH	Ken Phelps	1983–1988	M's purchased the Seattle native and minor-league slugger from Expos just prior to '83 season, and he gave them power and patience for six years.
C	Dave Valle	1984–1993	Had a touch of power and was at least adequate with the glove, but spent too much time on the DL to establish himself as one of the league's top catchers.
1B	John Olerud	2000–*2002*	Grew up near Seattle and matriculated at Washington State, finally came back home when he was 31, and brought fine glove and high OBP along with him.
2B	Julio Cruz	1977–1983	Essentially the first Mariner that anybody really noticed, as he finished among the league leaders in steals six straight years; totaled 290 SB with Mariners.
SS	Omar Vizquel	1989–1993	Not the hitter that he'd become in Cleveland, but every bit the fielder, which is to say excellent if not quite the second coming of Ozzie Smith; edges Spike Owen.
3B	Jim Presley	1984–1989	Okay, so he was a bit erratic in the field, and he posted a .293 OBP *(ack!)* with the M's. But he did hit 28 homers in 1985 and drove in 107 runs in '86.
LF	Greg Briley	1988–1992	The winner by default, because he was nominally the regular for three seasons, but only in 1989 was he even moderately productive with the stick.
CF	Mike Cameron	2000–*2002*	Replaced Griffey, was actually *better* than Junior after the deal, and did something great that Griffey never did, hitting 4 home runs in one game (5/2/02).
RF	Al Cowens	1982–1986	With the exception of a wretched '83 season, actually played better in his thirties with Mariners than he'd played with Royals in his twenties; cost $60K.
SP1	Erik Hanson	1988–1993	Featured three outstanding pitches—fastball, drop curve, change-up—but his best season came when he was 25, and he won his last major-league game at 31.
SP2	Floyd Bannister	1979–1982	Lefty with a beautiful delivery and all the pitches, did well in Seattle but never as well as everybody thought he should do; signed with White Sox as free agent.
SP3	Brian Holman	1989–1991	On April 20, 1990, only a home run by ex-Mariner Ken Phelps with two outs in ninth kept Holman from tossing perfect game; arm fell off after the '91 season.
SP4	Aaron Sele	2000–2001	Only two seasons in Seattle, but he grew up in the area and went 32-15 over those two seasons, and M's reached postseason both years.
RP	Mike Schooler	1988–1992	Big fastball/slider right-hander who didn't last long, but gave the Mariners solid work for three-and-a-half seasons before the roof caved in.

SINGLE SEASON			
		YEARS	NOTES
DH	Edgar Martinez	1995	Played every game, led AL with .356 batting average and .479 OBP, and crushed Yankees in Division Series.
C	Dan Wilson	1997	Not quite as good at the plate as in the previous season, but played nearly every day and did a great job with the glove.
1B	Alvin Davis	1984	Rookie hit from Day 1, and finished season with 27 homers and 116 RBI, the latter a team record that stood until 1995.
2B	Bret Boone	2001	At 32 and in first year with M's, obliterated previous career highs with 37 homers, 118 runs, and 141 RBI.
SS	Alex Rodriguez	2000	He was great in '96 but even better in 2000, including 41 homers (league-leading 28 on road) and great defense.
3B	Edgar Martinez	1992	In his last season as the more-or-less regular third baseman, smacked 46 doubles and hit .346 to annex batting title.
LF	Phil Bradley	1985	Not only the *best* season for an M's LF, but one of the few *good* seasons by an M's LF: 100 runs, 26 homers, All-Star.
CF	Ken Griffey, Jr.	1997	Bunch of great ones, but '97 is the clear choice: topped AL with 56 homers *and* 125 runs, 147 RBI and .646 slugging.
RF	Ichiro Suzuki	2001	Leadoff man, Gold Glove winner, and league MVP for the team that won 116 games.
SP	Randy Johnson	1997	The Big Unit's greatest season with the M's, as he went 20-4 with 2.28 ERA (though Clemens won the Cy Young).
RP	Bill Caudill	1982	Throwing almost exclusively high heat, bulky right-hander won 12 games, saved 26, and posted 2.35 ERA.

ALL-ROOKIE			
		YEARS	NOTES
DH	Ken Phelps	1983	Didn't play much or particularly well, but did well enough—7 homers in 127 at-bats—to earn a regular job in '84.
C	Scott Bradley	1986	Came from White Sox in late-June trade, played regularly the rest of the way, and batted .302 with power in 68 games.
1B	Alvin Davis	1984	Completely polished when he reached the majors; outpointed teammate Mark Langston for Rookie of the Year honors.
2B	Vacant	—	No Mariners rookie has played anything close to regularly at second base, let alone played well.
SS	Omar Vizquel	1989	Absolute zero at the plate—.273 OBP, .261 slugging—but he was already flashing the glove that would make him famous.
3B	Vacant	—	Martinez, Presley, and Russ Davis all played both sparingly and poorly as rookies . . . and they're the *best* candidates.
LF	Greg Briley	1989	Converted infielder played a few games at second base, and slugged .442 with 13 homers in his rookie/best season.
CF	Ken Griffey, Jr.	1989	Only 19, but he could already hit (.264-16-61) and would win his first Gold Glove the next season.
RF	Ichiro Suzuki	2001	Only the second Rookie of the Year to garner MVP honors, too, thanks to batting title and scintillating work in right field.
SP	Mark Langston	1984	Won 17 games and topped AL with 204 K's; finished second in Rookie of the Year balloting to teammate Alvin Davis.
RP	Kazuhiro Sasaki	2000	Like Ichiro, Japanese veteran walked off with Rookie of the Year award after his first summer this side of the Pacific.

In 2000 and 2001, at least a few baseball writers—one of them a very famous baseball writer—were upset because the top candidates for the American League's Rookie of the Year Award had both previously established themselves as stars in Japan.

The NHL has a rule: if you're not twenty-six or younger when the hockey season starts, you're simply not eligible to win the Calder Trophy. Indeed, such a rule in baseball would have kept Ichiro from winning, as he was twenty-seven on Opening Day of the 2001 season. Of course, such a rule would also have disqualified Jackie Robinson, Sam Jethroe, and Joe Black, all of whom reached the majors when they did due to the circumstances of their birth, rather than any particular choices they might have made. And I, for one, am not eager to repossess Jackie Robinson's Rookie of the Year award from his family.

Some writers would like the BBWAA to change its rules, to prohibit an experienced Japanese player from winning the Rookie of the Year Award. But why stop there? What about Cuba, and Mexico, and Australia? What about the American Association and the Pacific Coast League?

The Rookie of the Year Award, after all, is just a plaque that's given to the best first-year player in each league. Let's leave it alone.

It's funny, the things you remember.

The Mariners won a division title in 1997, but in 1998 they slid all the way to third place with a 76-85 record. If you're looking for a scapegoat, the obvious choice is Randy Johnson. He was working on the last year of his contract, and he basically pouted for four months. Johnson started twenty-three games and went 9-10. That finally got him traded to Houston, and—poof!—he turned into Randy Johnson again: eleven starts, ten wins, and a 1.28 ERA.

But what I always remember is a home run in the Mariners' ninth game of the season. Playing at Fenway Park, the M's owned a 7–2 lead heading into the bottom of the ninth, thanks to eight strong innings from Johnson and Edgar Martinez's 3 RBI.

Enter the bullpen (gasp!), which allowed seven runs without recording even a single out. The crowning blow was provided by Mo Vaughn, who won the game with a grand slam against Paul Spoljaric.

Of the four relievers involved, three of them—Spoljaric, Mike Timlin, and Heathcliff Slocumb—had come over in trades the previous July 31. Trades that cost the Mariners three good players. And listening to the radio that afternoon, hearing them blow yet another big lead, we—I was living in Seattle at the time—just had the feeling, "Here we go again."

And so we did.

		YEARS	NOTES
HOMEGROWN			
DH	Edgar Martinez	1987–*2002*	Born in New York, but grew up in Puerto Rico and signed as free agent just before his 20th birthday.
C	Dave Valle	1984–1993	New York native taken in second round of '78 draft, chugged his way through minors one step at a time.
1B	Tino Martinez	1990–1996	Tampa native was 14th overall pick in '88 draft; began pro career in Class AA and spent an extra year in AAA.
2B	Bret Boone	1992–1993 2001–*2002*	Played at USC for three seasons before signing as M's 5th draft pick in 1990; later reacquired as free agent.
SS	Alex Rodriguez	1994–2000	First player selected in 1993 draft; reached majors the next year in his first season as a professional.
3B	Jim Presley	1984–1989	Fourth-round pick in 1979, and one of the franchise's first draft picks to establish himself in the majors.
LF	Phil Bradley	1983–1987	Third-round pick in 1981, signed with M's before starring at QB in senior season at Univ. of Missouri.
CF	Ken Griffey, Jr.	1989–1999	Like Alex, Junior was No. 1 overall pick, and like Alex he reached the majors before he turned 20.
RF	Danny Tartabull	1984–1986	Swiped from Reds in (short-lived) compensation draft after two seasons in low minors, so we'll count him.
SP	Mark Langston	1984–1989	San Jose State University product was third-round pick in 1981, then blew through the minors in three years.
RP	Jeff Nelson	1992–1995 2001–*2002*	Started with Dodgers, but M's grabbed giant slider artist in Rule 5 draft after his first two pro seasons.

		TRADED	NOTES
TRADED AWAY			
DH	Ken Phelps	July 21, 1988	Gave the Yankees only two months of Phelpsian power, and he cost them Jay Buhner.
C	Jason Varitek	July 31, 1997	M's sent Varitek *and* Derek Lowe to Red Sox for . . . Heathcliff Slocumb (see All-Bust Team).
1B	Tino Martinez	December 7, 1995	Sent to Yankees, along with Jeff Nelson and Jim Mecir, for Sterling Hitchcock and Russ Davis.
2B	Bret Boone	November 2, 1993	At that point in his career, wanted to pull everything and didn't get along with Lou, so off he went to Reds.
SS	Omar Vizquel	December 20, 1993	Got ugly for a while, with Felix Fermin and Luis Sojo playing short, but everything worked out in the end.
3B	Dave Magadan	November 9, 1993	Acquired from Marlins for Jeff Darwin and Henry Cotto; sent back to Marlins for Darwin and dollars.
LF	José Cruz, Jr.	July 31, 1997	Third pick in '95 draft traded, in rookie season, to "solve" seemingly interminable bullpen problems.
CF	Dave Henderson	August 19, 1986	Sent with Spike Owen to Red Sox in bad deal; Hendu key player on pennant winners in Boston and Oakland.
RF	Danny Tartabull	December 10, 1986	The worst trade in the franchise's first decade: Tartabull to Royals for Scott Bankhead and Mike Kingery.
SP	Randy Johnson	July 31, 1998	Great after he left, but M's did get Freddy Garcia, John Halama, and Carlos Guillen in forced deal with Astros.
RP	Mike Jackson	December 11, 1991	Another terrible trade: Jackson, Bill Swift, and Dave Burba to S.F. for Kevin Mitchell and Mike Remlinger.

GOLD GLOVE		YEARS	NOTES
C	Dan Wilson	1994–*2002*	Piniella managed him in Cincinnati and loved his glove, so got him in Seattle as soon as he could.
1B	John Olerud	2000–*2002*	Wasn't that flashy but made all the plays; David Segui also outstanding, but didn't last two seasons in Seattle.
2B	Harold Reynolds	1983–1992	Three-time Gold Glove winner whose outstanding range compensated for high number of errors.
SS	Omar Vizquel	1989–1993	Became famous in Cleveland but won the first of his many Gold Gloves in 1993, his last year in Seattle.
3B	David Bell	1998–2001	He wasn't great but he was good, and there hasn't been a lot of goodness at third base in Seattle.
LF	Phil Bradley	1983–1987	Didn't throw well, but was a great running quarterback at Mizzou and had decent range in the field.
CF	Mike Cameron	2000–*2002*	Most would argue for Griffey, but Cameron's got Junior's great instincts *and* he's faster.
RF	Ichiro Suzuki	2001–*2002*	Amazing throw to 3B in April 11 game vs. A's sewed up Gold Glove for speedy Suzuki in his first season.
P	Mark Langston	1984–1989	Quick off the mound to cover bunts and possessor of great move to first base, won two Gold Gloves as Mariner.

IRON GLOVE		YEARS	NOTES
C	Scott Bradley	1986–1992	Played because he was versatile and could hit a little; considered subpar throwing and blocking low pitches.
1B	Paul Sorrento	1996–1997	Had pretty soft hands so he wasn't horrible, but lacked both quickness and any sort of speed, and thus range.
2B	Joey Cora	1995–1998	Cora was truly terrible, the worst defensive 2B in the majors, and had the stats and reputation to prove it.
SS	Rey Quiñones	1986–1989	Everybody thought he had a world of talent, but it showed up only in brief flashes; erratic in the field.
3B	Russ Davis	1996–1999	Posted .905 fielding percentage at 3B in '98; fielding woes resulted in ill-advised, ugly experiment in LF.
LF	Glenallen Hill	1998	There are plenty of candidates here, but Hill got dumped even though he was doing great with the bat.
CF	Joe Simpson	1979–1982	He wasn't *bad*, but he's probably the worst defensive center fielder who's played regularly for the M's.
RF	Jeff Burroughs	1981	Never a good outfielder, by the time he got to Seattle he was slow *and* he couldn't throw.
SP	Matt Young	1983–1986	Hands down, the worst-fielding pitcher of his time; finished 10-year career with *.878 fielding percentage.*

Many of you will be surprised, and some of you will be angered, to see that I've selected Mike Cameron rather than Ken Griffey, Jr., as the Mariners' greatest defensive center fielder. After all, Junior won ten Gold Gloves in his eleven years in Seattle.

But did he deserve them? Maybe yes, maybe no. The strange thing was that Griffey's defensive stats never matched his reputation. I was working at STATS, Inc., in the mid-1990s, when STATS published a book called *Baseball Scoreboard*. And every year, the same thing: we'd run our annual article on zone ratings—essentially the percentage of balls into a player's "area" that were fielded—and Griffey wouldn't come out anywhere near the top of the center-field rankings. In 1995, STATS CEO John Dewan made it a personal mission to figure out if we were missing something, if perhaps Griffey really *was* as good as everyone said. So we came up with all sorts of possible biases in our typical analysis, all sorts of mitigating factors . . . and we didn't find a single thing. I should also mention that I actually saw both Griffey and Cameron play hundreds of games. And while I believe that Griffey was good, I also believe that he wasn't quick enough, nor did he play shallow enough, to be great.

Mickey Brantley never actually started an Opening Day game in left field for the Mariners, but he was supposed to be a long-term solution at the position. That didn't work out, which is why he makes the All-Bust Team. But there are plenty of candidates for that slot, because since Phil Bradley virtually everybody who's played left field has been a bust. In the 1990s, "left field" became a running joke in Seattle, nearly as popular as the tired old groaners about Tacoma that tired old tour guides keep telling.

Ken Griffey's first game with the Mariners was Opening Day of the 1989 season. He would eventually start a dozen straight Opening Day games for the club. And alongside him in left field? Nine different left fielders.

Even that understates things, though, because few of those Opening Day starters held the job for long, which meant that Griffey played with a *lot* of left fielders. And some of them—Marc Newfield and Pat Lennon, for example—actually came to the majors with a great deal of hitting ability; unfortunately, none of them ever showed it when Junior was showing his. And the franchise's "left-field problem" resulted in a couple of horrible trades—one for Kevin Mitchell, the other for Eric Anthony—that cost the club some damn good pitchers.

ALL-BUST			
		YEARS	NOTES
DH	Al Chambers	1983–1985	The first player selected in 1979 draft, showed talent in minors but slugged .292 in his 57-game MLB career.
C	Mackey Sasser	1993–1994	Actually caught only 4 games, due to strange inability to throw the ball; showed inability to hit, too.
1B	Pete O'Brien	1990–1993	M's finally spent some big money on a free agent . . . and they got a flop, as O'Brien took up space for four years.
2B	Mark McLemore	2000	Pretty awful as regular 2B with .316 slugging pct., but did bounce back as utility man in 2001.
SS	Rey Quiñones	1986–1989	Everybody said he had great range at shortstop and he certainly had power, but quickly wore out his welcome.
3B	Jamie Allen	1983	No. 2 draft pick got just one chance in the majors: 86 games, 273 at-bats, .309 OBP, .304 slugging average.
LF	Mickey Brantley	1986–1989	Showed some promise in 1987 (843 OPS), but struggled as regular in '88 and was gone a year later.
CF	Alex Diaz	1995–1996	Not really a bust, but the M's couldn't find anybody better when Griffey got hurt in '95; .283 OBP with M's.
RF	Glenn Wilson	1988	Came from Phils, traded the following July after worst five months of his career (including .286 OBP).
SP	Greg Hibbard	1994	One of first big free-agent pitchers signed by M's, went 1-5 with 6.69 ERA before torn rotator cuff ended career.
RP	Heathcliff Slocumb	1997–1998	Came to M's in horrible trade, then lost job as closer shortly into '98 season and finished with 3 saves.

USED-TO-BE-GREAT			
		YEARS	NOTES
DH	Willie Horton	1979–1980	Longtime Tigers left fielder finished with M's; in 1979 he DH'd in all 162 games and drove in 106 runs.
C	Lance Parrish	1992	Ex–Tigers great came to M's during season, beginning four-year stretch with a different team every year.
1B	Pete O'Brien	1990–1993	Still had the glove, but the ex-Ranger's bat was mostly gone: pitiful .304 OBP and .371 slugging with Seattle.
2B	Wally Backman	1993	A poor defensive player with zero power, Backman played only 10 games in his last season, and batted .138.
SS	Dale Sveum	1994	Once hit 25 homers in a season for Milwaukee; with M's at end of three-year stretch in which he hit .192.
3B	Lenny Randle	1981–1982	Never actually great, but he's still famous in Seattle for dropping to his knees and blowing a bunt foul.
LF	Rickey Henderson	2000	He was 41, but came to M's in June, posted .362 OBP and stole 31 bases in 92 games for Wild Card winner.
CF	Gorman Thomas	1984–1986	Never actually played CF for M's—DH mostly, with a bit of LF—but once starred in center for Brewers.
RF	Jeff Burroughs	1981	Played well for the Braves in '80 and for the A's in '82, but former MVP didn't do much at all for M's.
SP	Gaylord Perry	1982–1983	His 300th victory, gained on May 6, 1982, was for a long time the biggest moment in franchise history.
RP	Goose Gossage	1994	Fastball a mere shadow of its former self, but at 43 he could still pitch: 3-0 with 4.18 ERA in 47 innings.

FAMILY TIES

		YEARS	NOTES
C	Steve Yeager	1986	His uncle is Chuck Yeager; sadly, the character of "Little Nephew Stevie" got cut from *The Right Stuff*.
1B	David Segui	1998–1999	David's father, Diego, pitched in the Seattle Pilots' first game and started the Mariners' first game.
2B	Bret Boone	1992–1993 2001–*2002*	When he debuted on 8/19/92, Boones became the first three-generation family in MLB history.
SS	David Bell	1998–2001	Like Boone, latest in the line of a three-generation MLB family, with father Buddy and grandpa Gus.
3B	Dave Magadan	1993	A native of Tampa, just like his manager, Piniella . . . who also happened to be his cousin.
LF	Kevin Mitchell Keith Mitchell	1992 1994	Both brothers—Kevin is seven years older—were Mariners for one season, mostly in left field.
CF	Ken Griffey, Jr.	1989–1999	Played with his old man for a few months, and his little brother Craig was in the system for years.
RF	Jay Buhner	1988–2001	Maybe M's didn't want to play favorites . . . Why else did they employ Jay's brother Shawn for six seasons?
SP	Jamie Moyer	1996–*2002*	Moyer is married to the former Karen Phelps, which makes him Digger Phelps's son-in-law.
RP	Brad Holman	1993	His brother Brian, a nice by-product of deal for Randy Johnson, pitched well before getting hurt.

TOP FIVE TEAMS

YEAR 2001 **RECORD** 116-46
BEST HITTERS Ichiro, Bret Boone
BEST PITCHER Freddy Garcia
NOTES M's set major-league record for wins in a season.

YEAR 1995 **RECORD** 79-66
BEST HITTERS Edgar Martinez
BEST PITCHER Randy Johnson (Cy Young)
NOTES Beat Angels in playoff for West title, then shocked Yankees in Division Series.

YEAR 2000 **RECORD** 91-71
BEST HITTERS Alex Rodriguez
BEST PITCHERS Aaron Sele, Kazu Sasaki
NOTES Swept White Sox in Division Series before running into Rocket.

YEAR 1997 **RECORD** 90-72
BEST HITTER Ken Griffey (MVP)
BEST PITCHER Randy Johnson
NOTES Lost Division Series to O's as Big Unit got hammered.

YEAR 1991 **RECORD** 83-79
BEST HITTER Ken Griffey
BEST PITCHER Bill Swift
NOTES In their fifteenth season, M's finally won more than they lost.

TOP FIVE MANAGERS

MANAGER Lou Piniella
YEARS 1993–2002
RECORD 840–711 (.542)
NOTES Great success came when a great pitching coach arrived.

MANAGER Jim Lefebvre
YEARS 1989–1991
RECORD 233-253 (.479)
NOTES One of only two M's managers *not* to finish last.

MANAGER Dick Williams
YEARS 1986–1988
RECORD 159-192 (.453)
NOTES M's were his sixth team, and seemed out of energy.

MANAGER Rene Lachemann
YEARS 1981–1983
RECORD 140-180 (.438)
NOTES M's second manager and Marlins' first, with similar success.

MANAGER Darrell Johnson
YEARS 1977–1980
RECORD 226-362 (.384)
NOTES Big comedown for manager of '75 Red Sox.

On August 31, 1989, the Seattle Mariners made some history. Thirty-nine-year-old George Kenneth Griffey, Sr., just acquired from Cincinnati, opened the Mariners' game against Kansas City in left field. And in center field? Nineteen-year-old George Kenneth Griffey, Jr.

It was the first time in major-league history that a father and son had played in the same game, let alone for the same team. In the bottom of the first, the Griffeys hit back-to-back singles and both later scored. But the highlight for father and son came on September 14. In the bottom of the first inning, facing Kirk McCaskill, Senior homered on an 0-2 pitch. And just a few moments later, Junior drove a 3-0 pitch over the fence.

The M's made history again a few years later, when Bret Boone made his major-league debut in a game against the Orioles in Baltimore. Boone was the son of Bob Boone and the grandson of Ray Boone, thus winning the "race" to become the first three-generation baseball family in the major leagues. (It wasn't until 1995 that the Bells joined this exclusive club, with the Hairstons coming aboard three years later.)

Though the Mariners are obviously a young franchise, they just might have the most interesting family connections of any franchise.

FOR WANT OF A FEW NAILS . . .

For the first decade of their existence, the Mariners stumbled along like any number of expansion franchises before them. The M's didn't win even 70 games until their sixth season, and then they settled into a comfortable sort of mediocrity: 74 wins this year, 67 next year, 78 the year after . . .

But beginning in the summer of 1987, in a period just short of two years the Seattle Mariners built the foundation for a dynasty.

On June 2, 1987, the Mariners spent the first pick in the draft on George Kenneth Griffey, Jr.

On July 21, 1988, the Mariners stole Jay Buhner from the Yankees.

On April 3, 1989, Edgar Martinez was in the lineup, playing third base and batting eighth, in the Mariners' first game of the season, as somebody finally figured out that Edgar just might be a major-league ballplayer.

And on May 25, 1989, the Mariners traded Mark Langston and a player to be named later to the Montreal Expos, and received Randy Johnson (and two other young pitchers).

Griffey. Buhner. Martinez. Johnson. Any number of World Series teams have been fashioned atop weaker underpinnings. Yet it's now more than a decade later, and neither Griffey nor Buhner nor Martinez has ever played in a World Series. Johnson did pitch in a World Series, but it was two teams removed from the Mariners. Seattle won 764 games in the 1990s, which ranked third in the American League West. Among four teams.

So what happened?

Two things. One, the Mariners essentially failed to find good or average players to play the positions not manned by great players. And two, they pissed away an incredible amount of pitching talent.

Beginning with the pissing away . . .

In a two-year span, Seattle traded Mike Hampton, Bill Swift, Dave Burba, Shawn Estes, Jeff Nelson, Mike Jackson, and Jim Mecir. In other words, they traded away a pretty good rotation and one hell of a bullpen.

In return for those seven pitchers, the M's received Sterling Hitchcock, Russ Davis, Eric Anthony, Salomon Torres, Kevin Mitchell, and Mike Remlinger. Hitchcock spent one season (13-9, 5.35) in Seattle, then was traded for Scott Sanders, who went 3-6 with a 6.47 ERA for the M's. Davis was supposed to fill the gap at third base, but never established himself as a quality player. Anthony and Torres were both complete washouts. Mitchell wasn't horrible, but after playing 99 games was traded to Cincinnati for Norm Charlton, who pitched 35 innings for the M's before leaving as a free agent (he would later come back twice, first in 1995 and then again in 2001). And Mike Remlinger never pitched in the majors for Seattle, departing after two seasons as a minor-league free agent.

In other words, for all those pitchers, the Mariners received little, *very* little, in return.

Of course, it's customary in essays like this one to focus on the negative while ignoring the positive. But while it's true that every team makes bad trades, they all make good ones, too, right? Not the Mariners in the 1990s. All of those *terrible* trades weren't balanced by even one *great* trade.

And they needed to make some great trades, or at least a few good ones, because the players they had simply weren't doing enough behind the big stars. And so what probably should have been four or five division titles in the 1990s instead became two.

I'm especially grateful to Mariners fans David Schoenfield, Ted Bishop, and Brandon Funston for their editorial suggestions.

Tampa Bay Devil Rays

		ALL-TIME	
		YEARS	NOTES
DH	José Canseco	1999–2000	Cuban-born slugger was supposed to be a big draw; that didn't happen, but Canseco *was* a productive hitter in 1999, finishing with 34 homers and a .563 slugging pct.
C	John Flaherty	1998–*2002*	Closest thing the Rays have had to a constant over the years, and beloved by the Tampa–St. Pete baseball writers; broke up Pedro's no-hit bid in September of 2000.
1B	Fred McGriff	1998–2001	Tampa native acquired, at least in part, as a gate attraction; struggled some in his first season home, but exploded with big '99 season.
2B	Miguel Cairo	1998–2000	Ran well and played solid defense, but he rarely walked and after three seasons the Devil Rays got tired of waiting for him to get better.
SS	Kevin Stocker	1998–2000	Solid with the glove and actually hit pretty well as part-timer after a disastrous (595 OPS) season with the stick in '98; too bad Rays gave up Bobby Abreu to get him. ✎
3B	Wade Boggs	1998–1999	He turned 40 midway through his first season in St. Pete, but Tampa native hit the first homer in franchise history and collected career hit No. 3,000 in August of '99.
LF	Greg Vaughn	2000–*2002*	The result of a typical Devil Rays move; after hitting 95 homers in '98 and '99 combined, joined Rays when he was 34 and hit 52 homers in 2000 and '01.
CF	Randy Winn	1998–*2002*	Never a *regular* until 2002 but a fine defender, and he came up with the biggest hit in franchise history, a three-run homer to end a 15-game losing streak (5/11/2002).
RF	Dave Martinez	1998–2000	Played for nine teams in his career (so far), and the Devil Rays were the sixth of them; right field's been a bad position for Rays, but Martinez not bad in 1999.
SP1	Rolando Arrojo	1998–1999	Throwing a variety of pitches from a variety of angles, recorded franchise's first victory, was franchise's first All-Star, and won 21 games in his two seasons with club.
SP2	Tanyon Sturtze	2000–*2002*	With all due respect to Sturtze—a good-looking fellow with a solid fastball and diving splitter—we're already scraping the bottom of the barrel here.
SP3	Bryan Rekar	1998–2001	From the frying pan into the fire, as Rekar joined Rays after three years with Rockies; only pitcher to start a game in each of franchise's first four seasons.
SP4	Albie Lopez	1998–2001	Big power pitcher won only 14 games as starter for Devil Rays, but he had a nice year (1998) as a reliever and pitched well for four months of 2000 as a starter.
RP	Roberto Hernandez	1998–2000	His 101 saves likely to stand as franchise record for at least a few more years; 320 career saves tops the list for pitchers born outside the United States.

✎ Historically, expansion drafts haven't been much help in stocking franchises. The Senators and Angels did okay in the first one . . . so good that the rules were changed for the next one, to keep new teams from actually acquiring any useful players. There wasn't much talent available in 1968 or 1976, either. But in 1992, the Rockies and Marlins both found some good players, as did the Diamondbacks and Devil Rays in 1997.

The problem for the Devil Rays was that as soon as they got a good player, they turned around and traded him. And then he became a great player.

Of course, I'm talking about Bobby Abreu. The Astros had a lot of young outfielders, and so they didn't protect Abreu, who was coming off an injury-plagued season in the minors. Everybody knew the guy could hit, though, and the Devil Rays grabbed him with their third pick in the expansion draft. Great move. But was it general manager Chuck LaMar's idea, or was LaMar just a proxy? Because moments later, Lamar traded Abreu to the Phillies for shortstop Kevin Stocker.

Stocker was a nice little player, played pretty good defense and got on base reasonably well. But he was twenty-seven years old and wasn't going to get any better. If you're trying to build a team, he's one of the *last* pieces of the puzzle. Not one of the first.

Among the many bad things that have happened to the Tampa Bay Devil Rays is this: they've had horrible luck matching up good seasons from their hitters with good seasons from their pitchers. In 1998, the Devil Rays enjoyed what may well have been the most effective first-year pitching staff in major-league history; by one method that adjusts for the fact that Tropicana Field played as a great hitter's park that season, Tampa Bay's pitchers were the third best in the league, behind only the Yankees and the Red Sox. Starters Rolando Arrojo, Julio Santana, and Tony Saunders were good, and relievers Albie Lopez (7-4, 2.60) and Jim Mecir (7-2, 3.11) were both excellent.

Tampa Bay's hitters sucked, though. Despite that great hitter's park, the Devil Rays scored fewer runs than any team in the league. By far. And the next year (with the fences pushed out), the hitters improved some . . . but the pitchers were terrible. Well, not terrible, but certainly nowhere near as good as they'd been the year before. In 2000, the Devil Rays pitchers were quite good—better than the Yankees, believe it or not—but again the hitters were terrible.

And since then, it's been a true team effort.

SINGLE SEASON

		YEARS	NOTES
DH	José Canseco	1999	Missed six weeks with back woes, but still hit 34 homers and was just 9th American Leaguer to have 30+ at All-Star break.
C	John Flaherty	1999	"Flash" improved his batting average by 71 points (to .278), the biggest jump in the league, and hit 14 homers.
1B	Fred McGriff	1999	After subpar '98, led club in hitting (.310), total bases (292), doubles (30), RBI (104), walks (86), and OBP (.405).
2B	Miguel Cairo	1999	Despite two stints on DL totaling five weeks, stole 22 bases, batted .295, and played excellent defense.
SS	Chris Gomez	2001	Played 58 games after coming from Padres in trade, and shocked the world with 8 homers!
3B	Bobby Smith	1998	Batting .310 in late August, but went into a month-long slump and finished up with a .276 average and 11 homers as rookie.
LF	Greg Vaughn	2000	Just missed becoming the third player in history to hit 30+ HR with 4 teams; first 2 were teammates Canseco and McGriff.
CF	Randy Winn	2002	With 821 OPS and good glove, rivaled McGriff's '99 season as the best in team history . . . and yes, that's faint praise.
RF	Dave Martinez	1999	Led Devil Rays with 79 runs scored and 8 outfield assists, and set career high with 68 RBI . . . whither Ben Grieve, though?
SP	Rolando Arrojo	1998	Defected from Cuba in 1996, and finished second in Rookie of the Year voting in '98 with 14 wins and 3.56 ERA.
RP	Roberto Hernandez	1999	Saved 43 of Rays' 69 wins—for a 62.3 percentage that broke the AL record—and failed to convert only 4 save chances.

GOLD GLOVE

		YEARS	NOTES
C	John Flaherty	1998–2002	Improved his footwork after joining club and became solid thrower; already a good receiver when he arrived.
1B	Fred McGriff	1998–2001	Not nearly as mobile as he'd been at the height of his days in the National League, but who else is there?
2B	Miguel Cairo	1998–2000	Consistency the only issue, as he seemed to match every highlight play with an error on a routine play.
SS	Felix Martínez	2000–2001	As Devil Ray, batted .228 with little power and modicum of walks . . . so yes, he could pick it at shortstop.
3B	Vinny Castilla	2000–2001	Ex-shortstop with good arm was particularly good at charging the slow rollers.
LF	Quinton McCracken	1998–2000	Like his teammate Mike Kelly (below), McCracken had the speed to play center field, and knew how to use it.
CF	Gerald Williams	2000–2001	He and his .298 OBP were generally a disaster, but Williams was an outstanding defensive player.
RF	Mike Kelly	1998	Close to a zero with the bat, but speedy onetime center fielder did the job in the outfield.
P	Tanyon Sturtze	2000–2002	Not much of a move, but he's a tremendous athlete who fields everything hit toward him and covers the bases.

STEP RIGHT UP, FOLKS . . .

Jim Morris represents everything that's gone wrong with the Tampa Bay Devil Rays.

Don't get me wrong. I'm not saying the Devil Rays shouldn't have given Morris a shot. He pitched to his first major-league hitter (Royce Clayton) on September 19. The Rays won that game 15–2, which left them still in fifth place, 25½ games behind the Yankees. So it's not like they had anything to lose. It was a wonderful story, and wonderful stories help make baseball what it is.

My point is that Jim Morris, rather than being just a nice little sidelight—and fodder for a Disney movie—is actually representative of the franchise's mindset. The Devil Rays don't make moves because they're trying to win. They make moves because they're trying to attract reluctant customers to their crummy ballpark.

Why did the Devil Rays acquire José Canseco? No, not because he looked like a building block for the future. They picked up Canseco because he was born in Cuba, and there are a lot of Cuban-Americans in Florida.

Why did the Devil Rays acquire Wade Boggs? No, not because he looked like a building block for the future. They picked up Boggs because he grew up in Florida, and was chasing 3,000 hits. He got there, too, on August 7 . . . and praise the Lord and pass the ammo, 39,512 fans showed up at Tropicana Field to see it.

Why did the Devil Rays acquire Fred McGriff? No, not because he looked like a building block for the future (though, as it happened, he actually had plenty left). They picked up McGriff because he grew up in Florida. Same for Dwight Gooden, and probably a few other native Floridians.

Why did the Devil Rays acquire Greg Vaughn? No, not because he looked like a building block for the future. Actually, I'm not sure *why* they acquired Vaughn . . . though, come to think of it, Vaughn did attend the University of Miami.

And then there's the story of one Greg "Toe" Nash, the amazing double threat from the swamps of Louisiana with a police record longer than his size-18 foot . . . *Don't be shy, folks! Step right up! See the 220-pound sugar-cane worker who can hit a baseball 500 FEET and throw it one HUNDRED miles per hour!* I don't fault the Devil Rays for signing Nash—who hasn't come close to reaching the majors—but I do fault them for not doing anything *important* that made positive headlines.

You see, from the very beginning, the Devil Rays operated under the assumption that if they could just get the fans in the ballpark, winning would follow. They even hired Mike Veeck, who's so good at getting people to show up for games in minor-league ballparks. But as Veeck discovered—and his old man knew—all the silly promotions in the world don't make a damn bit of difference if the team stinks.

People will come to the ballpark for two things, and two things only: free stuff, and baseball. Winning baseball. You can throw the grandest buffalo-milking contest in the history of Organized Baseball, and all you'll get from the fans is one big yawn. And that's exactly what the Devil Rays have received. In their second, third, and fourth seasons, the D-Rays finished tenth, thirteenth, and fourteenth (last) in American League attendance.

I don't know how much of the blame goes to owner Vince Naimoli, and how much goes to general manager Chuck LaMar. I suppose there's plenty for everyone.

Texas Rangers

Frank Howard barely played for the Texas Rangers. He did, however, play quite a lot for the second edition of the Washington Senators, which *became* the Texas Rangers in 1972. Since the Senators only lasted eleven seasons, it made sense to consider the two teams as one.

Frank Howard was never the best hitter in the American League, but for five or six years he might have been the *scariest* hitter in the American League.

The Dodgers paid Howard, a two-sport star at Ohio State, a $108,000 signing bonus in 1958, and he was worth every penny. In his first season as a pro, he hit thirty-seven home runs. In his second season as a pro, he was named Minor League Player of the Year by *The Sporting News*. And in his third season as a pro, he reached the majors and was named Rookie of the Year in the National League.

Frank Howard certainly wasn't the first man his size to reach the major leagues, but he *was* the first man his size who could actually play. At six-seven and 250-some pounds, he looked like he could bunt the ball out of the ballpark.

The Dodgers never really knew what to do with Howard, and anyway they always had more players than they could really use. So prior to the '65 season, the Dodgers traded Howard to the Senators in a deal that worked out for both clubs. From 1967 through 1970, "The Capital Punisher" hit 172 home runs, and nobody else in the majors—not Harmon Killebrew or Willie McCovey or Hank Aaron—was even close.

	ALL-TIME		
		YEARS	**NOTES**
DH	Larry Parrish	1982–1988	Big fella miscast as 3B with Expos and outfielder with Rangers; finally found his natural position in 1986, when he was 33, and thrived for a couple of years.
C	Ivan Rodriguez	1991–2002	If Pudge could have hit like Piazza or Piazza could have fielded like Pudge, you'd have the greatest player since Babe Ruth; not that Pudge wasn't a very *good* hitter.
1B	Rafael Palmeiro	1990–1993 1999–*2002*	Great hitter and one of the game's best defensive first basemen; getting him from the Cubs for Mitch Williams was the best move the Rangers ever made.
2B	Julio Franco	1989–1993	No sort of defensive player—he DH'd his last two years with Rangers—but all those line drives more than compensated before knee injury in 1992.
SS	Alex Rodriguez	2001–*2002*	Despite only two seasons with Rangers, Alex takes this spot because 1) there's not much competition, and 2) at this moment, he's the second-greatest shortstop ever.
3B	Buddy Bell	1979–1985	Widely regarded as the AL's top defensive third baseman in the early 1980s, and a pretty good hitter during his five full seasons with the Rangers.
LF	Frank Howard	1965–1972	From '68 through '70, the immensely strong "Hondo" was one of the AL's three best hitters; if he hadn't spent so many years in L.A., he might be in the Hall of Fame.
CF	Don Lock	1962–1966	Wichita native had big ears and a bigger swing, led two minor leagues in HR and RBI before graduating to majors; known for making spectacular catches in CF.
RF	Juan González	1989–1999 *2002*	I don't believe that he deserved either of them, but González did win MVP Awards in 1996 (.314-47-144) and 1998 (.318-45-157), and hit 348 HR with club (so far).
SP1	Charlie Hough	1980–1990	Bought from Dodgers for a pittance, knuckleballer is easily Rangers' all-time leader in wins (139) and innings (2,308), and led club in victories for seven straight years.
SP2	Fergie Jenkins	1974–1975 1978–1981	Hall of Famer set still-standing franchise record with 25 victories in '74, then slumped in '75; came back for second stint and again ranked as staff ace.
SP3	Kevin Brown	1986–1994	Gained his fame with other clubs, but put in four fine seasons for the Rangers, too; Brown's hard sinker was one of the game's least-hittable pitches.
SP4	Nolan Ryan	1989–1993	Even at 45, still one of the game's hardest throwers, able to dominate (if not always for 9 innings) with two pitches, and tossed 6th and 7th no-hitters for Texas.
RP	Jeff Russell	1985–1992 1995–1996	Nothing fancy about power pitcher Russell, who became solid closer after moving to bullpen for good in 1989, when he led AL with 38 saves.

		YEARS	NOTES
DH	Brian Downing	1991–1992	He was 40 when he arrived and nearly 42 when he left, but Downing could still get on base and he could still hit the ball out of the ballpark.
C	Jim Sundberg	1974–1983 1988–1989	Retired as Rangers leader in games, at-bats, hits, and triples, and also finished career with 1,927 games caught, then No. 2 on all-time list.
1B	Mike Hargrove	1974–1978	Rookie of the Year in '74 and an All-Star in '75, and arguably the first real star developed by the franchise; not much power, but .399 OBP as Ranger.
2B	Bump Wills	1977–1981	Outstanding defensively with great wheels, and only a so-so OBP kept him from being a great leadoff man; still holds franchise record with 161 steals.
SS	Toby Harrah	1969–1978 1985–1986	Not much with the glove at shortstop or third, but from 1975 onward he was something of an on-base machine; still ranks No. 2 on franchise list with 708 walks.
3B	Ken McMullen	1965–1970	Along with Frank Howard—with whom he was traded from Dodgers—one of the few bright spots on the awful Senators teams of the late '60s; solid all-around player.
LF	Rusty Greer	1994–2002	Beloved in Metroplex for willingness to get dirty, but his real value is described by his .387 career OBP; in 1995, cracked 2 walk-off homers as pinch hitter.
CF	Oddibe McDowell	1985–1988 1994	Only 5'9" and 160 pounds, but packed some pop with his great speed, and a lot of people thought he should have become a superstar (he didn't).
RF	Ruben Sierra	1986–1991 2000–2001	Aside from one season, Sierra never seemed to play quite as well as everybody thought he should; jump-started his career with bizarre comeback in 2001.
SP1	Kenny Rogers	1989–1995 2000–2002	With 101 victories, easily tops team list for wins by LHP, and leads *all* Rangers with 463 appearances; one of two Rangers to lead club in wins at least four times.
SP2	Rick Helling	1994–1996 1997–2001	Exceedingly durable, Helling started 137 games from 1998 through 2001, tops in the American League; first Ranger to win 10+ in four straight seasons since Hough.
SP3	Jon Matlack	1978–1983	Ex-Met enjoyed his best season—15-13 with brilliant 2.27 ERA—after joining Rangers, but 270 innings apparently took toll, and it was all downhill from there.
SP4	Dick Bosman	1966–1973	For one season, he was as good as anybody, going 14-5 with American League–best 2.19 ERA to earn a big raise; never approached that level afterward, though.
RP	John Wetteland	1997–2000	Tops franchise's all-time list with 150 saves, a mark likely to stand for at least a few more years; quit when he was 31, in decline but could still pitch effectively.

It's funny how quickly we forget. In 1988, the Rangers and their fans welcomed Jim Sundberg back into the fold with open arms, after a four-and-a-half-year exile with the Brewers, Royals, and Cubs (actually, "exile" probably isn't the right word; in 1985 with the Royals, Sundberg got a chance to do something he'd never done, or would do, with the Rangers: play in the postseason). But he'd first left the Rangers under something of a cloud.

In December of 1982, the Rangers worked out a trade with the Dodgers: Sundberg would go to Los Angeles, and the Rangers would get Dave Stewart, Burt Hooton . . . and Orel Hershiser.

Sundberg had a no-trade clause in his contract, though, and he exercised it.

Hooton didn't have much left, but Hershiser would win 204 games after *not* getting traded to the Rangers. And while Texas did eventually acquire Dave Stewart, they had to give up Rick Honeycutt in the deal.

The next season, Sundberg butted heads with new manager Dave Rader. At one point, Sundberg blamed some opposition stolen bases on a sore throwing arm, leading Rader to suggest that Sundberg must be either a whiner or a liar.

Of course, Sundberg had every right to veto the trade, and history will remember Rader as something of a lout. And so our memories of Sundberg are nothing less than positive.

In this franchise's first forty-two seasons, only one Senator or Ranger has been named the American League's Rookie of the Year. In 1974, Mike Hargrove won the award in a walk, thanks to a .323 batting average that would have ranked second in the league if he'd played enough to qualify.

Del Unser finished second in 1968, but it was a distant second to Yankees pitcher Stan Bahnsen. Pat Putnam tied for third in 1979. Oddibe McDowell finished fourth in 1985. Ivan Rodríguez finished a distant fourth in 1991 (granted, he didn't play his first game until June 20). Rusty Greer finished third in 1994. Jeff Zimmerman finished third in 1999.

And that's it. Not a horrible showing, perhaps, but where the Rangers have really fallen short has been with young pitchers. Since 1961, only one of the franchise's rookie pitchers has even drawn a single point in the voting. That was Kevin Brown in 1989, when he finished sixth (and last) by garnering a pair of third-place votes.

The Rangers have developed a fair number of good hitters, especially in the last dozen or so years, and at this writing they've got a number of fine hitting prospects in the minor leagues. But if there's one thing that defines the franchise, it's an inability to come up with its own pitchers.

SINGLE SEASON

		YEARS	NOTES
DH	Rafael Palmeiro	1999	After five years away, returned to Rangers and finished second in AL with 47 homers, 148 RBI, .630 slugging pct.
C	Ivan Rodriguez	1999	Batted .332 with 35 homers and won his first MVP; was almost exactly as good in each of the two previous seasons.
1B	Rafael Palmeiro	1993	In last year of first stint with club, established himself as power hitter with 37 homers, and led AL with 124 runs.
2B	Julio Franco	1991	Hit .341 (and stole 36 bases) to become the first—and so far, only—member of the franchise to win a batting title.
SS	Alex Rodriguez	2002	Don't blame Alex for the last-place finish; he hit 57 homers to break his own MLB record for a shortstop.
3B	Buddy Bell	1984	Last season, and the best, in a five-year peak that placed Bell behind only George Brett among AL third basemen.
LF	Juan González	1993	Didn't win MVP award, as he would twice later, but this was actually his best year: AL-best 46 homers and .632 slugging.
CF	Oddibe McDowell	1986	Could have gone with any of four players, but we're picking McDowell because he set a franchise record with 105 runs.
RF	Ruben Sierra	1989	After three years of potential, Sierra broke through to lead AL in triples (14), RBI (119), and slugging percentage (.543).
SP	Fergie Jenkins	1974	The single biggest reason for Rangers' amazing turnaround, as he went 25-12 with 29 CG in his first season with the club.
RP	Jim Kern	1979	At 30, joined Rangers and came through with one of *the* great relief seasons: 13 wins, 29 saves, and 1.57 ERA in 143 IP.

ALL-ROOKIE

		YEARS	NOTES
C	Ivan Rodriguez	1991	Let history remember 6/20/1991 as the day Pudge arrived; he was 19 and couldn't hit, but he already had the famous arm.
1B	Mike Hargrove	1974	His 4 homers weren't so hot for a first baseman, but the .323 batting average (and 49 walks) made him Rookie of the Year.
2B	Bump Wills	1977	Unfortunately, his first season—.287 batting average, career highs in OBP and slugging—would turn out to be his best.
SS	Toby Harrah	1971	Didn't hit at all—even in '71, a 590 OPS wasn't getting it done—but the other "candidate" (Curt Wilkerson) was worse.
3B	Roy Howell	1975	Poor defensive player but did some nice things at the plate; traded in '77 and was one of few bright spots for Blue Jays.
LF	Ruben Sierra	1986	Actually played more in RF, but did log 44 games in left; poor OBP and .476 slugging percentage a sign of things to come.
CF	Oddibe McDowell	1985	A summer after playing in the Olympics, reached majors after only 31 minor-league games; 18 homers and great defense.
RF	Rusty Greer	1994	Only 80 games because of strike, but posted .410 OBP that still ranks as best mark of his career.
SP	Kevin Brown	1989	Following cups of coffee in '86 and '88, stuck for good in '89 with a dozen wins and 3.35 ERA in 28 starts.
RP	Jeff Zimmerman	1999	Great story: not drafted out of college, signs with Northern League team, pitching in All-Star Game two seasons later.

HOMEGROWN

		YEARS	NOTES
C	Ivan Rodriguez	1991–2002	Puerto Rican signed as free agent, then spent only two full seasons in minors before reaching majors at 19.
1B	Pete O'Brien	1982–1988	Fifteenth-round pick hit zero home runs as a first-year pro, but hit 17 homers the next year and then advanced steadily.
2B	Bump Wills	1977–1981	Debuted five seasons after his old man's last game, and for a few years actually looked *better* than his dad.
SS	Toby Harrah	1969–1978 1985–1986	Actually signed by Phillies, but drafted by Senators after a so-so season in the Northern League.
3B	Dean Palmer	1989 1991–1997	The Rangers' third-round pick in 1986 struggled for three years, but finally found his power stroke in '89.
LF	Rusty Greer	1994–*2002*	Tenth-round pick out of tiny Alabama college, but quickly established himself by batting .345 in first year as pro.
CF	Oddibe McDowell	1985–1988 1994	The 12th player selected in the '84 draft spent just 31 games in the minors before reaching majors.
RF	Juan Gonzàlez	1989–1999 2002	Like Pudge Rodriguez, a native of Vega Baja, Puerto Rico; and like Pudge, tore up the minor leagues.
SP	Kevin Brown	1986–1994	Georgia Tech star was fourth overall pick in the '86 draft, sandwiched between Matt Williams and Kent Mercker.
RP	Robb Nen	1993	32nd-round draft pick in '87 struggled as starter in minors, and Rangers weren't smart enough to try him in the pen.

TRADED AWAY

		TRADED	NOTES
C	Mike Heath	June 15, 1979	Heath and Dave Chalk and cash to A's for pitcher John Henry Johnson, who totaled 13 more victories.
1B	Carlos Peña	January 14, 2002	Considered one of crown jewels of system, but sent to the Athletics, who soon traded him to the Tigers.
2B	Warren Morris	July 17, 1998	His career petered out quickly, but Morris did bat .288 with 15 homers as rookie with Pirates in 1999.
SS	Rich Aurilia	December 24, 1994	Even after a down year in Double-A, still a hot prospect and sent to Giants in package for Burkett.
3B	Bill Madlock	October 25, 1973	Madlock batted .338 with 22 homers in his last minor-league season, but he netted Fergie Jenkins.
LF	Lou Piniella	August 4, 1964	Senators were Piniella's second organization; he'd finally stick with his fourth, the Royals in 1969.
CF	Elliott Maddox	March 23, 1974	Actually sold to the Yankees for $35,000, after which he became a high-OBP guy before tearing up a knee.
RF	Sammy Sosa	July 29, 1989	Trading Sosa and Wilson Alvarez to the Sox for Harold Baines might be dumbest thing Dubya ever did.
SP	Dave Righetti	November 10, 1978	Rookie of the Year for Yankees in '81; they also traded Dave Stewart, Ron Darling, and released Jamie Moyer.
RP	Robb Nen	July 7, 1993	Traded to Marlins with 6.35 ERA in 23 MLB innings, then became one of game's best relievers a year later.

Too many of the good players the Rangers have developed—and let's be honest, there haven't been nearly enough of them—were discarded too early or simply didn't develop as they might have.

First baseman Mike Hargrove won the Rookie of the Year award in 1974, and played even better in 1975, firmly establishing himself as an on-base machine. He slumped a bit in 1978, though, and shortly after the season was traded to San Diego for, among other things, Oscar Gamble and a big pile of cash.

Third baseman Roy Howell played well as a rookie in 1975, took a step backward in 1976, and was traded early in the '77 season. Howell never did become a star or anything close to a star, but he was a pretty decent player for a decade (granted, the Rangers needed to make a spot for Toby Harrah).

Second baseman Bump Wills looked like a future star as a rookie in 1977, but his career petered out in just a few years.

All of which is to say, in the middle 1970s the Rangers had the makings of a pretty fine infield, but it just didn't work out. And in the middle 1980s it happened in the outfield, as neither Oddibe McDowell nor Ruben Sierra developed into the players their tools suggested they would.

For all that's gone wrong for this franchise in four decades, one thing that hasn't gone wrong is defense behind the plate, at least for the last twenty-five years or so.

Ivan Rodriguez has to be the catcher on the Rangers' all-defensive team, of course. But before him there was Jim Sundberg, and Jim Sundberg was great. I mean, really great. Beginning in 1976, Sundberg was baseball's top defensive catcher for six years, and nobody else was close. He combined excellent arm strength and accuracy with good mechanics, and in the late 1970s that mattered quite a bit more than it does now.

Sundberg set the standard in his league. He won six Gold Gloves, and nobody in the American League won more of them . . . until Pudge Rodriguez came along. After a four-year detour, Sundberg finished his career with the Rangers in 1989. And after a year of Geno Petralli—nobody's idea of a great defensive catcher—Rodriguez arrived in 1991. And Pudge was even better than Sunny. From 1991 through 2001, Pudge routinely posted the highest caught-stealing percentages in the major leagues, year after year. I could never understand why teams bothered trying to steal at all, but some of them did, and so year after year, runners with larceny in their hearts kept finding the ball waiting for them at second base.

GOLD GLOVE			
		YEARS	NOTES
C	Ivan Rodriguez	1991–2002	May not have been the best in the world at calling pitches, but *nobody* has ever thrown better than Pudge.
1B	Pete O'Brien	1982–1988	Never won a Gold Glove but should have; excellent range and particularly adept at starting the 3-6-3 DP.
2B	Bump Wills	1977–1981	Better known for his wheels and his dad; Jeff Frye also very good afield, but never played a whole season.
SS	Ed Brinkman	1961–1970	Longtime Senators regular one of the best in the business; no Rangers shortstop has been outstanding for long.
3B	Buddy Bell	1979–1985	Rangers reliever Jim Kern said Bell was "so smooth he makes everything look simple." Six Gold Gloves.
LF	Al Oliver	1978–1980	Eventually became a 1B/DH type, but he played a lot of CF early in his career and was better than fine in LF.
CF	Cecil Espy	1987–1990	He looked fast, his name *sounds* fast, and he was fast, with good instincts and decent arm; couldn't hit, though.
RF	Bobby Bonds	1978	Played only 130 games for Rangers but he could still run and throw, and ranks as the best of the lot.
P	Kenny Rogers	1989–1995 2000–*2002*	In addition to obvious athleticism, had a great pickoff move and generally shut down the running game.

IRON GLOVE			
		YEARS	NOTES
C	Mike Stanley	1986–1991	Eventually became a decent defender and a fine hitter, but unfortunately both happened after he left Texas.
1B	Dave Hostetler	1982–1984	Briefly famous for hitting a bunch of homers, but nobody ever said anything nice about his work around the bag.
2B	Wayne Tolleson	1981–1985	Actually a pretty decent shortstop, but didn't handle the DP pivot well and was a liability at second base.
SS	Nelson Norman	1978–1981	The regular in '79; didn't hit at all, and somehow managed to be even worse with the glove.
3B	Dean Palmer	1989–1997	Take your pick; Dave Nelson (1971–1972) and Mike Lamb (2000–2001) were both pretty brutal, too.
LF	Kevin Reimer	1988–1992	Talented hitter but never quite hit like he was supposed to, and defensively he was a complete disaster.
CF	Joe Lovitto	1972–1975	Rangers came out of nowhere to finish second; Lovitto did as much as anybody to keep them out of first.
RF	Jeff Burroughs	1970–1976	Won the MVP Award in '74, which just goes to prove that baseball writers don't *really* care about defense.
P	Nolan Ryan	1989–1993	As a young man, he was terrible; at the end of the line in Texas, he didn't even bother covering first base.

ALL-BUST

		YEARS	NOTES
DH	Andres Galarraga	2001	After missing '99 season with cancer, returned to Braves in 2000 and was great; did little for Rangers, though.
C	Donnie Scott	1983–1984	Good minor-league hitter got a shot when he was 23, but didn't hit at all *or* impress anybody with the glove.
1B	Dave Hostetler	1982–1984	As rookie in '82, hit 10 homers in June and 8 in August, but inability to make contact and bad defense did him in.
2B	Lenny Randle	1971–1976	Played horribly in '76, then assaulted his manager the next spring and had to be traded to Mets for peanuts.
SS	Bucky Dent	1982–1983	There was a time when Bucky's glove could carry his bat, but by 1983 that time had passed.
3B	Ken Caminiti	2001	Key part of a brilliant strategy that made the Rangers older, more expensive, and the West's laughingstock.
LF	Rico Carty	1973	Liked to say of himself, "When the bell rings, the Beeg Boy will hit," but he slugged teeny .301 in 86 games.
CF	Ruben Mateo	1999–2001	Supposed to be a star, but broken leg and lack of plate discipline wound up getting him traded to Cincinnati.
RF	George Wright	1982–1986	After a few decent years in CF, shifted to right in '85 and fell off the earth, batting .196 in '85 and '86.
SP	David Clyde	1973–1975	First pick in '73 draft went straight from high school to beating the Twins, but it was mostly downhill from there.
RP	Mike Henneman	1996	Saved 31 games but went 0-7 with 5.79 ERA and gave up big hit to Yankees in Game 3 of the Division Series.

USED-TO-BE-GREAT

		YEARS	NOTES
DH	Brian Downing	1991–1992	After a great career with the Angels, he finished up with the Rangers . . . and even at 41, he could still hit.
C	Jim Sundberg	1988–1989	After four-plus seasons with Brewers, Royals, and Cubs, came back to finish his career where it started.
1B	Andres Galarraga	2001	Turned 40 on June 18, and batting just .235 when traded to the Giants on July 24, after which he surged.
2B	Billy Ripken	1997	Hey, what do you want? He was a pretty decent defensive player, and he had a famous brother.
SS	Mario Mendoza	1981–1982	Okay, so he was never great or even good, but they *did* name the Mendoza Line after him; regular shortstop in '81.
3B	Ken Caminiti	2001	In 2000 he was productive for Astros when healthy, but wasn't either after signing as free agent with Rangers.
LF	Minnie Minoso	1963	His last hurrah; at 40 or thereabouts, played in 109 games for Senators but batted just .229 with 4 homers.
CF	Willie Davis	1975	Spent just 42 games with Rangers, traded to Cardinals after a clubhouse fistfight with manager Billy Martin.
RF	Ellis Valentine	1985	After a year in Japan, the man with the great arm gave it one more shot but lasted only 11 games.
SP	Camilo Pascual	1967–1969	After 13 years with Nationals/Twins, returned to Wash. and pitched well (25-22, 2.95) before collapsing in '69.
RP	Rich Gossage	1991	Returned from a year in Japan and proved that he could still pitch: 4 wins and a 3.57 ERA in 40 innings.

Doug Melvin is living proof that smart people are capable of doing stupid things.

After many years of futility, beginning in 1996 the Rangers won three division titles in four seasons. But after going from 95 wins and first place in 1999 to 91 losses and last place in 2000, owner Tom Hicks broke the bank, with the help of GM Melvin.

The Rangers committed nearly $35 million in 2001 salaries to four free agents: Alex Rodriguez, Andres Galarraga, Randy Velarde, and Ken Caminiti. When the Rangers flopped, a fair number of idiots shouted, "See, that's what happens when you spend all that money on hitting"—read: Alex Rodriguez—"and ignore the pitching!"

Which couldn't be more wrong. Yes, Melvin should have spent some of Tom Hicks' money on pitching. But the problem wasn't Alex Rodriguez. The problem was committing more than twelve million dollars to those other three guys. All three were old, all three were injury risks, and none of the three offered anything the Rangers didn't already have.

Popular opinion aside, Tom Hicks was quite happy with Alex Rodriguez, who spurred ticket sales and, oh yeah, hit fifty-two home runs. Hicks wasn't so happy with Melvin's three old geezers. And he wasn't so happy with Melvin, who got fired after the season.

In 1973, the Texas Rangers finished in last place with a 57-105 record.

In 1974, the Texas Rangers finished in second place with an 84-76 record.

The difference? Two men, one of whom is in the Hall of Fame, and one of whom probably should be.

The Hall of Famer is Ferguson Jenkins. In '73, Jenkins had posted his first losing record (14-16) since joining the Cubs' rotation in 1967. So on October 25, the Cubs sent Jenkins to the Rangers for Bill Madlock, who'd played brilliantly that summer in the Pacific Coast League. The deal worked out for both clubs. Madlock spent three seasons in Chicago and won two batting titles. Jenkins, it must be said, wasn't quite that good, but he did lead the American League with twenty-five wins in '74.

The non–Hall of Famer is Billy Martin, the greatest turnaround artist in baseball history. In the spring of 1974, Martin plucked both Mike Hargrove and Jim Sundberg from the minor leagues, giving them spots in the major-league lineup. Most of all, Martin convinced the Rangers that they weren't nearly as bad as everybody thought . . . and as it turned out, they weren't.

Martin eventually wore out his welcome, as he did in so many other cities. But in 1974 there wasn't a better baseball manager in the world.

ALL-NAME				
			YEARS	NOTES
M	"Little Dago" Billy Martin		1974–1975	Self-anointed by man who wanted more than anything to be a Yankee (Joe DiMaggio was the "Big Dago").
C	"Pudge" Ivan Rodriguez		1991–2002	Okay, what are the odds that two of the ten greatest catchers everwould have the same nickname?
1B	"Human Rain Delay" Mike Hargrove		1974–1978	Before Nomar Garciaparra, there was Mike Hargrove, who took his sweet time getting ready to hit.
2B	"The Governor" Jerry Browne		1986–1988	Native of Virgin Islands came to be nicknamed after the longtime governor of California.
SS	"Scooter" Scott Fletcher		1986–1989	He was just one of those guys who *look* like a "Scooter," you know?
3B	"Popeye" Don Zimmer		1963–1965	The difference was, Zimmer had tobacco in his cheeks, where the real Popeye had spinach.
LF	"The Capital Punisher" Frank Howard		1965–1972	A media nickname, of course; Howard's "real" nickname was "Hondo," after a John Wayne character.
CF	"The Strange Ranger" Willie Davis		1975	A yoga advocate who chanted mantras in his hotel room; got this in spring training, traded soon after.
RF	"Cap" Charles Peterson		1967–1968	His middle name was Andrew . . . get it? Charles *Andrew Peterson* . . . "Cap."
SP	"Fontay O'Rooney" Jim Bibby		1973–1975 1975	Nobody knew why fastballer called himself this strange name; also called Mr. Ed by those who knew him well.
RP	"Emu" Jim Kern		1979–1981	Invented by teammates in 1976, when he was 6'6" and 180 pounds; he read books, so also called "Airhead."

TOP FIVE SEASONS		
YEAR 1999	**RECORD**	95-67
BEST HITTER Rafael Palmeiro		
BEST PITCHERS Jeff Zimmerman, Aaron Sele		
NOTES Swept by Yankees in Division Series . . . again (see below).		
YEAR 1996	**RECORD**	90-72
BEST HITTER Ivan Rodriguez		
BEST PITCHER Ken Hill		
NOTES Lost to Yankees in Division Series, but they did win a game.		
YEAR 1998	**RECORD**	88-74
BEST HITTER Ivan Rodriguez		
BEST PITCHERS Rick Helling, John Wetteland		
NOTES Swept by Yankees in Division Series.		
YEAR 1974	**RECORD**	84-76
BEST HITTER Jeff Burroughs (MVP)		
BEST PITCHERS Fergie Jenkins		
NOTES Finally, respectability, thanks largely to Billy Martin.		
YEAR 1977	**RECORD**	94-68
BEST HITTERS Mike Hargrove, Toby Harrah		
BEST PITCHER Bert Blyleven		
NOTES Still no postseason, as Royals enjoy their best season.		

TOP FIVE MANAGERS	
MANAGER Johnny Oates	
YEARS 1995–2001	
RECORD 506-476 (.515)	
NOTES Managed club to all three of their postseason berths.	
MANAGER Billy Hunter	
YEARS 1977–1978	
RECORD 146-108 (.575)	
NOTES Rangers 60-33 under Hunter down stretch in '77.	
MANAGER Billy Martin	
YEARS 1973–1975	
RECORD 137-141 (.493)	
NOTES His third team, and his third big turnaround.	
MANAGER Bobby Valentine	
YEARS 1985–1992	
RECORD 581-605 (.490)	
NOTES Never could quite get them over the hump	
MANAGER Pat Corrales	
YEARS 1978–1980	
RECORD 160-164 (.494)	
NOTES Competitive, but worked Comer and Kern awful hard.	

LIKE THERE'S NO TOMORROW

Maybe David Clyde only had eighteen wins in that strong left arm, and maybe he had 218. All we'll ever know for sure is that he did, in fact, win exactly eighteen games in the major leagues.

And that wasn't nearly as many as people thought he would win.

Thanks to their 54-100 record in 1972, the Texas Rangers owned the first pick in the 1973 amateur draft. And on June 7, the Rangers used that precious pick to select David Clyde, an eighteen-year-old Texan who'd gone 18-0 with five no-hitters in his senior season for a suburban Houston high school. The Brewers had the third pick and selected Robin Yount; the Padres had the fourth pick and selected Dave Winfield.

Typically, of course, you first negotiate with the player you've drafted, then you pay him more money than he and his parents have ever seen in their lives, and then you send him off to the Lickskillet League for some seasoning. The Rangers weren't your typical team, though, and Bob Short wasn't your typical owner. The ball club was horrible—the Rangers would eventually lose 105 games in 1973—and Short was desperate as desperate gets to somehow get fannies into the seats.

According to Whitey Herzog, then managing the Rangers, Short called him as the negotiations with Clyde were heating up. Short told Herzog that Clyde was ready to sign, if only the Rangers would agree to let him start two major-league games before sending him to the minors.

Herzog would later write, "I agreed to pitch Clyde two games, then farm him out to the minors, where he could build his arm and confidence over a couple of years. I figured you'd pitch him a little, let him get a few big-leaguers out, then send him home in August. You'd ship him to the instructional league that fall, where he could get good coaching and pitching with guys his age. Next year, 200 innings at Double-A; the year after that, 150 or so at Triple-A. *Then* you bring him up to stay. I don't give a damn how good he is, that's how you develop a young pitcher."

Indeed. But Clyde actually pitched well in his two starts, and *at the time*, Herzog told writers, "In two starts the kid has shown that he's not just some two-headed calf we're putting out there as a drawing card. I don't see any reason now why we can't count on him to give us six good innings at least, and get a lot of people out while he's doing it."

Defenders of Herzog might suggest that he was merely toeing the company line, but if there's one thing that's always characterized Whitey Herzog, it's been a willingness to speak his mind. I'm sure he believes now that Clyde should have been shipped off to Gastonia, where he'd have presumably dominated hitters in the Western Carolinas League. But in 1973, Herzog was managing the worst team in the major leagues, and he was pretty thrilled to have a starting pitcher who could actually get people out, no matter how old he was.

Bob Short and the fans were thrilled, too. Nearly 37,000 fannies were in the seats for Clyde's debut, and while the excitement cooled off, the Rangers wound up averaging approximately 27,000 fans per game in Clyde's six home starts. And 27,000 was a *lot* for the Rangers; in games Clyde did *not* start, the Rangers averaged only six thousand per game that season.

So David Clyde remained a Ranger long enough to make a third start, and got hammered in Milwaukee. He lost to the Red Sox, and then he lost to the Brewers again. And still David Clyde remained a Ranger. He did pitch well in his next two starts, and apparently that was good enough; Clyde would not spend a single day of his first professional season in the minor leagues.

And like nearly every other eighteen-year-old pitcher in the twentieth century, David Clyde wasn't ready. He finished 1973 with a 5.01 ERA . . . and still, he spent all of 1974 in the majors, going 3-9 with a respectable 4.38 ERA. In 1975, Clyde finally went to the minors, and pitched fairly well in the Eastern League.

When the 1976 season opened, David Clyde was not quite twenty-one years old. He still had his whole life ahead of him. Unfortunately, he also had shoulder surgery ahead of him, and pitched only twenty-seven innings that season (for Sacramento). He came back in 1977, but racked up a 5.84 ERA in thirty-four games with Tucson. And then the Rangers traded David Clyde to the Indians.

It was in Cleveland that Clyde enjoyed his best major-league season, going 8-11 with a 4.29 ERA in 1978. He was still only twenty-three. Unfortunately, he spent the first three months of the 1979 season on the disabled list, undergoing treatment for alcoholism and (not coincidentally) gastritis. He came back in June, pitched for a couple of months, and went back on the disabled list with pain in his lower back.

The Rangers got Clyde back in 1980 . . . just in time for another shoulder surgery, after which they released him. In 1981, the Astros gave Clyde a tryout, and signed him (it didn't hurt that Clyde had grown up in Houston). In May, while pitching in Double-A, he said, "Going to the minors was what I should have done. But when you're 18 and somebody says, 'You can go pitch in the majors right now,' it's pretty hard to say, 'No, I want to go to Sarasota.'"

Indeed, it is hard. Which is why no eighteen-year-old pitcher should be put in that position. But David Clyde was, and what might have become a long and productive career instead ended when some pitchers are just getting started. Clyde won his last big-league game on July 27, 1979. He was twenty-four years old.

I'm grateful to Jamey Newberg for his editorial assistance. Sources for this chapter include Mark Shropshire's Seasons in Hell *(Donald I. Fine, 1996) and Whitey Herzog and Jonathan Pitts's* You're Missin' a Great Game *(Simon & Schuster, 1999).*

TORONTO BLUE JAYS

		YEARS	NOTES
DH	Paul Molitor	1993–1995	Slumped in '95, but Molly was brilliant in '93 and '94, leading MLB with 211 hits in '93, and winning World Series MVP honors that fall with 10 runs and 8 RBI.
C	Ernie Whitt	1977–1989	Roy Hartsfield, the club's first manager, told Whitt, "I just don't think you can catch at the big-league level. . . ." Whitt, who idolized Bill Freehan, proved otherwise.
1B	Carlos Delgado	1993–2002	In the minors, he was a "catcher" with fantastic hitting stats; though it took longer than we thought it would, he became fantastic in majors after switching to first base.
2B	Roberto Alomar	1991–1995	Hands down, the best all-around second baseman in the league; in five seasons with Jays, posted .384 OBP, .451 slugging percentage, and stole 206 bases.
SS	Tony Fernandez	1983–1990 1993	Fine, and occasionally brilliant, defensive shortstop with good speed and solid bat for the position; switch-hitter returned later for stints at second and third base.
3B	Kelly Gruber	1984–1992	From 1989 through '91, hit 69 home runs and played in two All-Star Games; career disintegrated abruptly due to serious—and for a time, mysterious—neck problem.
LF	George Bell	1981–1990	Not much of an outfielder and didn't draw many walks, but for six years he was one hell of a hitter; still the only American Leaguer to hit 3 home runs on Opening Day.
CF	Lloyd Moseby	1980–1989	Never won a Gold Glove but did have great range, which was good because Bell and Barfield, for all their gifts, didn't; tops club's all-time list in walks and runs.
RF	Jesse Barfield	1981–1989	Remembered for his amazing arm, but he was an immensely strong hitter who slugged .526 from 1983 through '86; franchise's first 20/20 man (1985).
SP1	Dave Stieb	1979–1992	Converted outfielder went 8-8 as rookie in '79, then pitched in All-Star Game the next summer; goes on All-Underrated team of '80s.
SP2	Jimmy Key	1984–1992	Didn't throw real hard, but usually knew where the fastball was going and featured one of the best curves in the game; 116-81 with 3.42 ERA with Jays.
SP3	Pat Hentgen	1991–1999	Fastballing workhorse led American League in innings pitched and complete games in 1996 and '97, and in '97 also won 20 games and the Cy Young Award.
SP4	Jim Clancy	1977–1988	Fastball-slider pitcher and world-class stoic won 128 games, behind only Stieb on franchise list; *does* hold club record with 140 losses.
RP	Tom Henke	1985–1992	Had everything a great closer needs: an overpowering fastball and killer forkball (as change-up); eventually retired when he was 37, still at the top of his game.

I remember thinking, back in 1985, that Toronto's outfield must be one of the great outfields in baseball history. Of course, now I realize that my "analysis" said a lot more about my lack of historical perspective than it did about the Jays' outfield. And it wasn't just me, either. In his book, Ernie Whitt wrote, "Some . . . thought it was the best outfield of all time."

Don't get me wrong, it was a fine outfield. But not only did those three guys not constitute a *great* outfield, it's hard to argue that they were great for even one season.

Bell, Moseby, and Barfield played regularly together for four seasons, 1985 through 1988. Their best season together was probably their first, when they combined for sixty-eight Win Shares; twenty-six for Barfield, twenty-one each for Bell and Moseby. Sixty-eight is very good, but it's nowhere near the top outfields in history. The "record" is held by the 1915 Detroit Tigers, when Bobby Veach, Ty Cobb, and Sam Crawford totaled *107* Win Shares. The 1948 Cardinals and 1962 Dodgers are tied for twenty-fourth place . . . with 85 Win Shares.

So it's pretty obvious that sixty-eight Win Shares ain't cutting the mustard. And in the next three seasons, Toronto's three outfielders combined for sixty-eight (again), sixty-seven, and forty-one Win Shares. They were very good (and very consistent) for three years. But they weren't great.

It seems hard to believe now, but after Roger Clemens's 1996 season there were actually people who thought he might be just about washed up. And though I don't have any evidence at hand, I'm afraid that I might have been one of those people.

That was the Rocket's last season with the Red Sox, and it was his second losing season in four years. After going 18-10 in 1991 and 18-11 in 1992, Clemens went 11-14, 9-7, 10-5, and 10-13 over the next four seasons. You have to admit, it's odd for a premier starting pitcher to go four straight seasons without winning even a dozen games.

On the other hand, in 1996 Clemens had led the American League with 257 strikeouts and posted a 2.09 ERA over his last ten starts.

And all he did in 1997, after signing as a free agent with the Blue Jays, was open the season 11-0, end it 21-7, and in between become the first pitcher since 1945 to lead the American League in wins, ERA, and strikeouts—the so-called pitcher's Triple Crown.

Ah, but 'twas just a fluke, one last great season from a future Hall of Famer. Not a bad theory, and—again, I don't have any evidence—I might have subscribed to it myself.

And then he went out and did it again.

		YEARS	NOTES
		NO. 2	
DH	Cliff Johnson	1983–1984 1985–1986	Veteran slugger's best position was always the batter's box; on June 29, 1986, he hit his 20th career pinch-hit homer, still the all-time record.
C	Pat Borders	1988–1994 1999	Minor-league infielder became solid defender thanks to hard work and Ernie Whitt's tutelage; no OBP at all, but had some pop.
1B	Fred McGriff	1986–1990	You know it's a strong position when Olerud doesn't even rank among the top two, but Olerud enjoyed just one season with Jays as good as McGriff's three best.
2B	Damaso García	1981–1986	"When he was healthy and wanted to play, he was the best second baseman in the game. But there were days when [he] simply didn't want to play."—Ernie Whitt
SS	Alfredo Griffin	1979–1984 1992–1993	Along with Willie Upshaw, he was one of the first quality major leaguers to play regularly for Jays; good defense, but little better than Rey Ordoñez with stick.
3B	Rance Mulliniks	1982–1992	For the first five years of his tenure with Jays, he and Garth Iorg constituted productive platoon; enjoyed his best year after becoming platoon DH in 1988.
LF	Joe Carter	1991–1997	Actually saw more action in right field, but we had to get him in the book and didn't want to bump Barfield or Green; five-time All-Star with six 100-RBI seasons.
CF	Devon White	1991–1995	With career on brink after three poor years with Angels, joined Jays and became a fine player; great glove in center field, speedy hitter with occasional power.
RF	Shawn Green	1993–1999	In three years playing for Cito Gaston, never could quite win an everyday job and never knew quite why; when Gaston was finally fired, Green became a big star.
SP1	David Wells	1987–1992 1999–2000	During first stint with Jays, portly portsider spent parts of all six seasons in bullpen; in second stint, won 20 games for the first time in '99, when he was 36.
SP2	Juan Guzmán	1991–1998	Injuries and inconsistency plagued Guzmán, but he *did* go 40-11 in his first three seasons *and* lead the American League with a 2.93 ERA in 1996.
SP3	Todd Stottlemyre	1988–1994	Threw in the mid-90s but didn't really learn to *pitch* until he left the Blue Jays, signing with Athletics after '94 season; 69-70 in seven Toronto seasons.
SP4	Roger Clemens	1997–1998	Only a Blue Jay for two seasons, but you have to make an exception for a pitcher who led the league in wins *and* strikeouts *and* ERA in *both* of those two seasons.
RP	Duane Ward	1986–1995	From 1988 through '92, threw 100-plus relief innings in each season, then saved 45 games in 1993 before torn rotator cuff ended his career; great slider and fastball.

	SINGLE SEASON		
		YEARS	NOTES
DH	Paul Molitor	1993	Last great season in a great career, as Molly led league with 211 hits and scored 121 runs for World Champions.
C	Ernie Whitt	1987	His biggest year in many ways, but really no different than his '88 and '89 seasons; very consistent player, obviously.
1B	John Olerud	1993	Topped .400 as late as August 2, finished at .363, and thanks to his glove, just edges Carlos Delgado in 2000.
2B	Roberto Alomar	1993	Alomar's first *great* season as he established (then) career highs with 17 homers, 109 runs, 93 RBI and 55 steals.
SS	Tony Fernandez	1988	Just as with Whitt, it's not easy picking Fernandez's best, as he enjoyed four or five seasons at essentially this level.
3B	Kelly Gruber	1990	Hit 31 homers and drove in 118 runs; plate discipline fell apart in '91, and by '93 he was gone.
LF	George Bell	1987	He had a fine year, with AL-leading 134 RBI, but the truth is that this "MVP" wasn't one of the five best in the league.
CF	Lloyd Moseby	1984	Nearly identical in many ways to his '83 season, but a bit better with the glove and deserved a Gold one.
RF	Jesse Barfield	1986	Question: Who led the American League in home runs in 1986? Answer: Jesse Barfield, with 40 (20 outfield assists, too).
SP	Roger Clemens	1997	First pitcher to lead AL in wins (21), ERA (2.05), and K's (292) since Newhouser in 1945 . . . and he did it again in '98.
RP	Mark Eichhorn	1986	As rookie, submarining reliever went 14-6 with 10 saves and 1.72 ERA, striking out 166 hitters in 157 innings.

	ALL-ROOKIE		
		YEARS	NOTES
DH	Fred McGriff	1987	With Willie Upshaw and Cecil Fielder on hand, McGriff limited to 107 games, but he still hit 20 HR and slugged .505.
C	Josh Phelps	2002	Not really a serious choice; he could certainly hit, but by 2002 the Jays had given up on Phelps as a catcher.
1B	John Olerud	1989	Like McGriff, Olerud DH'd in 90 games and played 1B just sparingly; didn't have McGriff's power, but '89 wasn't '87.
2B	Damaso García	1980	No plate discipline at all, but did bat .278 with 30 doubles and played the best defense in the league.
SS	Alfredo Griffin	1979	Swiped from Indians in one-sided trade, moved right into lineup, batted .287 and scored 81 runs.
3B	Eric Hinske	2002	And just think . . . if Billy Beane and J. P. Ricciardi weren't such good friends, he'd never have become a Blue Jay.
LF	Shannon Stewart	1997	Played only 44 games but slugged .446 and, again, this is as good as it gets.
CF	José Cruz, Jr.	1997	Third pick in '95 draft acquired from M's on July 31 and eventually finished second in Rookie of the Year vote.
RF	Shawn Green	1995	Won International League batting title in '94, then batted .288 with 15 homers as platoon player in '95.
SP	Juan Guzmán	1991	Didn't debut until June 7, but still finished second in Rookie of the Year vote after going 10-3 with 2.99 ERA.
RP	Mark Eichhorn	1986	Finished third in RoY balloting behind Canseco and Wally World, but I'd argue that he actually deserved the award.

I'm usually the first to downplay the value of relief pitchers. It's not that they're not valuable, it's just that they're not as valuable as everyday players, or starters, or visitors' clubhouse attendants.

I jest, of course. But it's difficult to remember a relief pitcher who deserved to win a Cy Young Award, let alone an MVP.

All that said, I think Mark Eichhorn should have been Rookie of the Year in 1986. Or maybe not. But he certainly should have finished better than a *distant* third behind Canseco and Joyner. Don't chalk it up to anti–Blue Jays bias, though. Because just one year later, George Bell won an MVP Award that he obviously didn't deserve.

Yes, Bell led the American League with 134 RBI in 1987. And his .605 slugging percentage ranked second (to Mark McGwire).

But what else did he do, exactly? Bell's .352 OBP wasn't anywhere near the league leaders. He played terrible defense in left field. And his team didn't even win, which blows the rationale that a lot of baseball writers use when they vote for one-dimensional power hitters.

Bell had a fine year, but he simply wasn't the best player, or even the most valuable player, in the league. The best, most valuable player in the league was Alan Trammell.

You know about baseball's Rule 5 draft, right? During the off-season, if a player has three years of professional service time and isn't placed on the forty-man roster, another club can draft that player for $50,000 (prior to 1985, it was $25,000).

Well, it's likely that no team has used the Rule 5 draft to better advantage than the Blue Jays. In the space of just eight years, 1977 through 1984, the Jays acquired six players who wound up playing key roles for the team.

Is six a lot? To be fair, I checked ten years of the draft, 1976 through 1985, looking for drafted players who enjoyed significant careers afterward. I found thirteen players drafted in those ten years who later got at least a thousand at-bats in the majors.

Four of them—George Bell, Willie Upshaw, Kelly Gruber, Manny Lee—were drafted by the Blue Jays. And those were four of the top six; Bobby Bonilla's on top, with 7,213 at-bats in the majors, and Jody Davis is fourth with 3,585 at-bats.

The Jays also picked up, in Jim Gott and Jim Acker, two of the top five or six pitchers. By my count, then, Toronto picked up six good players in the Rule 5 draft . . . and no other club got more than two.

HOMEGROWN			
		YEARS	NOTES
DH	Carlos Delgado	1993–*2002*	Signed out of Puerto Rico when he was 16, and batted .180 with zero homers in his first pro season.
C	Pat Borders	1988–1994 1999	Sixth-round pick in '82 spent four years in minors playing 3B and 1B, then two more learning to catch.
1B	John Olerud	1989–1996	Outstanding pitcher at Wash. State, lasted until third round because nobody thought he'd come out early.
2B	Jeff Kent	1992	A steal in the 20th round of the '89 draft; too bad he played only 65 games for the Jays (see below).
SS	Tony Fernandez	1983–1990 1993, 1998–1999	Stuck behind Alfredo Griffin, another Dominican, for two-plus years, otherwise he might have Hall shot.
3B	Ed Sprague	1991–1998	Stanford product was 25th overall pick in 1988; hit 36 homers in '96 and one *big* homer in '92 World Series.
LF	Shannon Stewart	1995–*2002*	Miami product taken with 19th pick in '92 draft, which the Jays got because the Dodgers signed Tom Candiotti.
CF	Lloyd Moseby	1980–1989	Second player selected in '78 draft batted .322 in three minor-league seasons before arriving in majors.
RF	Jesse Barfield	1981–1989	He won't stay here forever, but at this moment he's still a season or two ahead of Shawn Green.
SP	Dave Stieb	1979–1992 1998	Pitched only 17 innings in college and officially drafted as OF, but Jays knew he was a pitcher; signed for $28K.
RP	Mark Eichhorn	1986–1988 1992–1993	Actually started 7 games in '82, then struggled in the minors for a few years before making it back in '86.

TRADED AWAY			
		TRADED	NOTES
DH	Cecil Fielder	December 22, 1988	After two years of not quite getting it done, Fielder found himself sold to the Hanshin Tigers.
C	Alan Ashby	November 27, 1978	Astros got their regular catcher for the better part of a decade; Jays got three guys you never heard of.
1B	Fred McGriff	December 5, 1990	Second-best player in blockbuster that also included Tony Fernandez, Roberto Alomar, and Joe Carter.
2B	Jeff Kent	August 27, 1992	Sent to Mets because Jays wanted David Cone for stretch run; two other teams traded him later.
SS	Tony Fernandez	December 5, 1990	Of the four players in the blockbuster deal, Fernandez suffered most, and later returned to Jays twice.
3B	Chris Stynes	April 6, 1995	One of three minor leaguers, but the only good one, sent to Royals when Jays picked up Cone again.
LF	John Lowenstein	March 29, 1977	Traded to Tribe before he played a game for Jays, and eventually became most famous platooner in history.
CF	Derek Bell	March 30, 1993	Before the clown pants, before the moderate success in Houston, Bell traded to Padres for Darrin Jackson.
RF	Shawn Green	November 8, 1999	Wanted to play in a city with more Jews, so off he went to Los Angeles for Raul Mondesi.
SP	Pete Vuckovich	December 6, 1977	He's the best? Yep, though they've also traded Robert Person, David Cone, and Woody Williams.
RP	Billy Koch	December 7, 2001	With A's looking to replace Isringhausen and Jays looking to clear salary, off he went for Eric Hinske.

GOLD GLOVE

		YEARS	NOTES
C	Ernie Whitt	1977–1989	Pitchers liked working with him, and he handled throws from the outfield well; just okay throwing to bases.
1B	John Olerud	1989–1996	Didn't win his first Gold Glove until 2000, years removed from Jays, but he was outstanding in Toronto.
2B	Roberto Alomar	1991–1995	Alomar didn't take over as the league's best until he moved to Baltimore, but does edge Damaso García here.
SS	Tony Fernandez	1983–1990	Alex Gonzalez was very good, but Fernandez had style, amazing range, and garnered four Gold Gloves.
3B	Kelly Gruber	1984–1992	Considered a great athlete, showed great range and a powerful, if sometimes erratic, throwing arm.
LF	Barry Bonnell	1980–1982	Speed and arm made him a fine defensive left fielder; didn't hit anywhere near enough, though.
CF	Devon White	1991–1995	Won Gold Gloves all five seasons, and in 1991 was about as good as anybody has *ever* been.
RF	Jesse Barfield	1981–1989	Didn't have great or even good range, but what an arm; led American League in outfield assists four times.
P	Jerry Garvin	1977–1982	May have had the game's best move to first base, and picked off 22 runners in 1977; solid fielder, too.

IRON GLOVE

		YEARS	NOTES
C	Darrin Fletcher	1998–2002	He wasn't terrible, but his arm wasn't strong and good footwork could only make up for so much.
1B	Carlos Delgado	1993–*2002*	He worked hard, but was the worst glove man among the six first basemen to play regularly for the Jays.
2B	Dave McKay	1977–1979	Born a utility infielder, but for some reason the Jays gave him the everyday job at second base in '78.
SS	Hector Torres	1977	Not a bad defensive shortstop years earlier, but didn't have much left by '77 and one of the worst hitters *ever*.
3B	Roy Howell	1977–1980	Decent range but error-prone; Ed Sprague wasn't any great shakes, either.
LF	George Bell	1981–1990	Just edges Candy Maldonado, who also didn't run well but did have a great arm.
CF	Bob Bailor	1977	Neither he nor Barry Bonnell were really center fielders, and neither actually played there regularly for a season.
RF	Otto Velez	1977–1980	Fine hitter wasted away for years in Yankees system, then stumbled around in the outfield before settling in as DH.
P	Juan Guzmán	1991–1998	He wasn't horrible with the glove, but he never did figure out how to hold runners halfway close.

It's funny. Sometimes you're just as well off with the inmates running the asylum.

In spring training of 1988, Blue Jays manager Jimy Williams announced a lineup change. George Bell would shift from left field to DH, and rookie Sil Campusano would take over in left field. Made sense, considering that Bell's knees were hurting him, and he was always pretty lousy with the glove, anyway.

Bell didn't want to move, and one of the big stories that spring came when he refused to take the field as DH in a spring-training game. When Opening Day came around, though, Bell was in the lineup as DH and blasted three home runs off Bret Saberhagen (I was there). He didn't last long in that slot, though, and wound up playing only six more games as the DH all season.

Why? Because Campusano didn't hit, and lost his job. And looking back, it's hard to understand why anybody *thought* he would hit. He was fast and he'd take a walk, but he'd also been a .260 hitter in the minors, he didn't actually steal many bases, and there's no telling how old he was. What we do know is that he never did hit major-league pitching (and wound up with a .202 batting average in 154 major-league games). Fortunately, Rance Mulliniks gave the Jays a great year as a platoon DH, and they damn near won the pennant.

For a team that's been around for only twenty-six seasons, the Blue Jays can boast some pretty impressive busts among their starting pitchers. I selected Joey Hamilton because the Jays gave up Woody Williams to get him, but any of three other guys would have been arguable, too.

First, there's Mike Sirotka. In 2000, pitching for the White Sox, he looked like one of the better southpaws in the league. So the Jays traded David Wells to the Sox, received Sirotka in return . . . and discovered that Sirotka was damaged goods, suffering significant shoulder problems. The Jays complained to Major League Baseball, but to no avail, so they (and their insurers) got stuck paying three million bucks to Sirotka while he rehabilitated in 2001 *and* 2002.

In 1978, the Jays acquired a minor-league pitcher named Phil Huffman, who'd pitched fairly well (7-6, 3.88) with Oakland's Triple-A club. In 1979, the fans wanted him in the majors, and they got him. Unfortunately, he went 6-18 with a 5.77 ERA, and next appeared in the majors six years later, briefly with the Orioles.

And then there's Mark Lemongello, another 1979 fiasco. When the Jays got Lemongello from the Astros, he said he'd rather drive a truck than pitch in another country. As it happened, he did pitch, but like a truck driver: 1-9 with a 6.29 ERA.

		YEARS	NOTES
ALL-BUST			
DH	Willie Greene	1999	Long considered a hitter without a position, got a chance to DH regularly and batted .204 (albeit with power).
C	Benito Santiago	1997–1998	After great year in Philly, posted .279 OBP in '97, then missed most of '98 after wrecking his car and his knee.
1B	Doug Ault	1977–1978 1980	The worst of the franchise's six regulars at first base, but he did crack the first home run in franchise history.
2B	Danny Ainge	1979–1981	Great basketball player, of course, but had absolutely no business in the major leagues; .220 lifetime hitter.
SS	Eddie Zosky	1991–1992	Jays' first-round pick in '88 draft started pro career in Double-A, but wound up batting .160 in majors.
3B	Tony Batista	2001	In 2000, hit 45 homers and played in All-Star Game; in 2001, batted .207 in 72 games and traded to Orioles.
LF	Rickey Henderson	1993	Acquired in August for stretch drive, batted just .215 in 44 games, then batted .170 in 12 postseason games.
CF	Sil Campusano	1988	Supposed to continue the line of great Blue Jay outfielders, but batted .218 and never got another shot.
RF	Mark Whiten	1990–1991	Supposed to be hard-hittin' (rhymes with Whiten!), but punchless in '91 and got traded to Tribe.
SP	Joey Hamilton	1999–2001	Dave Stewart thought he could fix him, so Jays traded Woody Williams; 14-17 with 5.83 ERA in 50 games.
RP	Darren Hall	1994–1995	Won closer job with 17 saves as rookie, then saved just 3 more games for Jays before elbow surgery and trade.

		YEARS	NOTES
USED-TO-BE-GREAT			
DH	Dave Parker	1991	Last 13 games of his career; other candidates include Ron Fairly, Willie Horton, Dave Winfield, Rico Carty.
C	Lance Parrish	1995	Would be the final stop in Parrish's wonderful career, as he batted .202 with 4 homers in 70 games.
1B	Ron Fairly	1977	Longtime Dodger played in two All-Star Games: one as an Expo (1973) and one as a Blue Jay.
2B	Juan Samuel	1996–1998	He was never actually great and he played only 6 games at second for the Jays, but he's as good as it gets.
SS	Dick Schofield	1993–1994	Got his last regular duty in the majors as Jays' everyday shortstop, and enjoyed one of better seasons with bat.
3B	Tony Fernandez	1998–1999 2001	Somehow a better hitter as a third baseman in his late 30s than he'd ever been as a shortstop in his 20s.
LF	Rickey Henderson	1993	Doesn't fit the bill exactly, because of course he could still play, and spent another nine years in the majors.
CF	Mookie Wilson	1989–1991	Ex-Met could still run, but if he wasn't hitting .300 he couldn't help you, and Mookie batted .267 for Toronto.
RF	Dave Winfield	1992	Mostly a DH, but played a big part in Jays' first World Championship, and did play 26 games in right field.
SP	Phil Niekro	1987	Acquired in August for stretch run, but winless in 3 starts and Jays wound up 2 games out of first.
RP	John Candeleria	1990	Candy Man got knocked around in 13 games with Jays, then thrived as situational lefty for the Dodgers.

ALL-NAME		YEARS	NOTES
DH	"Big Daddy" Cecil Fielder	1985–1988	As you probably remember, Fielder was a big man: 240-ish at the beginning, and God knows how much later.
C	"Bigfoot" Ernie Whitt	1977–1989	Riddle me this: Is Whitt the worst *catcher* to dictate an autobiography? Or does Joe Garagiola count?
1B	"Crime Dog" Fred McGriff	1986–1990	One of Chris Berman's only "real" nicknames, tied to TV cartoon character McGruff the Crime Dog.
2B	"Little Hurt" Craig Grebeck	1998–2000	5'7" middle infielder got this one from Hawk Harrelson in Chicago, where he played with Big Hurt.
SS	"Professor Gadget" Tony Fernandez	1983–1990 1993, 1998–1999	He could turn seemingly anything—marbles, grips, broken bats—into strength-conditioning tools.
3B	"Razor" Rance Mulliniks	1982–1992	Not that it's got anything to do with the nickname, but his dad Harvey pitched (briefly) in the minors.
LF	"Thrill" Glenallen Hill	1989–1991	He was quite a thrill for minor-league pitchers, as he led his league in strikeouts four straight seasons.
CF	"Devo" Devon White	1991–1995	Not the most thrilling of nicknames, but "Whitey" wasn't going to work (and I was a big fan of the band).
RF	"Buffalo" Raul Mondesi	2000–2002	Not exactly an unqualified success, but did get off to a great start in 2001 and was briefly the toast of Toronto.
SP	"Pee Wee" Jimmy Key	1984–1992	Hung on Key by his teammates because he bore at least a passing resemblance to Pee Wee Herman.
RP	"The Terminator" Tom Henke	1985–1992	His first big year was 1987, three years after Arnold Schwarzenegger's and James Cameron's big year.

TOP FIVE SEASONS

YEAR 1992 **RECORD** 96-66
BEST HITTER Roberto Alomar
BEST PITCHERS Juan Guzmán, Duane Ward
NOTES After 15 years, the sweetness of a Championship.

YEAR 1993 **RECORD** 95-67
BEST HITTER John Olerud
BEST PITCHERS Duane Ward, Pat Hentgen
NOTES Joe Carter comes up big in the clutch.

YEAR 1985 **RECORD** 99-62
BEST HITTER Jesse Barfield
BEST PITCHER Dave Stieb
NOTES Still the franchise record for wins, but a bad ending.

YEAR 1989 **RECORD** 89-73
BEST HITTER Fred McGriff
BEST PITCHER Tom Henke
NOTES Ran into dynastic Athletics in ALCS.

YEAR 1991 **RECORD** 91-71
BEST HITTERS Roberto Alomar, Devon White
BEST PITCHERS Duane Ward, Jimmy Key
NOTES Steamrolled by Twins in ALCS.

TOP FIVE MANAGERS

MANAGER Cito Gaston
YEARS 1989–1997
RECORD 683-636 (.518)
NOTES Didn't get much credit for two straight Championships.

MANAGER Bobby Cox
YEARS 1982–1985
RECORD 355-292 (.549)
NOTES Did everything right until the 1985 ALCS.

MANAGER Jimy Williams
YEARS 1986–1989
RECORD 281-241 (.538)
NOTES Cox's protégé came oh-so-close to pennant in '87.

MANAGER Jim Fregosi
YEARS 1999–2000
RECORD 167-157 (.515)
NOTES Poor performance of young pitchers killed him.

MANAGER Tim Johnson
YEAR 1998
RECORD 88-74 (.543)
NOTES Might still be there if he'd actually seen some combat.

Ernie Whitt became a free agent after the 1986 season, and the Blue Jays played hardball. They could, because with the owners conspiring—now it's called Collusion, and it wound up costing the Lords of Baseball a few hundred million bucks—the Jays knew that Whitt wouldn't get a big offer anywhere else. Anyway, I don't want to write about something so distasteful as owners' perfidy and players' greed.

Instead, I want to write about man's inability to see his own shortcomings. In his autobiography—yes, Ernie Whitt has an autobiography—Whitt "wrote" at length about his contract negotiations, which became acrimonious. According to Whitt, Jays general manager Pat Gillick told him, "Look, you're just a platoon player. You can't hit left-handed pitchers. You're lucky to be getting what we're offering you."

To which Whitt responded, "It's not my idea to be a platoon player. I've told you . . . that I want to play every day. And if you look at my numbers, I do quite well against left-handed pitchers."

I looked at his numbers. It's true, Whitt had just batted .370 against left-handed pitchers in 1986. But that was only forty-six at-bats. Whitt's *career* batting average against lefties through the '86 season was just .227, with on-base and slugging percentages barely clearing .300. Gillick was right.

WOULD YOU RATHER BE PERFECT, OR LUCKY?

Nobody's going to remember how great Dave Stieb really was.

Well, maybe Stieb will; as he freely admitted, modesty wasn't one of his strong suits. But as a wise man once said, it ain't braggin' if you can do it. And Dave Stieb could do it.

Amazingly, Stieb came within one batter of throwing a no-hitter *three different times*. What's more, all three near no-nos came within a year . . . and two of them came within a week.

On September 24, 1988, Stieb had a no-hitter against the Indians until Julio Franco hit a bad-hop single with two outs in the ninth. In Stieb's very next start, on September 30, he lost his no-hitter when Orioles pinch hitter Jim Traber singled to right field with two outs in the ninth. And on August 4, 1989, Stieb had a perfect game against the Yankees with two outs in the ninth. This time the villain was Roberto Kelly, who doubled to left field. I *know* that no other pitcher has come within one batter of throwing a no-hitter, three different times. What's more, in those two seasons alone, Stieb threw three one-hitters in which the lone safety came before the ninth inning.

I'm happy to report that Dave Stieb did finally throw a no-hitter. On September 2, 1990, he no-hit the Indians, 3–0, in Cleveland.

One no-hitter is nice, but two or three (or four) probably would have left Stieb with a reputation better than the one he's got. Then again, Virgil Trucks threw two no-nos in one season, and nobody talks about him anymore. No, Stieb's real problem is that he didn't win enough games. That's due, in part, to the relative brevity of Stieb's career; he started twenty-five or more games in only ten seasons. But it's also due to the fact that Stieb just might be, *even aside from the lost no-hitters*, the game's unluckiest great pitcher.

Consider:

- In 1981, he posted a 3.19 ERA but went just 11-10.
- In 1982, he led the American League with nineteen complete games, five shutouts, and 288 innings, all while posting a 3.25 ERA . . . and went just 17-14.
- In 1985, he started thirty-six games, led the American League with a 2.48 ERA . . . and barely posted a winning record (14-13).

Those are just the highlights. Here's another one: Stieb pitched in seven All-Star Games, yet never won more than eighteen games in one season. Without checking, I'd be shocked to discover that another starting pitcher appeared in so many All-Star Games without ever winning twenty.

I'm sure that somebody reading this will dutifully send me an e-mail arguing that Stieb "didn't know how to win," which is about as ridiculous as suggesting that Stieb "didn't know how to finish no-hitters."

The title of Stieb's memoirs was *Tomorrow I'll Be Perfect*, but one can't help but think it should have been *Maybe Tomorrow I'll Be Lucky*.

I'm grateful to Dan Shulman for his editorial suggestions. Sources for this chapter include Ernie Whitt and Greg Cable's Catch: A Major League Life *(McGraw-Hill, 1989) and Dave Stieb and Kevin Boland's* Tomorrow I'll Be Perfect *(Doubleday, 1986).*

PART TWO

YESTERDAY'S SIX

Philadelphia/Kansas City/ Oakland Athletics

		YEARS	NOTES
ALL-TIME			
C	Mickey Cochrane	1925–1933	"More than any other player, Mickey Cochrane was responsible for the three pennants the Athletics won . . . He was Ty Cobb wearing a mask."—Connie Mack
1B	Jimmie Foxx	1925–1935	Foxx hit 534 home runs (302 with Athletics), and now it's easy to forget that he trailed only Ruth on the all-time list for many years, until Mays passed him in 1966.
2B	Eddie Collins	1906–1914 1927–1930	Frankie Frisch, himself one of the game's great second basemen, said, "Eddie Collins was the greatest infielder I ever saw. He could do everything."
SS	Eddie Joost	1947–1954	Tough choice between Joost and Campaneris (1964–1976), but Joost's excellence trumps Campy's longevity; Tejada still another year or two from consideration here.
3B	Frank Baker	1908–1914	Good fielder, great hitter, and AL's best third baseman until George Brett and Wade Boggs; famous, of course, for homering in consecutive Series games in 1911.
LF	Rickey Henderson	1979–1984 1989–1993 1994–1995	Also played 152 games for the A's in 1998, when he was 39; tough competition here in Al Simmons and Topsy Hartsel (1902–1911), an outstanding leadoff man.
CF	Dwayne Murphy	1978–1987	A's have never had a *great* center fielder, but they've enjoyed a number of very good ones, including Dave Henderson, Billy North, Sam Chapman, and Amos Strunk.
RF	Reggie Jackson	1967–1975 1987	No. 2 on franchise list is Socks Seybold (1901–08), who never played brilliantly but was consistently excellent until an injury finished his career, when he was only 27.
SP1	Lefty Grove	1925–1933	Including his years with Red Sox, led his league in ERA nine times, three times more than any other major-league pitcher; cost A's $100,600, and worth every penny.
SP2	Eddie Plank	1901–1914	"Plank was not the fastest, not the trickiest and not the possessor of the most stuff. He was just the greatest."—Eddie Collins; Plank won 284 games with Athletics.
SP3	Rube Waddell	1902–1907	Grove led AL in strikeouts seven straight seasons (1925–31), and Waddell did it in all six of his seasons with A's; Rube also won 131 games, including 27 in 1905.
SP4	Catfish Hunter	1965–1974	Reputation based largely on his durability—he topped 230 innings in 10 straight seasons—and October success; with A's, went 7-2 with 2.55 ERA in postseason.
RP	Dennis Eckersley	1987–1995	After Eckersley and Fingers (and Grove), the franchise's greatest relief pitcher was probably Paul Lindblad (1965–71, 1973–76), who posted 3.29 ERA in 479 games.

Who was the franchise's greatest relief pitcher before Rollie Fingers and Dennis Eckersley?

Would you believe Lefty Grove?

Grove arrived in 1925 with great fanfare—he cost Connie Mack $100,600, a record at the time—but didn't pitch particularly well, going 10-12 with a 4.75 ERA. The very next season, though, Grove significantly lowered his walks while significantly increasing his strikeouts, and he led the American League with a 2.51 ERA. Grove started thirty-three games that season . . . and he relieved in a dozen more, saving six of those. In 1929, suffering an injury to his pitching fingers, Grove didn't start in the World Series . . . but he did save Games 1 and 5 as the A's won their first World Championship since 1913.

Over the eight-year period beginning in 1926 and ending in 1933, only three American League pitchers saved more than thirty-two games. Two of them were famous relievers, Firpo Marberry (sixty-eight saves) and Wilcy Moore (forty-nine). And the other? The best *starter* in the league, Lefty Grove, with fifty saves. Also, according to *The Baseball Encyclopedia,* Grove's record as a reliever with the Athletics was 28-16 (including 1925, when he went 5-3 out of the pen). As a starter, Grove threw harder than anybody in the league. As a reliever, he must have been scary.

It's often assumed that in the good old days, before Marvin Miller created a profession full of very wealthy men, the owners paid the players whatever they wanted to pay them.

Technically, it's true. But practically, it wasn't. While it's true that owners could, according to the rules, pay players whatever they liked, it didn't work that way in practice. If a player felt that he wasn't being fairly compensated, he could often find lucrative work elsewhere, sometimes playing for a sandlot team not part of Organized Baseball.

To avoid this unhappy situation, the magnates would generally wind up paying their players something close to the going rate, even if it took a few months of negotiating. As a result, good players were occasionally traded simply because their cash-strapped employers couldn't afford the going rate. And if you believe Connie Mack, that's what happened with third baseman George Kell in 1946. He'd played decently for the A's in 1944 and '45, then batted .299 in his first twenty-six games in '46.

At which point, Mack traded him to the Tigers for outfielder Barney McCosky. Supposedly, Mack told Kell, "You're going to be a great one, but I'm trading you because I won't be able to afford to pay your salary." And Mack was right, at least about Kell being a great one. Today, George Kell is in the Hall of Fame. Barney McCosky is not.

SINGLE SEASON			
		YEARS	NOTES
C	Mickey Cochrane	Pick	Impossible to choose, as he was brilliant each season from '29 through '33; batted .357 in 1930, but struggled in World Series.
1B	Jimmie Foxx	1932 1933	Among first basemen, only Gehrig had two straight seasons as good, as Foxx blasted 106 homers and drove in 332 runs.
2B	Eddie Collins	1909	How can I omit Lajoie and his .426 batting average in 1901? Because the American League wasn't all that good in 1901.
SS	Eddie Joost	1949	Best season you never heard of, as Joost batted .263 with 23 homers, drew 149 walks, and was brilliant with the glove.
3B	Frank Baker	1912	Coming off the World Series that got him his nickname, batted .347 and led AL with 10 home runs and 130 RBI.
LF	Rickey Henderson	1990	Rickey aside, Al Simmons is the man, with great seasons in each of A's World Series pennant campaigns, 1929 through '31.
CF	Al Simmons	1925	Batted .384 and topped AL with 253 hits, but actually enjoyed bigger seasons later, when he played left field.
RF	José Canseco	1988	Just edges Reggie, who in 1969 led AL with 123 runs and .608 slugging percentage (it was an expansion year, though).
SP	Lefty Grove	1931	The best of the best, as the greatest left-hander of them all won 31 games, lost 4, and posted 2.06 ERA in hitter's year.
RP	Dennis Eckersley	1990	Wondering which was Fingers's best? My vote goes to 1973, when he posted 1.92 ERA and saved two World Series games.

TRADED AWAY			
		TRADED	NOTES
C	Mickey Cochrane	December 12, 1933	The fire sale continues—most components of the dynasty were already gone—as Mike sold to Tigers.
1B	Jimmie Foxx	December 10, 1935	Sent to Red Sox for a couple of forgotten players and a very large sum of Depression-era money: $150,000.
2B	Eddie Collins	December 8, 1914	Sold to White Sox for $50,000 in fire sale; in 1949, Mack traded Nellie Fox to Sox for Joe Tipton.
SS	Walt Weiss	November 17, 1992	Traded to Florida after a couple of poor seasons, and enjoyed nice years with Marlins, Rockies, and Braves.
3B	George Kell	May 18, 1946	Straight up for Detroit's Barney McCosky, a solid singles-hitting outfielder five years older than Kell.
LF	Joe Jackson	July 25, 1910	Mack traded Jackson soon after he spent an afternoon in a burlesque house instead of at the ballpark.
CF	Chet Lemon	June 15, 1975	Runner-up Doc Cramer did play 13 more seasons after going to the Red Sox, but not particularly well.
RF	Roger Maris	December 11, 1959	Okay, so it didn't work out . . . but the A's did get Norm Siebern, their best player for four years.
SP	Lefty Grove	December 12, 1933	Nine years earlier, Mack had paid $100K for Grove; now he sold him (and others) to Red Sox for $125K.
RP	Ryne Duren	June 15, 1957	Just another of many deals with Yankees; Duren didn't last long, but was brilliant in 1958 and '59.

ALL-BUST			
		YEARS	NOTES
C	Gidge Brucker	1948	A's first bonus baby—$30,000 worth—just happened to be son of longtime A's pitching coach.
1B	Dick Burruss	1919–1920	Mack spent $10,000, saying, "I have bought the greatest young player in the country." 18 RBI in 141 games.
2B	Benny McCoy	1946	He'd been a solid performer before the war, but came back in '46, at 30, and couldn't even make the roster.
SS	Dick Howser	1962–1963	The league's top leadoff man as rookie in '61, but suffered broken leg in '62 and was never the same afterward.
3B	Brook Jacoby	1991	Came over from Tribe in late July, and did as much as anybody to sink defending AL champs to fourth place.
LF	Don Baylor	1976	Hit on the left hand by a Dick Drago pitch on the second day of the season, and wound up slugging just .368.
CF	Paul Strand	1924	Mack paid $100,000 for Strand—who'd hit .394 for Salt Lake City—but he batted .228 in 47 games with A's.
RF	Claudell Washington	1976	Played in 1975 All-Star Game when he was 20, but slumped in '76 and traded in '77.
SP	Vida Blue	1972	And then there's Todd Van Poppel (1991–96), who was supposed to be a star but racked up 5.75 ERA as A.
RP	Luis Vizcaíno	1999–2001	With great stuff, supposed to be the closer of the future, but racked up 5.61 ERA in 49 games over 3 seasons.

USED-TO-BE-GREAT			
		YEARS	NOTES
C	Manny Sanguillen	1977	Came over in trade for *manager* Chuck Tanner, then returned to Steel City after one so-so season.
1B	Willie McCovey	1976	After spending most of a lousy season in San Diego, moved back to the Bay and hit 5 singles in 11 games.
2B	Joe Morgan	1984	All the great second basemen finish as Athletics; Nap Lajoie (1916) and Eddie Collins (1930) did, too.
SS	Granny Hamner	1962	By the time the A's got the former Phillies stalwart, they were in Kansas City and he was a knuckleball pitcher.
3B	Jimmy Collins	1907–1908	Players didn't age as well back then; at 37 and 38, Collins' power and speed were completely gone.
LF	Al Simmons	1940–1941 1944	Simmons returned, far past his prime, but he's got stiff competition in Zack Wheat (1927) and Tim Raines ('99).
CF	Tris Speaker	1928	The "Gray Eagle" turned 40 shortly before Opening Day, but today he could easily pass for 50 or even 60.
RF	Ty Cobb	1927–1928	With Speaker and Cobb cleared (officially, at least) of old game-fixing charges, Mack wound up with both.
SP	Satchel Paige	1965	Twelve years after his last MLB appearance and 59 years old, pitched three innings for A's and allowed one hit.
RP	Rich Gossage	1992–1993	Tom Burgmeier, who'd enjoyed big seasons with Royals, Twins, and Red Sox, turned 40 while pitching for A's.

In 1928, the Athletics featured no fewer than *seven* future Hall of Famers . . . and I've always wondered if that was two or three too many.

See, three of those future Hall of Famers could account for 122 years of age between them. Tris Speaker was forty, while Ty Cobb and Eddie Collins were both forty-one. It's hard to find fault with Collins—he hit .303 in just thirty-three at-bats—but Speaker and Cobb both saw significant action.

Just looking at their numbers, you'd think that they were actually pretty good; Speaker batted .267 and slugged .450 in sixty-seven games, while Cobb batted .323 and slugged .431 in ninety-five games. But those numbers were *not* particularly good for the time; Cobb was a bit better than league average, Speaker a bit worse. At their advanced ages, it's hard to think they contributed much on defense, either.

And here's the thing . . . the Athletics finished only two-and-a-half games behind the pennant-winning Yankees that season. I think it's reasonable to at least *suggest* the possibility that Connie Mack's momentary obsession with former greatness cost him the pennant.

Then again, Mack would probably argue that he needed the veterans to teach the kids how to win. And seeing as how they won three straight flags beginning in 1929, maybe he'd be right.

Oakland owned the old American League West from 1971 through 1975 (the Twins won in 1970, the Royals in '76). Here are the wins posted by those five teams during their regular seasons: 93, 94, 98, 101, 90.

No big surprises, right? They were pretty good in 1971 and 1975, but they were great from 1972 through '74 when they won all those World Series.

Except I pulled a fast one on you. Here's the *real* order: 101, 93, 94, 90, 98.

The A's actually won more games in the seasons in which they did *not* win the World Series.

In 1971, virtually all of the pieces were in place for the coming dynasty, and the A's won 101 games. Problem was, they ran into a fantastic Baltimore club in the playoffs and got swept.

In 1975, Catfish Hunter escaped to New York, but the A's did win ninety-eight games. They ran into a fine Red Sox team in the playoffs, though, and got swept. Shortly after the A's had been eliminated, a reporter asked Sal Bando if letting Hunter get away was the biggest blunder by a franchise in baseball history. "If it wasn't the biggest," replied Bando, "I haven't heard of any bigger."

That was a common sentiment, and the A's certainly missed Hunter, especially in the postseason. But they were just as good without him as they'd been with him. They just didn't get the same breaks in October.

ALL-NAME		YEARS	NOTES
C	"Black Mike" Mickey Cochrane	1925–1933	Due to his dark hair and complexion; "Mickey" itself was a nickname, and inspired Mickey Mantle's father.
1B	"Double X" Jimmie Foxx	1925–1935	Nickname to remind people that his name was *not* "Fox" with one x; burly Foxx also known as "The Beast."
2B	"Camera Eye" Max Bishop	1924–1933	Friends called him "Tilly," but the media invented this one as Bishop drew more than 100 walks in seven seasons.
SS	"Chicken" Fred Stanley	1981–1982	Never what you'd call a great hitter, Stanley managed to bat exactly .193 in both of his seasons in Oakland.
3B	"Home Run" Frank Baker	1908–1914	Led AL in homers four straight seasons, but got nickname for hitting two key blasts in 1911 World Series.
LF	"Bucketfoot Al" Al Simmons	1924–1932 1940–1941	Stepped in the bucket when he hit, but of course it worked for him; Simmons absolutely despised the nickname.
CF	"Hendu" Dave Henderson	1988–1993	When I lived in Seattle, I worked on my softball swing at Hendu's Ballyard; never saw Hendu himself, though.
RF	"Buck" Reggie Jackson	1967–1975 1987	"Mr. October" didn't come until later, when (according to Reggie) Thurman Munson came up with it.
SP	"Catfish" Jim Hunter	1965–1974	Invented by Charlie Finley out of whole cloth, on the day Hunter agreed to sign; his baseball name was just "Cat."
RP	"Chief" Jack Aker	1964–1968	Like virtually every baseball-playing Native American, got this imaginative moniker; led AL with 32 saves in '66.

TOP FIVE SEASONS

YEAR 1910 **RECORD** 102-48
BEST HITTER Eddie Collins
BEST PITCHER Jack Coombs
NOTES First of three World Championships in four years.

YEAR 1929 **RECORD** 104-46
BEST HITTERS Jimmie Foxx, Al Simmons
BEST PITCHER Lefty Grove
NOTES A's dethrone Yanks, win first of three straight pennants.

YEAR 1989 **RECORD** 99-63
BEST HITTERS Carney Lansford, Mark McGwire
BEST PITCHERS Mike Moore, Dave Stewart
NOTES Beat Giants in Bay Series interrupted by earthquake.

YEAR 1972 **RECORD** 93-62
BEST HITTER Joe Rudi
BEST PITCHER Catfish Hunter
NOTES First World Championship since 1930.

YEAR 1974 **RECORD** 90-72
BEST HITTER Reggie Jackson
BEST PITCHER Catfish Hunter
NOTES Mustache gang makes it three straight World Series.

TOP FIVE MANAGERS

MANAGER Connie Mack
YEARS 1901–1950
RECORD 3582-3814 (.414)
NOTES Fifty years, and paid attention until the last six or seven.

MANAGER Tony La Russa
YEARS 1986–1995
RECORD 798-673 (.542)
NOTES Loved veteran starters, one-out relievers, and utility men.

MANAGER Dick Williams
YEARS 1971–1973
RECORD 288-190 (.603)
NOTES Two World Championships in three seasons.

MANAGER Billy Martin
YEARS 1980–1982
RECORD 215-218 (.497)
NOTES In 1980, Oakland starters completed *94 games.*

MANAGER Art Howe
YEARS 1996–2002
RECORD 600-533 (.530)
NOTES No genius, but smart enough to go along with the program.

CORRECTED VISION

If Eddie Joost had played nearly as well in his twenties as he did in his thirties, he would be in the Hall of Fame.

The young Joost couldn't hit, but Reds manager Bill McKechnie loved great defense up the middle, and Joost played great defense up the middle. He took over as Cincinnati's everyday shortstop in the second half of the 1940 season, and held the job through 1942. In 1943, he joined the Boston Braves and batted .185, even though many of the good pitchers had, by then, been drafted. Joost didn't play baseball in 1944—instead, he worked in a meat-packing plant—but came back in '45 to play thirty-five games for the Braves before his season was cut short by a broken wrist.

For a variety of reasons, most of which have now been lost in the mists of time, Joost had acquired a reputation for being hard to get along with. This, coupled with his lousy track record as a hitter, made it hard for him to find a good job in his chosen profession. So in 1946, Joost 1) turned thirty, and 2) spent the entire season playing for Rochester in the International League.

So let's see here . . . thirty-year-old player in the *minor* leagues, with a .225 career batting average in the *major* leagues. Ninety-nine times out of a hundred, this guy's career would be over. However, the shortstop position had been a disaster for the last-place Athletics in 1946—three different A's had played at least thirty games at short, but none of them was any good with the glove—and Connie Mack, after personally checking out the stories about Joost, took a flyer and picked him up.

Joost batted just .206 in 1947, but that .206 was accompanied by thirteen home runs and 114 walks. Both of those figures were career highs by hefty margins . . . but the best was yet to come. As Joost would later recall,

The 1947 season went by and I wasn't having the type of year I wanted. The reason was that I had astigmatism, but I didn't want Mr. Mack to know it because only Bob Dillinger, the Browns' third baseman, wore glasses. But it got worse. When we played night games, I'd see two balls coming at me. I struck out 110 times. I finally got up the nerve to tell Mr. Mack that I'd probably have to wear glasses. He said, "So?" So I got my glasses. The first time I came up to the plate at Shibe Park, the pitcher looked 10 feet away. I couldn't believe my eyes had been that bad . . .

If not for the prejudice against baseball players—especially nonpitchers—wearing glasses, there's no telling what kind of hitter Joost might have been earlier in his career. What we do know is that *with* the glasses, he was one *hell* of a hitter. In 1948, Joost turned thirty-two. From that season through 1952, his last season as an everyday player, he batted .257 (a big improvement over what he'd done before) and, more to the point, he averaged nineteen home runs and 120 walks per season.

A primary source for this chapter is David M. Jordan's The Athletics of Philadelphia *(McFarland & Co., 1999).*

Eddie Joost in 1949. Just happy to be there.
National Baseball Library, Cooperstown, New York

If there's one *significant* subject in baseball history that's almost completely ignored, it's the impact of the Korean War on the careers of major-league baseball players. World War II gets all the glory, of course, and in more ways than one. But while many, many players spent two or three years in the service during World War II, is that any reason to forget that a number of players also spent a couple of seasons in the service during the Korean Conflict?

And when people do remember, all they remember is Ted Williams (who spent most of 1952 and '53 flying jets in the Marines). But Williams wasn't the only one, not by a long shot. Like Williams, Yankees infielder Jerry Coleman served during both wars. Whitey Ford missed all of the 1951 and 1952 seasons while serving in the army, and Willie Mays missed most of 1952 and all of 1953.

But there's also Del Crandall, not to mention Ed Bailey and Ken Boyer, and Tito Francona, Elston Howard, Jim Lemon, Danny O'Connell, Bubba Phillips, Daryl Spencer, Gus Triandos, and Preston Ward, all of whom missed two entire seasons during or shortly after the Korean War. And these are just the guys who enjoyed substantial careers afterward. There must have been many players whose professional careers were sidetracked to the point that they simply never reached the majors.

BOSTON/MILWAUKEE/ATLANTA BRAVES

		YEARS	NOTES
ALL-TIME			
C	Del Crandall	1949–1950 1953–1963	Reached majors when he was 19, but didn't establish himself as regular until 1953 because of military service; eight-time All-Star brought power and defense.
1B	Joe Adcock	1953–1962	Suffice to say, not a strong position over the years, as Adcock was a fine hitter but often platooned; Fred Tenney would be No. 1 if we considered 19th century.
2B	Glenn Hubbard	1978–1987	Another weak position, with very few players holding the job for more than a few years, let alone holding it and playing better than adequately.
SS	Rabbit Maranville	1912–1920 1929–1935	Not much of a hitter most years, but an outstanding defensive player well into his late thirties; one of the game's famous "characters."
3B	Eddie Mathews	1952–1966	Blasted 370 homers before he turned 30, but only 142 afterward; only man to play for Braves in Boston, Milwaukee, and Atlanta; just adequate with the glove.
LF	Rico Carty	1963–1972	Yet another trouble spot; once you get past Carty and Ryan Klesko, the only other candidate worthy of even moderate consideration is Sid Gordon (1950–53).
CF	Dale Murphy	1976–1990	Finally, a position of real strength, with Murphy joined by Andruw Jones, four-time All-Star Wally Berger (1930–37), and solid Bill Bruton (1953–60).
RF	Henry Aaron	1954–1974	As Phillies pitcher Curt Simmons somewhat famously said, "Trying to sneak a fastball past him is like trying to sneak a sunrise past a rooster."
SP1	Greg Maddux	1993–*2002*	Among his many fine feats, in 2002 Maddux became the second pitcher—and the first since Cy Young—to win at least 15 games in 15 straight seasons.
SP2	Warren Spahn	1942 1946–1964	Pitching well into his 40s, he won 363 games; "I don't think Spahn will ever get into the Hall of Fame. He'll never stop pitching."—Stan Musial, 1965
SP3	Phil Niekro	1964–1983 1987	"It was great. I got to meet a lot of important people. They all sit behind home plate."—Bob Uecker, on trying to catch Niekro's dancing knuckleball
SP4	Tom Glavine	1987–2002	Through 2002, *still* hadn't allowed even one grand slam over 16 seasons and 505 games; all 505 of those games were starts (Clemens has one relief job).
RP	Gene Garber	1978–1987	Braves' best pre-Atlanta reliever was Don McMahon (1957–62), who led club in saves for five straight years beginning in 1957 and tossed 5 shutout innings in '57 Series.

		SINGLE SEASON	
		YEARS	**NOTES**
C	Javy López	1998	One could reasonably argue for Joe Torre in 1964 or '66, but he played quite a bit of first base in both seasons.
1B	Earl Torgeson	1950	Making good on promise he'd shown as rookie in '47, drew 119 walks and scored league-best 120 runs.
2B	Rogers Hornsby	1928	Braves lost 103 games despite Hornsby's brilliant, lone season with club; led NL in all three hitting percentages.
SS	Jeff Blauser	1997	Other top seasons by Brave shortstops turned in by Rabbit Maranville, Johnny Logan, and Denis Menke.
3B	Eddie Mathews	1953	Still only 21, he batted .302, drove in 135 runs, and topped NL with 47 homers; he'd have other great years, of course.
LF	Rico Carty	1970	Strong contender is Sid Gordon's 1950; in his first season after coming over from Giants, slugged .557 with 103 RBI.
CF	Wally Berger	1935	Choice isn't really supported by the numbers, but I just can't ignore a player with 130 RBI for a team that lost 115 games.
RF	Hank Aaron	1963	Just one of many similarly brilliant seasons, but what sets this one apart is career-high 31 steals (with only 5 times caught).
SP	Bill James	1914	Easy choice is Gregory Maddux . . . but James won 26 to propel Miracle Braves to pennant, then two more in World Series.
RP	John Smoltz	2002	Got off to a shaky start, but wound up setting National League record with 55 saves in his first season as a closer.

		TRADED AWAY	
		TRADED	**NOTES**
C	Shanty Hogan	January 10, 1928	Prodigious eater sent to NYC in deal for Hornsby, then batted .311 in four seasons before returning to Braves.
1B	Darrell Evans	June 13, 1976	Two other good ones that got away: Elbie Fletcher (who would thrice lead NL in OBP) and Ryan Klesko.
2B	Bret Boone	December 22, 1999	Went to S.D. with Klesko in blockbuster that netted Reggie Sanders, Quilvio Veras, and Wally Joyner.
SS	Alvin Dark	December 14, 1949	Off to Giants because he and manager Billy Southworth didn't get along; Maranville and Joost also dealt.
3B	Joe Torre	March 17, 1969	Cards got Torre (whose stats skyrocketed) and Braves got Cepeda (who did have one big year left in him).
LF	Dusty Baker	November 17, 1975	Deal looked great in '76, as Dusty played terribly for Dodgers; not so good afterward, when he starred.
CF	Brett Butler	October 21, 1983	Part of a terrible deal—maybe their worst—that sent Butler *and* Brook Jacoby to Cleveland for Len Barker.
RF	Gary Matthews	March 25, 1981	Traded straight up to Phillies for young Bob Walk, and both players still had plenty of good ball to play.
SP	Juan Pizarro & Joey Jay	December 15, 1960	Also, Braves traded veteran Vic Willis in 1905 and kid Johnny Antonelli in 1954, and both deals went awry.
RP	Ron Reed	May 28, 1975	Runner-up is Steve Bedrosian (December 10, 1985), who won a Cy Young Award with the Phillies in 1987.

Neither Juan Pizarro nor Joey Jay ever became big stars. However, for a few years in the early '60s they both ranked among the better starters in their leagues. Before that, though, the Braves basically gave both of them away.

It happened on December 15, 1960. Johnny Logan, the Braves' longtime shortstop, hadn't played particularly well that season, and the club was looking to get better defensively at the position. So they traded pitchers Pizzaro and Jay to Cincinnati for Roy McMillan, the greatest defensive shortstop of the 1950s.

Two problems, though. One, Pizarro and Jay were both talented young pitchers, and the Braves weren't blessed with a number of *other* talented young pitchers. Two, being great in the 1950s doesn't mean you'll be great in the 1960s.

McMillan wasn't. Meanwhile, both Pizarro and Jay developed after leaving Milwaukee and getting real chances to pitch. Jay won twenty-games in both 1961 *and* 1962 for the Reds (his career went downhill soon afterward, though). And Pizarro, traded to the White Sox immediately upon going to the Reds, won sixty-one games with a 2.93 ERA from 1961 through 1964, and pitched in the 1963 All-Star Game.

It wasn't the first time this happened, either. Back in 1954, the Braves traded $50,000 and four players to the Giants for Bobby Thomson. One of those four players was a young pitcher named Johnny Antonelli, who would win 102 games for the Giants over the next six seasons.

What a story it was.

After fifteen seasons in New York, Babe Ruth would return to Boston, where he'd started his major-league career. If everything worked out, Ruth's presence would boost attendance enough to let owner Judge Emil Fuchs hold on to his team.

For this, Fuchs agreed to pay Ruth $35,000, along with a twenty-five percent share of the club's receipts from exhibition games.

Contrary to the accepted wisdom these days, in 1935 there was reason to think that Ruth, even though he was fat and forty, could still play a little. After all, in 1934 Ruth had slugged .537 and drawn 104 walks in 125 games. The old Babe wasn't the Babe of old, but even at forty he was one of the best hitters in the American League.

But what a difference a year can make. In 1935, Ruth didn't want to be anywhere but New York, and he resisted Fuchs's various efforts to capitalize on his fame. Heavier than he'd ever been, Ruth couldn't really play the field at all, leading some Braves pitchers to threaten a strike if Ruth again took the field. Oh, and he couldn't hit, either.

On May 25, the Babe blasted three home runs, one of them supposedly the longest in Forbes Field history. Eight days later, he quit. And the Braves, who had won seventy-eight games in 1934 and would win seventy-one in 1936, lost 115 games in 1935.

		YEARS	NOTES
ALL-BUST			
C	Jody Davis	1988–1990	An All-Star with the Cubs in 1984 and '86, came to the other superstation team and batted .161 in 92 games.
1B	Nick Esasky	1990	Signed as free agent after solid 1989 with Red Sox, then played only 9 more MLB games because of vertigo.
2B	Danny O'Connell	1954–1957	Braves paid six players and $100K for him, but he batted just .248 with 11 homers in three-and-a-half seasons.
SS	Larvell Blanks	1975	He played 141 games, including 129 at SS; spent another five seasons in majors, but never played that much again.
3B	Vinny Castilla	*2002*	More proof that Schuerholz ain't perfect; they moved Chipper to LF, and gave Castilla *eight million dollars?*
LF	Brad Komminsk	1983–1986	Fourth overall pick in '79 draft ran up impeccable track record in minors, but never found his stroke in majors.
CF	Oddibe McDowell	1990	Hit like gangbusters after coming over in mid-season '89, batting average dropped 61 points in '90.
RF	Brian Jordan	1999–2001	Some will quibble, but the Braves signed Jordan for an immense amount of money and got an average player.
SP	Len Barker	1983–1985	Getting hammered in Cleveland, but Braves gave up Brett Butler and Brook Jacoby for him anyway.
RP	Bruce Sutter	1985–1988	Close runner-up is John Rocker, who pitched well but had his— ummm—*problems* off the field.

		YEARS	NOTES
USED-TO-BE-GREAT			
C	Ted Simmons	1986–1988	Just a part-time player by then, but he did get behind the plate in 45 games over the three seasons.
1B	George Sisler	1928–1930	Batted .326 over his three seasons, which looks great until you remember that *everybody* was batting .326.
2B	Billy Herman	1946	Turned 37 shortly after coming over from Brooklyn in trade, but could still play and batted .306 in 75 games.
SS	Bill Dahlen	1908–1909	Longtime star for Cubs, Dodgers, and Giants last played regularly with Braves, in 1908 when he was 37.
3B	Darrell Evans	1989	Also, Bobby Bonilla spent the 2000 season with Braves (though he played only a few games at third base).
LF	Babe Ruth	1935	Batted .181 for Braves in 28 games and finally quit in June, but not before hitting three homers in one game.
CF	Jimmy Wynn	1976	In 1941, Earl Averill, suffering serious back pain, ended his career with two singles in eight games with Braves.
RF	Paul Waner	1941–1942	Best years behind him, but hung on through the war years and collected his 3,000th hit while with this Tribe.
SP	Cy Young	1911	Returned to Boston for final 11 starts of his career, and pitched shutout on September 22 for his very last win.
RP	Hoyt Wilhelm	1969–1970 1971	Two all-time greats, Bruce Sutter and Jeff Reardon, finished with Braves, and both somewhat less than happily.

ALL-NAME

		YEARS	NOTES
C	"Heavy" Earl Williams	1970–1972 1975–1976	One of the worst defensive catchers ever, Williams had "issues" with his weight but didn't mind the nickname.
1B	"Crime Dog" Fred McGriff	1993–1997	In era mostly bereft of fun nicknames, this one was both good and lasting; from TV's McGruff, the Crime Dog.
2B	"The Cat" Felix Millan	1966–1972	From the cartoon character "Felix the Cat" . . . did this mean anything to Millan's fellow Puerto Ricans?
SS	"Rabbit" Walter Maranville	1912–1920 1929–1935	There are at least four explanations for origin of "Rabbit," but all we know for sure is that he *could* wiggle his ears.
3B	"Chipper" Larry Jones	1993–*2002*	It seems a little strange, now, to call a man in his 30s "Chipper" . . . but then, he *does* hate "Larry."
LF	"Road Runner" Ralph Garr	1968–1975	Like McGriff and Millan, speedy Garr got his lasting moniker from a cartoon character.
CF	"Dusty" Johnnie Baker	1968–1975	He and his dog, Dusty, both preferred dirt to grass, and both would come home when someone called, "Dusty!"
RF	"Hammer" Hank Aaron	1954–1974	Media came up with "Hammerin' Henry" early on, but his teammates just called him "Hammer."
SP	"Knucksie" Phil Niekro	1966–1983 1987	My favorite nicknames are those that tell you something *about* the player, and this one certainly fits the bill.
RP	"Bedrock" Steve Bedrosian	1981–1985 1993–1995	A play on his last name, of course, and I can still hear Skip Caray using it almost exclusively.

TOP FIVE SEASONS

YEAR	1914	**RECORD**	94-59
BEST HITTERS	Joe Connolly, Johnny Evers, Rabbit Maranville		
BEST PITCHER	Bill James		
NOTES	Braves pull off Miracle *and* sweep A's in Series.		
YEAR	1957	**RECORD**	95-59
BEST HITTERS	Hank Aaron, Eddie Mathews		
BEST PITCHER	Warren Spahn		
NOTES	Upstarts top Yankees, thanks to Burdette.		
YEAR	1995	**RECORD**	90-54
BEST HITTERS	Chipper Jones, Fred McGriff, David Justice		
BEST PITCHER	Greg Maddux (Cy Young)		
NOTES	Beat Indians in World Series; 1990s weren't *completely* fruitless.		
YEAR	1991	**RECORD**	94-68
BEST HITTER	Terry Pendleton (MVP)		
BEST PITCHER	Tom Glavine		
NOTES	Lost to Twins in World Series; thanks a lot, Metrodome.		
YEAR	1948	**RECORD**	91-62
BEST HITTER	Bob Elliott		
BEST PITCHER	Johnny Sain		
NOTES	After 34 years, Braves finally return to World Series.		

TOP FIVE MANAGERS

MANAGER	Bobby Cox
YEARS	1978–1981, 1990–*2002*
RECORD	1,450-1,112 (.566)
NOTES	Greatest manager of the 1990s . . . until October.
MANAGER	Billy Southworth
YEARS	1946–1951
RECORD	424-358 (.542)
NOTES	Lured by big contract, brought first flag since 1914.
MANAGER	George Stallings
YEARS	1913–1920
RECORD	579-597 (.492)
NOTES	Pioneer of platooning, engineered a Miracle.
MANAGER	Joe Torre
YEARS	1982–1984
RECORD	257-229 (.529)
NOTES	Rehabilitated career after five awful seasons in Flushing.
MANAGER	Ted Turner
YEARS	1977
RECORD	0-1 (.000)
NOTES	Not really a manager, of course . . . but he lost just once!

Long before the XFL and He Hate Me, one major-league baseball team made a standard practice of putting nicknames on the backs of jerseys.

The Atlanta Braves didn't come up with the idea. It's thought that Ken Harrelson was the first player to replace his given name with a nickname; upon joining the Indians in 1969, he instructed the equipment manager to put HAWK above his number.

It wasn't until 1976, though, that a team grabbed the idea and ran with it. Speedy Ralph Garr's nickname was "Roadrunner," so that's what went on the jersey. Catcher Earl Williams's nickname was "Heavy," so that's what went above the numbers on his jersey. Jimmy Wynn, at the end of the line but still popularly known as "The Toy Cannon," batted .207 with CANNON stitched above the *24* on the back of his shirt.

The Braves had recently been purchased by Ted Turner, who also owned WTCG, which occupied channel 17 on the local cable system. Pitcher Andy Messersmith wore number seventeen, and so Turner came up with the bright idea of giving Messersmith a new nickname: "Channel." Get it?

Turner's free advertising didn't last long. National League president Chub Feeney found out, and ordered "Channel" stripped from Messersmith's uniform. He chose "Bluto" instead.

McKECHNIE & STENGEL

For fourteen straight seasons, the Boston Braves were managed by men who would eventually be elected to the Hall of Fame, purely because of their achievements as managers. Yet in all of those fourteen seasons, the Braves managed to finish as high as fourth place only twice.

In 1930, Braves owner Emil "Judge" Fuchs fired himself as manager and hired Bill McKechnie. This was, I can say without exaggerating, probably the smartest thing that Judge Fuchs ever did. McKechnie had already won pennants while managing the Pirates and the Cardinals, and was available only because the owner of the Cardinals was a petulant fellow with very little patience. The Cards won the pennant in 1928, but got off to a 34-29 start in '29 and so off went McKechnie's head.

That same season, Fuchs—with a lot of help from coach Johnny Evers—managed the Braves to a last-place finish, at which point he wisely decided that maybe managing wasn't his bag.

It certainly was McKechnie's, though. He managed the Braves for eight seasons, then took over as skipper in Cincinnati. In his first season, the Reds went from 56-98 to 82-68 and vaulted from eighth place to fourth place. In his second season, the Reds won their first National League pennant in twenty years. And in his third season, the Reds won the World Series.

Back in Beantown . . . McKechnie was replaced as Braves manager by an amusing character named Charles Dillon Stengel. Casey, for short. Stengel had managed the Dodgers from 1934 through '36, without a lot of success. His first season with the Braves was 1938, and they did about what they'd done the year before: a few games better than .500, good enough for fifth place. Unfortunately, that was as good as it got for Stengel's Braves. The next four seasons, the Tribe finished seventh, seventh, seventh, and seventh. In 1943, Stengel's last season, they jumped all the way to sixth.

In 1944, Casey went back to the minor leagues. In 1949, the Yankees shocked everybody by hiring Stengel to manage the club, and that same year he led them to the first of five straight World Championships.

I haven't rated either McKechnie or Stengel among the Braves' top five managers, because they didn't win a lot of games. But McKechnie's non-Braves teams won fifty-six percent of the games he managed, and Stengel's non-Braves and non-Mets teams won fifty-nine percent of the games *he* managed. That McKechnie's Braves won forty-six percent of their games, and Stengel's Braves won forty-three percent of theirs . . . well, we probably shouldn't hold it against them.

Casey Stengel
National Baseball Library, Cooperstown, New York

St. Louis Browns/Baltimore Orioles

		YEARS	NOTES
		ALL-TIME	
C	Rick Dempsey	1976–1986 1992	The best of the old Browns catchers was Hank Severeid (1915–1925), who topped .300 in five straight seasons and played professionally into his mid-40s.
1B	Eddie Murray	1977–1988 1996	George Sisler (1915–22, 1924–28) is in the Hall of Fame, and was an outstanding player before suffering eye malady, but quite an ordinary one after.
2B	Bobby Grich	1970–1976	Del Pratt (1912–1917) was a fine player, but Grich was one of the best players in the league in *each* season from 1973 through '76, and he remains obscenely underrated.
SS	Cal Ripken	1981–2001	Nobody's close to Ripken, of course, but Hall of Famer Bobby Wallace joined the Browns in 1902 and ranked among the club's better players for the entire decade.
3B	Brooks Robinson	1955–1977	Brooks's only competition is Harlond Clift (1934–43), a sabermetrician's dream who played brilliantly for eight seasons but petered out while still in his mid-30s.
LF	Ken Williams	1918–1927	His peak was short—1921 through '23—but for those 3 seasons he was one of the best in the league; in '22, led AL with 39 homers and 155 RBI, *and* stole 37 bases.
CF	Brady Anderson	1988–2001	Paul Blair (1964–1976) and Baby Doll Jacobson (1915–1926) were both damn good, too; Jacobson part of a great outfield including Ken Williams and Jack Tobin.
RF	Frank Robinson	1966–1971	Before Robinson and then Ken Singleton, Jack Tobin (1918–25) was the closest thing to an outstanding right fielder the franchise ever had.
SP1	Jim Palmer	1965–1984	"Jim had one of the most beautiful deliveries I've ever seen. It was almost like watching ballet."—longtime Orioles pitching coach Ray Miller
SP2	Urban Shocker	1918–1924	Spitballer only a Brown for seven seasons, but he never had a bad season and went 126-80 with 3.19 ERA before club foolishly traded him to Yankees.
SP3	Mike Mussina	1991–2000	One chink in Moose's armor: he won 18 or 19 games four times, but never got to 20; also, after going 18-5 with 2.54 ERA in first full season, never quite as good.
SP4	Dave McNally	1962–1974	Other candidates for this last spot on the list include the Orioles' Mike Cuellar and Brownies fastballer Jack Powell (1902–03, 1905–12).
RP	Gregg Olson	1988–1993	Olson certainly isn't the best closer who ever lived, but he just might have thrown the best curveball of any closer who ever lived.

Just about everybody has a bad year. Roger Clemens once went 11-14 with a 4.46 ERA. Greg Maddux once went 6-14 with a 5.61 ERA. Tom Seaver once went 5-13 with a 5.50 ERA.

Urban Shocker never had a bad year, though. Not even one.

Urbain Jacques Schockcor reached the majors with the Yankees in 1916. After two seasons in which he pitched well but sparingly, Shocker was dealt to the Browns in a big trade. In 1918, his first season with St. Louis, Shocker went just 6-5 but posted a 1.81 ERA. In 1919, he went 13-11. In 1920, Shocker went 20-10 to establish himself as one of the league's best pitchers. From that season through 1923, Shocker and his spitball won ninety-one games and lost fifty-one.

In 1924, Shocker pitched well again, but not quite up to his own standards. After the season, the Browns traded him back to the Yankees. He pitched well over the next three seasons, going 19-11 in 1926 and then 18-6 for the famed '27 squad.

That would be his last season. In 1928, Shocker pitched only two innings—scoreless, of course—but was ill the rest of the season and died of pneumonia on September 9, a few weeks before the Yankees played another World Series. He'd pitched in thirteen seasons, and not even once had he lost more than he won, or posted an ERA worse than league average.

In 1922, left fielder Ken Williams led the American League with thirty-nine home runs and 155 RBI, *and* he stole thirty-seven bases. Williams was the first thirty-thirty player, and he would remain the *only* thirty-thirty man until 1956, when Willie Mays turned the trick.

Actually, what's really interesting is that nobody in 1922 seems to have cared.

For one thing, Williams didn't garner even a single point in the MVP balloting, even though his team very nearly won the pennant.

Yes, there is a catch. The eight MVP voters were instructed to list eight players on their ballots: one player from each team, ranked one through eight. And that left Williams in the cold, because nearly all of the voters chose George Sisler as the most valuable Brown. This was no surprise, as Sisler led the American League with 134 runs and a .420 batting average. At least one writer did think that Sisler wasn't the most valuable Brown, but what little non-Sisler support there was went to Urban Shocker, who won twenty-four games.

Actually, what's *really* interesting is that nobody in 1922 seems to have *noticed.* The 1923 edition of the *Reach Official American League Base Ball Guide* runs 520 pages, and yet there's not even a single hint that Williams's combination of power and speed was anything special.

SINGLE SEASON			
		YEARS	NOTES
C	Chris Hoiles	1993	Yes, Chris Hoiles; what's more, no other catcher in the team's long history is really close to Hoiles and his 1004 OPS.
1B	Eddie Murray	1984	One could argue for one of George Sisler's .400 seasons—he did it twice—but Murray played in a tougher time to excel.
2B	Bobby Grich	1974	Del Pratt played outstanding ball in 1914 and 1916, but Grich's four best seasons beat anybody's in franchise history.
SS	Cal Ripken	1983	Vern Stephens equaled Ripken's best seasons in 1944, but of course most of the good pitchers were gone by then.
3B	Brooks Robinson	1964	Brooks's MVP season easily outdistances not only all of the franchise's other third sackers, but his other best seasons, too.
LF	George Stone	1906	One of the great forgotten seasons, as Stone led American League in batting (.358), OBP (.417), and slugging (.501).
CF	Brady Anderson	1996	Other notable seasons include Baby Doll Jacobson's 1920, Paul Blair's 1969, and (especially) Al Bumbry's 1980.
RF	Frank Robinson	1966	Frank's the Man, of course, but in 1977 Ken Singleton was awesome, batting .328 with 24 homers and 107 walks.
SP	Jim Palmer	1975	In their long history, the Browns/Orioles have never seen an amazing, drop-your-jaw season from one of their pitchers.
RP	Stu Miller	1965	In the Closer Era, honors go to Gregg Olson for his brilliant rookie campaign in 1989: 27 saves, 1.69 ERA in 85 innings.

TRADED AWAY			
		TRADED	NOTES
C	Sherm Lollar	November 27, 1951	In 1951, the Browns traded *20 players in 14 deals,* but Lollar was easily the best player who got dealt.
1B	Mike Epstein	May 29, 1967	O's traded Vic Wertz in 1954, in time for him to make history against Mays *and* play well for a few years.
2B	Del Pratt	January 22, 1918	The Brownies lost a great player in Pratt, but they got a great one (from the Yankees) in Urban Shocker.
SS	Vern Stephens	November 17, 1947	Sent their best hitter (Stephens) and an All-Star pitcher (Jack Kramer) to BoSox for five bodies and $310,000.
3B	Doug DeCinces	January 28, 1982	Also, Wayne Causey was a bust as O's bonus baby, but enjoyed a few nice seasons after going to A's in trade.
LF	Heinie Manush	June 13, 1930	In exchange of Hall of Famers, the Nationals got Manush and the Browns got Goose Goslin.
CF	Steve Finley	January 10, 1991	With Browns taking big chunk of SluFeds roster in 1916, Tilly Walker expendable and sold to Red Sox.
RF	Roy Cullenbine	June 7, 1942	After a huge 1941, he got off to a lousy start in '42 and so they shipped him off to Washington.
SP	Curt Schilling	January 10, 1991	Honorable mention goes to Bobo Newsom, whom the Browns sold or traded three different times.
RP	José Mesa	July 14, 1992	Ryne Duren spent eight seasons in organization and pitched in one MLB game before finally going to A's.

USED-TO-BE-GREAT

		YEARS	NOTES
C	Terry Kennedy	1987–1988	Former Padres All-Star posted .289 OBP in two seasons, and played his part in Orioles' 0-21 start in '88.
1B	Jim Bottomley	1936–1937	Built Hall of Fame credentials with Cardinals in '20s, and finished career as player-manager with Browns.
2B	Delino DeShields	1999–2001	Just edges Harold Reynolds, who played with O's for one season (1993) before finishing up in Anaheim.
SS	Marty Marion	1952–1953	Like Bottomley, this former Cardinal great finished his career as a player while managing the Brownies.
3B	Vern Stephens	1953–1955	Longtime Brownie came back for a spell, but his decline had started in 1952 and it was precipitous.
LF	Jesse Burkett	1902–1904	Ex–National League star was still pretty good after jumping from Cardinals to Browns.
CF	Hugh Duffy	1901	Duffy—two-time National League batting champ—is the only original (1901) Milwaukee Brewer in this book.
RF	Albert Belle	1999–2000	It's a shame that Dwight Evans (1991) didn't finish in Fenway, but Dewey did post .393 OBP with Orioles.
SP	Eddie Plank	1916–1917	After a year with St. Louis Federals, pitched quite well for Browns—21-21, 2.14—in last major-league action.
RP	Satchel Paige	1951–1953	Still crazy after all those years, Paige didn't pitch well in '51 but made All-Star team in both '52 and '53.

ALL-NAME

		YEARS	NOTES
M	"Captain Hook" Earl Weaver	1968–1982 1985–1986	Before Sparky Anderson immortalized the nickname, Weaver had it because of his affection for the bullpen.
C	"Tubby" Edward Spencer	1905–1908	He stood 5'10" and weighed 215 pounds; 'twas said that he could down a quart of whiskey and still play ball.
1B	"Boog" John Powell	1961–1974	I'll skip the explanation because it's boring; isn't it enough to say that "Boog"—given him as a child—*fit?*
2B	"Ski" Oscar Melillo	1926–1935	Of more interest, he was also nicknamed "Spinach" after being ordered by doctors to eat a lot of the green stuff.
SS	"Junior" Vernon Stephens	1941–1947 1953–1955	His dad was also Vernon, so his family called him "Junior" to avoid confusion; also "Buster" for his power.
3B	"Hoover" Brooks Robinson	1955–1977	For the way he sucked up ground balls, just like a vacuum cleaner; also "The Head" for receding hairline.
LF	"Captain Midnight" John Lowenstein	1979–1985	He loved to wear sunglasses, even at night; also fondly called "Brother Low."
CF	"Baby Doll" William Jacobson	1915, 1917 1919–1926	After he hit a homer in the minors, the band struck up a popular song of the day called "Oh You Beautiful Doll."
RF	Drungo Hazewood	1980	Wait, it gets better . . . his middle name was La Rue . . . *Drungo La Rue Hazewood* went 0-for-5 in 6 games.
SP	"Elmer the Great" Walter Beck	1924 1927–1928	Later became "Boom-Boom"; first got this one because he reminded people of a character in a Ring Lardner story.
RP	"Full Pack" Don Stanhouse	1978–1979 1982	Dubbed by Earl Weaver, who said he smoked that much when Stanhouse pitched; also "Stan the Man Unusual."

Satchel Paige turned forty-six years old on July 7, 1952.

And he was still pitching in the major leagues. Pitching well, too.

Paige joined the Cleveland Indians in 1948, and was one of the biggest stories of the year. He pitched well that season, and again in 1949, but wasn't asked back in 1950 and went back to barnstorming with the Kansas City Monarchs.

Bill Veeck had brought Paige to the majors when he owned the Indians; in 1951 he owned the Browns, and brought Paige to the majors again.

Paige pitched poorly that year, but he came back in 1952 because Veeck considered Paige a good drawing card. He opened the season in the bullpen, and pitched well enough to make the All-Star team.

Then came August 6. It was Paige's second start of the season. He hadn't pitched a complete game since 1949. But Paige locked up with Detroit's Virgil Trucks, and both of them pitched and pitched and pitched, shutout inning after shutout inning.

Finally, in the bottom of the twelfth, the Browns pushed across the winning run. Ol' Satchel had his twelve-inning shutout. It just might be the greatest game ever pitched by a man closer to sixty than thirty, and afterward Paige said, "Man, I'm a hundred years old, and I can still strike these guys out."

In July of 1987, when Billy Ripken got called up, manager Cal Ripken, Sr., became the first father to manage two sons at the same time in the major leagues. And according to the Orioles, Billy and Cal Jr. were just the fourth brother keystone combination in major-league history; Billy and Cal stuck together for the better part of five seasons. There was a middle brother, Fred. He was a motorcycle mechanic. (Did you know that Cal Sr.'s big brother Bill also played professional ball? In three seasons, mostly in the low minors, Bill batted .318 and showed a good batting eye and decent power.)

Second baseman Jerry Hairston, Jr., is part of the third three-generation family in the majors (the Boones and Bells came before). Jerry Sr. played in the majors for fourteen seasons, and *his* father Sam played for the White Sox in 1951.

My favorite Orioles family story, though, is that of the Raineses. Tim Sr. missed most of 1999 while battling lupus, then retired the following spring. He unretired in 2001, though, and batted .308 for the Expos. On October 3, the Expos essentially gave him to the Orioles so he could play with his son. And they played together twice—on October 4 and 5—with Senior in left and Junior in center field.

And people say there's no room for sentiment in baseball.

FAMILY TIES

		YEARS	NOTES
M	Cal Ripken, Sr.	1987–1988	An Orioles employee for 36 years, and still the only man to manage two sons (Cal Jr. and Billy) at once.
DH	Lee May	1975–1980	Lee got the power (.492 career slugging pct.) and little brother Carlos got the patience (.360 career OBP).
C	Rick Dempsey	1976–1986 1992	Dad was a vaudeville performer, mom was a Broadway star, and nephew Gregg Zaun was a catcher.
1B	Eddie Murray	1977–1988 1996	His brothers Rich, Leon, Charles, and Venice *all* played pro ball, with 1B Rich making it to majors with Giants.
2B	Jerry Hairston, Jr.	1998–2002	In 1998, Hairstons joined Bells and Boones as third three-generation MLB family.
SS	Luis Aparicio, Jr.	1964–1967	Luis Sr. was Venezuela's greatest shortstop in the late '30s and '40s, and could have signed with Senators.
3B	Ray Knight	1987	For at least a few years, his wife—golfer Nancy Lopez—was quite a bit more famous than he was.
LF	Pat Kelly	1977–1980	Brother Leroy was a Hall of Fame running back for the Cleveland Browns from 1964 through 1973.
CF	Tim Raines, Jr.	2001–2002	Got to play alongside his dad twice in 2001, as the Raineses joined the Griffeys in an exclusive club.
RF	Tito Francona	1956–1957	Batted just .249 for O's, didn't become star until going to Cleveland; son Terry nowhere near as good.
SP	Storm Davis	1982–1986 1992	Glenn Davis was adopted by Storm's parents, and the two got to play together with Orioles in 1992.
RP	Dan Boone	1990	Knuckleballer supposedly a descendant of *the* Daniel Boone (described by *TSN* as "American Pioneer").

TOP FIVE SEASONS

YEAR 1970 **RECORD** 108-54
BEST HITTER Boog Powell (MVP)
BEST PITCHERS Jim Palmer, Dave McNally (Cy Young)
NOTES After big letdown in '69, beat Reds in World Series.

YEAR 1966 **RECORD** 97-63
BEST HITTER Frank Robinson (MVP)
BEST PITCHER Stu Miller
NOTES Shockingly, swept Koufax's Dodgers in World Series.

YEAR 1983 **RECORD** 98-64
BEST HITTER Cal Ripken (MVP)
BEST PITCHER Scott McGregor
NOTES With Weaver gone, O's beat Phillies in World Series.

YEAR 1969 **RECORD** 109-53
BEST HITTER Frank Robinson
BEST PITCHER Mike Cuellar
NOTES Shockingly, lost World Series to the 'mazin's in five games.

YEAR 1944 **RECORD** 89-65
BEST HITTER Vern Stephens
BEST PITCHER Jack Kramer
NOTES It took a world war for Browns to win only pennant in their history.

TOP FIVE MANAGERS

MANAGER Earl Weaver
YEARS 1968–1982, 1985–1986
RECORD 1480-1060 (.583)
NOTES Greatest of his era, and it's not even close.

MANAGER Davey Johnson
YEARS 1996–1997
RECORD 186-138 (.574)
NOTES Two division titles in two seasons before he ran afoul of owner.

MANAGER Hank Bauer
YEARS 1964–1968
RECORD 407-318 (.561)
NOTES Guided O's to Series sweep in third season, dumped two years later.

MANAGER Paul Richards
YEARS 1955–1961
RECORD 517-539 (.490)
NOTES Like Weaver, wrote an excellent book on managing.

MANAGER Luke Sewell
YEARS 1941–1946
RECORD 432-410 (.513)
NOTES Managed Brownies to their only pennant in fifty-two seasons.

"CAN YOU SEND THE CHECK TODAY?"

I wonder what it was like to be a fan of the St. Louis Browns in the late 1940s and early '50s.

In 1922, the Browns very nearly beat out the Yankees for the American League pennant. It was the first time they'd been serious contenders, and it would be the last until 1944, when they did win the pennant before losing to the Cardinals in the World Series.

That year, 1944, the Browns traded two players and sold one. In 1945, they traded one player. In 1946, they traded three players.

And then in 1947, the floodgates busted wide open. In the space of two days, November 17 and 18, the Browns traded their best player (Vern Stephens), two of their best pitchers (Jack Kramer and Ellis Kinder), and part-time third baseman Billy Hitchcock to the Red Sox. The Browns got plenty of players in return; they gave up four, and received nine. But for the Browns, the deal wasn't about players, it was about money. In addition to those nine players, the Red Sox sent along $375,000, quite a tidy sum for the time. And by year's end, the Browns had traded four more players and realized another $90,000.

See, the Browns were always just *this close* from going bankrupt. In 1948, they traded or sold seven players, and received more than $250,000 in the deals. The sales continued in 1949 and '50, with the Browns getting some big money for some players who really weren't very good . . . which was a good thing, because they'd already dumped most of their players who were actually *worth* big money.

There just wasn't room in St. Louis for two teams, and after the war the Browns were losing huge amounts of money. Bill Veeck bought the club in 1951 with plans to drive the Cardinals out of town, but Veeck changed his mind when Gussie Busch bought the Redbirds in 1953. He realized that the Cardinals, backed up by Busch's substantial fortune, weren't going anywhere for quite some time. Shortly thereafter, Veeck sold the Browns, who were immediately moved to Baltimore, where they became the Orioles.

What was it like to be a fan of the St. Louis Browns in the late '40s and early '50s? My guess is that it was a little worse than being a fan, today, of the Kansas City Royals, and a little better than being a fan of the Montreal Expos.

Vern Stephens
National Baseball Library, Cooperstown, New York

In 1947, Jackie Robinson won the first Rookie of the Year Award. Since the inception of the prize, fifty-eight of them have been available to Dodgers . . . and Dodgers won fifteen of them, which is a pretty amazing percentage.

And they've come in bunches. Robinson, Don Newcombe, Joe Black, and Jim Gilliam won theirs in a seven-year span beginning in 1947. Rick Sutcliffe, Steve Howe, Fernando Valenzuela, and Steve Sax gave the Dodgers four straight Rookies of the Year, beginning in 1979. And then in 1992 the Dodgers began a run of *five* straight Rookies of the Year: Eric Karros, Mike Piazza, Raul Mondesi, Hideo Nomo, and Todd Hollandsworth.

Did Robinson begin the trend, or did he just continue one? Well, the Dodgers didn't churn out a *lot* of rookie talent prior to 1947, but they did enjoy slightly more than their fair share. Bill Deane is the expert in award voting. He's picked hypothetical Rookies of the Year from 1900 through 1946, and there are eight Dodgers: outfielder Harry Lumley (1904), pitcher Nap Rucker (1907), pitcher Jeff Pfeffer (1914), pitcher Leon Cadore (1917), first baseman Del Bissonette (1928), outfielder Johnny Frederick (1929), and pitcher Hugh Casey (1939).

BROOKLYN/LOS ANGELES DODGERS

		YEARS	ALL-TIME NOTES
C	Roy Campanella	1948–1957	Not quite the hitter that Piazza was, but he won three MVP Awards, played better defense, and spent 10 years with the club compared to Piazza's five.
1B	Steve Garvey	1969–1982	There's certainly an argument for Gil Hodges here, but Hodges was *not* widely considered a great player while active; and never finished higher than seventh in MVP vote.
2B	Jackie Robinson	1947–1956	What's too often missed is that Jackie was not only a great base runner but a great *player*, a fantastic fielder who hit for average and power and drew a ton of walks.
SS	Pee Wee Reese	1940–1942 1946–1958	Fine leadoff man with great skills, and only human to play in all 44 World Series games between Brooklyn Dodgers and New York Yankees.
3B	Ron Cey	1971–1982	The second-most famous third baseman in Dodgers history is Billy Cox, but Cookie Lavagetto and Joe Stripp were just as good, and Jim Gilliam was a lot better.
LF	Zack Wheat	1909–1926	Hall of Famer still tops franchise list in games (2,322), hits (2,804), doubles (464), and triples (171), and there aren't any challengers on the horizon.
CF	Duke Snider	1947–1962	From 1953 through '57, right up there with Willie Mays among the league's best players, but move to Los Angeles and knee injury brought on premature decline.
RF	Dixie Walker	1939–1947	No Hall of Famers, but a strong position over the years, with players like Harry Lumley, Babe Herman, Carl Furillo, Reggie Smith, and now Shawn Green.
SP1	Sandy Koufax	1955–1966	"I never saw those old-timers, but he must have the greatest stuff of any pitcher in history."—Phillies pitcher Ray Culp in 1964; Koufax was 9-10 before move West.
SP2	Dazzy Vance	1922–1932 1935	Dodgers picked up Vance as part of a package—they *really* wanted his minor-league teammate—and he led National League in strikeouts seven straight seasons.
SP3	Don Drysdale	1956–1969	In the Department of What Might Have Been, how about "What if Koufax and Drysdale had pitched into their late 30's?" Big D basically done at just 32.
SP4	Don Sutton	1966–1980 1988	People forget that the Korean War affected players other than Ted Williams; if Don Newcombe hadn't missed two prime seasons, he might edge Sutton here.
RP	Clem Labine	1950–1960	Supposedly retired Stan Musial 49 straight times; that's a myth, but lefty with the great sinker and curve did hold Musial to 10 hits, 1 homer in 42 at-bats.

		SINGLE SEASON	
		YEARS	**NOTES**
C	Mike Piazza	1997	Campanella won three MVPs, but he never came close to doing what Piazza did in his best season.
1B	Eddie Murray	1990	Yeah, Murray's best really was better than Steve Garvey's or Gil Hodges's or Dolph Camilli's best (but not by much).
2B	Jackie Robinson	1949	He may have played just a hair better in 1951, but in '49 he won the MVP and his team won the pennant by one game.
SS	Maury Wills	1962	Wills gets extra credit for winning the MVP, but then, Pee Wee Reese did bat .316 with a homer in the '49 Series.
3B	Pedro Guerrero	1983	If you just can't believe in Pete, your best bet is any one of four Ron Cey seasons in the middle and late '70s.
LF	Tommy Davis	1962	Zack Wheat was a fine player for a long, long time, but he never quite matched Tommy Davis's one great season. 🐚
CF	Duke Snider	1955	Just as good and maybe better in '53 and '54, but in '55 he also led all World Series players with 4 homers and 7 RBI.
RF	Shawn Green	2001	Other great seasons for Dodger right fielders include Harry Lumley's 1906 and Reggie Smith's 1977.
SP	Sandy Koufax	1966	Only other contender is Dazzy Vance, who in 1924 won 28 games and registered 262 K's, 127 more than anybody else.
RP	Mike Marshall	1974	Joe Black (1952) also a candidate; rookie went 15-4 with 2.15 ERA in relief, then pitched well in 3 World Series *starts*.

		TRADED AWAY	
		TRADED	**NOTES**
C	Mike Piazza	May 15, 1998	Dodgers also traded Ernie Lombardi, shortly after the *beginning* of his Hall of Fame career.
1B	Frank Howard	December 4, 1964	Take your pick, as Dodgers also traded away Jim Gentile, Dick Allen, Bill Buckner, and Paul Konerko.
2B	Eddie Stanky	March 6, 1948	Still a fine player but expendable, what with Jackie Robinson shifting from first base to second.
SS	Bill Dahlen	December 12, 1903	McGraw figured Dahlen as last piece of the puzzle, and sure enough the Giants won pennants in '04 and '05.
3B	Don Hoak	December 9, 1955	Traded to Cubs in five-player deal, later become something of a star with Pirates for a few years.
LF	Tommy Davis	November 29, 1966	Only 27 but his big years were far behind him; did hang around for another decade, though.
CF	Larry Hisle	October 26, 1972	Dodgers parked Hisle in Albuquerque for a season before trading him to Cards, who traded him to Twins.
RF	Roy Cullenbine	May 27, 1940	Cullenbine was traded five times in five years—anybody know why?—and this was the first.
SP	Burleigh Grimes	January 9, 1927	Longtime ace stumbled in '25 and '26, but bounced back after trade and won 94 games over next 5 years.
RP	John Wetteland	November 25, 1991	Ron Perranoski enjoyed some fine seasons after going to Twins, and Mike Marshall got traded too early.

🐚 In 1962, Tommy Davis batted .346, hit twenty-seven homers, and wound up with *153 RBI*; the homers and RBI were career highs, by far.

Davis played fourteen more seasons, and never drove in even ninety runs in one of those seasons. However, he did hit .326 in 1963 to win another batting title, and he would top .300 in four other seasons. So he wasn't a one-year wonder. Still, he was never anything like a star after 1963. He did miss most of 1965 after he broke his leg, and this injury is often the explanation for why Davis never won a batting title after 1963, when he was still only twenty-four years old.

There's a problem with this explanation, though . . . Davis played slightly *better* in the season after he broke his leg than he had the season before. In 1964, Davis batted .275 with a 708 OPS. In 1966, he batted .313 with a 730 OPS. And in 1967 with the Mets, he batted .302 with a 782 OPS.

Davis's power numbers went way down in 1968, and over the next eight seasons he played for seven different teams. He kept getting shots because he could always hit for average and people still remembered the great year. But I believe that his inability to control the strike zone—he never drew more than 38 walks in a season—cost a very talented man a great career.

On June 29, 1971, the Atlanta Braves released ancient knuckleballer Hoyt Wilhelm. It looked like Wilhelm's professional career, which had begun nearly thirty years earlier, was over.

Except Tommy Lasorda, managing the Dodgers' Triple-A farm club in Spokane, got a bright idea.

"I wanted to sign Hoyt Wilhelm to pitch for the Spokane Indians . . . I believed he could still pitch. I knew he would be a tremendous gate attraction. I thought he would really be able to help Charlie Hough, who was continuing to have problems controlling his own knuckleball. And finally, I liked the idea of managing a player who was older than I was."

So Lasorda signed his old buddy for $2,000 per month. Wilhelm could still pitch, and he did help Hough. In that order. As Hough recalled, "I listened to him and started pitching better than ever. And . . . when the Dodgers needed a relief pitcher, they called up Wilhelm. I had lost my job to a forty-seven-year-old man."

Forty-nine, actually. Wilhelm had been lying about his age for a long time. He was forty-eight when he signed with Spokane, and forty-nine when the Dodgers purchased his contract. He pitched well down the stretch, but struggled in 1972 and pitched his last game on July 10, just a few weeks shy of his fiftieth birthday.

		ALL-BUST	
		YEARS	NOTES
C	Todd Hundley	1999–2000	Batted .207 in '99, came back with solid numbers in 2000, but throwing woes drove fans to distraction.
1B	Greg Brock	1982–1986	Slugged .600 in four minor-league seasons, but never came close to filling Garvey's big spikes.
2B	Juan Samuel	1990–1992	He was what he was, but his "great tools" led people to expect so much more. . . .
SS	José Offerman	1990–1995	Dodgers did a lot of dumb things in the 1990s, and force-feeding Offerman was one of the dumbest.
3B	Bob Bailey	1967–1968	Decent hitter with Pirates and Expos before and after, but batted exactly .227 in both seasons as Dodger.
LF	Billy Ashley	1992–1997	In 1994, batted .345 with 37 homers in Triple-A, but strikeouts ate him alive in the majors.
CF	Pete Reiser	1940–1942 1946–1948	Best player in the league at 22, but couldn't stop running into walls and it killed his career.
RF	Darryl Strawberry	1991–1993	L.A. native signed big five-year deal as free agent, then gave the Dodgers one good year and two poor ones.
SP	Darren Dreifort	1994–2002	Dodgers gave him crazy contract after 2000, and then he missed half of 2001 and all of 2002.
RP	Steve Howe	1980–1985	One of game's great relievers, but drugs cost him entire 1984 season, and Dodgers finally dumped him in '85.

		USED-TO-BE-GREAT	
		YEARS	NOTES
C	Gary Carter	1991	Easy choice, but Chief Meyers (1916–17) had been NL's best-hitting catcher just a few years before Dodger stint.
1B	Eddie Murray	1997	Boog Powell (1977), Ed Konetchy (1919–21), and George Kelly (1932) all spent some golden years as Dodgers.
2B	Tony Lazzeri	1939	Supposed to bring some of "that old Yankee spirit," but released in the spring after playing only 14 games.
SS	Arky Vaughan	1942–1943 1947–1948	Still playing well in 1943, when he was 31, but quit after an argument with manager Leo Durocher.
3B	Ken Boyer	1968–1969	In 1936, Hall of Famer Freddie Lindstrom finished his career with 26 games as left fielder for Dodgers.
LF	Cesar Cedeño	1986	Just two years removed from 191 RBI, Hack Wilson (1932–34) looked good for a while, but tailed off quickly.
CF	Eric Davis	1992–1993	Devon White and Marquis Grissom recently held the job, and Lloyd Waner got into 15 games in wartime '44.
RF	Paul Waner	1941 1943–1944	Though 40 and 41 in second stint, showed great eye and posted .406 OBP; briefly reunited with brother Lloyd.
SP	Juan Marichal	1975	Other ex-greats to pitch for Dodgers: Waite Hoyt (1937–38), Jim Bunning (1969), and Ed Reulbach (1913–14).
RP	Hoyt Wilhelm	1971–1972	Also, Jesse Orosco played key role for '88 champs, returned in '01 and pitched well at 44 and 45!

ALL-NAME		YEARS	NOTES
M	"The Lip" Leo Durocher	1939–1946 1948	His Yankee teammates called him "Lippy" (among other, less savory things), and sportswriters shortened it.
C	"Gabby" John Roseboro	1957–1967	They named him "Gabby" because he didn't talk much; also known as "Mr. Cool" and (of course) "Rosy."
1B	"Mr. Perfect" Steve Garvey	1969–1982	Used derisively by teammates; took on new meaning when the world learned about all those offspring. . . .
2B	"Junior" Jim Gilliam	1953–1966	Nicknamed by his teammates on the Baltimore Elite Giants because he was the youngest player on the squad.
SS	"Mousey" Maury Wills	1959–1966 1969–1972	Weighed 165, and "Mousey" was short for "Mighty Mouse," which is what fans called him.
3B	"Penguin" Ron Cey	1971–1982	He picked this up in college, and it stuck because he had that low center of gravity and did run like a penguin.
LF	"Ducky" Joe Medwick	1940–1943 1946	Because a girl thought he swam like a duck; he preferred "Mickey," and players called him "Muscles."
CF	"Comet" Willie Davis	1960–1973	Overshadowed by Wills, but speedy Davis covered a lot of ground in center and stole 398 bases in his career.
RF	"Skoonj" Carl Furillo	1946–1960	Furillo was something less than fast, and "Skoonj" was short for *scungilli* . . . or "snail" in Italian.
SP	"Super Jew" Sandy Koufax	1956–1966	Also on the mid-'60s Dodgers, Larry Sherry was "Rude Jew" and his brother Norm was "Happy Jew."
RP	"The Vulture" Phil Regan	1966–1968	Went 14-1 in '66, which led Koufax to come up with this; Regan received rubber vultures in the mail.

TOP FIVE SEASONS

YEAR 1955 **RECORD** 98-55
BEST HITTER Duke Snider, Roy Campanella (MVP)
BEST PITCHER Don Newcombe
NOTES When waiting 'til next year finally paid off.

YEAR 1963 **RECORD** 99-63
BEST HITTER Tommy Davis, Jim Gilliam, Maury Wills
BEST PITCHER Sandy Koufax (Cy Young, MVP)
NOTES In new Dodgers' first shot at Yankees, they sweep.

YEAR 1988 **RECORD** 94-67
BEST HITTER Kirk Gibson (MVP)
BEST PITCHER Orel Hershiser (Cy Young)
NOTES Gibby and Bulldog help Dodgers shock Athletics.

YEAR 1965 **RECORD** 97-65
BEST HITTERS Maury Wills, Ron Fairly
BEST PITCHER Sandy Koufax (Cy Young)
NOTES Observant Koufax shuts out Twins in Game 7.

YEAR 1981 **RECORD** 63-47
BEST HITTER Dusty Baker, Ron Cey
BEST PITCHER Fernando Valenzuela (Cy Young, Rookie of the Year)
NOTES Third time's a charm, as Dodgers beat Yankees.

TOP FIVE MANAGERS

MANAGER Walt Alston
YEARS 1954–1976
RECORD 2040-1613 (.558)
NOTES Twenty-three seasons, twenty-three one-year contracts, and seven pennants.

MANAGER Tommy Lasorda
YEARS 1976–1996
RECORD 1599-1439 (.526)
NOTES A master motivator who didn't worry about pitch counts.

MANAGER Wilbert Robinson
YEARS 1914–1931
RECORD 1375-1341 (.506)
NOTES From day one until he left, the Dodgers were the "Robins."

MANAGER Leo Durocher
YEARS 1939–1946, 1948
RECORD 738-565 (.566)
NOTES Never played for McGraw, but managed like him.

MANAGER Charlie Dressen
YEARS 1951–1953
RECORD 298-166 (.642)
NOTES Figured he could manage his way out of anything.

These days when we say that a reliever "vultured" a win, we usually mean that he blew a lead, but got credited—thanks to our brilliantly conceived scoring rules—with a victory when his team went ahead while he was still the pitcher of record.

However, any suggestion that Phil Regan didn't *earn* nearly all fourteen of his wins in 1966 is ridiculous. In those fourteen victories, Regan pitched twenty-eight innings, and in those twenty-eight innings he allowed fourteen hits, four walks, two runs, and *one* earned run.

Only two of Regan's wins came in games that Koufax started, but it was Koufax who gave Regan the nickname. On July 27, Koufax pitched eleven innings against the Phillies but left with the score tied at one. Regan pitched a scoreless twelfth, and the Dodgers won in the bottom of the inning. After which Koufax came up with "Vulture."

And then five days later, it happened again. Koufax was losing 1–0 after seven and got bumped for a pinch hitter. The Dodgers tied the game that inning, then scored four more in the ninth. Another *W* for the Vulture.

Phil Regan and his sinker (or spitter, depending on whom you believe) were great in 1966. Bill James ranks him as the second-most valuable pitcher on the staff, behind only Koufax, and I think that's just about right.

CAMPY

Bill James says that Roy Campanella was the fourth-greatest catcher who ever played in the major leagues, and I'm not going to tell you that Bill was wrong.

Still, you look at Campanella's entry in *Total Baseball,* and it doesn't look like the entry for the fourth-greatest anything. Only ten seasons, and a few of those were stinkers. Aside from the stinkers, there were a couple of other seasons that were less than scintillating. So Campanella's status as one of the all-time greatest catchers is based, essentially, on five seasons.

They were five damn good seasons, though. After three of them—1951, 1953, 1955—he was named the National League's Most Valuable Player. Throw in the other two—1949 and '50—and in those five seasons Campanella hit 159 homers and drove in 528 runs.

Campanella's career was very brief by Hall of Fame standards. The aforementioned ten seasons included only 1,161 hits which, again, is very low by Hall of Fame standards. It's possible that despite those five brilliant seasons and those three MVP Awards, Campanella might not be in the Hall of Fame if not for some mitigating circumstances.

Which there were, of course. Campanella didn't play his first game for the Dodgers until he was twenty-six years old. Why? Because while his father was of Italian heritage, his mother was black. Campanella looked like he was somewhere in between, and of course that was enough to keep a man out of Organized Baseball until 1946, when Jackie Robinson signed with the Dodgers and joined their Montreal farm club.

Would Campanella have reached the majors before 1948, if not for segregation? Given what he accomplished once he got there, you have to think that if not for the color line, Campanella would have reached the majors at least four years before he actually did. He joined the Baltimore Elite Giants—one of the better all-black teams around—when he was still a teenager, and at twenty-two and twenty-three he ranked as one of the stars in the Negro National League. I doubt if Campanella would have been a star in *the* National League when he was that young, but he certainly would have been able to pad his career stats.

Then there's the way his career ended. As most of you know, Campanella's car slid off the road and he was paralyzed for the rest of his life. This happened after he'd picked out a house in California, but before he had a chance to actually play a game in Los Angeles. And he was going to play in Los Angeles. Though he was thirty-six, Campanella was still considered a big star and a big part of the team.

That said, I don't think the accident had a major impact on Campanella's career numbers. Thirty-six is old for a catcher, he was coming off two straight poor seasons, and the Dodgers had John Roseboro waiting in the wings. What's more, the Dodgers' new temporary home, Memorial Coliseum, would likely have been a very tough place for Campanella to hit. If anything—and I don't mean to sound callous or anything—getting paralyzed may have helped Campy's image, as his decline phase lasted two seasons instead of four or five.

Bill has him fourth, and I've got him fifth. My list: Bench, Berra, Cochrane, Piazza, and Campanella.

Roy Campanella
National Baseball Library, Cooperstown, New York

New York / San Francisco Giants

		ALL-TIME	
		YEARS	NOTES
C	Roger Bresnahan	1902–1908	Mostly remembered for introducing shin guards to the major leagues, but also experimented with a batting helmet and was a hell of a player besides.
1B	Willie McCovey	1959–1973 1977–1980	A fantastic position for the franchise, with McCovey joined by greats George Kelly, Bill Terry, Johnny Mize, Orlando Cepeda, and Will Clark.
2B	Jeff Kent	1997–2002	The best of the Giants' old-time second basemen was Frankie Frisch, but I'm partial to Larry Doyle, who said, "Gee, it's great to be young and a Giant."
SS	Travis Jackson	1922–1936	Have to go with the Hall of Famer who spent his entire career as a Giant, but Dick Bartell (1935–38) was better than Jackson at his best.
3B	Matt Williams	1987–1996	Freddy Lindstrom is in the Hall of Fame, but the Giants also have a great "lost" third baseman in Art Devlin (1904–1911), a speedy hitter with an outstanding glove.
LF	Barry Bonds	1993–2002	Great spot for the Giants until the early 1940s, with George Burns, Irish Meusel, and Jo-Jo Moore doing excellent work for long stretches.
CF	Willie Mays	1951–1972	A testament to what made Mays so great: he's the only player in history to hit 4 home runs in one game (4/30/1961) and three triples in another (9/15/1960).
RF	Mel Ott	1926–1947	He wasn't Willie Mays or Barry Bonds, but he was a great player, behind only Ruth, Aaron, and Robinson among the game's greatest right fielders.
SP1	Christy Mathewson	1900–1916	Between them, the Mathewson brothers won 372 games for Giants: 0 for Henry, 372 for Christy; that's just trivia, of course, and not befitting the great Matty.
SP2	Carl Hubbell	1928–1943	From 1933 through '37, the southpaw screwball artist won 115 games, lost 50, and in the process earned two MVP Awards and the nickname "Meal Ticket."
SP3	Juan Marichal	1960–1973	"This guy is a natural. He's got ideas about what he wants to do and then he goes and does it. He amazes me."—Carl Hubbell; Marichal thrice won 25 or 26 games
SP4	Freddy Fitzsimmons	1925–1937	Ranks seventh on franchise list with 173 wins, behind the three guys above and a trio of 19th-century fellows; pushed here by Hal Schumacher and Joe McGinnity.
RP	Robb Nen	1998–2002	During World War II, a fellow named Ace Adams pitched in 261 games and twice led the NL in saves, but in '46 he got hammered and went to Mexico.

They don't make 'em like Roger Bresnahan anymore.

Bresnahan first played in the major leagues on August 27, 1897. He was barely eighteen years old, and he was a pitcher. He did well for Washington's National League club, going 4–0 with a 3.95 ERA in a big year for hitters.

And then Bresnahan disappeared for two years, supposedly because he and the Washington club couldn't come to an agreement on his salary. Bresnahan surfaced again in 1900 with the Cubs . . . as a catcher. He would pitch in only three games, for a total of nine innings, over the rest of his long career.

In 1901, Bresnahan jumped to the new American League, with John McGraw's Baltimore Orioles. He was still a catcher. But in 1902, when he jumped, with McGraw and a few other Orioles, back to the National League to play for the Giants, he was playing a lot of third base and outfield. In 1903 and '04, Bresnahan established himself as one of the league's better hitters . . . while playing center field, mostly.

And then in 1905, he became a catcher again. It's been said that McGraw made Bresnahan a catcher at the suggestion of Christy Mathewson. Sounds awfully convenient to me—baseball writers would have given Matty credit for the sun coming up each day, if they thought they could get away with it—but if it *was* Matty's idea, it was one of the best he ever had. Because for the next few years, Bresnahan was the best in the business.

As the 2001 season neared its conclusion, David Schoenfield, my wonderful editor at ESPN.com, asked me to write something about a popular question: "Is Barry Bonds having the greatest season by any player, *ever?*"

Without going back to check, I honestly don't have any idea what I wrote. So what follows is, as far as I know, completely original. . . .

The answer? I don't have any earthly idea, and nobody else does, either. This book, of course, is almost entirely devoted to figuring out if Player A was better than Player B, or Season C was better than Season D. And for the most part, I'm fairly confident in my conclusions. But what I'm saying here is that it's close to impossible to choose between Barry Bonds in 2001 and Babe Ruth in his best season.

For one thing, it's difficult to pick Ruth's best season. Most analysts think it was 1920 or 1921, but there's reason to think that he was just as good in 1923. Bonds certainly has time on his side—it's theoretically more difficult to dominate now than then, plus there's the whole segregation issue—but Babe has the schedule on his side, as he got eight games fewer per season to show his stuff. Basically, I rate them as dead even.

But you know what? Honus Wagner in 1908 might have been better than both of them.

		SINGLE SEASON	
		YEARS	NOTES
C	Roger Bresnahan	1908	His shin guards and padded mask allowed him to catch 139 games; fine hitter topped NL with 83 walks.
1B	Will Clark	1989	Bill Terry and Johnny Mize enjoyed some big years, but the non-Clark campaigns are topped by McCovey's 1969.
2B	Rogers Hornsby	1927	In his one season as Giant, batted .361 with 125 RBI and nearly led club to pennant while serving as interim manager.
SS	Rich Aurilia	2001	Runner-up a battle between Dave Bancroft (1921), Art Fletcher (1917), Dick Bartell (1937), and Alvin Dark (1951).
3B	Art Devlin	1906	Like a lot of players, Devlin's greatness masked by the era in which he played; .299 average with 74 walks and 54 steals.
LF	Barry Bonds	2001	It's all Bonds . . . Barry Bonds. Even leaving aside 2001 and '02, Bonds's 1993 season is the third-best for any Giant ever.
CF	Willie Mays	1954	Could pick any one of five Say Hey! seasons, but we'll go with '54 because of The Catch.
RF	Mel Ott	1934	Or 1935, or 1936, or 1942; analysis doesn't really allow us to choose between Ott's many wonderful, similar seasons.
SP	Christy Mathewson	1905	Great season—league-leading 31 wins and 1.28 ERA—capped by *three* shutouts against A's in World Series.
RP	Robb Nen	1998	In 1952, 30-year-old rookie Hoyt Wilhelm went 15-3 and paced NL with 2.43 ERA in 71 games, all in relief.

		TRADED AWAY	
		TRADED	NOTES
C	Randy Hundley	December 2, 1965	Paul Richards wasn't much of a hitter, but his smarts would have been good to have around in the early '40s.
1B	George Kelly	July 25, 1917	What's going on here? Nine days after losing Kelly to Pirates on waivers, Giants got him *back* the same way.
2B	Rogers Hornsby	January 10, 1928	Traded to Braves for two run-of-the-mill players because the owner got sick of all the hassles.
SS	Dick Bartell	December 6, 1938	Didn't actually have a lot left, but he played every day for another few years and played well.
3B	Heinie Groh	May 22, 1913	Became a star after leaving Giants, returned 10 years later and immediately stopped being a star.
LF	Lefty O'Doul	October 29, 1928	Batted .319 but was a lousy outfielder, got dumped, then batted .373 over four seasons following trade.
CF	Edd Roush	July 20, 1916	Like Groh, was traded to the Reds, became a big star, and wound up with the Giants again toward the end.
RF	Felipe Alou	December 3, 1963	You could also argue for Bobby Bonds, who enjoyed four good seasons after going to Yanks for Murcer.
SP	Burleigh Grimes	February 11, 1928	Straight up for Vic Aldridge; Grimes won 25 games the next season, Aldridge won 4 more games in his *career.*
RP	Hoyt Wilhelm	February 26, 1957	To the Cardinals for Whitey Lockman; Wilhelm was 34, Lockman only 30 . . . and you know the rest.

		YEARS	NOTES
		ALL-BUST	
C	Steve Decker	1990–1992 1996	Heralded prospect batted just .215 in first go-round with club, then .230 with no power in second shot.
1B	J. R. Phillips	1993–1996	We might also consider Gail Harris (1955–1957), who had some power but posted .292 OBP in 181 games.
2B	Rennie Stennett	1980–1981	Coming off two horrible seasons with Pirates, but got a shot with Giants anyway; change of scenery didn't help.
SS	Rich Aurilia	1996	Solid prospect, but got the job before he was ready and didn't manage even .300 in OBP or slugging pct.
3B	Bob Elliott	1952	Coming off All-Star season with Braves, purchased by Giants and batted .228 in the worst season of his career.
LF	Mark Leonard	1990–1992 1994–1995	Impeccable minor-league track record—average, walks, power—but he never got a real shot and didn't hit much.
CF	Jim Thorpe	1913–1915 1917–1919	King of Sweden called him "the greatest athlete in the world," but he wasn't much in the Polo Grounds.
RF	Mose Solomon	1923	Set minor-league record with 49 HR, leading McGraw to hope he'd become the "Jewish Babe Ruth" (he didn't).
SP	Clint Hartung	1947–1952	Based on very little evidence, supposed to be an all-around threat, but didn't threaten much of anything.
RP	Jim Poole	1996–1998	Pitched well down stretch in '96 to earn hefty two-year deal, then posted 6.39 ERA to earn his outright release.

		YEARS	NOTES
		USED-TO-BE-GREAT	
C	Gabby Hartnett	1941	After 19 years with Cubs, joined Giants and batted .300 on the nose as Harry Danning's backup.
1B	Reggie Smith	1982	Al Oliver could roll out of bed and hit line drives, but by the time (1984) he joined the Giants his power was gone.
2B	Joe Morgan	1981–1982	After season in Chicago, Tony Lazzeri returned to NYC in '39 and closed out career with Dodgers *and* Giants.
SS	Dick Groat	1967	In 1930, Dave Bancroft returned to Giants as coach and occasional manager, and also got into 8 games.
3B	Bob Elliott	1952	Coming off All-Star season with Braves, purchased by Giants and batted .228 in 98 games.
LF	Hank Sauer	1957–1959	Joe Carter played brilliantly down stretch in '98, but ended his career with last at-bat in Wild Card playoff.
CF	Duke Snider	1964	Like Snider, Eric Davis (2001) used to be a great center fielder but played right field as part-timer with Giants.
RF	Darryl Strawberry	1994	After nightmare season in L.A., Strawberry started his comeback with 29 productive games with Giants in 1994.
SP	Warren Spahn	1965	Others: Steve Carlton (1986), Carl Mays (1929), Orel Hershiser (1998), and Bobo Newsom (1948).
RP	Rich Gossage	1989	Other notables include Firpo Marberry (1936) and Dan Quisenberry (1990).

To Giants fans, Steve Decker will always be the great catcher who wasn't so great after all. But to Rob Neyer, Steve Decker will always be the guy who broke through the fourth wall at Cheney Stadium.

Let me explain.

On May 12, 1999, I headed down to Tacoma to see the Rainiers host the Edmonton Trappers. The lure was Trappers starter Paul Morse, a knuckleball pitcher (who, I'm sad to say, pitched poorly that evening, and never reached the majors). But playing first base for the Trappers that night was Steve Decker, who'd traveled far past his prospect days and was, by then, just trying to keep his career going.

Decker doubled in the sixth, but he also struck out three times. After the third whiff, one of the local rowdies—he must have been all of twelve years old—sent a happy heckle Decker's way.

Decker was supposed to be in the big leagues, of course, and in the big leagues you just grit your teeth and do your job. But Decker wasn't in the big leagues, and so he said something. And I know what he said, because I wrote it down on my scorecard: *If you weren't sitting with your fat mother, I'd come over there and kick your ass.* Second-funniest thing I've ever heard a player say at the ballpark (first-funniest was when Jeff Huson told me to go fuck myself).

I've got all the World Series participants memorized. I'm not bragging. If anything, I'm embarrassed, because for some reason it took me a long time to memorize the 1913 and 1933 Series. I finally got 'em, though.

Still, I had to think a couple of times . . . have the Giants *really* not won a single World Series since they moved to San Francisco in 1958?

They haven't. In what's now been forty-five seasons, the Giants have played in only two World Series but didn't win either of them. They came very close to winning in 1962, they were swept in the Bay Series in 1989, and of course they came *oh* so close in 2002.

The Giants are not alone. Of the sixteen original Major League Baseball franchises, four others haven't won a World Series since 1958: the Cubs, the White Sox, the Indians, and of course the Red Sox.

The Red Sox have played in three World Series since 1958, and lost all of them. The Indians, like the Giants, have played in two World Series since 1958 and lost both of them. The White Sox played in one World Series since 1958, and lost. And the Cubs . . . well, you know about the Cubs.

So the Giants aren't historically unsuccessful or anything. I was just surprised to see that *all* of their best seasons came before the move west.

ALL-NAME

		YEARS	NOTES
M	"Little Napoleon" John McGraw	1902–1932	In 1891, he played some games in Cuba and became fondly known as *El mono amarillo:* the yellow monkey.
C	"Mule" Dick Dietz	1966–1971	The man with one long, thin eyebrow was stubborn, and played with bandaged head down the stretch in 1971.
1B	"Stretch" Willie McCovey	1959–1973 1977–1980	He was 6'4" with long arms . . . which only proves that a long reach doesn't necessarily make a good first baseman.
2B	"The Brat" Eddie Stanky	1950–1951	John McGraw would have been proud of the combative Stanky, who never met a fight he didn't like.
SS	"Rowdy Richard" Dick Bartell	1935–1938 1941–1943	Another McGraw type, and also known as "Pepper Pot" and "Shortwave" for all of his talking.
3B	"Dirty Al" Al Gallagher	1970–1973	Full name was Alan Mitchell Edward George Patrick Henry Gallagher; also "Pig Pen" and "Filthy McNasty."
LF	"Irish" Emil Meusel	1921–1926	Ah, the power of old-time sportswriters . . . a scribe thought he looked Irish—he wasn't—and the name stuck forever.
CF	"Say Hey" Willie Mays	1951–1972	Invented by sportswriter Barney Kremenko and made popular by broadcaster Russ Hodges; "Buck" to friends.
RF	"Moonlight" Archibald Graham	1905	Nobody knows the meaning of "Moonlight" . . . but Kinsella sure spins a hell of a story, doesn't he?
SP	"Woody" Kirk Rueter	1997–2002	Based on his resemblance to Tom Hanks–voiced character in the *Toy Story* movies (cartoon Woody has more hair).
RP	"Ace" Ace Adams	1941–1946	Giants' wartime relief ace was born that way: Ace Townsend Adams, way back in 1912.

TOP FIVE SEASONS

YEAR 1905	**RECORD** 105-48		
BEST HITTER	Turkey Mike Donlin		
BEST PITCHER	Christy Mathewson		
NOTES	After skipping World Series in '04, Giants win in '05.		

YEAR 1921	**RECORD** 94-59		
BEST HITTERS	Dave Bancroft, Frankie Frisch		
BEST PITCHERS	Art Nehf, Jesse Barnes		
NOTES	"Inside baseball" triumphs over Ruth's clouts.		

YEAR 1954	**RECORD** 97-57		
BEST HITTER	Willie Mays (MVP)		
BEST PITCHER	Johnny Antonelli		
NOTES	Indians won 111 games, but Giants swept Series.		

YEAR 1917	**RECORD** 98-56		
BEST HITTER	George Burns		
BEST PITCHER	Ferdie Schupp		
NOTES	After twelve years and three Series losses, finally a Championship.		

YEAR 1922	**RECORD** 93-61		
BEST HITTER	Dave Bancroft		
BEST PITCHER	Art Nehf		
NOTES	Two straight for Giants over their tenants, the Yankees.		

TOP FIVE MANAGERS

MANAGER	John McGraw
YEARS	1902–1932
RECORD	2583-1790 (.591)
NOTES	Ruled with a strong mind and an iron fist.

MANAGER	Leo Durocher
YEARS	1948–1955
RECORD	637-523 (.549)
NOTES	Never played for McGraw, but managed just like him.

MANAGER	Dusty Baker
YEARS	1993–2002
RECORD	840-715 (.540)
NOTES	Sure, he had Bonds and Kent, but not a lot else.

MANAGER	Bill Terry
YEARS	1932–1941
RECORD	823-661 (.555)
NOTES	Remembered for offhand comment, but managed in three World Series.

MANAGER	Alvin Dark
YEARS	1961–1964
RECORD	366-277 (.569)
NOTES	Was he prejudiced or wasn't he? Only he knows.

THE GREATEST BASEBALL PLAYER IN THE WORLD?

Jim Thorpe's baseball career is always, and I mean *always*, boiled down to five words: "He couldn't hit the curveball."

But I'm allowed more than five words, so if you'll indulge me for a moment . . .

I'm sure you know the story about Thorpe and his gold medals. At the 1912 Summer Olympics, Thorpe won both the pentathlon and the decathlon, leading Sweden's King Gustav V to describe him as "the greatest athlete in the world." However, the following January, the news broke that Thorpe had played professional baseball a few years earlier. Initially, Thorpe claimed that it was only a couple of games, for which he'd been paid barely a pittance. He was forced to return his medals anyway. Later, it was discovered that Thorpe had actually played two seasons in the Eastern Carolina League: forty-four games with Rocky Mount in 1909, forty-five games with Rocky Mount and Fayetteville in 1910.

The funny thing about all the subterfuge in 1913 is that there wasn't any subterfuge when Thorpe actually played. Right there in the 1910 *Reach Guide* is Thorpe's name and his 1909 stat line: 138 at-bats, eleven runs, thirty-five hits, and a .253 batting average. That doesn't sound good, but he actually ranked eleventh in hitting, as the ECL was apparently a wonderful place for pitchers.

Despite Thorpe's lack of experience and his two-year absence from professional baseball, he had many major-league suitors, including the Reds, Pirates, Cardinals . . . and Giants. And the Giants got him, thanks to a contract that supposedly made Thorpe the wealthiest rookie in baseball history.

In *The Days of Mr. McGraw*, Joe Durso wrote that John McGraw "wasn't sure Thorpe could play baseball, but he was very sure that people would pay to find out.

"He was right. People did pay, and they kept paying as the Giants racked up 103 victories against 48 defeats. In the American League, meanwhile, the Boston Red Sox were racking up 105 against 47 defeats. . . ."

Durso's strong suit as a writer was never accuracy, and this passage is certainly no exception. True, the Giants went 103-48 and the Red Sox 105-47 in 1912, but Thorpe didn't join the Giants until 1913. And there's no good evidence to suggest that Thorpe did anything for attendance. Coming off their 1912 pennant and playing nearly as well in 1913, the Giants actually drew slightly fewer fans in Thorpe's first season. And anyway, Thorpe hardly played: nineteen games and thirty-five at-bats. He saw similarly limited action over the next two seasons, mostly as a pinch hitter in 1914, then as a center fielder in 1915.

Actually, Thorpe spent most of the 1915 season playing in the International League, with Jersey City and Harrisburg. Shortly after Jersey City let him go, one scribe wrote, "Thorpe did well at the start and looked mighty good until the pitchers got on to his weakness—curve balls. From that moment the poor Indian never looked at anything else. His batting average shrunk to the size of his hat."

Thorpe spent the entire 1916 season in the minors, this time with Milwaukee in the American Association, and for the first time he showed the speed and strength that had won him so much fame as a football player and track-and-field star. In addition to batting .274, Thorpe hit fourteen triples and ten home runs, and he stole forty-eight bases.

That performance earned him a ticket back to the major leagues. He played for the Giants, then the Reds, then the Giants again, but still didn't hit. In May of 1919, McGraw finally gave up, trading Thorpe to the Braves for pitcher Pat Ragan. In *The Boston Braves*, Harold Kaese wrote of the deal, "Jim Thorpe, a great athlete but ordinary ballplayer, was sent over from New York to finish his brief and unspectacular big-league career by waving weakly at curves."

Well, it wasn't exactly brief. Thorpe spent six seasons—granted, not all of them were full seasons—in the majors. But what's really interesting is that Thorpe played *well* for the

Braves in 1919, batting .327 over the course of sixty games in a year when the league batted .258.

And so ended Jim Thorpe's major-league career.

But here's where it gets interesting. Thorpe did *not* stop playing baseball. In 1920 he played for Akron in the International League, and batted .360. In 1921 he played for Toledo in the American Association, and batted .358. In 1922, he played briefly in the Pacific Coast League, batting .308 in thirty-five games, then dropped down to Hartford-Waterbury in the Eastern League and batted .335 in ninety-six games.

And so ended Thorpe's career as a professional baseball player. But look at those three seasons. He was in his early thirties by then, but if you add up what he did in those four advanced minor leagues, you find that Thorpe batted .351 with a .535 slugging percentage. And so it's very difficult for me to believe that he couldn't have been at least a decent player in the majors during those years.

I'll tell you what I think. I think that Thorpe struggled in the National League for most of his career because he didn't learn to play baseball like most players do. But his athletic skills were so amazing that he *did* eventually learn to play, and probably could have been a pretty good major leaguer for a number of years if he'd been treated as a baseball player rather than a circus freak.

Then again, Thorpe essentially got what he wanted. With various clubs bidding for his services, he signed with the Giants because they offered him more money—three years at $6,000 per season—than anybody else did. And throughout his baseball career, he also played professional football, and was the most famous player in the game. Jim Thorpe was the original Bo Jackson, and for at least a decade he probably *was* the greatest athlete in the world.

Jim Thorpe
National Baseball Library, Cooperstown, New York

WASHINGTON SENATORS / MINNESOTA TWINS

		ALL-TIME	
		YEARS	**NOTES**
C	Earl Battey	1961–1967	Not a strong position for the franchise; Rick Ferrell was the regular for six seasons in separate stints, but his best seasons had already come with Browns and Red Sox.
1B	Harmon Killebrew	1954–1974	And then there's Joe Judge, who manned the initial sack for 15 straight seasons, followed by Joe Kuhel and Mickey Vernon for about 25 years . . . nice stability here.
2B	Rod Carew	1967–1978	Buddy Myer (1925–27, 1929–41) was an outstanding player, one of the 25 greatest second basemen of all time, and after trading him the Senators got him back quickly.
SS	Joe Cronin	1928–1934	It was the era of player-managers, and in 1933 Cronin started at shortstop in the first All-Star Game *and* led the Nationals to the World Series that fall.
3B	Ed Yost	1944 1946–1958	Perhaps a surprise to see Yost instead of Gaetti, but Gaetti just had too many seasons where he wasn't very good; Koskie still a few years away from consideration.
LF	Goose Goslin	1921–1930 1933, 1938	Played in all three of the Senators' World Series—1924, '25, and '33—and hit 7 homers; topped AL with 129 RBI in '24 and .379 batting average in '28.
CF	Kirby Puckett	1984–1995	You know, Stan Spence (1942–44, '46–47) was a hell of a player, but he stopped hitting immediately upon leaving Nats; Clyde Milan also a fine player and for a long time.
RF	Tony Oliva	1962–1976	Oliva *just* edges Hall of Famer Sam Rice, who spent all but one of his 20 seasons with club, batted .349 in 1930 when he was 40, and finished 13 hits short of 3,000.
SP1	Walter Johnson	1907–1927	"He was the only pitcher I ever faced who made the ball whistle . . . Sounded like a bullet from a rifle, sort of a zing, and it made you shaky in the knees."—Ty Cobb
SP2	Bert Blyleven	1970–1976 1985–1988	He pitched brilliantly for lousy teams during his first stint, then returned and played a big part (15-12, 4.01) in '87 when Twins finally won their first World Series.
SP3	Jim Kaat	1959–1973	Might be in the Hall of Fame if not for season-ending injury, suffered while sliding, in early July of 1972, after starting the season 10-2 with a 2.07 ERA.
SP4	Camilo Pascual	1954–1966	Cuban right-hander with Koufax-like stuff struggled in his first few seasons, but from 1959 through '64 he won 100 games and was named to five All-Star teams.
RP	Firpo Marberry	1923–1932 1936	He's one of only seven pitchers with at least 100 career saves and 100 career starts, but the *only* pitcher to serve in both roles at the same time for much of his career.

In 1954, W. W. Norton & Company published a new novel by a writer named Douglas Wallop. Wallop's book was titled *The Year the Yankees Lost the Pennant,* and that title was apt; the Yankees hadn't lost a pennant, or for that matter a World Series, since way back in 1948.

You probably know the premise of Wallop's novel, because it was later turned into a hit Broadway musical and then a popular film. But just in case you haven't seen the movie, an aging Senators fan named Joe Boyd is approached by Satan himself, who offers to transform Joe Boyd into Joe Hardy, the greatest player the game has ever seen. And the Senators, thus fortified, will finally win the pennant (and beat out the Yankees).

And so the story goes.

As it happened, in real life the Yankees *did* lose the pennant in 1954 . . . but not, of course, to the Washington Senators. The Yanks won 103 games that season, but still finished well behind the Indians, who won 111.

Wallop's novel is a lot of fun, but there's one question it never tackles: Would even Joe Hardy have been enough to make contenders out of the Senators? And the answer is, pretty clearly, that he would not. The *closest* the Nats got to first place in those years was seventeen games, in 1952. And friends, the greatest player in the world ain't worth seventeen games.

My friend Rany Jazayerli has argued that Jesse Orosco belongs in the Hall of Fame. If Rany's right, that would arguably make Orosco the *best* reliever traded before the prime of his career.

Granted, it's been a few years and I don't actually remember exactly what Rany's argument *was*. But just looking at Orosco's career, I don't see it.

Sure, he's had some great years. In 1983, he went 13-7 with seventeen saves and a 1.47 ERA in 110 innings. In 1984, he went 10-6 with thirty-one saves. In 1986, he saved twenty-one games during the regular season, then two more in the World Series, including Game 7.

But Orosco didn't pitch well for the Mets in 1987, which cost him his reputation as the sort of pitcher who can finish games. As a result, he hasn't saved ten games in a season since then (at this writing, Orosco hopes to pitch in 2003, when he'll be forty-six). Not that it's hurt his career much, as Orosco spent the next fifteen seasons as a setup man and situational lefty. And for most of those fifteen seasons, he's been quite effective.

But effective enough to earn a plaque in the Hall of Fame? To my way of thinking, it takes more than fifty innings per season for a ticket to Cooperstown, no matter how good those fifty innings were. And you know, they haven't been *that* good.

		SINGLE SEASON		
		YEARS	NOTES	
C	Earl Battey	1963	Not exactly a distinguished spot for the franchise; in 1923, Muddy Ruel batted .316 and posted a .394 OBP.	
1B	Rod Carew	1977	MVP just *barely* edges 1967 edition of Killebrew, who topped loop with 44 homers and 131 walks.	
2B	Chuck Knoblauch	1996	Knoblauch's got stiff competition from batting titlists Carew (still playing second base in 1974) and Buddy Myer (1935).	
SS	Zoilo Versalles	1965	In 1941, Cecil Travis batted .359 and led MLB with 218 hits . . . but nobody noticed because of Williams and DiMaggio.	
3B	Ed Yost	1951	"The Walking Man" did *not* lead league in walks, but he made up for that with 36 doubles; four other seasons about as good.	
LF	Roy Sievers	1957	One of very few players to lead his league in homers (42) and RBI (114) while playing for a last-place team.	
CF	Kirby Puckett	1988	Battle for best non-Kirby season is a dead heat between Clyde Milan (1912) and Stan Spence (1944).	
RF	Tony Oliva	1965	Hall of Famer Sam Rice enjoyed more than a dozen good seasons . . . but never came close to having a great one.	
SP	Walter Johnson	1913	Greatest season of many great seasons: career bests in wins (36), winning pct. (.837), shutouts (11), and ERA (1.14).	
RP	Doug Corbett	1980	Just the year before, Mike Marshall pitched brilliantly: 10 wins and league bests in saves (32) and games (90).	

		TRADED AWAY		
		TRADED	NOTES	
C	Rick Dempsey	October 27, 1972	In the 1990s, the Twins somehow let both Jeff Reed and Damian Miller get away.	
1B	Mickey Vernon	December 14, 1948	Sent to Indians in same lousy deal as Wynn (see below), but at least the Nats got him back before long.	
2B	Chuck Knoblauch	February 6, 1998	Sent to Yankees in exchange for four minor leaguers—including Eric Milton and Cristian Guzmán—and cash.	
SS	Jay Bell	August 1, 1985	Part of deal that brought Blyleven back; anyway, who knew that Bell would hit nearly 200 homers?	
3B	Graig Nettles	December 10, 1969	In Twins' defense, they weren't the only team dumb enough to trade Nettles, and they did get Tiant in return.	
LF	Goose Goslin	June 13, 1930	Just two seasons removed from .379 and batting title, got off to slow start and swapped to Browns for two stars.	
CF	Albie Pearson	May 26, 1959	Posted .354 OBP and took RoY honors in '58, but hit .188 in first 25 games in '59 and was sent off to Orioles.	
RF	Jackie Jensen	December 9, 1953	Nats were smart enough to get him from the Yankees, and dumb enough to trade him to the Red Sox.	
SP	Early Wynn	December 14, 1948	Deemed expendable after 8-19 season, but became one of baseball's best after going to Cleveland.	
RP	Jesse Orosco	December 8, 1978	Traded to Mets before he got a chance to pitch for Twins . . . and *24 years later*, still pitching in the majors.	

		ALL-BUST	
		YEARS	NOTES
C	Butch Wynegar	1978–1982	Looked like a future superstar his first two years, but injuries and mysteries made him huge disappointment.
1B	David McCarty	1993–1995	Third overall pick in '91 draft reached majors in just two years, then batted .226 with 3 homers in 167 games.
2B	Todd Walker	1996–2000	Eighth pick in '94 draft blew through minors, but struggled defensively and didn't get along with T.K.
SS	Cecil Travis	1945–1947	In 1942, he went into the army with a .327 lifetime batting average; after the war, batted just .241.
3B	Harlond Clift	1943–1945	First he got the mumps, then he got thrown from a horse and hurt his shoulder; result was some awful numbers.
LF	Mickey Hatcher	1985–1986	Lousy as part-timer in '81 and '82, earned regular job in '83 and '84, then combined for 678 OPS in '85 and '86.
CF	Darrell Brown	1983–1984	He didn't draw walks, or hit for power, or play great defense . . . but he did keep the position warm for Kirby.
RF	Dave Engle	1981–1982	After two seasons and .285 OBP, Twins realized that his "skills" might be more at home behind the plate.
SP	LaTroy Hawkins	1995–1999	Heralded prospect went 26-44 with *6.11 ERA* as starter before Twins finally sent him to the bullpen in 2000.
RP	Steve Howe	1985	Still had the amazing left arm, but also still had the coke problem and posted 6.16 ERA before relapse and release.

		USED-TO-BE-GREAT	
		YEARS	NOTES
C	John Roseboro	1968–1969	Other candidates are Randy Hundley (1974) and Minnesotan Terry Steinbach (1997–99).
1B	George Sisler	1928	Played just 20 games—and scored 1 run—before moving on to Braves, for whom he enjoyed his last good season.
2B	Johnny Pesky	1954	Lifetime .307 hitter closed out fine career with Nats, batting .253 in 49 games.
SS	Kid Elberfeld	1910–1911	Former star with Tigers and Highlanders put in a couple of good years with Senators before calling it quits.
3B	Harlond Clift	1943–1945	Longtime Browns stalwart finished with Senators, batting .211 in '45 as club finished just shy of pennant.
LF	Goose Goslin	1938	Didn't age nearly as well as Sam Rice; in third stay with Nats, was only 37 but batted .158 in last season.
CF	Tris Speaker	1927	"The Grey Eagle" was 39 but looked 10 years older; batted .327 with 43 doubles in 19th full season.
RF	Dave Winfield	1993–1994	Wally Post, who'd enjoyed some fine seasons in Cincy, played 21 games for the Twins in '63 and batted .191.
SP	Steve Carlton	1987–1988	Only other solid candidates are Lefty Gomez (1943), who pitched just five innings, and Joe Niekro (1987–88).
RP	Firpo Marberry	1936	Owner Clark Griffith loved to bring back his old stars, and so Fred went out with 5 games and 14 innings.

It's true that most ballplayers who served in the military during World War II didn't come under enemy fire. But you know, a lot of them did. And it may be that no major leaguer's career suffered more because of the war than Cecil Travis.

Travis came up with the Senators in 1933, and from day one he could hit for average. From 1934 through 1940, he batted at least .317 in every season but one. Entering the '41 season, Travis owned a .322 lifetime average.

In 1941, he went nuts, batting .359 with a league-best 218 hits and career highs in doubles (thirty-nine), triples (nineteen), and home runs (seven). In some (most?) seasons, Travis's performance would have made him a serious MVP candidate. But of course, 1941 was the year of DiMaggio and Williams, so nobody really noticed the .359-hitting shortstop on the fifth-place team.

Then came the war, and Travis didn't spend it in Hawaii, playing baseball to entertain the troops. It's been said many times that he suffered frozen feet during the Battle of the Bulge, but Travis himself said he got medical attention before actually suffering frostbite. What can't be disputed is that when Travis came back, he just wasn't the same. The war cost him nearly four full seasons, and he could manage only a .252 average in his only postwar season as a regular.

It's a story, like many stories, that was reported and then quickly forgotten. But if it happened today . . .

Albert Williams was born in 1954, in Nicaragua. He started playing baseball when he was seventeen and eventually caught the eye of Pirates scout Calvin Byron. In 1975, he arrived in the States to play for Pittsburgh's Class A team in Charleston, South Carolina. He spent two seasons with Charleston, and didn't pitch particularly well.

At that point, Al's baseball future didn't look too bright . . . and it looked a lot less bright the following winter, when he couldn't get a visa to return to the States from Nicaragua.

So Williams joined, and fought with, the Sandinistas.

For those of you too young to remember, the Sandinistas were fighting to liberate the country from a sick bastard named General Anastasio Somoza. In 1979, the Sandinistas deposed Somoza's regime, and Williams soon left Nicaragua for Panama, where he signed on with a team in the Inter-American League. Williams later played in Venezuela . . . where the Twins found him. He opened the 1980 season with Minnesota's farm club in Toledo, and on May 7 he made his major-league debut. He pitched well for that season and the next three, but his career petered out in 1984.

Oh, I almost forgot . . . they called him "Sandinista Al."

ALL-NAME			
		YEARS	NOTES
M	"Skip" Gene Mauch	1976–1980	"Skip" is, of course, a universal nickname for managers . . . but Mauch's dad called him "Skipper" early on.
C	"Boileryard" William Clarke	1901–1904	Regrettably, the origin of this wonderful moniker has been lost to time; the franchise's first regular catcher.
1B	"Killer" Harmon Killebrew	1954–1974	Referred only to his power, as Harm was considered one of the nicest guys in the game.
2B	"Al Newman" Albert Newman	1987–1991	I'm sad to report that his first name was not Alfred, nor was his middle initial *E*; still, it's fun to think about.
SS	"Zorro" Zoilo Versalles	1959–1967	Like TV's Zorro, popular at the time, Versalles was a bandit; in his case, stealing base hits with his glove.
3B	"The Walking Man" Ed Yost	1944 1946–1958	Only four men—all power hitters—drew more walks in a season than Yost: Bonds, Ruth, Williams, McGwire.
LF	"Goose" Leon Goslin	1921–1930 1933, 1938	He had a big nose, and sportswriter Denmar Thompson thought Goslin looked like a goose; also, it sounds good.
CF	"Deerfoot" Clyde Milan	1907–1922	Topped AL with 88 steals in 1912 and 75 in 1913, and he finished his long career with 495 bags.
RF	"Show Boat" George Fisher	1923–1924	Got the reputation as a showboat in the minor leagues, and supposedly once hit safely in 10 straight at-bats.
SP	"Big Train" Walter Johnson	1907–1927	Invented in 1915 by *Wash. Post*'s Bud Milliken; called "Barney" by friends, after auto racer Barney Oldfield.
RP	"Everyday Eddie" Eddie Guardado	1993–*2002*	Led the American League with 83 appearances in 1996; workload dropped off afterward, but nickname stuck.

TOP FIVE SEASONS	
YEAR	1987 RECORD 85-77
BEST HITTER	Kirby Puckett
BEST PITCHER	Frank Viola (Cy Young)
NOTES	Homer Hankies help Twins beat Cardinals in Series.
YEAR	1991 RECORD 95-67
BEST HITTERS	Chili Davis, Kirby Puckett
BEST PITCHER	Kevin Tapani
NOTES	Great Game 7 leaves Twins atop Braves.
YEAR	1965 RECORD 102-60
BEST HITTERS	Zoilo Versalles (MVP), Tony Oliva
BEST PITCHERS	Mudcat Grant, Jim Kaat
NOTES	In only their fifth year, Twins reach World Series.
YEAR	2002 RECORD 94-67
BEST HITTERS	Torii Hunter, Jacque Jones
BEST PITCHERS	Rick Reed, J. C. Romero
NOTES	From contraction to the ALCS in less than a year.
YEAR	1969 RECORD 97-65
BEST HITTER	Harmon Killebrew
BEST PITCHERS	Jim Perry, Ron Perranoski
NOTES	Swept by powerhouse Orioles in first ALCS.

TOP FIVE MANAGERS	
MANAGER	Tom Kelly
YEARS	1986–2001
RECORD	1140-1244 (.478)
NOTES	Two Championships . . . followed by a long dry spell.
MANAGER	Sam Mele
YEARS	1961–1967
RECORD	524-436 (.546)
NOTES	Did a fine job, but never managed another club.
MANAGER	Bucky Harris
YEARS	1924–1928, 1935–1942, 1950–1954
RECORD	1,336-1,416 (.485)
NOTES	If nothing else, the Boy Wonder has time on his side.
MANAGER	Bill Rigney
YEARS	1970–1972
RECORD	208-184
NOTES	Great 1970 season ended by Orioles in LCS.
MANAGER	Gene Mauch
YEARS	1976–1980
RECORD	378-394 (.490)
NOTES	Handicapped by an owner who wouldn't play ball.

. . . SECOND IN THE AMERICAN LEAGUE

The Washington Senators were, for most of their history, *not* a joke.

That's the perception, though. Why? I think it's because the most recent editions of the team were pretty bad. Before moving to Minnesota in 1961, the Senators had finished below .500 (far below .500, most of the time) for seven straight seasons. And the "new" Senators—the expansion team that moved in when the old Senators moved—finished below .500 (far below .500, most of the time) every season but one before moving to Texas in 1972. From 1954 through 1971, the two different Senators won forty-one percent of their games, which of course is pretty awful.

Then there's the little ditty about the Senators: "First in peace, first in war, last in the American League."

You know what's funny about that, though? From 1910 through 1943, the Washingtons didn't finish last in the American League even once. From 1910 through 1954—that's forty-five seasons—the Nats finished last three times. Things did get ugly in 1955, and they stayed that way for a long time. But for nearly half a century, Washington was a perfectly respectable American League franchise, right up there with everybody except the Yankees.

So where did the ditty come from?

The Senators—by the way, in 1906 the club was officially named the "Nationals," but the names were used interchangeably until the 1950s, when "Nationals" was discarded—were truly awful for the first nine seasons of their existence. After finishing sixth in 1901 and 1902, the club finished last, last, next to last, next to last, last, next to last, and last. Over those seven seasons, 1903 through 1909, the Washington club won 358 games and lost 686, "good" for a .343 winning percentage.

The Nationals returned to modest respectability in 1910 (66-85), and in 1912, under new manager Clark Griffith, they vaulted all the way to second place with a 91-61 record (their first ever above .500). But it was too late to avoid the line. In 1909, sportswriter Charles Dryden had come up with the "First in peace, first in war" line, and it stuck, even though it would be another thirty-five years until the Senators would actually finish last in the American League again.

We tend to remember beginnings and ends, and it's certainly true that the American League's first Washington baseball club had a lousy beginning and a lousy end. But the middle lasted quite a lot of years, and it wasn't so bad at all.

Goose Goslin, Heinie Manush, and Fred Schulte in 1933. They scored 310 runs, and the Nats won the pennant.
National Baseball Library, Cooperstown, New York

Sources for this chapter include Tom Deveaux's The Washington Senators, 1901–1971 *(McFarland & Co., 2001) and Shirley Povich's* The Washington Senators: An Informal History *(G. P. Putnam's Sons, 1954).*

APPENDIX
YEAR-BY-YEAR
LINEUPS

APPENDIX

Los Angeles Angels (American League), 1961–1964
California Angels (American League), 1965–1996
Anaheim Angels (American League), 1997–Present

YEAR	MANAGER	C	1B	2B	SS	3B	LF	CF	RF	DH
1961	Bill Rigney	Earl Averill	Steve Bilko	K. Aspromonte	Joe Koppe	Ed Yost	Leon Wagner	Ken Hunt	Albie Pearson	
1962	Bill Rigney	Buck Rodgers	Lee Thomas	Billy Moran	Joe Koppe	Felix Torres	Leon Wagner	Albie Pearson	G. Thomas	
1963	Bill Rigney	Buck Rodgers	Lee Thomas	Billy Moran	Jim Fregosi	Felix Torres	Leon Wagner	Albie Pearson	Bob Perry	
1964	Bill Rigney	Buck Rodgers	Joe Adcock	Bobby Knoop	Jim Fregosi	Felix Torres	Willie Smith	Jim Piersall	Lou Clinton	
1965	Bill Rigney	Buck Rodgers	Vic Power	Bobby Knoop	Jim Fregosi	Paul Schaal	Willie Smith	Jose Cardenal	Albie Pearson	
1966	Bill Rigney	Buck Rodgers	Norm Siebern	Bobby Knoop	Jim Fregosi	Paul Schaal	R. Reichardt	Jose Cardenal	E. Kirkpatrick	
1967	Bill Rigney	Buck Rodgers	Don Mincher	Bobby Knoop	Jim Fregosi	Paul Schaal	R. Reichardt	Jose Cardenal	Jimmie Hall	
1968	Bill Rigney	Buck Rodgers	Don Mincher	Bobby Knoop	Jim Fregosi	A. Rodriguez	R. Reichardt	Vic Davalillo	Roger Repoz	
1969	Lefty Phillips	Joe Azcue	Jim Spencer	Sandy Alomar	Jim Fregosi	A. Rodriguez	R. Reichardt	Jay Johnstone	Bill Voss	
1970	Lefty Phillips	Joe Azcue	Jim Spencer	Sandy Alomar	Jim Fregosi	K. McMullen	Alex Johnson	Jay Johnstone	Roger Repoz	
1971	Lefty Phillips	Buck Rodgers	Jim Spencer	Sandy Alomar	Jim Fregosi	K. McMullen	T. Gonzalez	Ken Berry	Roger Repoz	
1972	Del Rice	Art Kusnyer	Bob Oliver	Sandy Alomar	Leo Cardenas	K. McMullen	Vada Pinson	Ken Berry	Lee Stanton	
1973	Bob Winkles	Jeff Torborg	Mike Epstein	Sandy Alomar	Rudy Meoli	Al Gallagher	Vada Pinson	Ken Berry	Lee Stanton	F. Robinson
1974	D. Williams	E. Rodriguez	John Doherty	Denny Doyle	Dave Chalk	Paul Schaal	Joe Lahoud	Mi. Rivers	Lee Stanton	F. Robinson
1975	D. Williams	E. Rodriguez	Bruce Bochte	Jerry Remy	Mike Miley	Dave Chalk	Morris Nettles	Mi. Rivers	Lee Stanton	Tom Harper
1976	D. Williams	A. Etchebarren	Bruce Bochte	Jerry Remy	Dave Chalk	Ron Jackson	Lee Stanton	Rusty Torres	Bobby Bonds	Tommy Davis
1977	Sherry/Garcia	T. Humphrey	Tony Solaita	Jerry Remy	R. Mulliniks	Dave Chalk	Joe Rudi	Gil Flores	Bobby Bonds	Don Baylor
1978	Jim Fregosi	B. Downing	Ron Fairly	Bobby Grich	Dave Chalk	C. Lansford	Joe Rudi	Rick Miller	L. Bostock	Don Baylor
1979	Jim Fregosi	B. Downing	Rod Carew	Bobby Grich	B. Campaneris	C. Lansford	Joe Rudi	Rick Miller	Dan Ford	Don Baylor
1980	Jim Fregosi	Tom Donohue	Rod Carew	Bobby Grich	Fred Patek	C. Lansford	Joe Rudi	Rick Miller	Larry Harlow	J. Thompson
1981	Gene Mauch	Ed Ott	Rod Carew	Bobby Grich	Rick Burleson	Butch Hobson	B. Downing	Fred Lynn	Dan Ford	Don Baylor
1982	Gene Mauch	Bob Boone	Rod Carew	Bobby Grich	Tim Foli	D. DeCinces	B. Downing	Fred Lynn	R. Jackson	Don Baylor
1983	J. McNamara	Bob Boone	Rod Carew	Bobby Grich	Tim Foli	D. DeCinces	B. Downing	Fred Lynn	E. Valentine	R. Jackson
1984	J. McNamara	Bob Boone	Rod Carew	Rob Wilfong	D. Schofield	D. DeCinces	B. Downing	Gary Pettis	Fred Lynn	R. Jackson
1985	Gene Mauch	Bob Boone	Rod Carew	Bobby Grich	D. Schofield	D. DeCinces	B. Downing	Gary Pettis	Ruppert Jones	R. Jackson
1986	Gene Mauch	Bob Boone	Wally Joyner	Rob Wilfong	D. Schofield	D. DeCinces	B. Downing	Gary Pettis	Ruppert Jones	R. Jackson
1987	Gene Mauch	Bob Boone	Wally Joyner	M. McLemore	D. Schofield	D. DeCinces	Jack Howell	Gary Pettis	Devon White	B. Downing
1988	Cookie Rojas	Bob Boone	Wally Joyner	Johnny Ray	D. Schofield	Jack Howell	Tony Armas	Devon White	Chili Davis	B. Downing
1989	Doug Rader	Lance Parrish	Wally Joyner	Johnny Ray	D. Schofield	Jack Howell	Chili Davis	Devon White	C. Washington	B. Downing
1990	Doug Rader	Lance Parrish	Wally Joyner	Johnny Ray	D. Schofield	Jack Howell	D. Bichette	Devon White	D. Winfield	B. Downing
1991	Doug Rader	Lance Parrish	Wally Joyner	Luis Sojo	D. Schofield	Gary Gaetti	Luis Polonia	D. Gallagher	D. Winfield	Dave Parker
1992	Buck Rodgers	M. Fitzgerald	Lee Stevens	Luis Sojo	G. DiSarcina	Gary Gaetti	Luis Polonia	Junior Felix	Chad Curtis	Hubie Brooks
1993	Buck Rodgers	Greg Myers	J.T. Snow	Torey Lovullo	G. DiSarcina	R. Gonzales	Luis Polonia	Chad Curtis	Tim Salmon	Chili Davis
1994	M. Lachemann	Chris Turner	J.T. Snow	H. Reynolds	G. DiSarcina	Spike Owen	Jim Edmonds	Chad Curtis	Tim Salmon	Chili Davis
1995	M. Lachemann	J. Fabregas	J.T. Snow	D. Easley	G. DiSarcina	Tony Phillips	G. Anderson	Jim Edmonds	Tim Salmon	Chili Davis

YEAR	MANAGER	C	1B	2B	SS	3B	LF	CF	RF	DH
1996	M. Lachemann	J. Fabregas	J.T. Snow	R. Velarde	G. DiSarcina	George Arias	G. Anderson	Jim Edmonds	Tim Salmon	Chili Davis
1997	Terry Collins	Chad Kreuter	Darin Erstad	Luis Alicea	G. DiSarcina	Dave Hollins	G. Anderson	Jim Edmonds	Tim Salmon	Eddie Murray
1998	Terry Collins	Matt Walbeck	Cecil Fielder	J. Baughman	G. DiSarcina	Dave Hollins	Darin Erstad	Jim Edmonds	G. Anderson	Tim Salmon
1999	Terry Collins	Matt Walbeck	Darin Erstad	R. Velarde	G. DiSarcina	Troy Glaus	O. Palmeiro	G. Anderson	Tim Salmon	Mo Vaughn
2000	Mike Scioscia	Bengie Molina	Mo Vaughn	A. Kennedy	Benji Gil	Troy Glaus	Darin Erstad	G. Anderson	Tim Salmon	Scott Spiezio
2001	Mike Scioscia	Bengie Molina	Scott Spiezio	A. Kennedy	D. Eckstein	Troy Glaus	Darin Erstad	G. Anderson	Tim Salmon	O. Palmeiro
2002	Mike Scioscia	Bengie Molina	Scott Spiezio	A. Kennedy	D. Eckstein	Troy Glaus	G. Anderson	Darin Erstad	Tim Salmon	Brad Fullmer

ASTROS BY POSITION, YEAR BY YEAR

Houston Colt '45s a.k.a. Colts (National League), 1962–1964
Houston Astros (National League), 1965–Present

YEAR	MANAGER	C	1B	2B	SS	3B	LF	CF	RF
1962	Harry Craft	Hal Smith	Norm Larker	J. Amalfitano	Bob Lillis	Aspromonte	Al Spangler	Carl Warwick	R. Mejias
1963	Harry Craft	John Bateman	Rusty Staub	Ernie Fazio	Bob Lillis	Aspromonte	Al Spangler	Howie Goss	Carl Warwick
1964	Harry Craft	Jerry Grote	Walt Bond	Nellie Fox	Eddie Kasko	Aspromonte	Al Spangler	Mike White	Joe Gaines
1965	Lum Harris	Ron Brand	Walt Bond	Joe Morgan	Bob Lillis	Aspromonte	Lee Maye	Jimmy Wynn	Rusty Staub
1966	Grady Hatton	John Bateman	C. Harrison	Joe Morgan	S. Jackson	Aspromonte	Lee Maye	Jimmy Wynn	Rusty Staub
1967	Grady Hatton	John Bateman	E. Mathews	Joe Morgan	S. Jackson	Aspromonte	Ron Davis	Jimmy Wynn	Rusty Staub
1968	Harry Walker	John Bateman	Rusty Staub	Denis Menke	Hector Torres	Doug Rader	Jimmy Wynn	Ron Davis	Norm Miller
1969	Harry Walker	J. Edwards	Curt Blefary	Joe Morgan	Denis Menke	Doug Rader	Jesus Alou	Jimmy Wynn	Norm Miller
1970	Harry Walker	J. Edwards	Bob Watson	Joe Morgan	Denis Menke	Doug Rader	Jimmy Wynn	Cesar Cedeno	Jesus Alou
1971	Harry Walker	J. Edwards	Denis Menke	Joe Morgan	R. Metzger	Doug Rader	Jesus Alou	Cesar Cedeno	Jimmy Wynn
1972	Harry Walker	J. Edwards	Lee May	Tom Helms	R. Metzger	Doug Rader	Bob Watson	Cesar Cedeno	Jimmy Wynn
1973	Leo Durocher	Skip Jutze	Lee May	Tom Helms	R. Metzger	Doug Rader	Bob Watson	Cesar Cedeno	Jimmy Wynn
1974	Pr. Gomez	Milt May	Lee May	Tom Helms	R. Metzger	Doug Rader	Bob Watson	Cesar Cedeno	Greg Gross
1975	Pr. Gomez	Milt May	Bob Watson	Rob Andrews	R. Metzger	Doug Rader	W. Howard	Cesar Cedeno	Greg Gross
1976	Bill Virdon	Ed Herrmann	Bob Watson	Rob Andrews	R. Metzger	Enos Cabell	Jose Cruz	Cesar Cedeno	Greg Gross
1977	Bill Virdon	Joe Ferguson	Bob Watson	Art Howe	R. Metzger	Enos Cabell	Terry Puhl	Cesar Cedeno	Jose Cruz
1978	Bill Virdon	Luis Pujols	Bob Watson	Art Howe	R. Landestoy	Enos Cabell	D. Walling	Terry Puhl	Jose Cruz
1979	Bill Virdon	Alan Ashby	Cesar Cedeno	R. Landestoy	C. Reynolds	Enos Cabell	Jose Cruz	Terry Puhl	Jeff Leonard
1980	Bill Virdon	Alan Ashby	Art Howe	Joe Morgan	C. Reynolds	Enos Cabell	Jose Cruz	Cesar Cedeno	Terry Puhl
1981	Bill Virdon	Alan Ashby	Cesar Cedeno	Joe Pittman	C. Reynolds	Art Howe	Jose Cruz	Tony Scott	Terry Puhl
1982	Bill Virdon	Alan Ashby	Ray Knight	Phil Garner	Dickie Thon	Art Howe	Jose Cruz	Tony Scott	Terry Puhl
1983	Bob Lillis	Alan Ashby	Ray Knight	Bill Doran	Dickie Thon	Phil Garner	Jose Cruz	Omar Moreno	Terry Puhl
1984	Bob Lillis	Mark Bailey	Enos Cabell	Bill Doran	C. Reynolds	Phil Garner	Jose Cruz	J. Mumphrey	Terry Puhl
1985	Bob Lillis	Mark Bailey	Glenn Davis	Bill Doran	C. Reynolds	Phil Garner	Jose Cruz	Kevin Bass	J. Mumphrey
1986	Hal Lanier	Alan Ashby	Glenn Davis	Bill Doran	Dickie Thon	D. Walling	Jose Cruz	Billy Hatcher	Kevin Bass
1987	Hal Lanier	Alan Ashby	Glenn Davis	Bill Doran	C. Reynolds	D. Walling	Jose Cruz	Billy Hatcher	Kevin Bass
1988	Hal Lanier	Alex Trevino	Glenn Davis	Bill Doran	R. Ramirez	Buddy Bell	Billy Hatcher	Gerald Young	Kevin Bass
1989	Art Howe	Craig Biggio	Glenn Davis	Bill Doran	R. Ramirez	Ken Caminiti	Billy Hatcher	Gerald Young	Terry Puhl
1990	Art Howe	Craig Biggio	Glenn Davis	Bill Doran	R. Ramirez	Ken Caminiti	F. Stubbs	Eric Yelding	Glenn Wilson
1991	Art Howe	Craig Biggio	Jeff Bagwell	C. Candaele	Eric Yelding	Ken Caminiti	L. Gonzalez	Gerald Young	Steve Finley
1992	Art Howe	E. Taubensee	Jeff Bagwell	Craig Biggio	A. Cedeno	Ken Caminiti	L. Gonzalez	Steve Finley	Eric Anthony
1993	Art Howe	E. Taubensee	Jeff Bagwell	Craig Biggio	A. Cedeno	Ken Caminiti	L. Gonzalez	Steve Finley	Eric Anthony
1994	Terry Collins	Scott Servais	Jeff Bagwell	Craig Biggio	A. Cedeno	Ken Caminiti	L. Gonzalez	Steve Finley	J. Mouton
1995	Terry Collins	Tony Eusebio	Jeff Bagwell	Craig Biggio	O. Miller	D. Magadan	J. Mouton	Brian Hunter	Derek Bell
1996	Terry Collins	Rick Wilkins	Jeff Bagwell	Craig Biggio	O. Miller	Sean Berry	J. Mouton	Brian Hunter	Derek Bell
1997	Larry Dierker	Brad Ausmus	Jeff Bagwell	Craig Biggio	Tim Bogar	Sean Berry	L. Gonzalez	T. Howard	Derek Bell

YEAR	MANAGER	C	1B	2B	SS	3B	LF	CF	RF
1998	Larry Dierker	Brad Ausmus	Jeff Bagwell	Craig Biggio	R. Gutierrez	Bill Spiers	Moises Alou	Carl Everett	Derek Bell
1999	Larry Dierker	Tony Eusebio	Jeff Bagwell	Craig Biggio	Tim Bogar	Ken Caminiti	R. Hidalgo	Carl Everett	Derek Bell
2000	Larry Dierker	M. Meluskey	Jeff Bagwell	Craig Biggio	Tim Bogar	Chris Truby	Moises Alou	R. Hidalgo	L. Berkman
2001	Larry Dierker	Brad Ausmus	Jeff Bagwell	Craig Biggio	Julio Lugo	Vinny Castilla	L. Berkman	R. Hidalgo	Moises Alou
2002	Ji. Williams	Brad Ausmus	Jeff Bagwell	Craig Biggio	Julio Lugo	Geoff Blum	Daryle Ward	L. Berkman	R. Hidalgo

ATHLETICS BY POSITION, YEAR BY YEAR

Philadelphia Athletics (American League), 1901–1954
Kansas City Athletics (American League), 1955–1961
Kansas City A's (American League), 1962–1967
Oakland A's (American League), 1968–1986
Oakland Athletics (American League), 1987–Present

YEAR	MANAGER	C	1B	2B	SS	3B	LF	CF	RF
1901	Connie Mack	Doc Powers	Harry Davis	Nap Lajoie	Joe Dolan	Lave Cross	M. McIntyre	Dave Fultz	S. Seybold
1902	Connie Mack	Schreckengost	Harry Davis	Dan Murphy	Monte Cross	Lave Cross	Topsy Hartsel	Dave Fultz	S. Seybold
1903	Connie Mack	Schreckengost	Harry Davis	Dan Murphy	Monte Cross	Lave Cross	Topsy Hartsel	O. Pickering	S. Seybold
1904	Connie Mack	Schreckengost	Harry Davis	Dan Murphy	Monte Cross	Lave Cross	Topsy Hartsel	O. Pickering	S. Seybold
1905	Connie Mack	Schreckengost	Harry Davis	Dan Murphy	Jack Knight	Lave Cross	Topsy Hartsel	Dan Hoffman	S. Seybold
1906	Connie Mack	Schreckengost	Harry Davis	Dan Murphy	Monte Cross	Jack Knight	Topsy Hartsel	Bris Lord	S. Seybold
1907	Connie Mack	Schreckengost	Harry Davis	Dan Murphy	S. Nicholls	Jim Collins	Topsy Hartsel	Rube Oldring	S. Seybold
1908	Connie Mack	Schreckengost	Harry Davis	Eddie Collins	S. Nicholls	Jim Collins	Topsy Hartsel	Rube Oldring	Dan Murphy
1909	Connie Mack	Ira Thomas	Harry Davis	Eddie Collins	Jack Barry	Frank Baker	Topsy Hartsel	Rube Oldring	Dan Murphy
1910	Connie Mack	Jack Lapp	Harry Davis	Eddie Collins	Jack Barry	Frank Baker	Topsy Hartsel	Rube Oldring	Dan Murphy
1911	Connie Mack	Ira Thomas	S. McInnis	Eddie Collins	Jack Barry	Frank Baker	Bris Lord	Rube Oldring	Dan Murphy
1912	Connie Mack	Jack Lapp	S. McInnis	Eddie Collins	Jack Barry	Frank Baker	Amos Strunk	Rube Oldring	Bris Lord
1913	Connie Mack	Jack Lapp	S. McInnis	Eddie Collins	Jack Barry	Frank Baker	Rube Oldring	Jimmy Walsh	Eddie Murphy
1914	Connie Mack	Wally Schang	S. McInnis	Eddie Collins	Jack Barry	Frank Baker	Rube Oldring	Amos Strunk	Eddie Murphy
1915	Connie Mack	Jack Lapp	S. McInnis	Nap Lajoie	Larry Kopf	Wally Schang	Rube Oldring	Jimmy Walsh	Amos Strunk
1916	Connie Mack	Billy Meyer	S. McInnis	Nap Lajoie	Whitey Witt	Charlie Pick	Wally Schang	Amos Strunk	Jimmy Walsh
1917	Connie Mack	Wally Schang	S. McInnis	Roy Grover	Whitey Witt	Ray Bates	Ping Bodie	Amos Strunk	C. Jamieson
1918	Connie Mack	W. McAvoy	George Burns	Jimmy Dykes	Joe Dugan	Larry Gardner	Merlin Kopp	Tilly Walker	C. Jamieson
1919	Connie Mack	Cy Perkins	George Burns	Whitey Witt	Joe Dugan	Fred Thomas	Merlin Kopp	Tilly Walker	Amos Strunk
1920	Connie Mack	Cy Perkins	Ivy Griffin	Jimmy Dykes	C. Galloway	Fred Thomas	Tilly Walker	Frank Welch	Amos Strunk
1921	Connie Mack	Cy Perkins	John Walker	Jimmy Dykes	C. Galloway	Joe Dugan	Tilly Walker	Frank Welch	Whitey Witt
1922	Connie Mack	Cy Perkins	Joe Hauser	Ralph Young	C. Galloway	Jimmy Dykes	Tilly Walker	Bing Miller	Frank Welch
1923	Connie Mack	Cy Perkins	Joe Hauser	Jimmy Dykes	C. Galloway	Sammy Hale	Bing Miller	W. Matthews	Frank Welch
1924	Connie Mack	Cy Perkins	Joe Hauser	Max Bishop	C. Galloway	H. Riconda	Bill Lamar	Al Simmons	Bing Miller
1925	Connie Mack	M. Cochrane	Jim Poole	Max Bishop	C. Galloway	Sammy Hale	Bill Lamar	Al Simmons	Bing Miller
1926	Connie Mack	M. Cochrane	Jim Poole	Max Bishop	C. Galloway	Jimmy Dykes	Bill Lamar	Al Simmons	Walter French
1927	Connie Mack	M. Cochrane	Jimmy Dykes	Max Bishop	Joe Boley	Sammy Hale	Bill Lamar	Al Simmons	Ty Cobb
1928	Connie Mack	M. Cochrane	Joe Hauser	Max Bishop	Joe Boley	Sammy Hale	Al Simmons	Bing Miller	Ty Cobb
1929	Connie Mack	M. Cochrane	Jimmie Foxx	Max Bishop	Joe Boley	Sammy Hale	Al Simmons	Mule Haas	Bing Miller
1930	Connie Mack	M. Cochrane	Jimmie Foxx	Max Bishop	Joe Boley	Jimmy Dykes	Al Simmons	Mule Haas	Bing Miller
1931	Connie Mack	M. Cochrane	Jimmie Foxx	Max Bishop	Dib Williams	Jimmy Dykes	Al Simmons	Mule Haas	Bing Miller
1932	Connie Mack	M. Cochrane	Jimmie Foxx	Max Bishop	Eric McNair	Jimmy Dykes	Al Simmons	Mule Haas	Doc Cramer
1933	Connie Mack	M. Cochrane	Jimmie Foxx	Max Bishop	Dib Williams	Pinky Higgins	Bob Johnson	Doc Cramer	Ed Coleman
1934	Connie Mack	Charlie Berry	Jimmie Foxx	R. Warstler	Eric McNair	Pinky Higgins	Bob Johnson	Doc Cramer	Ed Coleman
1935	Connie Mack	Paul Richards	Jimmie Foxx	R. Warstler	Eric McNair	Pinky Higgins	Bob Johnson	Doc Cramer	Wally Moses

YEAR	MANAGER	C	1B	2B	SS	3B	LF	CF	RF	DH
1936	Connie Mack	Frankie Hayes	Lou Finney	R. Warstler	S. Newsome	Pinky Higgins	Bob Johnson	Wally Moses	G. Puccinelli	
1937	Connie Mack	Earle Brucker	Chubby Dean	Rusty Peters	S. Newsome	Billy Werber	Bob Johnson	Jesse Hill	Wally Moses	
1938	Connie Mack	Frankie Hayes	Lou Finney	D. Lodigiani	W. Ambler	Billy Werber	S. Chapman	Bob Johnson	Wally Moses	
1939	Connie Mack	Frankie Hayes	Dick Siebert	J. Gantenbein	S. Newsome	D. Lodigiani	Bob Johnson	S. Chapman	Wally Moses	
1940	Connie Mack	Frankie Hayes	Dick Siebert	Ben McCoy	Al Brancato	Al Rubeling	Bob Johnson	S. Chapman	Wally Moses	
1941	Connie Mack	Frankie Hayes	Dick Siebert	Ben McCoy	Al Brancato	Pete Suder	Bob Johnson	S. Chapman	Wally Moses	
1942	Connie Mack	Hal Wagner	Dick Siebert	Knickerbocker	Pete Suder	Buddy Blair	Bob Johnson	M. Kreevich	Elmer Valo	
1943	Connie Mack	Hal Wagner	Dick Siebert	Pete Suder	Irv Hall	Eddie Mayo	Bob Estalella	Jo-Jo White	Johnny Welaj	
1944	Connie Mack	Frankie Hayes	Bill McGhee	Irv Hall	Ed Busch	George Kell	Ford Garrison	Bob Estalella	Jo Jo White	
1945	Connie Mack	Buddy Rosar	Dick Siebert	Irv Hall	Ed Busch	George Kell	Mayo Smith	Bob Estalella	Hal Peck	
1946	Connie Mack	Buddy Rosar	G. McQuinn	Gene Handley	Pete Suder	Hank Majeski	S. Chapman	B. McCosky	Elmer Valo	
1947	Connie Mack	Buddy Rosar	Ferris Fain	Pete Suder	Eddie Joost	Hank Majeski	B. McCosky	S. Chapman	Elmer Valo	
1948	Connie Mack	Buddy Rosar	Ferris Fain	Pete Suder	Eddie Joost	Hank Majeski	B. McCosky	S. Chapman	Elmer Valo	
1949	Connie Mack	Mike Guerra	Ferris Fain	Pete Suder	Eddie Joost	Hank Majeski	Elmer Valo	S. Chapman	Wally Moses	
1950	Connie Mack	Mike Guerra	Ferris Fain	B. Hitchcock	Eddie Joost	Bob Dillinger	Paul Lehner	S. Chapman	Elmer Valo	
1951	Jimmy Dykes	Joe Tipton	Ferris Fain	Pete Suder	Eddie Joost	Hank Majeski	Gus Zernial	Dave Philley	Elmer Valo	
1952	Jimmy Dykes	Joe Astroth	Ferris Fain	Skeeter Kell	Eddie Joost	B. Hitchcock	Gus Zernial	Dave Philley	Elmer Valo	
1953	Jimmy Dykes	Joe Astroth	Ed Robinson	Cass Michaels	Joe DeMaestri	Loren Babe	Gus Zernial	Ed McGhee	Dave Philley	
1954	Eddie Joost	Joe Astroth	Lou Limmer	Spook Jacobs	Joe DeMaestri	Jim Finigan	Gus Zernial	Vic Power	Bill Renna	
1955	Lou Boudreau	Joe Astroth	Vic Power	Jim Finigan	Joe DeMaestri	Hector Lopez	Gus Zernial	H. Simpson	E. Slaughter	
1956	Lou Boudreau	T. Thompson	Vic Power	Jim Finigan	Joe DeMaestri	Hector Lopez	Lou Skizas	Johnny Groth	H. Simpson	
1957	Lou Boudreau	Hal Smith	Vic Power	Billy Hunter	Joe DeMaestri	Hector Lopez	Gus Zernial	Woody Held	Lou Skizas	
1958	Harry Craft	Harry Chiti	Vic Power	Mike Baxes	Joe DeMaestri	Hector Lopez	Bob Cerv	Bill Tuttle	Roger Maris	
1959	Harry Craft	Frank House	Kent Hadley	W. Terwilliger	Joe DeMaestri	D. Williams	Bob Cerv	Bill Tuttle	Roger Maris	
1960	Bob Elliott	Pete Daley	M. Thornberry	Jerry Lumpe	Ken Hamlin	Andy Carey	Norm Siebern	Bill Tuttle	Russ Snyder	
1961	Hank Bauer	H. Sullivan	Norm Siebern	Jerry Lumpe	Dick Howser	W. Causey	Leo Posada	B. Del Greco	D. Johnson	
1962	Hank Bauer	H. Sullivan	Norm Siebern	Jerry Lumpe	Dick Howser	Ed Charles	M. Jimenez	B. Del Greco	Gino Cimoli	
1963	Ed Lopat	Doc Edwards	Norm Siebern	Jerry Lumpe	W. Causey	Ed Charles	B. Del Greco	Jose Tartabull	Gino Cimoli	
1964	Mel McGaha	Doc Edwards	Jim Gentile	Dick Green	W. Causey	Ed Charles	Jose Tartabull	N. Mathews	R. Colavito	
1965	H. Sullivan	Billy Bryan	K. Harrelson	Dick Green	B. Campaneris	Ed Charles	T. Reynolds	Jim Landis	Hershberger	
1966	Alvin Dark	Phil Roof	K. Harrelson	Dick Green	B. Campaneris	Ed Charles	Larry Stahl	Joe Nossek	Hershberger	
1967	Alvin Dark	Phil Roof	Ray Webster	J. Donaldson	B. Campaneris	Dick Green	Jim Gosger	Rick Monday	Hershberger	
1968	Bob Kennedy	Dave Duncan	Danny Cater	J. Donaldson	B. Campaneris	Sal Bando	Hershberger	Rick Monday	R. Jackson	
1969	Hank Bauer	Phil Roof	Danny Cater	Dick Green	B. Campaneris	Sal Bando	T. Reynolds	Rick Monday	R. Jackson	
1970	J. McNamara	F. Fernandez	Don Mincher	Dick Green	B. Campaneris	Sal Bando	Felipe Alou	Rick Monday	R. Jackson	
1971	D. Williams	Dave Duncan	Mike Epstein	Dick Green	B. Campaneris	Sal Bando	Joe Rudi	Rick Monday	R. Jackson	
1972	D. Williams	Dave Duncan	Mike Epstein	Tim Cullen	B. Campaneris	Sal Bando	Joe Rudi	R. Jackson	A. Mangual	
1973	D. Williams	Ray Fosse	Gene Tenace	Dick Green	B. Campaneris	Sal Bando	Joe Rudi	Bill North	R. Jackson	D. Johnson
1974	Al Dark	Larry Haney	Gene Tenace	Dick Green	B. Campaneris	Sal Bando	Joe Rudi	Bill North	R. Jackson	Jesus Alou
1975	Al Dark	Gene Tenace	Joe Rudi	Phil Garner	B. Campaneris	Sal Bando	C. Washington	Bill North	R. Jackson	B. Williams
1976	Chuck Tanner	Larry Haney	Gene Tenace	Phil Garner	B. Campaneris	Sal Bando	Joe Rudi	Bill North	C. Washington	B. Williams
1977	Bob Winkles	Jeff Newman	Dick Allen	Marty Perez	Rob Picciolo	Wayne Gross	Mitchell Page	Tony Armas	Jim Tyrone	M. Sanguillen
1978	Jack McKeon	Jim Essian	D. Revering	M. Edwards	M. Guerrero	Wayne Gross	Mitchell Page	M. Dilone	Tony Armas	G. Alexander
1979	Jim Marshall	Jeff Newman	D. Revering	M. Edwards	Rob Picciolo	Wayne Gross	R. Henderson	D. Murphy	Larry Murray	Mitchell Page
1980	Billy Martin	Jim Essian	D. Revering	Dave McKay	M. Guerrero	Wayne Gross	R. Henderson	D. Murphy	Tony Armas	Mitchell Page
1981	Billy Martin	Mike Heath	Jim Spencer	Shooty Babitt	Rob Picciolo	Wayne Gross	R. Henderson	D. Murphy	Tony Armas	Cliff Johnson
1982	Billy Martin	Mike Heath	Dave Meyer	Davey Lopes	Fred Stanley	Wayne Gross	R. Henderson	D. Murphy	Tony Armas	Cliff Johnson
1983	Steve Boros	Bob Kearney	Wayne Gross	Davey Lopes	Tony Phillips	C. Lansford	R. Henderson	D. Murphy	Mike Davis	J. Burroughs
1984	Jackie Moore	Mike Heath	Bruce Bochte	Joe Morgan	Tony Phillips	C. Lansford	R. Henderson	D. Murphy	Mike Davis	D. Kingman

YEAR	MANAGER	C	1B	2B	SS	3B	LF	CF	RF	DH
1985	Jackie Moore	Mike Heath	Bruce Bochte	Donnie Hill	A. Griffin	C. Lansford	Dave Collins	D. Murphy	Mike Davis	D. Kingman
1986	T. La Russa	M. Tettleton	Bruce Bochte	Tony Phillips	A. Griffin	C. Lansford	Jose Canseco	D. Murphy	Mike Davis	D. Kingman
1987	T. La Russa	T. Steinbach	M. McGwire	Tony Phillips	A. Griffin	C. Lansford	Jose Canseco	Luis Polonia	Mike Davis	R. Jackson
1988	T. La Russa	Ron Hassey	M. McGwire	G. Hubbard	Walt Weiss	C. Lansford	Stan Javier	D. Henderson	Jose Canseco	Don Baylor
1989	T. La Russa	T. Steinbach	M. McGwire	Tony Phillips	Mike Gallego	C. Lansford	R. Henderson	D. Henderson	Stan Javier	Dave Parker
1990	T. La Russa	T. Steinbach	M. McGwire	W. Randolph	Walt Weiss	C. Lansford	R. Henderson	D. Henderson	Felix Jose	Jose Canseco
1991	T. La Russa	T. Steinbach	M. McGwire	Mike Gallego	Mike Bordick	Ernie Riles	R. Henderson	D. Henderson	Jose Canseco	Harold Baines
1992	T. La Russa	T. Steinbach	M. McGwire	Mike Bordick	Walt Weiss	C. Lansford	R. Henderson	Willie Wilson	Jose Canseco	Harold Baines
1993	T. La Russa	T. Steinbach	Mike Aldrete	Brent Gates	Mike Bordick	C. Paquette	R. Henderson	D. Henderson	Ruben Sierra	Troy Neel
1994	T. La Russa	T. Steinbach	Troy Neel	Brent Gates	Mike Bordick	Scott Brosius	R. Henderson	Stan Javier	Ruben Sierra	G. Berroa
1995	T. La Russa	T. Steinbach	M. McGwire	Brent Gates	Mike Bordick	C. Paquette	R. Henderson	Stan Javier	Ruben Sierra	G. Berroa
1996	Art Howe	T. Steinbach	M. McGwire	R. Bournigal	Mike Bordick	Scott Brosius	Phil Plantier	Ernie Young	Jose Herrera	G. Berroa
1997	Art Howe	Brent Mayne	M. McGwire	Scott Spiezio	R. Bournigal	Scott Brosius	Jason Giambi	D. Mashore	Matt Stairs	Jose Canseco
1998	Art Howe	A.J. Hinch	Jason Giambi	Scott Spiezio	M. Tejada	Mike Blowers	R. Henderson	R. Christenson	Ben Grieve	Matt Stairs
1999	Art Howe	M. Macfarlane	Jason Giambi	Tony Phillips	M. Tejada	Eric Chavez	Ben Grieve	R. Christenson	Matt Stairs	John Jaha
2000	Art Howe	R. Hernandez	Jason Giambi	R. Velarde	M. Tejada	Eric Chavez	Ben Grieve	Ter. Long	Matt Stairs	Je. Giambi
2001	Art Howe	R. Hernandez	Jason Giambi	F. Menechino	M. Tejada	Eric Chavez	Ter. Long	John Damon	Jermaine Dye	Je. Giambi
2002	Art Howe	R. Hernandez	S. Hatteberg	Mark Ellis	M. Tejada	Eric Chavez	David Justice	Ter. Long	Jermaine Dye	Ray Durham

BLUE JAYS BY POSITION, YEAR BY YEAR

Toronto Blue Jays (American League), 1977–Present

YEAR	MANAGER	C	1B	2B	SS	3B	LF	CF	RF	DH
1977	R. Hartsfield	Alan Ashby	Doug Ault	Steve Staggs	Hector Torres	Roy Howell	Al Woods	Bob Bailor	Otto Velez	Ron Fairly
1978	R. Hartsfield	Rick Cerone	J. Mayberry	Dave McKay	Luis Gomez	Roy Howell	Otto Velez	Rick Bosetti	Bob Bailor	Rico Carty
1979	R. Hartsfield	Rick Cerone	J. Mayberry	Danny Ainge	Al Griffin	Roy Howell	Al Woods	Rick Bosetti	Bob Bailor	Rico Carty
1980	B. Mattick	Ernie Whitt	J. Mayberry	D. Garcia	Al Griffin	Roy Howell	Bob Bailor	Barry Bonnell	L. Moseby	Otto Velez
1981	B. Mattick	Ernie Whitt	J. Mayberry	D. Garcia	Al Griffin	Danny Ainge	Al Woods	L. Moseby	Barry Bonnell	Otto Velez
1982	Bobby Cox	Ernie Whitt	W. Upshaw	D. Garcia	Al Griffin	R. Mulliniks	Barry Bonnell	L. Moseby	Jesse Barfield	D. Revering
1983	Bobby Cox	Ernie Whitt	W. Upshaw	D. Garcia	Al Griffin	R. Mulliniks	Barry Bonnell	L. Moseby	Jesse Barfield	C. Johnson
1984	Bobby Cox	Ernie Whitt	W. Upshaw	D. Garcia	Al Griffin	R. Mulliniks	Dave Collins	L. Moseby	George Bell	C. Johnson
1985	Bobby Cox	Ernie Whitt	W. Upshaw	D. Garcia	T. Fernandez	R. Mulliniks	George Bell	L. Moseby	Jesse Barfield	J. Burroughs
1986	J. Williams	Ernie Whitt	W. Upshaw	D. Garcia	T. Fernandez	R. Mulliniks	George Bell	L. Moseby	Jesse Barfield	C. Johnson
1987	J. Williams	Ernie Whitt	W. Upshaw	Garth Iorg	T. Fernandez	Kelly Gruber	George Bell	L. Moseby	Jesse Barfield	Fred McGriff
1988	J. Williams	Ernie Whitt	Fred McGriff	Manny Lee	T. Fernandez	Kelly Gruber	George Bell	L. Moseby	Jesse Barfield	R. Mulliniks
1989	J. Williams	Ernie Whitt	Fred McGriff	N. Liriano	T. Fernandez	Kelly Gruber	George Bell	L. Moseby	Junior Felix	R. Mulliniks
1990	Cito Gaston	Pat Borders	Fred McGriff	Manny Lee	T. Fernandez	Kelly Gruber	George Bell	M. Wilson	Junior Felix	John Olerud
1991	Cito Gaston	Greg Myers	John Olerud	R. Alomar	Manny Lee	Kelly Gruber	C. Maldonado	Devon White	Joe Carter	R. Mulliniks
1992	Cito Gaston	Pat Borders	John Olerud	R. Alomar	Manny Lee	Kelly Gruber	C. Maldonado	Devon White	Joe Carter	D. Winfield
1993	Cito Gaston	Pat Borders	John Olerud	R. Alomar	T. Fernandez	Ed Sprague	Turner Ward	Devon White	Joe Carter	Paul Molitor
1994	Cito Gaston	Pat Borders	John Olerud	R. Alomar	D. Schofield	Ed Sprague	Mike Huff	Devon White	Joe Carter	Paul Molitor
1995	Cito Gaston	Lance Parrish	John Olerud	R. Alomar	Al Gonzalez	Ed Sprague	Joe Carter	Devon White	Shawn Green	Paul Molitor
1996	Cito Gaston	C. O'Brien	John Olerud	Tomas Perez	Al Gonzalez	Ed Sprague	Joe Carter	Otis Nixon	Shawn Green	C. Delgado
1997	Cito Gaston	B. Santiago	C. Delgado	Carlos Garcia	Al Gonzalez	Ed Sprague	Shawn Green	Otis Nixon	O. Merced	Joe Carter
1998	Tim Johnson	D. Fletcher	C. Delgado	C. Grebeck	Al Gonzalez	Ed Sprague	S. Stewart	Jose Cruz	Shawn Green	Jose Canseco
1999	Jim Fregosi	D. Fletcher	C. Delgado	Homer Bush	Tony Batista	T. Fernandez	S. Stewart	Jose Cruz	Shawn Green	Willie Greene
2000	Jim Fregosi	D. Fletcher	C. Delgado	Homer Bush	Al Gonzalez	Tony Batista	S. Stewart	Jose Cruz	Raul Mondesi	Brad Fullmer
2001	B. Martinez	D. Fletcher	C. Delgado	Homer Bush	Al Gonzalez	Tony Batista	S. Stewart	Jose Cruz	Raul Mondesi	Brad Fullmer
2002	Carlos Tosca	Tom Wilson	C. Delgado	Dave Berg	C. Woodward	Eric Hinske	S. Stewart	Vernon Wells	Jose Cruz	Josh Phelps

BRAVES BY POSITION, YEAR BY YEAR

Boston Red Caps (National League), 1876–1882
Boston Beaneaters (National League), 1883–1906
Boston Doves (National League), 1907–1910
Boston Rustlers (National League), 1911
Boston Braves (National League), 1912–1935
Boston Bees (National League), 1936–1940
Boston Braves (National League), 1941–1952
Milwaukee Braves (National League), 1953–1965
Atlanta Braves (National League), 1966–Present

YEAR	MANAGER	C	1B	2B	SS	3B	LF	CF	RF
1901	Frank Selee	M. Kittridge	Fred Tenney	D'Montreville	Herman Long	Bobby Lowe	Duff Cooley	B. Hamilton	Jimmy Slagle
1902	Buckenberger	M. Kittridge	Fred Tenney	D'Montreville	Herman Long	Gremminger	Duff Cooley	Billy Lush	Pat Carney
1903	Buckenberger	Pat Moran	Fred Tenney	E. Abbaticchio	Harry Aubrey	Gremminger	Duff Cooley	C. Dexter	Pat Carney
1904	Buckenberger	T. Needham	Fred Tenney	Fred Raymer	E. Abbaticchio	Jim Delahanty	Duff Cooley	Phil Geier	Rip Cannell
1905	Fred Tenney	Pat Moran	Fred Tenney	Fred Raymer	E. Abbaticchio	H. Wolverton	Jim Delahanty	Rip Cannell	Cozy Dolan
1906	Fred Tenney	T. Needham	Fred Tenney	Allie Strobel	Al Bridwell	Dave Brain	Del Howard	Johnny Bates	Cozy Dolan
1907	Fred Tenney	T. Needham	Fred Tenney	C. Ritchey	Al Bridwell	Dave Brain	Newt Randall	G. Beaumont	Johnny Bates
1908	Joe Kelley	F. Bowerman	Dan McGann	C. Ritchey	Bill Dahlen	B. Sweeney	Johnny Bates	G. Beaumont	G. Browne
1909	F. Bowerman	P. Graham	Fred Stern	Dave Shean	Jack Coffey	B. Sweeney	Roy Thomas	G. Beaumont	Beals Becker
1910	Fred Lake	P. Graham	Bud Sharpe	Dave Shean	Bill Sweeney	Buck Herzog	Bill Collins	Fred Beck	Doc Miller
1911	Fred Tenney	Johnny Kling	Fred Tenney	Bill Sweeney	Buck Herzog	S. Ingerton	Al Kaiser	Mike Donlin	Doc Miller
1912	Johnny Kling	Johnny Kling	Ben Houser	Bill Sweeney	F. O'Rourke	E. McDonald	G. Jackson	Vin Campbell	John Titus
1913	G. Stallings	Bill Rariden	Hap Myers	Bill Sweeney	R. Maranville	Art Devlin	Joe Connolly	Les Mann	John Titus
1914	G. Stallings	Hank Gowdy	B. Schmidt	Johnny Evers	R. Maranville	Charlie Deal	Joe Connolly	Les Mann	Larry Gilbert
1915	G. Stallings	Hank Gowdy	B. Schmidt	Johnny Evers	R. Maranville	Red Smith	Joe Connolly	Sherry Magee	Herbie Moran
1916	G. Stallings	Hank Gowdy	Ed Konetchy	Johnny Evers	R. Maranville	Red Smith	Sherry Magee	F. Snodgrass	Joe Wilhoit
1917	G. Stallings	W. Tragesser	Ed Konetchy	J. Rawlings	R. Maranville	Red Smith	Joe Kelly	Ray Powell	Wally Rehg
1918	G. Stallings	Art Wilson	Ed Konetchy	Buck Herzog	J. Rawlings	Red Smith	Roy Massey	Ray Powell	Al Wickland
1919	G. Stallings	Hank Gowdy	Walter Holke	Buck Herzog	R. Maranville	Tony Boeckel	Walton Cruise	Joe Riggert	Ray Powell
1920	G. Stallings	Mi. O'Neill	Walter Holke	Charlie Pick	R. Maranville	Tony Boeckel	Les Mann	Ray Powell	Walter Cruise
1921	Fred Mitchell	Mi. O'Neill	Walter Holke	Hod Ford	W. Barbare	Tony Boeckel	Walter Cruise	Ray Powell	B. Southworth
1922	Fred Mitchell	Mi. O'Neill	Walter Holke	Larry Kopf	Hod Ford	Tony Boeckel	Al Nixon	Ray Powell	Walter Cruise
1923	Fred Mitchell	Mi. O'Neill	S. McInnis	Hod Ford	Bob Smith	Tony Boeckel	Gus Felix	Ray Powell	B. Southworth
1924	D. Bancroft	Mi. O'Neill	S. McInnis	C. Tierney	Bob Smith	Ernie Padgett	Cunningham	Gus Felix	Casey Stengel
1925	D. Bancroft	Frank Gibson	Dick Burrus	Doc Gautreau	D. Bancroft	W. Marriott	Dave Harris	Gus Felix	Jimmy Welsh
1926	D. Bancroft	Zack Taylor	Dick Burrus	Doc Gautreau	D. Bancroft	Andy High	Eddie Brown	Jack Smith	Jimmy Welsh
1927	D. Bancroft	Shanty Hogan	Jack Fournier	Doc Gautreau	D. Bancroft	Andy High	Eddie Brown	Jimmy Welsh	L. Richbourg
1928	R. Hornsby	Zack Taylor	George Sisler	R. Hornsby	Doc Farrell	Les Bell	Eddie Brown	Jack Smith	L. Richbourg
1929	Emil Fuchs	Al Spohrer	George Sisler	Fred Maguire	R. Maranville	Les Bell	G. Harper	Earl Clark	L. Richbourg
1930	B. McKechnie	Al Spohrer	George Sisler	Fred Maguire	R. Maranville	B. Chatham	Wally Berger	Jimmy Welsh	L. Richbourg
1931	B. McKechnie	Al Spohrer	Earl Sheely	Fred Maguire	R. Maranville	B. Urbanski	Worthington	Wally Berger	Schulmerich
1932	B. McKechnie	Al Spohrer	Art Shires	R. Maranville	B. Urbanski	Fritz Knothe	Worthington	Wally Berger	Schulmerich
1933	B. McKechnie	Shanty Hogan	Buck Jordan	R. Maranville	B. Urbanski	P. Whitney	Hal Lee	Wally Berger	Randy Moore
1934	B. McKechnie	Al Spohrer	Buck Jordan	M. McManus	B. Urbanski	P. Whitney	Hal Lee	Wally Berger	T. Thompson
1935	B. McKechnie	Al Spohrer	Buck Jordan	Les Mallon	B. Urbanski	P. Whitney	Hal Lee	Wally Berger	T. Thompson
1936	B. McKechnie	Al Lopez	Buck Jordan	T. Cuccinello	B. Urbanski	Joe Coscarart	Hal Lee	Wally Berger	Gene Moore
1937	B. McKechnie	Al Lopez	Elbie Fletcher	T. Cuccinello	R. Warstler	Gil English	Debs Garms	V. DiMaggio	Gene Moore
1938	Casey Stengel	Ray Mueller	Elbie Fletcher	T. Cuccinello	R. Warstler	Joe Stripp	Max West	V. DiMaggio	John Cooney
1939	Casey Stengel	Al Lopez	Bud Hassett	T. Cuccinello	Eddie Miller	Hank Majeski	Max West	John Cooney	Debs Garms

YEAR	MANAGER	C	1B	2B	SS	3B	LF	CF	RF
1940	Casey Stengel	Ray Berres	Bud Hassett	Bama Rowell	Eddie Miller	Sibby Sisti	Chet Ross	John Cooney	Max West
1941	Casey Stengel	Ray Berres	Bud Hassett	Bama Rowell	Eddie Miller	Sibby Sisti	Max West	John Cooney	Gene Moore
1942	Casey Stengel	E. Lombardi	Max West	Sibby Sisti	Eddie Miller	N. Fernandez	Chet Ross	Tom Holmes	Paul Waner
1943	Casey Stengel	Phil Masi	J. McCarthy	Connie Ryan	Wietelmann	Eddie Joost	Bob Nieman	Tom Holmes	C. Workman
1944	Bob Coleman	Phil Masi	B. Etchison	Connie Ryan	Wietelmann	D. Phillips	Bob Nieman	Tom Holmes	C. Workman
1945	Bob Coleman	Phil Masi	Vince Shupe	Wietelmann	Dick Culler	C. Workman	Bob Nieman	C. Gillenwater	Tom Holmes
1946	B. Southworth	Phil Masi	Ray Sanders	Connie Ryan	Dick Culler	N. Fernandez	Bama Rowell	C. Gillenwater	Tom Holmes
1947	B. Southworth	Phil Masi	Earl Torgeson	Connie Ryan	Dick Culler	Bob Elliott	Bama Rowell	Johnny Hopp	Tom Holmes
1948	B. Southworth	Phil Masi	Earl Torgeson	Eddie Stanky	Alvin Dark	Bob Elliott	Jeff Heath	Jim Russell	Tom Holmes
1949	B. Southworth	Bill Salkeld	Elbie Fletcher	Eddie Stanky	Alvin Dark	Bob Elliott	Marv Rickert	Jim Russell	Tom Holmes
1950	B. Southworth	Wa. Cooper	Earl Torgeson	R. Hartsfield	Buddy Kerr	Bob Elliott	Sid Gordon	Sam Jethroe	Tom Holmes
1951	Tom Holmes	Wa. Cooper	Earl Torgeson	R. Hartsfield	Buddy Kerr	Bob Elliott	Sid Gordon	Sam Jethroe	W. Marshall
1952	Tom Holmes	Wa. Cooper	Earl Torgeson	Jack Dittmer	Johnny Logan	Ed Mathews	Sid Gordon	Sam Jethroe	Jack Daniels
1953	Ch. Grimm	Del Crandall	Joe Adcock	Jack Dittmer	Johnny Logan	Ed Mathews	Sid Gordon	Bill Bruton	Andy Pafko
1954	Ch. Grimm	Del Crandall	Joe Adcock	D. O'Connell	Johnny Logan	Ed Mathews	Hank Aaron	Bill Bruton	Andy Pafko
1955	Ch. Grimm	Del Crandall	G. Crowe	D. O'Connell	Johnny Logan	Ed Mathews	B. Thomson	Bill Bruton	Hank Aaron
1956	Fred Haney	Del Crandall	Joe Adcock	D. O'Connell	Johnny Logan	Ed Mathews	B. Thomson	Bill Bruton	Hank Aaron
1957	Fred Haney	Del Crandall	Frank Torre	Schoendienst	Johnny Logan	Ed Mathews	W. Covington	Bill Bruton	Hank Aaron
1958	Fred Haney	Del Crandall	Frank Torre	Schoendienst	Johnny Logan	Ed Mathews	Andy Pafko	Bill Bruton	Hank Aaron
1959	Fred Haney	Del Crandall	Joe Adcock	Felix Mantilla	Johnny Logan	Ed Mathews	W. Covington	Bill Bruton	Hank Aaron
1960	C. Dressen	Del Crandall	Joe Adcock	Chuck Cottier	Johnny Logan	Ed Mathews	Al Spangler	Bill Bruton	Hank Aaron
1961	C. Dressen	Joe Torre	Joe Adcock	Frank Bolling	R. McMillan	Ed Mathews	Frank Thomas	Hank Aaron	Lee Maye
1962	B. Tebbets	Del Crandall	Joe Adcock	Frank Bolling	R. McMillan	Ed Mathews	Lee Maye	Hank Aaron	Mack Jones
1963	Bobby Bragan	Joe Torre	Gene Oliver	Frank Bolling	R. McMillan	Ed Mathews	Lee Maye	Mack Jones	Hank Aaron
1964	Bobby Bragan	Joe Torre	Gene Oliver	Frank Bolling	Denis Menke	Ed Mathews	Rico Carty	Lee Maye	Hank Aaron
1965	Bobby Bragan	Joe Torre	Felipe Alou	Frank Bolling	W. Woodward	Ed Mathews	Rico Carty	Mack Jones	Hank Aaron
1966	Bobby Bragan	Joe Torre	Felipe Alou	W. Woodward	Denis Menke	Ed Mathews	Rico Carty	Mack Jones	Hank Aaron
1967	B. Hitchcock	Joe Torre	Felipe Alou	W. Woodward	Denis Menke	Clete Boyer	Rico Carty	Mack Jones	Hank Aaron
1968	Lum Harris	Joe Torre	D. Johnson	Felix Millan	So. Jackson	Clete Boyer	Mike Lum	Felipe Alou	Hank Aaron
1969	Lum Harris	Bob Didier	O. Cepeda	Felix Millan	So. Jackson	Clete Boyer	T. Gonzalez	Felipe Alou	Hank Aaron
1970	Lum Harris	Bob Tillman	O. Cepeda	Felix Millan	So. Jackson	Clete Boyer	Rico Carty	T. Gonzalez	Hank Aaron
1971	Lum Harris	Earl Williams	Hank Aaron	Felix Millan	Marty Perez	Darrell Evans	Ralph Garr	S. Jackson	Mike Lum
1972	Lum Harris	Earl Williams	Hank Aaron	Felix Millan	Marty Perez	Darrell Evans	Rico Carty	Dusty Baker	Ralph Garr
1973	Ed Mathews	Johnny Oates	Mike Lum	D. Johnson	Marty Perez	Darrell Evans	Hank Aaron	Dusty Baker	Ralph Garr
1974	Ed Mathews	Johnny Oates	D. Johnson	Marty Perez	C. Robinson	Darrell Evans	Hank Aaron	Dusty Baker	Ralph Garr
1975	Clyde King	Vic Correll	Earl Williams	Marty Perez	L. Blanks	Darrell Evans	Ralph Garr	R. Office	Dusty Baker
1976	Dave Bristol	Vic Correll	W. Montanez	Rod Gilbreath	D. Chaney	Jerry Royster	Jimmy Wynn	R. Office	K. Henderson
1977	Dave Bristol	Biff Pocoroba	W. Montanez	Rod Gilbreath	Pat Rockett	Junior Moore	G. Matthews	R. Office	J. Burroughs
1978	Bobby Cox	Biff Pocoroba	Dale Murphy	Jerry Royster	D. Chaney	Bob Horner	J. Burroughs	R. Office	G. Matthews
1979	Bobby Cox	B. Benedict	Dale Murphy	G. Hubbard	Pepe Frias	Bob Horner	J. Burroughs	R. Office	G. Matthews
1980	Bobby Cox	B. Benedict	C. Chambliss	G. Hubbard	Luis Gomez	Bob Horner	J. Burroughs	Dale Murphy	G. Matthews
1981	Bobby Cox	B. Benedict	C. Chambliss	G. Hubbard	R. Ramirez	Bob Horner	R. Linares	Dale Murphy	C. Washington
1982	Joe Torre	B. Benedict	C. Chambliss	G. Hubbard	R. Ramirez	Bob Horner	R. Linares	Dale Murphy	C. Washington
1983	Joe Torre	B. Benedict	C. Chambliss	G. Hubbard	R. Ramirez	Bob Horner	Brett Butler	Dale Murphy	C. Washington
1984	Joe Torre	B. Benedict	C. Chambliss	G. Hubbard	R. Ramirez	R. Johnson	B. Komminsk	Dale Murphy	C. Washington
1985	Eddie Haas	Rick Cerone	Bob Horner	G. Hubbard	R. Ramirez	K. Oberkfell	Terry Harper	Dale Murphy	C. Washington
1986	Chuck Tanner	Ozzie Virgil	Bob Horner	G. Hubbard	A. Thomas	K. Oberkfell	Terry Harper	Dale Murphy	Omar Moreno
1987	Chuck Tanner	Ozzie Virgil	Gerald Perry	G. Hubbard	A. Thomas	K. Oberkfell	Ken Griffey	Dion James	Dale Murphy
1988	Chuck Tanner	Ozzie Virgil	Gerald Perry	Ron Gant	A. Thomas	K. Oberkfell	Dion James	Albert Hall	Dale Murphy

YEAR	MANAGER	C	1B	2B	SS	3B	LF	CF	RF
1989	Russ Nixon	Jody Davis	Gerald Perry	J. Treadway	A. Thomas	Jeff Blauser	Lonnie Smith	O. McDowell	Dale Murphy
1990	Bobby Cox	Greg Olson	Dave Justice	J. Treadway	Jeff Blauser	Jim Presley	Lonnie Smith	Ron Gant	Dale Murphy
1991	Bobby Cox	Greg Olson	Brian Hunter	Mark Lemke	R. Belliard	T. Pendleton	Otis Nixon	Ron Gant	Dave Justice
1992	Bobby Cox	Greg Olson	Sid Bream	Mark Lemke	R. Belliard	T. Pendleton	Ron Gant	Otis Nixon	Dave Justice
1993	Bobby Cox	D. Berryhill	Sid Bream	Mark Lemke	Jeff Blauser	T. Pendleton	Ron Gant	Otis Nixon	Dave Justice
1994	Bobby Cox	Javy Lopez	Fred McGriff	Mark Lemke	Jeff Blauser	T. Pendleton	Ryan Klesko	Roberto Kelly	Dave Justice
1995	Bobby Cox	Javy Lopez	Fred McGriff	Mark Lemke	Jeff Blauser	Chipper Jones	Ryan Klesko	M. Grissom	Dave Justice
1996	Bobby Cox	Javy Lopez	Fred McGriff	Mark Lemke	Jeff Blauser	Chipper Jones	Ryan Klesko	M. Grissom	Jermaine Dye
1997	Bobby Cox	Javy Lopez	Fred McGriff	Mark Lemke	Jeff Blauser	Chipper Jones	Ryan Klesko	Andruw Jones	M. Tucker
1998	Bobby Cox	Javy Lopez	A. Galarraga	K. Lockhart	Walt Weiss	Chipper Jones	Ryan Klesko	Andruw Jones	G. Williams
1999	Bobby Cox	Eddie Perez	Brian Hunter	Bret Boone	Walt Weiss	Chipper Jones	G. Williams	Andruw Jones	Brian Jordan
2000	Bobby Cox	Javy Lopez	A. Galarraga	Quilvio Veras	Rafael Furcal	Chipper Jones	R. Sanders	Andruw Jones	Brian Jordan
2001	Bobby Cox	Javy Lopez	Wes Helms	Marcus Giles	Rafael Furcal	Chipper Jones	B.J. Surhoff	Andruw Jones	Brian Jordan
2002	Bobby Cox	Javy Lopez	Julio Franco	K. Lockhart	Rafael Furcal	Vinny Castilla	Chipper Jones	Andruw Jones	G. Sheffield

BREWERS BY POSITION, YEAR BY YEAR

Seattle Pilots (American League), 1969
Milwaukee Brewers (American League), 1970–1997
Milwaukee Brewers (National League), 1998-Present

YEAR	MANAGER	C	1B	2B	SS	3B	LF	CF	RF	DH
1969	Joe Schultz	J. McNertney	Don Mincher	J. Donaldson	Ray Oyler	Tom Harper	Tommy Davis	Wayne Comer	Steve Hovley	
1970	Dave Bristol	Phil Roof	Mike Hegan	Ted Kubiak	Roberto Pena	Tom Harper	D. Walton	Davey May	Russ Snyder	
1971	Dave Bristol	E. Rodriguez	Roberto Pena	R. Theobald	R. Auerbach	Tom Harper	Johnny Briggs	Davey May	Bill Voss	
1972	Dave Bristol	E. Rodriguez	George Scott	R. Theobald	R. Auerbach	Mike Ferraro	Johnny Briggs	Davey May	Joe Lahoud	
1973	Del Crandall	Darrell Porter	George Scott	Pedro Garcia	Tim Johnson	Don Money	Johnny Briggs	Davey May	Bob Coluccio	Ollie Brown
1974	Del Crandall	Darrell Porter	George Scott	Pedro Garcia	Robin Yount	Don Money	Johnny Briggs	Bob Coluccio	Davey May	B. Mitchell
1975	Del Crandall	Darrell Porter	George Scott	Pedro Garcia	Robin Yount	Don Money	Bill Sharp	G. Thomas	S. Lezcano	Hank Aaron
1976	Al Grammas	Darrell Porter	George Scott	Tim Johnson	Robin Yount	Don Money	S. Lezcano	Von Joshua	G. Thomas	Hank Aaron
1977	Al Grammas	C. Moore	Cecil Cooper	Don Money	Robin Yount	Sal Bando	Jim Wohlford	Von Joshua	S. Lezcano	Jamie Quirk
1978	G. Bamberger	C. Moore	Cecil Cooper	Paul Molitor	Robin Yount	Sal Bando	Ben Oglivie	G. Thomas	S. Lezcano	Larry Hisle
1979	G. Bamberger	C. Moore	Cecil Cooper	Paul Molitor	Robin Yount	Sal Bando	Ben Oglivie	G. Thomas	S. Lezcano	Dick Davis
1980	G. Bamberger	C. Moore	Cecil Cooper	Paul Molitor	Robin Yount	Jim Gantner	Ben Oglivie	G. Thomas	S. Lezcano	Dick Davis
1981	Buck Rodgers	Ted Simmons	Cecil Cooper	Jim Gantner	Robin Yount	Don Money	Ben Oglivie	G. Thomas	M. Brouhard	Larry Hisle
1982	Buck Rodgers	Ted Simmons	Cecil Cooper	Jim Gantner	Robin Yount	Paul Molitor	Ben Oglivie	G. Thomas	C. Moore	Roy Howell
1983	H. Kuenn	Ted Simmons	Cecil Cooper	Jim Gantner	Robin Yount	Paul Molitor	Ben Oglivie	Rick Manning	C. Moore	Roy Howell
1984	R. Lachemann	Jim Sundberg	Cecil Cooper	Jim Gantner	Robin Yount	Ed Romero	Ben Oglivie	Rick Manning	Dion James	Ted Simmons
1985	G. Bamberger	C. Moore	Cecil Cooper	Jim Gantner	Ernie Riles	Paul Molitor	Ben Oglivie	Robin Yount	Householder	Ted Simmons
1986	G. Bamberger	C. Moore	B. Robidoux	Jim Gantner	Ernie Riles	Paul Molitor	Rick Manning	Robin Yount	Rob Deer	Cecil Cooper
1987	T. Trebelhorn	B.J. Surhoff	Greg Brock	Juan Castillo	Dale Sveum	Ernie Riles	Rob Deer	Robin Yount	Glenn Braggs	Cecil Cooper
1988	T. Trebelhorn	B.J. Surhoff	Greg Brock	Jim Gantner	Dale Sveum	Paul Molitor	Jeff Leonard	Robin Yount	Rob Deer	Joey Meyer
1989	T. Trebelhorn	B.J. Surhoff	Greg Brock	Jim Gantner	Bill Spiers	Paul Molitor	Glenn Braggs	Robin Yount	Rob Deer	Joey Meyer
1990	T. Trebelhorn	B.J. Surhoff	Greg Brock	Jim Gantner	Bill Spiers	G. Sheffield	Mike Felder	Robin Yount	Rob Deer	Dave Parker
1991	T. Trebelhorn	B.J. Surhoff	F. Stubbs	W. Randolph	Bill Spiers	Jim Gantner	Greg Vaughn	Robin Yount	D. Bichette	Paul Molitor
1992	Phil Garner	B.J. Surhoff	F. Stubbs	Scott Fletcher	Pat Listach	Kevin Seitzer	Greg Vaughn	Robin Yount	D. Hamilton	Paul Molitor
1993	Phil Garner	Dave Nilsson	John Jaha	Bill Spiers	Pat Listach	B.J. Surhoff	Greg Vaughn	Robin Yount	D. Hamilton	Kevin Reimer
1994	Phil Garner	Dave Nilsson	John Jaha	Jody Reed	Jose Valentin	Kevin Seitzer	Greg Vaughn	Turner Ward	Matt Mieske	Brian Harper
1995	Phil Garner	Joe Oliver	John Jaha	Fe. Vina	Jose Valentin	Jeff Cirillo	David Hulse	D. Hamilton	Matt Mieske	Greg Vaughn
1996	Phil Garner	M. Matheny	Kevin Seitzer	Fe. Vina	Jose Valentin	Jeff Cirillo	Greg Vaughn	Pat Listach	Matt Mieske	John Jaha

YEAR	MANAGER	C	1B	2B	SS	3B	LF	CF	RF	DH
1997	Phil Garner	M. Matheny	Dave Nilsson	Fe. Vina	Jose Valentin	Jeff Cirillo	Matt Mieske	G. Williams	J. Burnitz	Julio Franco
1998	Phil Garner	M. Matheny	Mark Loretta	Fe. Vina	Jose Valentin	Jeff Cirillo	D. Jackson	M. Grissom	J. Burnitz	
1999	Phil Garner	Dave Nilsson	Mark Loretta	R. Belliard	Jose Valentin	Jeff Cirillo	Geoff Jenkins	M. Grissom	J. Burnitz	
2000	Davey Lopes	Henry Blanco	Richie Sexson	R. Belliard	Mark Loretta	J. Hernandez	Geoff Jenkins	M. Grissom	J. Burnitz	
2001	Davey Lopes	Henry Blanco	Richie Sexson	R. Belliard	J. Hernandez	Mark Loretta	Geoff Jenkins	Devon White	J. Burnitz	
2002	Jerry Royster	J. Fabregas	Richie Sexson	Eric Young	J. Hernandez	Ron Belliard	Matt Stairs	Alex Sanchez	J. Hammonds	

CARDINALS BY POSITION, YEAR BY YEAR

St. Louis Browns (American Association), 1884–1891
St. Louis Browns (National League), 1892–1898
St. Louis Perfectos (National League), 1899
St. Louis Cardinals (National League), 1900–Present

YEAR	MANAGER	C	1B	2B	SS	3B	LF	CF	RF
1901	P. Donovan	Jack Ryan	Dan McGann	Dick Padden	Bob Wallace	Otto Krueger	Jesse Burkett	E. Heidrick	P. Donovan
1902	P. Donovan	Jack Ryan	Roy Brashear	John Farrell	Otto Krueger	Fred Hartman	G. Barclay	Homer Smoot	P. Donovan
1903	P. Donovan	Jack O'Neill	Jim Hackett	John Farrell	Dave Brain	Jimmy Burke	G. Barclay	Homer Smoot	P. Donovan
1904	Kid Nichols	Mike Grady	Jake Beckley	John Farrell	Danny Shay	Jimmy Burke	G. Barclay	Homer Smoot	S. Shannon
1905	S. Robison	Mike Grady	Jake Beckley	Harry Arndt	G. McBride	Jimmy Burke	S. Shannon	Homer Smoot	J. Dunleavy
1906	J. McCloskey	Mike Grady	Jake Beckley	Pug Bennett	G. McBride	Harry Arndt	S. Shannon	Homer Smoot	Al Burch
1907	J. McCloskey	Doc Marshall	Ed Konetchy	Pug Bennett	Ed Holly	Bobby Byrne	Red Murray	Jack Burnett	Shad Barry
1908	J. McCloskey	Bill Ludwig	Ed Konetchy	Billy Gilbert	P. O'Rourke	Bobby Byrne	J. Delahanty	Al Shaw	Red Murray
1909	R. Bresnahan	Ed Phelps	Ed Konetchy	C. Charles	R. Hulswitt	Bobby Byrne	Rube Ellis	Al Shaw	Steve Evans
1910	R. Bresnahan	Ed Phelps	Ed Konetchy	M. Huggins	A. Hauser	Mike Mowrey	Rube Ellis	Rebel Oakes	Steve Evans
1911	R. Bresnahan	Jack Bliss	Ed Konetchy	M. Huggins	A. Hauser	Mike Mowrey	Rube Ellis	Rebel Oakes	Steve Evans
1912	R. Bresnahan	Ivey Wingo	Ed Konetchy	M. Huggins	A. Hauser	Mike Mowrey	Lee Magee	Rebel Oakes	Steve Evans
1913	M. Huggins	Ivey Wingo	Ed Konetchy	M. Huggins	C. O'Leary	Mike Mowrey	Lee Magee	Rebel Oakes	Steve Evans
1914	M. Huggins	Frank Snyder	Dots Miller	M. Huggins	Art Butler	Zinn Beck	Cozy Dolan	Lee Magee	Chief Wilson
1915	M. Huggins	Frank Snyder	Dots Miller	M. Huggins	Art Butler	Bruno Betzel	Bob Bescher	Chief Wilson	Tom Long
1916	M. Huggins	M. Gonzalez	Dots Miller	Bruno Betzel	Roy Corhan	R. Hornsby	Bob Bescher	Jack Smith	Tom Long
1917	M. Huggins	Frank Snyder	Gene Paulette	Dots Miller	R. Hornsby	Doug Baird	Walton Cruise	Jack Smith	Tom Long
1918	J. Hendricks	M. Gonzalez	Gene Paulette	Bob Fisher	R. Hornsby	Doug Baird	A. McHenry	C. Heathcoate	Wa. Cruise
1919	B. Rickey	V. Clemons	Dots Miller	Milt Stock	Doc Lavan	R. Hornsby	A. McHenry	C. Heathcoate	Jack Smith
1920	B. Rickey	V. Clemons	Jack Fournier	R. Hornsby	Doc Lavan	Milt Stock	A. McHenry	Jack Smith	C. Heathcoate
1921	B. Rickey	V. Clemons	Jack Fournier	R. Hornsby	Doc Lavan	Milt Stock	A. McHenry	Les Mann	Jack Smith
1922	B. Rickey	Ed Ainsmith	Jack Fournier	R. Hornsby	S. Toporcer	Milt Stock	Joe Schultz	Jack Smith	Max Flack
1923	B. Rickey	Ed Ainsmith	J. Bottomley	R. Hornsby	H. Freigau	Milt Stock	Jack Smith	Hy Myers	Max Flack
1924	B. Rickey	M. Gonzalez	J. Bottomley	R. Hornsby	J. Cooney	H. Freigau	Ray Blades	Wattie Holm	Jack Smith
1925	R. Hornsby	B. O'Farrell	J. Bottomley	R. Hornsby	S. Toporcer	Les Bell	Ray Blades	H. Mueller	Chick Hafey
1926	R. Hornsby	B. O'Farrell	J. Bottomley	R. Hornsby	T. Thevenow	Les Bell	Ray Blades	T. Douthit	B. Southworth
1927	B. O'Farrell	Frank Snyder	J. Bottomley	Frankie Frisch	H. Schuble	Les Bell	Chick Hafey	T. Douthit	B. Southworth
1928	B. McKechnie	J. Wilson	J. Bottomley	Frankie Frisch	R. Maranville	Wattie Holm	Chick Hafey	T. Douthit	G. Harper
1929	B. Southworth	J. Wilson	J. Bottomley	Frankie Frisch	C. Gelbert	Andy High	Chick Hafey	T. Douthit	Ernie Orsatti
1930	Gabby Street	J. Wilson	J. Bottomley	Frankie Frisch	C. Gelbert	S. Adams	Chick Hafey	T. Douthit	G. Watkins
1931	Gabby Street	J. Wilson	J. Bottomley	Frankie Frisch	C. Gelbert	S. Adams	Chick Hafey	Pepper Martin	G. Watkins
1932	Gabby Street	Gus Mancuso	R. Collins	Jimmie Reese	C. Gelbert	Jake Flowers	Ernie Orsatti	Pepper Martin	G. Watkins
1933	Gabby Street	J. Wilson	R. Collins	Frankie Frisch	Leo Durocher	Pepper Martin	Joe Medwick	Ernie Orsatti	G. Watkins
1934	Frankie Frisch	Spud Davis	R. Collins	Frankie Frisch	Leo Durocher	Pepper Martin	Joe Medwick	Ernie Orsatti	Jack Rothrock
1935	Frankie Frisch	B. DeLancey	R. Collins	Frankie Frisch	Leo Durocher	Pepper Martin	Joe Medwick	Terry Moore	Jack Rothrock

YEAR	MANAGER	C	1B	2B	SS	3B	LF	CF	RF
1936	Frankie Frisch	Spud Davis	Johnny Mize	Stu Martin	Leo Durocher	C. Gelbert	Joe Medwick	Terry Moore	Pepper Martin
1937	Frankie Frisch	Ogrodowski	Johnny Mize	Jimmy Brown	Leo Durocher	D. Gutteridge	Joe Medwick	Terry Moore	Don Padgett
1938	Frankie Frisch	Mickey Owen	Johnny Mize	Stu Martin	Lynn Myers	D. Gutteridge	Joe Medwick	Terry Moore	E. Slaughter
1939	Ray Blades	Mickey Owen	Johnny Mize	Stu Martin	Jimmy Brown	D. Gutteridge	Joe Medwick	Terry Moore	E. Slaughter
1940	B. Southworth	Mickey Owen	Johnny Mize	Joe Orengo	Marty Marion	Stu Martin	Ernie Koy	Terry Moore	E. Slaughter
1941	B. Southworth	Gus Mancuso	Johnny Mize	Creepy Crespi	Marty Marion	Jimmy Brown	Johnny Hopp	Terry Moore	E. Slaughter
1942	B. Southworth	Walk Cooper	Johnny Hopp	Creepy Crespi	Marty Marion	W. Kurowski	Stan Musial	Terry Moore	E. Slaughter
1943	B. Southworth	Walk Cooper	Ray Sanders	Lou Klein	Marty Marion	W. Kurowski	D. Litwhiler	Harry Walker	Stan Musial
1944	B. Southworth	Walk Cooper	Ray Sanders	Emil Verban	Marty Marion	W. Kurowski	D. Litwhiler	Johnny Hopp	Stan Musial
1945	B. Southworth	Ken O'Dea	Ray Sanders	Emil Verban	Marty Marion	W. Kurowski	Schoendienst	Buster Adams	Johnny Hopp
1946	Eddie Dyer	Joe Garagiola	Stan Musial	Schoendienst	Marty Marion	W. Kurowski	Erv Dusak	Harry Walker	E. Slaughter
1947	Eddie Dyer	Del Rice	Stan Musial	Schoendienst	Marty Marion	W. Kurowski	E. Slaughter	Terry Moore	Ron Northey
1948	Eddie Dyer	Del Rice	Nippy Jones	Schoendienst	Marty Marion	Don Lang	E. Slaughter	Terry Moore	Stan Musial
1949	Eddie Dyer	Del Rice	Nippy Jones	Schoendienst	Marty Marion	Eddie Kazak	E. Slaughter	C. Diering	Stan Musial
1950	Eddie Dyer	Del Rice	Rocky Nelson	Schoendienst	Marty Marion	T. Glaviano	Stan Musial	Bill Howerton	E. Slaughter
1951	Marty Marion	Del Rice	Nippy Jones	Schoendienst	Solly Hemus	Billy Johnson	Stan Musial	P. Lowrey	E. Slaughter
1952	Eddie Stanky	Del Rice	Dick Sisler	Schoendienst	Solly Hemus	Billy Johnson	P. Lowrey	Stan Musial	E. Slaughter
1953	Eddie Stanky	Del Rice	Steve Bilko	Schoendienst	Solly Hemus	Ray Jablonski	Stan Musial	Rip Repulski	E. Slaughter
1954	Eddie Stanky	Bill Sarni	Cunningham	Schoendienst	Al Grammas	Ray Jablonski	Rip Repulski	Wally Moon	Stan Musial
1955	Harry Walker	Bill Sarni	Stan Musial	Schoendienst	Al Grammas	Ken Boyer	Rip Repulski	Bill Virdon	Wally Moon
1956	F. Hutchinson	Hal Smith	Stan Musial	Blasingame	Alvin Dark	Ken Boyer	Rip Repulski	B. Del Greco	Wally Moon
1957	F. Hutchinson	Hal Smith	Stan Musial	Blasingame	Alvin Dark	Eddie Kasko	Wally Moon	Ken Boyer	Del Ennis
1958	F. Hutchinson	Hal Smith	Stan Musial	Blasingame	Eddie Kasko	Ken Boyer	Del Ennis	Curt Flood	Wally Moon
1959	Solly Hemus	Hal Smith	Stan Musial	Blasingame	Al Grammas	Ken Boyer	Gino Cimoli	Curt Flood	Cunningham
1960	Solly Hemus	Hal Smith	Bill White	Julian Javier	Daryl Spencer	Ken Boyer	Stan Musial	Curt Flood	Cunningham
1961	Johnny Keane	J. Schaffer	Bill White	Julian Javier	Al Grammas	Ken Boyer	Stan Musial	Curt Flood	Charlie James
1962	Johnny Keane	Gene Oliver	Bill White	Julian Javier	Julio Gotay	Ken Boyer	Stan Musial	Curt Flood	Charlie James
1963	Johnny Keane	T. McCarver	Bill White	Julian Javier	Dick Groat	Ken Boyer	Charlie James	Curt Flood	G. Altman
1964	Johnny Keane	T. McCarver	Bill White	Julian Javier	Dick Groat	Ken Boyer	Lou Brock	Curt Flood	M. Shannon
1965	Schoendienst	T. McCarver	Bill White	Julian Javier	Dick Groat	Ken Boyer	Lou Brock	Curt Flood	M. Shannon
1966	Schoendienst	T. McCarver	O. Cepeda	Julian Javier	Dal Maxvill	Charlie Smith	Lou Brock	Curt Flood	M. Shannon
1967	Schoendienst	T. McCarver	O. Cepeda	Julian Javier	Dal Maxvill	M. Shannon	Lou Brock	Curt Flood	Roger Maris
1968	Schoendienst	T. McCarver	O. Cepeda	Julian Javier	Dal Maxvill	M. Shannon	Lou Brock	Curt Flood	Roger Maris
1969	Schoendienst	T. McCarver	Joe Torre	Julian Javier	Dal Maxvill	M. Shannon	Lou Brock	Curt Flood	Vada Pinson
1970	Schoendienst	Ted Simmons	Joe Hague	Julian Javier	Dal Maxvill	Joe Torre	Lou Brock	Jose Cardenal	Leron Lee
1971	Schoendienst	Ted Simmons	Joe Hague	T. Sizemore	Dal Maxvill	Joe Torre	Lou Brock	Matty Alou	Jose Cardenal
1972	Schoendienst	Ted Simmons	Matty Alou	T. Sizemore	Dal Maxvill	Ken Reitz	Lou Brock	Jose Cruz	L. Melendez
1973	Schoendienst	Ted Simmons	Joe Torre	T. Sizemore	Mike Tyson	Ken Reitz	Lou Brock	L. Melendez	Jose Cruz
1974	Schoendienst	Ted Simmons	Joe Torre	T. Sizemore	Mike Tyson	Ken Reitz	Lou Brock	B. McBride	Jose Cruz
1975	Schoendienst	Ted Simmons	Reggie Smith	T. Sizemore	Mike Tyson	Ken Reitz	Lou Brock	B. McBride	Reggie Smith
1976	Schoendienst	Ted Simmons	K. Hernandez	Mike Tyson	D. Kessinger	Hector Cruz	Lou Brock	J. Mumphrey	W. Crawford
1977	Vern Rapp	Ted Simmons	K. Hernandez	Mike Tyson	G. Templeton	Ken Reitz	Lou Brock	J. Mumphrey	Hector Cruz
1978	Ken Boyer	Ted Simmons	K. Hernandez	Mike Tyson	G. Templeton	Ken Reitz	Lou Brock	G. Hendrick	Jerry Morales
1979	Ken Boyer	Ted Simmons	K. Hernandez	K. Oberkfell	G. Templeton	Ken Reitz	Lou Brock	Tony Scott	G. Hendrick
1980	W. Herzog	Ted Simmons	K. Hernandez	K. Oberkfell	G. Templeton	Ken Reitz	Bobby Bonds	Tony Scott	G. Hendrick
1981	W. Herzog	Darrell Porter	K. Hernandez	Tommy Herr	G. Templeton	K. Oberkfell	Dane Iorg	G. Hendrick	Sixto Lezcano
1982	W. Herzog	Darrell Porter	K. Hernandez	Tommy Herr	Ozzie Smith	K. Oberkfell	Lonnie Smith	Willie McGee	G. Hendrick
1983	W. Herzog	Darrell Porter	G. Hendrick	Tommy Herr	Ozzie Smith	K. Oberkfell	Lonnie Smith	Willie McGee	David Green
1984	W. Herzog	Darrell Porter	David Green	Tommy Herr	Ozzie Smith	T. Pendleton	Lonnie Smith	Willie McGee	G. Hendrick

YEAR	MANAGER	C	1B	2B	SS	3B	LF	CF	RF
1985	W. Herzog	Tom Nieto	Jack Clark	Tommy Herr	Ozzie Smith	T. Pendleton	V. Coleman	Willie McGee	A. Van Slyke
1986	W. Herzog	M. LaValliere	Jack Clark	Tommy Herr	Ozzie Smith	T. Pendleton	V. Coleman	Willie McGee	A. Van Slyke
1987	W. Herzog	Tony Pena	Jack Clark	Tommy Herr	Ozzie Smith	T. Pendleton	V. Coleman	Willie McGee	Curt Ford
1988	W. Herzog	Tony Pena	Bob Horner	Luis Alicea	Ozzie Smith	T. Pendleton	V. Coleman	Willie McGee	T. Brunansky
1989	W. Herzog	Tony Pena	P. Guerrero	Jose Oquendo	Ozzie Smith	T. Pendleton	V. Coleman	M. Thompson	T. Brunansky
1990	W. Herzog	Todd Zeile	P. Guerrero	Jose Oquendo	Ozzie Smith	T. Pendleton	V. Coleman	Willie McGee	M. Thompson
1991	Joe Torre	Tom Pagnozzi	P. Guerrero	Jose Oquendo	Ozzie Smith	Todd Zeile	M. Thompson	Ray Lankford	Felix Jose
1992	Joe Torre	Tom Pagnozzi	A. Galarraga	Luis Alicea	Ozzie Smith	Todd Zeile	B. Gilkey	Ray Lankford	Felix Jose
1993	Joe Torre	Tom Pagnozzi	G. Jefferies	Luis Alicea	Ozzie Smith	Todd Zeile	B. Gilkey	Ray Lankford	Mark Whiten
1994	Joe Torre	Tom Pagnozzi	G. Jefferies	G. Pena	Ozzie Smith	Todd Zeile	B. Gilkey	Ray Lankford	Mark Whiten
1995	M. Jorgensen	D. Sheaffer	John Mabry	Jose Oquendo	Tripp Cromer	Scott Cooper	B. Gilkey	Ray Lankford	Brian Jordan
1996	T. La Russa	Tom Pagnozzi	John Mabry	Luis Alicea	R. Clayton	Gary Gaetti	Ron Gant	Ray Lankford	Brian Jordan
1997	T. La Russa	M. DiFelice	Dmitri Young	D. DeShields	R. Clayton	Gary Gaetti	Ron Gant	Ray Lankford	Willie McGee
1998	T. La Russa	Eli Marrero	M. McGwire	D. DeShields	R. Clayton	Gary Gaetti	Ron Gant	Ray Lankford	Brian Jordan
1999	T. La Russa	Eli Marrero	M. McGwire	Joe McEwing	Ed Renteria	F. Tatis	Ray Lankford	J.D. Drew	Willie McGee
2000	T. La Russa	M. Matheny	M. McGwire	Fern. Vina	Ed Renteria	F. Tatis	Ray Lankford	Jim Edmonds	J.D. Drew
2001	T. La Russa	M. Matheny	M. McGwire	Fern. Vina	Ed Renteria	P. Polanco	Albert Pujols	Jim Edmonds	J.D. Drew
2002	T. La Russa	M. Matheny	Tino Martinez	Fern. Vina	Ed Renteria	P. Polanco	Albert Pujols	Jim Edmonds	J.D. Drew

CUBS BY POSITION, YEAR BY YEAR

Chicago White Stockings (National League), 1876–1889
Chicago Colts (National League), 1890–1897
Chicago Orphans (National League), 1898–1901
Chicago Cubs (National League), 1902–Present

YEAR	MANAGER	C	1B	2B	SS	3B	LF	CF	RF
1901	Tom Loftus	Johnny Kling	Jack Doyle	Cupid Childs	B. McCormick	Fred Raymer	Topsy Hartsel	Danny Green	Frank Chance
1902	Frank Selee	Johnny Kling	Frank Chance	Bobby Lowe	Joe Tinker	G. Schaefer	Jimmy Slagle	Johnny Dobbs	Davy Jones
1903	Frank Selee	Johnny Kling	Frank Chance	Johnny Evers	Joe Tinker	Doc Casey	Jimmy Slagle	Davy Jones	Dick Harley
1904	Frank Selee	Johnny Kling	Frank Chance	Johnny Evers	Joe Tinker	Doc Casey	Jimmy Slagle	J. McCarthy	Davy Jones
1905	Frank Selee	Johnny Kling	Frank Chance	Johnny Evers	Joe Tinker	Doc Casey	Fred Schulte	Jimmy Slagle	B. Maloney
1906	Frank Chance	Johnny Kling	Frank Chance	Johnny Evers	Joe Tinker	H. Steinfeldt	Jim Sheckard	Jimmy Slagle	Frank Schulte
1907	Frank Chance	Johnny Kling	Frank Chance	Johnny Evers	Joe Tinker	H. Steinfeldt	Jim Sheckard	Jimmy Slagle	Frank Schulte
1908	Frank Chance	Johnny Kling	Frank Chance	Johnny Evers	Joe Tinker	H. Steinfeldt	Jim Sheckard	Jimmy Slagle	Frank Schulte
1909	Frank Chance	Jimmy Archer	Frank Chance	Johnny Evers	Joe Tinker	H. Steinfeldt	Jim Sheckard	Solly Hofman	Frank Schulte
1910	Frank Chance	Johnny Kling	Frank Chance	Johnny Evers	Joe Tinker	H. Steinfeldt	Jim Sheckard	Solly Hofman	Frank Schulte
1911	Frank Chance	Jimmy Archer	Vic Saier	H. Zimmerman	Joe Tinker	Jim Doyle	Jim Sheckard	Solly Hofman	Frank Schulte
1912	Frank Chance	Jimmy Archer	Vic Saier	Johnny Evers	Joe Tinker	H. Zimmerman	Jim Sheckard	Tommy Leach	Frank Schulte
1913	Johnny Evers	Jimmy Archer	Vic Saier	Johnny Evers	Al Bridwell	H. Zimmerman	Mike Mitchell	Tommy Leach	Frank Schulte
1914	Hank O'Day	R. Bresnahan	Vic Saier	Bill Sweeney	Red Corriden	H. Zimmerman	Fred Schulte	Tommy Leach	Wilbur Good
1915	R. Bresnahan	Jimmy Archer	Vic Saier	H. Zimmerman	Bobby Fisher	Art Phelan	Fred Schulte	Cy Williams	Wilbur Good
1916	Joe Tinker	Jimmy Archer	Vic Saier	Otto Knabe	C. Wortman	H. Zimmerman	Les Mann	Cy Williams	Max Flack
1917	Fred Mitchell	Art Wilson	Fred Merkle	Larry Doyle	C. Wortman	Charlie Deal	Les Mann	Cy Williams	Max Flack
1918	Fred Mitchell	Bill Killefer	Fred Merkle	Rollie Zeider	C. Hollocher	Charlie Deal	Les Mann	Dode Paskert	Max Flack
1919	Fred Mitchell	Bill Killefer	Fred Merkle	Charlie Pick	C. Hollocher	Charlie Deal	Les Mann	Dode Paskert	Max Flack
1920	Fred Mitchell	Bob O'Farrell	Fred Merkle	Zeb Terry	C. Hollocher	Charlie Deal	D. Robertson	Dode Paskert	Max Flack
1921	Johnny Evers	Bob O'Farrell	Ray Grimes	Zeb Terry	C. Hollocher	Charlie Deal	Turner Barber	Geo. Maisel	Max Flack
1922	Bill Killefer	Bob O'Farrell	Ray Grimes	Zeb Terry	C. Hollocher	Marty Krug	Hack Miller	Jigger Statz	Bernie Friberg
1923	Bill Killefer	Bob O'Farrell	Ray Grimes	G. Grantham	Sparky Adams	Bernie Friberg	Hack Miller	Jigger Statz	C. Heathcote

YEAR	MANAGER	C	1B	2B	SS	3B	LF	CF	RF
1924	Bill Killefer	G. Hartnett	Harvey Cotter	G. Grantham	Sparky Adams	Bernie Friberg	D. Grigsby	Jigger Statz	C. Heathcote
1925	Bill Killefer	G. Hartnett	Ch. Grimm	Sparky Adams	R. Maranville	H. Freigau	Art Jahn	Mandy Brooks	C. Heathcote
1926	Joe McCarthy	G. Hartnett	Ch. Grimm	Sparky Adams	Jim Cooney	H. Freigau	R. Stephenson	Hack Wilson	C. Heathcote
1927	Joe McCarthy	G. Hartnett	Ch. Grimm	Clyde Beck	W. English	Sparky Adams	R. Stephenson	Hack Wilson	Earl Webb
1928	Joe McCarthy	G. Hartnett	Ch. Grimm	Fred Maguire	W. English	Clyde Beck	R. Stephenson	Hack Wilson	Kiki Cuyler
1929	Joe McCarthy	Zack Taylor	Ch. Grimm	R. Hornsby	W. English	N. McMillan	R. Stephenson	Hack Wilson	Kiki Cuyler
1930	Joe McCarthy	G. Hartnett	Ch. Grimm	Footsie Blair	W. English	Les Bell	R. Stephenson	Hack Wilson	Kiki Cuyler
1931	R. Hornsby	G. Hartnett	Ch. Grimm	R. Hornsby	W. English	Les Bell	Danny Taylor	Hack Wilson	Kiki Cuyler
1932	R. Hornsby	G. Hartnett	Ch. Grimm	Billy Herman	Billy Jurges	W. English	R. Stephenson	Johnny Moore	Kiki Cuyler
1933	Ch. Grimm	G. Hartnett	Ch. Grimm	Billy Herman	Billy Jurges	W. English	R. Stephenson	F. Demaree	Babe Herman
1934	Ch. Grimm	G. Hartnett	Ch. Grimm	Billy Herman	Billy Jurges	Stan Hack	Chuck Klein	Kiki Cuyler	Babe Herman
1935	Ch. Grimm	G. Hartnett	P. Cavaretta	Billy Herman	Billy Jurges	Stan Hack	Augie Galan	F. Demaree	Chuck Klein
1936	Ch. Grimm	G. Hartnett	P. Cavaretta	Billy Herman	Billy Jurges	Stan Hack	Ethan Allen	Augie Galan	F. Demaree
1937	Ch. Grimm	G. Hartnett	Ripper Collins	Billy Herman	Billy Jurges	Stan Hack	Augie Galan	Joe Marty	F. Demaree
1938	Ch. Grimm	G. Hartnett	Ripper Collins	Billy Herman	Billy Jurges	Stan Hack	Augie Galan	Carl Reynolds	F. Demaree
1939	G. Hartnett	G. Hartnett	Rip Russell	Billy Herman	Dick Bartell	Stan Hack	Augie Galan	Hank Leiber	Jim Gleeson
1940	G. Hartnett	Al Todd	P. Cavaretta	Billy Herman	B. Mattick	Stan Hack	B. Nicholson	Jim Gleeson	Hank Leiber
1941	Jimmy Wilson	C. McCullough	B. Dahlgren	Lou Stringer	Bob Sturgeon	Stan Hack	Dallessandro	P. Cavaretta	B. Nicholson
1942	Jimmy Wilson	C. McCullough	P. Cavaretta	Lou Stringer	L. Merullo	Stan Hack	Lou Novikoff	Dallessandro	B. Nicholson
1943	Jimmy Wilson	C. McCullough	P. Cavaretta	Eddie Stanky	L. Merullo	Stan Hack	Lou Novikoff	P. Lowrey	B. Nicholson
1944	Ch. Grimm	D. Williams	P. Cavaretta	Don Johnson	L. Merullo	Stan Hack	Dallessandro	Andy Pafko	B. Nicholson
1945	Ch. Grimm	M Livingston	P. Cavaretta	Don Johnson	L. Merullo	Stan Hack	P. Lowrey	Andy Pafko	B. Nicholson
1946	Ch. Grimm	C. McCullough	Eddie Waitkus	Don Johnson	Billy Jurges	Stan Hack	Marv Rickert	P. Lowrey	P. Cavaretta
1947	Ch. Grimm	Bob Scheffing	Eddie Waitkus	Don Johnson	L. Merullo	P. Lowrey	P. Cavaretta	Andy Pafko	B. Nicholson
1948	Ch. Grimm	Bob Scheffing	Eddie Waitkus	Hank Schenz	Roy Smalley	Andy Pafko	P. Lowrey	Hal Jeffcoat	B. Nicholson
1949	Frank Frisch	Mickey Owen	Herm Reich	Evil Verban	Roy Smalley	Frank Gustine	Hank Sauer	Andy Pafko	Hal Jeffcoat
1950	Frank Frisch	Mickey Owen	Preston Ward	W. Terwilliger	Roy Smalley	Bill Serena	Hank Sauer	Andy Pafko	B. Borkowski
1951	Frank Frisch	S. Burgess	C. Connors	Eddie Miksis	Roy Smalley	R. Jackson	Hank Sauer	Hal Jeffcoat	F. Baumholtz
1952	P. Cavaretta	Toby Atwell	Dee Fondy	Eddie Miksis	Roy Smalley	R. Jackson	Hank Sauer	Hal Jeffcoat	F. Baumholtz
1953	P. Cavaretta	C. McCullough	Dee Fondy	Eddie Miksis	Roy Smalley	R. Jackson	Ralph Kiner	F. Baumholtz	Hank Sauer
1954	Stan Hack	Joe Garagiola	Dee Fondy	Gene Baker	Ernie Banks	R. Jackson	Ralph Kiner	Dale Talbot	Hank Sauer
1955	Stan Hack	Harry Chiti	Dee Fondy	Gene Baker	Ernie Banks	R. Jackson	Hank Sauer	Eddie Miksis	Jim King
1956	Stan Hack	H. Landrith	Dee Fondy	Gene Baker	Ernie Banks	Don Hoak	Monte Irvin	P. Whisenant	Walt Moryn
1957	Bob Scheffing	Cal Neeman	Dale Long	Bob Morgan	Ernie Banks	Bobby Adams	Lee Walls	Bob Speake	Walt Moryn
1958	Bob Scheffing	Sammy Taylor	Dale Long	Tony Taylor	Ernie Banks	Alvin Dark	Walt Moryn	B. Thomson	Lee Walls
1959	Bob Scheffing	Sammy Taylor	Dale Long	Tony Taylor	Ernie Banks	Alvin Dark	B. Thomson	G. Altman	Lee Walls
1960	Lou Boudreau	El Tappe	Ed Bouchee	Jerry Kindall	Ernie Banks	Ron Santo	R. Ashburn	G. Altman	Bob Will
1961	El Tappe	Dick Bertell	Ed Bouchee	Don Zimmer	Ernie Banks	Ron Santo	Billy Williams	Al Heist	G. Altman
1962	Charlie Metro	Dick Bertell	Ernie Banks	Ken Hubbs	A. Rodgers	Ron Santo	Billy Williams	Lou Brock	G. Altman
1963	Bob Kennedy	Dick Bertell	Ernie Banks	Ken Hubbs	A. Rodgers	Ron Santo	Billy Williams	Ellis Burton	Lou Brock
1964	Bob Kennedy	Dick Bertell	Ernie Banks	J. Amalfitano	A. Rodgers	Ron Santo	Billy Williams	Billy Cowan	L. Gabrielson
1965	Lou Klein	V. Roznofsky	Ernie Banks	Glenn Beckert	Don Kessinger	Ron Santo	Doug Clemens	D. Landrum	Billy Williams
1966	Leo Durocher	R. Hundley	Ernie Banks	Glenn Beckert	Don Kessinger	Ron Santo	Byron Browne	A. Phillips	Billy Williams
1967	Leo Durocher	R. Hundley	Ernie Banks	Glenn Beckert	Don Kessinger	Ron Santo	Billy Williams	A. Phillips	Ted Savage
1968	Leo Durocher	R. Hundley	Ernie Banks	Glenn Beckert	Don Kessinger	Ron Santo	Billy Williams	A. Phillips	Jim Hickman
1969	Leo Durocher	R. Hundley	Ernie Banks	Glenn Beckert	Don Kessinger	Ron Santo	Billy Williams	Don Young	Jim Hickman
1970	Leo Durocher	R. Hundley	Ernie Banks	Glenn Beckert	Don Kessinger	Ron Santo	Billy Williams	Jim Hickman	J. Callison
1971	Leo Durocher	C. Cannizzaro	Joe Pepitone	Glenn Beckert	Don Kessinger	Ron Santo	Billy Williams	Brock Davis	J. Callison
1972	Leo Durocher	R. Hundley	Jim Hickman	Glenn Beckert	Don Kessinger	Ron Santo	Billy Williams	Rick Monday	Jose Cardenal

YEAR	MANAGER	C	1B	2B	SS	3B	LF	CF	RF
1973	W. Lockman	R. Hundley	Jim Hickman	Glenn Beckert	Don Kessinger	Ron Santo	Billy Williams	Rick Monday	Jose Cardenal
1974	W. Lockman	Steve Swisher	A. Thornton	Vic Harris	Don Kessinger	Bill Madlock	Jerry Morales	Rick Monday	Jose Cardenal
1975	Jim Marshall	Steve Swisher	A. Thornton	Manny Trillo	Don Kessinger	Bill Madlock	Jose Cardenal	Rick Monday	Jerry Morales
1976	Jim Marshall	Steve Swisher	Pete LaCock	Manny Trillo	Mick Kelleher	Bill Madlock	Jose Cardenal	Rick Monday	Jerry Morales
1977	H. Franks	G. Mitterwald	Bill Buckner	Manny Trillo	Ivan DeJesus	S. Ontiveros	Jose Cardenal	Jerry Morales	Bobby Murcer
1978	H. Franks	Dave Rader	Bill Buckner	Manny Trillo	Ivan DeJesus	S. Ontiveros	D. Kingman	Greg Gross	Bobby Murcer
1979	H. Franks	Barry Foote	Bill Buckner	Ted Sizemore	Ivan DeJesus	S. Ontiveros	D. Kingman	Jerry Martin	S. Thompson
1980	P. Gomez	Tim Blackwell	Bill Buckner	Mike Tyson	Ivan DeJesus	Lenny Randle	D. Kingman	Jerry Martin	Mike Vail
1981	J. Amalfitano	Jody Davis	Bill Buckner	Mike Tyson	Ivan DeJesus	Ken Reitz	S. Henderson	Jerry Morales	Leon Durham
1982	Lee Elia	Jody Davis	Bill Buckner	Bump Wills	Larry Bowa	R. Sandberg	K. Moreland	Gary Woods	Leon Durham
1983	Lee Elia	Jody Davis	Bill Buckner	R. Sandberg	Larry Bowa	Ron Cey	Leon Durham	Mel Hall	K. Moreland
1984	Jim Frey	Jody Davis	Leon Durham	R. Sandberg	Larry Bowa	Ron Cey	G. Matthews	Bob Dernier	K. Moreland
1985	Jim Frey	Jody Davis	Leon Durham	R. Sandberg	S. Dunston	Ron Cey	G. Matthews	Bob Dernier	K. Moreland
1986	Gene Michael	Jody Davis	Leon Durham	R. Sandberg	S. Dunston	Ron Cey	G. Matthews	Bob Dernier	K. Moreland
1987	Gene Michael	Jody Davis	Leon Durham	R. Sandberg	S. Dunston	K. Moreland	J. Mumphrey	Dave Martinez	A. Dawson
1988	Don Zimmer	D. Berryhill	Mark Grace	R. Sandberg	S. Dunston	Vance Law	R. Palmeiro	D. Jackson	A. Dawson
1989	Don Zimmer	D. Berryhill	Mark Grace	R. Sandberg	S. Dunston	Vance Law	Dwight Smith	J. Walton	A. Dawson
1990	Don Zimmer	Joe Girardi	Mark Grace	R. Sandberg	S. Dunston	Luis Salazar	D. Dascenzo	J. Walton	A. Dawson
1991	Jim Essian	Rick Wilkins	Mark Grace	R. Sandberg	S. Dunston	Luis Salazar	George Bell	J. Walton	A. Dawson
1992	Jim Lefebvre	Joe Girardi	Mark Grace	R. Sandberg	Rey Sanchez	S. Buechele	Derrick May	D. Dasczenzo	A. Dawson
1993	Jim Lefebvre	Rick Wilkins	Mark Grace	R. Sandberg	Rey Sanchez	S. Buechele	Derrick May	Dwight Smith	Sammy Sosa
1994	T. Trebelhorn	Rick Wilkins	Mark Grace	R. Sandberg	S. Dunston	S. Buechele	Derrick May	Glenallen Hill	Sammy Sosa
1995	J. Riggleman	Scott Servais	Mark Grace	Rey Sanchez	S. Dunston	Todd Zeile	Luis Gonzalez	Brian McRae	Sammy Sosa
1996	J. Riggleman	Scott Servais	Mark Grace	R. Sandberg	Rey Sanchez	Leo Gomez	Luis Gonzalez	Brian McRae	Sammy Sosa
1997	J. Riggleman	Scott Servais	Mark Grace	R. Sandberg	S. Dunston	Kevin Orie	D. Glanville	Brian McRae	Sammy Sosa
1998	J. Riggleman	Scott Servais	Mark Grace	M. Morandini	Jeff Blauser	Gary Gaetti	H. Rodriguez	Brant Brown	Sammy Sosa
1999	J. Riggleman	Ben Santiago	Mark Grace	M. Morandini	J. Hernandez	Gary Gaetti	H. Rodriguez	Lance Johnson	Sammy Sosa
2000	Don Baylor	Joe Girardi	Mark Grace	Eric Young	R. Gutierrez	Willie Greene	H. Rodriguez	D. Buford	Sammy Sosa
2001	Don Baylor	Todd Hundley	Matt Stairs	Eric Young	R. Gutierrez	Ron Coomer	Rondell White	G. Matthews	Sammy Sosa
2002	Don Baylor	Todd Hundley	Fred McGriff	Mark Bellhorn	A. Gonzalez	Bill Mueller	Moises Alou	C. Patterson	Sammy Sosa

DEVIL RAYS BY POSITION, YEAR BY YEAR

Tampa Bay Devil Rays (American League), 1998–Present

YEAR	MANAGER	C	1B	2B	SS	3B	LF	CF	RF	DH
1998	L. Rothschild	John Flaherty	Fred McGriff	Miguel Cairo	K. Stocker	Bobby Smith	Q. McCracken	Randy Winn	Mike Kelly	Paul Sorrento
1999	L. Rothschild	John Flaherty	Fred McGriff	Miguel Cairo	K. Stocker	Wade Boggs	B. Trammell	Randy Winn	D. Martinez	Jose Canseco
2000	L. Rothschild	John Flaherty	Fred McGriff	Miguel Cairo	F. Martinez	Vinny Castilla	Greg Vaughn	G. Williams	Jose Guillen	Jose Canseco
2001	Hal McRae	John Flaherty	Steve Cox	B. Abernathy	F. Martinez	Aubrey Huff	Jason Tyner	Jason Tyner	Ben Grieve	Greg Vaughn
2002	Hal McRae	Toby Hall	Steve Cox	B. Abernathy	Chris Gomez	J. Sandberg	Greg Vaughn	Randy Winn	Ben Grieve	Aubrey Huff

DIAMONDBACKS BY POSITION, YEAR BY YEAR

Arizona Diamondbacks (National League), 1998–Present

YEAR	MANAGER	C	1B	2B	SS	3B	LF	CF	RF
1998	B. Showalter	K. Stinnett	Travis Lee	Stankiewicz	Jay Bell	M. Williams	D. Dellucci	Devon White	Karim Garcia
1999	B. Showalter	K. Stinnett	Travis Lee	Jay Bell	Andy Fox	M. Williams	Luis Gonzalez	Steve Finley	T. Womack
2000	B. Showalter	D. Miller	G. Colbrunn	Jay Bell	T. Womack	M. Williams	Luis Gonzalez	Steve Finley	D. Bautista

YEAR	MANAGER	C	1B	2B	SS	3B	LF	CF	RF
2001	Bob Brenly	D. Miller	Mark Grace	Jay Bell	T. Womack	M. Williams	Luis Gonzalez	Steve Finley	R. Sanders
2002	Bob Brenly	D. Miller	Mark Grace	Junior Spivey	T. Womack	C. Counsell	Luis Gonzalez	Steve Finley	Q. McCracken

DODGERS BY POSITION, YEAR BY YEAR

Brooklyn Bridegrooms (National League), 1890–1898
Brooklyn Superbas (National League), 1899–1910
Brooklyn Dodgers (National League), 1911–1913
Brooklyn Robins (National League), 1914–1931
Brooklyn Dodgers (National League), 1932–1957
Los Angeles Dodgers (National League), 1958–Present

YEAR	MANAGER	C	1B	2B	SS	3B	LF	CF	RF
1901	Ned Hanlon	D. McGuire	Joe Kelley	Tom Daly	Bill Dahlen	Charlie Irwin	Jim Sheckard	T. McCreery	Willie Keeler
1902	Ned Hanlon	Hugh Hearne	T. McCreery	Tim Flood	Bill Dahlen	Charlie Irwin	Jim Sheckard	Cozy Dolan	Willie Keeler
1903	Ned Hanlon	Lew Ritter	Jack Doyle	Tim Flood	Bill Dahlen	Sammy Strang	Jim Sheckard	Johnny Dobbs	J. McCredie
1904	Ned Hanlon	Bill Bergen	Pop Dillon	Dutch Jordan	Charlie Babb	M. McCormick	Jim Sheckard	Johnny Dobbs	Harry Lumley
1905	Ned Hanlon	Lew Ritter	Doc Gessler	Charlie Malay	Phil Lewis	Heinie Batch	Jim Sheckard	Johnny Dobbs	Harry Lumley
1906	Pat Donovan	Bill Bergen	Tim Jordan	W. Alperman	Phil Lewis	Doc Casey	J. McCarthy	Billy Maloney	Harry Lumley
1907	Pat Donovan	Lew Ritter	Tim Jordan	W. Alperman	Phil Lewis	Doc Casey	Heinie Batch	Billy Maloney	Harry Lumley
1908	Harry Lumley	Bill Bergen	Tim Jordan	Harry Pattee	Phil Lewis	Tom Sheehan	Al Burch	Billy Maloney	Harry Lumley
1909	Harry Lumley	Bill Bergen	Tim Jordan	W. Alperman	T. McMillan	Ed Lennox	W. Clement	Al Burch	Harry Lumley
1910	Bill Dahlen	Bill Bergen	Jake Daubert	John Hummel	Tony Smith	Ed Lennox	Zack Wheat	Bill Davidson	Jack Dalton
1911	Bill Dahlen	Bill Bergen	Jake Daubert	John Hummel	Bert Tooley	E. Zimmerman	Zack Wheat	Bill Davidson	Bob Coulson
1912	Bill Dahlen	Otto Miller	Jake Daubert	G. Cutshaw	Bert Tooley	Red Smith	Zack Wheat	Herbie Moran	Hub Northen
1913	Bill Dahlen	Otto Miller	Jake Daubert	G. Cutshaw	Bobby Fisher	Red Smith	Zack Wheat	Casey Stengel	Herbie Moran
1914	W. Robinson	Lew McCarty	Jake Daubert	G. Cutshaw	Dick Egan	Red Smith	Zack Wheat	Jack Dalton	Casey Stengel
1915	W. Robinson	Otto Miller	Jake Daubert	G. Cutshaw	Ollie O'Mara	Gus Getz	Zack Wheat	Hy Myers	Casey Stengel
1916	W. Robinson	Chief Meyers	Jake Daubert	G. Cutshaw	Ivy Olson	Mike Mowrey	Zack Wheat	Hy Myers	Casey Stengel
1917	W. Robinson	Otto Miller	Jake Daubert	G. Cutshaw	Ivy Olson	Mike Mowrey	Zack Wheat	Jim Hickman	Casey Stengel
1918	W. Robinson	Otto Miller	Jake Daubert	Mi. Doolan	Ivy Olson	Ollie O'Mara	Zack Wheat	Hy Myers	Jim Johnston
1919	W. Robinson	Ernie Krueger	Ed Konetchy	Jim Johnston	Ivy Olson	Lew Malone	Zack Wheat	Hy Myers	T. Griffith
1920	W. Robinson	Otto Miller	Ed Konetchy	Pete Kilduff	Ivy Olson	Jim Johnston	Zack Wheat	Hy Myers	T. Griffith
1921	W. Robinson	Otto Miller	Ray Schmandt	Pete Kilduff	Ivy Olson	Jim Johnston	Zack Wheat	Hy Myers	T. Griffith
1922	W. Robinson	Hank DeBerry	Ray Schmandt	Jim Johnston	Ivy Olson	Andy High	Zack Wheat	Hy Myers	T. Griffith
1923	W. Robinson	Zack Taylor	Jack Fournier	Ivy Olson	Jim Johnston	Andy High	Gene Bailey	Bernie Neis	T. Griffith
1924	W. Robinson	Zack Taylor	Jack Fournier	Andy High	John Mitchell	Milt Stock	Zack Wheat	Eddie Brown	T. Griffith
1925	W. Robinson	Zack Taylor	Jack Fournier	Milt Stock	John Mitchell	Jim Johnston	Zack Wheat	Eddie Brown	Dick Cox
1926	W. Robinson	Mi. O'Neill	Babe Herman	Chick Fewster	Johnny Butler	Bill Marriott	Zack Wheat	Gus Felix	Dick Cox
1927	W. Robinson	Hank DeBerry	Babe Herman	Jay Partridge	Johnny Butler	Bob Barrett	Gus Felix	Jigger Statz	Max Carey
1928	W. Robinson	Hank DeBerry	Del Bissonette	Jake Flowers	Dave Bancroft	H. Hendrick	Rube Bressler	Max Carey	Babe Herman
1929	W. Robinson	Val Picinich	Del Bissonette	Eddie Moore	Dave Bancroft	Wally Gilbert	Rube Bressler	J. Frederick	Babe Herman
1930	W. Robinson	Al Lopez	Del Bissonette	Neal Finn	Glenn Wright	Wally Gilbert	Rube Bressler	J. Frederick	Babe Herman
1931	W. Robinson	Al Lopez	Del Bissonette	Neal Finn	Gordon Slade	Wally Gilbert	Lefty O'Doul	J. Frederick	Babe Herman
1932	Max Carey	Al Lopez	George Kelly	T. Cuccinello	Glenn Wright	Joe Stripp	Lefty O'Doul	Danny Taylor	Hack Wilson
1933	Max Carey	Al Lopez	Sam Leslie	T. Cuccinello	Glenn Wright	Joe Stripp	Hack Wilson	Danny Taylor	J. Frederick
1934	Casey Stengel	Al Lopez	Sam Leslie	T. Cuccinello	Lonny Frey	Joe Stripp	Danny Taylor	Len Koenecke	Buzz Boyle
1935	Casey Stengel	Al Lopez	Sam Leslie	T. Cuccinello	Lonny Frey	Joe Stripp	Danny Taylor	F. Bordagaray	Buzz Boyle
1936	Casey Stengel	Ray Berres	Buddy Hassett	Jimmy Jordan	Lonny Frey	Joe Stripp	G. Watkins	John Cooney	F. Bordagaray
1937	Bu. Grimes	Babe Phelps	Buddy Hassett	C. Lavagetto	W. English	Joe Stripp	Gib Brack	John Cooney	H. Manush

YEAR	MANAGER	C	1B	2B	SS	3B	LF	CF	RF
1938	Bu. Grimes	Babe Phelps	Dolph Camilli	John Hudson	Leo Durocher	C. Lavagetto	Buddy Hassett	Ernie Koy	Goody Rosen
1939	Leo Durocher	Babe Phelps	Dolph Camilli	Pete Coscarart	Leo Durocher	C. Lavagetto	Ernie Koy	Dixie Walker	Gene Moore
1940	Leo Durocher	Babe Phelps	Dolph Camilli	Pete Coscarart	Pee W. Reese	C. Lavagetto	Joe Medwick	Dixie Walker	Joe Vosmik
1941	Leo Durocher	Mickey Owen	Dolph Camilli	Billy Herman	Pee W. Reese	C. Lavagetto	Joe Medwick	Pete Reiser	Dixie Walker
1942	Leo Durocher	Mickey Owen	Dolph Camilli	Billy Herman	Pee W. Reese	Arky Vaughan	Joe Medwick	Pete Reiser	Dixie Walker
1943	Leo Durocher	Mickey Owen	Dolph Camilli	Billy Herman	Arky Vaughan	Arky Vaughan	Dixie Walker	Augie Galan	Paul Waner
1944	Leo Durocher	Mickey Owen	Howie Schultz	Eddie Stanky	Bobby Bragan	F. Bordagaray	Augie Galan	Goody Rosen	Dixie Walker
1945	Leo Durocher	M. Sandlock	Augie Galan	Eddie Stanky	Ed Basinski	F. Bordagaray	Luis Olmo	Goody Rosen	Dixie Walker
1946	Leo Durocher	B. Edwards	Ed Stevens	Eddie Stanky	Pee W. Reese	C. Lavagetto	Pete Reiser	Carl Furillo	Dixie Walker
1947	Burt Shotton	B. Edwards	J. Robinson	Eddie Stanky	Pee W. Reese	S. Jorgensen	Pete Reiser	Carl Furillo	Dixie Walker
1948	Burt Shotton	R. Campanella	Gil Hodges	J. Robinson	Pee W. Reese	Billy Cox	Marv Rackley	Carl Furillo	G. Hermanski
1949	Burt Shotton	R. Campanella	Gil Hodges	J. Robinson	Pee W. Reese	Billy Cox	G. Hermanski	Duke Snider	Carl Furillo
1950	Burt Shotton	R. Campanella	Gil Hodges	J. Robinson	Pee W. Reese	Billy Cox	G. Hermanski	Duke Snider	Carl Furillo
1951	C. Dressen	R. Campanella	Gil Hodges	J. Robinson	Pee W. Reese	Billy Cox	Andy Pafko	Duke Snider	Carl Furillo
1952	C. Dressen	R. Campanella	Gil Hodges	J. Robinson	Pee W. Reese	Billy Cox	Andy Pafko	Duke Snider	Carl Furillo
1953	C. Dressen	R. Campanella	Gil Hodges	Jim Gilliam	Pee W. Reese	Billy Cox	J. Robinson	Duke Snider	Carl Furillo
1954	Walter Alston	R. Campanella	Gil Hodges	Jim Gilliam	Pee W. Reese	Don Hoak	J. Robinson	Duke Snider	Carl Furillo
1955	Walter Alston	R. Campanella	Gil Hodges	Jim Gilliam	Pee W. Reese	J. Robinson	Sandy Amoros	Duke Snider	Carl Furillo
1956	Walter Alston	R. Campanella	Gil Hodges	Jim Gilliam	Pee W. Reese	J. Robinson	Sandy Amoros	Duke Snider	Carl Furillo
1957	Walter Alston	R. Campanella	Gil Hodges	Jim Gilliam	Charlie Neal	Pee W. Reese	Gino Cimoli	Duke Snider	Carl Furillo
1958	Walter Alston	John Roseboro	Gil Hodges	Charlie Neal	Don Zimmer	Dick Gray	Jim Gilliam	Gino Cimoli	Carl Furillo
1959	Walter Alston	John Roseboro	Gil Hodges	Charlie Neal	Don Zimmer	Jim Gilliam	Wally Moon	Don Demeter	Duke Snider
1960	Walter Alston	John Roseboro	Norm Larker	Charlie Neal	Maury Wills	Jim Gilliam	Wally Moon	Tommy Davis	Frank Howard
1961	Walter Alston	John Roseboro	Gil Hodges	Charlie Neal	Maury Wills	Jim Gilliam	Wally Moon	Willie Davis	Tommy Davis
1962	Walter Alston	John Roseboro	Ron Fairly	L. Burright	Maury Wills	Jim Gilliam	Tommy Davis	Willie Davis	Frank Howard
1963	Walter Alston	John Roseboro	Ron Fairly	Jim Gilliam	Maury Wills	K. McMullen	Tommy Davis	Willie Davis	Frank Howard
1964	Walter Alston	John Roseboro	Ron Fairly	Nate Oliver	Maury Wills	Jim Gilliam	Tommy Davis	Willie Davis	Frank Howard
1965	Walter Alston	John Roseboro	Wes Parker	Jim Lefebvre	Maury Wills	Jim Gilliam	Lou Johnson	Willie Davis	Ron Fairly
1966	Walter Alston	John Roseboro	Wes Parker	Jim Lefebvre	Maury Wills	John Kennedy	Lou Johnson	Willie Davis	Ron Fairly
1967	Walter Alston	John Roseboro	Wes Parker	Ron Hunt	Gene Michael	Jim Lefebvre	Lou Johnson	Willie Davis	Ron Fairly
1968	Walter Alston	Tom Haller	Wes Parker	Paul Popovich	Z. Versalles	Bob Bailey	L. Gabrielson	Willie Davis	Ron Fairly
1969	Walter Alston	Tom Haller	Wes Parker	Ted Sizemore	Maury Wills	Bill Sudakis	W. Crawford	Willie Davis	Andy Kosco
1970	Walter Alston	Tom Haller	Wes Parker	Ted Sizemore	Maury Wills	Grabarkewitz	Manny Mota	Willie Davis	W. Crawford
1971	Walter Alston	Duke Sims	Wes Parker	Jim Lefebvre	Maury Wills	Steve Garvey	Dick Allen	Willie Davis	Bill Buckner
1972	Walter Alston	C. Cannizzaro	Wes Parker	Lee Lacy	Bill Russell	Steve Garvey	Manny Mota	Willie Davis	F. Robinson
1973	Walter Alston	Joe Ferguson	Bill Buckner	Davey Lopes	Bill Russell	Ron Cey	Manny Mota	Willie Davis	W. Crawford
1974	Walter Alston	Steve Yeager	Steve Garvey	Davey Lopes	Bill Russell	Ron Cey	Bill Buckner	Jimmy Wynn	W. Crawford
1975	Walter Alston	Steve Yeager	Steve Garvey	Davey Lopes	Bill Russell	Ron Cey	Bill Buckner	Jimmy Wynn	W. Crawford
1976	Walter Alston	Steve Yeager	Steve Garvey	Davey Lopes	Bill Russell	Ron Cey	Bill Buckner	Dusty Baker	Reggie Smith
1977	Tom Lasorda	Steve Yeager	Steve Garvey	Davey Lopes	Bill Russell	Ron Cey	Dusty Baker	Rick Monday	Reggie Smith
1978	Tom Lasorda	Steve Yeager	Steve Garvey	Davey Lopes	Bill Russell	Ron Cey	Dusty Baker	Billy North	Reggie Smith
1979	Tom Lasorda	Steve Yeager	Steve Garvey	Davey Lopes	Bill Russell	Ron Cey	Dusty Baker	D. Thomas	G. Thomasson
1980	Tom Lasorda	Steve Yeager	Steve Garvey	Davey Lopes	Bill Russell	Ron Cey	Dusty Baker	Rudy Law	Reggie Smith
1981	Tom Lasorda	Mike Scioscia	Steve Garvey	Davey Lopes	Bill Russell	Ron Cey	Dusty Baker	K. Landreaux	P. Guerrero
1982	Tom Lasorda	Mike Scioscia	Steve Garvey	Steve Sax	Bill Russell	Ron Cey	Dusty Baker	K. Landreaux	P. Guerrero
1983	Tom Lasorda	Steve Yeager	Greg Brock	Steve Sax	Bill Russell	P. Guerrero	Dusty Baker	K. Landreaux	Mike Marshall
1984	Tom Lasorda	Mike Scioscia	Greg Brock	Steve Sax	D. Anderson	P. Guerrero	Mike Marshall	K. Landreaux	C. Maldonado
1985	Tom Lasorda	Mike Scioscia	Greg Brock	Steve Sax	M. Duncan	D. Anderson	P. Guerrero	K. Landreaux	Mike Marshall
1986	Tom Lasorda	Mike Scioscia	Greg Brock	Steve Sax	M. Duncan	Bill Madlock	F. Stubbs	R. Williams	Mike Marshall

YEAR	MANAGER	C	1B	2B	SS	3B	LF	CF	RF
1987	Tom Lasorda	Mike Scioscia	F. Stubbs	Steve Sax	M. Duncan	Mick Hatcher	P. Guerrero	John Shelby	Mike Marshall
1988	Tom Lasorda	Mike Scioscia	F. Stubbs	Steve Sax	A. Griffin	Jeff Hamilton	Kirk Gibson	John Shelby	Mike Marshall
1989	Tom Lasorda	Mike Scioscia	Eddie Murray	W. Randolph	A. Griffin	Jeff Hamilton	Kirk Gibson	John Shelby	Mike Marshall
1990	Tom Lasorda	Mike Scioscia	Eddie Murray	Juan Samuel	A. Griffin	M. Sharperson	Kal Daniels	Stan Javier	Hubie Brooks
1991	Tom Lasorda	Mike Scioscia	Eddie Murray	Juan Samuel	A. Griffin	Lenny Harris	Kal Daniels	Brett Butler	D. Strawberry
1992	Tom Lasorda	Mike Scioscia	Eric Karros	Lenny Harris	Jose Offerman	Dave Hansen	Eric Davis	Brett Butler	M. Webster
1993	Tom Lasorda	Mike Piazza	Eric Karros	Jody Reed	Jose Offerman	Tim Wallach	Eric Davis	Brett Butler	Cory Snyder
1994	Tom Lasorda	Mike Piazza	Eric Karros	D. DeShields	Jose Offerman	Tim Wallach	H. Rodriguez	Brett Butler	Raul Mondesi
1995	Tom Lasorda	Mike Piazza	Eric Karros	D. DeShields	Jose Offerman	Tim Wallach	Billy Ashley	Roberto Kelly	Raul Mondesi
1996	Bill Russell	Mike Piazza	Eric Karros	D. DeShields	Greg Gagne	Mike Blowers	Hollandsworth	Roger Cedeno	Raul Mondesi
1997	Bill Russell	Mike Piazza	Eric Karros	W. Guerrero	Greg Gagne	Todd Zeile	Hollandsworth	Brett Butler	Raul Mondesi
1998	G. Hoffman	C. Johnson	Eric Karros	Eric Young	J. Vizcaino	Adrian Beltre	T. Hubbard	Raul Mondesi	Gary Sheffield
1999	Dave Johnson	Todd Hundley	Eric Karros	Eric Young	Grudzielanek	Adrian Beltre	Gary Sheffield	Devon White	Raul Mondesi
2000	Dave Johnson	Todd Hundley	Eric Karros	Grudzielanek	Alex Cora	Adrian Beltre	Gary Sheffield	Hollandsworth	Shawn Green
2001	Jim Tracy	Paul LoDuca	Eric Karros	Grudzielanek	Alex Cora	Adrian Beltre	Gary Sheffield	M. Grissom	Shawn Green
2002	Jim Tracy	Paul LoDuca	Eric Karros	Grudzielanek	Cesar Izturis	Adrian Beltre	Brian Jordan	Dave Roberts	Shawn Green

EXPOS BY POSITION, YEAR BY YEAR

Montreal Expos (National League), 1969–Present

YEAR	MANAGER	C	1B	2B	SS	3B	LF	CF	RF
1969	Gene Mauch	Ron Brand	Bob Bailey	G. Sutherland	Bobby Wine	Coco Laboy	Mack Jones	A. Phillips	Rusty Staub
1970	Gene Mauch	John Bateman	Ron Fairly	G. Sutherland	Bobby Wine	Coco Laboy	Mack Jones	A. Phillips	Rusty Staub
1971	Gene Mauch	John Bateman	Ron Fairly	Ron Hunt	Bobby Wine	Bob Bailey	Jim Fairey	Boots Day	Rusty Staub
1972	Gene Mauch	J. Boccabella	M. Jorgensen	Ron Hunt	Tim Foli	Bob Bailey	K. Singleton	Boots Day	C. Mashore
1973	Gene Mauch	J. Boccabella	M. Jorgensen	Ron Hunt	Tim Foli	Bob Bailey	Ron Fairly	Ron Woods	K. Singleton
1974	Gene Mauch	Barry Foote	M. Jorgensen	Jim Cox	Tim Foli	Ron Hunt	Bob Bailey	Willie Davis	K. Singleton
1975	Gene Mauch	Barry Foote	M. Jorgensen	P. Mackanin	Tim Foli	Larry Parrish	Larry Biittner	Pepe Mangual	Gary Carter
1976	Karl Kuehl	Barry Foote	M. Jorgensen	P. Mackanin	Tim Foli	Larry Parrish	Del Unser	Jerry White	E. Valentine
1977	D. Williams	Gary Carter	Tony Perez	Dave Cash	Chris Speier	Larry Parrish	W. Cromartie	A. Dawson	E. Valentine
1978	D. Williams	Gary Carter	Tony Perez	Dave Cash	Chris Speier	Larry Parrish	W. Cromartie	A. Dawson	E. Valentine
1979	D. Williams	Gary Carter	Tony Perez	Rodney Scott	Chris Speier	Larry Parrish	W. Cromartie	A. Dawson	E. Valentine
1980	D. Williams	Gary Carter	W. Cromartie	Rodney Scott	Chris Speier	Larry Parrish	Ron LeFlore	A. Dawson	R. Office
1981	D. Williams	Gary Carter	W. Cromartie	Rodney Scott	Chris Speier	Larry Parrish	Tim Raines	A. Dawson	Jerry White
1982	Jim Fanning	Gary Carter	Al Oliver	Doug Flynn	Chris Speier	Tim Wallach	Tim Raines	A. Dawson	W. Cromartie
1983	Bill Virdon	Gary Carter	Al Oliver	Doug Flynn	Chris Speier	Tim Wallach	Tim Raines	A. Dawson	W. Cromartie
1984	Buck Rodgers	Gary Carter	T. Francona	Doug Flynn	Angel Salazar	Tim Wallach	J. Wohlford	Tim Raines	A. Dawson
1985	Buck Rodgers	M. Fitzgerald	Dan Driessen	Vance Law	Hubie Brooks	Tim Wallach	Tim Raines	Winningham	A. Dawson
1986	Buck Rodgers	D. Bilardello	A. Galarraga	Vance Law	Hubie Brooks	Tim Wallach	Tim Raines	M. Webster	A. Dawson
1987	Buck Rodgers	M. Fitzgerald	A. Galarraga	Vance Law	Hubie Brooks	Tim Wallach	Tim Raines	Winningham	M. Webster
1988	Buck Rodgers	N. Santovenia	A. Galarraga	Tom Foley	Luis Rivera	Tim Wallach	Tim Raines	Otis Nixon	Hubie Brooks
1989	Buck Rodgers	N. Santovenia	A. Galarraga	Tom Foley	Spike Owen	Tim Wallach	Tim Raines	D. Martinez	Hubie Brooks
1990	Buck Rodgers	M. Fitzgerald	A. Galarraga	D. DeShields	Spike Owen	Tim Wallach	Tim Raines	D. Martinez	Larry Walker
1991	Tom Runnells	Gil Reyes	A. Galarraga	D. DeShields	Spike Owen	Tim Wallach	Ivan Calderon	M. Grissom	Larry Walker
1992	Felipe Alou	Gary Carter	Tim Wallach	D. DeShields	Spike Owen	Bret Barberie	Moises Alou	M. Grissom	Larry Walker
1993	Felipe Alou	D. Fletcher	G. Colbrunn	D. DeShields	Wil Cordero	Sean Berry	Moises Alou	M. Grissom	Larry Walker
1994	Felipe Alou	D. Fletcher	Cliff Floyd	Mike Lansing	Wil Cordero	Sean Berry	Moises Alou	M. Grissom	Larry Walker
1995	Felipe Alou	D. Fletcher	David Segui	Mike Lansing	Wil Cordero	Sean Berry	Moises Alou	R. White	Tony Tarasco
1996	Felipe Alou	D. Fletcher	David Segui	Mike Lansing	Grudzielanek	S. Andrews	H. Rodriguez	F. Santangelo	Moises Alou

YEAR	MANAGER	C	1B	2B	SS	3B	LF	CF	RF
1997	Felipe Alou	Chris Widger	David Segui	Mike Lansing	Grudzielanek	Doug Strange	H. Rodriguez	R. White	F. Santangelo
1998	Felipe Alou	Chris Widger	Brad Fullmer	Jose Vidro	Grudzielanek	S. Andrews	F. Santangelo	R. White	V. Guerrero
1999	Felipe Alou	Chris Widger	Brad Fullmer	Jose Vidro	O. Cabrera	S. Andrews	R. White	M. Martinez	V. Guerrero
2000	Felipe Alou	Chris Widger	Lee Stevens	Jose Vidro	O. Cabrera	M. Mordecai	Terry Jones	P. Bergeron	V. Guerrero
2001	Jeff Torborg	M. Barrett	Lee Stevens	Jose Vidro	O. Cabrera	Geoff Blum	Mark Smith	P. Bergeron	V. Guerrero
2002	F. Robinson	M. Barrett	A. Galarraga	Jose Vidro	O. Cabrera	F. Tatis	B. Wilkerson	Jose Macias	V. Guerrero

GIANTS BY POSITION, YEAR BY YEAR

New York Gothams (National League), 1883–1884
New York Giants (National League), 1885–1957
San Francisco Giants (National League), 1958–Present

YEAR	MANAGER	C	1B	2B	SS	3B	LF	CF	RF
1901	George Davis	John Warner	John Ganzel	Ray Nelson	George Davis	Sam Strang	Kip Selbach	Van Haltren	Algie McBride
1902	John McGraw	F. Bowerman	Dan McGann	Heinie Smith	Joe Bean	Billy Lauder	Jim Jones	Steve Brodie	Jack Dunn
1903	John McGraw	John Warner	Dan McGann	Billy Gilbert	Charlie Babb	Billy Lauder	Sam Mertes	R. Bresnahan	G. Browne
1904	John McGraw	John Warner	Dan McGann	Billy Gilbert	Bill Dahlen	Art Devlin	Sam Mertes	R. Bresnahan	G. Browne
1905	John McGraw	R. Bresnahan	Dan McGann	Billy Gilbert	Bill Dahlen	Art Devlin	Sam Mertes	Mike Donlin	G. Browne
1906	John McGraw	R. Bresnahan	Dan McGann	Billy Gilbert	Bill Dahlen	Art Devlin	S. Shannon	Cy Ceymour	G. Browne
1907	John McGraw	R. Bresnahan	Dan McGann	Larry Doyle	Bill Dahlen	Art Devlin	S. Shannon	Cy Seymour	G. Browne
1908	John McGraw	R. Bresnahan	Fred Tenney	Larry Doyle	Al Bridwell	Art Devlin	S. Shannon	Cy Seymour	Mike Donlin
1909	John McGraw	A. Schlei	Fred Tenney	Larry Doyle	Al Bridwell	Art Devlin	McCormick	Bill O'Hara	Red Murray
1910	John McGraw	Chief Meyers	Fred Merkle	Larry Doyle	Al Bridwell	Art Devlin	Josh Devore	F. Snodgrass	Red Murray
1911	John McGraw	Chief Meyers	Fred Merkle	Larry Doyle	Al Bridwell	Art Devlin	Josh Devore	F. Snodgrass	Red Murray
1912	John McGraw	Chief Meyers	Fred Merkle	Larry Doyle	Art Fletcher	Buck Herzog	F. Snodgrass	Beals Becker	Red Murray
1913	John McGraw	Chief Meyers	Fred Merkle	Larry Doyle	Art Fletcher	Buck Herzog	George Burns	F. Snodgrass	Red Murray
1914	John McGraw	Chief Meyers	Fred Merkle	Larry Doyle	Art Fletcher	Milt Stock	George Burns	Bob Bescher	F. Snodgrass
1915	John McGraw	Chief Meyers	Fred Merkle	Larry Doyle	Art Fletcher	Hans Lobert	George Burns	F. Snodgrass	D. Robertson
1916	John McGraw	Bill Rariden	Fred Merkle	Larry Doyle	Art Fletcher	B. McKechnie	George Burns	Benny Kauff	D. Robertson
1917	John McGraw	Bill Rariden	Walter Holke	Buck Herzog	Art Fletcher	Zimmerman	George Burns	Benny Kauff	D. Robertson
1918	John McGraw	Lew McCarty	Walter Holke	Larry Doyle	Art Fletcher	Zimmerman	George Burns	Benny Kauff	Ross Youngs
1919	John McGraw	Lew McCarty	Hal Chase	Larry Doyle	Art Fletcher	Zimmerman	George Burns	Benny Kauff	Ross Youngs
1920	John McGraw	Frank Snyder	George Kelly	Larry Doyle	D. Bancroft	Frankie Frisch	George Burns	Lee King	Ross Youngs
1921	John McGraw	Frank Snyder	George Kelly	J. Rawlings	D. Bancroft	Frankie Frisch	Irish Meusel	George Burns	Ross Youngs
1922	John McGraw	Frank Snyder	George Kelly	Frankie Frisch	D. Bancroft	Heinie Groh	Irish Meusel	Casey Stengel	Ross Youngs
1923	John McGraw	Frank Snyder	George Kelly	Frankie Frisch	D. Bancroft	Heinie Groh	Irish Meusel	Cunningham	Ross Youngs
1924	John McGraw	Frank Snyder	George Kelly	Frankie Frisch	T. Jackson	Heinie Groh	Irish Meusel	Hack Wilson	Ross Youngs
1925	John McGraw	Frank Snyder	Bill Terry	George Kelly	T. Jackson	F. Lindstrom	Irish Meusel	B. Southworth	Ross Youngs
1926	John McGraw	Paul Florence	George Kelly	Frankie Frisch	T. Jackson	F. Lindstrom	Irish Meusel	Ty Tyson	Ross Youngs
1927	John McGraw	Zack Taylor	Bill Terry	R. Hornsby	T. Jackson	F. Lindstrom	H. Mueller	Edd Roush	George Harper
1928	John McGraw	Shanty Hogan	Bill Terry	Andy Cohen	T. Jackson	F. Lindstrom	Lefty O'Doul	Jimmy Welsh	Mel Ott
1929	John McGraw	Shanty Hogan	Bill Terry	Andy Cohen	T. Jackson	F. Lindstrom	Freddy Leach	Edd Roush	Mel Ott
1930	John McGraw	Shanty Hogan	Bill Terry	Hughie Critz	T. Jackson	F. Lindstrom	Freddy Leach	W. Roettger	Mel Ott
1931	John McGraw	Shanty Hogan	Bill Terry	B. Hunnefield	T. Jackson	John Vergez	Freddy Leach	Ethan Allen	Mel Ott
1932	Bill Terry	Shanty Hogan	Bill Terry	Hughie Critz	Doc Marshall	John Vergez	Jo-Jo Moore	F. Lindstrom	Mel Ott
1933	Bill Terry	Gus Mancuso	Bill Terry	Hughie Critz	Blondy Ryan	John Vergez	Jo-Jo Moore	Kiddo Davis	Mel Ott
1934	Bill Terry	Gus Mancuso	Bill Terry	Hughie Critz	T. Jackson	John Vergez	Jo-Jo Moore	G. Watkins	Mel Ott
1935	Bill Terry	Gus Mancuso	Sam Leslie	Mark Koenig	Dick Bartell	T. Jackson	Jo-Jo Moore	Hank Leiber	Mel Ott
1936	Bill Terry	Gus Mancuso	Sam Leslie	B. Whitehead	Dick Bartell	T. Jackson	Jo-Jo Moore	Hank Lieber	Mel Ott

YEAR	MANAGER	C	1B	2B	SS	3B	LF	CF	RF
1937	Bill Terry	H. Danning	J. McCarthy	B. Whitehead	Dick Bartell	L. Chiozza	Jo-Jo Moore	Jimmy Ripple	Mel Ott
1938	Bill Terry	H. Danning	J. McCarthy	A. Kampouris	Dick Bartell	Mel Ott	Jo-Jo Moore	Hank Leiber	Jimmy Ripple
1939	Bill Terry	H. Danning	Zeke Bonura	B. Whitehead	Billy Jurges	Tom Hafey	Jo-Jo Moore	F. Demaree	Mel Ott
1940	Bill Terry	H. Danning	Babe Young	T. Cuccinello	Mickey Witek	B. Whitehead	Jo-Jo Moore	F. Demaree	Mel Ott
1941	Bill Terry	H. Danning	Babe Young	B. Whitehead	Billy Jurges	Dick Bartell	Jo-Jo Moore	John Rucker	Mel Ott
1942	Mel Ott	H. Danning	Johnny Mize	Mickey Witek	Billy Jurges	Billy Werber	Babe Barna	W. Marshall	Mel Ott
1943	Mel Ott	Gus Mancuso	Joe Orengo	Mickey Witek	Billy Jurges	Dick Bartell	Joe Medwick	John Rucker	Mel Ott
1944	Mel Ott	E. Lombardi	P. Weintraub	G. Hausman	Buddy Kerr	Hal Luby	Joe Medwick	John Rucker	Mel Ott
1945	Mel Ott	E. Lombardi	P. Weintraub	G. Hausman	Buddy Kerr	Nap Reyes	Dan Gardella	John Rucker	Mel Ott
1946	Mel Ott	Walk Cooper	Johnny Mize	Bud Blattner	Buddy Kerr	Bill Rigney	Sid Gordon	W. Marshall	Goody Rosen
1947	Mel Ott	Walk Cooper	Johnny Mize	Bill Rigney	Buddy Kerr	Jack Lohrke	Sid Gordon	B. Thomson	W. Marshall
1948	Leo Durocher	Walk Cooper	Johnny Mize	Bill Rigney	Buddy Kerr	Sid Gordon	B. Thomson	W. Lockman	W. Marshall
1949	Leo Durocher	Wes Westrum	Johnny Mize	H. Thompson	Buddy Kerr	Sid Gordon	W. Lockman	B. Thomson	W. Marshall
1950	Leo Durocher	Wes Westrum	T. Gilbert	Eddie Stanky	Alvin Dark	H. Thompson	W. Lockman	B. Thomson	Don Mueller
1951	Leo Durocher	Wes Westrum	W. Lockman	Eddie Stanky	Alvin Dark	H. Thompson	Monte Irvin	Willie Mays	Don Mueller
1952	Leo Durocher	Wes Westrum	W. Lockman	D. Williams	Alvin Dark	B. Thomson	Bob Elliott	H. Thompson	Don Mueller
1953	Leo Durocher	Wes Westrum	W. Lockman	D. Williams	Alvin Dark	H. Thompson	Monte Irvin	B. Thomson	Don Mueller
1954	Leo Durocher	Wes Westrum	W. Lockman	D. Williams	Alvin Dark	H. Thompson	Monte Irvin	Willie Mays	Don Mueller
1955	Leo Durocher	Ray Katt	Gail Harris	W. Terwilliger	Alvin Dark	H. Thompson	W. Lockman	Willie Mays	Don Mueller
1956	Bill Rigney	Bill Sarni	Bill White	R. Shoendienst	Daryl Spencer	F. Castleman	Jackie Brandt	Willie Mays	Don Mueller
1957	Bill Rigney	Val Thomas	W. Lockman	D. O'Connell	Daryl Spencer	Ray Jablonski	Hank Sauer	Willie Mays	Don Mueller
1958	Bill Rigney	Bob Schmidt	O. Cepeda	D. O'Connell	Daryl Spencer	J. Davenport	Hank Sauer	Willie Mays	W. Kirkland
1959	Bill Rigney	H. Landrith	O. Cepeda	J. Davenport	Ed Bressoud	J. Davenport	Jack Brandt	Willie Mays	W. Kirkland
1960	Tom Sheehan	Bob Schmidt	W. McCovey	D. Blasingame	Ed Bressoud	J. Davenport	Felipe Alou	Willie Mays	W. Kirkland
1961	Alvin Dark	Ed Bailey	W. McCovey	J. Amalfitano	Jose Pagan	J. Davenport	H. Kuenn	Willie Mays	Felipe Alou
1962	Alvin Dark	Tom Haller	O. Cepeda	Chuck Hiller	Jose Pagan	J. Davenport	H. Kuenn	Willie Mays	Felipe Alou
1963	Alvin Dark	Ed Bailey	O. Cepeda	Chuck Hiller	Jose Pagan	J. Davenport	W. McCovey	Willie Mays	Felipe Alou
1964	Alvin Dark	Tom Haller	O. Cepeda	Hal Lanier	Jose Pagan	Jim Ray Hart	H. Kuenn	Willie Mays	Jesus Alou
1965	H. Franks	Tom Haller	W. McCovey	Hal Lanier	D. Schofield	Jim Ray Hart	Matty Alou	Willie Mays	Jesus Alou
1966	H. Franks	Tom Haller	W. McCovey	Hal Lanier	Tito Fuentes	Jim Ray Hart	Jesus Alou	Willie Mays	Ollie Brown
1967	H. Franks	Tom Haller	W. McCovey	Tito Fuentes	Hal Lanier	Jim Ray Hart	Jesus Alou	Willie Mays	Ollie Brown
1968	H. Franks	Dick Dietz	W. McCovey	Ron Hunt	Hal Lanier	J. Davenport	Jesus Alou	Willie Mays	Bobby Bonds
1969	Charlie Fox	Dick Dietz	W. McCovey	Ron Hunt	Hal Lanier	J. Davenport	K. Henderson	Willie Mays	Bobby Bonds
1970	Charlie Fox	Dick Dietz	W. McCovey	Ron Hunt	Hal Lanier	Al Gallagher	K. Henderson	Willie Mays	Bobby Bonds
1971	Charlie Fox	Dick Dietz	W. McCovey	Tito Fuentes	Chris Speier	Al Gallagher	K. Henderson	Willie Mays	Bobby Bonds
1972	Charlie Fox	Dave Rader	W. McCovey	Tito Fuentes	Chris Speier	Al Gallagher	K. Henderson	G. Maddox	Bobby Bonds
1973	Charlie Fox	Dave Rader	W. McCovey	Tito Fuentes	Chris Speier	Ed Goodson	G. Matthews	G. Maddox	Bobby Bonds
1974	Wes Westrum	Dave Rader	D. Kingman	Tito Fuentes	Chris Speier	S. Ontiveros	G. Matthews	G. Maddox	Bobby Bonds
1975	Wes Westrum	Dave Rader	W. Montanez	D. Thomas	Chris Speier	S. Ontiveros	G. Matthews	Von Joshua	Bobby Murcer
1976	Bill Rigney	Dave Rader	Darrell Evans	Marty Perez	Chris Speier	Ken Reitz	G. Matthews	L. Herndon	Bobby Murcer
1977	Joe Altobelli	Marc Hill	W. McCovey	Rob Andrews	Tim Foli	Bill Madlock	G. Thomasson	D. Thomas	Jack Clark
1978	Joe Altobelli	Marc Hill	W. McCovey	Bill Madlock	J. LeMaster	Darrell Evans	T. Whitfield	L. Herndon	Jack Clark
1979	Joe Altobelli	D. Littlejohn	Mike Ivie	Joe Strain	J. LeMaster	Darrell Evans	L. Herndon	Bill North	Jack Clark
1980	Dave Bristol	Milt May	Mike Ivie	R. Stennett	J. LeMaster	Darrell Evans	L. Herndon	Bill North	Jack Clark
1981	F. Robinson	Milt May	Enos Cabell	Joe Morgan	J. LeMaster	Darrell Evans	L. Herndon	Jerry Martin	Jack Clark
1982	F. Robinson	Milt May	Reggie Smith	Joe Morgan	J. LeMaster	Darrell Evans	Jeff Leonard	Chili Davis	Jack Clark
1983	F. Robinson	Bob Brenly	Darrell Evans	B. Wellman	J. LeMaster	T. O'Malley	Jeff Leonard	Chili Davis	Jack Clark
1984	F. Robinson	Bob Brenly	S. Thompson	Manny Trillo	J. LeMaster	J. Youngblood	Jeff Leonard	Dan Gladden	Chili Davis
1985	J. Davenport	Bob Brenly	David Green	Manny Trillo	Jose Uribe	Chris Brown	Jeff Leonard	Dan Gladden	Chili Davis

YEAR	MANAGER	C	1B	2B	SS	3B	LF	CF	RF
1986	Roger Craig	Bob Brenly	Will Clark	R. Thompson	Jose Uribe	Chris Brown	C. Maldonado	Dan Gladden	Chili Davis
1987	Roger Craig	Bob Brenly	Will Clark	R. Thompson	Jose Uribe	K. Mitchell	Jeff Leonard	Chili Davis	C. Maldonado
1988	Roger Craig	Bob Melvin	Will Clark	R. Thompson	Jose Uribe	K. Mitchell	Mike Aldrete	Brett Butler	C. Maldonado
1989	Roger Craig	T. Kennedy	Will Clark	R. Thompson	Jose Uribe	Ernie Riles	K. Mitchell	Brett Butler	C. Maldonado
1990	Roger Craig	T. Kennedy	Will Clark	R. Thompson	Jose Uribe	Matt Williams	K. Mitchell	Brett Butler	Mike Kingery
1991	Roger Craig	Steve Decker	Will Clark	R. Thompson	Jose Uribe	Matt Williams	K. Mitchell	Willie McGee	Kevin Bass
1992	Roger Craig	K. Manwaring	Will Clark	R. Thompson	Roy Clayton	Matt Williams	Mike Felder	Darren Lewis	Willie McGee
1993	Dusty Baker	K. Manwaring	Will Clark	R. Thompson	Roy Clayton	Matt Williams	Barry Bonds	Darren Lewis	Willie McGee
1994	Dusty Baker	K. Manwaring	T. Benzinger	J. Patterson	Roy Clayton	Matt Williams	Barry Bonds	Darren Lewis	Dave Martinez
1995	Dusty Baker	K. Manwaring	Mark Carreon	R. Thompson	Roy Clayton	Matt Williams	Barry Bonds	Darren Lewis	Glenallen Hill
1996	Dusty Baker	Tom Lampkin	Mark Carreon	S. Scarsone	Rich Aurilia	Matt Williams	Barry Bonds	Marv Benard	Glenallen Hill
1997	Dusty Baker	Rick Wilkins	J.T. Snow	Jeff Kent	Jose Vizcaino	Bill Mueller	Barry Bonds	D. Hamilton	Stan Javier
1998	Dusty Baker	Brian Johnson	J.T. Snow	Jeff Kent	Rich Aurilia	Bill Mueller	Barry Bonds	D. Hamilton	Stan Javier
1999	Dusty Baker	Brent Mayne	J.T. Snow	Jeff Kent	Rich Aurilia	Bill Mueller	Barry Bonds	Marv Benard	Ellis Burks
2000	Dusty Baker	Bob Estalella	J.T. Snow	Jeff Kent	Rich Aurilia	Bill Mueller	Barry Bonds	Marv Benard	Ellis Burks
2001	Dusty Baker	Be. Santiago	J.T. Snow	Jeff Kent	Rich Aurilia	R. Martinez	Barry Bonds	Marv Benard	Armando Rios
2002	Dusty Baker	Be. Santiago	J.T. Snow	Jeff Kent	Rich Aurilia	David Bell	Barry Bonds	T. Shinjo	R. Sanders

INDIANS BY POSITION, YEAR BY YEAR

Cleveland Bluebirds a.k.a. Blues (American League), 1901–1902
Cleveland Naps (American League), 1903–1911
Cleveland Molly McGuires (American League), 1912–1914
Cleveland Indians (American League), 1915–Present

YEAR	MANAGER	C	1B	2B	SS	3B	LF	CF	RF
1901	Jim McAleer	Bob Wood	C. LaChance	Erve Beck	F. Scheibeck	Bill Bradley	J. McCarthy	O. Pickering	Jack O'Brien
1902	Bill Armour	Harry Bemis	C. Hickman	Nap Lajoie	J. Gochnauer	Bill Bradley	J. McCarthy	Harry Bay	Elmer Flick
1903	Bill Armour	Harry Bemis	C. Hickman	Nap Lajoie	J. Gochnauer	Bill Bradley	J. McCarthy	Harry Bay	Elmer Flick
1904	Bill Armour	Harry Bemis	C. Hickman	Nap Lajoie	Terry Turner	Bill Bradley	Billy Lush	Harry Bay	Elmer Flick
1905	Nap Lajoie	Fritz Buelow	Charlie Carr	Nap Lajoie	Terry Turner	Bill Bradley	Jim Jackson	Harry Bay	Elmer Flick
1906	Nap Lajoie	Harry Bemis	C. Rossman	Nap Lajoie	Terry Turner	Bill Bradley	Jim Jackson	Elmer Flick	B. Congalton
1907	Nap Lajoie	Nig Clarke	G. Stovall	Nap Lajoie	Terry Turner	Bill Bradley	B. Hinchman	J. Birmingham	Elmer Flick
1908	Nap Lajoie	Nig Clarke	G. Stovall	Nap Lajoie	G. Perring	Bill Bradley	Josh Clarke	J. Birmingham	B. Hinchman
1909	Nap Lajoie	Ted Easterly	G. Stovall	Nap Lajoie	Neal Ball	Bill Bradley	B. Hinchman	J. Birmingham	Wilbur Good
1910	Dan McGuire	Ted Easterly	G. Stovall	Nap Lajoie	Terry Turner	Bill Bradley	Jack Graney	J. Birmingham	Bris Lord
1911	G. Stovall	Gus Fisher	G. Stovall	Neal Ball	Ivy Olson	Terry Turner	Jack Graney	J. Birmingham	Joe Jackson
1912	Harry Davis	Steve O'Neill	Art Griggs	Nap Lajoie	Peckinpaugh	Terry Turner	Buddy Ryan	J. Birmingham	Joe Jackson
1913	J. Birmingham	Steve O'Neill	Doc Johnston	Nap Lajoie	Ray Chapman	Terry Turner	Jack Graney	Nemo Leibold	Joe Jackson
1914	J. Birmingham	Steve O'Neill	Doc Johnston	Nap Lajoie	Ray Chapman	Terry Turner	Jack Graney	Nemo Leibold	Joe Jackson
1915	Lee Fohl	Steve O'Neill	Jay Kirke	Wambsganss	Ray Chapman	W. Barbare	Jack Graney	Nemo Leibold	Elmer Smith
1916	Lee Fohl	Steve O'Neill	Chick Gandil	Ivon Howard	Wambsganss	Terry Turner	Jack Graney	Tris Speaker	Braggo Roth
1917	Lee Fohl	Steve O'Neill	Joe Harris	Wambsganss	Ray Chapman	Joe Evans	Jack Graney	Tris Speaker	Braggo Roth
1918	Lee Fohl	Steve O'Neill	Doc Johnston	Wambsganss	Ray Chapman	Joe Evans	Joe Wood	Tris Speaker	Braggo Roth
1919	Lee Fohl	Steve O'Neill	Doc Johnston	Wambsganss	Ray Chapman	Larry Gardner	Jack Graney	Tris Speaker	Elmer Smith
1920	Tris Speaker	Steve O'Neill	Doc Johnston	Wambsganss	Ray Chapman	Larry Gardner	C. Jamieson	Tris Speaker	Elmer Smith
1921	Tris Speaker	Steve O'Neill	Doc Johnston	Wambsganss	Joe Sewell	Larry Gardner	C. Jamieson	Tris Speaker	Elmer Smith
1922	Tris Speaker	Steve O'Neill	Stu McInnis	Wambsganss	Joe Sewell	Larry Gardner	C. Jamieson	Tris Speaker	Joe Wood
1923	Tris Speaker	Steve O'Neill	Frank Brower	Wambsganss	Joe Sewell	Rube Lutzke	C. Jamieson	Tris Speaker	H. Summa
1924	Tris Speaker	George Myatt	George Burns	Chick Fewster	Joe Sewell	Rube Lutzke	C. Jamieson	Tris Speaker	H. Summa

YEAR	MANAGER	C	1B	2B	SS	3B	LF	CF	RF	DH
1925	Tris Speaker	George Myatt	George Burns	Chick Fewster	Joe Sewell	Rube Lutzke	C. Jamieson	Tris Speaker	Pat McNulty	
1926	Tris Speaker	Luke Sewell	George Burns	F. Spurgeon	Joe Sewell	Rube Lutzke	C. Jamieson	Tris Speaker	H. Summa	
1927	J. McCallister	Luke Sewell	George Burns	Lew Fonseca	Joe Sewell	Rube Lutzke	C. Jamieson	Ike Eichrodt	H. Summa	
1928	Peckinpaugh	Luke Sewell	Lew Fonseca	Carl Lind	Joe Sewell	John Hodapp	C. Jamieson	Sam Langford	H. Summa	
1929	Peckinpaugh	Luke Sewell	Lew Fonseca	John Hodapp	Jack Tavener	Joe Sewell	C. Jamieson	Earl Averill	Bibb Falk	
1930	Peckinpaugh	Luke Sewell	Eddie Morgan	John Hodapp	J. Goldman	Joe Sewell	C. Jamieson	Earl Averill	Dick Porter	
1931	Peckinpaugh	Luke Sewell	Eddie Morgan	John Hodapp	Ed Montague	Willie Kamm	Joe Vosmik	Earl Averill	Dick Porter	
1932	Peckinpaugh	Luke Sewell	Eddie Morgan	Bill Cissell	John Burnett	Willie Kamm	Joe Vosmik	Earl Averill	Dick Porter	
1933	W. Johnson	Roy Spencer	Harley Boss	Odell Hale	Knickerbocker	Willie Kamm	Joe Vosmik	Earl Averill	Dick Porter	
1934	W. Johnson	Frank Pytlak	Hal Trosky	Odell Hale	Knickerbocker	Willie Kamm	Joe Vosmik	Earl Averill	Sam Rice	
1935	W. Johnson	Ed Phillips	Hal Trosky	Boze Berger	Knickerbocker	Odell Hale	Joe Vosmik	Earl Averill	Milt Galatzer	
1936	Steve O'Neill	Billy Sullivan	Hal Trosky	Roy Hughes	Knickerbocker	Odell Hale	Joe Vosmik	Earl Averill	R. Weatherly	
1937	Steve O'Neill	Frank Pytlak	Hal Trosky	John Kroner	Lyn Lary	Odell Hale	Moose Solters	Earl Averill	B. Campbell	
1938	Ossie Vitt	Frank Pytlak	Hal Trosky	Odell Hale	Lyn Lary	Ken Keltner	Jeff Heath	Earl Averill	B. Campbell	
1939	Ossie Vitt	R. Hemsley	Hal Trosky	Odell Hale	Skeeter Webb	Ken Keltner	Jeff Heath	Ben Chapman	B. Campbell	
1940	Ossie Vitt	R. Hemsley	Hal Trosky	Ray Mack	Lou Boudreau	Ken Keltner	Ben Chapman	R. Weatherly	Beau Bell	
1941	Peckinpaugh	R. Hemsley	Hal Trosky	Ray Mack	Lou Boudreau	Ken Keltner	Gee Walker	R. Weatherly	Jeff Heath	
1942	Lou Boudreau	Otto Denning	Les Fleming	Ray Mack	Lou Boudreau	Ken Keltner	Jeff Heath	R. Weatherly	Oris Hockett	
1943	Lou Boudreau	Buddy Rosar	Mickey Rocco	Ray Mack	Lou Boudreau	Ken Keltner	Jeff Heath	Oris Hockett	R. Cullenbine	
1944	Lou Boudreau	Buddy Rosar	Mickey Rocco	Ray Mack	Lou Boudreau	Ken Keltner	Pat Seerey	Oris Hockett	R. Cullenbine	
1945	Lou Boudreau	Frank Hayes	Mickey Rocco	Dutch Meyer	Lou Boudreau	Don Ross	Jeff Heath	F. Mackiewicz	Pat Seerey	
1946	Lou Boudreau	Jim Hegan	Les Fleming	Dutch Meyer	Lou Boudreau	Ken Keltner	George Case	Pat Seerey	H. Edwards	
1947	Lou Boudreau	Jim Hegan	Ed Robinson	Joe Gordon	Lou Boudreau	Ken Keltner	Dale Mitchell	C. Metkovich	H. Edwards	
1948	Lou Boudreau	Jim Hegan	Ed Robinson	Joe Gordon	Lou Boudreau	Ken Keltner	Dale Mitchell	T. Tucker	Larry Doby	
1949	Lou Boudreau	Jim Hegan	Mick Vernon	Joe Gordon	Lou Boudreau	Ken Keltner	Dale Mitchell	Larry Doby	Bob Kennedy	
1950	Lou Boudreau	Jim Hegan	Luke Easter	Joe Gordon	Ray Boone	Al Rosen	Dale Mitchell	Larry Doby	Bob Kennedy	
1951	Al Lopez	Jim Hegan	Luke Easter	Bobby Avila	Ray Boone	Al Rosen	Dale Mitchell	Larry Doby	Bob Kennedy	
1952	Al Lopez	Jim Hegan	Luke Easter	Bobby Avila	Ray Boone	Al Rosen	Dale Mitchell	Larry Doby	H. Simpson	
1953	Al Lopez	Jim Hegan	Bill Glynn	Bobby Avila	G. Strickland	Al Rosen	Dale Mitchell	Larry Doby	Bob Kennedy	
1954	Al Lopez	Jim Hegan	Vic Wertz	Bobby Avila	G. Strickland	Al Rosen	Al Smith	Larry Doby	Dave Philley	
1955	Al Lopez	Jim Hegan	Vic Wertz	Bobby Avila	G. Strickland	Al Rosen	Ralph Kiner	Larry Doby	Al Smith	
1956	Al Lopez	Jim Hegan	Vic Wertz	Bobby Avila	C. Carrasquel	Al Rosen	Al Smith	Jim Busby	R. Colavito	
1957	Kerby Farrell	Jim Hegan	Vic Wertz	Bobby Avila	C. Carrasquel	Al Smith	G. Woodling	Roger Maris	R. Colavito	
1958	Joe Gordon	Russ Nixon	Mick Vernon	Bobby Avila	Billy Hunter	Billy Harrell	M. Minoso	Larry Doby	R. Colavito	
1959	Joe Gordon	Russ Nixon	Vic Power	Billy Martin	Woody Held	G. Strickland	M. Minoso	Jim Piersall	R. Colavito	
1960	Joe Gordon	J. Romano	Vic Power	K. Aspromonte	Woody Held	B. Phillips	Tito Francona	Jim Piersall	H. Kuenn	
1961	Jimmy Dykes	J. Romano	Vic Power	John Temple	Woody Held	B. Phillips	Tito Francona	Jim Piersall	W. Kirkland	
1962	Mel McGaha	J. Romano	Tito Francona	Jerry Kindall	Woody Held	B. Phillips	C. Essegian	Ty Cline	W. Kirkland	
1963	B. Tebbetts	Joe Azcue	Fred Whitfield	Woody Held	Jerry Kindall	Max Alvis	Tito Francona	Vic Davalillo	W. Kirkland	
1964	B. Tebbetts	J. Romano	Bob Chance	Larry Brown	Jerry Kindall	Max Alvis	Leon Wagner	Vic Davalillo	Tito Francona	
1965	B. Tebbetts	Joe Azcue	Fred Whitfield	P. Gonzalez	Larry Brown	Max Alvis	Leon Wagner	Vic Davalillo	R. Colavito	
1966	B. Tebbetts	Joe Azcue	Fred Whitfield	P. Gonzalez	Larry Brown	Max Alvis	Leon Wagner	Vic Davalillo	R. Colavito	
1967	Joe Adcock	Joe Azcue	Tony Horton	P. Gonzalez	Larry Brown	Max Alvis	Leon Wagner	Vic Davalillo	Chuck Hinton	
1968	Alvin Dark	Joe Azcue	Tony Horton	Vern Fuller	Larry Brown	Max Alvis	Lee Maye	Jose Cardenal	Tom Harper	
1969	Alvin Dark	Duke Sims	Tony Horton	Vern Fuller	Larry Brown	Max Alvis	Russ Snyder	Jose Cardenal	K. Harrelson	
1970	Alvin Dark	Ray Fosse	Tony Horton	Eddie Leon	J. Heidemann	Graig Nettles	Roy Foster	T. Uhlaender	Vada Pinson	
1971	Alvin Dark	Ray Fosse	C. Chambliss	Eddie Leon	J. Heidemann	Graig Nettles	T. Uhlaender	Vada Pinson	Roy Foster	
1972	Aspromonte	Ray Fosse	C. Chambliss	J. Brohamer	Frank Duffy	Graig Nettles	Alex Johnson	Del Unser	Buddy Bell	
1973	Aspromonte	Dave Duncan	C. Chambliss	J. Brohamer	Frank Duffy	Buddy Bell	C. Spikes	G. Hendrick	Rusty Torres	Oscar Gamble

YEAR	MANAGER	C	1B	2B	SS	3B	LF	CF	RF	DH
1974	Aspromonte	Dave Duncan	Johnny Ellis	J. Brohamer	Frank Duffy	Buddy Bell	J. Lowenstein	G. Hendrick	C. Spikes	Oscar Gamble
1975	F. Robinson	Alan Ashby	Boog Powell	Duane Kuiper	Frank Duffy	Buddy Bell	Oscar Gamble	Rick Manning	G. Hendrick	Rico Carty
1976	F. Robinson	Alan Ashby	Boog Powell	Duane Kuiper	Frank Duffy	Buddy Bell	G. Hendrick	Rick Manning	C. Spikes	Rico Carty
1977	Jeff Torborg	Fred Kendall	A. Thornton	Duane Kuiper	Frank Duffy	Buddy Bell	Bruce Bochte	Jim Norris	Paul Dade	Rico Carty
1978	Jeff Torborg	G. Alexander	A. Thornton	Duane Kuiper	Tom Veryzer	Buddy Bell	John Grubb	Rick Manning	Paul Dade	Bernie Carbo
1979	Jeff Torborg	G. Alexander	A. Thornton	Duane Kuiper	Tom Veryzer	Toby Harrah	Jim Norris	Rick Manning	Bobby Bonds	Cliff Johnson
1980	Dave Garcia	Ron Hassey	M. Hargrove	J. Brohamer	Tom Veryzer	Toby Harrah	M. Dilone	Rick Manning	Jorge Orta	J. Charboneau
1981	Dave Garcia	Ron Hassey	M. Hargrove	Duane Kuiper	Tom Veryzer	Toby Harrah	M. Dilone	Rick Manning	Jorge Orta	A. Thornton
1982	Dave Garcia	Ron Hassey	M. Hargrove	Jack Perconte	Mike Fischlin	Toby Harrah	M. Dilone	Rick Manning	Von Hayes	A. Thornton
1983	Mike Ferraro	Ron Hassey	M. Hargrove	Manny Trillo	Julio Franco	Toby Harrah	A. Bannister	G. Thomas	G. Vukovich	A. Thornton
1984	Pat Corrales	Jerry Willard	M. Hargrove	T. Bernazard	Julio Franco	Brook Jacoby	Mel Hall	Brett Butler	G. Vukovich	A. Thornton
1985	Pat Corrales	Jerry Willard	Pat Tabler	T. Bernazard	Julio Franco	Brook Jacoby	Joe Carter	Brett Butler	G. Vukovich	A. Thornton
1986	Pat Corrales	A. Allanson	Pat Tabler	T. Bernazard	Julio Franco	Brook Jacoby	Mel Hall	Brett Butler	Joe Carter	A. Thornton
1987	Pat Corrales	Chris Bando	Joe Carter	T. Bernazard	Julio Franco	Brook Jacoby	Mel Hall	Brett Butler	Cory Snyder	Pat Tabler
1988	Doc Edwards	A. Allanson	Willie Upshaw	Julio Franco	Jay Bell	Brook Jacoby	Mel Hall	Joe Carter	Cory Snyder	Ron Kittle
1989	Doc Edwards	A. Allanson	Pete O'Brien	Jerry Browne	Felix Fermin	Brook Jacoby	Joe Carter	B. Komminsk	Cory Snyder	Dave Clark
1990	J. McNamara	S. Alomar	Brook Jacoby	Jerry Browne	Felix Fermin	Carlos Baerga	C. Maldonado	M. Webster	Cory Snyder	Chris James
1991	M. Hargrove	Joel Skinner	Brook Jacoby	Mark Lewis	Felix Fermin	Carlos Baerga	Albert Belle	Alex Cole	Mark Whiten	Chris James
1992	M. Hargrove	S. Alomar	Paul Sorrento	Carlos Baerga	Mark Lewis	Brook Jacoby	T. Howard	Kenny Lofton	Mark Whiten	Albert Belle
1993	M. Hargrove	Junior Ortiz	Paul Sorrento	Carlos Baerga	Felix Fermin	A. Espinoza	Albert Belle	Kenny Lofton	Wayne Kirby	R. Jefferson
1994	M. Hargrove	S. Alomar	Paul Sorrento	Carlos Baerga	Omar Vizquel	Jim Thome	Albert Belle	Kenny Lofton	M. Ramirez	Eddie Murray
1995	M. Hargrove	Tony Pena	Paul Sorrento	Carlos Baerga	Omar Vizquel	Jim Thome	Albert Belle	Kenny Lofton	M. Ramirez	Eddie Murray
1996	M. Hargrove	S. Alomar	Julio Franco	Carlos Baerga	Omar Vizquel	Jim Thome	Albert Belle	Kenny Lofton	M. Ramirez	Eddie Murray
1997	M. Hargrove	S. Alomar	Jim Thome	T. Fernandez	Omar Vizquel	Matt Williams	Brian Giles	M. Grissom	M. Ramirez	Dave Justice
1998	M. Hargrove	S. Alomar	Jim Thome	David Bell	Omar Vizquel	T. Fryman	Brian Giles	Kenny Lofton	M. Ramirez	Dave Justice
1999	M. Hargrove	Einar Diaz	Richie Sexson	R. Alomar	Omar Vizquel	T. Fryman	Dave Justice	Kenny Lofton	M. Ramirez	Jim Thome
2000	C. Manuel	S. Alomar	David Segui	R. Alomar	Omar Vizquel	T. Fryman	R. Sexson	Kenny Lofton	M. Ramirez	Jim Thome
2001	C. Manuel	Einar Diaz	Jim Thome	R. Alomar	Omar Vizquel	T. Fryman	M. Cordova	Kenny Lofton	J. Gonzalez	Ellis Burks
2002	C. Manuel	Einar Diaz	Jim Thome	R. Gutierrez	Omar Vizquel	T. Fryman	C. Magruder	M. Bradley	Matt Lawton	Ellis Burks

MARINERS BY POSITION, YEAR BY YEAR

Seattle Mariners (American League), 1977–Present

YEAR	MANAGER	C	1B	2B	SS	3B	LF	CF	RF	DH
1977	D. Johnson	Bob Stinson	Dan Meyer	Jose Baez	C. Reynolds	Bill Stein	Steve Braun	Ruppert Jones	Lee Stanton	J. Bernhardt
1978	D. Johnson	Bob Stinson	Dan Meyer	Julio Cruz	C. Reynolds	Bill Stein	Bruce Bochte	Ruppert Jones	Leon Roberts	Lee Stanton
1979	D. Johnson	Larry Cox	Bruce Bochte	Julio Cruz	M. Mendoza	Dan Meyer	Leon Roberts	Ruppert Jones	Joe Simpson	Willie Horton
1980	D. Johnson	Larry Cox	Bruce Bochte	Julio Cruz	M. Mendoza	Ted Cox	Dan Meyer	Joe Simpson	Leon Roberts	Willie Horton
1981	R. Lachemann	Jerry Narron	Bruce Bochte	Julio Cruz	Jim Anderson	Lenny Randle	Tom Paciorek	Joe Simpson	J. Burroughs	Richie Zisk
1982	R. Lachemann	Rick Sweet	Gary Gray	Julio Cruz	Todd Cruz	M. Castillo	Bruce Bochte	D. Henderson	Al Cowens	Richie Zisk
1983	Del Crandall	Rick Sweet	Pat Putnam	T. Bernazard	Spike Owen	Jamie Allen	S. Henderson	D. Henderson	Al Cowens	Richie Zisk
1984	Del Crandall	Bob Kearney	Alvin Davis	Jack Perconte	Spike Owen	Jim Presley	Phil Bradley	D. Henderson	Al Cowens	Ken Phelps
1985	Chuck Cottier	Bob Kearney	Alvin Davis	Jack Perconte	Spike Owen	Jim Presley	Phil Bradley	D. Henderson	Al Cowens	G. Thomas
1986	D. Williams	Bob Kearney	Alvin Davis	H. Reynolds	Spike Owen	Jim Presley	Phil Bradley	John Moses	Dan Tartabull	G. Thomas
1987	D. Williams	Scott Bradley	Alvin Davis	H. Reynolds	Rey Quinones	Jim Presley	Phil Bradley	John Moses	Mike Kingery	Ken Phelps
1988	Jimmy Snyder	Scott Bradley	Alvin Davis	H. Reynolds	Rey Quinones	Jim Presley	M. Brantley	Henry Cotto	Glenn Wilson	Ken Phelps
1989	Jim Lefebvre	Dave Valle	Alvin Davis	H. Reynolds	Omar Vizquel	Jim Presley	Greg Briley	Ken Griffey	Darnell Coles	Jeff Leonard
1990	Jim Lefebvre	Dave Valle	Pete O'Brien	H. Reynolds	Omar Vizquel	E. Martinez	Greg Briley	Ken Griffey	Henry Cotto	Alvin Davis
1991	Jim Lefebvre	Dave Valle	Pete O'Brien	H. Reynolds	Omar Vizquel	E. Martinez	Greg Briley	Ken Griffey	Jay Buhner	Alvin Davis

YEAR	MANAGER	C	1B	2B	SS	3B	LF	CF	RF	DH
1992	Bill Plummer	Dave Valle	Pete O'Brien	H. Reynolds	Omar Vizquel	E. Martinez	Henry Cotto	Ken Griffey	Jay Buhner	Tino Martinez
1993	Lou Piniella	Dave Valle	Tino Martinez	Rich Amaral	Omar Vizquel	Mike Blowers	Mike Felder	Ken Griffey	Jay Buhner	Pete O'Brien
1994	Lou Piniella	Dan Wilson	Tino Martinez	Rich Amaral	Felix Fermin	E. Martinez	Eric Anthony	Ken Griffey	Jay Buhner	R. Jefferson
1995	Lou Piniella	Dan Wilson	Tino Martinez	Joey Cora	Luis Sojo	Mike Blowers	Rich Amaral	Alex Diaz	Jay Buhner	E. Martinez
1996	Lou Piniella	Dan Wilson	Paul Sorrento	Joey Cora	Al Rodriguez	Russ Davis	Rich Amaral	Ken Griffey	Jay Buhner	E. Martinez
1997	Lou Piniella	Dan Wilson	Paul Sorrento	Joey Cora	Al Rodriguez	Russ Davis	Rob Ducey	Ken Griffey	Jay Buhner	E. Martinez
1998	Lou Piniella	Dan Wilson	David Segui	Joey Cora	Al Rodriguez	Russ Davis	Glenallen Hill	Ken Griffey	Rob Ducey	E. Martinez
1999	Lou Piniella	Dan Wilson	David Segui	David Bell	Al Rodriguez	Russ Davis	Brian Hunter	Ken Griffey	Jay Buhner	E. Martinez
2000	Lou Piniella	Dan Wilson	John Olerud	M. McLemore	Al Rodriguez	David Bell	Stan Javier	M. Cameron	Jay Buhner	E. Martinez
2001	Lou Piniella	Dan Wilson	John Olerud	Bret Boone	C. Guillen	David Bell	McLemore	M. Cameron	Ichiro Suzuki	E. Martinez
2002	Lou Piniella	Dan Wilson	John Olerud	Bret Boone	C. Guillen	Jeff Cirillo	Ruben Sierra	M. Cameron	Ichiro Suzuki	E. Martinez

MARLINS BY POSITION, YEAR BY YEAR

Florida Marlins (National League), 1997–Present

YEAR	MANAGER	C	1B	2B	SS	3B	LF	CF	RF
1993	R. Lachemann	Ben Santiago	O. Destrade	Bret Barberie	Walt Weiss	G. Sheffield	Jeff Conine	Chuck Carr	D. Whitmore
1994	R. Lachemann	Ben Santiago	G. Colbrunn	Bret Barberie	Kurt Abbott	Jerry Browne	Jeff Conine	Chuck Carr	G. Sheffield
1995	R. Lachemann	C. Johnson	G. Colbrunn	Quilvio Veras	Kurt Abbott	T. Pendleton	Jeff Conine	Chuck Carr	G. Sheffield
1996	R. Lachemann	C. Johnson	G. Colbrunn	Quilvio Veras	Ed Renteria	T. Pendleton	Jeff Conine	Devon White	G. Sheffield
1997	Jim Leyland	C. Johnson	Jeff Conine	Luis Castillo	Ed Renteria	Bob Bonilla	Moises Alou	Devon White	G. Sheffield
1998	Jim Leyland	Gregg Zaun	Derrek Lee	C. Counsell	Ed Renteria	Todd Zeile	Cliff Floyd	T. Dunwoody	Mark Kotsay
1999	John Boles	M. Redmond	Kevin Millar	Luis Castillo	Al Gonzalez	Mike Lowell	Bruce Aven	Pr. Wilson	Mark Kotsay
2000	John Boles	M. Redmond	Derrek Lee	Luis Castillo	Al Gonzalez	Mike Lowell	Cliff Floyd	Pr. Wilson	Mark Kotsay
2001	Tony Perez	C. Johnson	Derrek Lee	Luis Castillo	Al Gonzalez	Mike Lowell	Cliff Floyd	Pr. Wilson	Kevin Millar
2002	Jeff Torborg	C. Johnson	Derrek Lee	Luis Castillo	Andy Fox	Mike Lowell	Kevin Millar	Pr. Wilson	Eric Owens

METS BY POSITION, YEAR BY YEAR

New York Mets (National League), 1962–Present

YEAR	MANAGER	C	1B	2B	SS	3B	LF	CF	RF
1962	Casey Stengel	C. Cannizzaro	Throneberry	Charlie Neal	Elio Chacon	Felix Mantilla	Frank Thomas	Jim Hickman	R. Ashburn
1963	Casey Stengel	C. Coleman	Tim Harkness	Ron Hunt	Al Moran	Charlie Neal	Frank Thomas	Jim Hickman	Duke Snider
1964	Casey Stengel	Jesse Gonder	Ed Kranepool	Ron Hunt	R. McMillan	Charley Smith	G. Altman	Jim Hickman	J. Christopher
1965	Casey Stengel	C. Cannizzaro	Ed Kranepool	Chuck Hiller	R. McMillan	Charley Smith	Ron Swoboda	Jim Hickman	Johnny Lewis
1966	Wes Westrum	Jerry Grote	Ed Kranepool	Ron Hunt	Ed Bressoud	Ken Boyer	Ron Swoboda	Cleon Jones	Al Luplow
1967	Wes Westrum	Jerry Grote	Ed Kranepool	Jerry Buchek	B. Harrelson	Ed Charles	Tommy Davis	Cleon Jones	Ron Swoboda
1968	Gil Hodges	Jerry Grote	Ed Kranepool	Phil Linz	B. Harrelson	Ed Charles	Cleon Jones	Tommie Agee	Ron Swoboda
1969	Gil Hodges	Jerry Grote	Ed Kranepool	Ken Boswell	B. Harrelson	W. Garrett	Cleon Jones	Tommie Agee	Ron Swoboda
1970	Gil Hodges	Jerry Grote	D. Clendenon	Ken Boswell	B. Harrelson	Joe Foy	Cleon Jones	Tommie Agee	Ron Swoboda
1971	Gil Hodges	Jerry Grote	Ed Kranepool	Ken Boswell	B. Harrelson	B. Aspromonte	Cleon Jones	Tommie Agee	Ken Singleton
1972	Yogi Berra	Duffy Dyer	Ed Kranepool	Ken Boswell	B. Harrelson	Jim Fregosi	John Milner	Tommie Agee	Rusty Staub
1973	Yogi Berra	Jerry Grote	John Milner	Felix Millan	B. Harrelson	W. Garrett	Cleon Jones	Don Hahn	Rusty Staub
1974	Yogi Berra	Jerry Grote	John Milner	Felix Millan	B. Harrelson	W. Garrett	Cleon Jones	Don Hahn	Rusty Staub
1975	Yogi Berra	Jerry Grote	Ed Kranepool	Felix Millan	Mike Phillips	W. Garrett	D. Kingman	Del Unser	Rusty Staub
1976	Joe Frazier	Jerry Grote	Ed Kranepool	Felix Millan	B. Harrelson	Roy Staiger	John Milner	Del Unser	D. Kingman
1977	Joe Torre	John Stearns	John Milner	Felix Millan	B. Harrelson	Lenny Randle	S. Henderson	Lee Mazzilli	Mike Vail
1978	Joe Torre	John Stearns	W. Montanez	Doug Flynn	Tim Foli	Lenny Randle	S. Henderson	Lee Mazzilli	E. Maddox
1979	Joe Torre	John Stearns	W. Montanez	Doug Flynn	Frank Taveras	R. Hebner	S. Henderson	Lee Mazzilli	J. Youngblood

YEAR	MANAGER	C	1B	2B	SS	3B	LF	CF	RF
1980	Joe Torre	Alex Trevino	Lee Mazzilli	Doug Flynn	Frank Taveras	E. Maddox	S. Henderson	J. Youngblood	C. Washington
1981	Joe Torre	John Stearns	D. Kingman	Doug Flynn	Frank Taveras	Hubie Brooks	Lee Mazzilli	M. Wilson	E. Valentine
1982	G. Bamberger	John Stearns	D. Kingman	W. Backman	R. Gardenhire	Hubie Brooks	George Foster	M. Wilson	E. Valentine
1983	Frank Howard	Ron Hodges	K. Hernandez	Brian Giles	Jose Oquendo	Hubie Brooks	George Foster	M. Wilson	D. Strawberry
1984	D. Johnson	M. Fitzgerald	K. Hernandez	W. Backman	Jose Oquendo	Hubie Brooks	George Foster	M. Wilson	D. Strawberry
1985	D. Johnson	Gary Carter	K. Hernandez	W. Backman	R. Santana	H. Johnson	George Foster	M. Wilson	D. Strawberry
1986	D. Johnson	Gary Carter	K. Hernandez	W. Backman	R. Santana	Ray Knight	M. Wilson	Len Dykstra	D. Strawberry
1987	D. Johnson	Gary Carter	K. Hernandez	Tim Teufel	R. Santana	H. Johnson	K. McReynolds	Len Dykstra	D. Strawberry
1988	D. Johnson	Gary Carter	K. Hernandez	W. Backman	Kevin Elster	H. Johnson	K. McReynolds	Len Dykstra	D. Strawberry
1989	D. Johnson	Barry Lyons	D. Magadan	G. Jefferies	Kevin Elster	H. Johnson	K. McReynolds	Juan Samuel	D. Strawberry
1990	B. Harrelson	M. Sasser	D. Magadan	G. Jefferies	Kevin Elster	H. Johnson	K. McReynolds	Daryl Boston	D. Strawberry
1991	B. Harrelson	Rick Cerone	D. Magadan	G. Jefferies	Kevin Elster	H. Johnson	K. McReynolds	Daryl Boston	Hubie Brooks
1992	Jeff Torborg	Todd Hundley	Eddie Murray	W. Randolph	D. Schofield	D. Magadan	Daryl Boston	H. Johnson	Bob Bonilla
1993	Dallas Green	Todd Hundley	Eddie Murray	Jeff Kent	Tim Bogar	H. Johnson	V. Coleman	Joe Orsulak	Bob Bonilla
1994	Dallas Green	Todd Hundley	David Segui	Jeff Kent	Jose Vizcaino	Bob Bonilla	J. Cangelosi	R. Thompson	Joe Orsulak
1995	Dallas Green	Todd Hundley	Rico Brogna	Jeff Kent	Jose Vizcaino	E. Alfonzo	Joe Orsulak	Brett Butler	Carl Everett
1996	Dallas Green	Todd Hundley	Butch Huskey	Jose Vizcaino	Rey Ordonez	Jeff Kent	B. Gilkey	L. Johnson	Alex Ochoa
1997	B. Valentine	Todd Hundley	John Olerud	Carlos Baerga	Rey Ordonez	E. Alfonzo	B. Gilkey	Carl Everett	Butch Huskey
1998	B. Valentine	Mike Piazza	John Olerud	Carlos Baerga	Rey Ordonez	E. Alfonzo	B. Gilkey	Brian McRae	Butch Huskey
1999	B. Valentine	Mike Piazza	John Olerud	E. Alfonzo	Rey Ordonez	R. Ventura	R. Henderson	Brian McRae	Roger Cedeno
2000	B. Valentine	Mike Piazza	Todd Zeile	E. Alfonzo	Mike Bordick	R. Ventura	B. Agbayani	Jay Payton	Derek Bell
2001	B. Valentine	Mike Piazza	Todd Zeile	E. Alfonzo	Rey Ordonez	R. Ventura	B. Agbayani	Jay Payton	T. Shinjo
2002	B. Valentine	Mike Piazza	Mo Vaughn	R. Alomar	Rey Ordonez	E. Alfonzo	Roger Cedeno	Timo Perez	J. Burnitz

ORIOLES BY POSITION, YEAR BY YEAR

Milwaukee Brewers (American League), 1901
St. Louis Browns (American League), 1902–1953
Baltimore Orioles (American League), 1954–Present

YEAR	MANAGER	C	1B	2B	SS	3B	LF	CF	RF
1901	Hugh Duffy	Billy Maloney	J. Anderson	Billy Gilbert	Wid Conroy	Jimmy Burke	Bill Hallman	Hugh Duffy	Irv Waldron
1902	Jim McAleer	Joe Sugden	J. Anderson	Dick Padden	Bob Wallace	B. McCormick	Jesse Burkett	E. Heidrick	C. Hemphill
1903	Jim McAleer	Mike Kahoe	J. Anderson	Bill Friel	Bob Wallace	Hunter Hill	Jesse Burkett	E. Heidrick	C. Hemphill
1904	Jim McAleer	Joe Sugden	Tom Jones	Dick Padden	Bob Wallace	C. Moran	Jesse Burkett	E. Heidrick	C. Hemphill
1905	Jim McAleer	Joe Sugden	Tom Jones	I. Rockenfield	Bob Wallace	H. Gleason	George Stone	Ben Koehler	Emil Frisk
1906	Jim McAleer	B. Rickey	Tom Jones	Pete O'Brien	Bob Wallace	Roy Hartzell	George Stone	C. Hemphill	Harry Niles
1907	Jim McAleer	T. Spencer	Tom Jones	Harry Niles	Bob Wallace	Joe Yeager	George Stone	C. Hemphill	O. Pickering
1908	Jim McAleer	T. Spencer	Tom Jones	Jim Williams	Bob Wallace	Hobe Ferris	George Stone	Dan Hoffman	Roy Hartzell
1909	Jim McAleer	Lou Criger	Tom Jones	Jim Williams	Bob Wallace	Hobe Ferris	George Stone	Dan Hoffman	Roy Hartzell
1910	J. O'Connor	Jim Stephens	Pat Newnam	F. Truesdale	Bob Wallace	Roy Hartzell	George Stone	Dan Hoffman	A. Schweitzer
1911	Bob Wallace	Nig Clarke	Jack Black	Frank LaPorte	Bob Wallace	Jimmy Austin	Willie Hogan	Burt Shotton	A. Schweitzer
1912	G. Stovall	Jim Stephens	G. Stovall	Del Pratt	Bob Wallace	Jimmy Austin	Willie Hogan	Burt Shotton	Gus Williams
1913	G. Stovall	Sam Agnew	G. Stovall	Del Pratt	Mike Balenti	Jimmy Austin	J. Johnston	Burt Shotton	Gus Williams
1914	B. Rickey	Sam Agnew	John Leary	Del Pratt	Doc Lavan	Jimmy Austin	Tilly Walker	Burt Shotton	Gus Williams
1915	B. Rickey	Sam Agnew	John Leary	Del Pratt	Doc Lavan	Jimmy Austin	Burt Shotton	Tilly Walker	Dee Walsh
1916	Fielder Jones	H. Severeid	George Sisler	Del Pratt	Doc Lavan	Jimmy Austin	Burt Shotton	A. Marsans	Ward Miller
1917	Fielder Jones	H. Severeid	George Sisler	Del Pratt	Doc Lavan	Jimmy Austin	Burt Shotton	B. Jacobson	Tod Sloan
1918	Jimmy Burke	Ray Demmitt	George Sisler	Joe Gedeon	Jimmy Austin	Fritz Maisel	Earl Smith	Jim Tobin	Ray Demmitt
1919	Jimmy Burke	H. Severeid	George Sisler	Joe Gedeon	Wally Gerber	Jimmy Austin	Jim Tobin	B. Jacobson	Earl Smith

YEAR	MANAGER	C	1B	2B	SS	3B	LF	CF	RF
1920	Jimmy Burke	H. Severeid	George Sisler	Joe Gedeon	Wally Gerber	Jimmy Austin	K. Williams	B. Jacobson	Jim Tobin
1921	Lee Fohl	H. Severeid	George Sisler	M. McManus	Wally Gerber	Frank Ellerbe	K. Williams	B. Jacobson	Jim Tobin
1922	Lee Fohl	H. Severeid	George Sisler	M. McManus	Wally Gerber	Frank Ellerbe	K. Williams	B. Jacobson	Jim Tobin
1923	Lee Fohl	H. Severeid	D. Schliebner	M. McManus	Wally Gerber	Homer Ezell	K. Williams	B. Jacobson	Jim Tobin
1924	George Sisler	H. Severeid	George Sisler	M. McManus	Wally Gerber	G. Robertson	K. Williams	B. Jacobson	Jim Tobin
1925	George Sisler	Leo Dixon	George Sisler	M. McManus	Bob LaMotte	G. Robertson	K. Williams	B. Jacobson	Harry Rice
1926	George Sisler	Wally Schang	George Sisler	Ski Melillo	Wally Gerber	M. McManus	K. Williams	Harry Rice	Bing Miller
1927	Dan Howley	Wally Schang	George Sisler	Ski Melillo	Wally Gerber	F. O'Rourke	K. Williams	Bing Miller	Harry Rice
1928	Dan Howley	Wally Schang	Lu Blue	Otis Brannan	Red Kress	F. O'Rourke	H. Manush	Fred Schulte	E. McNeely
1929	Dan Howley	Wally Schang	Lu Blue	Ski Melillo	Red Kress	F. O'Rourke	H. Manush	Fred Schulte	B. McGowan
1930	Bill Killefer	Rick Ferrell	Lu Blue	Ski Melillo	Red Kress	F. O'Rourke	Goose Goslin	Fred Schulte	Ted Gullic
1931	Bill Killefer	Rick Ferrell	Jack Burns	Ski Melillo	Jim Levey	Red Kress	Goose Goslin	Fred Schulte	Tom Jenkins
1932	Bill Killefer	Rick Ferrell	Jack Burns	Ski Melillo	Jim Levey	Art Scharein	Goose Goslin	Fred Schulte	B. Campbell
1933	Bill Killefer	Merv Shea	Jack Burns	Ski Melillo	Jim Levey	Art Scharein	Carl Reynolds	Sammy West	B. Campbell
1934	R. Hornsby	R. Hemsley	Jack Burns	Ski Melillo	Alan Strange	Harlond Clift	Ray Pepper	Sammy West	B. Campbell
1935	R. Hornsby	R. Hemsley	Jack Burns	Tom Carey	Lyn Lary	Harlond Clift	Moose Solters	Sammy West	Ed Coleman
1936	R. Hornsby	R. Hemsley	J. Bottomley	Tom Carey	Lyn Lary	Harlond Clift	Moose Solters	Sammy West	Beau Bell
1937	J. Bottomley	R. Hemsley	Harry Davis	Tom Carey	Knickerbocker	Harlond Clift	Joe Vosmik	Sammy West	Beau Bell
1938	Gabby Street	Billy Sullivan	G. McQuinn	Don Heffner	Red Kress	Harlond Clift	Buster Mills	Mel Almada	Beau Bell
1939	Fred Haney	Joe Glenn	G. McQuinn	J. Berardino	Don Heffner	Harlond Clift	Joe Gallagher	Chet Laabs	Myril Hoag
1940	Fred Haney	Bob Swift	G. McQuinn	Don Heffner	J. Berardino	Harlond Clift	Rip Radcliff	Walt Judnich	R. Cullenbine
1941	Luke Sewell	Rick Ferrell	G. McQuinn	Don Heffner	J. Berardino	Harlond Clift	R. Cullenbine	Walt Judnich	Chet Laabs
1942	Luke Sewell	Rick Ferrell	G. McQuinn	D. Gutteridge	V. Stephens	Harlond Clift	G. McQuillen	Walt Judnich	Chet Laabs
1943	Luke Sewell	Frankie Hayes	G. McQuinn	D. Gutteridge	V. Stephens	Harlond Clift	Chet Laabs	Milt Byrnes	Mike Chartak
1944	Luke Sewell	F. Mancuso	G. McQuinn	D. Gutteridge	V. Stephens	M. Christman	Milt Byrnes	M. Kreevich	Gene Moore
1945	Luke Sewell	F. Mancuso	G. McQuinn	D. Gutteridge	V. Stephens	M. Christman	Milt Byrnes	M. Kreevich	Gene Moore
1946	Luke Sewell	F. Mancuso	C. Stevens	J. Berardino	V. Stephens	M. Christman	Jeff Heath	Walt Judnich	Al Zarilla
1947	Muddy Ruel	Les Moss	Walt Judnich	J. Berardino	V. Stephens	Bob Dillinger	Jeff Heath	Paul Lehner	Al Zarilla
1948	Zack Taylor	Les Moss	C. Stevens	Jerry Priddy	Ed Pellagrini	Bob Dillinger	Whitey Platt	Paul Lehner	Al Zarilla
1949	Zack Taylor	Sherm Lollar	Jack Graham	Jerry Priddy	Ed Pellagrini	Bob Dillinger	Roy Sievers	Stan Spence	Dick Kokos
1950	Zack Taylor	Sherm Lollar	Don Lenhardt	Owen Friend	Tom Upton	Bill Sommers	Dick Kokos	Ray Coleman	Ken Wood
1951	Zack Taylor	Sherm Lollar	Hank Arft	Bobby Young	Bill Jennings	Fred Marsh	Ray Coleman	Jim Delsing	Ken Wood
1952	Marty Marion	C. Courtney	D. Kryhoski	Bobby Young	Joe DeMaestri	Jim Dyck	Jim Delsing	Jim Rivera	Bob Nieman
1953	Marty Marion	C. Courtney	D. Kryhoski	Bobby Young	Billy Hunter	Jim Dyck	Dick Kokos	Johnny Groth	Vic Wertz
1954	Jimmy Dykes	C. Courtney	Ed Waitkus	Bobby Young	Billy Hunter	V. Stephens	Jim Fridley	C. Diering	Cal Abrams
1955	Paul Richards	Hal Smith	Gus Triandos	Fred Marsh	W. Miranda	W. Causey	Dave Philley	C. Diering	Cal Abrams
1956	Paul Richards	Gus Triandos	Bob Boyd	Billy Gardner	W. Miranda	George Kell	Bob Nieman	D. Williams	Tito Francona
1957	Paul Richards	Gus Triandos	Bob Boyd	Billy Gardner	W. Miranda	George Kell	Bob Nieman	Jim Busby	Al Pilarcik
1958	Paul Richards	Gus Triandos	Bob Boyd	Billy Gardner	W. Miranda	B. Robinson	Bob Nieman	D. Williams	G. Woodling
1959	Paul Richards	Gus Triandos	Bob Boyd	Billy Gardner	C. Carrasquel	B. Robinson	Bob Nieman	Willie Tasby	G. Woodling
1960	Paul Richards	Gus Triandos	Jim Gentile	M. Breeding	Ron Hansen	B. Robinson	G. Woodling	Jackie Brandt	G. Stephens
1961	Paul Richards	Gus Triandos	Jim Gentile	Jerry Adair	Ron Hansen	B. Robinson	Russ Snyder	Jackie Brandt	W. Herzog
1962	B. Hitchcock	Gus Triandos	Jim Gentile	M. Breeding	Jerry Adair	B. Robinson	Boog Powell	Jackie Brandt	Russ Snyder
1963	B. Hitchcock	John Orsino	Jim Gentile	Jerry Adair	Luis Aparicio	B. Robinson	Boog Powell	Jackie Brandt	Russ Snyder
1964	Hank Bauer	Dick Brown	Norm Siebern	Jerry Adair	Luis Aparicio	B. Robinson	Boog Powell	Jackie Brandt	Sam Bowens
1965	Hank Bauer	Dick Brown	Boog Powell	Jerry Adair	Luis Aparicio	B. Robinson	Curt Blefary	Paul Blair	Russ Snyder
1966	Hank Bauer	A. Etchebarren	Boog Powell	D. Johnson	Luis Aparicio	B. Robinson	Curt Blefary	Paul Blair	F. Robinson
1967	Hank Bauer	A. Etchebarren	Boog Powell	D. Johnson	Luis Aparicio	B. Robinson	Curt Blefary	Paul Blair	F. Robinson
1968	Earl Weaver	A. Etchebarren	Boog Powell	D. Johnson	M. Belanger	B. Robinson	Curt Blefary	Paul Blair	F. Robinson

YEAR	MANAGER	C	1B	2B	SS	3B	LF	CF	RF	DH
1969	Earl Weaver	E. Hendricks	Boog Powell	D. Johnson	M. Belanger	B. Robinson	Don Buford	Paul Blair	F. Robinson	
1970	Earl Weaver	E. Hendricks	Boog Powell	D. Johnson	M. Belanger	B. Robinson	Don Buford	Paul Blair	F. Robinson	
1971	Earl Weaver	E. Hendricks	Boog Powell	D. Johnson	M. Belanger	B. Robinson	Don Buford	Paul Blair	F. Robinson	
1972	Earl Weaver	Johnny Oates	Boog Powell	D. Johnson	M. Belanger	B. Robinson	Don Buford	Paul Blair	Rettenmund	
1973	Earl Weaver	Earl Williams	Boog Powell	Bobby Grich	M. Belanger	B. Robinson	Don Baylor	Paul Blair	Rich Coggins	Tommy Davis
1974	Earl Weaver	Earl Williams	Boog Powell	Bobby Grich	M. Belanger	B. Robinson	Don Baylor	Paul Blair	Rich Coggins	Tommy Davis
1975	Earl Weaver	Dave Duncan	Lee May	Bobby Grich	M. Belanger	B. Robinson	Don Baylor	Paul Blair	K. Singleton	Tommy Davis
1976	Earl Weaver	Dave Duncan	Tony Muser	Bobby Grich	M. Belanger	D. DeCinces	K. Singleton	Paul Blair	R. Jackson	Lee May
1977	Earl Weaver	R. Dempsey	Lee May	Billy Smith	M. Belanger	D. DeCinces	Pat Kelly	Al Bumbry	K. Singleton	Eddie Murray
1978	Earl Weaver	R. Dempsey	Eddie Murray	Rich Dauer	M. Belanger	D. DeCinces	Pat Kelly	Larry Harlow	K. Singleton	Lee May
1979	Earl Weaver	R. Dempsey	Eddie Murray	Rich Dauer	Kiko Garcia	D. DeCinces	G. Roenicke	Al Bumbry	K. Singleton	Lee May
1980	Earl Weaver	R. Dempsey	Eddie Murray	Rich Dauer	M. Belanger	D. DeCinces	G. Roenicke	Al Bumbry	K. Singleton	T. Crowley
1981	Earl Weaver	R. Dempsey	Eddie Murray	Rich Dauer	M. Belanger	D. DeCinces	J. Lowenstein	Al Bumbry	G. Roenicke	T. Crowley
1982	Earl Weaver	R. Dempsey	Eddie Murray	Rich Dauer	Lenn Sakata	Cal Ripken	G. Roenicke	Al Bumbry	Dan Ford	K. Singleton
1983	Joe Altobelli	R. Dempsey	Eddie Murray	Rich Dauer	Cal Ripken	Todd Cruz	J. Lowenstein	John Shelby	Dan Ford	K. Singleton
1984	Joe Altobelli	R. Dempsey	Eddie Murray	Rich Dauer	Cal Ripken	Wayne Gross	G. Roenicke	John Shelby	Mike Young	K. Singleton
1985	Earl Weaver	R. Dempsey	Eddie Murray	Alan Wiggins	Cal Ripken	Fl. Rayford	Mike Young	Fred Lynn	Lee Lacy	Larry Sheets
1986	Earl Weaver	R. Dempsey	Eddie Murray	Juan Bonilla	Cal Ripken	Fl. Rayford	John Shelby	Fred Lynn	Lee Lacy	Larry Sheets
1987	C. Ripken Sr.	T. Kennedy	Eddie Murray	Billy Ripken	Cal Ripken	Ray Knight	Ken Gerhart	Fred Lynn	Larry Sheets	Mike Young
1988	F. Robinson	M. Tettleton	Eddie Murray	Billy Ripken	Cal Ripken	R. Gonzales	Pete Stanicek	Fred Lynn	Joe Orsulak	Eddie Murray
1989	F. Robinson	M. Tettleton	R. Milligan	Billy Ripken	Cal Ripken	Worthington	Phil Bradley	M. Devereaux	Joe Orsulak	Larry Sheets
1990	F. Robinson	M. Tettleton	R. Milligan	Billy Ripken	Cal Ripken	Worthington	Phil Bradley	M. Devereaux	Steve Finley	Sam Horn
1991	Johnny Oates	Chris Hoiles	R. Milligan	Billy Ripken	Cal Ripken	Leo Gomez	B. Anderson	M. Devereaux	Joe Orsulak	Sam Horn
1992	Johnny Oates	Chris Hoiles	R. Milligan	Billy Ripken	Cal Ripken	Leo Gomez	B. Anderson	M. Devereaux	Joe Orsulak	Glenn Davis
1993	Johnny Oates	Chris Hoiles	David Segui	H. Reynolds	Cal Ripken	Tim Hulett	B. Anderson	M. Devereaux	M. McLemore	Harold Baines
1994	Johnny Oates	Chris Hoiles	R. Palmeiro	M. McLemore	Cal Ripken	Leo Gomez	B. Anderson	M. Devereaux	J. Hammonds	Harold Baines
1995	Phil Regan	Chris Hoiles	R. Palmeiro	M. Alexander	Cal Ripken	Jeff Manto	B. Anderson	C. Goodwin	Kevin Bass	Harold Baines
1996	D. Johnson	Chris Hoiles	R. Palmeiro	R. Alomar	Cal Ripken	B.J. Surhoff	M. Devereaux	B. Anderson	Bob Bonilla	Eddie Murray
1997	D. Johnson	L. Webster	R. Palmeiro	R. Alomar	Mike Bordick	Cal Ripken	B.J. Surhoff	B. Anderson	J. Hammonds	G. Berroa
1998	Ray Miller	L. Webster	R. Palmeiro	R. Alomar	Mike Bordick	Cal Ripken	B.J. Surhoff	B. Anderson	Eric Davis	Harold Baines
1999	Ray Miller	C. Johnson	Jeff Conine	D. DeShields	Mike Bordick	Cal Ripken	B.J. Surhoff	B. Anderson	Albert Belle	Harold Baines
2000	M. Hargrove	C. Johnson	Will Clark	D. DeShields	Mike Bordick	Cal Ripken	B.J. Surhoff	B. Anderson	Albert Belle	Harold Baines
2001	M. Hargrove	B. Fordyce	Jeff Conine	Jerry Hairston	Mike Bordick	Cal Ripken	B. Anderson	Melvin Mora	Chris Richard	Tony Batista
2002	M. Hargrove	Geronimo Gil	Jeff Conine	Jerry Hairston	Mike Bordick	Tony Batista	Melvin Mora	C. Singleton	Jay Gibbons	M. Cordova

PADRES BY POSITION, YEAR BY YEAR

San Diego Padres (National League), 1969–Present

YEAR	MANAGER	C	1B	2B	SS	3B	LF	CF	RF
1969	Pr. Gomez	C. Cannizzaro	Nate Colbert	Jose Arcia	Tommy Dean	Ed Spiezio	Al Ferrara	Cito Gaston	Ollie Brown
1970	Pr. Gomez	C. Cannizzaro	Nate Colbert	D. Campbell	Jose Arcia	Ed Spiezio	Al Ferrara	Cito Gaston	Ollie Brown
1971	Pr. Gomez	Bob Barton	Nate Colbert	Dave Mason	E. Hernandez	Ed Spiezio	Larry Stahl	Cito Gaston	Ollie Brown
1972	Don Zimmer	Fred Kendall	Nate Colbert	Rich Morales	E. Hernandez	Dave Roberts	Leron Lee	Johnny Jeter	Cito Gaston
1973	Don Zimmer	Fred Kendall	Nate Colbert	D. Thomas	D. Thomas	Dave Roberts	Leron Lee	John Grubb	Cito Gaston
1974	J. McNamara	Fred Kendall	W. McCovey	D. Thomas	E. Hernandez	Dave Roberts	D. Winfield	John Grubb	Bobby Tolan
1975	J. McNamara	Fred Kendall	W. McCovey	Tito Fuentes	E. Hernandez	Ted Kubiak	Bobby Tolan	John Grubb	D. Winfield
1976	J. McNamara	Fred Kendall	Mike Ivie	Tito Fuentes	E. Hernandez	Doug Rader	John Grubb	Willie Davis	D. Winfield
1977	Al Dark	Gene Tenace	Mike Ivie	M. Champion	Bill Almon	T. Ashford	G. Richards	G. Hendrick	D. Winfield
1978	Roger Craig	Rick Sweet	Gene Tenace	F. Gonzalez	Ozzie Smith	Bill Almon	G. Richards	D. Winfield	Oscar Gamble

YEAR	MANAGER	C	1B	2B	SS	3B	LF	CF	RF
1979	Roger Craig	Bill Fahey	Gene Tenace	Dave Cash	Ozzie Smith	Paul Dade	Jerry Turner	G. Richards	D. Winfield
1980	J. Coleman	Gene Tenace	W. Montanez	Juan Bonilla	Ozzie Smith	A. Rodriguez	G. Richards	J. Mumphrey	D. Winfield
1981	Frank Howard	T. Kennedy	Br. Perkins	Juan Bonilla	Ozzie Smith	Luis Salazar	G. Richards	Ruppert Jones	Joe Lefebvre
1982	D. Williams	T. Kennedy	Br. Perkins	Tim Flannery	G. Templeton	Luis Salazar	G. Richards	Ruppert Jones	Sixto Lezcano
1983	D. Williams	T. Kennedy	Steve Garvey	Juan Bonilla	G. Templeton	Luis Salazar	Al Wiggins	Ruppert Jones	Sixto Lezcano
1984	D. Williams	T. Kennedy	Steve Garvey	Al Wiggins	G. Templeton	Graig Nettles	C. Martinez	McReynolds	Tony Gwynn
1985	D. Williams	T. Kennedy	Steve Garvey	Tim Flannery	G. Templeton	Graig Nettles	C. Martinez	McReynolds	Tony Gwynn
1986	Steve Boros	T. Kennedy	Steve Garvey	Tim Flannery	G. Templeton	Graig Nettles	McReynolds	M. Wynne	Tony Gwynn
1987	Larry Bowa	B. Santiago	John Kruk	Tim Flannery	G. Templeton	Randy Ready	S. Jefferson	Shane Mack	Tony Gwynn
1988	Jack McKeon	B. Santiago	K. Moreland	R. Alomar	G. Templeton	Chris Brown	C. Martinez	M. Wynne	Tony Gwynn
1989	Jack McKeon	B. Santiago	Jack Clark	R. Alomar	G. Templeton	Luis Salazar	Chris James	M. Wynne	Tony Gwynn
1990	Greg Riddoch	B. Santiago	Jack Clark	R. Alomar	G. Templeton	M. Pagliarulo	Bip Roberts	Joe Carter	Tony Gwynn
1991	Greg Riddoch	B. Santiago	Fred McGriff	Bip Roberts	T. Fernandez	Jack Howell	Jerald Clark	D. Jackson	Tony Gwynn
1992	Greg Riddoch	B. Santiago	Fred McGriff	Kurt Stillwell	T. Fernandez	G. Sheffield	Jerald Clark	D. Jackson	Tony Gwynn
1993	J. Riggleman	K. Higgins	Fred McGriff	Jeff Gardner	R. Gutierrez	G. Sheffield	Phil Plantier	Derek Bell	Tony Gwynn
1994	J. Riggleman	Brad Ausmus	Ed Williams	Bip Roberts	R. Gutierrez	Craig Shipley	Phil Plantier	Derek Bell	Tony Gwynn
1995	Bruce Bochy	Brad Ausmus	Ed Williams	Jody Reed	A. Cedeno	Ken Caminiti	Mel Nieves	Steve Finley	Tony Gwynn
1996	Bruce Bochy	John Flaherty	Wally Joyner	Jody Reed	Chris Gomez	Ken Caminiti	R. Henderson	Steve Finley	Tony Gwynn
1997	Bruce Bochy	John Flaherty	Wally Joyner	Quilvio Veras	Chris Gomez	Ken Caminiti	Greg Vaughn	Steve Finley	Tony Gwynn
1998	Bruce Bochy	C. Hernandez	Wally Joyner	Quilvio Veras	Chris Gomez	Ken Caminiti	Greg Vaughn	Steve Finley	Tony Gwynn
1999	Bruce Bochy	Ben Davis	Wally Joyner	Quilvio Veras	D. Jackson	Phil Nevin	Eric Owens	Ruben Rivera	R. Sanders
2000	Bruce Bochy	W. Gonzalez	Ryan Klesko	Bret Boone	D. Jackson	Phil Nevin	Al Martin	Ruben Rivera	Eric Owens
2001	Bruce Bochy	Ben Davis	Ryan Klesko	D. Jackson	D. Jimenez	Phil Nevin	R. Henderson	Mark Kotsay	B. Trammell
2002	Bruce Bochy	Tom Lampkin	Ryan Klesko	R. Vazquez	Deivi Cruz	Phil Nevin	Ron Gant	Mark Kotsay	B. Trammell

PHILLIES BY POSITION, YEAR BY YEAR

Worcester Brown Stockings (National League), 1880–1882
Philadelphia Phillies (National League), 1890–1941
Philadelphia Phils (National League), 1942
Philadelphia Phillies (National League), 1943
Philadelphia Blue Jays (National League), 1944–1945
Philadelphia Phillies (National League), 1946–Present

YEAR	MANAGER	C	1B	2B	SS	3B	LF	CF	RF
1901	B. Shettsline	Ed McFarland	H. Jennings	Billy Hallman	Monte Cross	H. Wolverton	Ed Delahanty	Roy Thomas	Elmer Flick
1902	B. Shettsline	Red Dooin	H. Jennings	Pete Childs	Rudy Hulswitt	Billy Hallman	G. Browne	Roy Thomas	Shad Barry
1903	Chief Zimmer	Frank Roth	K. Douglass	Kid Gleason	Rudy Hulswitt	H. Wolverton	Shad Barry	Roy Thomas	Bill Keister
1904	Hugh Duffy	Red Dooin	Jack Doyle	Kid Gleason	Rudy Hulswitt	H. Wolverton	John Titus	Roy Thomas	Sherry Magee
1905	Hugh Duffy	Red Dooin	K. Bransfield	Kid Gleason	Mi. Doolan	E. Courtney	Sherry Magee	Roy Thomas	John Titus
1906	Hugh Duffy	Red Dooin	K. Bransfield	Kid Gleason	Mi. Doolan	E. Courtney	Sherry Magee	Roy Thomas	John Titus
1907	Billy Murray	Red Dooin	K. Bransfield	Otto Knabe	Mi. Doolan	E. Courtney	Sherry Magee	Roy Thomas	John Titus
1908	Billy Murray	Red Dooin	K. Bransfield	Otto Knabe	Mi. Doolan	Eddie Grant	Sherry Magee	Ossie Osborn	John Titus
1909	Billy Murray	Red Dooin	K. Bransfield	Otto Knabe	Mi. Doolan	Eddie Grant	Sherry Magee	Johnny Bates	John Titus
1910	Red Dooin	Red Dooin	K. Bransfield	Otto Knabe	Mi. Doolan	Eddie Grant	Sherry Magee	Johnny Bates	John Titus
1911	Red Dooin	Red Dooin	Fred Luderus	Otto Knabe	Mi. Doolan	Hans Lobert	Sherry Magee	Dode Paskert	John Titus
1912	Red Dooin	Red Dooin	Fred Luderus	Otto Knabe	Mi. Doolan	Hans Lobert	Sherry Magee	Dode Paskert	Gavy Cravath
1913	Red Dooin	Bill Killefer	Fred Luderus	Otto Knabe	Mi. Doolan	Hans Lobert	Sherry Magee	Dode Paskert	Gavy Cravath
1914	Red Dooin	Bill Killefer	Fred Luderus	Bobby Byrne	Jack Martin	Hans Lobert	Beals Becker	Dode Paskert	Gavy Cravath
1915	Pat Moran	Bill Killefer	Fred Luderus	Bert Niehoff	Dave Bancroft	Bobby Byrne	Beals Becker	P. Whitted	Gavy Cravath

YEAR	MANAGER	C	1B	2B	SS	3B	LF	CF	RF
1916	Pat Moran	Bill Killefer	Fred Luderus	Bert Niehoff	Dave Bancroft	Milt Stock	P. Whitted	Dode Paskert	Gavy Cravath
1917	Pat Moran	Bill Killefer	Fred Luderus	Bert Niehoff	Dave Bancroft	Milt Stock	P. Whitted	Dode Paskert	Gavy Cravath
1918	Pat Moran	Bert Adams	Fred Luderus	P. McGaffigan	Dave Bancroft	Milt Stock	Irish Meusel	Cy Williams	Gavy Cravath
1919	Gavy Cravath	Bert Adams	Fred Luderus	Gene Paulette	Dave Bancroft	L. Blackburne	Irish Meusel	Cy Williams	Leo Callahan
1920	Gavy Cravath	Mack Wheat	Gene Paulette	J. Rawlings	Art Fletcher	Ralph Miller	Irish Meusel	Cy Williams	Casey Stengel
1921	Bill Donovan	Frank Bruggy	Ed Konetchy	Jimmy Smith	F. Parkinson	Wrightstone	Irish Meusel	Cy Williams	B. LeBourveau
1922	K. Wilhelm	Butch Henline	Roy Leslie	F. Parkinson	Art Fletcher	Goldie Rapp	Cliff Lee	Cy Williams	Curt Walker
1923	Art Fletcher	Butch Henline	Walter Holke	C. Tierney	Heinie Sand	Wrightstone	John Mokan	Cy Williams	Curt Walker
1924	Art Fletcher	Butch Henline	Walter Holke	Hod Ford	Heinie Sand	Wrightstone	John Mokan	Cy Williams	G. Harper
1925	Art Fletcher	Jim Wilson	C. Hawks	B. Friberg	Heinie Sand	Cl. Huber	George Burns	G. Harper	Cy Williams
1926	Art Fletcher	Jim Wilson	Jack Bentley	B. Friberg	Heinie Sand	Cl. Huber	John Mokan	Freddy Leach	Cy Williams
1927	S. McInnis	Jim Wilson	Wrightstone	F. Thompson	Heinie Sand	B. Friberg	Dick Spalding	Freddy Leach	Cy Williams
1928	Burt Shotton	Walt Lerian	Don Hurst	F. Thompson	Heinie Sand	P. Whitney	Freddy Leach	D. Sothern	Cy Williams
1929	Burt Shotton	Walt Lerian	Don Hurst	F. Thompson	T. Thevenow	P. Whitney	Lefty O'Doul	D. Sothern	Chuck Klein
1930	Burt Shotton	Spud Davis	Don Hurst	F. Thompson	T. Thevenow	P. Whitney	Lefty O'Doul	D. Sothern	Chuck Klein
1931	Burt Shotton	Spud Davis	Don Hurst	Les Mallon	Dick Bartell	P. Whitney	Chuck Klein	Fred Brickell	Buzz Arlett
1932	Burt Shotton	Spud Davis	Don Hurst	Les Mallon	Dick Bartell	P. Whitney	Hal Lee	Kiddo Davis	Chuck Klein
1933	Burt Shotton	Spud Davis	Don Hurst	Jack Warner	Dick Bartell	Jim McLeod	Schulmerich	Chick Fullis	Chuck Klein
1934	Jim Wilson	Al Todd	Dolph Camilli	Lou Chiozza	Dick Bartell	Bu. Walters	Ethan Allen	Kiddo Davis	Johnny Moore
1935	Jim Wilson	Al Todd	Dolph Camilli	Lou Chiozza	Mickey Haslin	John Vergez	G. Watkins	Ethan Allen	Johnny Moore
1936	Jim Wilson	Earl Grace	Dolph Camilli	Chile Gomez	Leo Norris	P. Whitney	Johnny Moore	Lou Chiozza	Chuck Klein
1937	Jim Wilson	Bill Atwood	Dolph Camilli	Del Young	G. Scharein	P. Whitney	M. Arnovich	Hersh Martin	Chuck Klein
1938	Jim Wilson	Bill Atwood	P. Weintraub	H. Mueller	Del Young	P. Whitney	M. Arnovich	Hersh Martin	Chuck Klein
1939	Doc Prothro	Spud Davis	Gus Suhr	Roy Hughes	G. Scharein	Pinky May	M. Arnovich	Hersh Martin	Le Grant Scott
1940	Doc Prothro	Ben Warren	Art Mahan	Ham Schulte	Bobby Bragan	Pinky May	Johnny Rizzo	Joe Marty	Chuck Klein
1941	Doc Prothro	Ben Warren	Nick Etten	D. Murtaugh	Bobby Bragan	Pinky May	Dan Litwhiler	Joe Marty	S. Benjamin
1942	Hans Lobert	Ben Warren	Nick Etten	Al Glossop	Bobby Bragan	Pinky May	Dan Litwhiler	Ernie Koy	Ron Northey
1943	Bucky Harris	M. Livingston	Jim Wasdell	D. Murtaugh	Glen Stewart	Pinky May	Coker Triplett	Buster Adams	Ron Northey
1944	Fitzsimmons	Bob Finley	Tony Lupien	Moon Mullen	Ray Hamrick	Glen Stewart	Jim Wasdell	Buster Adams	Ron Northey
1945	Ben Chapman	A. Seminick	Jim Wasdell	Tony Daniels	Bitsy Mott	John Antonelli	Coker Triplett	V. DiMaggio	Vance Dinges
1946	Ben Chapman	A. Seminick	F. McCormick	Emil Verban	S. Newsome	Jim Tabor	Del Ennis	J. Wyrostek	Ron Northey
1947	Ben Chapman	A. Seminick	Howie Schultz	Emil Verban	S. Newsome	Lee Handley	Del Ennis	Harry Walker	J. Wyrostek
1948	Ben Chapman	A. Seminick	Dick Sisler	G. Hamner	Eddie Miller	P. Caballero	John Blatnik	R. Ashburn	Del Ennis
1949	Eddie Sawyer	A. Seminick	Dick Sisler	Eddie Miller	G. Hamner	Willie Jones	Del Ennis	R. Ashburn	B. Nicholson
1950	Eddie Sawyer	A. Seminick	Eddie Waitkus	Mike Goliat	G. Hamner	Willie Jones	Dick Sisler	R. Ashburn	Del Ennis
1951	Eddie Sawyer	A. Seminick	Eddie Waitkus	P. Caballero	G. Hamner	Willie Jones	Dick Sisler	R. Ashburn	Del Ennis
1952	Steve O'Neill	S. Burgess	Eddie Waitkus	Connie Ryan	G. Hamner	Willie Jones	Del Ennis	R. Ashburn	J. Wyrostek
1953	Steve O'Neill	S. Burgess	Earl Torgeson	G. Hamner	Ted Kazanski	Willie Jones	Del Ennis	R. Ashburn	J. Wyrostek
1954	Terry Moore	S. Burgess	Earl Torgeson	G. Hamner	Bob Morgan	Willie Jones	Danny Schell	R. Ashburn	Del Ennis
1955	Mayo Smith	A. Seminick	M. Blaylock	Bob Morgan	Roy Smalley	Willie Jones	Del Ennis	R. Ashburn	J. Greengrass
1956	Mayo Smith	Stan Lopata	M. Blaylock	Ted Kazanski	G. Hamner	Willie Jones	Del Ennis	R. Ashburn	Elmer Valo
1957	Mayo Smith	Stan Lopata	Ed Bouchee	G. Hamner	C. Fernandez	Willie Jones	H. Anderson	R. Ashburn	Rip Repulski
1958	Terry Moore	Stan Lopata	Ed Bouchee	Solly Hemus	C. Fernandez	Willie Jones	H. Anderson	R. Ashburn	Wally Post
1959	Eddie Sawyer	Carl Sawatski	Ed Bouchee	S. Anderson	Joe Koppe	Gene Freese	H. Anderson	R. Ashburn	Wally Post
1960	Gene Mauch	Jimmie Coker	P. Herrera	Tony Taylor	Ruben Amaro	Alvin Dark	John Callison	B. Del Greco	Ken Walters
1961	Gene Mauch	C. Dalrymple	P. Herrera	Tony Taylor	Ruben Amaro	Charlie Smith	John Callison	T. Gonzalez	Ken Walters
1962	Gene Mauch	C. Dalrymple	Roy Sievers	Tony Taylor	Bobby Wine	Don Demeter	Ted Savage	T. Gonzalez	John Callison
1963	Gene Mauch	C. Dalrymple	Roy Sievers	Tony Taylor	Bobby Wine	Don Hoak	T. Gonzalez	Don Demeter	John Callison
1964	Gene Mauch	C. Dalrymple	J. Herrnstein	Tony Taylor	Bobby Wine	Dick Allen	W. Covington	T. Gonzalez	John Callison

YEAR	MANAGER	C	1B	2B	SS	3B	LF	CF	RF
1965	Gene Mauch	C. Dalrymple	Dick Stuart	Tony Taylor	Bobby Wine	Dick Allen	Alex Johnson	T. Gonzalez	John Callison
1966	Gene Mauch	C. Dalrymple	Bill White	Cookie Rojas	Dick Groat	Dick Allen	T. Gonzalez	Johnny Briggs	John Callison
1967	Gene Mauch	C. Dalrymple	Bill White	Cookie Rojas	Bobby Wine	Dick Allen	T. Gonzalez	Johnny Briggs	John Callison
1968	Bob Skinner	Mike Ryan	Bill White	Cookie Rojas	Roberto Pena	Tony Taylor	Dick Allen	T. Gonzalez	John Callison
1969	Bob Skinner	Mike Ryan	Dick Allen	Cookie Rojas	Don Money	Tony Taylor	Johnny Briggs	Larry Hisle	John Callison
1970	F. Lucchesi	Mike Ryan	D. Johnson	Denny Doyle	Larry Bowa	Don Money	Johnny Briggs	Larry Hisle	Ron Stone
1971	F. Lucchesi	T. McCarver	D. Johnson	Denny Doyle	Larry Bowa	J. Vukovich	Oscar Gamble	W. Montanez	Roger Freed
1972	Danny Ozark	John Bateman	Tom Hutton	Denny Doyle	Larry Bowa	Don Money	Greg Luzinski	W. Montanez	Bill Robinson
1973	Danny Ozark	Bob Boone	W. Montanez	Denny Doyle	Larry Bowa	Mike Schmidt	Greg Luzinski	Del Unser	Bill Robinson
1974	Danny Ozark	Bob Boone	W. Montanez	Dave Cash	Larry Bowa	Mike Schmidt	Greg Luzinski	Del Unser	M. Anderson
1975	Danny Ozark	Bob Boone	Dick Allen	Dave Cash	Larry Bowa	Mike Schmidt	Greg Luzinski	Gary Maddox	M. Anderson
1976	Danny Ozark	Bob Boone	Dick Allen	Dave Cash	Larry Bowa	Mike Schmidt	Greg Luzinski	Gary Maddox	Jay Johnstone
1977	Danny Ozark	Bob Boone	Richie Hebner	Ted Sizemore	Larry Bowa	Mike Schmidt	Greg Luzinski	Gary Maddox	Jay Johnstone
1978	Danny Ozark	Bob Boone	Richie Hebner	Ted Sizemore	Larry Bowa	Mike Schmidt	Greg Luzinski	Gary Maddox	Bake McBride
1979	Danny Ozark	Bob Boone	Pete Rose	Manny Trillo	Larry Bowa	Mike Schmidt	Greg Luzinski	Gary Maddox	Bake McBride
1980	Dallas Green	Bob Boone	Pete Rose	Manny Trillo	Larry Bowa	Mike Schmidt	Greg Luzinski	Gary Maddox	Bake McBride
1981	Dallas Green	Bob Boone	Pete Rose	Manny Trillo	Larry Bowa	Mike Schmidt	G. Matthews	Gary Maddox	Bake McBride
1982	Pat Corrales	Bo Diaz	Pete Rose	Manny Trillo	Ivan DeJesus	Mike Schmidt	G. Matthews	Gary Maddox	G. Vukovich
1983	Pat Corrales	Bo Diaz	Pete Rose	Joe Morgan	Ivan DeJesus	Mike Schmidt	G. Matthews	Gary Maddox	Von Hayes
1984	Paul Owens	Ozzie Virgil	Len Matuszek	Juan Samuel	Ivan DeJesus	Mike Schmidt	Glenn Wilson	Von Hayes	Sixto Lezcano
1985	John Felske	Ozzie Virgil	Mike Schmidt	Juan Samuel	Steve Jeltz	Rick Schu	Von Hayes	Gary Maddox	Glenn Wilson
1986	John Felske	John Russell	Von Hayes	Juan Samuel	Steve Jeltz	Mike Schmidt	Gary Redus	M. Thompson	Glenn Wilson
1987	Lee Elia	Lance Parrish	Von Hayes	Juan Samuel	Steve Jeltz	Mike Schmidt	Chris James	M. Thompson	Glenn Wilson
1988	Lee Elia	Lance Parrish	Von Hayes	Juan Samuel	Steve Jeltz	Mike Schmidt	Chris James	M. Thompson	Chris James
1989	Nick Leyva	D. Daulton	Ricky Jordan	Tommy Herr	Dickie Thon	Charlie Hayes	Phil Bradley	L. Dykstra	Von Hayes
1990	Nick Leyva	D. Daulton	Ricky Jordan	Tommy Herr	Dickie Thon	Charlie Hayes	John Kruk	L. Dykstra	Von Hayes
1991	Jim Fregosi	D. Daulton	John Kruk	M. Morandini	Dickie Thon	Charlie Hayes	Chamberlain	Von Hayes	Dale Murphy
1992	Jim Fregosi	D. Daulton	John Kruk	M. Morandini	Juan Bell	Dave Hollins	M. Duncan	L. Dykstra	Ruben Amaro
1993	Jim Fregosi	D. Daulton	John Kruk	M. Morandini	Kevin Stocker	Dave Hollins	M. Thompson	L. Dykstra	J. Eisenreich
1994	Jim Fregosi	D. Daulton	John Kruk	M. Morandini	Kevin Stocker	Dave Hollins	M. Thompson	L. Dykstra	J. Eisenreich
1995	Jim Fregosi	D. Daulton	Dave Hollins	M. Morandini	Kevin Stocker	Charlie Hayes	G. Jefferies	A. Van Slyke	J. Eisenreich
1996	Jim Fregosi	Be. Santiago	G. Jefferies	M. Morandini	Kevin Stocker	Todd Zeile	P. Incaviglia	Ricky Otero	J. Eisenreich
1997	T. Francona	M. Lieberthal	Rico Brogna	M. Morandini	Kevin Stocker	Scott Rolen	G. Jefferies	Ruben Amaro	D. Daulton
1998	T. Francona	M. Lieberthal	Rico Brogna	Mark Lewis	Desi Relaford	Scott Rolen	G. Jefferies	D. Glanville	Bobby Abreu
1999	T. Francona	M. Lieberthal	Rico Brogna	M. Anderson	Alex Arias	Scott Rolen	Ron Gant	D. Glanville	Bobby Abreu
2000	T. Francona	M. Lieberthal	Pat Burrell	M. Morandini	Desi Relaford	Scott Rolen	Ron Gant	D. Glanville	Bobby Abreu
2001	Larry Bowa	John Estrada	Travis Lee	M. Anderson	Jimmy Rollins	Scott Rolen	Pat Burrell	D. Glanville	Bobby Abreu
2002	Larry Bowa	M. Lieberthal	Travis Lee	M. Anderson	Jimmy Rollins	Scott Rolen	Pat Burrell	D. Glanville	Bobby Abreu

PIRATES BY POSITION, YEAR BY YEAR

Pittsburgh Alleghenies (National League), 1887–1889
Pittsburgh Innocents (National League), 1890
Pittsburgh Pirates (National League), 1891–Present

YEAR	MANAGER	C	1B	2B	SS	3B	LF	CF	RF
1901	Fred Clarke	Chief Zimmer	K. Bransfield	C. Ritchey	Bones Ely	Tommy Leach	Fred Clarke	G. Beaumont	Lefty Davis
1902	Fred Clarke	Harry Smith	K. Bransfield	C. Ritchey	Wid Conroy	Tommy Leach	Fred Clarke	G. Beaumont	H. Wagner
1903	Fred Clarke	Ed Phelps	K. Bransfield	C. Ritchey	H. Wagner	Tommy Leach	Fred Clarke	G. Beaumont	Jim Sebring
1904	Fred Clarke	Ed Phelps	K. Bransfield	C. Ritchey	H. Wagner	Tommy Leach	Fred Clarke	G. Beaumont	Jim Sebring

YEAR	MANAGER	C	1B	2B	SS	3B	LF	CF	RF
1905	Fred Clarke	Heinie Peitz	Del Howard	C. Ritchey	H. Wagner	Dave Brain	Fred Clarke	G. Beaumont	Otis Clymer
1906	Fred Clarke	G. Gibson	Jim Nealon	C. Ritchey	H. Wagner	Tom Sheehan	Fred Clarke	G. Beaumont	Bob Ganley
1907	Fred Clarke	G. Gibson	Jim Nealon	Abbaticchio	H. Wagner	Alan Storke	Fred Clarke	Tom Leach	G. Anderson
1908	Fred Clarke	G. Gibson	H. Swacina	Abbaticchio	H. Wagner	Tom Leach	Fred Clarke	Roy Thomas	Chief Wilson
1909	Fred Clarke	G. Gibson	Bill Abstein	Dots Miller	H. Wagner	Jap Barbeau	Fred Clarke	Tom Leach	Chief Wilson
1910	Fred Clarke	G. Gibson	John Flynn	Dots Miller	H. Wagner	Bobby Byrne	Fred Clarke	Tom Leach	Chief Wilson
1911	Fred Clarke	G. Gibson	Newt Hunter	Dots Miller	H. Wagner	Bobby Byrne	Fred Clarke	Max Carey	Chief Wilson
1912	Fred Clarke	G. Gibson	Dots Miller	Al McCarthy	H. Wagner	Bobby Byrne	Max Carey	Chief Wilson	Mike Donlin
1913	Fred Clarke	Mike Simon	Dots Miller	Jim Viox	H. Wagner	Bobby Byrne	Max Carey	Mike Mitchell	Chief Wilson
1914	Fred Clarke	G. Gibson	Ed Konetchy	Jim Viox	H. Wagner	Mike Mowrey	Max Carey	Joe Kelly	Mike Mitchell
1915	Fred Clarke	G. Gibson	Doc Johnston	Jim Viox	H. Wagner	Dave Baird	Max Carey	Zip Collins	Bill Hinchman
1916	N. Callahan	W. Schmidt	Doc Johnston	Jack Farmer	H. Wagner	Dave Baird	W. Schulte	Max Carey	Bill Hinchman
1917	N. Callahan	Bill Fischer	H. Wagner	Jake Pitler	Chuck Ward	Tony Boeckel	C. Bigbee	Max Carey	Lee King
1918	Hugo Bezdek	W. Schmidt	Fritz Mollwitz	G. Cutshaw	Buster Caton	B. McKechnie	C. Bigbee	Max Carey	B. Southworth
1919	Hugo Bezdek	W. Schmidt	Fritz Mollwitz	G. Cutshaw	Zeb Terry	W. Barbare	B. Southworth	C. Bigbee	Casey Stengel
1920	G. Gibson	W. Schmidt	Ch. Grimm	G. Cutshaw	Buster Caton	P. Whitted	C. Bigbee	Max Carey	B. Southworth
1921	G. Gibson	W. Schmidt	Ch. Grimm	G. Cutshaw	R. Maranville	C. Barnhart	C. Bigbee	Max Carey	P. Whitted
1922	B. McKechnie	Johnny Gooch	Ch. Grimm	C. Tierney	R. Maranville	Pie Traynor	C. Bigbee	Max Carey	Reb Russell
1923	B. McKechnie	W. Schmidt	Ch. Grimm	J. Rawlings	R. Maranville	Pie Traynor	C. Bigbee	Max Carey	C. Barnhart
1924	B. McKechnie	Johnny Gooch	Ch. Grimm	R. Maranville	Glenn Wright	Pie Traynor	Kiki Cuyler	Max Carey	C. Barnhart
1925	B. McKechnie	Earl Smith	G. Grantham	Eddie Moore	Glenn Wright	Pie Traynor	C. Barnhart	Max Carey	Kiki Cuyler
1926	B. McKechnie	Earl Smith	G. Grantham	Hal Rhyne	Glenn Wright	Pie Traynor	Kiki Cuyler	Max Carey	Paul Waner
1927	Donie Bush	Johnny Gooch	Joe Harris	G. Grantham	Glenn Wright	Pie Traynor	C. Barnhart	Lloyd Waner	Paul Waner
1928	Donie Bush	C. Hargreaves	G. Grantham	Sp. Adams	Glenn Wright	Pie Traynor	Fred Brickell	Lloyd Waner	Paul Waner
1929	Donie Bush	C. Hargreaves	Earl Sheely	G. Grantham	Dick Bartell	Pie Traynor	A. Comorosky	Lloyd Waner	Paul Waner
1930	Jewel Ens	R. Hemsley	Gus Suhr	G. Grantham	Dick Bartell	Pie Traynor	A. Comorosky	Lloyd Waner	Paul Waner
1931	Jewel Ens	Eddie Phillips	Gus Suhr	G. Grantham	T. Thevenow	Pie Traynor	A. Comorosky	Lloyd Waner	Paul Waner
1932	G. Gibson	Earl Grace	Gus Suhr	Tony Piet	A. Vaughan	Pie Traynor	A. Comorosky	Lloyd Waner	Paul Waner
1933	G. Gibson	Earl Grace	Gus Suhr	Tony Piet	A. Vaughan	Pie Traynor	Lloyd Waner	F. Lindstrom	Paul Waner
1934	Pie Traynor	Earl Grace	Gus Suhr	C. Lavagetto	A. Vaughan	Pie Traynor	F. Lindstrom	Lloyd Waner	Paul Waner
1935	Pie Traynor	Tom Padden	Gus Suhr	Pep Young	A. Vaughan	T. Thevenow	Woody Jensen	Lloyd Waner	Paul Waner
1936	Pie Traynor	Tom Padden	Gus Suhr	Pep Young	A. Vaughan	Bill Brubaker	Woody Jensen	Lloyd Waner	Paul Waner
1937	Pie Traynor	Al Todd	Gus Suhr	Lee Handley	A. Vaughan	Bill Brubaker	Woody Jensen	Lloyd Waner	Paul Waner
1938	Pie Traynor	Al Todd	Gus Suhr	Pep Young	A. Vaughan	Lee Handley	Johnny Rizzo	Lloyd Waner	Paul Waner
1939	Pie Traynor	Ray Berres	Elbie Fletcher	Pep Young	A. Vaughan	Lee Handley	Johnny Rizzo	Lloyd Waner	Paul Waner
1940	Frank Frisch	Spud Davis	Elbie Fletcher	Frank Gustine	A. Vaughan	Lee Handley	Van Robays	V. DiMaggio	Bob Elliott
1941	Frank Frisch	Al Lopez	Elbie Fletcher	Frank Gustine	A. Vaughan	Lee Handley	Van Robays	V. DiMaggio	Bob Elliott
1942	Frank Frisch	Al Lopez	Elbie Fletcher	Frank Gustine	Pete Coscarart	Bob Elliott	Jim Wasdell	V. DiMaggio	John Barrett
1943	Frank Frisch	Al Lopez	Elbie Fletcher	P. Coscarart	Frank Gustine	Bob Elliott	Jim Russell	V. DiMaggio	John Barrett
1944	Frank Frisch	Al Lopez	B. Dahlgren	P. Coscarart	Frank Gustine	Bob Elliott	Jim Russell	V. DiMaggio	John Barrett
1945	Frank Frisch	Al Lopez	B. Dahlgren	P. Coscarart	Frank Gustine	Bob Elliott	Jim Russell	Al Gionfriddo	John Barrett
1946	Frank Frisch	Al Lopez	Elbie Fletcher	Frank Gustine	Frank Gustine	Lee Handley	Jim Russell	Ralph Kiner	Bob Elliott
1947	Billy Herman	Dixie Howell	H. Greenberg	J. Bloodworth	Billy Cox	Frank Gustine	Ralph Kiner	Jim Russell	W. Westlake
1948	Billy Meyer	E. Fitz Gerald	Ed Stevens	D. Murtaugh	Stan Rojek	Frank Gustine	Ralph Kiner	W. Westlake	Dixie Walker
1949	Billy Meyer	McCullough	Johnny Hopp	Monty Basgall	Stan Rojek	P. Castiglione	Ralph Kiner	Dino Restelli	W. Westlake
1950	Billy Meyer	McCullough	Johnny Hopp	D. Murtaugh	Stan Rojek	Bob Dillinger	Ralph Kiner	W. Westlake	Gus Bell
1951	Billy Meyer	McCullough	Jack Phillips	D. Murtaugh	G. Strickland	P. Castiglione	Ralph Kiner	C. Metkovich	Gus Bell
1952	Billy Meyer	Joe Garagiola	T. Bartirome	Jack Merson	Dick Groat	P. Castiglione	Ralph Kiner	B. Del Greco	Gus Bell
1953	Fred Haney	M. Sandlock	Pete Ward	Jim O'Brien	Ed O'Brien	D. O'Connell	Hal Rice	Frank Thomas	Cal Abrams

YEAR	MANAGER	C	1B	2B	SS	3B	LF	CF	RF
1954	Fred Haney	Toby Atwell	Bob Skinner	Curt Roberts	Gair Allie	Dick Cole	Dick Hall	Frank Thomas	Sid Gordon
1955	Fred Haney	Jack Shepard	Dale Long	Jim O'Brien	Dick Groat	Gene Freese	Jerry Lynch	Frank Thomas	R. Clemente
1956	Bobby Bragan	Jack Shepard	Dale Long	B. Mazeroski	Dick Groat	Frank Thomas	Lee Walls	Bill Virdon	R. Clemente
1957	Bobby Bragan	Hank Foiles	Dee Fondy	B. Mazeroski	Dick Groat	Gene Freese	Bob Skinner	Bill Virdon	R. Clemente
1958	D. Murtaugh	Hank Foiles	T. Kluszewski	B. Mazeroski	Dick Groat	Frank Thomas	Bob Skinner	Bill Virdon	R. Clemente
1959	D. Murtaugh	S. Burgess	Dick Stuart	B. Mazeroski	Dick Groat	Don Hoak	Bob Skinner	Bill Virdon	R. Clemente
1960	D. Murtaugh	S. Burgess	Dick Stuart	B. Mazeroski	Dick Groat	Don Hoak	Bob Skinner	Bill Virdon	R. Clemente
1961	D. Murtaugh	S. Burgess	Dick Stuart	B. Mazeroski	Dick Groat	Don Hoak	Bob Skinner	Bill Virdon	R. Clemente
1962	D. Murtaugh	S. Burgess	Dick Stuart	B. Mazeroski	Dick Groat	Don Hoak	Bob Skinner	Bill Virdon	R. Clemente
1963	D. Murtaugh	Jim Pagliaroni	D. Clendenon	B. Mazeroski	D. Schofield	Bob Bailey	W. Stargell	Bill Virdon	R. Clemente
1964	D. Murtaugh	Jim Pagliaroni	D. Clendenon	B. Mazeroski	D. Schofield	Bob Bailey	Manny Mota	Bill Virdon	R. Clemente
1965	Harry Walker	Jim Pagliaroni	D. Clendenon	B. Mazeroski	Gene Alley	Bob Bailey	W. Stargell	Bill Virdon	R. Clemente
1966	Harry Walker	Jim Pagliaroni	D. Clendenon	B. Mazeroski	Gene Alley	Bob Bailey	W. Stargell	Matty Alou	R. Clemente
1967	Harry Walker	Jerry May	D. Clendenon	B. Mazeroski	Gene Alley	Maury Wills	W. Stargell	Matty Alou	R. Clemente
1968	Larry Shepard	Jerry May	D. Clendenon	B. Mazeroski	Gene Alley	Maury Wills	W. Stargell	Matty Alou	R. Clemente
1969	Larry Shepard	M. Sanguillen	Al Oliver	B. Mazeroski	Fred Patek	Richie Hebner	W. Stargell	Matty Alou	R. Clemente
1970	D. Murtaugh	M. Sanguillen	B. Robertson	B. Mazeroski	Gene Alley	Richie Hebner	W. Stargell	Matty Alou	R. Clemente
1971	D. Murtaugh	M. Sanguillen	B. Robertson	Dave Cash	Gene Alley	Richie Hebner	W. Stargell	Al Oliver	R. Clemente
1972	Bill Virdon	M. Sanguillen	W. Stargell	Dave Cash	Gene Alley	Richie Hebner	Vic Davalillo	Al Oliver	R. Clemente
1973	Bill Virdon	M. Sanguillen	B. Robertson	Dave Cash	Dal Maxvill	Richie Hebner	W. Stargell	Al Oliver	Richie Zisk
1974	D. Murtaugh	M. Sanguillen	B. Robertson	R. Stennett	Frank Taveras	Richie Hebner	W. Stargell	Al Oliver	Richie Zisk
1975	D. Murtaugh	M. Sanguillen	W. Stargell	R. Stennett	Frank Taveras	Richie Hebner	Richie Zisk	Al Oliver	Dave Parker
1976	D. Murtaugh	M. Sanguillen	W. Stargell	R. Stennett	Frank Taveras	Richie Hebner	Richie Zisk	Al Oliver	Dave Parker
1977	Chuck Tanner	Duffy Dyer	Bill Robinson	R. Stennett	Frank Taveras	Phil Garner	Al Oliver	Omar Moreno	Dave Parker
1978	Chuck Tanner	Ed Ott	W. Stargell	R. Stennett	Frank Taveras	Phil Garner	Bill Robinson	Omar Moreno	Dave Parker
1979	Chuck Tanner	Ed Ott	W. Stargell	R. Stennett	Tim Foli	Bill Madlock	Bill Robinson	Omar Moreno	Dave Parker
1980	Chuck Tanner	Ed Ott	John Milner	Phil Garner	Tim Foli	Bill Madlock	Mike Easler	Omar Moreno	Dave Parker
1981	Chuck Tanner	Tony Pena	J. Thompson	Phil Garner	Tim Foli	Bill Madlock	Mike Easler	Omar Moreno	Dave Parker
1982	Chuck Tanner	Tony Pena	J. Thompson	Johnny Ray	Dale Berra	Bill Madlock	Mike Easler	Omar Moreno	Lee Lacy
1983	Chuck Tanner	Tony Pena	J. Thompson	Johnny Ray	Dale Berra	Bill Madlock	Mike Easler	Marv Wynne	Dave Parker
1984	Chuck Tanner	Tony Pena	J. Thompson	Johnny Ray	Dale Berra	Bill Madlock	Lee Lacy	Marv Wynne	Doug Frobel
1985	Chuck Tanner	Tony Pena	J. Thompson	Johnny Ray	Sam Khalifa	Bill Madlock	Joe Orsulak	Marv Wynne	G. Hendrick
1986	Jim Leyland	Tony Pena	Sid Bream	Johnny Ray	R. Belliard	Jim Morrison	R.J. Reynolds	Barry Bonds	Joe Orsulak
1987	Jim Leyland	M. LaValliere	Sid Bream	Johnny Ray	Al Pedrique	Bobby Bonilla	Barry Bonds	A. Van Slyke	R.J. Reynolds
1988	Jim Leyland	M. LaValliere	Sid Bream	Jose Lind	R. Belliard	Bobby Bonilla	Barry Bonds	A. Van Slyke	R.J. Reynolds
1989	Jim Leyland	Junior Ortiz	Gary Redus	Jose Lind	Jay Bell	Bobby Bonilla	Barry Bonds	A. Van Slyke	R.J. Reynolds
1990	Jim Leyland	M. LaValliere	Sid Bream	Jose Lind	Jay Bell	Jeff King	Barry Bonds	A. Van Slyke	Bobby Bonilla
1991	Jim Leyland	M. LaValliere	O. Merced	Jose Lind	Jay Bell	Bobby Bonilla	Barry Bonds	A. Van Slyke	Gary Varsho
1992	Jim Leyland	M. LaValliere	O. Merced	Jose Lind	Jay Bell	S. Buechele	Barry Bonds	A. Van Slyke	Cecil Espy
1993	Jim Leyland	Don Slaught	Kevin Young	Carlos Garcia	Jay Bell	Jeff King	Al Martin	A. Van Slyke	O. Merced
1994	Jim Leyland	Don Slaught	Brian Hunter	Carlos Garcia	Jay Bell	Jeff King	Al Martin	A. Van Slyke	O. Merced
1995	Jim Leyland	Mark Parent	Mark Johnson	Carlos Garcia	Jay Bell	Jeff King	Al Martin	J. Brumfield	O. Merced
1996	Jim Leyland	Jason Kendall	Mark Johnson	Carlos Garcia	Jay Bell	Charlie Hayes	Al Martin	Mike Kingery	O. Merced
1997	Gene Lamont	Jason Kendall	Kevin Young	T. Womack	K. Polcovich	Joe Randa	Al Martin	J. Allensworth	Jose Guillen
1998	Gene Lamont	Jason Kendall	Kevin Young	T. Womack	Lou Collier	A. Ramirez	Al Martin	Turner Ward	Jose Guillen
1999	Gene Lamont	Jason Kendall	Kevin Young	W. Morris	M. Benjamin	Ed Sprague	Al Martin	Brian Giles	Adrian Brown
2000	Gene Lamont	Jason Kendall	Kevin Young	W. Morris	Pat Meares	A. Ramirez	Wil Cordero	Adrian Brown	Brian Giles
2001	L. McClendon	Jason Kendall	Kevin Young	Pat Meares	Jack Wilson	A. Ramirez	Brian Giles	G. Matthews	J. Vander Wal
2002	L. McClendon	Jason Kendall	Kevin Young	Pokey Reese	Jack Wilson	A. Ramirez	Brian Giles	R. Mackowiak	Craig Wilson

RANGERS BY POSITION, YEAR BY YEAR

Washington Senators (American League), 1961–1971
Texas Rangers (American League), 1972–Present

YEAR	MANAGER	C	1B	2B	SS	3B	LF	CF	RF	DH
1961	Mi. Vernon	Gene Green	Dale Long	Chuck Cottier	Coot Veal	D. O'Connell	M. Keough	Willie Tasby	G. Woodling	
1962	Mi. Vernon	Ken Retzer	Harry Bright	Chuck Cottier	Ken Hamlin	Bob Johnson	Chuck Hinton	Jim Piersall	Jim King	
1963	Gil Hodges	Ken Retzer	Bobo Osborne	Chuck Cottier	Ed Brinkman	Don Zimmer	Chuck Hinton	Don Lock	Jim King	
1964	Gil Hodges	M. Brumley	M. Skowron	Blasingame	Ed Brinkman	John Kennedy	Chuck Hinton	Don Lock	Jim King	
1965	Gil Hodges	M. Brumley	Dick Nen	Blasingame	Ed Brinkman	K. McMullen	Frank Howard	Don Lock	Woody Held	
1966	Gil Hodges	P. Casanova	Dick Nen	Bob Saverine	Ed Brinkman	K. McMullen	Frank Howard	Don Lock	F. Valentine	
1967	Gil Hodges	P. Casanova	Mike Epstein	Bernie Allen	Ed Brinkman	K. McMullen	Frank Howard	F. Valentine	Cap Peterson	
1968	Jim Lemon	P. Casanova	Mike Epstein	Bernie Allen	Ron Hansen	K. McMullen	Frank Howard	Del Unser	Ed Stroud	
1969	Ted Williams	P. Casanova	Mike Epstein	Bernie Allen	Ed Brinkman	K. McMullen	Frank Howard	Del Unser	Hank Allen	
1970	Ted Williams	P. Casanova	Mike Epstein	Tim Cullen	Ed Brinkman	A. Rodriguez	Frank Howard	Ed Stroud	Del Unser	
1971	Ted Williams	P. Casanova	Don Mincher	Tim Cullen	Toby Harrah	Dave Nelson	Frank Howard	E. Maddox	Del Unser	
1972	Ted Williams	Dick Billings	Frank Howard	Lenny Randle	Toby Harrah	Dave Nelson	Larry Biittner	Joe Lovitto	Ted Ford	
1973	W. Herzog	Ken Suarez	Jim Spencer	Dave Nelson	Jim Mason	Toby Harrah	Rico Carty	Vic Harris	J. Burroughs	Alex Johnson
1974	Billy Martin	Jim Sundberg	M. Hargrove	Dave Nelson	Toby Harrah	Lenny Randle	Alex Johnson	Cesar Tovar	J. Burroughs	Jim Spencer
1975	Billy Martin	Jim Sundberg	Jim Spencer	Lenny Randle	Toby Harrah	Roy Howell	M. Hargrove	Dave Moates	J. Burroughs	Cesar Tovar
1976	F. Lucchesi	Jim Sundberg	M. Hargrove	Lenny Randle	Toby Harrah	Roy Howell	Gene Clines	J. Beniquez	J. Burroughs	Tom Grieve
1977	Billy Hunter	Jim Sundberg	M. Hargrove	Bump Wills	B. Campaneris	Toby Harrah	C. Washington	J. Beniquez	Dave May	Willie Horton
1978	Pat Corrales	Jim Sundberg	M. Hargrove	Bump Wills	B. Campaneris	Toby Harrah	Al Oliver	J. Beniquez	Bobby Bonds	Richie Zisk
1979	Pat Corrales	Jim Sundberg	Pat Putnam	Bump Wills	N. Norman	Buddy Bell	Billy Sample	Al Oliver	Richie Zisk	John Ellis
1980	Pat Corrales	Jim Sundberg	Pat Putnam	Bump Wills	Pepe Frias	Buddy Bell	Al Oliver	Mi. Rivers	John Grubb	Richie Zisk
1981	Don Zimmer	Jim Sundberg	Pat Putnam	Bump Wills	M. Mendoza	Buddy Bell	Billy Sample	Mi. Rivers	Leon Roberts	Al Oliver
1982	Don Zimmer	Jim Sundberg	D. Hostetler	Mike Richardt	Mark Wagner	Buddy Bell	Billy Sample	G. Wright	Larry Parrish	L. Johnson
1983	Doug Rader	Jim Sundberg	Pete O'Brien	W. Tolleson	Bucky Dent	Buddy Bell	Billy Sample	G. Wright	Larry Parrish	D. Hostetler
1984	Doug Rader	Donnie Scott	Pete O'Brien	W. Tolleson	C. Wilkerson	Buddy Bell	Billy Sample	G. Wright	Gary Ward	Larry Parrish
1985	B. Valentine	Don Slaught	Pete O'Brien	Toby Harrah	C. Wilkerson	Buddy Bell	Gary Ward	O. McDowell	G. Wright	Cliff Johnson
1986	B. Valentine	Don Slaught	Pete O'Brien	Toby Harrah	Scott Fletcher	S. Buechele	Ruben Sierra	O. McDowell	P. Incaviglia	Larry Parrish
1987	B. Valentine	Don Slaught	Pete O'Brien	Jerry Browne	Scott Fletcher	S. Buechele	P. Incaviglia	O. McDowell	Ruben Sierra	Larry Parrish
1988	B. Valentine	Geno Petralli	Pete O'Brien	C. Wilkerson	Scott Fletcher	S. Buechele	Cecil Espy	O. McDowell	Ruben Sierra	Larry Parrish
1989	B. Valentine	Chad Kreuter	R. Palmeiro	Julio Franco	Scott Fletcher	S. Buechele	P. Incaviglia	Cecil Espy	Ruben Sierra	Harold Baines
1990	B. Valentine	Geno Petralli	R. Palmeiro	Julio Franco	Jeff Huson	S. Buechele	P. Incaviglia	Gary Pettis	Ruben Sierra	Harold Baines
1991	B. Valentine	I. Rodriguez	R. Palmeiro	Julio Franco	Jeff Huson	S. Buechele	J. Gonzalez	Gary Pettis	Ruben Sierra	B. Downing
1992	B. Valentine	I. Rodriguez	R. Palmeiro	Al Newman	Dickie Thon	Dean Palmer	Kevin Reimer	J. Gonzalez	Ruben Sierra	B. Downing
1993	K. Kennedy	I. Rodriguez	R. Palmeiro	Doug Strange	Manny Lee	Dean Palmer	J. Gonzalez	David Hulse	Jose Canseco	Julio Franco
1994	K. Kennedy	I. Rodriguez	Will Clark	Jeff Frye	Manny Lee	Dean Palmer	J. Gonzalez	David Hulse	Rusty Greer	Jose Canseco
1995	Johnny Oates	I. Rodriguez	Will Clark	Jeff Frye	Benji Gil	M. Pagliarulo	M. McLemore	Otis Nixon	Rusty Greer	J. Gonzalez
1996	Johnny Oates	I. Rodriguez	Will Clark	M. McLemore	Kevin Elster	Dean Palmer	Rusty Greer	D. Hamilton	J. Gonzalez	M. Tettleton
1997	Johnny Oates	I. Rodriguez	Will Clark	M. McLemore	Benji Gil	Dean Palmer	Rusty Greer	D. Buford	W. Newson	J. Gonzalez
1998	Johnny Oates	I. Rodriguez	Will Clark	M. McLemore	Kevin Elster	F. Tatis	Rusty Greer	T. Goodwin	J. Gonzalez	Lee Stevens
1999	Johnny Oates	I. Rodriguez	Lee Stevens	M. McLemore	R. Clayton	Todd Zeile	Rusty Greer	T. Goodwin	J. Gonzalez	R. Palmeiro
2000	Johnny Oates	I. Rodriguez	R. Palmeiro	Luis Alicea	R. Clayton	Mike Lamb	Rusty Greer	Gabe Kapler	Chad Curtis	David Segui
2001	Johnny Oates	I. Rodriguez	R. Palmeiro	M. Young	Al Rodriguez	Mike Lamb	F. Catalanotto	Gabe Kapler	Ricky Ledee	Ruben Sierra
2002	Jerry Narron	I. Rodriguez	Mike Lamb	M. Young	Al Rodriguez	Herb Perry	Kevin Mench	Carl Everett	J. Gonzalez	R. Palmeiro

Cincinnati Reds (National League), 1890–1943
Cincinnati Redlegs (National League), 1944–1945
Cincinnati Reds (National League), 1946–1953
Cincinnati Redlegs (National League), 1954–1960
Cincinnati Reds (National League), 1961–Present

YEAR	MANAGER	C	1B	2B	SS	3B	LF	CF	RF
1901	Bid McPhee	Bill Bergen	Jake Beckley	H. Steinfeldt	M. Magoon	Charlie Irwin	Dick Harley	Johnny Dobbs	Sam Crawford
1902	Bid McPhee	Bill Bergen	Jake Beckley	Heinie Peitz	T. Corcoran	H. Steinfeldt	Johnny Dobbs	Dummy Hoy	Sam Crawford
1903	Joe Kelley	Heinie Peitz	Jake Beckley	Tom Daly	T. Corcoran	H. Steinfeldt	Mike Donlin	Cy Seymour	Cozy Dolan
1904	Joe Kelley	A. Schlei	Joe Kelley	M. Huggins	T. Corcoran	H. Steinfeldt	Fred Odwell	Cy Seymour	Cozy Dolan
1905	Joe Kelley	A. Schlei	Shad Barry	M. Huggins	T. Corcoran	H. Steinfeldt	Joe Kelley	Cy Seymour	Fred Odwell
1906	Ned Hanlon	A. Schlei	Snake Deal	M. Huggins	T. Corcoran	Jim Delahanty	Joe Kelley	Cy Seymour	Frank Jude
1907	Ned Hanlon	Larry McLean	John Ganzel	M. Huggins	Hans Lobert	Mike Mowrey	Fred Odwell	Art Kruger	Mike Mitchell
1908	John Ganzel	A. Schlei	John Ganzel	M. Huggins	R. Hulswitt	Hans Lobert	Dode Paskert	John Kane	Mike Mitchell
1909	Clark Griffith	Larry McLean	D. Hoblitzel	Dick Egan	Tom Downey	Hans Lobert	Bob Bescher	Rebel Oakes	Mike Mitchell
1910	Clark Griffith	Larry McLean	D. Hoblitzel	Dick Egan	T. McMillan	Hans Lobert	Bob Bescher	Dode Paskert	Mike Mitchell
1911	Clark Griffith	Larry McLean	D. Hoblitzel	Dick Egan	Tom Downey	Eddie Grant	Bob Bescher	Johnny Bates	Mike Mitchell
1912	Hank O'Day	Larry McLean	D. Hoblitzel	Dick Egan	Jim Esmond	Art Phelan	Bob Bescher	A. Marsans	Mike Mitchell
1913	Joe Tinker	Tom Clarke	D. Hoblitzel	Heinie Groh	Joe Tinker	John Dodge	Bob Bescher	A. Marsans	Johnny Bates
1914	Buck Herzog	Tom Clarke	D. Hoblitzel	Heinie Groh	Buck Herzog	Bert Niehoff	G. Twombly	Bert Daniels	Herbie Moran
1915	Buck Herzog	Ivey Wingo	Fritz Mollwitz	Bill Rodgers	Buck Herzog	Heinie Groh	Red Killefer	Tom Leach	Tom Griffith
1916	Buck Herzog	Ivey Wingo	Hal Chase	Baldy Louden	Buck Herzog	Heinie Groh	Greasy Neale	Edd Roush	Tom Griffith
1917	C. Mathewson	Ivey Wingo	Hal Chase	Dave Shean	Larry Kopf	Heinie Groh	Greasy Neale	Edd Roush	Tom Griffith
1918	C. Mathewson	Ivey Wingo	Hal Chase	Lee Magee	L. Blackburne	Heinie Groh	Greasy Neale	Edd Roush	Tom Griffith
1919	Pat Moran	Ivey Wingo	Jake Daubert	Morrie Rath	Larry Kopf	Heinie Groh	Rube Bressler	Edd Roush	Greasy Neale
1920	Pat Moran	Ivey Wingo	Jake Daubert	Morrie Rath	Larry Kopf	Heinie Groh	Pat Duncan	Edd Roush	Greasy Neale
1921	Pat Moran	Ivey Wingo	Jake Daubert	Sam Bohne	Larry Kopf	Heinie Groh	Pat Duncan	Edd Roush	Rube Bressler
1922	Pat Moran	B. Hargrave	Jake Daubert	Sam Bohne	Ike Caveney	Babe Pinelli	Pat Duncan	George Burns	George Harper
1923	Pat Moran	B. Hargrave	Jake Daubert	Sam Bohne	Ike Caveney	Babe Pinelli	Pat Duncan	Edd Roush	George Burns
1924	J. Hendricks	B. Hargrave	Jake Daubert	Hughie Critz	Ike Caveney	Babe Pinelli	Pat Duncan	Edd Roush	Curt Walker
1925	J. Hendricks	B. Hargrave	Walter Holke	Hughie Critz	Ike Caveney	Babe Pinelli	Billy Zitzman	Edd Roush	Curt Walker
1926	J. Hendricks	B. Hargrave	Wally Pipp	Hughie Critz	Frank Emmer	C. Dressen	C. Christensen	Edd Roush	Curt Walker
1927	J. Hendricks	B. Hargrave	Wally Pipp	Hughie Critz	Hod Ford	C. Dressen	Rube Bressler	Ethan Allen	Curt Walker
1928	J. Hendricks	Val Picinich	George Kelly	Hughie Critz	Hod Ford	C. Dressen	Billy Zitzman	Ethan Allen	Curt Walker
1929	J. Hendricks	Johnny Gooch	George Kelly	Hughie Critz	Hod Ford	C. Dressen	Ever Swanson	Ethan Allen	Curt Walker
1930	Dan Howley	C. Sukeforth	Joe Stripp	Hod Ford	Leo Durocher	T. Cuccinello	Curt Walker	Bob Meusel	H. Heilmann
1931	Dan Howley	C. Sukeforth	H. Hendrick	T. Cuccinello	Leo Durocher	Joe Stripp	Edd Roush	T. Douthit	Estel Crabtree
1932	Dan Howley	E. Lombardi	H. Hendrick	G. Grantham	Leo Durocher	Wally Gilbert	W. Roettger	Estel Crabtree	Babe Herman
1933	Donie Bush	E. Lombardi	J. Bottomley	J. Morrissey	Otto Bluege	Sp. Adams	Johnny Moore	Chick Hafey	Harry Rice
1934	B. O'Farrell	E. Lombardi	J. Bottomley	Tony Piet	Gordon Slade	Mark Koenig	Harlin Pool	Chick Hafey	A. Comorosky
1935	C. Dressen	E. Lombardi	J. Bottomley	A. Kampouris	Billy Myers	Lew Riggs	Babe Herman	Sammy Byrd	Ival Goodman
1936	C. Dressen	E. Lombardi	Les Scarsella	A. Kampouris	Billy Myers	Lew Riggs	Babe Herman	Kiki Cuyler	Ival Goodman
1937	C. Dressen	E. Lombardi	Buck Jordan	A. Kampouris	Billy Myers	Lew Riggs	Kiki Cuyler	Chick Hafey	Ival Goodman
1938	B. McKechnie	E. Lombardi	F. McCormick	Lonnie Frey	Billy Myers	Lew Riggs	Wally Berger	Harry Craft	Ival Goodman
1939	B. McKechnie	E. Lombardi	F. McCormick	Lonnie Frey	Billy Myers	Bill Werber	Wally Berger	Harry Craft	Ival Goodman
1940	B. McKechnie	E. Lombardi	F. McCormick	Lonnie Frey	Billy Myers	Bill Werber	McCormick	Harry Craft	Ival Goodman
1941	B. McKechnie	E. Lombardi	F. McCormick	Lonnie Frey	Eddie Joost	Bill Werber	McCormick	Harry Craft	Jim Gleeson
1942	B. McKechnie	Ray Lamanno	F. McCormick	Lonnie Frey	Eddie Joost	Bert Haas	Eric Tipton	Gee Walker	Max Marshall
1943	B. McKechnie	Ray Mueller	F. McCormick	Lonnie Frey	Eddie Miller	Steve Mesner	Eric Tipton	Gee Walker	Max Marshall

YEAR	MANAGER	C	1B	2B	SS	3B	LF	CF	RF
1944	B. McKechnie	Ray Mueller	F. McCormick	W. Williams	Eddie Miller	Steve Mesner	Eric Tipton	Dain Clay	Gee Walker
1945	B. McKechnie	Al Lakeman	F. McCormick	W. Williams	Eddie Miller	Steve Mesner	Eric Tipton	Dain Clay	Al Libke
1946	B. McKechnie	Ray Mueller	Bert Haas	Bobby Adams	Eddie Miller	Grady Hatton	Eddie Lukon	Dain Clay	Al Libke
1947	Johnny Neun	Ray Lamanno	Babe Young	Ben Zientara	Eddie Miller	Grady Hatton	Augie Galan	Bert Haas	F. Baumholtz
1948	Johnny Neun	Ray Lamanno	T. Kluszewski	Bobby Adams	V. Stallcup	Grady Hatton	Hank Sauer	J. Wyrostek	F. Baumholtz
1949	Buck Walters	Walk Cooper	T. Kluszewski	J. Bloodworth	V. Stallcup	Grady Hatton	P. Lowrey	L. Merriman	J. Wyrostek
1950	Luke Sewell	Dixie Howell	T. Kluszewski	Connie Ryan	V. Stallcup	Grady Hatton	Joe Adcock	Bob Usher	J. Wyrostek
1951	Luke Sewell	Dixie Howell	T. Kluszewski	Connie Ryan	V. Stallcup	Grady Hatton	Joe Adcock	L. Merriman	J. Wyrostek
1952	Luke Sewell	A. Seminick	T. Kluszewski	Grady Hatton	R. McMillan	Bobby Adams	Joe Adcock	B. Borkowski	W. Marshall
1953	R. Hornsby	A. Seminick	T. Kluszewski	R. Bridges	R. McMillan	Bobby Adams	J. Greengrass	Gus Bell	W. Marshall
1954	B. Tebbetts	A. Seminick	T. Kluszewski	John Temple	R. McMillan	Bobby Adams	J. Greengrass	Gus Bell	Wally Post
1955	B. Tebbetts	S. Burgess	T. Kluszewski	John Temple	R. McMillan	R. Bridges	Stan Palys	Gus Bell	Wally Post
1956	B. Tebbetts	Ed Bailey	T. Kluszewski	John Temple	R. McMillan	Ray Jablonski	F. Robinson	Gus Bell	Wally Post
1957	B. Tebbetts	Ed Bailey	G. Crowe	John Temple	R. McMillan	Don Hoak	F. Robinson	Gus Bell	Wally Post
1958	B. Tebbetts	Ed Bailey	G. Crowe	John Temple	R. McMillan	Don Hoak	F. Robinson	Gus Bell	Jerry Lynch
1959	Mayo Smith	Ed Bailey	F. Robinson	John Temple	Eddie Kasko	Willie Jones	Jerry Lynch	Vada Pinson	Gus Bell
1960	F. Hutchinson	Ed Bailey	F. Robinson	Billy Martin	R. McMillan	Eddie Kasko	Wally Post	Vada Pinson	Gus Bell
1961	F. Hutchinson	J. Zimmerman	G. Coleman	D. Blasingame	Eddie Kasko	Gene Freese	Wally Post	Vada Pinson	F. Robinson
1962	F. Hutchinson	J. Edwards	G. Coleman	D. Blasingame	Leo Cardenas	Eddie Kasko	Wally Post	Vada Pinson	F. Robinson
1963	F. Hutchinson	J. Edwards	G. Coleman	Pete Rose	Leo Cardenas	Gene Freese	F. Robinson	Vada Pinson	Tom Harper
1964	F. Hutchinson	J. Edwards	D. Johnson	Pete Rose	Leo Cardenas	Steve Boros	Tom Harper	Vada Pinson	F. Robinson
1965	Dick Sisler	J. Edwards	Tony Perez	Pete Rose	Leo Cardenas	D. Johnson	Tom Harper	Vada Pinson	F. Robinson
1966	Don Heffner	J. Edwards	Tony Perez	Pete Rose	Leo Cardenas	Tom Helms	D. Johnson	Vada Pinson	Tom Harper
1967	Dave Bristol	J. Edwards	Lee May	Tom Helms	Leo Cardenas	Tony Perez	Pete Rose	Vada Pinson	Tom Harper
1968	Dave Bristol	Johnny Bench	Lee May	Tom Helms	Leo Cardenas	Tony Perez	Alex Johnson	Vada Pinson	Pete Rose
1969	Dave Bristol	Johnny Bench	Lee May	Tom Helms	W. Woodward	Tony Perez	Alex Johnson	Bobby Tolan	Pete Rose
1970	S. Anderson	Johnny Bench	Lee May	Tom Helms	D. Concepcion	Tony Perez	Bernie Carbo	Bobby Tolan	Pete Rose
1971	S. Anderson	Johnny Bench	Lee May	Tom Helms	D. Concepcion	Tony Perez	Hal McRae	George Foster	Pete Rose
1972	S. Anderson	Johnny Bench	Tony Perez	Joe Morgan	D. Concepcion	Denis Menke	Pete Rose	Bobby Tolan	C. Geronimo
1973	S. Anderson	Johnny Bench	Tony Perez	Joe Morgan	D. Concepcion	Denis Menke	Pete Rose	C. Geronimo	Bobby Tolan
1974	S. Anderson	Johnny Bench	Tony Perez	Joe Morgan	D. Concepcion	Dan Driessen	Pete Rose	C. Geronimo	George Foster
1975	S. Anderson	Johnny Bench	Tony Perez	Joe Morgan	D. Concepcion	Pete Rose	George Foster	C. Geronimo	Ken Griffey
1976	S. Anderson	Johnny Bench	Tony Perez	Joe Morgan	D. Concepcion	Pete Rose	George Foster	C. Geronimo	Ken Griffey
1977	S. Anderson	Johnny Bench	Dan Driessen	Joe Morgan	D. Concepcion	Pete Rose	George Foster	C. Geronimo	Ken Griffey
1978	S. Anderson	Johnny Bench	Dan Driessen	Joe Morgan	D. Concepcion	Pete Rose	George Foster	C. Geronimo	Ken Griffey
1979	J. McNamara	Johnny Bench	Dan Driessen	Joe Morgan	D. Concepcion	Ray Knight	George Foster	C. Geronimo	Ken Griffey
1980	J. McNamara	Johnny Bench	Dan Driessen	J. Kennedy	D. Concepcion	Ray Knight	George Foster	Dave Collins	Ken Griffey
1981	J. McNamara	Joe Nolan	Dan Driessen	Ron Oester	D. Concepcion	Ray Knight	George Foster	Ken Griffey	Dave Collins
1982	J. McNamara	Alex Trevino	Dan Driessen	Ron Oester	D. Concepcion	Johnny Bench	Eddie Milner	Cesar Cedeno	P. Householder
1983	Russ Nixon	D. Bilardello	Dan Driessen	Ron Oester	D. Concepcion	Nick Esasky	Gary Redus	Eddie Milner	P. Householder
1984	Vern Rapp	Brad Gulden	Dan Driessen	Ron Oester	D. Concepcion	Nick Esasky	Gary Redus	Eddie Milner	Dave Parker
1985	Pete Rose	D. Van Gorder	Pete Rose	Ron Oester	D. Concepcion	Buddy Bell	Gary Redus	Eddie Milner	Dave Parker
1986	Pete Rose	Bo Diaz	Nick Esasky	Ron Oester	Kurt Stillwell	Buddy Bell	Eric Davis	Eddie Milner	Dave Parker
1987	Pete Rose	Bo Diaz	Nick Esasky	Ron Oester	Barry Larkin	Buddy Bell	Kal Daniels	Eric Davis	Dave Parker
1988	Pete Rose	Bo Diaz	Nick Esasky	Jeff Treadway	Barry Larkin	Chris Sabo	Kal Daniels	Eric Davis	Paul O'Neill
1989	Pete Rose	Jeff Reed	T. Benzinger	Ron Oester	Barry Larkin	Chris Sabo	R. Roomes	Eric Davis	Paul O'Neill
1990	Lou Piniella	Joe Oliver	T. Benzinger	M. Duncan	Barry Larkin	Chris Sabo	Billy Hatcher	Eric Davis	Paul O'Neill
1991	Lou Piniella	Joe Oliver	Hal Morris	Bill Doran	Barry Larkin	Chris Sabo	Billy Hatcher	Eric Davis	Paul O'Neill
1992	Lou Piniella	Joe Oliver	Hal Morris	Bill Doran	Barry Larkin	Chris Sabo	R. Sanders	D. Martinez	Paul O'Neill

YEAR	MANAGER	C	1B	2B	SS	3B	LF	CF	RF
1993	D. Johnson	Joe Oliver	Hal Morris	Bip Roberts	Barry Larkin	Chris Sabo	K. Mitchell	J. Brumfield	R. Sanders
1994	D. Johnson	Brian Dorsett	Hal Morris	Bret Boone	Barry Larkin	T. Fernandez	K. Mitchell	D. Sanders	R. Sanders
1995	D. Johnson	B. Santiago	Hal Morris	Bret Boone	Barry Larkin	Jeff Branson	Ron Gant	J. Walton	R. Sanders
1996	Ray Knight	E. Taubensee	Hal Morris	Bret Boone	Barry Larkin	Willie Greene	T. Howard	Eric Davis	R. Sanders
1997	Ray Knight	Joe Oliver	Hal Morris	Bret Boone	Pokey Reese	Willie Greene	C. Goodwin	D. Sanders	R. Sanders
1998	Jack McKeon	E. Taubensee	Sean Casey	Bret Boone	Barry Larkin	Willie Greene	Dmitri Young	R. Sanders	Jon Nunnally
1999	Jack McKeon	E. Taubensee	Sean Casey	Pokey Reese	Barry Larkin	Aaron Boone	Greg Vaughn	M. Cameron	M. Tucker
2000	Jack McKeon	B. Santiago	Sean Casey	Pokey Reese	Barry Larkin	Aaron Boone	Dmitri Young	Ken Griffey	Dante Bichette
2001	Bob Boone	Jason LaRue	Sean Casey	Todd Walker	Pokey Reese	Aaron Boone	Dmitri Young	Ken Griffey	Alex Ochoa
2002	Bob Boone	Jason LaRue	Sean Casey	Todd Walker	Barry Larkin	Aaron Boone	Adam Dunn	J. Encarnacion	Austin Kearns

RED SOX BY POSITION, YEAR BY YEAR

Boston Americans (American League), 1901–1907
Boston Red Sox (American League), 1908–Present

YEAR	MANAGER	C	1B	2B	SS	3B	LF	CF	RF
1901	Ji. Collins	Schreckengost	B. Freeman	Hobe Ferris	Freddy Parent	Jim Collins	Tom Dowd	Chick Stahl	C. Hemphill
1902	Ji. Collins	Lou Criger	C. LaChance	Hobe Ferris	Freddy Parent	Jim Collins	P. Dougherty	Chick Stahl	B. Freeman
1903	Ji. Collins	Lou Criger	C. LaChance	Hobe Ferris	Freddy Parent	Jim Collins	Kip Selbach	Chick Stahl	B. Freeman
1904	Ji. Collins	Lou Criger	C. LaChance	Hobe Ferris	Freddy Parent	Jim Collins	Kip Selbach	Chick Stahl	B. Freeman
1905	Ji. Collins	Lou Criger	M. Grimshaw	Hobe Ferris	Freddy Parent	Jim Collins	Jesse Burkett	Chick Stahl	Kip Selbach
1906	Ji. Collins	C. Armbruster	M. Grimshaw	Hobe Ferris	Freddy Parent	Red Morgan	Jack Hoey	Chick Stahl	Jack Hayden
1907	D. McGuire	Lou Criger	Bob Unglaub	Hobe Ferris	H. Wagner	Jack Knight	Jimmy Barrett	D. Sullivan	B. Congalton
1908	D. McGuire	Lou Criger	Jake Stahl	A. McConnell	H. Wagner	Harry Lord	Jack Thoney	D. Sullivan	Doc Gessler
1909	Fred Lake	Bill Carrigan	Jake Stahl	A. McConnell	H. Wagner	Harry Lord	Harry Niles	Tris Speaker	Doc Gessler
1910	Pat Donovan	Bill Carrigan	Jake Stahl	L. Gardner	H. Wagner	Harry Lord	Duffy Lewis	Tris Speaker	Harry Hooper
1911	Pat Donovan	Bill Carrigan	Clyde Engle	H. Wagner	Steve Yerkes	Larry Gardner	Duffy Lewis	Tris Speaker	Harry Hooper
1912	Jake Stahl	Bill Carrigan	Jake Stahl	Steve Yerkes	H. Wagner	Larry Gardner	Duffy Lewis	Tris Speaker	Harry Hooper
1913	Jake Stahl	Bill Carrigan	Clyde Engle	Steve Yerkes	H. Wagner	Larry Gardner	Duffy Lewis	Tris Speaker	Harry Hooper
1914	Bill Carrigan	Bill Carrigan	D. Hoblitzel	Steve Yerkes	Everett Scott	Larry Gardner	Duffy Lewis	Tris Speaker	Harry Hooper
1915	Bill Carrigan	Pinch Thomas	D. Hoblitzel	H. Wagner	Everett Scott	Larry Gardner	Duffy Lewis	Tris Speaker	Harry Hooper
1916	Bill Carrigan	Pinch Thomas	D. Hoblitzel	Jack Barry	Everett Scott	Larry Gardner	Duffy Lewis	Tilly Walker	Harry Hooper
1917	Jack Barry	Sam Agnew	D. Hoblitzel	Jack Barry	Everett Scott	Larry Gardner	Duffy Lewis	Tilly Walker	Harry Hooper
1918	Ed Barrow	Sam Agnew	Stu McInnis	Dave Shean	Everett Scott	Fred Thomas	Babe Ruth	Amos Strunk	Harry Hooper
1919	Ed Barrow	Wally Schang	Stu McInnis	Red Shannon	Everett Scott	Ossie Vitt	Babe Ruth	Braggo Roth	Harry Hooper
1920	Ed Barrow	Roxy Walters	Stu McInnis	M. McNally	Everett Scott	Eddie Foster	M. Menosky	Jim Hendryx	Harry Hooper
1921	Hugh Duffy	Muddy Ruel	Stu McInnis	Del Pratt	Everett Scott	Eddie Foster	M. Menosky	Nemo Leibold	Shano Collins
1922	Hugh Duffy	Muddy Ruel	George Burns	Del Pratt	John Mitchell	Joe Dugan	M. Menosky	Nemo Leibold	Shano Collins
1923	Frank Chance	Val Picinich	George Burns	Chick Fewster	John Mitchell	H. Shanks	Joe Harris	Dick Reichle	Ira Flagstead
1924	Lee Fohl	Steve O'Neill	Joe Harris	Wambsganss	Dud Lee	Danny Clark	Bobby Veach	Ira Flagstead	Ike Boone
1925	Lee Fohl	Val Picinich	Phil Todt	Wambsganss	Dud Lee	Doc Prothro	Roy Carlyle	Ira Flagstead	Ike Boone
1926	Lee Fohl	Alex Gaston	Phil Todt	Bill Regan	T. Rigney	Fred Haney	Si Rosenthal	Ira Flagstead	B.D. Jacobson
1927	Bill Carrigan	G. Hartley	Phil Todt	Bill Regan	Buddy Myer	Billy Rogell	Wally Shaner	Ira Flagstead	Jack Tobin
1928	Bill Carrigan	F. Hofmann	Phil Todt	Bill Regan	Wally Gerber	Buddy Myer	Ken Williams	Ira Flagstead	Doug Taitt
1929	Bill Carrigan	Charlie Berry	Phil Todt	Bill Regan	Hal Rhyne	Bobby Reeves	Russ Scarritt	Jack Rothrock	Bill Barrett
1930	H. Wagner	Charlie Berry	Phil Todt	Bill Regan	Hal Rhyne	Otto Miller	Russ Scarritt	Tom Oliver	Earl Webb
1931	Shano Collins	Charlie Berry	Bill Sweeney	R. Warstler	Hal Rhyne	Otto Miller	Jack Rothrock	Tom Oliver	Earl Webb
1932	M. McManus	Bennie Tate	D. Alexander	Marv Olson	R. Warstler	U. Pickering	Smead Jolley	Tom Oliver	Roy Johnson
1933	M. McManus	Rick Ferrell	D. Alexander	John Hodapp	R. Warstler	M. McManus	Smead Jolley	Dusty Cooke	Roy Johnson

YEAR	MANAGER	C	1B	2B	SS	3B	LF	CF	RF	DH
1934	Bucky Harris	Rick Ferrell	Eddie Morgan	Bill Cissell	Lyn Lary	Bill Werber	Roy Johnson	Carl Reynolds	M. Solters	
1935	Joe Cronin	Rick Ferrell	B. Dahlgren	Ski Melillo	Joe Cronin	Bill Werber	Roy Johnson	Mel Almada	Dusty Cooke	
1936	Joe Cronin	Rick Ferrell	Jimmie Foxx	Ski Melillo	Eric McNair	Bill Werber	H. Manush	Doc Cramer	Dusty Cooke	
1937	Joe Cronin	G. Desautels	Jimmie Foxx	Eric McNair	Joe Cronin	Pinky Higgins	Buster Mills	Doc Cramer	Ben Chapman	
1938	Joe Cronin	G. Desautels	Jimmie Foxx	Bobby Doerr	Joe Cronin	Pinky Higgins	Joe Vosmik	Doc Cramer	Ben Chapman	
1939	Joe Cronin	John Peacock	Jimmie Foxx	Bobby Doerr	Joe Cronin	Jim Tabor	Joe Vosmik	Doc Cramer	Ted Williams	
1940	Joe Cronin	G. Desautels	Jimmie Foxx	Bobby Doerr	Joe Cronin	Jim Tabor	Ted Williams	D. DiMaggio	Doc Cramer	
1941	Joe Cronin	Frank Pytlak	Jimmie Foxx	Bobby Doerr	Joe Cronin	Jim Tabor	Ted Williams	D. DiMaggio	Lou Finney	
1942	Joe Cronin	Bill Conroy	Ted Lupien	Bobby Doerr	Johnny Pesky	Jim Tabor	Ted Williams	D. DiMaggio	Lou Finney	
1943	Joe Cronin	Roy Partee	Ted Lupien	Bobby Doerr	S. Newsome	Jim Tabor	L. Culberson	C. Metkovich	Pete Fox	
1944	Joe Cronin	Roy Partee	Lou Finney	Bobby Doerr	S. Newsome	Jim Tabor	Bob Johnson	C. Metkovich	Pete Fox	
1945	Joe Cronin	Bob Garbark	C. Metkovich	S. Newsome	Eddie Lake	Jack Tobin	Bob Johnson	L. Culberson	Johnny Lazor	
1946	Joe Cronin	Hal Wagner	Rudy York	Bobby Doerr	Johnny Pesky	Rip Russell	Ted Williams	D. DiMaggio	C. Metkovich	
1947	Joe Cronin	B. Tebbetts	Jake Jones	Bobby Doerr	Johnny Pesky	Ed Pellegrini	Ted Williams	D. DiMaggio	Sam Mele	
1948	Joe McCarthy	B. Tebbetts	B. Goodman	Bobby Doerr	V. Stephens	Johnny Pesky	Ted Williams	D. DiMaggio	S. Spence	
1949	Joe McCarthy	B. Tebbetts	B. Goodman	Bobby Doerr	V. Stephens	Johnny Pesky	Ted Williams	D. DiMaggio	Al Zarilla	
1950	Steve O'Neill	B. Tebbetts	Walt Dropo	Bobby Doerr	V. Stephens	Johnny Pesky	Ted Williams	D. DiMaggio	Al Zarilla	
1951	Steve O'Neill	Les Moss	Walt Dropo	Bobby Doerr	Johnny Pesky	V. Stephens	Ted Williams	D. DiMaggio	C. Vollmer	
1952	Lou Boudreau	Sammy White	Dick Gernert	B. Goodman	V. Stephens	George Kell	Hoot Evers	D. DiMaggio	F. Throneberry	
1953	Lou Boudreau	Sammy White	Dick Gernert	B. Goodman	Milt Bolling	George Kell	Hoot Evers	T. Umphlett	Jim Piersall	
1954	Lou Boudreau	Sammy White	H. Agganis	Ted Lepcio	Milt Bolling	Grady Hatton	Ted Williams	Jackie Jensen	Jim Piersall	
1955	Pinky Higgins	Sammy White	N. Zauchin	B. Goodman	Billy Klaus	Grady Hatton	Ted Williams	Jim Piersall	Jackie Jensen	
1956	Pinky Higgins	Sammy White	Mick Vernon	B. Goodman	Don Buddin	Billy Klaus	Ted Williams	Jim Piersall	Jackie Jensen	
1957	Pinky Higgins	Sammy White	Dick Gernert	Ted Lepcio	Billy Klaus	F. Malzone	Ted Williams	Jim Piersall	Jackie Jensen	
1958	Pinky Higgins	Sammy White	Dick Gernert	Pete Runnels	Don Buddin	F. Malzone	Ted Williams	Jim Piersall	Jackie Jensen	
1959	Billy Jurges	Sammy White	Dick Gernert	Pete Runnels	Don Buddin	F. Malzone	G. Stephens	Gary Geiger	Jackie Jensen	
1960	Pinky Higgins	Russ Nixon	Vic Wertz	Pete Runnels	Don Buddin	F. Malzone	Ted Williams	Willie Tasby	Lou Clinton	
1961	Pinky Higgins	Jim Pagliaroni	Pete Runnels	C. Schilling	Don Buddin	F. Malzone	Yastrzemski	Gary Geiger	Jackie Jensen	
1962	Pinky Higgins	Jim Pagliaroni	Pete Runnels	C. Schilling	Ed Bressoud	F. Malzone	Yastrzemski	Gary Geiger	Lou Clinton	
1963	Johnny Pesky	Bob Tillman	Dick Stuart	C. Schilling	Ed Bressoud	F. Malzone	Yastrzemski	Gary Geiger	Lou Clinton	
1964	Johnny Pesky	Bob Tillman	Dick Stuart	Dalton Jones	Ed Bressoud	F. Malzone	T. Conigliaro	Yastrzemski	Lee Thomas	
1965	Billy Herman	Bob Tillman	Lee Thomas	Felix Mantilla	R. Petrocelli	F. Malzone	Yastrzemski	Lenny Green	T. Conigliaro	
1966	Billy Herman	Mike Ryan	George Scott	George Smith	R. Petrocelli	Joe Foy	Yastrzemski	Don Demeter	T. Conigliaro	
1967	D. Williams	Mike Ryan	George Scott	M. Andrews	R. Petrocelli	Joe Foy	Yastrzemski	Reggie Smith	T. Conigliaro	
1968	D. Williams	Russ Gibson	George Scott	M. Andrews	R. Petrocelli	Joe Foy	Yastrzemski	Reggie Smith	K. Harrelson	
1969	D. Williams	Russ Gibson	Dalton Jones	M. Andrews	R. Petrocelli	George Scott	Yastrzemski	Reggie Smith	T. Conigliaro	
1970	Eddie Kasko	Jerry Moses	Yastrzemski	M. Andrews	R. Petrocelli	George Scott	B. Conigliaro	Reggie Smith	T. Conigliaro	
1971	Eddie Kasko	D. Josephson	George Scott	Doug Griffin	Luis Aparicio	R. Petrocelli	Yastrzemski	B. Conigliaro	Reggie Smith	
1972	Eddie Kasko	Carlton Fisk	Danny Cater	Doug Griffin	Luis Aparicio	R. Petrocelli	Yastrzemski	Tom Harper	Reggie Smith	
1973	Eddie Kasko	Carlton Fisk	Yastrzemski	Doug Griffin	Luis Aparicio	R. Petrocelli	Tom Harper	Rick Miller	Dwight Evans	
1974	D. Johnson	Montgomery	Yastrzemski	Doug Griffin	M. Guerrero	R. Petrocelli	Bernie Carbo	J. Beniquez	Dwight Evans	
1975	D. Johnson	Carlton Fisk	Yastrzemski	Doug Griffin	Rick Burleson	R. Petrocelli	Bernie Carbo	Fred Lynn	Dwight Evans	Jim Rice
1976	D. Johnson	Carlton Fisk	Yastrzemski	Denny Doyle	Rick Burleson	Butch Hobson	Jim Rice	Fred Lynn	Dwight Evans	Cecil Cooper
1977	Don Zimmer	Carlton Fisk	George Scott	Denny Doyle	Rick Burleson	Butch Hobson	Yastrzemski	Fred Lynn	Rick Miller	Jim Rice
1978	Don Zimmer	Carlton Fisk	George Scott	Jerry Remy	Rick Burleson	Butch Hobson	Yastrzemski	Fred Lynn	Dwight Evans	Jim Rice
1979	Don Zimmer	G. Allenson	Bob Watson	Jerry Remy	Rick Burleson	Butch Hobson	Jim Rice	Fred Lynn	Dwight Evans	Yastrzemski
1980	Don Zimmer	Carlton Fisk	Tony Perez	D. Stapleton	Rick Burleson	G. Hoffman	Jim Rice	Fred Lynn	Dwight Evans	Yastrzemski
1981	Ralph Houk	Rich Gedman	Tony Perez	Jerry Remy	G. Hoffman	C. Lansford	Jim Rice	Rick Miller	Dwight Evans	Yastrzemski
1982	Ralph Houk	G. Allenson	D. Stapleton	Jerry Remy	G. Hoffman	C. Lansford	Jim Rice	Rick Miller	Dwight Evans	Yastrzemski

YEAR	MANAGER	C	1B	2B	SS	3B	LF	CF	RF	DH
1983	Ralph Houk	G. Allenson	D. Stapleton	Jerry Remy	G. Hoffman	Wade Boggs	Jim Rice	Tony Armas	Dwight Evans	Yastrzemski
1984	Ralph Houk	Rich Gedman	Bill Buckner	M. Barrett	J. Gutierrez	Wade Boggs	Jim Rice	Tony Armas	Dwight Evans	Mike Easler
1985	J. McNamara	Rich Gedman	Bill Buckner	M. Barrett	J. Gutierrez	Wade Boggs	Jim Rice	Steve Lyons	Dwight Evans	Mike Easler
1986	J. McNamara	Rich Gedman	Bill Buckner	M. Barrett	Ed Romero	Wade Boggs	Jim Rice	Tony Armas	Dwight Evans	Don Baylor
1987	J. McNamara	Marc Sullivan	Dwight Evans	M. Barrett	Spike Owen	Wade Boggs	Jim Rice	Ellis Burks	M. Greenwell	Don Baylor
1988	J. McNamara	Rich Gedman	T. Benzinger	M. Barrett	Jody Reed	Wade Boggs	M. Greenwell	Ellis Burks	Dwight Evans	Jim Rice
1989	Joe Morgan	Rick Cerone	Nick Esasky	M. Barrett	Luis Rivera	Wade Boggs	M. Greenwell	Ellis Burks	K. Romine	Dwight Evans
1990	Joe Morgan	Tony Pena	C. Quintana	Jody Reed	Luis Rivera	Wade Boggs	M. Greenwell	Ellis Burks	T. Brunansky	Dwight Evans
1991	Joe Morgan	Tony Pena	C. Quintana	Jody Reed	Luis Rivera	Wade Boggs	M. Greenwell	Ellis Burks	T. Brunansky	Jack Clark
1992	Butch Hobson	Tony Pena	Mo Vaughn	Jody Reed	Luis Rivera	Wade Boggs	Billy Hatcher	Bob Zupcic	T. Brunansky	Jack Clark
1993	Butch Hobson	Tony Pena	Mo Vaughn	Scott Fletcher	John Valentin	Scott Cooper	M. Greenwell	Billy Hatcher	Bob Zupcic	A. Dawson
1994	Butch Hobson	D. Berryhill	Mo Vaughn	Scott Fletcher	John Valentin	Scott Cooper	M. Greenwell	Otis Nixon	T. Brunansky	A. Dawson
1995	K. Kennedy	M. Macfarlane	Mo Vaughn	Luis Alicea	John Valentin	Tim Naehring	M. Greenwell	Lee Tinsley	Troy O'Leary	Jose Canseco
1996	K. Kennedy	Mike Stanley	Mo Vaughn	Jeff Frye	John Valentin	Tim Naehring	M. Greenwell	Lee Tinsley	Troy O'Leary	Jose Canseco
1997	Jim Williams	S. Hatteberg	Mo Vaughn	Jeff Frye	N. Garciaparra	Tim Naehring	Wil Cordero	Darren Bragg	Troy O'Leary	R. Jefferson
1998	Jim Williams	S. Hatteberg	Mo Vaughn	M. Benjamin	N. Garciaparra	John Valentin	Troy O'Leary	Darren Lewis	Darren Bragg	R. Jefferson
1999	Jim Williams	Jason Varitek	Mike Stanley	J. Offerman	N. Garciaparra	John Valentin	Troy O'Leary	Darren Lewis	Trot Nixon	R. Jefferson
2000	Jim Williams	Jason Varitek	Mike Stanley	J. Offerman	N. Garciaparra	M. Alexander	Troy O'Leary	Carl Everett	Trot Nixon	B. Daubach
2001	Jim Williams	S. Hatteberg	B. Daubach	J. Offerman	Mike Lansing	S. Hillenbrand	Troy O'Leary	Carl Everett	Trot Nixon	M. Ramirez
2002	Grady Little	Jason Varitek	Tony Clark	Rey Sanchez	N. Garciaparra	S. Hillenbrand	M. Ramirez	Jo. Damon	Trot Nixon	B. Daubach

ROCKIES BY POSITION, YEAR BY YEAR

Colorado Rockies (National League), 1993–Present

YEAR	MANAGER	C	1B	2B	SS	3B	LF	CF	RF
1993	Don Baylor	Joe Girardi	A. Galarraga	Eric Young	Vinny Castilla	Charlie Hayes	Jerald Clark	Alex Cole	D. Bichette
1994	Don Baylor	Joe Girardi	A. Galarraga	N. Liriano	Walt Weiss	Charlie Hayes	H. Johnson	Mike Kingery	D. Bichette
1995	Don Baylor	Joe Girardi	A. Galarraga	Jason Bates	Walt Weiss	Vinny Castilla	D. Bichette	Mike Kingery	Larry Walker
1996	Don Baylor	Jeff Reed	A. Galarraga	Eric Young	Walt Weiss	Vinny Castilla	Ellis Burks	Q. McCracken	D. Bichette
1997	Don Baylor	K. Manwaring	A. Galarraga	Eric Young	Walt Weiss	Vinny Castilla	D. Bichette	Q. McCracken	Larry Walker
1998	Jim Leyland	K. Manwaring	Todd Helton	Mike Lansing	Neifi Perez	Vinny Castilla	D. Bichette	Ellis Burks	Larry Walker
1999	Buddy Bell	Henry Blanco	Todd Helton	Kurt Abbott	Neifi Perez	Vinny Castilla	D. Bichette	D. Hamilton	Larry Walker
2000	Buddy Bell	Brent Mayne	Todd Helton	Mike Lansing	Neifi Perez	Jeff Cirillo	J. Hammonds	T. Goodwin	Larry Walker
2001	Buddy Bell	Ben Petrick	Todd Helton	Todd Walker	Neifi Perez	Jeff Cirillo	Ron Gant	Juan Pierre	Larry Walker
2002	Clint Hurdle	Gary Bennett	Todd Helton	Brent Butler	Juan Uribe	Todd Zeile	Hollandsworth	Juan Pierre	Larry Walker

ROYALS BY POSITION, YEAR BY YEAR

Kansas City Royals (American League), 1969–Present

YEAR	MANAGER	C	1B	2B	SS	3B	LF	CF	RF	DH
1969	Joe Gordon	E. Rodriguez	Mike Fiore	Jerry Adair	J. Hernandez	Joe Foy	Lou Piniella	Bob Oliver	Pat Kelly	
1970	Bob Lemon	E. Kirkpatrick	Bob Oliver	Cookie Rojas	J. Hernandez	Paul Schaal	Lou Piniella	Amos Otis	Pat Kelly	
1971	Bob Lemon	J. May	Gail Hopkins	Cookie Rojas	Fred Patek	Paul Schaal	Lou Piniella	Amos Otis	Joe Keough	
1972	Bob Lemon	E. Kirkpatrick	J. Mayberry	Cookie Rojas	Fred Patek	Paul Schaal	Lou Piniella	Amos Otis	R. Scheinblum	
1973	Jack McKeon	Fran Healy	J. Mayberry	Cookie Rojas	Fred Patek	Paul Schaal	Lou Piniella	Amos Otis	E. Kirkpatrick	Hal McRae
1974	Jack McKeon	Fran Healy	J. Mayberry	Cookie Rojas	Fred Patek	George Brett	Jim Wohlford	Amos Otis	Vada Pinson	Hal McRae
1975	J. McKeon	B. Martinez	J. Mayberry	Cookie Rojas	Fred Patek	George Brett	Hal McRae	Amos Otis	Al Cowens	H. Killebrew
1976	W. Herzog	B. Martinez	J. Mayberry	Frank White	Fred Patek	George Brett	Tom Poquette	Amos Otis	Al Cowens	Hal McRae
1977	W. Herzog	Darrell Porter	J. Mayberry	Frank White	Fred Patek	George Brett	Tom Poquette	Amos Otis	Al Cowens	Hal McRae

YEAR	MANAGER	C	1B	2B	SS	3B	LF	CF	RF	DH
1978	W. Herzog	Darrell Porter	Pete LaCock	Frank White	Fred Patek	George Brett	Willie Wilson	Amos Otis	Al Cowens	Hal McRae
1979	W. Herzog	Darrell Porter	Pete LaCock	Frank White	Fred Patek	George Brett	Willie Wilson	Amos Otis	Al Cowens	Hal McRae
1980	Jim Frey	Darrell Porter	Willie Aikens	Frank White	U Washington	George Brett	Willie Wilson	Amos Otis	Clint Hurdle	Hal McRae
1981	Jim Frey	John Wathan	Willie Aikens	Frank White	U Washington	George Brett	Willie Wilson	Amos Otis	C. Geronimo	Hal McRae
1982	Dick Howser	John Wathan	Willie Aikens	Frank White	U Washington	George Brett	Willie Wilson	Amos Otis	Jerry Martin	Hal McRae
1983	Dick Howser	John Wathan	Willie Aikens	Frank White	U Washington	George Brett	Willie Wilson	Amos Otis	Pat Sheridan	Hal McRae
1984	Dick Howser	Don Slaught	Steve Balboni	Frank White	O. Concepcion	Greg Pryor	Darryl Motley	Willie Wilson	Pat Sheridan	Hal McRae
1985	Dick Howser	Jim Sundberg	Steve Balboni	Frank White	O. Concepcion	George Brett	Lonnie Smith	Willie Wilson	Darryl Motley	Hal McRae
1986	Dick Howser	Jim Sundberg	Steve Balboni	Frank White	Angel Salazar	George Brett	Lonnie Smith	Willie Wilson	Rudy Law	Jorge Orta
1987	Billy Gardner	Jamie Quirk	George Brett	Frank White	Angel Salazar	Kevin Seitzer	Bo Jackson	Willie Wilson	Dan Tartabull	Steve Balboni
1988	John Wathan	Jamie Quirk	George Brett	Frank White	Kurt Stillwell	Kevin Seitzer	Bo Jackson	Willie Wilson	Dan Tartabull	Bill Buckner
1989	John Wathan	Bob Boone	George Brett	Frank White	Kurt Stillwell	Kevin Seitzer	Bo Jackson	Willie Wilson	J. Eisenreich	Dan Tartabull
1990	John Wathan	M. Macfarlane	George Brett	Frank White	Kurt Stillwell	Kevin Seitzer	Willie Wilson	Bo Jackson	J. Eisenreich	Gerald Perry
1991	Hal McRae	Brent Mayne	T. Benzinger	T. Shumpert	Kurt Stillwell	Bill Pecota	J. Eisenreich	Brian McRae	Dan Tartabull	George Brett
1992	Hal McRae	M. Macfarlane	Wally Joyner	Keith Miller	D. Howard	G. Jefferies	McReynolds	Brian McRae	J. Eisenreich	George Brett
1993	Hal McRae	M. Macfarlane	Wally Joyner	Jose Lind	Greg Gagne	Gary Gaetti	McReynolds	Brian McRae	Felix Jose	George Brett
1994	Hal McRae	M. Macfarlane	Wally Joyner	Jose Lind	Greg Gagne	Gary Gaetti	V. Coleman	Brian McRae	Felix Jose	Bob Hamelin
1995	Bob Boone	Brent Mayne	Wally Joyner	K. Lockhart	Greg Gagne	Gary Gaetti	V. Coleman	T. Goodwin	Jon Nunnally	Bob Hamelin
1996	Bob Boone	M. Macfarlane	J. Offerman	K. Lockhart	D. Howard	Joe Randa	T. Goodwin	Jo. Damon	M. Tucker	Joe Vitiello
1997	Bob Boone	M. Macfarlane	Jeff King	J. Offerman	Jay Bell	C. Paquette	Bip Roberts	T. Goodwin	Jo. Damon	Chili Davis
1998	Tony Muser	M. Sweeney	Jeff King	J. Offerman	Mendy Lopez	Dean Palmer	Jeff Conine	Jo. Damon	Larry Sutton	T. Pendleton
1999	Tony Muser	Chad Kreuter	M. Sweeney	Carlos Febles	Rey Sanchez	Joe Randa	Jo. Damon	Carlos Beltran	Jermaine Dye	J. Giambi
2000	Tony Muser	Gregg Zaun	M. Sweeney	Carlos Febles	Rey Sanchez	Joe Randa	Jo. Damon	Carlos Beltran	Jermaine Dye	Mark Quinn
2001	Tony Muser	Brent Mayne	M. Sweeney	Carlos Febles	Rey Sanchez	Joe Randa	Mark Quinn	Carlos Beltran	Jermaine Dye	Raul Ibanez
2002	Tony Pena	Brent Mayne	M. Sweeney	Carlos Febles	Neifi Perez	Joe Randa	C. Knoblauch	Carlos Beltran	M. Tucker	Raul Ibanez

TIGERS BY POSITION, YEAR BY YEAR

Detroit Tigers (American League), 1901–Present

YEAR	MANAGER	C	1B	2B	SS	3B	LF	CF	RF
1901	G. Stallings	Fritz Buelow	Pop Dillon	Kid Gleason	Kid Elberfeld	Doc Casey	Doc Nance	Jimmy Barrett	D. Holmes
1902	Frank Dwyer	D. McGuire	Pop Dillon	Kid Gleason	Kid Elberfeld	Doc Casey	Dick Harley	Jimmy Barrett	D. Holmes
1903	Ed Barrow	D. McGuire	Charlie Carr	Heinie Smith	S. McAllister	Joe Yeager	Billy Lush	Jimmy Barrett	S. Crawford
1904	Ed Barrow	Lew Drill	Charlie Carr	Bobby Lowe	C. O'Leary	Gremminger	M. McIntyre	Jimmy Barrett	S. Crawford
1905	Bill Armour	Lew Drill	Chris Lindsay	G. Schaefer	C. O'Leary	Bill Coughlin	M. McIntyre	Duff Cooley	S. Crawford
1906	Bill Armour	Boss Schmidt	Chris Lindsay	G. Schaefer	C. O'Leary	Bill Coughlin	M. McIntyre	Ty Cobb	S. Crawford
1907	H. Jennings	Boss Schmidt	C. Rossman	Red Downs	C. O'Leary	Bill Coughlin	Davy Jones	S. Crawford	Ty Cobb
1908	H. Jennings	Boss Schmidt	C. Rossman	Red Downs	G. Schaefer	Bill Coughlin	M. McIntyre	S. Crawford	Ty Cobb
1909	H. Jennings	Boss Schmidt	C. Rossman	G. Schaefer	Donie Bush	G. Moriarty	M. McIntyre	S. Crawford	Ty Cobb
1910	H. Jennings	Oscar Stanage	Tom Jones	Jim Delahanty	Donie Bush	G. Moriarty	Davy Jones	Ty Cobb	S. Crawford
1911	H. Jennings	Oscar Stanage	Jim Delahanty	C. O'Leary	Donie Bush	G. Moriarty	Davy Jones	Ty Cobb	S. Crawford
1912	H. Jennings	Oscar Stanage	G. Moriarty	Baldy Louden	Donie Bush	Charlie Deal	Davy Jones	Ty Cobb	S. Crawford
1913	H. Jennings	Oscar Stanage	Del Gainer	Ossie Vitt	Donie Bush	G. Moriarty	Bobby Veach	Ty Cobb	S. Crawford
1914	H. Jennings	Oscar Stanage	George Burns	M. Kavanaugh	Donie Bush	G. Moriarty	Bobby Veach	Ty Cobb	S. Crawford
1915	H. Jennings	Oscar Stanage	George Burns	Ralph Young	Donie Bush	Ossie Vitt	Bobby Veach	Ty Cobb	S. Crawford
1916	H. Jennings	Oscar Stanage	George Burns	Ralph Young	Donie Bush	Ossie Vitt	Bobby Veach	Ty Cobb	S. Crawford
1917	H. Jennings	Oscar Stanage	George Burns	Ralph Young	Donie Bush	Ossie Vitt	Bobby Veach	Ty Cobb	H. Heilmann
1918	H. Jennings	Archie Yelle	H. Heilmann	Ralph Young	Donie Bush	Ossie Vitt	Bobby Veach	Ty Cobb	G. Harper
1919	H. Jennings	Ed Ainsmith	H. Heilmann	Ralph Young	Donie Bush	Bob Jones	Bobby Veach	Ty Cobb	Ira Flagstead

YEAR	MANAGER	C	1B	2B	SS	3B	LF	CF	RF
1920	H. Jennings	Oscar Stanage	H. Heilmann	Ralph Young	Donie Bush	Babe Pinelli	Bobby Veach	Ty Cobb	Chick Shorten
1921	Ty Cobb	John Bassler	Lu Blue	Ralph Young	Donie Bush	Bob Jones	Bobby Veach	Ty Cobb	H. Heilmann
1922	Ty Cobb	John Bassler	Lu Blue	G. Cutshaw	T. Rigney	Bob Jones	Bobby Veach	Ty Cobb	H. Heilmann
1923	Ty Cobb	John Bassler	Lu Blue	Fred Haney	T. Rigney	Bob Jones	Bobby Veach	Ty Cobb	H. Heilmann
1924	Ty Cobb	John Bassler	Lu Blue	Del Pratt	T. Rigney	Bob Jones	H. Manush	Ty Cobb	H. Heilmann
1925	Ty Cobb	John Bassler	Lu Blue	F. O'Rourke	Jack Tavener	Fred Haney	Al Wingo	Ty Cobb	H. Heilmann
1926	Ty Cobb	Clyde Manion	Lu Blue	C. Gehringer	Jack Tavener	Jack Warner	F. Fothergill	H. Manush	H. Heilmann
1927	G. Moriarty	L. Woodall	Lu Blue	C. Gehringer	Jack Tavener	Jack Warner	F. Fothergill	H. Manush	H. Heilmann
1928	G. Moriarty	P. Hargrave	Bill Sweeney	C. Gehringer	Jack Tavener	M. McManus	F. Fothergill	Harry Rice	H. Heilmann
1929	Bucky Harris	Eddie Phillips	D. Alexander	C. Gehringer	H. Schuble	M. McManus	Roy Johnson	Harry Rice	H. Heilmann
1930	Bucky Harris	R. Hayworth	D. Alexander	C. Gehringer	Mark Koenig	M. McManus	John Stone	Liz Funk	Roy Johnson
1931	Bucky Harris	R. Hayworth	D. Alexander	C. Gehringer	Billy Rogell	M. McManus	John Stone	Hub Walker	Roy Johnson
1932	Bucky Harris	R. Hayworth	Harry Davis	C. Gehringer	Billy Rogell	H. Schuble	John Stone	Gee Walker	Earl Webb
1933	Bucky Harris	R. Hayworth	H. Greenberg	C. Gehringer	Billy Rogell	Marv Owen	Gee Walker	Pete Fox	John Stone
1934	M. Cochrane	M. Cochrane	H. Greenberg	C. Gehringer	Billy Rogell	Marv Owen	Goose Goslin	Jo-Jo White	Pete Fox
1935	M. Cochrane	M. Cochrane	H. Greenberg	C. Gehringer	Billy Rogell	Marv Owen	Goose Goslin	Jo-Jo White	Pete Fox
1936	M. Cochrane	R. Hayworth	Jack Burns	C. Gehringer	Billy Rogell	Marv Owen	Goose Goslin	Al Simmons	G. Walker
1937	M. Cochrane	Rudy York	H. Greenberg	C. Gehringer	Billy Rogell	Marv Owen	Gee Walker	Jo-Jo White	Pete Fox
1938	M. Cochrane	Rudy York	H. Greenberg	C. Gehringer	Billy Rogell	Don Ross	Dixie Walker	Chet Morgan	Pete Fox
1939	Del Baker	B. Tebbetts	H. Greenberg	C. Gehringer	F. Croucher	Pinky Higgins	Earl Averill	B. McCosky	Pete Fox
1940	Del Baker	B. Tebbetts	Rudy York	C. Gehringer	Dick Bartell	Pinky Higgins	H. Greenberg	B. McCosky	Pete Fox
1941	Del Baker	B. Tebbetts	Rudy York	C. Gehringer	F. Croucher	Pinky Higgins	Rip Radcliff	B. McCosky	B. Campbell
1942	Del Baker	B. Tebbetts	Rudy York	J. Bloodworth	B. Hitchcock	Pinky Higgins	B. McCosky	Doc Cramer	Ned Harris
1943	Steve O'Neill	Paul Richards	Rudy York	J. Bloodworth	Joe Hoover	Pinky Higgins	D. Wakefield	Doc Cramer	Ned Harris
1944	Steve O'Neill	Paul Richards	Rudy York	Eddie Mayo	Joe Hoover	Pinky Higgins	D. Wakefield	Doc Cramer	Jim Outlaw
1945	Steve O'Neill	Bob Swift	Rudy York	Eddie Mayo	Skeeter Webb	Bob Maier	Jim Outlaw	Doc Cramer	R. Cullenbine
1946	Steve O'Neill	B. Tebbetts	H. Greenberg	J. Bloodworth	Eddie Lake	George Kell	D. Wakefield	Hoot Evers	R. Cullenbine
1947	Steve O'Neill	Bob Swift	R. Cullenbine	Eddie Mayo	Eddie Lake	George Kell	D. Wakefield	Hoot Evers	Pat Mullin
1948	Steve O'Neill	Bob Swift	George Vico	Eddie Mayo	Johnny Lipon	George Kell	Vic Wertz	Hoot Evers	Pat Mullin
1949	Red Rolfe	A. Robinson	P. Campbell	Neil Berry	Johnny Lipon	George Kell	Hoot Evers	Johnny Groth	Vic Wertz
1950	Red Rolfe	A. Robinson	D. Kolloway	Jerry Priddy	Johnny Lipon	George Kell	Hoot Evers	Johnny Groth	Vic Wertz
1951	Red Rolfe	Joe Ginsberg	D. Kryhoski	Jerry Priddy	Johnny Lipon	George Kell	Hoot Evers	Johnny Groth	Vic Wertz
1952	F. Hutchinson	Joe Ginsberg	Walt Dropo	Jerry Priddy	Neil Berry	Fred Hatfield	Pat Mullin	Johnny Groth	Vic Wertz
1953	F. Hutchinson	Matt Batts	Walt Dropo	Johnny Pesky	H. Kuenn	Ray Boone	Bob Nieman	Jim Delsing	Don Lund
1954	F. Hutchinson	Frank House	Walt Dropo	Frank Bolling	H. Kuenn	Ray Boone	Jim Delsing	Bill Tuttle	Al Kaline
1955	Bucky Harris	Frank House	Earl Torgeson	Fred Hatfield	H. Kuenn	Ray Boone	Jim Delsing	Bill Tuttle	Al Kaline
1956	Bucky Harris	Frank House	Earl Torgeson	Frank Bolling	H. Kuenn	Ray Boone	C. Maxwell	Bill Tuttle	Al Kaline
1957	Jack Tighe	Frank House	Ray Boone	Frank Bolling	H. Kuenn	Reno Bertoia	C. Maxwell	Bill Tuttle	Al Kaline
1958	Bill Norman	Red Wilson	Gail Harris	Frank Bolling	Billy Martin	Reno Bertoia	C. Maxwell	H. Kuenn	Al Kaline
1959	Jimmy Dykes	Lou Berberet	Gail Harris	Frank Bolling	R. Bridges	Ed Yost	C. Maxwell	Al Kaline	H. Kuenn
1960	Jimmy Dykes	Lou Berberet	Norm Cash	Frank Bolling	C. Fernandez	Ed Yost	C. Maxwell	Al Kaline	R. Colavito
1961	Bob Scheffing	Dick Brown	Norm Cash	Jake Wood	C. Fernandez	Steve Boros	R. Colavito	Bill Bruton	Al Kaline
1962	Bob Scheffing	Dick Brown	Norm Cash	Jake Wood	C. Fernandez	Steve Boros	R. Colavito	Bill Bruton	Al Kaline
1963	C. Dressen	Gus Triandos	Norm Cash	Jake Wood	D. McAuliffe	B. Phillips	R. Colavito	Bill Bruton	Al Kaline
1964	C. Dressen	Bill Freehan	Norm Cash	D. McAuliffe	D. McAuliffe	Don Wert	Gates Brown	G. Thomas	Al Kaline
1965	C. Dressen	Bill Freehan	Norm Cash	Jerry Lumpe	D. McAuliffe	Don Wert	Willie Horton	Don Demeter	Al Kaline
1966	Frank Skaff	Bill Freehan	Norm Cash	Jerry Lumpe	D. McAuliffe	Don Wert	Willie Horton	Al Kaline	Jim Northrup
1967	Mayo Smith	Bill Freehan	Norm Cash	D. McAuliffe	Ray Oyler	Don Wert	Jim Northrup	Mick Stanley	Al Kaline
1968	Mayo Smith	Bill Freehan	Norm Cash	D. McAuliffe	Ray Oyler	Don Wert	Willie Horton	Mick Stanley	Jim Northrup

YEAR	MANAGER	C	1B	2B	SS	3B	LF	CF	RF	DH
1969	Mayo Smith	Bill Freehan	Norm Cash	D. McAuliffe	Tom Tresh	Don Wert	Willie Horton	Jim Northrup	Al Kaline	
1970	Mayo Smith	Bill Freehan	Norm Cash	D. McAuliffe	C. Gutierrez	Don Wert	Willie Horton	Mick Stanley	Jim Northrup	
1971	Billy Martin	Bill Freehan	Norm Cash	D. McAuliffe	Ed Brinkman	A. Rodriguez	Willie Horton	Mick Stanley	Al Kaline	
1972	Billy Martin	Bill Freehan	Norm Cash	D. McAuliffe	Ed Brinkman	A. Rodriguez	Willie Horton	Mick Stanley	Jim Northrup	
1973	Billy Martin	Bill Freehan	Norm Cash	D. McAuliffe	Ed Brinkman	A. Rodriguez	Willie Horton	Mick Stanley	Jim Northrup	Gates Brown
1974	Ralph Houk	Jerry Moses	Bill Freehan	G. Sutherland	Ed Brinkman	A. Rodriguez	Willie Horton	Ben Oglivie	Jim Northrup	Al Kaline
1975	Ralph Houk	Bill Freehan	Jack Pierce	G. Sutherland	Tom Veryzer	A. Rodriguez	Ben Oglivie	Ron LeFlore	Leon Roberts	Willie Horton
1976	Ralph Houk	Bruce Kimm	J. Thompson	Pedro Garcia	Tom Veryzer	A. Rodriguez	Alex Johnson	Ron LeFlore	Rusty Staub	Willie Horton
1977	Ralph Houk	Milt May	J. Thompson	Tito Fuentes	Tom Veryzer	A. Rodriguez	Steve Kemp	Ron LeFlore	Ben Oglivie	Rusty Staub
1978	Ralph Houk	Milt May	J. Thompson	Lou Whitaker	Al Trammell	A. Rodriguez	Steve Kemp	Ron LeFlore	Tim Corcoran	Rusty Staub
1979	S. Anderson	Lance Parrish	J. Thompson	Lou Whitaker	Al Trammell	A. Rodriguez	Steve Kemp	Ron LeFlore	Jerry Morales	Rusty Staub
1980	S. Anderson	Lance Parrish	R. Hebner	Lou Whitaker	Al Trammell	T. Brookens	Steve Kemp	Rick Peters	Al Cowens	C. Summers
1981	S. Anderson	Lance Parrish	R. Hebner	Lou Whitaker	Al Trammell	T. Brookens	Steve Kemp	Al Cowens	Kirk Gibson	J. Wockenfuss
1982	S. Anderson	Lance Parrish	Enos Cabell	Lou Whitaker	Al Trammell	T. Brookens	L. Herndon	Glenn Wilson	Chet Lemon	Mike Ivie
1983	S. Anderson	Lance Parrish	Enos Cabell	Lou Whitaker	Al Trammell	T. Brookens	L. Herndon	Chet Lemon	Glenn Wilson	Kirk Gibson
1984	S. Anderson	Lance Parrish	D. Bergman	Lou Whitaker	Al Trammell	H. Johnson	L. Herndon	Chet Lemon	Kirk Gibson	Darrell Evans
1985	S. Anderson	Lance Parrish	Darrell Evans	Lou Whitaker	Al Trammell	T. Brookens	L. Herndon	Chet Lemon	Kirk Gibson	John Grubb
1986	S. Anderson	Lance Parrish	Darrell Evans	Lou Whitaker	Al Trammell	Darnell Coles	Dave Collins	Chet Lemon	Kirk Gibson	John Grubb
1987	S. Anderson	Matt Nokes	Darrell Evans	Lou Whitaker	Al Trammell	T. Brookens	Kirk Gibson	Chet Lemon	Pat Sheridan	Bill Madlock
1988	S. Anderson	Matt Nokes	Ray Knight	Lou Whitaker	Al Trammell	T. Brookens	Pat Sheridan	Gary Pettis	Chet Lemon	Darrell Evans
1989	S. Anderson	Mike Heath	D. Bergman	Lou Whitaker	Al Trammell	Rick Schu	Fred Lynn	Gary Pettis	Chet Lemon	K. Moreland
1990	S. Anderson	Mike Heath	Cecil Fielder	Lou Whitaker	Al Trammell	Tony Phillips	Gary Ward	L. Moseby	Chet Lemon	D. Bergman
1991	S. Anderson	M. Tettleton	Cecil Fielder	Lou Whitaker	Al Trammell	T. Fryman	L. Moseby	Milt Cuyler	Rob Deer	Tony Phillips
1992	S. Anderson	M. Tettleton	Cecil Fielder	Lou Whitaker	T. Fryman	S. Livingstone	Dan Gladden	Milt Cuyler	Rob Deer	Tony Phillips
1993	S. Anderson	Chad Kreuter	Cecil Fielder	Lou Whitaker	Al Trammell	T. Fryman	Tony Phillips	Milt Cuyler	Rob Deer	Kirk Gibson
1994	S. Anderson	Chad Kreuter	Cecil Fielder	Lou Whitaker	Al Trammell	T. Fryman	Tony Phillips	Milt Cuyler	Junior Felix	Kirk Gibson
1995	S. Anderson	John Flaherty	Cecil Fielder	Lou Whitaker	Chris Gomez	T. Fryman	B. Higginson	Chad Curtis	D. Bautista	Kirk Gibson
1996	Buddy Bell	Brad Ausmus	Tony Clark	Mark Lewis	A. Cedeno	T. Fryman	B. Higginson	Chad Curtis	Mel Nieves	Ed Williams
1997	Buddy Bell	R. Casanova	Tony Clark	D. Easley	Deivi Cruz	T. Fryman	B. Higginson	Brian Hunter	Mel Nieves	Bob Hamelin
1998	Buddy Bell	Paul Bako	Tony Clark	D. Easley	Deivi Cruz	Joe Randa	Luis Gonzalez	Brian Hunter	B. Higginson	G. Berroa
1999	Larry Parrish	Brad Ausmus	Tony Clark	D. Easley	Deivi Cruz	Dean Palmer	J. Encarnacion	Gabe Kapler	B. Higginson	Luis Polonia
2000	Phil Garner	Brad Ausmus	Tony Clark	D. Easley	Deivi Cruz	Dean Palmer	B. Higginson	J. Encarnacion	Rich Becker	J. Gonzalez
2001	Phil Garner	Robert Fick	Tony Clark	D. Easley	Deivi Cruz	Jose Macias	B. Higginson	Roger Cedeno	J. Encarnacion	Dean Palmer
2002	Luis Pujols	Brandon Inge	R. Simon	D. Easley	Shane Halter	Chris Truby	B. Higginson	W. Magee	Robert Fick	R. Simon

TWINS BY POSITION, YEAR BY YEAR

Washington Senators (American League), 1901–1905
Washington Nationals (American League), 1906–1956
Washington Senators (American League), 1957–1960
Minnesota Twins (American League), 1961–Present

YEAR	MANAGER	C	1B	2B	SS	3B	LF	CF	RF
1901	Jim Manning	B. Clarke	Mike Grady	John Farrell	B. Clingman	Bill Coughlin	Pop Foster	Irv Waldron	Sam Dungan
1902	Tom Loftus	B. Clarke	Scoops Carey	Jack Doyle	Bones Ely	Bill Coughlin	Ed Delahanty	Jimmy Ryan	Watty Lee
1903	Tom Loftus	M. Kittridge	B. Clarke	B. McCormick	C. Moran	Bill Coughlin	Kip Selbach	Jimmy Ryan	Watty Lee
1904	Pat Dovovan	M. Kittridge	Jake Stahl	B. McCormick	Joe Cassidy	Hunter Hill	F. Huelsman	Bill O'Neill	Pat Donovan
1905	Jake Stahl	Mike Heydon	Jake Stahl	C. Hickman	Joe Cassidy	Hunter Hill	F. Huelsman	Charlie Jones	J. Anderson
1906	Jake Stahl	H. Wakefield	Jake Stahl	Larry Schlafly	Dave Altizer	Lave Cross	J. Anderson	Charlie Jones	C. Hickman
1907	Joe Cantillon	John Warner	J. Anderson	Jim Delahanty	Dave Altizer	Bill Shipke	Otis Clymer	Charlie Jones	Bob Ganley

YEAR	MANAGER	C	1B	2B	SS	3B	LF	CF	RF
1908	Joe Cantillon	Gabby Street	Jerry Freeman	Jim Delahanty	G. McBride	Bill Shipke	Bob Ganley	Clyde Milan	O. Pickering
1909	Joe Cantillon	Gabby Street	J. Donahue	Jim Delahanty	G. McBride	Wid Conroy	Jack Lelivelt	Clyde Milan	G. Browne
1910	Jim McAleer	Gabby Street	Bob Unglaub	Red Killefer	G. McBride	Kid Elberfeld	Jack Lelivelt	Clyde Milan	Doc Gessler
1911	Jim McAleer	Gabby Street	G. Schaefer	Cunningham	G. McBride	Wid Conroy	Tilly Walker	Clyde Milan	Doc Gessler
1912	Clark Griffith	John Henry	Chick Gandil	Ray Morgan	G. McBride	Eddie Foster	Howie Shanks	Clyde Milan	Dan Moeller
1913	Clark Griffith	John Henry	Chick Gandil	Ray Morgan	G. McBride	Eddie Foster	Howie Shanks	Clyde Milan	Dan Moeller
1914	Clark Griffith	John Henry	Chick Gandil	Ray Morgan	G. McBride	Eddie Foster	Howie Shanks	Clyde Milan	Dan Moeller
1915	Clark Griffith	John Henry	Chick Gandil	Ray Morgan	G. McBride	Eddie Foster	Howie Shanks	Clyde Milan	Dan Moeller
1916	Clark Griffith	John Henry	Joe Judge	Ray Morgan	G. McBride	Eddie Foster	Howie Shanks	Clyde Milan	Dan Moeller
1917	Clark Griffith	E. Ainsmith	Joe Judge	Ray Morgan	Howie Shanks	Eddie Foster	M. Menosky	Clyde Milan	Sam Rice
1918	Clark Griffith	E. Ainsmith	Joe Judge	Ray Morgan	Doc Lavan	Eddie Foster	Burt Shotton	Clyde Milan	Frank Schulte
1919	Clark Griffith	Val Picinich	Joe Judge	Hal Janvrin	Howie Shanks	Eddie Foster	M. Menosky	Clyde Milan	Sam Rice
1920	Clark Griffith	Patsy Gharrity	Joe Judge	Bucky Harris	Jim O'Neill	Frank Ellerbe	Clyde Milan	Sam Rice	Braggo Roth
1921	G. McBride	Patsy Gharrity	Joe Judge	Bucky Harris	F. O'Rourke	Howie Shanks	Bing Miller	Sam Rice	Clyde Milan
1922	Clyde Milan	Patsy Gharrity	Joe Judge	Bucky Harris	Peckinpaugh	Bob LaMotte	Goose Goslin	Sam Rice	Frank Brower
1923	Donie Bush	Muddy Ruel	Joe Judge	Bucky Harris	Peckinpaugh	Ossie Bluege	Goose Goslin	Nemo Leibold	Sam Rice
1924	Bucky Harris	Muddy Ruel	Joe Judge	Bucky Harris	Peckinpaugh	Ossie Bluege	Goose Goslin	Nemo Leibold	Sam Rice
1925	Bucky Harris	Muddy Ruel	Joe Judge	Bucky Harris	Peckinpaugh	Ossie Bluege	Goose Goslin	Earl McNeely	Sam Rice
1926	Bucky Harris	Muddy Ruel	Joe Judge	Bucky Harris	Buddy Myer	Ossie Bluege	Earl McNeely	Goose Goslin	Sam Rice
1927	Bucky Harris	Muddy Ruel	Joe Judge	Bucky Harris	Bobby Reeves	Ossie Bluege	Goose Goslin	Tris Speaker	Sam Rice
1928	Bucky Harris	Muddy Ruel	Joe Judge	Bucky Harris	Bobby Reeves	Ossie Bluege	Goose Goslin	Sam West	Sam Rice
1929	W. Johnson	Bennie Tate	Joe Judge	Buddy Myer	Joe Cronin	Jackie Hayes	Goose Goslin	Sam West	Sam Rice
1930	W. Johnson	Roy Spencer	Joe Judge	Buddy Myer	Joe Cronin	Ossie Bluege	H. Manush	Sam West	Sam Rice
1931	W. Johnson	Roy Spencer	Joe Kuhel	Buddy Myer	Joe Cronin	Ossie Bluege	H. Manush	Sam West	Sam Rice
1932	W. Johnson	Roy Spencer	Joe Kuhel	Buddy Myer	Joe Cronin	Ossie Bluege	H. Manush	Sam West	Carl Reynolds
1933	Joe Cronin	Luke Sewell	Joe Kuhel	Buddy Myer	Joe Cronin	Ossie Bluege	H. Manush	Fred Schulte	Goose Goslin
1934	Joe Cronin	Eddie Phillips	Joe Kuhel	Buddy Myer	Joe Cronin	Cecil Travis	H. Manush	Fred Schulte	John Stone
1935	Bucky Harris	Cliff Bolton	Joe Kuhel	Buddy Myer	Ossie Bluege	Cecil Travis	H. Manush	Jake Powell	John Stone
1936	Bucky Harris	Cliff Bolton	Joe Kuhel	Ossie Bluege	Cecil Travis	Buddy Lewis	John Stone	Ben Chapman	Carl Reynolds
1937	Bucky Harris	Rick Ferrell	Joe Kuhel	Buddy Myer	Cecil Travis	Buddy Lewis	Al Simmons	Mel Almada	John Stone
1938	Bucky Harris	Rick Ferrell	Zeke Bonura	Buddy Myer	Cecil Travis	Buddy Lewis	Al Simmons	Sam West	George Case
1939	Bucky Harris	Rick Ferrell	Mick Vernon	J. Bloodworth	Cecil Travis	Buddy Lewis	Taffy Wright	Sam West	George Case
1940	Bucky Harris	Rick Ferrell	Zeke Bonura	J. Bloodworth	Jimmy Pofahl	Cecil Travis	Gee Walker	George Case	Buddy Lewis
1941	Bucky Harris	Jake Early	Mick Vernon	J. Bloodworth	Cecil Travis	G. Archie	George Case	Doc Cramer	Buddy Lewis
1942	Bucky Harris	Jake Early	Mick Vernon	Ellis Clary	John Sullivan	Bob Estalella	George Case	Stan Spence	B. Campbell
1943	Ossie Bluege	Jake Early	Mick Vernon	Jerry Priddy	John Sullivan	Ellis Clary	Bob Johnson	Stan Spence	George Case
1944	Ossie Bluege	Rick Ferrell	Joe Kuhel	George Myatt	John Sullivan	Gil Torres	George Case	Stan Spence	Roberto Ortiz
1945	Ossie Bluege	Rick Ferrell	Joe Kuhel	George Myatt	Gil Torres	Harlond Clift	George Case	George Binks	Buddy Lewis
1946	Ossie Bluege	Al Evans	Mick Vernon	Jerry Priddy	B. Hitchcock	Cecil Travis	Joe Grace	Stan Spence	Buddy Lewis
1947	Ossie Bluege	Al Evans	Mick Vernon	Jerry Priddy	M. Christman	Ed Yost	Joe Grace	Stan Spence	Buddy Lewis
1948	Joe Kuhel	Jake Early	Mick Vernon	Al Kozar	M. Christman	Ed Yost	Gil Coan	J. Wooten	Bud Stewart
1949	Joe Kuhel	Al Evans	Ed Robinson	Al Kozar	Sam Dente	Ed Yost	Bud Stewart	C. Vollmer	Buddy Lewis
1950	Bucky Harris	Al Evans	Mick Vernon	Cass Michaels	Sam Dente	Ed Yost	Bud Stewart	Irv Noren	Sam Mele
1951	Bucky Harris	Mike Guerra	Mick Vernon	Cass Michaels	Pete Runnels	Ed Yost	Gil Coan	Irv Noren	Sam Mele
1952	Bucky Harris	Mick Grasso	Mick Vernon	Floyd Baker	Pete Runnels	Ed Yost	Gil Coan	Jim Busby	Jackie Jensen
1953	Bucky Harris	E. Fitz Gerald	Mick Vernon	W. Terwilliger	Pete Runnels	Ed Yost	C. Vollmer	Jim Busby	Jackie Jensen
1954	Bucky Harris	E. Fitz Gerald	Mick Vernon	W. Terwilliger	Pete Runnels	Ed Yost	Roy Sievers	Jim Busby	T. Umphlett
1955	C. Dressen	E. Fitz Gerald	Mick Vernon	Pete Runnels	J. Valdivielso	Ed Yost	Roy Sievers	T. Umphlett	Carlos Paula
1956	C. Dressen	C. Courtney	Pete Runnels	Herb Plews	J. Valdivielso	Ed Yost	Roy Sievers	W. Herzog	Jim Lemon

YEAR	MANAGER	C	1B	2B	SS	3B	LF	CF	RF	DH
1957	C. Lavagetto	Lou Berberet	Pete Runnels	Herb Plews	R. Bridges	Ed Yost	Roy Sievers	Bob Usher	Jim Lemon	
1958	C. Lavagetto	C. Courtney	N. Zauchin	K. Aspromonte	R. Bridges	Ed Yost	Roy Sievers	Albie Pearson	Jim Lemon	
1959	C. Lavagetto	Hal Naragon	Roy Sievers	Reno Bertoia	Billy Consolo	H. Killebrew	Jim Lemon	Bob Allison	F. Throneberry	
1960	C. Lavagetto	Earl Battey	Julio Becquer	Billy Gardner	J. Valdivielso	Reno Bertoia	Jim Lemon	F. Throneberry	Bob Allison	
1961	Sam Mele	Earl Battey	H. Killebrew	Billy Martin	Z. Versalles	Bill Tuttle	Jim Lemon	Lenny Green	Bob Allison	
1962	Sam Mele	Earl Battey	Vic Power	Bernie Allen	Z. Versalles	Rich Rollins	H. Killebrew	Lenny Green	Bob Allison	
1963	Sam Mele	Earl Battey	Vic Power	Bernie Allen	Z. Versalles	Rich Rollins	H. Killebrew	Jimmie Hall	Bob Allison	
1964	Sam Mele	Earl Battey	Bob Allison	Bernie Allen	Z. Versalles	Rich Rollins	H. Killebrew	Jimmie Hall	Tony Oliva	
1965	Sam Mele	Earl Battey	Don Mincher	Jerry Kindall	Z. Versalles	Rich Rollins	Bob Allison	Jimmie Hall	Tony Oliva	
1966	Sam Mele	Earl Battey	Don Mincher	Bernie Allen	Z. Versalles	H. Killebrew	Jimmie Hall	T. Uhlaender	Tony Oliva	
1967	Cal Ermer	J. Zimmerman	H. Killebrew	Rod Carew	Z. Versalles	Rich Rollins	Bob Allison	T. Uhlaender	Tony Oliva	
1968	Cal Ermer	J. Roseboro	Rich Reese	Rod Carew	J. Hernandez	Cesar Tovar	Bob Allison	T. Uhlaender	Tony Oliva	
1969	Billy Martin	J. Roseboro	Rich Reese	Rod Carew	Leo Cardenas	H. Killebrew	T. Uhlaender	Cesar Tovar	Tony Oliva	
1970	Bill Rigney	G. Mitterwald	Rich Reese	D. Thompson	Leo Cardenas	H. Killebrew	Jim Holt	Cesar Tovar	Tony Oliva	
1971	Bill Rigney	G. Mitterwald	Rich Reese	Rod Carew	Leo Cardenas	Steve Braun	Cesar Tovar	Jim Holt	Tony Oliva	
1972	Frank Quilici	Phil Roof	H. Killebrew	Rod Carew	D. Thompson	E. Soderholm	Steve Brye	Bob Darwin	Cesar Tovar	
1973	Frank Quilici	G. Mitterwald	Joe Lis	Rod Carew	D. Thompson	Steve Braun	Jim Holt	Larry Hisle	Bob Darwin	Tony Oliva
1974	Frank Quilici	G. Borgmann	Craig Kusick	Rod Carew	D. Thompson	E. Soderholm	Larry Hisle	Steve Brye	Bob Darwin	Tony Oliva
1975	Frank Quilici	G. Borgmann	Craig Kusick	Rod Carew	D. Thompson	E. Soderholm	Steve Braun	Dan Ford	L. Bostock	Tony Oliva
1976	Gene Mauch	B. Wynegar	Rod Carew	Bob Randall	Roy Smalley	M. Cubbage	Larry Hisle	L. Bostock	Dan Ford	Craig Kusick
1977	Gene Mauch	B. Wynegar	Rod Carew	Bob Randall	Roy Smalley	M. Cubbage	Larry Hisle	L. Bostock	Dan Ford	Craig Kusick
1978	Gene Mauch	B. Wynegar	Rod Carew	Bob Randall	Roy Smalley	M. Cubbage	W. Norwood	Dan Ford	H. Powell	Glenn Adams
1979	Gene Mauch	B. Wynegar	Ron Jackson	Rob Wilfong	Roy Smalley	John Castino	B. Rivera	K. Landreux	H. Powell	Jose Morales
1980	Gene Mauch	B. Wynegar	Ron Jackson	Rob Wilfong	Roy Smalley	John Castino	Rick Sofield	K. Landreux	H. Powell	Jose Morales
1981	John Goryl	Sal Butera	D. Goodwin	Rob Wilfong	Roy Smalley	John Castino	Gary Ward	Mick Hatcher	Dave Engle	Glenn Adams
1982	Billy Gardner	Tim Laudner	Kent Hrbek	John Castino	R. Washington	Gary Gaetti	Gary Ward	Bob Mitchell	T. Brunansky	R. Johnson
1983	Billy Gardner	Dave Engle	Kent Hrbek	John Castino	R. Washington	Gary Gaetti	Gary Ward	Darrell Brown	T. Brunansky	Randy Bush
1984	Billy Gardner	Dave Engle	Kent Hrbek	Tim Teufel	H. Jimenez	Gary Gaetti	Mick Hatcher	Kirby Puckett	T. Brunansky	Randy Bush
1985	Ray Miller	Mike Salas	Kent Hrbek	Tim Teufel	Greg Gagne	Gary Gaetti	Mick Hatcher	Kirby Puckett	T. Brunansky	Roy Smalley
1986	Ray Miller	Mike Salas	Kent Hrbek	Lombardozzi	Greg Gagne	Gary Gaetti	Randy Bush	Kirby Puckett	T. Brunansky	Roy Smalley
1987	Tom Kelly	Tim Laudner	Kent Hrbek	Lombardozzi	Greg Gagne	Gary Gaetti	Dan Gladden	Kirby Puckett	T. Brunansky	Roy Smalley
1988	Tom Kelly	Tim Laudner	Kent Hrbek	Lombardozzi	Greg Gagne	Gary Gaetti	Dan Gladden	Kirby Puckett	Randy Bush	Gene Larkin
1989	Tom Kelly	Brian Harper	Kent Hrbek	Al Newman	Greg Gagne	Gary Gaetti	Dan Gladden	Kirby Puckett	Randy Bush	Jim Dwyer
1990	Tom Kelly	Brian Harper	Kent Hrbek	Al Newman	Greg Gagne	Gary Gaetti	Dan Gladden	Kirby Puckett	Shane Mack	Gene Larkin
1991	Tom Kelly	Brian Harper	Kent Hrbek	C. Knoblauch	Greg Gagne	M. Pagliarulo	Dan Gladden	Kirby Puckett	Shane Mack	Chili Davis
1992	Tom Kelly	Brian Harper	Kent Hrbek	C. Knoblauch	Greg Gagne	Scott Leius	Shane Mack	Kirby Puckett	Pedro Munoz	Chili Davis
1993	Tom Kelly	Brian Harper	Kent Hrbek	C. Knoblauch	Pat Meares	M. Pagliarulo	Pedro Munoz	Shane Mack	Kirby Puckett	D. Winfield
1994	Tom Kelly	Matt Walbeck	Kent Hrbek	C. Knoblauch	Pat Meares	Scott Leius	Shane Mack	Alex Cole	Kirby Puckett	D. Winfield
1995	Tom Kelly	Matt Walbeck	S. Stahoviak	C. Knoblauch	Pat Meares	Scott Leius	M. Cordova	Rich Becker	Kirby Puckett	Pedro Munoz
1996	Tom Kelly	Greg Myers	S. Stahoviak	C. Knoblauch	Pat Meares	Dave Hollins	M. Cordova	Rich Becker	Roberto Kelly	Paul Molitor
1997	Tom Kelly	T. Steinbach	S. Stahoviak	C. Knoblauch	Pat Meares	Ron Coomer	M. Cordova	Rich Becker	Matt Lawton	Paul Molitor
1998	Tom Kelly	T. Steinbach	David Ortiz	Todd Walker	Pat Meares	Brent Gates	M. Cordova	Otis Nixon	Matt Lawton	Paul Molitor
1999	Tom Kelly	T. Steinbach	Mientkiewicz	Todd Walker	C. Guzman	Corey Koskie	Chad Allen	Torii Hunter	Matt Lawton	M. Cordova
2000	Tom Kelly	Matt LeCroy	Ron Coomer	Jay Canizaro	C. Guzman	Corey Koskie	Jacque Jones	Torii Hunter	Matt Lawton	David Ortiz
2001	Tom Kelly	A. Pierzynski	Mientkiewicz	Luis Rivas	C. Guzman	Corey Koskie	Jacque Jones	Torii Hunter	Matt Lawton	David Ortiz
2002	R. Gardenhire	A. Pierzynski	Mientkiewicz	Luis Rivas	C. Guzman	Corey Koskie	Jacque Jones	Torii Hunter	Dustan Mohr	David Ortiz

WHITE SOX BY POSITION, YEAR BY YEAR

Chicago White Stockings (American League), 1901–1902
Chicago White Sox (American League), 1903–Present

YEAR	MANAGER	C	1B	2B	SS	3B	LF	CF	RF
1901	Clark Griffith	Billy Sullivan	Frank Isbell	Sam Mertes	Frank Shugart	Fred Hartman	H. McFarland	Dummy Hoy	Fielder Jones
1902	Clark Griffith	Billy Sullivan	Frank Isbell	Tom Daly	George Davis	Sam Strang	Sam Mertes	Fielder Jones	Danny Green
1903	N. Callahan	Jack Slattery	Frank Isbell	G. Maggoon	Lee Tannehill	N. Callahan	D. Holmes	Fielder Jones	Danny Green
1904	Fielder Jones	Billy Sullivan	J. Donahue	Gus Dundon	George Davis	Lee Tannehill	N. Callahan	Fielder Jones	Danny Green
1905	Fielder Jones	Billy Sullivan	J. Donahue	Gus Dundon	George Davis	Lee Tannehill	N. Callahan	Fielder Jones	Danny Green
1906	Fielder Jones	Billy Sullivan	J. Donahue	Frank Isbell	George Davis	Lee Tannehill	Ed Hahn	Fielder Jones	Bill O'Neill
1907	Fielder Jones	Billy Sullivan	J. Donahue	Frank Isbell	George Davis	George Rohe	P. Dougherty	Fielder Jones	Ed Hahn
1908	Fielder Jones	Billy Sullivan	J. Donahue	George Davis	Freddy Parent	Lee Tannehill	P. Dougherty	Fielder Jones	Ed Hahn
1909	Billy Sullivan	Billy Sullivan	Frank Isbell	Jake Atz	Freddy Parent	Lee Tannehill	P. Dougherty	Dave Altizer	Ed Hahn
1910	Hugh Duffy	Fred Payne	Chick Gandil	Rollie Zeider	L. Blackburne	Billy Purtell	P. Dougherty	Freddy Parent	Shano Collins
1911	Hugh Duffy	Billy Sullivan	Shano Collins	A. McConnell	Lee Tannehill	Harry Lord	N. Callahan	Ping Bodie	M. McIntyre
1912	N. Callahan	Walt Kuhn	Rollie Zeider	Morrie Rath	Buck Weaver	Harry Lord	N. Callahan	Ping Bodie	Shano Collins
1913	N. Callahan	Ray Schalk	Hal Chase	Morrie Rath	Buck Weaver	Harry Lord	Ping Bodie	Chick Mattick	Shano Collins
1914	N. Callahan	Ray Schalk	Jack Fournier	L. Blackburne	Buck Weaver	Jim Breton	Ray Demmitt	Ping Bodie	Shano Collins
1915	P. Rowland	Ray Schalk	Jack Fournier	Eddie Collins	Buck Weaver	L. Blackburne	Shano Collins	Happy Felsch	Eddie Murphy
1916	P. Rowland	Ray Schalk	Jack Fournier	Eddie Collins	Zeb Terry	Buck Weaver	Joe Jackson	Happy Felsch	Shano Collins
1917	P. Rowland	Ray Schalk	Chick Gandil	Eddie Collins	S. Risberg	Buck Weaver	Joe Jackson	Happy Felsch	Nemo Leibold
1918	P. Rowland	Ray Schalk	Chick Gandil	Eddie Collins	Buck Weaver	F. McMullin	Nemo Leibold	Shano Collins	Eddie Murphy
1919	Kid Gleason	Ray Schalk	Chick Gandil	Eddie Collins	S. Risberg	Buck Weaver	Joe Jackson	Happy Felsch	Nemo Leibold
1920	Kid Gleason	Ray Schalk	Shano Collins	Eddie Collins	S. Risberg	Buck Weaver	Joe Jackson	Happy Felsch	Nemo Leibold
1921	Kid Gleason	Ray Schalk	Earl Sheely	Eddie Collins	Ernie Johnson	E. Mulligan	Bibb Falk	Amos Strunk	Harry Hooper
1922	Kid Gleason	Ray Schalk	Earl Sheely	Eddie Collins	Ernie Johnson	E. Mulligan	Bibb Falk	Johnny Mostil	Harry Hooper
1923	Kid Gleason	Ray Schalk	Earl Sheely	Eddie Collins	H. McClellan	Willie Kamm	Bibb Falk	Johnny Mostil	Harry Hooper
1924	Johnny Evers	Buck Crouse	Earl Sheely	Eddie Collins	Bill Barrett	Willie Kamm	Bibb Falk	Johnny Mostil	Harry Hooper
1925	Eddie Collins	Ray Schalk	Earl Sheely	Eddie Collins	Ike Davis	Willie Kamm	Bibb Falk	Johnny Mostil	Harry Hooper
1926	Eddie Collins	Ray Schalk	Earl Sheely	Eddie Collins	B. Hunnefield	Willie Kamm	Bibb Falk	Johnny Mostil	Bill Barrett
1927	Ray Schalk	H. McCurdy	Bud Clancy	Aaron Ward	B. Hunnefield	Willie Kamm	Bibb Falk	Alex Metzler	Bill Barrett
1928	Ray Schalk	Buck Crouse	Bud Clancy	B. Hunnefield	Bill Cissell	Willie Kamm	Bibb Falk	Johnny Mostil	Alex Metzler
1929	L. Blackburne	Moe Berg	Art Shires	John Kerr	Bill Cissell	Willie Kamm	Alex Metzler	D. Hoffman	Carl Reynolds
1930	Donie Bush	Bennie Tate	J. Watwood	Bill Cissell	G. Mulleavy	Willie Kamm	Smead Jolley	Red Barnes	Carl Reynolds
1931	Donie Bush	Bennie Tate	Lu Blue	John Kerr	Bill Cissell	Billy Sullivan	Lew Fonseca	J. Watwood	Carl Reynolds
1932	Lew Fonseca	Frank Grube	Lu Blue	Jackie Hayes	Luke Appling	Carey Selph	B. Fothergill	Liz Funk	Bob Seeds
1933	Lew Fonseca	Frank Grube	Red Kress	Jackie Hayes	Luke Appling	Jimmy Dykes	Al Simmons	Mule Haas	Evar Swanson
1934	Jimmy Dykes	Ed Madjeski	Zeke Bonura	Jackie Hayes	Luke Appling	Jimmy Dykes	Al Simmons	Mule Haas	Evar Swanson
1935	Jimmy Dykes	Luke Sewell	Zeke Bonura	Jackie Hayes	Luke Appling	Jimmy Dykes	Rip Radcliff	Al Simmons	Mule Haas
1936	Jimmy Dykes	Luke Sewell	Zeke Bonura	Jackie Hayes	Luke Appling	Jimmy Dykes	Rip Radcliff	M. Kreevich	Mule Haas
1937	Jimmy Dykes	Luke Sewell	Zeke Bonura	Jackie Hayes	Luke Appling	Tony Piet	Rip Radcliff	M. Kreevich	Dixie Walker
1938	Jimmy Dykes	Luke Sewell	Joe Kuhel	Jackie Hayes	Luke Appling	Marv Owen	Gee Walker	M. Kreevich	H. Steinbacher
1939	Jimmy Dykes	Mike Tresh	Joe Kuhel	Ollie Bejma	Luke Appling	Eric McNair	Gee Walker	M. Kreevich	L. Rosenthal
1940	Jimmy Dykes	Mike Tresh	Joe Kuhel	Skeeter Webb	Luke Appling	Bob Kennedy	Moose Solters	M. Kreevich	Taffy Wright
1941	Jimmy Dykes	Mike Tresh	Joe Kuhel	Knickerbocker	Luke Appling	D. Lodigiani	Myril Hoag	M. Kreevich	Taffy Wright
1942	Jimmy Dykes	Mike Tresh	Joe Kuhel	D. Kolloway	Luke Appling	Bob Kennedy	Taffy Wright	Myril Hoag	Wally Moses
1943	Jimmy Dykes	Mike Tresh	Joe Kuhel	D. Kolloway	Luke Appling	Ralph Hodgin	Guy Curtright	T. Tucker	Wally Moses
1944	Jimmy Dykes	Mike Tresh	Hal Trosky	Roy Schalk	Skeeter Webb	Ralph Hodgin	Eddie Carnett	T. Tucker	Wally Moses
1945	Jimmy Dykes	Mike Tresh	Kerby Farrell	Roy Schalk	Cass Michaels	T. Cuccinello	J. Dickshot	Oris Hockett	Wally Moses
1946	Ted Lyons	Mike Tresh	Hal Trosky	D. Kolloway	Luke Appling	D. Lodigiani	Bob Kennedy	T. Tucker	Taffy Wright

YEAR	MANAGER	C	1B	2B	SS	3B	LF	CF	RF	DH
1947	Ted Lyons	Mike Tresh	Rudy York	D. Kolloway	Luke Appling	Floyd Baker	Taffy Wright	Dave Philley	Bob Kennedy	
1948	Ted Lyons	A. Robinson	Tony Lupien	D. Kolloway	Cass Michaels	Luke Appling	Pat Seerey	Dave Philley	Taffy Wright	
1949	Jack Onslow	Don Wheeler	Chuck Kress	Cass Michaels	Luke Appling	Floyd Baker	Gus Zernial	C. Metkovich	Dave Philley	Marv Rickert
1950	Paul Richards	Phil Masi	Ed Robinson	Nellie Fox	C. Carrasquel	Hank Majeski	Gus Zernial	Dave Philley		
1951	Paul Richards	Phil Masi	Ed Robinson	Nellie Fox	C. Carrasquel	Bob Dillinger	M. Minoso	Jim Busby	Al Zarilla	
1952	Paul Richards	Sherm Lollar	Ed Robinson	Nellie Fox	C. Carrasquel	H. Rodriguez	M. Minoso	Ray Coleman	Sam Mele	
1953	Paul Richards	Sherm Lollar	Ferris Fain	Nellie Fox	C. Carrasquel	Bob Elliott	M. Minoso	Jim Rivera	Sam Mele	
1954	Paul Richards	Sherm Lollar	Ferris Fain	Nellie Fox	C. Carrasquel	Cass Michaels	M. Minoso	Johnny Groth	Jim Rivera	
1955	Marty Marion	Sherm Lollar	Walt Dropo	Nellie Fox	C. Carrasquel	George Kell	M. Minoso	Jim Busby	Jim Rivera	
1956	Marty Marion	Sherm Lollar	Walt Dropo	Nellie Fox	Luis Aparicio	Fred Hatfield	M. Minoso	Larry Doby	Jim Rivera	
1957	Al Lopez	Sherm Lollar	E. Torgeson	Nellie Fox	Luis Aparicio	B. Phillips	M. Minoso	Larry Doby	Jim Landis	
1958	Al Lopez	Sherm Lollar	E. Torgeson	Nellie Fox	Luis Aparicio	B. Goodman	Jim Rivera	Jim Landis	Al Smith	
1959	Al Lopez	Sherm Lollar	E. Torgeson	Nellie Fox	Luis Aparicio	B. Phillips	Al Smith	Jim Landis	Jim Rivera	
1960	Al Lopez	Sherm Lollar	Roy Sievers	Nellie Fox	Luis Aparicio	Gene Freese	M. Minoso	Jim Landis	Al Smith	
1961	Al Lopez	Sherm Lollar	Roy Sievers	Nellie Fox	Luis Aparicio	Al Smith	M. Minoso	Jim Landis	F. Robinson	
1962	Al Lopez	Cam Carreon	J Cunningham	Nellie Fox	Luis Aparicio	Al Smith	F. Robinson	Jim Landis	Hershberger	
1963	Al Lopez	J.C. Martin	Tom McCraw	Nellie Fox	Ron Hansen	Pete Ward	D. Nicholson	Jim Landis	F. Robinson	
1964	Al Lopez	J.C. Martin	Tom McCraw	Al Weis	Ron Hansen	Pete Ward	F. Robinson	Jim Landis	Hershberger	
1965	Al Lopez	J.C. Martin	M. Skowron	Don Buford	Ron Hansen	Pete Ward	Danny Cater	Ken Berry	F. Robinson	
1966	Eddie Stanky	John Romano	Tom McCraw	Al Weis	Lee Elia	Don Buford	Ken Berry	Tommie Agee	F. Robinson	
1967	Eddie Stanky	J.C. Martin	Tom McCraw	W. Causey	Ron Hansen	Don Buford	Pete Ward	Tommie Agee	Ken Berry	
1968	Eddie Stanky	D. Josephson	Tom McCraw	S. Alomar	Luis Aparicio	Pete Ward	Tommy Davis	Ken Berry	Bud Bradford	
1969	D. Gutteridge	Ed Herrmann	Gail Hopkins	Bobby Knoop	Luis Aparicio	Bill Melton	Carlos May	Ken Berry	W. Williams	
1970	D. Gutteridge	Ed Herrmann	Gail Hopkins	Bobby Knoop	Luis Aparicio	Bill Melton	Carlos May	Ken Berry	W. Williams	
1971	Chuck Tanner	Ed Herrmann	Carlos May	M. Andrews	Luis Alvarado	Bill Melton	R. Reichardt	Jay Johnstone	W. Williams	
1972	Chuck Tanner	Ed Herrmann	Dick Allen	M. Andrews	Rich Morales	Ed Spiezio	Carlos May	Jay Johnstone	Pat Kelly	
1973	Chuck Tanner	Ed Herrmann	Tony Muser	Jorge Orta	Eddie Leon	Bill Melton	Carlos May	Johnny Jeter	Pat Kelly	K. Henderson
1974	Chuck Tanner	Ed Herrmann	Dick Allen	Jorge Orta	Bucky Dent	Bill Melton	Carlos May	K. Henderson	Bill Sharp	Pat Kelly
1975	Chuck Tanner	B. Downing	Carlos May	Jorge Orta	Bucky Dent	Bill Melton	Nyls Nyman	K. Henderson	Pat Kelly	D. Johnson
1976	Paul Richards	B. Downing	Jim Spencer	J. Brohamer	Bucky Dent	Kevin Bell	Jorge Orta	Chet Lemon	Ralph Garr	Pat Kelly
1977	Bob Lemon	Jim Essian	Jim Spencer	Jorge Orta	A. Bannister	E. Soderholm	Ralph Garr	Chet Lemon	Richie Zisk	Oscar Gamble
1978	Larry Doby	B. Nahorodny	Mike Squires	Jorge Orta	D. Kessinger	E. Soderholm	Ralph Garr	Chet Lemon	C. Washington	L. Johnson
1979	D. Kessinger	Milt May	Mike Squires	A. Bannister	Greg Pryor	Kevin Bell	Rusty Torres	Chet Lemon	C. Washington	Jorge Orta
1980	T. La Russa	Bruce Kimm	Mike Squires	Jim Morrison	Todd Cruz	Kevin Bell	W. Nordhagen	Chet Lemon	Harold Baines	L. Johnson
1981	T. La Russa	Carlton Fisk	Mike Squires	T. Bernazard	Bill Almon	Jim Morrison	Ron LeFlore	Chet Lemon	Harold Baines	Greg Luzinski
1982	T. La Russa	Carlton Fisk	Mike Squires	T. Bernazard	Bill Almon	A. Rodriguez	Steve Kemp	Rudy Law	Harold Baines	Greg Luzinski
1983	T. La Russa	Carlton Fisk	Mike Squires	Julio Cruz	J. Dybzinski	Vance Law	Ron Kittle	Rudy Law	Harold Baines	Greg Luzinski
1984	T. La Russa	Carlton Fisk	Greg Walker	Julio Cruz	Scott Fletcher	Vance Law	Ron Kittle	Rudy Law	Harold Baines	Greg Luzinski
1985	T. La Russa	Carlton Fisk	Greg Walker	Julio Cruz	Ozzie Guillen	Tim Hulett	Rudy Law	Daryl Boston	Harold Baines	Ron Kittle
1986	Jim Fregosi	Carlton Fisk	Greg Walker	Julio Cruz	Ozzie Guillen	Tim Hulett	Reid Nichols	J. Cangelosi	Harold Baines	Ron Kittle
1987	Jim Fregosi	Carlton Fisk	Greg Walker	F. Manrique	Ozzie Guillen	Tim Hulett	Gary Redus	Ken Williams	Ivan Calderon	Harold Baines
1988	Jim Fregosi	Carlton Fisk	Greg Walker	F. Manrique	Ozzie Guillen	Steve Lyons	Daryl Boston	D. Gallagher	Dan Pasqua	Harold Baines
1989	Jeff Torborg	Carlton Fisk	Greg Walker	Steve Lyons	Ozzie Guillen	C. Martinez	Daryl Boston	D. Gallagher	Ivan Calderon	Harold Baines
1990	Jeff Torborg	Carlton Fisk	C. Martinez	Scott Fletcher	Ozzie Guillen	R. Ventura	Ivan Calderon	L. Johnson	Sammy Sosa	Dan Pasqua
1991	Jeff Torborg	Carlton Fisk	Dan Pasqua	Scott Fletcher	Ozzie Guillen	R. Ventura	Tim Raines	L. Johnson	Sammy Sosa	Frank Thomas
1992	Gene Lamont	R. Karkovice	Frank Thomas	Steve Sax	C. Grebeck	R. Ventura	Tim Raines	L. Johnson	Shawn Abner	George Bell
1993	Gene Lamont	R. Karkovice	Frank Thomas	Joey Cora	Ozzie Guillen	R. Ventura	Tim Raines	L. Johnson	Ellis Burks	George Bell
1994	Gene Lamont	R. Karkovice	Frank Thomas	Joey Cora	Ozzie Guillen	R. Ventura	Tim Raines	L. Johnson	D. Jackson	Julio Franco
1995	T. Bevington	R. Karkovice	D. Martinez	Ray Durham	Ozzie Guillen	R. Ventura	Tim Raines	L. Johnson	M. Devereaux	Frank Thomas

YEAR	MANAGER	C	1B	2B	SS	3B	LF	CF	RF	DH
1996	T. Bevington	R. Karkovice	Frank Thomas	Ray Durham	Ozzie Guillen	R. Ventura	Tony Phillips	Darren Lewis	D. Tartabull	Harold Baines
1997	T. Bevington	J. Fabregas	Frank Thomas	Ray Durham	Ozzie Guillen	Chris Snopek	Albert Belle	M. Cameron	D. Martinez	Harold Baines
1998	Jerry Manuel	Chad Kreuter	Wil Cordero	Ray Durham	Mike Caruso	R. Ventura	Albert Belle	M. Cameron	M. Ordonez	Frank Thomas
1999	Jerry Manuel	B. Fordyce	Paul Konerko	Ray Durham	Mike Caruso	Greg Norton	Carlos Lee	C. Singleton	M. Ordonez	Frank Thomas
2000	Jerry Manuel	Mark Johnson	Paul Konerko	Ray Durham	Jose Valentin	Herb Perry	Carlos Lee	C. Singleton	M. Ordonez	Frank Thomas
2001	Jerry Manuel	Sandy Alomar	Paul Konerko	Ray Durham	R. Clayton	Jose Valentin	Carlos Lee	C. Singleton	M. Ordonez	Jose Canseco
2002	Jerry Manuel	Mark Johnson	Paul Konerko	Ray Durham	R. Clayton	Jose Valentin	Carlos Lee	Kenny Lofton	M. Ordonez	Frank Thomas

YANKEES BY POSITION, YEAR BY YEAR

Baltimore Orioles (American League), 1901–1902
New York Highlanders (American League), 1903–1912
New York Highlanders a.k.a. Yankees (American League), 1905–1912
New York Yankees (American League), 1913–Present

YEAR	MANAGER	C	1B	2B	SS	3B	LF	CF	RF
1901	John McGraw	R. Bresnahan	Burt Hart	Jim Williams	Bill Keister	John McGraw	Jim Jackson	Steve Brodie	Cy Seymour
1902	W. Robinson	W. Robinson	Dan McGann	Jim Williams	Billy Gilbert	R. Bresnahan	Kip Selbach	H. McFarland	Cy Seymour
1903	Clark Griffith	Monte Beville	John Ganzel	Jim Williams	Kid Elberfeld	Wid Conroy	Lefty Davis	H. McFarland	Willie Keeler
1904	Clark Griffith	D. McGuire	John Ganzel	Jim Williams	Kid Elberfeld	Wid Conroy	P. Dougherty	J. Anderson	Willie Keeler
1905	Clark Griffith	Red Kleinow	Hal Chase	Jim Williams	Kid Elberfeld	Joe Yeager	P. Dougherty	Dave Fultz	Willie Keeler
1906	Clark Griffith	Red Kleinow	Hal Chase	Jim Williams	Kid Elberfeld	Frank LaPorte	Wid Conroy	Dan Hoffman	Willie Keeler
1907	Clark Griffith	Red Kleinow	Hal Chase	Jim Williams	Kid Elberfeld	G. Moriarty	Wid Conroy	Dan Hoffman	Willie Keeler
1908	Clark Griffith	Red Kleinow	Hal Chase	Harry Niles	Neal Ball	Wid Conroy	Jake Stahl	C. Hemphill	Willie Keeler
1909	G. Stallings	Red Kleinow	Hal Chase	Frank LaPorte	John Knight	Jimmy Austin	Clyde Engle	Ray Demmitt	Willie Keeler
1910	G. Stallings	Ed Sweeney	Hal Chase	Frank LaPorte	John Knight	Jimmy Austin	Birdie Cree	C. Hemphill	Harry Wolter
1911	Hal Chase	Walter Blair	Hal Chase	Earle Gardner	John Knight	Roy Hartzell	Birdie Cree	Bert Daniels	Harry Wolter
1912	H. Wolverton	Ed Sweeney	Hal Chase	H. Simmons	Jack Martin	Roy Hartzell	Bert Daniels	Dutch Sterrett	Guy Zinn
1913	Frank Chance	Ed Sweeney	John Knight	Roy Hartzell	Peckinpaugh	Ezra Midkiff	Birdie Cree	Harry Wolter	Bert Daniels
1914	Frank Chance	Ed Sweeney	C. Mullen	Lute Boone	Peckinpaugh	Fritz Maisel	Roy Hartzell	Birdie Cree	Doug Cook
1915	Bill Donovan	L. Nunamaker	Wally Pipp	Lute Boone	Peckinpaugh	Fritz Maisel	Roy Hartzell	Hugh High	Doug Cook
1916	Bill Donovan	L. Nunamaker	Wally Pipp	Joe Gedeon	Peckinpaugh	Frank Baker	Hugh High	Lee Magee	F. Gilhooley
1917	Bill Donovan	L. Nunamaker	Wally Pipp	Fritz Maisel	Peckinpaugh	Frank Baker	Hugh High	Elmer Miller	Tim Hendryx
1918	M. Huggins	Truck Hannah	Wally Pipp	Del Pratt	Peckinpaugh	Frank Baker	Ping Bodie	Elmer Miller	F. Gilhooley
1919	M. Huggins	Muddy Ruel	Wally Pipp	Del Pratt	Peckinpaugh	Frank Baker	Duffy Lewis	Ping Bodie	Sammy Vick
1920	M. Huggins	Muddy Ruel	Wally Pipp	Del Pratt	Peckinpaugh	Aaron Ward	Duffy Lewis	Ping Bodie	Babe Ruth
1921	M. Huggins	Wally Schang	Wally Pipp	Aaron Ward	Peckinpaugh	Frank Baker	Babe Ruth	Elmer Miller	Bob Meusel
1922	M. Huggins	Wally Schang	Wally Pipp	Aaron Ward	Everett Scott	Joe Dugan	Babe Ruth	Whitey Witt	Bob Meusel
1923	M. Huggins	Wally Schang	Wally Pipp	Aaron Ward	Everett Scott	Joe Dugan	Bob Meusel	Whitey Witt	Babe Ruth
1924	M. Huggins	Wally Schang	Wally Pipp	Aaron Ward	Everett Scott	Joe Dugan	Bob Meusel	Whitey Witt	Babe Ruth
1925	M. Huggins	B. Bengough	Lou Gehrig	Aaron Ward	P. Wanninger	Joe Dugan	Bob Meusel	Earle Combs	Babe Ruth
1926	M. Huggins	Pat Collins	Lou Gehrig	Tony Lazzeri	Mark Koenig	Joe Dugan	Bob Meusel	Earle Combs	Babe Ruth
1927	M. Huggins	Pat Collins	Lou Gehrig	Tony Lazzeri	Mark Koenig	Joe Dugan	Bob Meusel	Earle Combs	Babe Ruth
1928	M. Huggins	J. Grabowski	Lou Gehrig	Tony Lazzeri	Mark Koenig	Joe Dugan	Bob Meusel	Earle Combs	Babe Ruth
1929	M. Huggins	Bill Dickey	Lou Gehrig	Tony Lazzeri	Leo Durocher	G. Robertson	Bob Meusel	Earle Combs	Babe Ruth
1930	Bob Shawkey	Bill Dickey	Lou Gehrig	Tony Lazzeri	Lyn Lary	Ben Chapman	Earle Combs	Harry Rice	Babe Ruth
1931	Joe McCarthy	Bill Dickey	Lou Gehrig	Tony Lazzeri	Lyn Lary	Joe Sewell	Ben Chapman	Earle Combs	Babe Ruth
1932	Joe McCarthy	Bill Dickey	Lou Gehrig	Tony Lazzeri	Frank Crosetti	Joe Sewell	Ben Chapman	Earle Combs	Babe Ruth
1933	Joe McCarthy	Bill Dickey	Lou Gehrig	Tony Lazzeri	Frank Crosetti	Joe Sewell	Ben Chapman	Earle Combs	Babe Ruth
1934	Joe McCarthy	Bill Dickey	Lou Gehrig	Tony Lazzeri	Frank Crosetti	J. Saltzgaver	Myril Hoag	Ben Chapman	Babe Ruth

YEAR	MANAGER	C	1B	2B	SS	3B	LF	CF	RF	DH
1935	Joe McCarthy	Bill Dickey	Lou Gehrig	Tony Lazzeri	Frank Crosetti	Red Rolfe	Jesse Hill	Ben Chapman	G. Selkirk	
1936	Joe McCarthy	Bill Dickey	Lou Gehrig	Tony Lazzeri	Frank Crosetti	Red Rolfe	Joe DiMaggio	Jake Powell	G. Selkirk	
1937	Joe McCarthy	Bill Dickey	Lou Gehrig	Tony Lazzeri	Frank Crosetti	Red Rolfe	Jake Powell	Joe DiMaggio	Myril Hoag	
1938	Joe McCarthy	Bill Dickey	Lou Gehrig	Joe Gordon	Frank Crosetti	Red Rolfe	G. Selkirk	Joe DiMaggio	Tom Henrich	
1939	Joe McCarthy	Bill Dickey	B. Dahlgren	Joe Gordon	Frank Crosetti	Red Rolfe	G. Selkirk	Joe DiMaggio	Charlie Keller	
1940	Joe McCarthy	Bill Dickey	B. Dahlgren	Joe Gordon	Frank Crosetti	Red Rolfe	G. Selkirk	Joe DiMaggio	Charlie Keller	
1941	Joe McCarthy	Bill Dickey	Johnny Sturm	Joe Gordon	Phil Rizzuto	Red Rolfe	Charlie Keller	Joe DiMaggio	Tom Henrich	
1942	Joe McCarthy	Bill Dickey	Bud Hassett	Joe Gordon	Phil Rizzuto	Frank Crosetti	Charlie Keller	Joe DiMaggio	Tom Henrich	
1943	Joe McCarthy	Bill Dickey	Nick Etten	Joe Gordon	Frank Crosetti	Billy Johnson	Charlie Keller	John Lindell	Bud Metheny	
1944	Joe McCarthy	Mike Garbark	Nick Etten	S. Stirnweiss	M. Milosevich	Oscar Grimes	Hersh Martin	John Lindell	Bud Metheny	
1945	Joe McCarthy	Mike Garbark	Nick Etten	S. Stirnweiss	Frank Crosetti	Oscar Grimes	Hersh Martin	T. Stainback	Bud Metheny	
1946	Bill Dickey	A. Robinson	Nick Etten	Joe Gordon	Phil Rizzuto	S. Stirnweiss	Charlie Keller	Joe DiMaggio	Tom Henrich	
1947	Bucky Harris	A. Robinson	G. McQuinn	S. Stirnweiss	Phil Rizzuto	Billy Johnson	John Lindell	Joe DiMaggio	Tom Henrich	
1948	Bucky Harris	Gus Niarhos	G. McQuinn	S. Stirnweiss	Phil Rizzuto	Billy Johnson	John Lindell	Joe DiMaggio	Tom Henrich	
1949	Casey Stengel	Yogi Berra	T. Henrich	J. Coleman	Phil Rizzuto	Bobby Brown	G. Woodling	Cliff Mapes	Hank Bauer	
1950	Casey Stengel	Yogi Berra	Joe Collins	J. Coleman	Phil Rizzuto	Billy Johnson	G. Woodling	Joe DiMaggio	Hank Bauer	
1951	Casey Stengel	Yogi Berra	Joe Collins	J. Coleman	Phil Rizzuto	Bobby Brown	G. Woodling	Joe DiMaggio	Hank Bauer	
1952	Casey Stengel	Yogi Berra	Joe Collins	Billy Martin	Phil Rizzuto	G. McDougald	G. Woodling	Mi. Mantle	Hank Bauer	
1953	Casey Stengel	Yogi Berra	Joe Collins	Billy Martin	Phil Rizzuto	G. McDougald	G. Woodling	Mi. Mantle	Hank Bauer	
1954	Casey Stengel	Yogi Berra	Joe Collins	G. McDougald	Phil Rizzuto	Andy Carey	Irv Noren	Mi. Mantle	Hank Bauer	
1955	Casey Stengel	Yogi Berra	M. Skowron	G. McDougald	Billy Hunter	Andy Carey	Irv Noren	Mi. Mantle	Hank Bauer	
1956	Casey Stengel	Yogi Berra	M. Skowron	Billy Martin	G. McDougald	Andy Carey	E. Howard	Mi. Mantle	Hank Bauer	
1957	Casey Stengel	Yogi Berra	M. Skowron	B. Richardson	G. McDougald	Andy Carey	E. Howard	Mi. Mantle	Hank Bauer	
1958	Casey Stengel	Yogi Berra	M. Skowron	G. McDougald	Tony Kubek	Andy Carey	Norm Siebern	Mi. Mantle	Hank Bauer	
1959	Casey Stengel	Yogi Berra	M. Skowron	B. Richardson	Tony Kubek	Hector Lopez	Norm Siebern	Mi. Mantle	Hank Bauer	
1960	Casey Stengel	E. Howard	M. Skowron	B. Richardson	Tony Kubek	Clete Boyer	Hector Lopez	Mi. Mantle	Roger Maris	
1961	Ralph Houk	E. Howard	M. Skowron	B. Richardson	Tony Kubek	Clete Boyer	Yogi Berra	Mi. Mantle	Roger Maris	
1962	Ralph Houk	E. Howard	M. Skowron	B. Richardson	Tom Tresh	Clete Boyer	Hector Lopez	Mi. Mantle	Roger Maris	
1963	Ralph Houk	E. Howard	Joe Pepitone	B. Richardson	Tony Kubek	Clete Boyer	Hector Lopez	Tom Tresh	Roger Maris	
1964	Yogi Berra	E. Howard	Joe Pepitone	B. Richardson	Tony Kubek	Clete Boyer	Tom Tresh	Mi. Mantle	Roger Maris	
1965	Johnny Keane	E. Howard	Joe Pepitone	B. Richardson	Tony Kubek	Clete Boyer	Mi. Mantle	Tom Tresh	Hector Lopez	
1966	Ralph Houk	E. Howard	Joe Pepitone	B. Richardson	Horace Clarke	Clete Boyer	Tom Tresh	Mi. Mantle	Roger Maris	
1967	Ralph Houk	Jake Gibbs	Mi. Mantle	Horace Clarke	Ruben Amaro	Charley Smith	Tom Tresh	Joe Pepitone	S. Whitaker	
1968	Ralph Houk	Jake Gibbs	Mi. Mantle	Horace Clarke	Tom Tresh	Bobby Cox	Roy White	Joe Pepitone	Andy Kosco	
1969	Ralph Houk	Jake Gibbs	Joe Pepitone	Horace Clarke	Gene Michael	Jerry Kenney	Roy White	Ron Woods	Bo. Murcer	
1970	Ralph Houk	T. Munson	Danny Cater	Horace Clarke	Gene Michael	Jerry Kenney	Roy White	Bo. Murcer	Curt Blefary	
1971	Ralph Houk	T. Munson	Danny Cater	Horace Clarke	Gene Michael	Jerry Kenney	Roy White	Bo. Murcer	Felipe Alou	
1972	Ralph Houk	T. Munson	Felipe Alou	Horace Clarke	Gene Michael	C. Sanchez	Roy White	Bo. Murcer	John Callison	
1973	Ralph Houk	T. Munson	Felipe Alou	Horace Clarke	Gene Michael	Graig Nettles	Roy White	Bo. Murcer	Matty Alou	Jim Ray Hart
1974	Bill Virdon	T. Munson	C. Chambliss	Sandy Alomar	Jim Mason	Graig Nettles	Lou Piniella	E. Maddox	Bo. Murcer	R. Blomberg
1975	Bill Virdon	T. Munson	C. Chambliss	Sandy Alomar	Jim Mason	Graig Nettles	Roy White	E. Maddox	Bobby Bonds	Ed Herrmann
1976	Billy Martin	T. Munson	C. Chambliss	W. Randolph	Fred Stanley	Graig Nettles	Roy White	Mi. Rivers	Oscar Gamble	Carlos May
1977	Billy Martin	T. Munson	C. Chambliss	W. Randolph	Bucky Dent	Graig Nettles	Roy White	Mi. Rivers	R. Jackson	Carlos May
1978	Billy Martin	T. Munson	C. Chambliss	W. Randolph	Bucky Dent	Graig Nettles	Lou Piniella	Mi. Rivers	R. Jackson	Cliff Johnson
1979	Billy Martin	T. Munson	C. Chambliss	W. Randolph	Bucky Dent	Graig Nettles	Lou Piniella	Bo. Murcer	R. Jackson	Jim Spencer
1980	Dick Howser	Rick Cerone	Bob Watson	W. Randolph	Bucky Dent	Graig Nettles	Lou Piniella	Bobby Brown	R. Jackson	E. Soderholm
1981	Gene Michael	Rick Cerone	Bob Watson	W. Randolph	Bucky Dent	Graig Nettles	D. Winfield	J. Mumphrey	R. Jackson	Bo. Murcer
1982	Gene Michael	Rick Cerone	J. Mayberry	W. Randolph	Roy Smalley	Graig Nettles	D. Winfield	J. Mumphrey	Ken Griffey	Oscar Gamble
1983	Billy Martin	B. Wynegar	Ken Griffey	W. Randolph	Roy Smalley	Graig Nettles	D. Winfield	J. Mumphrey	Steve Kemp	Don Baylor

YEAR	MANAGER	C	1B	2B	SS	3B	LF	CF	RF	DH
1984	Yogi Berra	B. Wynegar	D. Mattingly	W. Randolph	B. Meacham	Toby Harrah	Ken Griffey	Omar Moreno	D. Winfield	Don Baylor
1985	Billy Martin	B. Wynegar	D. Mattingly	W. Randolph	B. Meacham	M. Pagliarulo	Ken Griffey	R. Henderson	D. Winfield	Don Baylor
1986	Lou Piniella	B. Wynegar	D. Mattingly	W. Randolph	W. Tolleson	M. Pagliarulo	Dan Pasqua	R. Henderson	D. Winfield	Mike Easler
1987	Lou Piniella	Rick Cerone	D. Mattingly	W. Randolph	W. Tolleson	M. Pagliarulo	Gary Ward	R. Henderson	D. Winfield	Ron Kittle
1988	Lou Piniella	Don Slaught	D. Mattingly	W. Randolph	R. Santana	M. Pagliarulo	R. Henderson	C. Washington	D. Winfield	Jack Clark
1989	Dallas Green	Don Slaught	D. Mattingly	Steve Sax	Al Espinoza	M. Pagliarulo	Mel Hall	Roberto Kelly	Jesse Barfield	Steve Balboni
1990	Stump Merrill	Bob Geren	D. Mattingly	Steve Sax	Al Espinoza	R. Velarde	Oscar Azocar	Roberto Kelly	Jesse Barfield	Steve Balboni
1991	Stump Merrill	Matt Nokes	D. Mattingly	Steve Sax	Al Espinoza	Pat Kelly	Roberto Kelly	B. Williams	Mel Hall	Kevin Maas
1992	B. Showalter	Matt Nokes	D. Mattingly	Pat Kelly	Stankiewicz	Charlie Hayes	Mel Hall	Roberto Kelly	Dan Tartabull	Kevin Maas
1993	B. Showalter	Mike Stanley	D. Mattingly	Pat Kelly	Spike Owen	Wade Boggs	Dion James	B. Williams	Paul O'Neill	Dan Tartabull
1994	B. Showalter	Mike Stanley	D. Mattingly	Pat Kelly	Mike Gallego	Wade Boggs	Luis Polonia	B. Williams	Paul O'Neill	Dan Tartabull
1995	B. Showalter	Mike Stanley	D. Mattingly	Pat Kelly	T. Fernandez	Wade Boggs	G. Williams	B. Williams	Paul O'Neill	Ruben Sierra
1996	Joe Torre	Joe Girardi	Tino Martinez	M. Duncan	Derek Jeter	Wade Boggs	G. Williams	B. Williams	Paul O'Neill	Ruben Sierra
1997	Joe Torre	Joe Girardi	Tino Martinez	Luis Sojo	Derek Jeter	Charlie Hayes	Chad Curtis	B. Williams	Paul O'Neill	Cecil Fielder
1998	Joe Torre	Jorge Posada	Tino Martinez	C. Knoblauch	Derek Jeter	Scott Brosius	Chad Curtis	B. Williams	Paul O'Neill	D. Strawberry
1999	Joe Torre	Jorge Posada	Tino Martinez	C. Knoblauch	Derek Jeter	Scott Brosius	Chad Curtis	B. Williams	Paul O'Neill	Chili Davis
2000	Joe Torre	Jorge Posada	Tino Martinez	C. Knoblauch	Derek Jeter	Scott Brosius	Dave Justice	B. Williams	Paul O'Neill	S. Spencer
2001	Joe Torre	Jorge Posada	Tino Martinez	A. Soriano	Derek Jeter	Scott Brosius	C. Knoblauch	B. Williams	Paul O'Neill	David Justice
2002	Joe Torre	Jorge Posada	Jason Giambi	A. Soriano	Derek Jeter	R. Ventura	R. White	B. Williams	Raul Mondesi	Nick Johnson

ACKNOWLEDGMENTS

I generally like to start this part of the book by thanking my agent and my editor, but this time around I must first extend my heartfelt gratitude to Geoff Reiss, for the compelling reason that this book was Geoff's idea. Geoff also wrote most of the player comments in the Mets chapter, he wrote some of the player comments in a number of other chapters, and he made hundreds of vital contributions elsewhere. So Geoff comes first.

My agent is Jay Mandel, at William Morris. This is my third book, but I would probably still be dreaming about my first if not for Jay. It was Jay who e-mailed me five or six years ago, wondering if I had any book ideas. I did, he told me to keep trying, and eventually Eddie Epstein and I came up with *Baseball Dynasties*. My career as an author has taken some strange twists and turns since, but Jay's always been there when I needed him. The way it works is, I come up with an idea for a book, and if Jay thinks the audience for the book would extend past my mom, somehow he figures a way to have a check in my grubby paws within a few months. It's really an amazing thing, what he does.

My editor is Brant Rumble, who just might be the most patient man in North America. I worked and I worked and I worked, and still I fell further and further and further behind schedule. And through it all, Brant kept telling me that the material was good, just keep plugging away. After all those months, I don't have any idea if the material really is good, but at least it was published on schedule. For that and many other things, I'm grateful to Brant.

I'm also grateful to all the other hardworking people at Fireside, including (but not limited to) Scott Gray, Cherlynne Li, Jennifer Love, and Joy O'Meara. This book looks amazingly close to what Geoff and I initially conceived, and that doesn't happen without a lot of help.

Billy Beane, Bill James, Michael Lewis, Jon Miller, and Joshua Prager were kind enough to read portions of the manuscript and respond with the words that you'll find on the cover, and I'm grateful to all of them, too.

David Schoenfield and Ted Bishop, my friends and colleagues at ESPN.com, contributed to this book in a variety of ways. Both are Mariners fans from the bad old days; their memories inform that chapter of the book, and they're credited there. But they deserve special mention here, too. Ted has been instrumental in getting me the teams' media guides over the last few years, without which this book would have been a lot harder to write. And Dave, who edited many hundreds of my columns with great patience and good humor before moving on to bigger and better things, is the main reason that I've now been gainfully employed by the same company for eight years (looking at those words leaves me in disbelief . . . *eight years*).

Which reminds me, I'm grateful to ESPN's John Marvel, Neal Scarbrough, John Walsh, and John Skipper for their roles in providing me with what I think is the single greatest platform a baseball columnist could have. As I tell people all the time, I have the best job in the world . . . and they *pay* me to do it.

Eric Enders and the staff at Triple E Productions were wonderful about answering my research requests in a timely and financially reasonable fashion. And, as always, I'm grateful to David Smith, Tom Ruane, and the other wonderful folks at Retrosheet for their amazing dedication and kindness. The intrepid researchers at the National Baseball Library, particularly Bruce Markusen, were of great help, too.

Speaking of Cooperstown, I'm particularly grateful to the Hall's Bill Burdick, who was his usual helpful self when it came to acquiring photographs. Thanks also to Jim Callis (and *Baseball America*), Jim Anderson (and the Detroit Tigers), Steve Copses (and the Florida Marlins), Debbie Gallas (and the Oakland Athletics), Molly Gallatin (and the Minnesota Twins), Chris Gutierrez (and the Los Angeles Dodgers), Jason Parry (and the Milwaukee Brewers), Susan Webner (and the Arizona Diamondbacks), and the good people at Tom DiPace Photography.

The scary thing about writing a book like this is the impossibility of learning enough about each team to come across as an expert to a knowledgeable fan of each particular team. The solution? Right, find my own knowledgeable fans to look at the chapters before they're actually published. I was able to do that for most teams, and I've mentioned those fans (along with a few pros) at the conclusion of those chapters. Without their help, I would be ashamed of this book.

I do a *lot* of radio interviews—"phoners," as they're called in the business—and there's not space here for all of the hosts and producers who have been kind to me over the years. But I would particularly like to thank hosts Bob Valvano, Bob Haynie, Ted Sarandis, Bill Hayes, Larry Krueger, Bruce Ciskie, and Mike Crowley, and producers Andy Elrick, Vince Kates, Ray Bachman, Jason Romano, and Shawn Page.

Finally, I thank Kristien (my wife) and Micah (my stepson). Every minute that I'm writing is a minute that I can't spend with Kristien the Wife and Micah the Boy (not to mention Terra the Dog), and I'm grateful to them. I could have written this book without their love and patience, but it wouldn't have been nearly as much fun.

Index